THE BIG TRIVIA QUIZ BOOK

DK LONDON

Senior Editor Victoria Heyworth-Dunne
Americanizers Heather Wilcox, Second Glance editorial; Kayla Dugger
US Executive Editor Lori Hand
Senior Art Editor Gadi Farfour
Managing Editor Gareth Jones
Senior Managing Art Editor Lee Griffiths
Senior Production Editor Andy Hilliard
Senior Production Controller Rachel Ng
Senior Jacket Designer Akiko Kato
Development Manager Sophia MTT
Publishing Director Jonathan Metcalf
Associate Publishing Director Liz Wheeler
Art Director Karen Self
Design Director Philip Ormerod

DK DELHI

Senior Editor Janashree Singha
Project Editor Dipika Dasgupta
Editors Nandini D. Tripathy, Devangana Ojha,
Rishi Bryan, Avanika
Assistant Editor Ankita Gupta
Senior Art Editor Chhaya Sajwan
Project Art Editor Sourabh Challariya
Managing Editor Soma B. Chowdhury
Senior Managing Art Editor Arunesh Talapatra
DTP Designer Anita Yadav
Pre-production Manager Balwant Singh

DYNAMO

Question selection and adaptation, and project management by
Dynamo Limited

First American Edition, 2020
Published in the United States by DK Publishing,
a division of Penguin Random House LLC
1745 Broadway, 20th Floor, New York, NY 10019

Copyright © 2020 Dorling Kindersley Limited
23 24 25 26 27 10 9 8 7
015–323118–Aug/2020

All rights reserved. Without limiting the rights under the copyright reserved above, no
part of this publication may be reproduced, stored in or introduced into a retrieval system,
or transmitted, in any form, or by any means (electronic, mechanical, photocopying,
recording, or otherwise), without the prior written permission of the copyright owner.
Published in Great Britain by Dorling Kindersley Limited

A catalog record for this book is available from the Library of Congress.
ISBN 978-0-7440-3583-4

DK books are available at special discounts when purchased in bulk
for sales promotions, premiums, fund-raising, or educational use.
For details, contact: DK Publishing Special Markets,
1745 Broadway, 20th Floor, New York, NY 10019
SpecialSales@dk.com

Printed and bound in the UK

www.dk.com

MIX
Paper | Supporting
responsible forestry
FSC™ C018179

This book was made with Forest
Stewardship Council™ certified
paper – one small step in DK's
commitment to a sustainable future.
Learn more at
www.dk.com/uk/information/sustainability

THE
BIG
TRIVIA
QUIZ
BOOK

10,000 QUESTIONS
FOR ALL AGES

CONTENTS

History 6

Science & Technology 52

Art & Literature 98

Geography 144

Music 190

The Natural World 236

Sports & Leisure 282

Food & Drink 328

Film & TV 374

Potluck 420

Answers 466

INTRODUCTION

Doing quizzes is a great way to learn facts, test your knowledge, and have fun. With 450 quizzes and 10,000 questions covering a wide range of topics from dinosaurs, inventors, and ancient history to comics, film, and food, there is something for everyone. Test yourself on your favorite subject or challenge your brain and try something completely new!

Each themed section has 45 quizzes. Each quiz has 15 Easy, 15 Medium, and 15 Difficult sets of questions. Half the quizzes have 20 questions, and half have 25 questions. The quizzes are numbered from 1 to 450. To find the answers, look up the number of the quiz in the Answers section.

HOW TO USE THIS BOOK

There are many ways to use the book. You can do the quizzes by yourself, in teams, or with another person. Here are a few suggestions, but you can create your own quiz games to play.

- **By yourself.** Work your way through the book from the beginning. See which is your best subject. Do one quiz from each section each time. Go back and do the quizzes again to test your memory. Then try the next quiz in the section until you have done all the quizzes in the book.

- **Quiz in pairs.** Each person can take turns choosing a number from 1 to 450 and then going to that quiz. Set a time limit to answer the questions. Score a point for each correct answer and another point for the person who got the most right answers. The first person to get a set number of points (say, 100) is the winner.

- **Play in teams.** Write the section names on a piece of paper and put them in a bowl. Each team takes turns selecting a piece of paper. Put the piece of paper back in the bowl. The teams do one quiz from the section (in the order they appear). Then select another piece of paper and so on. The team with the most correct answers at the end of a set number of quizzes is the winner.

CHAPTER 1

HISTORY

From ancient to modern history, check out the people, battles, and events that shaped our world. These quizzes will test your knowledge of dates, names, and places.

World War II

1. What was the operational name for the D-Day landings in June 1944?

2. Which Japanese city was hit by the first atomic bomb?

3. Which Battle of Britain fighter had the same name as a type of storm?

4. What was a "doodlebug"?

5. What does "blitzkrieg" mean?

6. Which British prime minister declared war on Germany in September 1939?

7. Who was in charge of the SS?

8. Stalin was the political leader of which country?

9. What was a "blimp"?

10. Men over 35 were too old for the draft in the US. True or False?

11. Where might you find an Anderson Shelter?

12. What sort of gun was a Sten?

13. Which nation sent its Red Army to war in Europe?

14. A "Sherman" was a type of what?

15. What was a B-29?

16. In which month did the Allies declare "Victory in Europe"?

17. What was the name of the German general who was in charge of the Afrika Korps?

18. What does "kamikaze" mean?

19. The invasion of which country prompted Britain's entry into the war?

20. Which winter-long battle for a Russian city began in 1942?

21. Was Italy one of the Allies?

22. What was the name of the machine used to create German secret codes?

23. Which event brought the United States into the war?

24. Which European country declared war on Germany alongside Britain in 1939?

25. Operation Barbarossa in 1941 was the name for Hitler's attack on which country?

(Answers on page 466)

The Vikings

1. In which centuries did the Vikings live?

2. What name is given to Viking stories and legends?

3. What were Viking warships called?

4. On a sword or dagger, where was the hilt?

5. Viking helmets had horns. True or False?

6. Which Viking god was considered the most important?

7. What were Viking combs made of?

8. The first known Viking raid on England was in 793 CE. Where did this attack take place?

9. A Viking woman could choose her own husband and demand divorce if he was unfaithful. True or False?

10. What is chain mail?

11. What was the ornamental carving on a ship's prow called?

12. Which Viking explorer was the son of Erik the Red?

13. The Viking cemetery in Lindholm Høje is one of the largest. It has how many graves: 300–400, 600–700, 1,000–2,000?

14. What farm tools did many Vikings take to battle?

15. By the 12th century CE, Viking raids across Europe had ended due to the Vikings' adoption of which religion?

16. Viking warriors believed that if they died in battle, they would go to a heavenly palace. What was its name?

17. Which Norse god had an ax and was associated with thunder and trees?

18. Does the Norse word "vik" mean a creek or inlet, a horned helmet, a ship?

19. Where did the Vikings come from?

20. The Vikings were the first Europeans to colonize North America. When did they land in what is now Canada? Around the year 800, 900, 1000, 1066?

(Answers on page 466)

Famous Ships and Commanders

1. Where in 1982 did Rear Admiral Sandy Woodward lead a British task force?

2. Which British admiral sent the famous signal "England expects that every man will do his duty"?

3. Which American aircraft carrier fought at the Coral Sea and Midway battles before being sunk? Was it USS *Yorktown*, *Nautilus*, or *Missouri*?

4. Which German pocket battleship was sunk following the Battle of the River Plate in December 1939?

5. Which famous Roman commanded the Egyptian Fleet and was defeated at the Battle of Actium?

6. Who commanded the Spanish Armada in 1588?

7. Who commanded the US Pacific Fleet in World War II? A famous US ship in the late 20th century carries his name. Was it Omar N. Bradley, Chester W. Nimitz, Douglas MacArthur?

8. Which famous ship sank in sight of Henry VIII and the attacking French fleet in 1545?

9. What was the name of the Argentine cruiser controversially sunk by the Royal Navy in 1982?

10. What was the name of the first nuclear-powered submarine?

11. Who commanded the British Grand Fleet at the Battle of Jutland: Haig, Jellicoe, Trenchard?

12. What was the British flagship at the Battle of Trafalgar?

13. Which American hero captured a British frigate off Scarborough in 1779?

14. What was the name of the ship heroically commanded by Sir Richard Grenville in the Azores in 1591?

15. The 16th-century North African Corsair Kheir-ed-Din was better known as: Barbarossa, Saladin, or Blackbeard?

16. The sinking of which British liner by a German U-boat off southern Ireland in May 1915 helped bring the US into World War I?

17. The Japanese naval officer who conceived the attack on Pearl Harbor was: Tojo, Yamaha, Yamamoto?

18. Who thought he could finish a game of lawn bowling before beating the Spaniards?

19. Which German battleship sank the British battlecruiser HMS *Hood* in 1941?

20. Who designed the giant iron sailing steamship SS *Great Eastern*, launched in 1858?

Kings and Queens

1. Who was the first Tudor monarch?

2. Which king of England was known as "the Confessor," because he was very religious?

3. Which king of England and Scotland has his name linked to a translation of the Bible?

4. Who reigned in Britain from 1837 to 1901?

5. Which English monarch faced an armada?

6. Which king of England was crowned in Westminster Abbey on Christmas Day, 1066?

7. Which king of England signed the Magna Carta in 1215?

8. Who became the first king of Scotland in 843?

9. Who was known as "Bloody Mary"?

10. Which king of England had to fight a civil war against his cousin Matilda?

11. What was the Christian name of all of the Hanoverian kings?

12. Which English king won a great victory at Agincourt?

13. Who was the Sixth who also became the First?

14. Which King Edward gave up the throne uncrowned?

15. Which English king was known as the Lionheart?

16. What was the original last name of the House of Windsor?

17. Who was last sovereign prince of Wales, killed in 1282 during the struggle against Edward I of England?

18. Which English king was known as both "Edward Longshanks" and "the hammer of the Scots"?

19. Which king of England and Wales had six wives?

20. Who was the last Yorkist king?

21. Queen Anne had 18 pregnancies. How many of her children survived?

22. Which king was known as "Unready"?

23. Who was the last British monarch to lead troops into battle?

24. Which king is said to have lost the crown jewels in the Wash in 1216?

25. Which monarch was also Empress of India?

Ancient Egypt

1. The pyramids were tombs for the Egyptian pharaohs. Is the oldest pyramid at Giza or the Valley of the Kings?

2. Pharaohs were believed to be "living gods." True or False?

3. What did the Nile do every year in ancient Egypt that enabled crops to be sown?

4. For how many years did the ancient Egyptian civilization last?

5. What original color were the pyramids at Giza?

6. The pharaoh wore the crown of Upper and Lower Egypt to symbolize the country's unity. True or False?

7. Which pharaoh commissioned the temple of Abu Simbel to be built?

8. What does the word "pharaoh" mean?

9. Which pharaoh commissioned the Great Pyramid?

10. How many limestone blocks are in the Great Pyramid? 1.3 million, 2.3 million, 3.3 million?

11. After the pyramids were raided by grave robbers, where were the pharaohs buried?

12. The tomb and treasure of which pharaoh was famously discovered in the Valley of the Kings in 1922?

13. What oval symbol was a pharaoh's name written on?

14. What was the form of writing used by the ancient Egyptians?

15. What stone helped scholars translate the Ancient Egyptian inscriptions?

16. Shabti figures were buried with the dead so they could serve them in the afterlife. True or False?

17. The jackal-headed Egyptian god of embalming was... ?

18. What is the name of the book that prepared ancient Egyptians for their journey to the afterlife?

19. The brain was pulled out through the nose as part of the mummification process. True or False?

20. Who was the last Egyptian pharaoh?

The Cold War

1. The Cold War is widely considered to have taken place between 1947 and: 1955, 1979, 1991?

2. What simple terms described the opposing sides (communist countries and democratic countries) in the Cold War? East/West or North/South?

3. Herbert B. Swope coined the term "Cold War." True or False?

4. What was the name of the communist alliance that opposed NATO?

5. Where did a missile crisis take place in 1962?

6. A blockade of which European city in 1948 resulted in supplies being airlifted in?

7. In which 1950s war did the USSR and the US fight each other indirectly?

8. What was the name of the group of countries that wished to stay neutral in the Cold War?

9. When was NATO formed?

10. Which US president was behind the "Star Wars" program?

11. Which "friendly" country did Soviet troops invade in 1956?

12. When was the Berlin Wall built to stop people from leaving East Germany?

13. The Cold War never featured any direct military action. True or False?

14. In 1947, US President Truman announced the "Truman Doctrine" to look at the benefits of communism for the US. True or False?

15. What was the name of the Soviet Union's secret police?

16. Which US secretary of state outlined a plan for rebuilding Europe?

17. What year did the Berlin Wall come down?

18. The Soviet invasion of Afghanistan in 1979 caused Cold War tensions to flare up. True or False?

19. Who was the first US president to visit Moscow?

20. What gift did President Nixon receive following his visit to China?

(Answers on page 466)

Castles

1. Which conquering people brought the first castles to England?

2. In which part of a castle were banquets held?

3. What were the private chambers of a castle lord called?

4. The Normans first built motte and bailey castles. True or False?

5. Which is the largest castle in England?

6. What is the name of the last castle built in England?

7. What part of a castle did a person called the "Gong-Farmer" have to clean out?

8. The fortified tower at the heart of a castle was called the… ?

9. What name is given to the ditch around a castle's walls?

10. What was often poured down "Murder Holes" onto attacking soldiers?

11. Castles provided protection to those inside, but they were cold, smoky, smelly places to live. True or False?

12. Most castles had a small private chapel beside the lord's chambers. True or False?

13. An "oubliette" was a small hole in a dungeon where prisoners were left and forgotten. True or False?

14. What were narrow vertical openings in the castle walls that allowed missiles to be fired called?

15. By the 15th century, the widespread use of gunpowder made castle fortifications less relevant. True or False?

16. The gaps in a castle's battlements are called what?

17. What was the spiked metal barrier that could be lowered over the castle gates?

18. A concentric castle can also be described as… ?

19. Where did the lord of a castle sit during a banquet?

20. King Henry VII was born in which Welsh castle?

Medieval Europe

1. Which English king started the Hundred Years' War with France?

2. The original intention of the Crusades was to capture which city?

3. The Medici family dominated life in which Italian city?

4. For what did Edward I raise funds by taxing moneylenders: churches, palaces, wars?

5. What killed 80 percent of the people who caught it?

6. What did Wat Tyler lead in England in 1381?

7. Who was the first monarch of the Plantagenet dynasty?

8. What caused the greatest loss of life for English forces in the Agincourt campaign?

9. What style of architecture describes Chartres Cathedral?

10. In medieval England, children drank beer because it was safer than water. True or False?

11. Which traveler said, "I have not told half of what I saw"?

12. Which German metalworker pioneered printing?

13. A trebuchet was a type of what?

14. Medieval peasants would consume up to how many calories per day?

15. What name is often given to the Islamic people who ruled much of Spain during the Middle Ages?

16. Animals were put on trial in medieval times. True or False?

17. King Edward III required which skill to be practiced every Sunday?

18. San Gimignano in Italy is famous for its: towers, tombs, torture chambers?

19. Which fish was sometimes used as currency: eels, sturgeon, or carp?

20. Which part of the body did armor called "greaves" protect?

 (Answers on page 466)

The Tudors

1. Which English monarch did Henry Tudor beat at the Battle of Bosworth?

2. How many of Henry VIII's wives were beheaded?

3. York was the capital of England during Tudor times. True or False?

4. Name the best-known Tudor theater.

5. Which American state was named after Elizabeth I?

6. What was the split with the Roman Catholic Church called?

7. Which country tried to invade England with the armada?

8. Which Englishman did the Spanish call "El Draco"?

9. Which playwright, possibly a spy, was killed in a tavern brawl?

10. Wolves still roamed parts of England during Tudor times. True or False?

11. What food was illegal to eat on a Friday?

12. At 11 in the morning in Tudor schools, what could children expect?

13. Elizabeth of England and Mary of Scotland were first cousins. True or False?

14. Which German artist was a famous painter in Tudor England?

15. Which Tudor monarch ruled for just nine days?

16. At the beginning of the Tudor dynasty, which event in 1486 united the rival Houses of Lancaster and York?

17. William Shakespeare once met Henry VIII. True or False?

18. Who were King Edward VI's parents?

19. What were the people who stood at the front of an Elizabethan theater known as?

20. Whom did Queen Mary I marry?

21. The Tudor rose was a combination of the York and Lancaster roses. True or False?

22. Tudors only ate with a fork. True or False?

23. How many times did Elizabeth I marry?

24. By tradition, what is Sir Walter Raleigh credited with bringing from the Americas?

25. How did Elizabethan theaters indicate that a play was going to be performed?

(Answers on page 467)

Famous People In History

1. Which English king had six wives?

2. Who wrote the plays *Romeo and Juliet* and *A Midsummer Night's Dream*?

3. Who was the first female prime minister of Britain?

4. Who developed a system of raised dots to help blind people to read using their sense of touch?

5. Which queen ruled England at the time of the Spanish Armada?

6. Which author wrote about Fagin and his gang of child thieves?

7. The Egyptian pharaoh Akhenaten had a beautiful wife whose sandstone bust has made her image famous. Her name was… ?

8. Who was Britain's prime minister throughout the majority of World War II?

9. Who wrote a diary describing life in London at the time of the plague in 1665 and the Great Fire in 1666?

10. Which king was believed to live at Camelot?

11. Who was the first president of the United States?

12. Florence Nightingale was named after the city where she was born. True or False?

13. Who was the warrior queen in Britain who fought against the Romans?

14. What did Guy Fawkes try to do?

15. Who painted the *Mona Lisa*?

16. Which philosopher famously said, "I think, therefore I am"?

17. Who became known as "Buddha"?

18. Buzz Aldrin was the second man to step on the moon. True or False?

19. Who lived in a secret room in Amsterdam because her family needed to hide from the Nazis?

20. Who was the first European to view the Victoria Falls?

21. Who is the only English monarch to have been beheaded?

22. Who led the Bolshevik Revolution in Russia in 1917?

23. Who led the first British expedition to reach the South Pole?

24. Who led the French resistance to the English invasion in the Hundred Years' War?

25. Who devoted her life to helping the poor and sick in Kolkata, India?

     (Answers on page 467)

Essential World War I

1. What was a Dreadnought?

2. Which two countries signed the Entente Cordiale?

3. In which year did World War I begin?

4. Whose assassination in Sarajevo in 1914 led to military mobilization and the outbreak of the war?

5. On which front did most of the fighting take place during World War I?

6. Which country left the war after a revolution in 1917?

7. Who was king of Great Britain during World War I?

8. What was the name of the earthworks that stretched all the way from the English Channel to Switzerland throughout the war?

9. What was the complaint suffered by many soldiers because of wet conditions in the trenches?

10. Turkey was an ally of which country: Britain or Germany?

11. What was the new weapon first developed by the British that changed the course of land warfare?

12. Which 1916 battle is usually considered to be the worst disaster in British military history due to the huge loss of life?

13. Why did Britain declare war on Germany?

14. Who was the famous German fighter ace whose "Flying Circus" unit terrorized Allied pilots?

15. What was the name of the only major naval battle of World War I?

16. What was the role of a sapper?

17. What was No Man's Land?

18. Which country joined the British and French in 1917? The huge resources of this nation helped to end the war within a year.

19. What was the Armistice?

20. In which year did World War I end?

21. How many horses were involved in the war?

22. What were the enormous German airships that carried out bombing raids on Britain called?

23. World War I pilots did not carry parachutes. True or False?

24. Troops from which country were led by General Pershing?

25. How old was the youngest British soldier to fight in the war: 12, 13, 14?

(Answers on page 467)   17

Living in Ancient Greece

1. What name describes the government of the first Greek city-states: oligarchy, monarchy, hierarchy?

2. What was a polis: police force, temple, or city-state?

3. Which Greek mathematician laid the foundations of geometry in his treatise called *The Elements*?

4. Ur was a Greek city-state. True or False?

5. What was the name of the main marketplace in a city-state of ancient Greece?

6. What activities took place in the gymnasium?

7. What was to be found in the Sanctuary of Athena at Delphi?

8. What was the original purpose of the Parthenon in Athens?

9. Which of the city-states was famed for its army and military training?

10. With which areas of knowledge is Aristotle principally associated?

11. Name the general who spread Greek culture via his conquests across the Middle East.

12. After which famous battle did a messenger run himself to death bringing news of a Greek victory?

13. Which city-state is considered to be the birthplace of democracy?

14. What was a chiton in ancient Greece?

15. Who wrote *The Odyssey*?

16. Between which city-states was the Peloponnesian War fought?

17. Which mathematician is famous for a law about right angles?

18. Where did ancient Greeks believe that their gods lived?

19. In whose honor were the original Olympic Games held near Mount Olympus?

20. Where would you expect to have found hoplites, peltasts, and phalanxes?

21. Both men and women could be full citizens in ancient Greece. True or False?

22. Which materials were used to build most houses in ancient Greece?

23. What did performers wear in ancient Greek theaters?

24. What first took place in 776 BCE?

25. Ancient Greeks believed the gods and goddesses had human qualities. True or False?

Britons and Invaders

1. In which country is the 5,000-year-old Stone Age passage tomb of Newgrange?

2. Modern humans first came to Britain around 40,000 BCE. True or False?

3. What metal was introduced into Britain around 4000 BCE?

4. Why were the Beaker People who arrived in 2400 BCE given this name?

5. Name the most famous prehistoric monument that comprises rings of standing stones.

6. Around 800 BCE, a new metal began to be widely used in Britain. What was it?

7. What type of Iron Age defended settlement was Maiden Castle?

8. Which Roman general attempted an invasion of Britain in 55 and 54 BCE?

9. Name the Roman emperor who succeeded in conquering parts of Britain in 43 CE.

10. By what name is the Roman defensive line across north Britain dating from 122 CE known?

11. Who was the leader of the Iceni who rebelled against Roman rule?

12. What place-name evidence today suggests that a modern town was once a Roman fort?

13. Which parts of the British Isles not conquered by the Romans later were settled by the Vikings?

14. Who is usually credited with converting Ireland to Christianity?

15. Which groups of people invaded Britain after the Romans withdrew their legions?

16. What is the name of the earthwork built by a Saxon king of Mercia to prevent a Welsh invasion?

17. What was the Danelaw?

18. From where in Europe did Viking raiders and settlers originate?

19. Which Anglo-Saxon king successfully stood up to the Viking invaders?

20. Who were the last people to successfully invade Britain, in 1066?

Great Leaders

1. George Washington was the first US president. True or False?

2. Which powerful military leader first established the Mongol Empire?

3. Who became the Prussian prime minister in 1862?

4. What was Mussolini's first name?

5. Which great leader rose to power during the French Revolution and later crowned himself the first emperor of France?

6. Who led the Muslim forces against the European crusaders?

7. Which Roman leader was the first to have his own image on a coin?

8. Which US president created the "New Deal"?

9. In which year did Margaret Thatcher become the prime minister of Great Britain?

10. Alexander the Great was Macedonian. True or False?

11. Which king led Scottish forces at the Battle of Bannockburn?

12. Which Indian lawyer led a successful nonviolent campaign for India's independence from British rule?

13. Who led the campaign to unify Italy in the 1860s?

14. Who led the Chinese Revolution of 1949?

15. Where was William the Conqueror born?

16. Richard I, king of England, spoke French better than English. True or False?

17. Schloss Bellevue is the official home of which country's president?

18. Anwar Sadat was president of which country?

19. There is a famous memorial to four US presidents on Mount… ?

20. In which city is the Lincoln Memorial?

21. What is the Duke of Wellington most famous for?

22. What did Nelson Mandela achieve in 1994?

23. Who led British and Allied forces to victory at Alamein in 1942?

24. Which empress enlarged and strengthened the Russian empire and was the country's longest-ruling female leader?

25. Who was the leader of Parliament's forces, known as "Roundheads," at the Battle of Naseby in 1645?

(Answers on page 467)

The Russian Revolution

1. In which year did the Russian Revolution begin?

2. What was the name of the political group led by Lenin in the October Revolution?

3. Which Russian leader was executed on July 16, 1918?

4. What did the Bolshevik militias turn into during the Russian Revolution?

5. Who succeeded Czar Nicholas II of Russia in 1917?

6. Which Russian revolutionary leader wrote a book in 1899 titled *The Development of Capitalism in Russia*?

7. Which battleship became an icon of revolution after a 1905 mutiny?

8. What was the name of the anti-communist forces who fought the Red Army during the revolution?

9. Name the founder of the Red Army who was assassinated in Mexico in 1940.

10. How was revolutionary leader Leon Trotsky killed?

11. What term describes the mass arrests, executions, and atrocities conducted by the Bolshevik government, announced in 1918?

12. What was the Russian Revolution's term for combining the country's agricultural land for shared ownership by the country's peasants?

13. What did the name "Stalin" mean?

14. What is the modern name for the city of Petrograd where food riots broke out?

15. Leon Trotsky said that socialism in Russia could not be realized without a world revolution. True or False?

16. Lenin wrote his book *State and Revolution* in which country: Sweden, Russia, Finland?

17. Who became the Russian prime minister in 1917 and tried to arrest Lenin?

18. In which country was there a knock-on revolution during 1918–1919, as a result of the Russian Revolution?

19. Who became leader of the USSR following Lenin's death in 1924?

20. The remains of executed Czar Nicholas II and his family were discovered in the 1970s. True or False?

(Answers on page 468)   **21**

The Victorians

1. Who was Queen Victoria married to?

2. Queen Victoria was the last of which dynasty?

3. What 1840 innovation is associated with Rowland Hill?

4. What was the color of the first postage stamp?

5. What does Boer, as in "Boer War," mean?

6. What did the Chartists campaign for from the 1830s to the 1850s?

7. Which country gained dominion status from the British Empire in 1867?

8. What famous waterway opened in 1869?

9. Who developed the Suez Canal?

10. Robert Peel repealed which laws in 1846?

11. Some Victorian pillar boxes have the initials "VR" on them. What do these initials stand for?

12. The Great Exhibition of 1851 was held in a converted railway station. True or False?

13. The Crystal Palace was moved in 1854 to which London suburb?

14. In which part of the British Isles did many thousands die in the 1845–1851 potato famine?

15. How many times was William Gladstone prime minister?

16. Who was William Gladstone's great Tory rival in the 1870s?

17. Who wrote *The Book of Household Management* in 1861 with recipes and advice for young wives?

18. Which political theorist moved to London in 1849?

19. The Clifton Suspension Bridge was designed by which engineer?

20. The monument dedicated to Prince Albert lies near which London park?

21. Who was the Victorian pioneer of nursing?

22. Which three sisters in this era wrote novels that have become classics?

23. Name the naturalist who wrote *On the Origin of Species*.

24. During this era, where were people who were poor and unable to work because of sickness or old age housed?

25. The first trains were pulled by horses. True or False?

Civil Wars

1. Who led the Parliamentarian forces during the English Civil War?

2. In which year did the southern states split from the American Union?

3. Why were supporters of Oliver Cromwell sometimes known as "Roundheads"?

4. What name was given to the reformed Parliamentarian forces?

5. Who led the Nationalist forces in the Spanish Civil War?

6. Which battle is regarded as the turning point in the American Civil War?

7. What name did the monarchs of the English Civil War share?

8. Name the capital of Bosnia, besieged during the Yugoslavian Civil War.

9. Which war in Southeast Asia began as an anti-colonial struggle and eventually drew in the United States?

10. When did the English Civil War begin?

11. Who was the leader of Yugoslavia who unified the country after World War II?

12. Which were the opposing sides in the Wars of the Roses?

13. The Battle of Edgehill in the English Civil War ended in a draw. True or False?

14. Who did the Cavaliers fight for?

15. What was the nickname of Confederate General Thomas Jackson?

16. With which civil war is the abolitionist John Brown associated?

17. The Battle of the Bulge was an American Civil War battle. True or False?

18. What was the name of General Lee's horse that he used for most of the American Civil War?

19. Which Union military commander became US president in 1869?

20. Which US president was assassinated in 1865?

Empires

1. Where did the Ottoman Empire originate?

2. In which part of the world was the Mayan Empire: Africa, India, Central America?

3. Which ancient empire was governed by provincial governors called *satraps*?

4. Which 1997 event has been said to mark the final curtain for the British Empire?

5. The Byzantine Empire is also known as the what?

6. In which empire did the Eighteenth Dynasty usher in its New Kingdom?

7. The Gupta Empire is associated with which country?

8. In which empire did the shogun rule from the city of Edo?

9. Who founded the Macedonian Empire in 334 BCE?

10. The Ptolemaic Dynasty is most associated with which empire?

11. When did the Ottoman Empire finally end, 623 years after it was formed?

12. The Mongol Empire began under which leader?

13. Remains of the Hittite Empire would be best seen in which modern-day country?

14. Who was the first Roman leader to be proclaimed emperor?

15. The Chinese Ming Dynasty began in which century CE?

16. Sargon the Great ruled over which empire in the 24th century BCE?

17. Tenochtitlan was the capital city of which empire?

18. Aqueducts provided fresh water to people in Roman cities. True or False?

19. Beginning in 1922, for how many years did the Soviet Empire last?

20. Which of these African cities was within the Songhai Empire: Timbuktu, Cairo, Lusaka?

21. Hammurabi, the sixth king of the Babylon Dynasty, is best known for creating what?

22. Which empire was founded by a warrior named Babur in 1526?

23. Who was the ruler when the Ottoman Empire reached the height of its power in the 16th century?

24. Who established his empire first: Cyrus the Great, Charlemagne, or Genghis Khan?

25. The capital of the Byzantine Empire was… ?

(Answers on page 468)

Plague and Pestilence

1. The Black Death reputedly first reached Europe in which modern-day country?

2. What disease was identified in the mummified remains of Pharaoh Ramesses V?

3. Hong Kong was struck by which virus in 2003?

4. Which Greek city suffered a devastating plague in 430–429 BCE?

5. Approximately how many Europeans died from the plague during the Black Death?

6. What percentage of the European population died from the plague during the 14th century?

7. The term "Black Death" arose because all victims died at night. True or False?

8. Which form of the Black Death plague was spread via air and inhaled?

9. King Charles II chose to stay in London during the Great Plague of 1665–1666. True or False?

10. The Lord Mayor of London ordered the extermination of which animals to combat the Great Plague?

11. What was the name of the Derbyshire village that sacrificed itself to halt the spread of plague?

12. The Spanish flu originated in Spain. True or False?

13. Use of sheep and horse hair increased the incidence of which disease in the 18th century?

14. What was the name of the 19th-century doctor who pioneered the use of clean water to prevent cholera in London?

15. How long did the Justinian plague that ravaged much of the Roman Empire last?

16. Where do historians think the plague originated?

17. Which disease numbered among its victims the gangster Al Capone?

18. Homes of medieval plague victims were branded with red crosses. True or False?

19. When did the Black Death first arrive in England?

20. Queen Elizabeth I caught and survived smallpox. True or False?

21. What were buboes?

22. Smallpox is caused by a virus. True or False?

23. Do male mosquitos spread malaria?

24. Where in the world did the first cholera pandemic begin in the 19th century?

25. Which disease killed 20 to 25 percent of the Inca population?

HISTORY

Historical Sports

1. What is the name of the 3,000-year-old Gaelic sport played with a stick and a ball?

2. Where was the ancient rugbylike ball game of *harpastum* played: China, Rome, Mexico?

3. The game of rugby was based on an ancient Greek sport called "Episkyros." True or False?

4. What is considered to be the oldest historical sport?

5. What were winners of ancient Olympics crowned with?

6. In which country did the equestrian sport of polo originate?

7. Bull-leaping is associated with which ancient civilization?

8. In which year were the first Olympic Games held?

9. What form of clothing did ancient Olympians wear?

10. During which Roman ceremonies were the first gladiator fights believed to have been held?

11. How many people could the Colosseum in Rome hold to watch gladiator fights?

12. Where were the ancient Roman chariot races held?

13. Where have some of the oldest images associated with boxing been discovered?

14. In what sport did James Figg become British champion in 1719?

15. Who lost to Muhammad Ali in the "Thrilla in Manila" world title bout in 1975?

16. Cricket can be traced back to which period of English history?

17. *Choule* was an ancient stick and ball game, roughly akin to what?

18. During which century did soccer begin to spread from England to the rest of the world?

19. When were the rules of baseball first codified in the US?

20. Married women were not allowed to watch or take part in the ancient Olympic Games. True or False?

Highwaymen

1. Complete this highwayman's saying: "Your money or your… ?

2. In Britain, robbery with violence was punishable by death. How were most captured highwaymen executed?

3. What is the name of the hat commonly associated with highwaymen?

4. When was the last recorded horseback robbery in Britain?

5. "Bushrangers" is the name for highwaymen in which country?

6. Which bushranger is famous for wearing a suit of homemade armor to protect him from bullets?

7. In which century was Dick Turpin active?

8. Immortalized in fiction, by what name is his horse popularly known?

9. Which dog breed was commonly used as "coach dogs" for show and even to ward off highwaymen?

10. Which ballad opera by John Gay features highwayman Captain Macheath as its hero?

11. What was the name of the type of cheap 19th-century publication of serialized stories that often featured tales of highwaymen?

12. Who wrote the popular narrative poem "The Highwayman" about a highwayman's love for "Bess, the landlord's daughter"?

13. The name for an unmounted roadside robber was a "Footpad." True or False?

14. Which British band had a hit with "Stand and Deliver" in 1981, with a music video featuring the lead singer dressed as a highwayman?

15. John "Swift Nick" Nevison was supposedly given his nickname by which monarch, after a 200-mile (320-km) dash from Kent to York to fake an alibi?

16. Now partly buried beneath Heathrow Airport's runways, which patch of land was a notorious highwayman haunt in the 17th and 18th centuries?

17. What was the main reason for the sharp decline in highway robberies in Britain after 1763?

18. Who was the "gentleman highwayman," known for his gallant behavior, fashionable clothes, and avoidance of violence?

19. The "Tyburn Tree," a set of gallows where many highwaymen were hanged and left on display, stood near which present-day London location?

20. Where was Dick Turpin hanged in 1739?

(Answers on page 468)

Famous Ships

1. In Herman Melville's book *Moby-Dick*, what is the name of Captain Ahab's ship?

2. What event made the HMS *Bounty* famous in the history of seafaring?

3. Which side of a boat is the starboard?

4. What was the name of the ship that first took British explorer Ernest Shackleton to the Antarctic?

5. Who sailed the ship known as the *Santa Maria*?

6. Name the ship that took the Pilgrim Fathers to America in 1620.

7. Which US ship is nicknamed "Old Ironsides"?

8. What is the name of the record-breaking tea clipper now preserved at Greenwich in London?

9. What was the name of the famous German battleship that was sunk in 1941?

10. What was the name of the world's first battle cruiser?

11. Who captained the *Jolly Roger*?

12. The world's first nuclear-powered submarine was called the USS *Nautilus*. True or False?

13. In Greek mythology, what was the name of Jason's ship?

14. Who was the captain of the RMS *Titanic*?

15. Who sailed the HMS *Endeavour* on his first voyage of exploration?

16. Why is the US battleship *Missouri* particularly remembered?

17. The back of a ship is called the bow. True or False?

18. Which famous explorer was the captain of the *Golden Hind*?

19. What was the name of the ship that rescued the survivors of the RMS *Titanic*?

20. What type of ship was the *Exxon Valdez*?

21. What was the name of Fulton's pioneer submersible of 1801?

22. The *Kon-Tiki* was sailed by which famous explorer?

23. Which organization is known for its ship called *Rainbow Warrior*?

24. Which ship is the subject of a famous painting by J. M. W. Turner?

25. Which ship was found sailing but deserted in the Atlantic Ocean in 1872?

Olympic Sports from the Past

1. What was the ancient Olympic sport of pankration?

2. Which track-and-field athletics event comprises a hop, a stride, and a jump?

3. What did athletes have to carry in each hand during the ancient Olympic event of jumping?

4. The ancient Olympic Games did not feature a marathon. When did the event become a part of the modern Olympics?

5. Cricket was only played once as an Olympic sport—in 1900, between England and France. Which team won?

6. Chariot races were included in the ancient Olympics. True or False?

7. *Jeu de paume* (real tennis) appeared twice as a modern Olympic demonstration sport. How many times was it played as a competitive Olympic event?

8. Golf appeared as an Olympic event during the 2016 Games. When was it previously played at the Olympics?

9. In which year did rackets make its first and last appearance as an Olympic event?

10. The discus was originally made of stone and later of iron, lead, or bronze. True or False?

11. Polo was played at six consecutive modern Olympic Games. In which year did it first appear on the program?

12. An ancient Olympic race was for chariots pulled by mules. True or False?

13. What is the oldest Olympic sport?

14. In whose honor were the ancient Olympic Games held?

15. After appearing as a competitive sport at the 1904 and 1908 Olympics, when was lacrosse once again played at the Olympics, this time as a demonstration sport?

16. In which year did the first separate Winter Games take place?

17. In 1900, which two sports included women competitors for the first time at the Olympic Games?

18. Which events did Jim Thorpe win at the 1912 Games, only to lose his medals on the grounds of ineligibility?

19. In ancient Greece, what kind of Olympic sport was pálē?

20. Rugby was played at four modern Olympic Games before being dropped. In what form did the game return in 2016?

(Answers on page 469)   **29**

Gunmen of the Old West

1. Who manufactured the single-action .44 and .45 revolvers favored by most Wild West gunmen?

2. Which gunman shot between 14 and 50 men and boasted he'd "shoot anyone for a fee"?

3. Bill Dalton and Bull Doolin led which 1890s outlaw gang?

4. What was the alternative occupation of Wild West gunman Doc Holliday?

5. What was Billy the Kid's real name?

6. Which gunman of the Old West shot a man for "snoring too loud"?

7. Which Wild West gunman had blond curly hair, spoke in a high-pitched voice, and wore frilly shirts?

8. Where did feuding gunmen Frank Loving and Levi Richardson have a famous shoot-out?

9. Which Earp was the town marshal of Tombstone at the time of the O. K. Corral shoot-out: Wyatt, Virgil, Morgan?

10. Robert Leroy Parker and Henry Longabaugh were better known as… ?

11. What name was given to the burial grounds of gunfighters?

12. What did Wild West gunmen commonly call their single-action revolvers?

13. Which gun is often known as "The gun that won the West"?

14. For which gunfight is Tombstone, Arizona, best known?

15. Phoebe Annie Moses is better known as… ?

16. Which Wild West gunman was easily identified by his green-banded sombrero?

17. Who committed the first bank robbery in the US?

18. Which sheriff shot and killed Billy the Kid in 1881?

19. How did Buffalo Bill get his nickname?

20. With which gang is "bandit queen" Belle Starr most associated?

21. In Dodge City, who had a showdown with Wyatt Earp?

22. Which gunfighter's death in 1882 looked like suicide?

23. By which name is Martha Jane Cannaray best known?

24. Who killed Jesse James?

25. How old was Billy the Kid when he killed his first man?

     (Answers on page 469)

Roman Gladiators

1. Which Roman emperor would dress as Hercules and fight in the Colosseum?

2. Early gladiator fights performed at Roman funerals were called… ?

3. Which type of gladiator would hunt down wild animals in the arena?

4. Criminals without gladiatorial training who fought blindfolded on horseback were called… ?

5. What kind of gladiator was a rudiarius?

6. This gladiator would finish off mortally wounded gladiators in the arena. As whom was he dressed up?

7. During a day at the Colosseum, when would the gladiator fights begin?

8. What lunchtime entertainment would precede the gladiator fights at the Colosseum?

9. For how many days in a row did Emperor Trajan hold gladiatorial games after conquering Dacia?

10. How many gladiators died in the games held by Emperor Trajan after his conquest of Dacia?

11. What did the crowd chant if they wanted a gladiator to be granted a reprieve after fighting?

12. How long was the average gladiator fight thought to have lasted?

13. There was no such thing as a female gladiator. True or False?

14. How many trapdoors were there in the Colosseum floor to bring up animals, gladiators, and pieces of scenery?

15. What would take place in front of the crowd before the gladiators of the Colosseum fought?

16. Where was the homeland of the slave gladiator Spartacus?

17. Which type of gladiator would a secutor traditionally fight?

18. What was a Roman gladiator school called?

19. Senator Titus Statilius Taurus erected the first stone amphitheater for gladiator fights in Rome. True or False?

20. Which Roman emperor was said to like watching the expressions of the gladiators as they died?

21. Some gladiators fought from chariots. True or False?

22. How did Equites fight in gladiatorial contests?

23. Emperor Septimius Severus banned women from gladiatorial contests in 200 CE. True or False?

24. What food did gladiators eat?

25. What kind of swords did trainees use?

(Answers on page 469)   **31**

Medieval Tournaments

1. Early medieval tournaments were bloody free-for-all brawls known as… ?

2. Which medieval tournament regular was once called "the greatest knight who ever lived"?

3. What was the "recess" at a medieval tournament?

4. At a medieval tournament, what was a *joust à l'outrance*?

5. The couched lance was new in which century: 10th, 11th, 12th?

6. What was the revolving target used by knights to practice for medieval tournaments?

7. Tournaments were held regularly in Greece. True or False?

8. Which pope issued an edict in 1130 that any knight killed at a tournament would be denied his funeral rights?

9. Which English county was not authorized by King Richard I to hold a medieval tournament under royal license?

10. Which French poet wrote about chivalric themes and so influenced medieval tournaments?

11. In later medieval tournaments, why were coronels fitted to lances?

12. In the 14th century, knights who had taken part in what could not participate in tournaments?

13. From the 14th century, for a knight to participate, how many generations did he have to prove that his family had been fighting in tournaments?

14. In France, violent tournaments were gradually replaced by a choreographed "carousel." True or False?

15. On what occasion would a medieval tournament often be held?

16. Which king issued a charter to stop knights from misbehaving on their way to tournaments?

17. In France, women sometimes fought in their own tournaments. True or False?

18. What did melee combatants try to do?

19. In which year did Pope John XXII lift the papal ban on medieval tournaments?

20. What weapons were used at a *joust à plaisance*, that is, "for pleasure"?

21. In jousting, what was the fence that separated the knights called?

22. What was an ecranche?

23. How long was a typical lance?

24. Tournaments were part of competitions called "hastiludes." True or False?

25. Which king was killed in a jousting competition?

Sea Battles

1. Why were fire arrows dangerous in the Age of Sail?

2. What was the name given to Venetian ships that used sails and oars but were floating gun platforms?

3. Who invented the self-propelled torpedo?

4. In the Age of Sail, what was the definition of a battleship?

5. What missiles from French suppliers did the Argentines use against British ships in 1982?

6. What much-feared weapon of war, deadly to ships, was reputedly invented by an engineer named Callanicus in Constantinople in 670 CE?

7. What unusual tactics did Nelson employ at the Battle of Trafalgar?

8. What was the Fairey Swordfish?

9. What name is given to the rear mast of a galleon?

10. How many guns did a "Third Rate" man-of-war have in the 18th-century British navy?

11. Why was a trireme, used by ancient Romans and Greeks among others, so called?

12. What was significant about the speedy vessel demonstrated to the British navy by Charles Parsons in 1897?

13. What name was given to disguised armed ships that were used by the British against German U-boats in World War I?

14. What were the largest naval guns in use in the 20th century?

15. What name was given to groups of attacking U-boats in World War II?

16. What was the name "destroyer" for a type of ship short for?

17. What is the range of a Trident ballistic missile fired from a submarine: 5,000 miles, 7,000 miles, 10,000 miles?

18. What powered U-boats when moving under water during World War II?

19. What did the phrase "holding the weather gage" mean in the Age of Sail?

20. What name was given to the simultaneous firing of all the cannons on one side of a man-of-war?

Commanders

1. Who led the Prussian forces to victory in the Franco-Prussian War in 1870–1871?

2. Which Egyptian pharaoh defeated the Hittites in the Battle of Kadesh?

3. Which Carthaginian general won the battle of Cannae and is known for taking elephants across the Alps?

4. Which Roman general crushed the slave revolt led by Spartacus but was later killed at the Battle of Carrhae?

5. Who commanded the US forces in Vietnam from 1964 to 1968?

6. What two major injuries did Admiral Nelson receive during his career?

7. Which Chinese emperor, notably successful as a war leader, was buried with a terra-cotta army in his mausoleum?

8. Who was the Byzantine general who recaptured Italy from the Ostrogoths and protected Constantinople from the Huns?

9. Who was the 9th-century-CE Frankish king who established an empire that stretched from northern Europe to Italy and Spain?

10. Which Norman duke's victory over Harold II in Sussex won him the crown of England?

11. Which king of England was known as "Richard the Lionheart" because of his leadership during the Third Crusade?

12. Who was the British hero of Atbara, Omdurman, and Paardeberg whose image appeared on recruitment posters in 1914?

13. Who was the 13th-century-CE Mongol khan who conquered an area from China to the Black Sea?

14. Which English king subdued Wales and Scotland and defeated the French at the Battle of Crécy?

15. Sir John Jellicoe commanded the British fleet at the Battle of Jutland. True or False?

16. Who was responsible for the planning and organization of the New Model Army during the English Civil War?

17. Which commander led his troops to victory at the Battle of Blenheim in 1704?

18. Which British military commander was responsible for victories at Arcot and Plassey?

19. Which German general commanded the Western Front armies on D-Day in 1944?

20. Who commanded the Confederate Army in the American Civil War?

Scottish History

1. Which historic declaration was signed in 1320?

2. Who led the Scottish Army at the Battle of Bannockburn in 1314?

3. What was King James II of Scotland known as?

4. What is the national flower of Scotland?

5. Rob Roy is sometimes known as the Scottish Robin Hood. True or False?

6. Macbeth wasn't actually a real Scottish king. True or False?

7. The "Auld Alliance" was between which two nations?

8. When was Scotland formally united with England to form Great Britain?

9. Which Scottish railway station is named after a book by Sir Walter Scott?

10. Who led the Jacobite Uprising in 1745?

11. Victims of the Massacre of Glencoe belonged to which Scottish clan?

12. Mary, Queen of Scots, was executed after being imprisoned. Where did she die?

13. Which battle was led and won by William Wallace in 1297?

14. The Battle of Flodden Field saw the defeat and killing of which monarch?

15. Who was Robert Burns?

16. What does the term "Picts" mean?

17. Who were Burke and Hare in Edinburgh in the early 19th century?

18. Who was the first husband of Mary, Queen of Scots?

19. What does "Holyrood" mean?

20. When is "Burns Night" or "Burns Supper" celebrated?

21. Who was known as "the Old Pretender"?

22. What were the Scots banned from wearing after the Battle of Culloden?

23. Who built Edinburgh Castle?

24. Why is Aberdeen known as the Granite City?

25. What color is the flag of St. Andrew, the patron saint of Scotland?

HISTORY

The Suffragist Movement

1. Which country was the first to give women the right to vote?

2. In what year were they given this right?

3. In what year were English women over 30 given the right to vote?

4. Women in the US were allowed to vote in presidential elections from… ?

5. What was the name of the famous suffragist who died by throwing herself under the king's horse in 1913?

6. Sylvia and Christabel were daughters of which famous British suffragist?

7. What does the word "suffrage" mean?

8. A slogan on a suffragist women's newspaper read: "Men, their rights, and nothing more; women, their rights, and nothing less." True or False?

9. What conflict showed that women were more than capable of performing in traditional male roles?

10. Militant suffragists from which country inspired suffragists in the US?

11. Which was the last European country to grant women the right to vote?

12. In which year were they given the right to vote?

13. Which English newspaper coined the term "suffragette"?

14. When did Saudi women get the right to vote?

15. The US National Woman's Party is still fighting for equal rights for women. True or False?

16. Many English suffragists performed what form of protest in prison?

17. As a result of their protest in prison, many English suffragists were force-fed through tubes stuck down their throats. True or False?

18. What did the Cat and Mouse Act of 1913 allow?

19. Some men argued that women should not have the right to vote because they were too emotional and could not think as logically as men. True or False?

20. In which year was the right to vote extended to all UK women over the age of 21?

　　　(Answers on page 470)

Architecture through the Ages

1. What is the name for the area in the dome of St. Paul's Cathedral, 257 steps above the main floor?

2. Which capital city has a name meaning "Place of the Gods" and is the ancestral home of the Dalai Lama?

3. One of the earliest Christian settlements is at Qadisha. In which country is Qadisha?

4. Which city developed on the site of the Aztec capital of Tenochtitlán?

5. In which country is the ancient ruined city of Petra, the "rose-red city half as old as time"?

6. The Golden Temple at Amritsar in India is a sacred shrine associated with which religion?

7. Which "lost city" was rediscovered by the American Hiram Bingham in 1911?

8. Which New York City skyscraper is famous for its art deco style?

9. This bridge is nicknamed "the Coat Hanger" due to its arched design.

10. The Grand Mosque at Djenné in Mali is the largest building in the world made of which material?

11. Which building was erected to commemorate the Great Fire of London?

12. Which art gallery in Paris was designed by the architect Richard Rogers and has all the pipes on the outside of the building?

13. What is the name of the bridge connecting the Petronas Towers in Kuala Lumpur?

14. After which saint is the cathedral in Moscow's Red Square named?

15. One of the largest buildings in the US is the VAB, or Vehicle Assembly Building, operated by which organization?

16. Which famous structure, built in 1889, was originally only supposed to stand for 20 years?

17. What was the original purpose of the Taj Mahal when it was built?

18. The Royal Albert Hall in London is a UNESCO World Heritage Site. True or False?

19. With which Spanish city is Antoni Gaudí associated?

20. The Great Pyramid holds the burial chamber for which pharaoh, also known as Khufu?

21. Which skyscraper, then the world's tallest, was climbed by King Kong?

22. In what architectural style was the Temple of Athena constructed?

23. What materials are most of the buildings in Timbuktu made of?

24. What types of rock did the Incas use to build their cities?

25. About 95 percent of the materials used to build the Shard in London are recycled. True or False?

(Answers on page 470)   **37**

HISTORY

Ancient Civilizations

1. Who was the first emperor of Rome?

2. What is the Great Sphinx of Giza?

3. Who was the god of the sea in ancient Greece?

4. What were aqueducts used for?

5. Who was the god of the sun in ancient Egypt?

6. What type of gladiator fought with a net and a trident?

7. Which Greek physician devised the "four humors" theory in medicine?

8. Which king built the Hanging Gardens of Babylon?

9. From which ancient civilization did Hippocrates come?

10. What was the Roman name for the English town of Bath?

11. What was papyrus used to make in ancient Egypt?

12. What was a "ziggurat" in Babylon?

13. What was the name of the famous slave who led a revolt against Rome?

14. What is considered to be the "cradle" of Chinese civilization?

15. Where is the Valley of the Kings?

16. Which army used the "testudo" as a military ploy?

17. Which ancient Greek philosopher died after drinking hemlock?

18. The famous "300 Spartans" fought at which battle?

19. Which Roman emperor ordered the invasion of Britain in 43 CE?

20. From which ancient civilization did the word "theater" originate?

21. Which sport was the most popular in the Mayan civilization?

22. What is the Kingdom of Benin most famous for?

23. Ancient Egyptian queen Hatshepsut is shown on official art wearing a beard. True or False?

24. Why did the ancient Romans sometimes flood the Colosseum or the Circus Maximus?

25. What medical technique did the Incas use to relieve pressure in the head and also to release demons?

Royals and Others

1. Which queen of England allegedly had six fingers on her right hand?

2. Pope John Paul II was Polish. Who, more than 400 years earlier, had been the previous non-Italian pontiff?

3. Which former ruler of England ended his days wandering around Europe under various aliases?

4. Which queen was the mother of both King John and King Richard I?

5. Who, in 1301, became the first English prince of Wales?

6. Who was the father of James I of England?

7. In 1975, Juan Carlos I became the king of Spain after a 44-year interregnum. Who preceded him on the throne?

8. After he was deposed, the last king of Portugal lived out his days in exile in England. Who was he?

9. Who became the king of England when he was only nine months old?

10. Who became the queen of France in 1774 and lost her head on the guillotine?

11. This cricket player was once offered the throne of Albania. Who was he?

12. Balmoral Castle is Queen Elizabeth's official residence in Scotland. True or False?

13. Prince Philip, duke of Edinburgh, was born on which Greek island?

14. Which Middle Eastern country's monarchy was set up in 1921?

15. What family name is shared by the rulers of Monaco and a famous clown?

16. King William II is the only king of England who never married. True or False?

17. Who, in 2001, became the first ex-monarch to be democratically elected as the prime minister?

18. Which country's royal house is called Orange?

19. Which king was known as the "Prince of Whales" because of his 54-inch (137-cm) waistline?

20. Founded, according to tradition, in 660 BCE, which is the world's oldest continuous hereditary monarchy?

History Year by Year

1. In which year did the Vikings capture the city of York in England?

2. In which year were the Knights Templar founded in Jerusalem?

3. In which year was the Magna Carta signed, following a brief civil war in England?

4. In which year did Benito Mussolini come into power in Italy?

5. In which year did King Henry IV of England die?

6. In which year did Nicolaus Copernicus suggest that Earth orbits the sun and not vice versa?

7. In which year was Joan of Arc burned as a witch?

8. In which year was the English colony of Connecticut established in North America?

9. In which year did the English playwright William Shakespeare die?

10. In which year did the Salem witch trials begin in New England?

11. In which year was St. Paul's Cathedral in London completed?

12. In which year was a vaccine for smallpox developed?

13. In which year did Marie Antoinette marry Louis XVI in France?

14. In which year was the New York Stock Exchange founded?

15. In which year was the Declaration of Independence signed in the British American colonies?

16. In which year were the Corn Laws abolished in Britain?

17. In which year was the attack on Fort Sumter that started the American Civil War?

18. In which year was the Night of the Long Knives in Germany?

19. In which year was the Communist Long March undertaken in China?

20. In which year was the Bloody Sunday Massacre in the Winter Palace in St. Petersburg?

21. In which year was there a general strike in England?

22. In which year was the Wall Street crash?

23. In which year was the first telephone call made?

24. In which year did Captain Matthew Webb become the first person to swim the English Channel?

25. When did the Great Plague of London start?

            (Answers on page 470)

Gladiators

1. On a daylong bill of bloodshed in the Arena, when were the gladiator fights held?

2. What was lunchtime reserved for?

3. Which type of gladiator would have carried a heavy net and a trident?

4. What event were the first gladiator fights associated with?

5. What were *munera* in ancient Rome?

6. Who first paid for public gladiator fights to bolster support among the people of Rome?

7. Who were the *bestiarii*?

8. Which type of gladiator wore an oval helmet, carried a large, curved rectangular shield and a short sword, had his right arm wrapped in leather or metal, and wore armor to protect his lower left leg?

9. What did Emperor Augustus do to make sure no gladiatorial games surpassed his own?

10. How long did the games last during the reign of Augustus?

11. What took place during the morning's events?

12. Who once remarked that he wished "the Roman people had but one neck"?

13. What type of gladiator was a Thracian?

14. Which emperor often walked the streets of Rome with an entourage of gladiators to help him win the fights he picked?

15. Which emperor fought in the arena as a gladiator?

16. The famous gladiator Flamma won four prized yet unusual trophies. What were they?

17. Which emperor is thought to have enjoyed watching the expressions of gladiators as they died?

18. Why did the Colosseum have a sand floor?

19. In which year were the first gladiator games held?

20. There was no such thing as a female gladiator. True or False?

Travel in Days Gone By

1. Which city did Marco Polo depart from when he began his travels to Asia?

2. The Silk Road takes its name from the production of the fabric in which modern-day country?

3. When did Thomas Cook organize his first travel excursion?

4. How many days would a stagecoach take to travel from Edinburgh to London in 1754 during a dry summer month?

5. Which kingdom did Portuguese explorer Ferdinand Magellan serve?

6. The first steam railway to carry passengers (in 1830) linked Liverpool to which destination?

7. The Persian Royal Road connected modern-day Iran to which other country?

8. The Way of St. James was a pilgrimage to a city in which Spanish region?

9. What was the name given to the journey that well-to-do young European men took between the 17th and w19th centuries?

10. On which ship did Columbus sail during his 1492 voyage to the Americas?

11. Who wrote the 18th-century *A Tour through the Whole Island of Great Britain*?

12. A barouche was a type of horse-drawn carriage. True or False?

13. How many men could sail on a Viking longship?

14. The Spice Islands were part of which modern-day country?

15. How far east did Alexander the Great travel to extend his empire?

16. In which year was the last recorded robbery by a horse-riding highwayman in England?

17. According to Julius Caesar, the most civilized ancient Britons lived in which modern-day county?

18. When did Lord Byron swim across the Dardanelles?

19. Which British railway did Isambard Kingdom Brunel design?

20. In the 18th century, people in British cities could be carried in what conveyance suspended on two poles?

The Aztecs

1. What modern-day country was home to the Aztecs?

2. What did the sun transform into at night, according to Aztec belief?

3. What did the Aztecs ban during sowing, harvesting, and at night?

4. What did Aztecs call gold?

5. The conquistadors came from which European country?

6. The Aztecs developed the wheel for use as a toy. True or False?

7. What was the Aztec city Tenochtitlán built on?

8. The name of the goddess "Coatlicue" translates as what?

9. What stone did the Aztecs use to make knives, spears, and arrowheads?

10. Tlaloc was the Aztec god of rain. True or False?

11. What did the Aztecs use for currency?

12. Tenochtitlán had as many as 300,000 citizens. True or False?

13. Who led the conquistadors?

14. The Aztecs thought Cortés was a god called "Quetzalcoatl." True or False?

15. Name the Aztec leader defeated by Cortés.

16. Up to what percentage of the Aztecs are believed to have succumbed to smallpox?

17. Aztec women who died in childbirth were accorded the same respect as those who died in battle. True or False?

18. What did the Aztecs use chinampas for?

19. How did Aztec couriers travel to relay messages?

20. Aztec society had collapsed by the middle of which century?

21. What was the name of the last Aztec emperor?

22. How many days are there in an Aztec month?

23. The Aztecs drank hot chocolate. True or False?

24. Which animal did Aztec warriors dress up as?

25. What did the chief priest of the Aztec god Xipe Totec wear?

(Answers on page 471)

Cathedrals and Churches

1. What is the name of the Spanish church on which construction began in 1882?

2. Who was the main architect of Barcelona's Sagrada Família?

3. What kind of mine is the Cathedral of Zipaquirá in Colombia built inside?

4. What is "the Felsenkirche" church in Germany otherwise known as?

5. What is Lalibela in Ethiopia famous for?

6. In which Parisian cathedral did Quasimodo ring his bell?

7. In which English cathedral was Thomas Becket murdered, probably as the result of a misunderstanding?

8. What is the name of the onion-domed cathedral that stands at one end of Moscow's Red Square?

9. Which cathedral in the English Midlands was famously bombed during World War II?

10. Which church in Venice contains the buried remains of its namesake?

11. What church lies at the heart of the Vatican in Rome?

12. Where were French kings traditionally crowned?

13. Which Italian cathedral's east doors are called "the Gates of Paradise"?

14. Which artist is responsible for the east doors of the baptistery in Florence?

15. Borgund Stave Church was built in the 12th century. In which country does it stand?

16. Which London cathedral was redesigned by Christopher Wren following the Great Fire of London?

17. St. Paul's received only minor damage during the bombing of London in World War II. True or False?

18. The Mezquita of Córdoba in Spain went from being a church, to a mosque, and back to being a church again. True or False?

19. Which church is the long-established location for the crowning of English kings and queens?

20. Christian churches and cathedrals are traditionally designed in what shape?

The American Civil War

1. Between which years was the American Civil War fought?

2. How many men fought in the war?

3. Three hundred women dressed up as men so they could join the fighting. True or False?

4. How many boys under the age of 14 fought for the Union?

5. The highest number of casualties during one battle was nearly 24,000. What was the battle?

6. What was the first ironclad warship to engage in the war?

7. The appearance of ironclad warships immediately made all existing wooden warships more useful. True or False?

8. In which year did Congress issue the first banknotes, called "Greenbacks"?

9. Which Confederate private survived capture and later undertook a search for Dr. Livingstone?

10. What did a bounty paid to new enlistees create large numbers of?

11. Approximately how many American Indians fought for the Union?

12. Name the woman who nursed wounded soldiers and founded the American Red Cross.

13. Twice as many soldiers died from disease than from battle injuries. True or False?

14. Approximately how many African American men enlisted in the Union Army?

15. In which year did the motto "In God We Trust" first appear on an American coin?

16. How many times a minute could an American Civil War musket be loaded and fired?

17. The first naval hospital ship was the *Red Rover*. True or False?

18. More than 80 percent of injuries sustained by soldiers were the a result of artillery fire. True or False?

19. About what percentage of soldiers wounded in the war ended up dying?

20. The number of Confederate generals born in the North was greater than the number of Union generals born in the South. True or False?

21. What is the period after the Civil War had ended called?

22. Which city in Virginia was the Confederate capital?

23. Who was the president of the Confederate States of America?

24. How many slave states remained part of the Union during the Civil War?

25. Which state did not have a battle fought in it during the Civil War?

HISTORY

Ancient Job Titles

1. What kind of metal was a "whitesmith" involved with?

2. What was an ancient "all spice"?

3. A goldsmith used to be known as a what?

4. An itinerant peddler who took his goods from town to town was called a what?

5. A "yeoman" referred to a farmer who owned his own land. True or False?

6. Originally from Córdoba in Spain, what type of leather worker was a "cordwainer"?

7. At one time, to seek medical help in Europe, you would have visited an "archiator." True or False?

8. "Tipstaff" referred to what?

9. A baker was sometimes known as a baxter. True or False?

10. What did a "fletcher" make?

11. A "pettifogger" refers to a what?

12. What would you have seen a "whitewing" doing in medieval times?

13. What did a "jagger" peddle?

14. What was an ironworker known as in the Middle Ages?

15. In England in the 1300s, who was hired to wash clothes?

16. One who used to put the tap in an ale cask was known as a what?

17. A bricklayer who specialized in making and repairing sewers was called a "sewer rat." True or False?

18. A "charwoman" did what job?

19. A "flauner" used to make what?

20. A "snobscat" was a shoe repairer. True or False?

The Conquest of the Ocean

1. Spanish Muslims called the Nordic Vikings *al-Madjus* because they were such capable sailors. What does this translate to?

2. The island of Greenland was discovered by Eric the Red. Why did he give it this name?

3. Admiral Lord Nelson died in 1805 during the Battle of Trafalgar. How was his body preserved so he could have a hero's funeral upon return to England?

4. Arab ships called dhows were made from flexible, light woods. How were these planks assembled?

5. Ancient Polynesian seafarers invented the catamaran and outrigger that are still used in sailing today. True or False?

6. Who led the first voyage to successfully circumnavigate the globe?

7. What is scurvy, a common disease on long sea journeys, caused by?

8. Where could baleen plates be found?

9. The Great Tea Race from China to England was won by the *Ariel* in 1866. It set a new record for the 15,000-miles (24,000-km) journey. How many days did it take?

10. What were "black ships"?

11. What was a "backstaff": a sailor's weapon, a grappling iron, a stern mast, a navigation aid?

12. What does the name of the famous clipper ship *Cutty Sark* mean?

13. Which European explorer rounded the Cape of Good Hope in 1497 and sailed on to land in India?

14. The astrolabe was invented by the ancient Greeks and refined by Arab sailors. What is it used for?

15. A Greek galley known as a "penteconter" required how many oarsmen?

16. The submarine *Fenian Ram* was first tested in 1881 in New York Harbor and sank 12 ft (3.6 m) before resurfacing. Who was the designer?

17. In the struggle for American independence, John Paul Jones set out to raid the British port of Whitehaven. Why did this attempt fail?

18. The *Susan Constant*, the *Godspeed,* and the *Discovery* sailed to America in the early 17th century, resulting in the founding of Jamestown, Virginia. True or False?

19. Who were privateers?

20. What nationality was the navigator Bartolomeu Diaz?

(Answers on page 471)

Famous Firsts

1. Who was Britain's first prime minister?

2. Who is usually accepted as "the father of History"?

3. Who invented the first working steam engine?

4. Who promised the American people a New Deal in the 1930s?

5. Which US president ordered the use of the atomic bomb?

6. Who is popularly accepted as having invented the Internet?

7. From which country did Christopher Columbus set sail in 1492 on the voyage during which he discovered the West Indies?

8. Who was the first black president of the United States?

9. Whose murder started World War I in 1914?

10. Who, in 1917, promised the Russian people "peace, bread, and land"?

11. Who led the Chinese Communist Revolution?

12. Which Mormon leader led the Latter-day Saints to the Great Salt Lake?

13. Who invented the electric battery in 1799?

14. Who invented the flush toilet?

15. Who invented and built the world's first successful airplane?

16. Which pope gave his name to a calendar?

17. The moon is Earth's only natural satellite: on what date did humans first walk on its surface?

18. Who founded the Red Cross?

19. Who performed the first human heart transplant?

20. Who invented a system of reading and writing for use by the blind?

21. Who founded the Boy Scout movement?

22. The lighting rod was invented by which American Founding Father?

23. Who made the first telephone call?

24. Who was the first man to orbit Earth in space?

25. Who invented the automobile in 1886?

(Answers on page 471)

Mapping History

1. How did the ancient Phoenicians navigate the oceans?

2. Which ancient Greek's map of Europe, the Mediterranean, and North Africa was in use until the end of the Middle Ages?

3. Camels enabled the Arabs to develop a trade in incense and spices from the 12th century CE. What was their trade route called?

4. In 600 BCE, Herodotus claimed that European traders had circumnavigated Africa. Who were they?

5. Which ocean was explored and settled by Polynesian navigators from around 1000 BCE?

6. Who set up a naval school at Sagres in 1416 to teach Portuguese sailors?

7. Which coast of Africa was first mapped after early Portuguese voyages of discovery?

8. Which innovation in the rigging of a sailing ship helped European sailors to make better use of the wind?

9. With what aspect of world discovery is Gerardus Mercator associated?

10. Which two European nations dominated the early voyages of discovery?

11. Which navigation aid used from the 18th century measures the angle between a heavenly body and the horizon?

12. Whose voyage to the Spice Islands was frustrated by finding the Americas in 1492?

13. European governments were anxious to find the Northwest Passage, in order to have a what?

14. Which invention of 1764 allowed sailors to accurately determine maritime longitude?

15. Who was the first person to map parts of New Holland, Tasmania, and New Zealand in the 17th century?

16. What was Captain Cook's mission on his second voyage?

17. Who led the first major European expedition into the Niger Valley in 1805?

18. Who were the first cartographers to cross the United States from east to west in 1805?

19. Which 19th-century explorer in central Africa was a Christian missionary and opponent of slavery?

20. Who led the first expedition to reach the South Pole in December 1911?

(Answers on page 472)

HISTORY

History of Britain and Ireland

1. When was the last person beheaded in Britain?

2. Britain went to war with Spain in 1739. What is the war known as?

3. Where did the Peterloo Massacre of 1819 take place: Manchester, Dublin, or Leeds?

4. Who went to quell rebellion in Ireland in 1649?

5. The biggest loss of life in a single day on English soil was 20,000 men. What was the name of the battle?

6. Which king abdicated the throne after reigning for only 327 days?

7. Which war did Britain join in 1854, in alliance with its old enemy France?

8. Who became a queen in 1542, when only six days old?

9. In which year did the Act of Union, which joined Britain and Ireland, come into effect?

10. London stepped up to host the Olympic Games in 1906 after Rome had to pull out. What made Rome pull out?

11. How long did the Republic of Connaught last in Ireland?

12. At which battle in Ireland was the army of James II defeated in 1690?

13. Who was the youngest person to become the UK prime minister in the 20th century?

14. Which famous battle is depicted on the Bayeux Tapestry?

15. Who designed the Clifton Suspension Bridge in Bristol?

16. In what year was the Welsh Assembly formed?

17. Oliver Cromwell is the only person other than a reigning monarch to have appeared on the obverse side of a British coin. True or False?

18. Which prime minister introduced income tax to Britain in 1799?

19. The period from the outbreak of World War II to the spring of 1940 was called what?

20. Which politician led the campaign in Britain to abolish the slave trade?

21. In which decade of the 19th century did the potato famine spread in Ireland?

22. After partition, how many counties formed Northern Ireland?

23. The uprising in Ireland in 1916 was named after which religious festival?

24. Who was the first queen of England to rule in her own right?

25. Which former archbishop of Canterbury was burned at the stake in 1556?

Ancient Rome

1. When was the city of Rome founded?

2. What are the names of the two brothers who founded Rome?

3. What neighboring earlier culture influenced Roman development?

4. What form of clothing was worn only by male Roman citizens?

5. Romans added volcanic ash to concrete, thus allowing it to do what?

6. What was the name of the group of people who governed the republic?

7. Early Rome was ruled by kings. The last king, Tarquin the Proud, was banished in 509 BCE. True or False?

8. Which organization had ten cohorts?

9. The Romans wore amber jewelry as a charm to prevent what?

10. How many people could sit in the Colosseum?

11. Who did the Romans defeat in the Punic Wars?

12. How many Roman legionaries were commanded by a centurion?

13. Septimus Severus was declared emperor in 195 BCE. "Severus" is Latin for what?

14. What was the name of the simple straight tunics often worn by women in ancient Rome?

15. What did the Roman Army build that helped them to control a huge empire?

16. How many vestal virgins served at any one time?

17. The Romans, above all, wanted to be "civitas." What did this mean?

18. Freed Roman slaves could vote. True or False?

19. Which Roman towns were destroyed by the eruption of Mount Vesuvius in August 79 BCE?

20. What did Romans use to heat large villas and public baths?

21. In which year did the Western Roman Empire come to an end?

22. Which leader became the dictator of Rome and put an end to the Roman Republic?

23. Which religious officials interpreted signs purporting to show the will of the gods?

24. Which monument in Rome shows the army on campaign and bears the name of an emperor?

25. What did the Eastern Roman Empire become known as?

CHAPTER 2

SCIENCE & TECHNOLOGY

Space, the human body, inventions, psychology, and engineering—there is something to test all science sleuths in these fact-filled quizzes. From ancient science to modern technology, test your science know-how.

Head to Toe

1. During the growth phase, hairs grow by how much each month?

2. Which part of the eye changes size to control light going into the eye?

3. What is the main organ of taste?

4. Where is gray matter found?

5. What bone is sometimes called "the funny bone"?

6. Which type of tissue can contract suddenly?

7. Where is bile produced?

8. The column of bones running from the neck to the pelvis is called what?

9. What type of joint does a hip have?

10. How many chambers are there in the heart?

11. The largest blood vessel in the body is the superior vena cava. True or False?

12. Which organ removes waste chemicals and water from the blood?

13. An 8-week-old human fetus is about the size of a: peanut, grape, orange?

14. Cells in the human body get their chemical energy from tiny powerhouses called what?

15. Which part or parts of the body consist largely of dead cells?

16. The eardrum is part of the nervous system. True or False?

17. In which part of the body are the hamstring muscles found?

18. The term "vaccine" comes from the Greek word for cow. True or False?

19. Where is the femur, the body's longest bone?

20. The medical term for the voicebox is the what?

21. Where are the small bones called "phalanges" found?

22. Where are the sclera?

23. Where in the body are the alveoli?

24. What does the Ishihara test indicate?

25. Which part of the body has four parts: ascending, descending, transverse, and sigmoid?

SCIENCE & TECHNOLOGY

Electrical Inventions

1. In electronics, what does "DC" stand for?

2. Electricity can be used to make things magnetic. What is the name given to something that uses electricity to make it magnetic?

3. Which renewable energy source makes hydroelectric power?

4. When did the first electric refrigerators begin to appear?

5. On a battery, what symbol marks the positive electrode or cathode?

6. Electric food mixers for homes were first available in 1910 but had been invented 4 years earlier for use in which type of shop?

7. In which year was the first electric lie detector used: 1900, 1921, 1946?

8. The first electronic computers were designed for what wartime purpose?

9. The discovery of what electrical component in 1947 signaled the Second Industrial Revolution and the development of computers?

10. When were the first microwave ovens patented?

11. Which 19th-century invention allowed messages to be sent as pulses of electric current along wires?

12. What kind of electricity can make your hair stand up?

13. The term "kWh" often appears on electricity bills. What does it stand for?

14. With what metal are some cars electroplated to protect them from rust?

15. What is measured in amps?

16. When was the first electric toothbrush made?

17. Why are plugs made of plastic?

18. An electrocardiogram (ECG) measures electric current in the body. What organ is making the electrical signals detected by the ECG?

19. Copper is a poor conductor of electricity. True or False?

20. What name is given to an unbroken loop through which electricity can flow?

(Answers on page 472)

SCIENCE & TECHNOLOGY

Energy Sources

1. The primary source of Earth's energy and all the energy in the solar system is what?

2. What is the typical form of renewable electricity generation used on spacecraft?

3. What name describes oil, natural gas, and coal as energy sources?

4. What does a solar furnace use to focus the sun's rays and thereby provide energy?

5. The burning of fossil fuels causes air pollution by releasing which gas?

6. Renewable resources are going to run out within the next 100 years. True or False?

7. What, besides tankers, is the main method for transporting natural gas?

8. Can crops like sugar cane and maize be used to generate energy?

9. Which sea provided Britain with much of its energy in the last decades of the 20th century?

10. Waste from nuclear power plants is difficult to dispose of. Why?

11. Tidal power systems are examples of renewable energy sourcing. True or False?

12. What name is given to the process of injecting liquid at high pressure into subterranean rocks o extract oil?

13. The burning of oil and natural gas can cause acid rain by releasing what?

14. Which European country has the most nuclear power stations?

15. Renewable resources can be used over and over again. True or False?

16. Hydroelectric power stations are often located on: highland regions, coastal regions, or islands?

17. One disadvantage of hydroelectric power is that: dams are expensive, rivers too often run dry, people protest at the noise?

18. Geothermal power involves extracting heat energy from beneath the surface of Earth. True or False?

19. Organic matter used as a fuel is referred to as what?

20. Can biogas be made from animal dung?

Space Race

1. Who was the first man in space?

2. Who was the first woman in space?

3. How long did Alan Shepard's space flight of 1961 last?

4. In which year did the US land a man on the moon?

5. Who was the second man on the moon?

6. Which American was the first to walk in space?

7. Which US astronaut was the only one to have been onboard Mercury-Atlas 6, Gemini 6, and Apollo 7?

8. How many people have walked on the moon?

9. What is the name of the Apollo 11 lunar module that made the first manned landing on the moon's surface?

10. What was Sputnik 1?

11. When was it launched?

12. What was the first animal to go into space orbit?

13. Where did the Russians send *Luna 2* in 1959?

14. What was Explorer 1?

15. What name was given to the unmanned US probes that landed on the moon in the 1960s?

16. What does "cosmonaut" mean?

17. What does "astronaut" mean?

18. Which US president started the race for the moon?

19. The cooperative Apollo-Soyuz Test Project spaceflight mission of 1975 eased tensions between the US and USSR. True or False?

20. Where is the Kennedy Space Center located?

21. What does "Sputnik" mean?

22. What was the name of the launch vehicle used to send Apollo craft to the moon?

23. When was NASA founded?

24. What does "NASA" stand for?

25. How many hours did the Apollo 11 astronauts spend on the moon on that first historic landing?

(Answers on page 472)

Incredible Bodies

1. Approximately how many dead skin cells fall off your body every minute?

2. Where are new blood cells made?

3. Babies are born with 300 bones, but adults only have how many?

4. How many bones do you have in each hand?

5. The surface area of the lungs is approximately the same size as a what?

6. How many times do your eyes blink every minute?

7. The main job of the colon is to absorb water, nutrients, and salts from partially digested food. True or False?

8. What are the smallest blood vessels called?

9. Approximately how many new cells do you create every second?

10. Is it true that humans have fewer muscles than caterpillars do?

11. How long does it take one red blood cell to travel around your entire body?

12. Does breathing require conscious or unconscious effort?

13. Do you use more muscles to frown or smile?

14. What carries oxygen around the body?

15. What is the biggest organ in your body?

16. What stops blood from flowing backward?

17. What is the fastest-growing hair on the human body?

18. What does the cranium protect?

19. Deoxyribonucleic acid (DNA) contains the instructions for a living thing to grow and to work. True or False?

20. Each human grows an entire new layer of skin every what?

21. How much food will you eat in your lifetime?

22. There are enough blood vessels in the human body to stretch around Earth's equator twice. True or False?

23. How many baby teeth does a baby have?

24. Which is the hardest-working muscle in the body?

25. Nose, windpipe, and lungs make up which system?

(Answers on page 473)

Wheels, Watches, and Widgets

SCIENCE & TECHNOLOGY

1. Roller skates were invented more than 200 years ago. True or False?

2. What is the name of the giant Ferris wheel beside the Thames River in England?

3. Maurice Gatsonides invented a speed camera. What was his profession?

4. Which parts of a car have discs and pads?

5. Why does a race car have a wing or airfoil?

6. Diesel engines have no spark plugs. True or False?

7. What is a 4x4?

8. What is a Swiss Army knife?

9. Every swing of a pendulum takes the same time. True or False?

10. What did Linus Yale invent?

11. When was the digital watch created?

12. What is a chronometer?

13. What became almost redundant when digital cameras came along?

14. What is the study of time called?

15. What name is given to the kind of wheels that have teeth or notches to engage with other wheels?

16. What vibrates inside a quartz watch?

17. What were old-fashioned baby buggies called?

18. Some canned drinks include a small device to improve the fizziness. What is this device called?

19. From 1974 to 1995, the US national speed limit for cars was 55 mph (89 kmph). True or False?

20. The famous clock in Wells Cathedral in England is more than 600 years old. True or False?

21. What is Big Ben?

22. In which century was the alarm clock invented?

23. What does "widget" mean?

24. Frederick Henry Royce and Charles Stewart Rolls first teamed up in 1904. True or False?

25. In which year did Ransom Olds make the first car using mass-production methods: 1896, 1901, 1918?

Plane to See

1. Most aircraft wheels are arranged like the wheels of a tricycle. True or False?

2. What is the place where an aircraft lands and takes off called?

3. Why is a biplane airplane called this?

4. Which branch of the US military would a prospective pilot join?

5. How were the first airplanes powered?

6. Orville and Wilbur Wright made flying history in 1903 with the first powered airplane. What was the name of their machine?

7. How many engines does a Boeing 747 jumbo jet have?

8. What is "jetlag"?

9. In an airliner, does the captain usually sit in the left- or right-hand seat?

10. The largest airplane to have flown was called the *Spruce Goose*. What was it made of?

11. What sort of aircraft uses an arrester hook?

12. By what name is an aircraft's flight recorder popularly known?

13. In 1910, Louis Blériot won a prize for flying over water. What did he fly across?

14. At what angle do helicopters land and take off?

15. Charles Lindbergh made the first solo flight across the Atlantic Ocean. What did he call his airplane?

16. In 1986, an airplane flew all the way around the world without stopping. What was the airplane called?

17. Airliners cruise in the stratosphere at 30,000 ft (9,144 m). What is the temperature of the outside air up there?

18. Airline pilots train using a computer flight simulator. True or False?

19. Which was the first supersonic airliner to fly transatlantic services?

20. Why are Alcock and Brown famous flyers?

SCIENCE & TECHNOLOGY

(Answers on page 473)

On the Road

1. What color traffic light means "stop"?

2. Some sedan chairs were used like taxis in 1700s London. True or False?

3. A juggernaut is a type of digger. True or False?

4. How far could an ox-cart travel on a Roman road in a day?

5. What does a turbo, or turbocharger, in a car do?

6. Some bikes are made of carbon fiber. What are the advantages of this material?

7. What kind of vehicle was a London Routemaster?

8. What is a "Gatso"?

9. What approximate braking distance should a driver allow when moving at 30 mph (48 kmph): about 16 ft (5 m), about 33 ft (10 m), or more than 65 ft (20 m)?

10. What is a "crumple zone"?

11. In which year did President Eisenhower sign the Federal-Aid Highway Act, allowing the construction of US interstate highways?

12. What was the power source in a hansom cab of the late 19th century?

13. Minibikes are allowed on all US public roads. True or False?

14. Percy Shaw invented a reflector to help with road safety at night. What is it called?

15. The Roman road from London to York was called: Watling Street, the Great North Road, Ermine Street?

16. Early cars were called horseless carriages. True or False?

17. The concept of traffic lights was first created for the railroads, not streets and roads. True or False?

18. Why do heavy trucks have lots of wheels?

19. Which engineer improved roads in Britain in the early 1800s by designing better-drained and hard-wearing surfaces?

20. The first cars had solid wheels. True or False?

 (Answers on page 473)

Meanwhile, Back on the Farm

1. Some of the first tractors used steam power. True or False?

2. We get a lot of our food from the wheat plant. Which part of it do we eat?

3. What does a tractor pull to dig rows in a field?

4. Farmers cut fresh grass and let it dry so that it does not spoil. What is the dried grass called?

5. A windmill is used to make flour from grain. True or False?

6. Why do sheep grow wool?

7. Is it true that Colorado beetles are good for farm crops?

8. What are "pesticides"?

9. Many vegetables are grown in polytunnels. How does covering the plants with transparent plastic help?

10. In cool regions, tomatoes are grown in greenhouses. How does the glass structure help the tomato plants?

11. Farm vehicles have very wide tires. What is the reason for this?

12. Some farm machines in the 19th century were steam-driven. True or False?

13. We get a lot of our food from the potato plant. Which part of the plant do we eat?

14. Why is fresh milk usually cooled as soon as possible?

15. Some farm machinery uses pressurized oil to provide a force for lifting. What is this system called?

16. In dry weather, farmers use artificial methods to water the fields. What is this technique called?

17. Farmers can improve the soil by adding chemicals containing nitrogen. Why would adding nitrogen help?

18. Farmers keep cattle from straying with an electric fence. What happens when the cattle touch the electric fence?

19. Can some animal manure be used an organic soil fertilizer?

20. All plants can make sugar. What is the main energy source for this?

(Answers on page 473)

Space is Ace

SCIENCE & TECHNOLOGY

1. Which is the smallest planet in our solar system?

2. How old is the sun?

3. Which galaxy are we in?

4. Which planet travels fastest around the sun?

5. Which planet is sometimes called "the red planet"?

6. Which missions took astronauts to the moon?

7. What is the closest star to Earth?

8. Yuri Gagarin was the first astronaut to walk on the moon. True or False?

9. Which is the smallest constellation?

10. What is the brightest star in the night sky?

11. Is the Starfish a constellation?

12. Which spacecraft gave astronauts their first look at the far side of the moon?

13. Which planets are at either side of the asteroid belt?

14. Which planet is completely covered by clouds?

15. On which planet did the rover Opportunity land and keep working from 2004 to 2018?

16. What is at the center of the Milky Way galaxy?

17. Which was the first comet seen in close-up?

18. What does "ISS" stand for?

19. The first spacewalk was made by Alexei Leonov. True or False?

20. Which planet has the most rings?

21. What do the planets in the solar system orbit around?

22. Which planet has now been downgraded to dwarf-planet status?

23. Which planet is usually closest to Earth?

24. After whom or what is Mars named?

25. Which planet is third in distance from the sun?

(Answers on page 473)

You Think You Know about Biology

1. What is produced during photosynthesis?

2. What substance in leaves makes them green?

3. A potato is a stem tuber. True or False?

4. What provides the energy for photosynthesis?

5. Which animal group has a pouch?

6. What are injections that protect you against diseases called?

7. What is the main component of the cardiovascular system?

8. How often is your skin replaced?

9. What did Daniel Gabriel Fahrenheit invent?

10. How are hormones transported around your body?

11. Would a microbiologist study psychology?

12. Invertebrates have a backbone. True or False?

13. What gives red blood cells their color?

14. In which continent has evidence been found of hominids' existence 7 million years ago?

15. Who invented a heating and cooling process that is used to sterilize food and liquids?

16. Which teeth tear food?

17. Who devised the scientific system for naming organisms?

18. What is the main purpose of a flower?

19. Which are the only animals with feathers?

20. The classification group for animals with mammary glands is what?

(Answers on page 473)

What's the Matter?

1. What type of substance can be picked up because its component atoms cannot move around?

2. Helium gas is an example of a substance that has no structure and whose atoms can move around freely. True or False?

3. Are diamonds hard or soft materials?

4. What is the melting point of ice?

5. What is the boiling point of water?

6. What are the two main types of solids?

7. What is an "LCD"?

8. Is syrup more viscous than milk?

9. What is evaporation?

10. What does the "H" in H_2O stand for?

11. What happens when you put an object that is more dense than water in the water?

12. What does "diffusion" mean?

13. Is the melting of an ice cube a reversible change?

14. Which is the most common substance in air?

15. Which element is needed for life as we know it to exist?

16. What happens to a candle if there is no oxygen?

17. A compound is a combination of two or more what?

18. What scale does the Universal Indicator use?

19. What is the pH value of a strong alkali?

20. Which of these is an example of a weak acid: lemon juice, sour milk, mashed potato?

21. Plasma is a state of matter. True or False?

22. What is "sublimation"?

23. When a gas condenses, what does it become?

24. Gases are hard to compress. True or False?

25. What is the term used to describe a liquid becoming solid?

SCIENCE & TECHNOLOGY

(Answers on page 473)

Are You a Science Sleuth?

1. What was pioneered by the surgeon Joseph Lister?

2. What was the name of Charles Darwin's ship?

3. What is a "newton"?

4. The first commercial telefax service was introduced in 1865, 11 years before the invention of telephones. True or False?

5. Which substance was discovered by the Polish-born scientist Marie Curie?

6. Which artist, who painted the *Mona Lisa*, also designed inventions?

7. Who formalized rules for nursing after her work at Scutari?

8. What garden observation is said to have inspired Isaac Newton's ideas about gravity?

9. What did Louis Pasteur study?

10. What is the chemical symbol for potassium?

11. Who was the first astronaut to walk on the moon?

12. The invention of the wheel occurred in the Iron Age. True or False?

13. Of what was Guglielmo Marconi a pioneer?

14. Who invented dynamite?

15. Who discovered the mold that led to penicillin?

16. Is lead magnetic?

17. What did an Austrian monk named Mendel research using pea plants?

18. Which New Zealand–born physicist discovered the atomic nucleus?

19. What material is used to make microchips?

20. Who created a code using dots and dashes?

SCIENCE & TECHNOLOGY

Powered by Oil

SCIENCE & TECHNOLOGY

1. The first internal combustion engines used gas as a fuel. True or False?

2. After whom did Karl Benz name the Mercedes-Benz car?

3. What was invented by John Boyd Dunlop in 1888, as a solution to uncomfortable bicycle rides?

4. Who invented the diesel engine in 1892?

5. In which year was the first ocean-going diesel ship launched: 1890, 1901, 1911?

6. Could you burn jet fuel in a kerosine heater?

7. What were the *R101*, the *Hindenburg*, and the *Graf Zeppelin*?

8. What was a "Short Sunderland"?

9. For what are John Alcock, Arthur Whitten Brown, and their Vickers Vimy bomber famous?

10. What type of ships competed for the Blue Riband for the fastest crossing of the Atlantic Ocean?

11. Which "unsinkable" passenger liner sank on its first voyage across the Atlantic in 1912?

12. What was a "charabanc"?

13. What was the name of Herbert Austin's mass-produced "baby" car, manufactured between 1922 and 1939?

14. Trolleys were powered by overhead electricity lines. True or False?

15. What was the first passenger jet?

16. Which new form of transportation was invented by Christopher Cockerell in 1955?

17. What are Scotts, Triumphs, and BSAs?

18. What was invented by Lambretta in 1947?

19. Which form of transportation has made international travel affordable?

20. A Boeing aircraft was nicknamed "the Jumbo" because of its size. By what series number is it properly known?

Robots

1. Who is the diminutive white and blue robot in *Star Wars*?

2. "Robot" comes from the Czech word for "slave." True or False?

3. Which science-fiction writer came up with the Laws of Robotics?

4. Nikola Tesla made a foray into robotics by designing what in 1898?

5. More than half of the world's robots are located in Asia. True or False?

6. Wakamaru is a Japanese domestic robot designed to help whom?

7. In which Fritz Lang movie can a robot be seen?

8. How many Laws of Robotics are there?

9. Built in 1961, Unimate was the first industrial robot. What work did it do?

10. What was the name of the robot in the 1956 film *Forbidden Planet*?

11. What were the names of the human-looking robots in the movie *Blade Runner*?

12. Japanese robot EveR-2 was the first android with the ability to do what?

13. Optimus Prime is a robot in which films?

14. Many industrial robots with fixed arms are used for what simple function?

15. The da Vinci multiarmed wonderbot was designed for use in: surgery, car manufacturing, warehouse handling?

16. Which robotic car was the star of the TV show *Knight Rider*?

17. Some robots went rogue in which futuristic movie starring Will Smith?

18. How many of the world's robots can be found in Africa?

19. What kind of robot is designed to look like a human?

20. There is a robot in *The Simpsons* TV show. True or False?

SCIENCE & TECHNOLOGY

SCIENCE & TECHNOLOGY

Heat, Light, and Sound

1. Heat is created by vibrating atoms. True or False?

2. What happens to light particles when light hits an uneven surface?

3. What is the name of the unit for energy?

4. What device do we use to measure heat energy?

5. What form of heat transfer causes a metal pan handle to get hot?

6. What happens to metals when they are heated?

7. What happens when gases are cooled?

8. What is the main way in which heat is transferred through a fluid?

9. What type of waves are sound waves?

10. Ultrasound waves can produce an image on a screen. True or False?

11. Does sound travel fastest through gas, air, or solids?

12. If a ray of light hits a mirror at 30 degrees, what angle will it be reflected at?

13. What happens to light rays that strike a convex mirror?

14. An endoscope uses total internal reflection. True or False?

15. What is happening when light waves bend?

16. What happens to light rays that strike a concave lens?

17. A rainbow results from refraction and what other action of light?

18. Onto what part of the human eye does the lens focus an image?

19. What part of a camera is like the pupil in our eyes?

20. What kind of lens would you find in a pair of binoculars?

Psychology

1. According to the ancient Greeks, what was the cause of hysteria?

2. What was Sigmund Freud's nationality?

3. What did the 19th-century discipline of phrenology study?

4. A "Freudian slip" is a term for an act or word that is close to but different than what is consciously intended and reflects unconscious motives or desires. True or False?

5. What discipline did Carl Jung found?

6. According to Freud, what three levels constitute the mind?

7. According to Galton, what are the two major influences on a person?

8. The origin of the word "schizophrenia" derives from the Egyptian "skezoz" for "torn." True or False?

9. What mental property was Hermann Ebbinghaus studying: memory, intuition, or intelligence?

10. Which psychologist proposed the idea of the "intelligence quotient" or IQ?

11. On what animals did Pavlov perform his famous conditioning experiments?

12. What did Stanley Milgram's experiments at Yale University aim to measure?

13. What method did Freud give up in favor of psychoanalysis?

14. The "collective unconscious" is a term coined by which psychologist?

15. With what group of people is the therapy of Melanie Klein associated?

16. Erich Fromm defined how many nonproductive personality types?

17. What does the Zeigarnik Effect claim to prove?

18. According to Endel Tulving, how many types of memory are there?

19. Who conducted the first experiments involving subliminal advertising?

20. What popular idea was disproved by Harry Harlow's experiments on monkeys?

(Answers on page 474)

A Voyage through the Solar System

1. What was the name of the first US reusable manned spacecraft?

2. Which planet in the solar system is similar in size to Earth?

3. Who was the second man to walk on the moon?

4. What is the name of the space station that was constructed in orbit around Earth between 1998 and 2012?

5. Which acid is found in the clouds of Venus?

6. Which planet has red dust over most of its surface?

7. What covers the surface of Mercury?

8. Which planet's name is the Roman version of the Greek Cronus?

9. What is the eighth and farthest planet from the sun?

10. What is the name of the spacecraft launched to explore Venus in 1989?

11. What was NASA's MER?

12. What is found in the solar system between Mars and Jupiter?

13. Most stars form in nebulae. What is a "nebula"?

14. At least 336 bodies in the solar system are formally classified as moons. True or False?

15. What covers the surface of Jupiter's moon Io?

16. Which planet has the largest set of rings?

17. Approximately how many stars are in the Milky Way galaxy?

18. What are the white areas that are visible on Neptune?

19. Is Ophelia a moon?

20. Which of Saturn's moons did the Cassini-Huygens probe visit?

(Answers on page 474)

So You Think You're a Science Sleuth

1. Who invented the first light bulb?

2. Where was Albert Einstein born?

3. What is Einstein's theory called?

4. Isaac Newton studied mathematics, physics, optics, and which other subject?

5. Who, in about 400 BCE, set up a medical school that sought physical causes for illnesses?

6. Who discovered that a body displaces its own volume in water?

7. A "dynamo" is a form of generator. True or False?

8. Copernicus asserted that the sun was the center of the universe. True or False?

9. What did Benjamin Franklin discover?

10. Who wrote: "Changing a magnetic field can generate an electric field"?

11. On which properties of gas did Robert Boyle concentrate his research?

12. What do cipher machines do?

13. Who won a Nobel Prize for his work on radiography?

14. Which modern cosmologist used an electronic voice?

15. What was the first successful vaccine to be developed?

16. In the 19th century, glass vacuum tubes proved useful in which area?

17. The Montgolfier brothers are credited with creating which flying machine?

18. Who sent the first wireless signal across the English Channel?

19. The printing press is widely regarded as the most important invention of the "modern period." Who invented it?

20. In which country did people first use gunpowder?

21. 50% of human DNA is the same as that in a banana. True or False?

22. How many chromosomes do humans have?

23. Which scientist did experiments on inheritance in pea plants?

24. DNA is a code using four bases. Which letters are used to represent this code?

25. A change in the structure of a gene is called what?

Can You Feel the Force?

1. What kind of compass do modern ships use to navigate?

2. In a homemade compass, why does the needle point to Earth's magnetic North Pole?

3. When particles emitted from the sun interact with Earth's magnetic field, what do we see near the North Pole?

4. What is the name of the naturally occurring magnetic material?

5. A battery will last longer if it is stored at a low temperature. True or False?

6. What type of medical scan uses a magnetic field to detect problems in our bodies?

7. Which scientist made the link between electricity and magnetism?

8. What type of electricity do we get at home?

9. In Fleming's right-hand rule, what does the first finger indicate?

10. In Fleming's left-hand rule, what does the thumb indicate?

11. What kind of electricity generators are used in power stations?

12. What drives a turbine in a coal-fired power station?

13. What type of transformer has more turns on the secondary coil than on the primary coil?

14. What characteristic of direct current is required for electrolysis to work?

15. What is the wire inside a light bulb called?

16. What is Ohm's law about?

17. How do n-type semiconductors conduct electricity?

18. Do conductors have a high or low resistance?

19. When was the transistor invented?

20. What can be defined as the speed of an object in a given direction?

(Answers on page 474)

SCIENCE & TECHNOLOGY

Engineers and Engineering: Past to Present

1. How long did the Step Pyramid of Djoser take to build, covering almost the duration of his reign?

2. The Pantheon in Rome is made of marble and what other material?

3. Engineers in which country first developed the water wheel?

4. Which device for detecting ground movements did Zhang Heng invent?

5. Which engineer was said to have shouted "Eureka!" after a bath?

6. Who built lighthouses in the 1700s and first used the term "civil engineer"?

7. In which century did Drebbel demonstrate a primitive submersible on the Thames River?

0. Who discovered the law of elasticity?

9. Of which familiar domestic appliance is American engineer Jacob Perkins said to be the "father"?

10. Which of the Founding Fathers devised bifocal glasses and designed an improved fireplace?

11. In which US state was the first-known metal suspension bridge built?

12. Over which river did the first hot-air balloon fly?

13. Who designed the Crystal Palace for the Exhibition of 1851?

14. Who made the world's first phone call in 1876?

15. The Greek sculptor Phidias supervised construction of which building?

16. A complete car left the Ford Model T assembly line every 10 seconds. True or False?

17. Which structure was the entrance to the 1889 World's Fair?

18. Where is the world's tallest building?

19. Who designed the Brooklyn Suspension Bridge in New York City?

20. How long is the Large Hadron Collider tunnel?

(Answers on page 475)

Mad Science

1. It is impossible for a person to sneeze with his or her eyes open. True or False?

2. Which birds can fly backward?

3. 89% of water is made up of which element?

4. Approximately how long would a metal ball take to fall from a ship to the deepest point in the ocean: 10 minutes, 1 hour, or 15 hours?

5. Approximately how much would a thimbleful of a neutron star weigh?

6. Approximately how many people in the world are estimated to carry parasitic hookworms?

7. The interstellar gas cloud Sagittarius B contains an enormous mass of what?

8. Fingernails grow faster than toenails. True or False?

9. Can oysters change their sex?

10. What is the hottest planet in the solar system?

11. If Earth was the size of a grain of sand, on the same scale, how far away would be the next closest star, Alpha Centauri: roughly ½ mile (1 km), 6 miles (10 km), 60 miles (100 km)?

12. Sound travels faster in water than air by how many times?

13. What part of the human body does not grow as an individual ages?

14. Which African mammal has no vocal cords?

15. How long does it take Earth to make one full rotation?

16. Approximately how many detectable earthquakes occur every year on Earth?

17. What gas is commonly produced by cows?

18. What animal can accelerate faster than a launching space shuttle?

19. Astronauts cannot belch in space. True or False?

20. How many years will elapse before our sun is expected to turn into a red giant?

21. What dinosaur do people associate with the Loch Ness monster?

22. What is the chemical name for "Laughing Gas," which Sir Humphry Davy found made people less aware of pain?

23. What set of huge stones may have been created as an early calendar?

24. What new branch of scientific knowledge was developed by Gregor Mendel in the 19th century, through his study of pea plants?

25. For what did scientist António Egas Moniz controversially win the Nobel Prize in 1949?

Cloning

1. Born on July 5 1996, what creature became the first cloned mammal in the world?

2. In 2004, South Korean scientists cloned the first human in history. True or False?

3. The word "clone" comes from the ancient Greek word for what?

4. Can a cow be cloned?

5. Approximately what percentage of cloning attempts succeed?

6. Somatic-cell nuclear transfer produces embryos for therapeutic purposes. True or False?

7. In 1952, what was the first species of creature to be cloned?

8. What was the name of the world's first commercially cloned cat?

9. The world's first cloned dog, an Afghan hound, was born in which Asian country?

10. Which extinct species did the Australian Museum attempt to clone in the early 2000s?

11. The first hybrid human clone was created from a man's leg cell and a cow's egg. True or False?

12. Which Aldous Huxley novel deals with the thorny issue of artificially producing humans?

13. In which year was the consumption of meat and other products from cloned animals approved in the US?

14. Do most studies reveal that cloned animals have increased risk of deformity at birth?

15. In which popular series of science-fiction movies is a cloned trooper army created?

16. Mewtwo is a clone character from which popular Japanese anime?

17. Russian scientists are attempting to clone a prehistoric woolly mammoth using DNA from elephants. True or False?

18. Which Steven Spielberg movie tells the story of extinct creatures cloned and brought back to life?

19. Do an animal and its clone share exactly the same DNA?

20. What was the name of the first cloned mammal in the world?

SCIENCE & TECHNOLOGY

MEDIUM

Technologic

SCIENCE & TECHNOLOGY

1. In which year was the first portable computer released?

2. What did Howard Aiken and Grace Hopper create in 1941?

3. In 1943, computer engineers at MIT began work on the "Project Whirlwind" flight simulator for the US Navy. When was the project completed?

4. Which British computer scientist led the team that cracked the Enigma code?

5. Which corporation was responsible for manufacturing the UNIVAC I in the early 1950s?

6. Approximately how much did a UNIVAC I cost to buy at that time?

7. When was IBM founded?

8. What does "IBM" stand for?

9. What was the name of the first video game, created for the DEC PDP-1 computer?

10. What did Douglas Engelbart create in 1964?

11. What was the Intel 1103, released in 1970?

12. In which year was the first email sent?

13. Who designed the Apple I in 1976?

14. What was the first portable computer called?

15. In 1940, what did the initials "CNC" refer to?

16. In which year did Microsoft launch Windows?

17. What is the best-selling computer of all time?

18. During which years was the best-selling computer of all time in production?

19. Who designed the Linux operating system?

20. What breakthrough first-person-shooter game was released in 1993?

 (Answers on page 475)

Great Scientists

SCIENCE & TECHNOLOGY

1. Which scientist was the first to see the moon through a telescope?

2. Which famous ancient Greek scientist contributed to the fields of physics, zoology, politics, and biology?

3. Which great scientist wrote *On the Origin of Species by Means of Natural Selection*?

4. Which New Zealand scientist is credited with splitting the atom?

5. Which principle concerning subatomic particles in the field of quantum mechanics was put forward by Werner Heisenberg?

6. For what was scientist Alessandro Giuseppe Antonio Anastasio Volta best known?

7. Which scientist pioneered electric light and had more than 1,000 patents to his name?

8. Whose germ research showed that viruses were not detectable through an optical microscope?

9. Which Polish scientist was awarded Nobel Prizes in both physics and chemistry?

10. Who is the English mathematician and logician widely considered to be the father of computer science?

11. Which female scientist who fled the Nazis invented the term "nuclear fission"?

12. Which Nobel laureate physicist was responsible for inventing radio?

13. Which astronomer proposed that the sun was at the center of the universe?

14. Which great ancient scientist invented the screw pump and siege machine?

15. Which self-taught scientist invented the dynamo in the 1830s and made breakthrough investigations into electrolysis?

16. The Renaissance Italian who conceptualized a helicopter, a tank, solar power, and the calculator was who?

17. Florey and Chain brought what discovery to the medical world in the 20th century?

18. Which French psychologist invented the first practical IQ test for students?

19. Which famous Cambridge professor wrote *A Brief History of Time*?

20. Which Englishman, described as "the greatest scientist who ever lived," is known for his groundbreaking discoveries in gravitation and motion?

(Answers on page 475)

SCIENCE & TECHNOLOGY

To Boldly Go

1. Soyuz, a type of spacecraft first used in the mid-1960s, is completely reusable. True or False?

2. In space exploration, what is a "fairing"?

3. Salyut was so named in whose honor?

4. The Mir Space Station was only a core unit when launched, so that more modules could be added later in space. True or False?

5. How many astronauts did each Apollo mission carry?

6. In 1962, *Mariner 2* found that Venus had a cold surface. True or False?

7. On January 6, 2005, the Mars Exploration Rover *Opportunity* found the first: water, meteorite, or uranium on another planet?

8. *Voyager 2* is the only spacecraft to have flown by which planet?

9. Spacesuits were originally made-to-measure but are now a standard size with adjustable leg lengths. True or False?

10. Between 1969 and 1972, around 200 samples were brought back by six Apollo missions. True or False?

11. Three lunar roving vehicles were taken to the moon by the US. What happened to them?

12. In which year was the Hubble Space Telescope launched into orbit?

13. Cometary nuclei are so small that they cannot be viewed by Earth-based telescopes. To be seen, they must be visited by spacecraft. True or False?

14. Which was the first planet, other than Earth, to be orbited by a spacecraft?

15. When were the first live TV signals relayed from the US to Britain with the use of satellites?

16. The rovers that went to Mars were designed so that their cameras are roughly the height of an astronaut's eyes. True or False?

17. Itokawa is an irregularly shaped asteroid made of silicate rock. Which country sent a craft to observe it?

18. Astronauts' bones grow faster during spaceflights. True or False?

19. What do these craft have in common: *Pioneer 10* and *11*, *Voyager 1* and *2*, and *Galileo*?

20. What was the name of the European Space Agency's first mission to a planet?

Supercars

1. What was allegedly the fastest car in the world in 2020?

2. What was the first road car to exceed 200 mph (322 kmph)?

3. The Dodge Viper SRT-10 (Mk II) has a larger engine than the Bugatti Veyron. True or False?

4. Which was the first production supercar to feature a mid-engine design?

5. Which was the last rear-wheel-drive Lamborghini supercar still being sold in the new millennium?

6. Which former Formula 1 champion was involved with the early development of the Ferrari 458 Italia?

7. Koenigsegg Automotive is based in which country?

8. Which supercar is capable of extracting more than 1,000 bhp from its Chrysler Viper engine?

9. What was the first road car to achieve 0–100 mph (0–161 kmph) in under 10 seconds?

10. Name the first supercar from Japan.

11. Which car's shape was based on more than 1,000 hours of research in a wind tunnel?

12. What is the Lamborghini Murcielago named after?

13. In 2006, which manufacturer entered the production supercar market with the launch of the R8?

14. Which supercar manufacturer has "For the tenacious, no road is impassable" as its motto?

15. In the film *Quantum of Solace*, the McLaren F1 replaced the Aston Martin DB7 Volante as James Bond's car of choice. True or False?

16. Which German car manufacturer owns Bugatti?

17. Which former Formula 1 champion was involved in the early development of the Pagani Zonda?

18. What was the first Aston Martin to be manufactured under Ford's ownership?

19. What replaced the McLaren F1 as the world's fastest road car in 2005?

20. What was the final model commissioned by Enzo Ferrari?

21. The Tesla Roadster electric car claims to do 0–100 mph (0–161 kmph) in 4.2 seconds. True or False?

22. What is Formula E?

23. Which animal does the Alfa Romeo logo feature?

24. What was the Porsche supercar from the 1980s?

25. Where is the Tesla company's US base?

(Answers on page 475)

Historic Medicine

1. Which ancient civilization was the first to use examination, diagnosis, treatment, and prognosis for medical ailments?

2. What became the anesthetic of choice after the 1840s?

3. X-ray-proof underwear for women appeared soon after the discovery of X-rays in 1895. True or False?

4. From which civilization does the diagnostic handbook *Sakikku* come?

5. Which ancient Greek is considered to be the father of modern medicine?

6. Some medieval physicians calculated the moon's position before performing what?

7. What was the greatest medical contribution of the Arab physician known in the West as Abulcasis?

8. What did English physician William Harvey describe to the medical world?

9. What radical medical practice did Ignaz Semmelweis prescribe for doctors attending women in labor?

10. An ancient Egyptian mummy was found buried with a wooden prosthesis for which body part?

11. During which decade was the disease smallpox eradicated?

12. During which war did Florence Nightingale's exploits give nursing a new respectability?

13. By linking microorganisms with disease, Louis Pasteur brought about a revolution in medicine. True or False?

14. In which decade did tobacco smoking first become linked to lung cancer?

15. Peseshet, the first-known woman physician, practiced in ancient Egypt in the Fourth Dynasty. True or False?

16. In which year was the World Health Organization founded?

17. During the American Civil War, more deaths were caused by disease than by battles. True or False?

18. Which mysterious disease that affected Anne Boleyn, among others, was prevalent until the 1550s, when it suddenly vanished?

19. Which people did ancient Greek writer Herodotus describe as "the healthiest of all men, next to the Libyans"?

20. Following the British cholera epidemic of 1854, what conclusion did John Snow reach?

SCIENCE & TECHNOLOGY

Solar System Challenge

1. Which is the second-largest planet in the solar system?

2. How many known moons does Jupiter have?

3. What are PHOs?

4. Which planet is famous for its Great Red Spot?

5. Which is the most abundant gas in Earth's atmosphere?

6. Which planet has the shortest orbit?

7. The missions that landed 12 men on the moon between 1969 and 1972 were part of which NASA space program?

8. The four largest planets in the solar system have what common features around all of them?

9. What is the largest solid body in the solar system?

10. What can be seen on the surface of the sun where strong magnetism prevents hot gas from reaching it?

11. Which atmospheric layer lies beneath Earth's stratosphere?

12. Which planet is sometimes described as Earth's twin because of its similarity in size?

13. Who was the last astronaut to walk on the moon?

14. What did William Herschel discover in March 1781?

15. When were the first satellite pictures of Earth seen?

16. There are two regions of space beyond Neptune filled with comets. What is the name of the innermost region?

17. Which of the four giant planets is the smallest?

18. Name the largest moon in our solar system.

19. Which was the first planet to be fully orbited by a spacecraft?

20. Titan is the largest of which planet's moons?

21. What kind of star would have a mass of approximately 20 solar masses?

22. How do stars produce energy?

23. What happens to a main sequence star at the end of its life?

24. What is a binary system?

25. What was NASA's Kepler Mission (2009–2018) designed to search for?

SCIENCE & TECHNOLOGY

(Answers on page 475)   **81**

SCIENCE & TECHNOLOGY

Trains

1. The word "train" originally comes from the Latin *trahere*. What did this word mean?

2. Who demonstrated the first steam locomotive in 1804?

3. What name is given to the minimum-friction train system that uses two sets of magnets?

4. Name the locomotive entered by George Stephenson for the Rainhill Trials of 1829.

5. In railway-speak, what is the name of the building where trains are stored and serviced?

6. On a US railroad train, what name was used for the car used as an office and as the crew's sleeping quarters?

7. In which year did London's first underground railway line open?

8. In railway jargon, what is "rolling stock"?

9. Which country has a high-speed-rail bridge that is more than 100 miles (160 km) long?

10. What can be put onto railway tracks to provide better grip?

11. In railway terms, what is a "bogie"?

12. Which type of railway wagon carries liquids?

13. A monorail train can travel on up to three railway tracks at the same time. True or False?

14. Which two cities did the original Orient Express travel between?

15. Which strip of sea do Eurostar trains cross using a tunnel?

16. The 1930 Beyer-Garratt was one of Europe's largest-ever steam locomotives. How many wheels did it have?

17. What was the TGV, introduced in France in 1981?

18. High-speed trains usually travel at speeds above 124 mph (200 kmph). True or False?

19. Which country has the biggest rail network in terms of track length?

20. Which steam train made the world's longest nonstop run (London to Edinburgh) in 1928?

(Answers on page 476)

The Good, the Bad, and the Body Part

1. What shape are the chromosomes that make up DNA?

2. Some strands of DNA are made up of ademine, guamine, thymine, and which other chemical?

3. What shape are muscle cells?

4. What are the protein units in DNA called?

5. How many chromosomes are in a human genome?

6. What is a biological catalyst called?

7. What is the term for the breaking down of complex molecules during energy production?

8. When the upper part of the stomach bulges through the esophageal opening in the diaphragm, the condition is called what?

9. What name is given to the disease that causes pouches to bulge out of the colon wall?

10. What is the function of the kidneys?

11. What is the average amount of urine produced by an adult every day?

12. Where in the body does cystic fibrosis occur?

13. What is stored in the gallbladder?

14. What name is given to the flap of elastic cartilage attached to the entrance of the larynx?

15. What name is given to cells that can divide through mitosis to become specialized?

16. Renal arteries carry blood to the kidneys from which major blood vessel?

17. What can endometriosis cause?

18. Where is the fontanelle?

19. What is a zygote?

20. What are eye teeth also known as?

21. What is the large intestine also known as?

22. What is the duodenum part of?

23. Where are your napes?

24. Which organ has a neck, body, and tail?

25. What connects the kidneys and the bladder?

The Development of Medicine

1. What was a doctor's *vade mecum*?

2. What did Banting and Best pioneer the use of?

3. What record did Robert Liston hold in 19th-century surgery?

4. Which drink was originally developed as patent medicine to cure sickness, headaches, neuralgia, hysteria, and melancholy?

5. What event, in 1858, prompted the building of a new sewer system for London?

6. What part of the human body did William Harvey deduce must exist but was unable to prove?

7. What is Adolf Gaston Eugen Fick associated with?

8. Why was thalidomide prescribed to pregnant women in the period 1959–1962?

9. What was a key ingredient of Godfrey's Cordial, which was also used as a cure for flatulence and insomnia?

10. What prosthetic limb was developed by the French surgeon Paré in the 16th century?

11. Which organization was founded in 1863 by Henry Dunant in Geneva?

12. Which medicine is a version of the chemical salicylic acid?

13. What did flagellants do to avoid catching the Black Death?

14. Who was the secretary to the Poor Law Board who said poor living conditions in towns and poor health of the workers were connected?

15. Digitalis flowers contain a substance that, although poisonous, can also be used in medicine for the heart. True or False?

16. In which decade did St. Vincent's School of Nursing in New York City begin to accept men?

17. Who became the first secretary of the US Department of Health, Education, and Welfare (HEW) in 1953?

18. What was used as a treatment for syphilis, which was painful and often led to madness?

19. What medical aid did René Laënnec invent in 1816?

20. When Florey and Chain were trying to purify penicillin, what technology was used by the scientists at Pfizer to help them?

21. What was "trepanning"?

22. When was St. Bartholomew's hospital in London founded?

23. Before modern medicine, doctors blamed disease on "miasma," or bad smells. True or False?

24. The acceptance of chloroform in childbirth was helped by which queen?

25. When were X-rays discovered?

Internet and IT Pioneers

1. ARPANET was the world's first operational packet switching network, and a precursor of the Internet. What do the letters stand for?

2. To which US government department was ARPANET attached?

3. Which event sparked ARPANET's creation?

4. Who suggested that a computer network be established to allow ARPA research contractors to communicate more easily?

5. The architect of ARPANET was Paul Baran. True or False?

6. Who improved networking technology with the invention of the Ethernet?

7. What was Hawaii's 1970s computer network called?

8. What was the American 1970s satellite network called?

9. Who wrote a Transmission Control Protocol in 1974 that meant different networks could communicate with each other?

10. What is "Vint Cerf" also known as?

11. In which decade did most universities and research-oriented institutions have computers that were connected to the Internet?

12. Who coined the term "Hypertext"?

13. What did hypertext go on to enable the creation of?

14. Who led the team that created one of the first WWW browsers, Netscape?

15. Where does a plaque commemorating the "Birth of the Internet" stand?

16. In which year did Robert Cailliau organize the first International WWW Conference?

17. Which year saw the rise in "dot-com" companies?

18. In which year did the dot-com bubble burst?

19. A new web model for the exchange of information in 2004 was called what?

20. In 2009, the Global Language Monitor declared "Web 2.0" to be the one-millionth English word. True or False?

SCIENCE & TECHNOLOGY

Chemistry

1. Who invented dynamite by combining unstable nitroglycerin and ground rock?

2. Which substance is H_2O the chemical structure for?

3. What is "laughing gas" also known as?

4. Which element must be present in a compound for it to be described as "organic"?

5. Which element has the atomic symbol "Co"?

6. What is the name of the process where a solid becomes a gas without first becoming a liquid?

7. Which element has the atomic symbol "K"?

8. What type of gas is helium?

9. What is the chemical formula for salt?

10. A pH level of 14 would indicate that a substance is highly acidic. True or False?

11. What is added to iron to make steel?

12. Electrons carry a positive charge. True or False?

13. What is the atomic symbol for gold?

14. What does "corrosive" mean?

15. What metal comes from bauxite?

16. What is the center of an atom called?

17. Which element has the atomic symbol "Sn"?

18. What is organic chemistry?

19. What is the only metal that exists in liquid form at room temperature?

20. How many Nobel prizes was Marie Curie awarded?

(Answers on page 476)

Observing the Universe

1. What do we call the path of the planets across the sky?

2. We measure the positions of the stars with the coordinate system, ascension, and declination. What are the units for declination?

3. Two astronomical coordinates are declination and RA. What does "RA" stand for?

4. How far above Earth does space start?

5. You can observe Pluto with the naked eye. True or False?

6. Mizor and Alcor form a double star in which constellation?

7. What is the brightest galaxy in Ursa Major, when viewed from Earth?

8. The stars Merak and Dubhe in Ursa Major point toward which other important star?

9. What is the name of the red supergiant star found in the constellation Orion?

10. What is the name of the blue supergiant star in the constellation Orion?

11. What is the catalog code for the Orion nebula?

12. The stars in Orion's belt point to which star?

13. What is the apparent magnitude of Sirius?

14. How many constellations are there in Earth's sky?

15. Which lunar phase is the best time to observe the moon?

16. Which meteor shower is best observed around mid-November?

17. Which is the largest planet in our solar system?

18. What is the main advantage of a catadioptric telescope?

19. What telescope aperture is needed to view objects of apparent magnitude of 14.7?

20. Where in the world is the largest single-aperture telescope?

21. The heaviest meteorite on Earth landed in Tanzania fewer than 80,000 years ago. True or False?

22. How many solar system planets have rings?

23. What percentage of stars are more luminous than the sun?

24. What wavelength does the Spitzer Space Telescope observe in?

25. Which five planets can you see with the naked eye?

SCIENCE & TECHNOLOGY

(Answers on page 476)   **87**

Science and Technology in History

1. Irene Joliot won the Nobel Prize for chemistry in 1935. Who was her mother?

2. Who set up the progressive academy called the Lyceum in the 4th century BCE?

3. Who wrote to the Royal Society in 1673 to tell them about his discovery of microscopic organisms, which he called "animalcules"?

4. Which Jewish scientist renounced his German citizenship in 1933?

5. Who used instruments called "astrolabes" and "sextants" during the Middle Ages?

6. Where was the second nuclear bomb to be used as a weapon dropped?

7. Who was responsible for construction of the underground sewer system that was opened in London in 1865?

8. Where did Darwin find a range of unique species that influenced his thinking on the theory of evolution?

9. What did Hermann Anschütz-Kaempfe design in 1906?

10. Who died from pneumonia in 1626 after going out in the snow to prove that freezing a chicken could preserve it?

11. What word describes Charles Goodyear's treatment of rubber to make it more elastic and weatherproof?

12. Which surgeon carried out the first heart transplant?

13. Who first developed the disposable razor?

14. What was the profession of Leon Battista Alberti, who in 1450 invented the first mechanical anemometer to measure wind speed?

15. With what technology is Thomas Savery associated?

16. Which piece of diving equipment was invented by Jacques Cousteau?

17. What did the Salk vaccine protect against?

18. What was a *shadoof* in ancient Egypt?

19. Which temperature-control device contains a bimetallic strip?

20. Which mathematician worked out the circumference and the diameter of Earth in 240 BCE?

21. Rosalind Franklin made a vital contribution to the discovery of what?

22. What recognition did Crick, Watson, and Wilkins get for working on the structure of DNA?

23. In which field of science did Ernest Rutherford work?

24. Who classified bacteria into rods, spheres, commas, and spirals?

25. The first Otis safety elevator was in a bed factory. True or False?

(Answers on page 476)

Under the Microscope

1. A flagellum helps a bacterium to do what?

2. Cyclops belongs to which group of animals?

3. Which tiny creature causes the skin disease scabies?

4. Bacillus are a type of what ?

5. A vaccine for the plague was first used in what year?

6. The liver disease hepatitis is usually caused by a virus. Which type of hepatitis is spread by contaminated food and water?

7. What do bacteriophage viruses do?

8. Which bacteria, found in unpasteurized milk, should pregnant women try to avoid?

9. Who performed the first successful vaccination?

10. In what year was the last death caused by the smallpox virus?

11. Which virus is associated with the common cold?

12. What illness is caused by the Bordetella pertussis bacterium?

13. To what class of organisms does the microorganism paramecium belong to?

14. What disease is named after the town in Connecticut in which it was first recognized in 1975?

15. Which tree has been used to treat malaria?

16. Alexander Fleming is credited with discovering penicillin. In what year did this happen?

17. What infective agent is thought to cause the disease BSE (mad cow disease)?

18. Robert Koch is associated with which animal disease?

19. Heliozoans live in fresh water and the sea. They are known by what other name?

20. Mosquitoes pass on which parasite?

(Answers on page 477)

Famous Formulas and Equations

1. Which scientist came up with the equation $E = mc^2$?

2. What is the mathematical formula $a^2 + b^2 = c^2$?

3. Of what is 3.14159 the most accurate approximation?

4. In math, e = 2.71828. But what is e?

5. Which mathematical formula expresses the fact that differentiation and integration are inverse operations of each other?

6. What is the scientific equation $F = -kx$?

7. What is $Ax = b$?

8. What scientific equation is $V = RI$?

9. Which famous mathematical principle did Archimedes come up with in the bath?

10. As what is Bernoulli's law of fluid dynamics more commonly known?

11. Scientist John Dalton once proposed that each chemical element is composed of atoms. What name was given to his theory?

12. In science, Fourier's law of heat conduction deals with the transmission of heat in materials. True or False?

13. Who used four equations to formulate a unified description of electricity and magnetism in 1862?

14. For what is this the formula: $C = 2\pi r$?

15. The cornerstone of classical mechanics is the formula $F = ma$; what is it known as?

16. How would this formula be written: Electrical Energy = Power (Kw) x Time (h)?

17. With which scientist are the mathematical constants α and δ associated?

18. The golden ratio φ is a number often used in the world of physics. True or False?

19. What object did Archimedes use to find out its correct volume in water?

20. For what does $E = mc^2$ stand?

(Answers on page 477)

Unnatural Disasters

1. What disaster took place on April 26, 1986, in Ukraine?

2. What is the size of the exclusion zone that still surrounds the site today?

3. The largest loss of life caused by a maritime disaster during peacetime was the loss of the Filipino ferry *Dona Paz* in 1987. How many people died?

4. What was the Bhopal disaster of 1984?

5. How many people did London's Great Smog of 1952 kill?

6. What form of disaster struck Fukushima, Japan, in 2011?

7. How long did the 2003 fire at the Iraqi Al-Mishraq sulfur plant burn for?

8. Which sea has shrunk by 90 percent since the Russian government diverted rivers in the 1960s?

9. In which year was a poisonous plume of the toxin tetrachlorodibenzoparadioxin released from a pesticide plant in Seveso, Italy?

10. How many animals were slaughtered to prevent the toxin from entering the food chain?

11. What happened in 1979 at the Three Mile Island nuclear reactor in Pennsylvania?

12. What caused the Halifax Explosion of December 6, 1917?

13. Which space shuttle disintegrated on re-entry into Earth's atmosphere, killing all seven astronauts on board?

14. What caused 1,426 deaths in a pedestrian tunnel in Mecca in 1990?

15. What caused more than 800 deaths in the Saint-Michel-de-Maurienne rail disaster of 1917?

16. Where did the Benxihu Colliery explosion take place, killing 1,549 people in 1942?

17. The biggest loss of life at sea was the sinking of the *Wilhelm Gustloff* during World War II. More than 9,500 people lost their lives. True or False?

18. More than 600 oil wells were set on fire in Kuwait during the 1991 Gulf War. How long did they burn?

19. In which body of water is the Gyre Garbage Patch, a swirling mass of mainly plastic trash that can be seen from space?

20. In which year did the tanker *Exxon Valdez* run aground in Alaska, spilling more than 10.8 million gallons (40.9 million liters) of oil?

SCIENCE & TECHNOLOGY

(Answers on page 477)   91

Expert Cars

1. In which year was the current Alfa Romeo logo introduced?

2. What motoring term did the Ford Mustang inspire?

3. In which year did Ford purchase Aston Martin?

4. What was the winner of the *Top Gear* Car of the Decade award for the 2000s?

5. Which constructor won World Champion team and driver in its first full Formula 1 season?

6. Juan Manuel Fangio is the only Argentine driver to have won the Argentine Grand Prix. True or False?

7. With which soccer team is Fiat traditionally associated?

8. Which manufacturer makes the Bentley car?

9. Which was the only major US car maker to increase sales during the 1958 recession?

10. How many Formula 1 drivers have won four or more World Championships?

11. Which car manufacturer makes the Yaris?

12. Which Citroën was styled as a successor to the classic Citroën DS?

13. What was the first turbocharged car to win a Grand Prix?

14. From 1987 to 1989, the Ferrari F40 was the world's fastest production car. True or False?

15. In the Toyota MR2, what does "MR2" stand for?

16. What was the winner of the *Top Gear* Car of the Decade award for the 1990s?

17. Which Italian car was featured in the *Miami Vice* TV series?

18. Which car was dubbed the "mini E-type"?

19. In which year was the Chevrolet Corvette first manufactured?

20. What was the first four-wheeled, gas-engine vehicle to reach 10 mph (16 kmph)?

21. In which county is the manufacturer of the Koenigsegg Agera RS based?

22. What was the first road car to exceed 200 mph (322 kmph)?

23. The Dodge Viper SRT-10 (Mk II) has a larger engine than the Bugatti Veyron. True or False?

24. The first Indianapolis 500 race took place in which year?

25. What was the last rear-wheel-drive Lamborghini supercar still being sold in the new millennium?

The Human Story

1. What period followed the extinction of the dinosaurs?

2. Which of our ancestors had the smallest proportion of body mass composed by the brain at just 1.2%?

3. Primates, the species that includes humans, are arboreal. What does this mean?

4. How different in DNA percentage terms are humans from chimpanzees?

5. One of the earliest species of two-legged hominin was the *Orrorin tugenensis*. What biological evidence suggests this?

6. When was *Australopithecus anamensis* declared a species?

7. The best preserved specimen of *Paranthropus aethiopicus* is known as what?

8. Why was *Paranthropus boisei* given the nickname "Nutcracker Man"?

9. Which hominin was known as the "Handy Man"?

10. Which species left 1.5-million-year-old footprint trails in Kenya, providing evidence for the oldest humanlike feet?

11. What tool first appears 1.65 million years ago in the record known as the Acheulean stone-tool industry?

12. What do anthropologists think the species *Homo georgicus* was the first to do?

13. Where was the first *Homo erectus* fossil found?

14. *Homo antecessor* may have been the first Western European hominin. What does this name mean?

15. When did *Homo heidelbergensis* colonize Europe?

16. Where is the site where the remains of *Homo floresiensis* were found?

17. What theory is given to explain the shrinking of *Homo florensiensis* compared to its mainland relatives?

18. Where is the Neander Valley, where the partial remains of a *Homo neanderthalensis* were found?

19. The first modern humans are known as *Homo sapiens*. What does this term mean?

20. What feature is present in no other hominin other than *Homo sapiens*?

(Answers on page 477)

To the South Pole

1. Which form of animal transportation is no longer used in Antarctica?

2. When did humans first see Antarctica?

3. A mountain range divides Antarctica. True or False?

4. What is the permanent population of Antarctica?

5. What percentage of Antarctic ice is contained in the Ross Ice Shelf?

6. What is the name of the natural light display in the sky that is only visible from South America, Antarctica, and Australia?

7. The largest Antarctic iceberg ever seen was bigger than Belgium. True or False?

8. The continent of Antarctica has always been at the South Pole? True or False?

9. Who led the first expedition to record a sighting of Antarctica?

10. By what percentage does the size of Antarctica increase when the sea around the continent freezes during winter?

11. How do ice cores help scientists to understand past climates?

12. When did the Antarctic Treaty, which provides for international cooperation and bans exploitation, go into effect?

13. Which type of ice does not occur at sea?

14. How many International Polar Years have there been to promote research and cooperation?

15. Which is the only penguin that breeds in the Antarctic winter?

16. There are more hours of sunshine in the Antarctic Peninsula over a year than in most equatorial countries. True or False?

17. At the South Pole, how many days per year does the sun not rise?

18. The South Geomagnetic Pole and the South Pole are at the same place. True or False?

19. Is Antarctica water surrounded by land or land surrounded by sea?

20. Which is colder, the Antarctic or the Arctic?

(Answers on page 477)

The Final Frontier

1. "I don't think the human race will survive the next thousand years, unless we spread into space." Who said this?

2. Used continuously since 1957, what is the world's largest launch site?

3. When did NASA's space shuttle first take to the air?

4. What does the acronym "PAM" stand for?

5. The laws of gravity mean that the farther out a satellite orbits, the slower it moves through space. True or False?

6. How many Langrarian points are there in the Earth-moon-sun system?

7. The American space station Skylab orbited Earth from 1973 to 1979. How long did its first crew stay on board?

8. Who or what are Zvezda and Kibo?

9. Approximately how many times a day does the International Space Station orbit Earth?

10. What is Alexei Leonov's claim to fame?

11. What was NASA's space satellite Explorer 6 the first to do in 1959?

12. In the Apollo spacecraft, there were three modules: the command module, the lunar module, and what?

13. Where was Apollo 11's *Eagle*'s landing site?

14. Which Apollo lunar mission took the first roving vehicle to the moon, in 1971?

15. What was the name of the first mission to take samples of comet particles?

16. What was Sojourner?

17. To which body in the solar system was the Huygens probe sent in 2005?

18. Voyager 2 launched in 1977 and was still active in 2020. True or False?

19. The New Horizons spacecraft completed its mission in 2015 with a flyby of which body?

20. ESA's Rosetta Mission to Comet 67P/C-G ended its mission of exploration in 2015 by crashing on the comet. True or False?

21. Which US president signed the National Aeronautics and Space Act, leading to the birth of NASA?

22. Who invented the term "Big Bang"?

23. About how many times bigger is the sun than the moon?

24. Which planet has been visited by the MESSENGER craft?

25. What was the average speed of the Mir Space Station?

(Answers on page 477)   **95**

It's Elementary

1. What is the chemical symbol of the element gold?

2. What is atomic mass?

3. What does "pH" mean?

4. What material were electrical insulators originally made from?

5. Carbon forms allotropes. True or False?

6. When hydrogen and nitrogen are mixed, what is produced?

7. Who won a Nobel Prize in 1954 for his work in quantum mechanics in chemistry?

8. Who drew up the first periodic table of elements?

9. Which element is the best conductor of electricity?

10. What is the most common element in Earth's crust?

11. When sodium and chlorine are combined, what sort of bond is created?

12. What three constituents do molecules contain?

13. Ammonia was used as an ingredient in explosives during World War I. True or False?

14. What is "oil of vitriol" known as today?

15. Whose law refers to the relationship between pressure and volume?

16. When hydrogen and carbon atoms are joined, what ending does the new compound have?

17. Which English chemist discovered oxygen?

18. To which metal group does iron belong: alkali, transition, or inner transition?

19. What is the most common element in the human body?

20. If a chemical's name ends in "-ide," how many elements is it made of?

(Answers on page 477)

Body of Knowledge

1. Which cells are found in your fingertips and help you feel light pressure?

2. You use only 10 percent of your brain. True or False?

3. Adrenaline makes you wide-eyed, alert, and ready for action. Where are the glands that make it?

4. What does peroxisome do inside cells?

5. Which part of your brain can you blame for putting you in a bad mood?

6. Which of your muscles is responsible for pulling up the rib cage when you breathe?

7. The unusual ability to see smells, hear colors, and smell sounds is known as what?

8. The three semicircular canals in the inner ear detect movement. Which part of the semicircular canals detects vertical movement?

9. The liver is the largest internal organ and performs more than 500 jobs. True or False?

10. When someone talks too much, what type of joint is he or she overusing?

11. The largest muscle in the human body can be found in the what?

12. The medical term for a "nose job" is what?

13. More than half of your blood is plasma. True or False?

14. Which metal has been found to have an antibacterial effect and is sometimes used in wound dressings?

15. Which part of the body is most sensitive to heat and cold?

16. What helps prevent us from suffering the same disease twice?

17. There are around 30 trillion red blood cells in the human body. True or False?

18. What cells secrete insulin?

19. What chemical causes a fever?

20. A dream can trigger a sneeze. True or False?

21. What else did medieval doctors do to the patient's urine when they were trying to diagnose an illness, beside study its color?

22. Blood transfusions did not work before the 20th century; what happened in 1901 that made them possible?

23. What medicine was discovered in mold in 1928?

24. From which flower do we get the drugs opium and morphine?

25. In which part of the body is the vena cava?

SCIENCE & TECHNOLOGY

CHAPTER 3

ART & LITERATURE

Discover how much of a culture vulture you are with these quizzes covering art and literature from the past to the present, the classic to the avant-garde. See if your favorites are here and learn about new favorites.

Shakespeare

1. In which town was William Shakespeare born?

2. William Shakespeare was born and died on April 26. True or False?

3. In which play do we meet Rosencrantz and Guildenstern?

4. Which monarch ruled England at the start of Shakespeare's career as a playwright?

5. How many plays were published in Shakespeare's first folio: 10, 34, 36, 50?

6. Complete the title of this play: *Much Ado About…*

7. Which Shakespearean theater was reconstructed on London's South Bank in 1997?

8. Which tragic play features the characters Iago and Desdemona?

9. Which play features two "star-crossed" lovers?

10. Shakespeare wrote three different types of plays: comedies, tragedies, and what else?

11. Which play was set on a remote island?

12. Shakespeare invented the word "assassination." True or False?

13. The average adult today uses only 3,000 words. How many did Shakespeare use across his plays?

14. Which Roman general neglects his soldierly duties after falling for Cleopatra's charms?

15. The Three Witches appear in which Shakespeare play?

16. Who falls in love with Nick Bottom in *A Midsummer Night's Dream*?

17. What is the unrhymed poetry in Shakespeare's plays called?

18. Which of Shakespeare's plays takes place in the "Forest of Arden"?

19. Which play includes the Battle of Agincourt?

20. How many lines does a sonnet have?

21. What is the name of Hamlet's mother?

22. What was the name of Shakespeare's wife?

23. How many sonnets did Shakespeare write?

24. Which of Shakespeare's plays is the shortest?

25. Which play does this quote come from: "If music be the food of love, play on"?

ART & LITERATURE

Best-Selling Novels

1. Which best-selling trilogy was inspired by competitive reality TV shows and news coverage of the war in Iraq?

2. Which British author won the Man Booker prize twice, for *Wolf Hall* (2009) and *Bring up the Bodies* (2012)?

3. Who is the author of the best-selling children's series *Diary of a Wimpy Kid*?

4. Which best-selling novel by Sally Rooney was made into a TV series in 2020?

5. *Snuff* is the 39th book in which long-running fantasy series?

6. Following the success of the Harry Potter series, J. K. Rowling wrote which best-selling novel for adults?

7. To date, the *Fifty Shades* trilogy has sold just under 50 million copies worldwide. True or False?

8. Bella, Edward, and Jacob are the main characters in which popular young-adult series?

9. *The Millennium Series*, a trilogy of crime-fiction novels focused on Lisbeth Salander and Mikael Blomkvist, was originally published in which language?

10. *The Guinness Book of World Records* holds the world record for best-selling copyrighted book series of all time. True or False?

11. Sara Gruen's *Water for Elephants* was written as part of the National Novel Writing Month online challenge. True or False?

12. David Nicholl's *One Day* was adapted into a film in 2011. Who played Emma?

13. What was the first blockbuster title written by Dan Brown?

14. Which celebrity chef's 15-minute-meal cookbook has topped best-seller charts?

15. Which Margaret Atwood novel was made into a popular TV series?

16. Originally published in 1937, which novel hit the best-sellers' list again following excitement about its movie release?

17. Who is the author of the best-selling *A Song of Ice and Fire* series?

18. Stephen King's *11/22/63* revisits the assassination of US President Abraham Lincoln. True or False?

19. Whose novels feature a forensic psychologist named Alex Cross?

20. Which political figure wrote a memoir called *Becoming*?

　　　　(Answers on page 478)

ART & LITERATURE

Word on the Street: Authors

1. Who wrote the thrillers in which the agent 007 appears?

2. Which 2001 book by Yann Martel was made into a film by Ang Lee in 2012?

3. Who is the author responsible for introducing the world in 2007 to vampires who sparkle in sunlight?

4. What is the name of the detective in Raymond Chandler's hard-boiled crime novel *The Big Sleep*?

5. Which American author's long list of international best-sellers have seen him become known as the king of the legal thriller genre?

6. Who wrote the novel *Atonement*, later turned into the multi-Oscar-nominated film starring Keira Knightley and James McAvoy?

7. Who wrote *The Catcher in the Rye*, a modern classic about angst-ridden teen Holden Caulfield?

8. Alice Walker became the first black woman to win the Pulitzer Prize for Fiction in 1983. With which novel did she win?

9. In which great novel will you find the line "all animals are equal, but some animals are more equal than others"?

10. Which magical land behind a wardrobe was created by C. S. Lewis?

11. Who is the author of the *Memory Man* series of thrillers?

12. Which novel by Cormac McCarthy was adapted into an Oscar-winning film in 2007?

13. In French literature, who caused a stir with his modern classic *L'Etranger*?

14. Which film was originally a novel by popular British author Nick Hornby?

15. Phillip Pullman's *His Dark Materials* trilogy begins with *Northern Lights* and is followed by which book?

16. Which murder-mystery writer created the legendary detective Hercule Poirot?

17. Which popular travel writer famously took a step into history writing with *A Short History of Nearly Everything*?

18. Which children's author wrote books about witches, peaches, chocolate, and twits?

19. Which work by J. R. R. Tolkien was published posthumously by his son Christopher in 1977?

20. Terry Pratchett is the author of one of the most popular and long-running fantasy series ever, but what is it called?

Famous Artists

ART & LITERATURE

1. Which Italian Renaissance artist sculpted *David*?

2. Which brand of soup was used in a screenprint by Andy Warhol?

3. A cottage in Suffolk was featured in a painting by which John?

4. Pablo Picasso was part of which artistic movement?

5. Which English artist produced the satirical work called *A Rake's Progress*?

6. Which ancient civilization was known for its red-figure vases?

7. Johannes Vermeer's most famous work, *Girl with a Pearl Earring,* was sold in Holland for the equivalent of 32 cents. True or False?

8. Vincent van Gogh was famous for painting which flowers?

9. Who painted the *Mona Lisa*?

10. Which surrealist artist was noted for his moustache?

11. J. M. W. Turner was a Pre-Raphaelite painter. True or False?

12. Who sculpted *The Kiss*?

13. When did the Romantic Movement start?

14. Antony Gormley's large sculpture in Gateshead, England, is called the *Angel in the North*. True or False?

15. *The Scream* was painted by which artist?

16. Who famously painted his garden?

17. Hans Holbein was most famous for which type of painting?

18. What nationality was artist Henri Matisse?

19. What form of art is Henry Moore famous for?

20. Mark Rothko is known for what style of painting?

21. Which artist had an exhibition of his iPad paintings?

22. Which artist is most associated with pointillism?

23. Which artist is nicknamed "Jack the Dripper"?

24. What is the artist Alphonse Mucha best known for?

25. Which artist is known for painting Parisian nightlife?

Roald Dahl

1. What shop did Mrs. Pratchett run?

2. What is Matilda's favorite pastime?

3. What is the BFG's favorite drink?

4. Name the three farmers in *Fantastic Mr. Fox*.

5. What animal is featured in *Esio Trot*?

6. What does Danny's father hunt?

7. Who runs the chocolate factory?

8. Name one of James Henry Trotter's aunts.

9. What did Roald Dahl always eat after lunch?

10. Name Roald Dahl's own favorite book.

11. Who is Matilda's headmistress?

12. Who illustrated many of Roald Dahl's books?

13. Which book (considered his first) was inspired by Dahl's Royal Air Force service?

14. What was Roald Dahl's favorite color?

15. What special language does the BFG speak?

16. In which book do the Oompa-Loompas appear?

17. Who is the terrifying ruler in *The Witches*?

18. What does Mr. Twit never wash?

19. Name the boy in *The Giraffe and The Pelly and Me*.

20. What is a Muggle-Wump?

21. In the *Magic Finger*, why is the Gregg family punished?

22. Who does George use his marvelous medicine on?

23. How do the aunts in *James and the Giant Peach* die?

24. In *Matilda*, how is Miss Honey related to Miss Trunchbull?

25. What do square sweets do?

ART & LITERATURE

The Lion, the Witch, and the Wardrobe

1. The Pevensie children are sent to the country to escape what?

2. Susan is the oldest of the Pevensie children. True or False?

3. The professor in *The Lion, the Witch and the Wardrobe* is called Professor Digory what?

4. When Lucy first meets Mr. Tumnus, what is he carrying?

5. In which year was *The Lion, the Witch and the Wardrobe* first published?

6. The children don't believe Lucy when she tells them about her visit to Narnia. True or False?

7. What does Edmund eat when he first meets the White Witch?

8. Which animal is the Chief of the Secret Police and sent to hunt the children?

9. Father Christmas gives all the children gifts. What gift does he give Peter?

10. Father Christmas also gives Mr. and Mrs. Beaver presents. What does Mrs. Beaver receive?

11. Whose life does Aslan bargain for with the White Witch?

12. What is the first indication that the White Witch's hold over Narnia is breaking?

13. What does the White Witch do to Mr. Tumnus?

14. What did the Beavers give the children for dessert at their first meeting?

15. Aslan sacrifices himself on the what?

16. Who eventually slays the White Witch?

17. Who does Peter save from being killed by a wolf?

18. After Edmund has been crowned, he is known as Edmund the Valiant. True or False?

19. Where are the children crowned as Kings and Queens of Narnia?

20. The children are chasing after which animal when they find themselves back in the wardrobe?

21. Who tells the children about Aslan?

22. What is a faun?

23. How many thrones are at Cair Paravel?

24. What is the spell that the White Witch casts on Narnia?

25. What color are the White Witch's reindeer?

(Answers on page 478)

Harry Potter

1. In the first book, how old is Harry when he discovers that he is a wizard?

2. What is the name of Ron's pet rat?

3. What is the emblem of Gryffindor house?

4. In which shop can wizards and witches buy their wands in Diagon Alley?

5. What is the name of the magical mirror that shows people the deepest desires of their hearts?

6. When is Harry Potter's birthday?

7. The *Hogwarts Express* departs from which platform at London's King's Cross station?

8. What is the name of the creature that feeds off positive human emotion?

9. What is the name of the magical plant that allows a wizard or witch to breathe underwater?

10. Hermione Granger's Patronus Charm is in the shape of which animal?

11. Who are the Muggle aunt and uncle with whom Harry lives every summer?

12. Who kills Dumbledore at the end of the sixth book?

13. Ron has seven siblings. True or False?

14. Who shows Harry Tom Riddle's diary?

15. Who was the prisoner of Azkaban?

16. Where did Peter Pettigrew kill Cedric Diggory?

17. "Avada Kedavra" is one of the Unforgivable Curses. True or False?

18. Who is Rita Skeeter?

19. How many staircases are there at Hogwarts?

20. Which language other than English can both Harry and Voldemort speak?

21. Which pets are not officially allowed at Hogwarts?

22. What kind of animal is Trevor?

23. Which book did Harry get the name of his owl from?

24. What was the name of Hermione's cat?

25. The word "muggle" is now in the *Oxford English Dictionary*. True or False?

ART & LITERATURE

Artists' Handbook

1. Which is NOT a primary color: blue, red, orange, yellow?

2. Which is NOT a secondary color: purple, green, blue, orange?

3. Which is not a paint: acrylics or pastels?

4. What term is used to describe the assembly of assorted materials to form a composition?

5. What color is the opposite of purple on the color wheel?

6. What was traditionally made from thin peeled willow twigs?

7. What do artists do with a medium?

8. What is the name of the object that artists traditionally use to mix paint on?

9. Mixing blue and yellow paint makes what color?

10. Intaglio is a type of what?

11. What must you do to a fabric canvas before you use it for painting?

12. What color is made by mixing red, yellow, and blue?

13. Crayons are soluble in water. True or False?

14. Which of these pencils' lead is harder: 2H or H?

15. Red, orange, and yellow are warm or cool colors?

16. Tempera, a principal painting medium before oil, was traditionally made from which food?

17. What are colors across from each other on the color wheel called?

18. The red pigment carmine comes from what?

19. What is the artistic tradition called that uses small ceramic tiles to create a pattern or picture?

20. What kind of gum is used as a binder for watercolor painting?

106   (Answers on page 479)

Books with Bite

1. Which is the second book in Stephenie Meyer's *Twilight* series?

2. Which of Anne Rice's vampire novels was made into a film starring Tom Cruise?

3. Does the Stephen King novel *Carrie* feature a vampire?

4. Who wrote *Dracula*?

5. The lyrics to "Moon Over Bourbon Street" by Sting were inspired by Anne Rice's *Interview with the Vampire*. True or False?

6. In Stephenie Meyer's *Twilight* series, which vampire falls in love with Bella Swan?

7. In which seaside town is Dracula's boat shipwrecked when it comes to England?

0. Which author wrote the books that inspired the TV series *True Blood*?

9. Which bloodthirsty real-life person is believed to have inspired the character Dracula?

10. Where are the book and TV series *The Vampire Diaries* set?

11. In the *Twilight* series, which type of animal blood does Edward Cullen enjoy drinking most (after human)?

12. In literature, many things are said to kill the average vampire. Which of these probably wouldn't: garlic bread, a crucifix, sunlight?

13. In *True Blood*, what is Sookie Stackhouse's "gift"?

14. Which classic novel is mentioned several times in Stephenie Meyer's *Eclipse*?

15. In Charlaine Harris's books, what is True Blood?

16. The character Frankenstein in the novel *Frankenstein* is a vampire. True or False?

17. In *Breaking Dawn*, what do Edward and Bella call their child?

18. Who created the fictional vampire Lestat de Lioncourt?

19. Bela Lugosi was famous for his film role in *Dracula* or *Frankenstein*?

20. Bram Stoker's Dracula slept in a four-poster bed, not a coffin. True or False?

Children's Classics

ART & LITERATURE

1. Which children's classic by J. M. Barrie features a boy who won't grow up?

2. Which animals are the main characters in *Watership Down*?

3. In Rudyard Kipling's *The Jungle Book*, who is the Man-Cub's best friend?

4. In *The Wonderful Wizard of Oz*, what does the Tin Woodman hope to get in Emerald City?

5. *What Katy Did…*? Complete the title of the book that follows *What Katy Did* and W*hat Katy Did at School.*

6. In *A Christmas Carol* by Dickens, Bob Cratchit says the words, "God bless us, everyone." True or False?

7. Which book features the character Christopher Robin?

8. Anne Shirley is the main character in which children's classic?

9. In *Peter Pan*, what does Peter have to sprinkle on the children before they can fly?

10. Which novel features Tweedledee and Tweedledum?

11. In *Gulliver's Travels* by Jonathan Swift, where does Gulliver find himself a giant?

12. *Treasure Island*'s Long John Silver is also known as the "Sea Cook" and what else?

13. Who wrote *The Railway Children*?

14. What creature is Jack London's White Fang?

15. Where does Peter Pan live?

16. In *King Solomon's Mines* by H. Rider Haggard, where are the mines?

17. In which book do Lucy, Edmund, Susan, and Peter Pevensie appear?

18. In *The Merry Adventures of Robin Hood*, what does the Sheriff of Nottingham offer as a prize to lure Robin Hood to the archery match?

19. Where is *Heidi* set?

20. Who wrote *The Water Babies*?

21. In which book does the Waterbury family star?

22. In *Little Women*, what does Jo sell to help her sick father?

23. Who wrote the *The Secret Garden*?

24. Which family does Mary Poppins go to work for?

25. Who wrote *Black Beauty*?

Contemporary Art

1. Tracey Emin was born in Margate. True or False?

2. Emin's *Everyone I Have Ever Slept with 1963–1995* features what?

3. Which Saatchi brother has been a key figure in contemporary art collection?

4. Which pop artist was famous for creating silkscreen "diptychs," or collages, of Marilyn Monroe?

5. Which band's video for "Country House" did Damien Hirst direct?

6. Grayson Perry is renowned for his work in which medium?

7. Who made a cast of his head using his own blood?

8. Which was the first US city to feature "CowParade"—colorful cow sculptures dotted around the streets—in 1999?

9. Hirst's *The Physical Impossibility of Death in the Mind of Someone Living* features which animal?

10. In which year did Tracey Emin make *My Bed*?

11. Which revolutionary did Gavin Turk cast himself as?

12. Which iconic art gallery in New York City was designed by architect Frank Lloyd Wright?

13. Sam Taylor-Wood directed a film about which Beatle?

14. What are the first names of the Chapman brothers?

15. Much of the Chapman brothers' work was destroyed by what in 2004?

16. The Turner Prize is named in honor of the artist J. M. W Turner. True or False?

17. When was the Turner Prize inaugurated?

18. Taylor-Wood made a video installation starring which sleeping soccer player?

19. Hirst's *For The Love of God* features 8,601 what embedded in a platinum skull?

20. Whose work is featured in a book called *Wall and Piece*?

ART & LITERATURE

Aesop's Fables

1. Which fable is associated with: "Slow and steady wins the race"?

2. Which tale ends with: "Even when liars tell the truth, they are never believed. The liar will lie once, twice, and then perish when he tells the truth"?

3. In which story does a bird drop pebbles into a jug to enable it to drink?

4. The moral of *Ant and the Grasshopper* is: "To work today is to eat tomorrow." True or False?

5. In which fable does the bird learn to: "Beware of flatterers"?

6. In which story do the characters learn they could achieve more by working together?

7. What is the moral of *The Bear and the Travelers*?

8. Who delivers the moral in *The Bear and the Travelers* fable?

9. "Honesty is the best policy" is usually associated with which fable?

10. Who was so busy planning what to do with her money that she dropped the pail?

11. The moral of the story *The Milkmaid and the Pail* is what?

12. In which fable does one character prevent the other characters from having something that he himself has no use for?

13. Androcles removes a thorn from the paw of which kind of animal?

14. Where does Androcles meet the animal again?

15. In *The Dog and Its Reflection*, what does the dog lose in the water?

16. Which fable suggests that: "Quality is better than quantity"?

17. After being unable to reach some tasty-looking grapes, what does the fox decide they are?

18. What popular expression is taken from the fable *The Fox and the Grapes*?

19. "Enemies' promises are made to be broken" comes from which fable?

20. Frauds and liars are always discovered eventually and pay for their actions accordingly. Which fable does this moral belong to?

(Answers on page 479)

Picasso

1. Picasso's father's name was Ruiz y Blasco. True or False?

2. How old was Picasso when his father felt he had surpassed him in artistic talent?

3. Which was Picasso's first "period"?

4. In which year was Picasso born?

5. Which Greek painter was a great early influence on Picasso?

6. With whom did Picasso share an apartment when he moved to Paris?

7. Where was Picasso born?

8. Of which magazine did Picasso publish five issues, featuring portraits of the poor?

9. What is the name of the painting Picasso did in response to the bombing of a Spanish town?

10. American art collectors Leo and Gertrude Stein were great admirers of Picasso's work. True or False?

11. Which artist developed Cubism alongside Picasso?

12. Which of Picasso's mistresses appears in many of his "Rose" paintings?

13. What alternative art form did Picasso pursue between 1935 and 1959?

14. In 1944, Picasso began a love affair with a young student named Françoise Gilot. What was the age difference between them?

15. What political ideology was Picasso associated with?

16. Who did Picasso always play in his film appearances?

17. During which years did Picasso produce most of his ceramics?

18. Picasso once said: "Art is a truth that makes us realize the lie." True or False?

19. Picasso's "African" period lasted for how long?

20. Where can Picasso's giant sculpture the *Bust of Sylvette* be found?

21. Which mythological creature did Picasso paint a lot in the 1930s?

22. Where is the Picasso Museum?

23. When and where did Picasso die?

24. Which artist did Picasso declare was his "one and only master"?

25. How old was Picasso when he finished his first painting?

(Answers on page 479)   **111**

Degas

1. One of the founders of Impressionism, Degas preferred to be called a what?

2. Hilaire-Germain-Edgar Degas was born into a middle-class family. What was the actual family name?

3. In which year was Degas born?

4. Degas was half French and half what?

5. What drink is shown being consumed in his 1875 masterpiece?

6. What was Degas's first masterpiece?

7. In what branch of the military did Degas enlist at the outbreak of the Franco-Prussian War in 1870?

8. Where in America did Degas begin an extended stay in 1872?

9. Degas painted ballerinas because such works sold well. True or False?

10. Why did Degas leave many of his late works unfinished?

11. Degas joined forces with which group of young artists in 1874?

12. Degas often painted horse races. True or False?

13. During which years did Degas develop a passion for photography?

14. In what kind of light would Degas often photograph his subjects?

15. In which European country did Degas spend a lot of time from 1854 to 1859?

16. *Little Dancer, Aged Fourteen* is a sculpture by Degas. What is it made of?

17. In which year did Degas die?

18. Impressionism originated in the 1860s. True or False?

19. What happened to Degas in his later years?

20. Degas painted half of his works on the subject of what?

21. Degas created a set of paintings about which American city?

22. Degas made many paintings of which animal?

23. Walter Sickert was a close friend of Degas. True or False?

24. Degas was greatly influenced by Japanese prints. True or False?

25. Degas married Mary Cassatt. True or False?

(Answers on page 479)

Which Novel Am I?

1. Which F. Scott Fitzgerald novel is mainly set in West Egg during the Roaring Twenties?

2. Which Miguel de Cervantes novel is about a gentle knight and his servant Sancho Panza?

3. Daniel Defoe's novel *Captain Singleton* describes the life of a shipwrecked sailor. True or False?

4. Which Mary Shelley title was written as the result of a competition?

5. Cathy and Heathcliff play out their destinies in which Gothic thriller?

6. "Call me Ishmael" begins which tale of maritime madness?

7. Which story sends its main character down a rabbit hole?

8. Which Fyodor Dostoyevsky novel details Rodion Raskolnikov's moral dilemma?

9. Which Mark Twain title recounts Jim and Huck's adventures on the Mississippi?

10. Evelyn Waugh's essay on Fleet Street is called what?

11. Winston Smith's struggle against totalitarianism is told in which novel by George Orwell?

12. Holden Caulfield goes on a personal journey for a week in this J. D. Salinger classic.

13. Which Joseph Heller novel details a no-win wartime situation?

14. Three stories about being down and out in the Big Smoke are featured in Paul Auster's what?

15. This savage story of boys on an island is William Golding's what?

16. V. S. Naipaul's uneasy novel set in revolutionary Africa is called what?

17. No literary list would be complete without this J. R. R. Tolkien trilogy.

18. A bleak allegory about apartheid is J. M. Coetzee's what?

19. Franz Kafka's enigmatic tale of Josef K is called what?

20. Leo Tolstoy's tortured tale of a married woman's passion for a younger man is called what?

21. What is Hilary Mantel's first novel in the trilogy about Thomas Cromwell?

22. What was Maya Angelou's debut novel?

23. This Jane Austen novel features the Woodhouse family.

24. This Alice Walker novel won the Pulitzer Prize for Fiction in 1983.

25. In which fictional English county are Anthony Trollope's clerical chronicles set?

ART & LITERATURE

Great Artists

1. Which artist famously damaged his ear?

2. Where was Leonardo da Vinci born?

3. Which Leonardo da Vinci work sold for $450 million in 2017, making it then the world's most expensive painting?

4. Which contemporary artist was commissioned to design the cover for the December 1985 issue of the French edition of *Vogue*?

5. The images we today associate with Tudor monarchs like Henry VIII come from portraits painted by which 16th-century artist?

6. Which 19th-century English artist is known for studies of the East Anglian landscape and rural scenes?

7. Which French artist is best known for his portraits of ballerinas?

8. Vincent van Gogh's most famous painting is known as *Starry* what?

9. Théothile Steinlen's 1896 advertisement for a Parisian cabaret has now been immortalized in a popular poster. What is it called?

10. Which 19th-century artist stated that "We all stem from Pissarro," referring to the French Impressionist artist Camille Pissarro?

11. Who painted *The Scream*?

12. Which artist is often credited with painting the first purely abstract works?

13. Which Russian's stained-glass windows and religious scenes helped him become one of the most successful 20th-century artists?

14. Which genre of art features colorful, brash paintings, often inspired by comic strips and advertising?

15. Whose abstract, dreamlike paintings often featured clocks, elephants, and eggs?

16. Urban landscapes and "matchstick men" populate the works of which English artist?

17. Monet and Renoir pioneered which 19th-century art movement featuring shimmering outdoor scenes, bold colors, and little detail?

18. Who painted the ceiling of the Sistine Chapel within the Vatican City?

19. How many paintings did Vincent van Gogh sell in his lifetime?

20. Which French artist left his home to paint in Polynesia?

All about Novels

1. Who wrote *Wuthering Heights*?

2. *The Woman in White* is considered to be one of the very first mystery novels. Who wrote it?

3. What are the names of the main lovers in *Doctor Zhivago*?

4. In which country is *Wide Sargasso Sea* set?

5. *Lady Chatterley's Lover* was not openly published in the UK until which year?

6. Jane Austen wrote a novel called *Ruth*. True or False?

7. Much of *The Wings of the Dove* is set in which Italian city?

8. Pip, a young orphan, is featured in which Dickens novel?

9. *The Picture of Dorian Gray* was Oscar Wilde's only adult novel. True or False?

10. Meg, Jo, Beth, and Amy are sisters in which 19th-century American novel?

11. In which year was *Nineteen Eighty-Four* published?

12. In *The Catcher in the Rye*, how does the protagonist Holden deal with difficult situations?

13. What is the name of Madame Bovary's husband?

14. Which novel is narrated by six-year-old Scout Finch?

15. Which novel, published in 1920, is a sequel to *The Rainbow*?

16. *The Count of Monte Cristo* was written by Benjamin Disraeli. True or False?

17. Edna Ferber won the Pulitzer Prize for which novel?

18. What was the title of the first version of *Pride and Prejudice* published in 1796?

19. In *Lord of the Flies*, who heads up the group of hunters?

20. How old was Mary Shelley when she wrote *Frankenstein*?

21. *The Modern Prometheus* is the subtitle of which novel?

22. Clara Peggotty appears in which Dickens novel?

23. In *The Handmaid's Tale*, what are the housekeepers called?

24. Who wrote *Brave New World*?

25. In which George Eliot novel do Dorothea Brooke and Edward Casaubon marry?

ART & LITERATURE

A Good Impression

1. Impressionism began in the 18th century. True or False?

2. In which year was the term "Impressionism" coined?

3. Which river was painted by Monet and Renoir?

4. What did the Impressionists initially set out to do?

5. "Unfinished" was used to describe the Impressionist style. True or False?

6. What effect did painting on white canvases have on Impressionist painting?

7. Monet was best known for his paintings of which sort of ponds?

8. Who painted *Luncheon at the Boating Party*, exhibited in 1882?

9. What is the French term "*plein air*" used to describe?

10. Which war did Monet escape from when he relocated to London in 1870?

11. Impressionism marked the birth of modern painting. True or False?

12. "Anyone can have a talent at 25. The difficulty is to have talent at 50": which artist said that?

13. Which Impressionist artist died at his home in Giverny, penniless and unknown?

14. *View from Louveciennes* is a painting by which Impressionist artist?

15. American Impressionist Childe Hassam was best known for painting what objects?

16. Which "forgotten" Impressionist born in France was a British citizen and said, "I always start a painting with the sky"?

17. Which Impressionist artist married Eugéne Manet, Édouard Manet's brother?

18. What term was used to describe the experimental nature of the Impressionist painters in Paris?

19. What "dotty" painting by Georges Seurat launched Neo-Impressionism in the 1880s?

20. The leader of the Post-Impressionist movement, Paul Gauguin, sought inspiration from communities in which South Pacific island?

21. Which movement reacted against the Impressionists?

22. Which art critic created the term "Impressionism"?

23. Who painted *At the Moulin Rouge*?

24. Photography had a big influence on the Impressionists. True or False?

25. Overall, what was the most popular subject in Impressionism?

(Answers on page 480)

Mad about Austen

1. In *Pride and Prejudice*, who is the youngest Bennet sister?

2. In *Persuasion*, how does Captain Wentworth let Anne know of his feelings for her?

3. *The Brothers* was the name of the original manuscript for which later Austen novel?

4. How many children were in Jane Austen's family?

5. What does Catherine think Henry's father has done with his wife in *Northanger Abbey*?

6. In which year was Jane Austen born?

7. In *Persuasion*, Anne Elliot is considered a spinster. How old is she in the novel?

8. How many novels did Jane Austen complete during her lifetime?

9. In *Pride and Prejudice*, how many truly accomplished women does Darcy claim to know?

10. It has been estimated that at any one time (around the world), there are more than 600 Jane Austen adaptations being produced. True or False?

11. Was *Villette* written by Jane Austen?

12. Jane once accepted a marriage proposal but changed her mind and turned the man down the following day. True or False?

13. Which pseudonym did Jane Austen go under when she was first published?

14. At which Surrey beauty spot is a picnic held in *Emma*?

15. Where does the Bennet family live?

16. Which modern-day book, inspired by *Pride and Prejudice*, features Mark Darcy?

17. In 1996, the actress Gwyneth Paltrow played which Austen heroine in a film adaptation?

18. In *Mansfield Park*, who does Fanny Price marry?

19. Where is Jane Austen buried?

20. *Lady Susan* is the title of an unpublished Austen novel. True or False?

21. In *Pride and Prejudice*, Elizabeth's best friend is whom?

22. *Sense and Sensibility* tells the story of two sisters. What are their names?

23. How many marriages take place in *Pride and Prejudice*?

24. How many novels did Jane Austen have published in her lifetime?

25. E. M. Forster was a huge fan of Jane Austen. True or False?

ART & LITERATURE

Take a Walk on the Dark Side

1. Who created the detective Alex Cross?

2. Betty Barnard is strangled with her own belt in which Agatha Christie book?

3. In Edgar Allan Poe's *The Murders in the Rue Morgue*, the murderer is which animal?

4. What is the name of P. D. James's female private detective?

5. Who created Inspector Wexford?

6. *The Woman in White* is by which author?

7. Which scheming and repellent character appears in five of Patricia Highsmith's novels?

8. Raymond Chandler forgets to tell us who murdered the chauffeur in *The Big Sleep*. True or False?

9. Who is the archenemy of Sherlock Holmes?

10. *Silver Bullet* is a horror film based on the Stephen King novella *Cycle of the Werewolf.* What is the Silver Bullet?

11. Which hilarious New Jersey bounty hunter was created by Janet Evanovich?

12. Crime author Patricia Highsmith kept snails as pets and carried them around in her handbag. True or False?

13. What is the first name of Agatha Christie's Miss Marple?

14. Which crusading Swedish journalist died in 2004, leaving behind the manuscripts of three now-famous thrillers?

15. Who created Philip Marlowe?

16. Which inspector is featured in Charles Dickens's *Bleak House*?

17. In which book does Sherlock Holmes first appear?

18. Which author's character is Dr. Temperance "Bones" Brennan from the TV series loosely based on?

19. Which career did Sara Paretsky's gritty V. I. Warshawski attempt before becoming a P.I.?

20. Which Agatha Christie "whodunit" opened in London's West End in 1952 and is still going, making it the world's longest-running play?

Harry Potter: Magical Creatures

1. The Grey Lady is the Ravenclaw House ghost. What is her real name?

2. What was Albus Dumbledore's boggart?

3. Goblins converse in a language known as what?

4. A Thestral is seen only by… ?

5. Lord Voldemort's pet snake Nagini is a Horcrux. True or False?

6. Which house-elf served the Crouch family?

7. Which magical creature lives in the attic of the Burrow, causing minor disruptions when things are too quiet?

8. Which musical instrument does Harry use to get past Fluffy, the three-headed dog that guards the Philosopher's Stone?

9. What is the name of Dumbledore's phoenix?

10. Who slays Nagini in the final book?

11. Dementors are invisible to Muggles but affect them in the same way. True or False?

12. Witherwings is the alias given to which magical creature to avoid suspicion from the Ministry of Magic?

13. How many Horcruxes were destroyed using Basilisk venom?

14. Aragog, an Acromantula, is the "Monster of Slytherin." True or False?

15. What color is Unicorn blood?

16. What kind of creature does Professor Lockhart let loose in his classroom in the second Harry Potter book?

17. What kind of owl is Harry's pet Hedwig?

18. Is Hedwig a female or male owl?

19. Which animal represents the school house Hufflepuff?

20. Who made Wolfsbane Potion for Professor Lupin to help him keep his human thoughts once he was transformed into a werewolf?

ART & LITERATURE

Know Your Books?

ART & LITERATURE

1. Which publisher is responsible for publishing J. K. Rowling's *Harry Potter* series?

2. Which author created the cannibalistic serial killer Hannibal Lecter?

3. Who wrote *The Tenant of Wildfell Hall*?

4. Which *Lord of the Rings* character is first described as "the Grey"?

5. *The Ghost Road* by Pat Barker won the Booker Prize. True or False?

6. Which of these Shakespeare plays is NOT a comedy: *Hamlet, Twelfth Night, A Midsummer's Nights Dream*?

7. Where did Adrian Mole grow up?

8. The book *Do Androids Dream of Electric Sheep?* served as the primary basis for the plot of which 1982 film?

9. In Enid Blyton's *The Famous Five*, Timmy the dog is actually a female. True or False?

10. In 1961, who was Holly Golightly in the film version of Truman Capote's *Breakfast at Tiffany's*?

11. Mary Shelley's *Frankenstein* was first published anonymously in which year?

12. In Rudyard Kipling's *The Jungle Book*, what animal is Shere Khan?

13. Nancy Mitford got the title of her book *Love in a Cold Climate* from George Orwell's novel *Keep the Aspidistra Flying*. True or False?

14. *Carte Blanche*, a new James Bond novel, was published in 2011. Who wrote it?

15. According to *The Hitchhiker's Guide to the Galaxy*, what is the answer to the "Ultimate Question of Life, The Universe, and Everything"?

16. In John Wyndham's *The Day of the Triffids*, what are the Triffids?

17. Complete the title of this book by John Buchan: *The…Steps*.

18. In which novel by Charles Dickens does Miss Havisham appear?

19. *The Quiet American* was written by…?

20. Which famous detective is featured in Dashiell Hammett's *The Maltese Falcon*?

21. Which Malorie Blackman novel about a state separated by color was made into a successful TV series?

22. Which author created private eye Cormoran Strike under a different name?

23. Which name did the author use to write the Cormoran Strike novels?

24. Who wrote the *Chaos Walking* trilogy?

25. *Some Assembly Required* and *Rethinking Normal* are autobiographies about what?

The Book That Became a Film

1. Which character does Kermit the Frog play in the Muppet version of Robert Louis Stevenson's *Treasure Island*?

2. Which infamous movie villain was originally created by American horror/thriller author Thomas Harris?

3. Complete the famous line from *The Lord of the Rings*: "One Ring to rule them all; One Ring to find them; One Ring to bring them all…"

4. What brand and model of car can be seen flying across London and the British countryside in the second *Harry Potter* film?

5. Alice Walker's *The Color Purple* became a hit Steven Spielberg–directed film in 1985. Which star got her big break in the lead role?

6. In Rudyard Kipling's and Disney's *The Jungle Book*, what is the name of the python?

7. In the Oscar-winning screen adaptation of the Winston Groom novel, where does Forrest Gump spend much of the film sitting?

8. After five nominations, Kate Winslet won her first Oscar in 2008 for her role in an adaptation of which book by Bernhard Schlink?

9. Which Disney film adaptation of a classic book features playing cards, hares, cats, rabbits, dodos, and doorknobs?

10. Which classic novel, twice adapted to film, is set on a desert island populated only by children?

11. *Breakfast at Tiffany's* has transitioned from novella to film to Broadway musical to famous song. Who wrote the original book?

12. What career has the actor who played Charlie in the original adaptation of Roald Dahl's *Charlie and the Chocolate Factory* gone on to?

13. Charles Dickens's *Oliver Twist* has proved popular with filmmakers: how many big screen adaptations have there been?

14. In the classic film *The Godfather* adapted from Mario Puzo's book, which Mafia boss is famously "gonna make him an offer he can't refuse"?

15. Which American literary courtroom classic, covering issues of racial inequality, became an Oscar-winning film in 1962?

16. What is the name of the book that became the influential Steven Spielberg film about the Holocaust, *Schindler's List*?

17. C. S. Lewis's *The Chronicles of Narnia* have now been made into three blockbuster movies, but how many books are there in the series?

18. Which was the first Bond book to be made into a film?

19. Who is the author of the James Bond books?

20. Which museum is featured in the film of Dan Brown's *The Da Vinci Code*?

ART & LITERATURE

Art for Art's Sake

1. In which decade did Francis Bacon die?

2. Who founded the Cubist movement with Picasso?

3. Which painting was stolen from the National Gallery in Oslo in 1994 and held for ransom?

4. Which sculptress is associated with Cornwall?

5. What does the term "impasto" mean?

6. William Blake was first trained and worked in which craft?

7. Who created *The Angel of the North*?

8. What type of art is Banksy known for?

9. Who painted Ophelia, depicting the suicide of the same character in *Hamlet*?

10. Which American artist painted *Christina's World* in 1948?

11. Where was Frida Kahlo born?

12. Which artist famously painted his mother?

13. Which artist is known for his giant balloon animals?

14. Rene Magritte was part of which art movement?

15. Canaletto is famous for painting which city?

16. Which animal did the painter Stubbs enjoy depicting?

17. Which name is Greek artist Doménikos Theotokópoulos better known by?

18. Who was the first president of the Royal Academy?

19. In which year did Tate Modern open?

20. The cave paintings in Lascaux, France, were made about 15,000 years ago. True or False?

21. Which Italian sculptor and architect is said to have created the Baroque style of sculpture?

22. Leonard Da Vinci's mural *The Last Supper* can be seen in which city?

23. Acrylic is made from pigment and plastic. True or False?

24. Which animal is often used in art to symbolize peace?

25. Which supermodel was painted naked by Lucian Freud in 2002?

Marvel Comics

1. In which year was *Marvel Comics #1* first published by Timely?

2. Stan Lee wrote his first story in 1941 for which Timely (soon to be Marvel) comic?

3. The *Fantastic Four #1* was first published in 1961. True or False?

4. Which issue of *The Amazing Spider-Man* first features Dr. Octopus?

5. Wolverine appears in the first issue of X-Men in 1963. True or False?

6. What is Daredevil's real name?

7. In which year did Susan Storm and Reed Richards get married?

8. Is Captain Planet a Marvel Comics hero?

9. 1978 saw the first graphic novel from Marvel. Written by Stan Lee and Jack Kirby, it was called *The Silver Surfer*. True or False?

10. In which year did *The Savage She-Hulk* first appear in print?

11. In 1986, the original X-Men returned in a new comic book titled *X-Factor*. True or False?

12. When does Gambit, known for his ability to supercharge objects with kinetic energy, first appear in *The Uncanny X-Men*?

13. Spider-Man's clone, Ben Reilly, goes by which superhero name?

14. Who are Arsenic, Sister Grimm, Lucy in the Sky, Talkback, and Bruiser?

15. Who wrote the miniseries *Civil War*?

16. Who is the odd one out: the Red Hulk, the Green Hulk, or the Blue Hulk?

17. One of the X-Men, Jean Grey, is also known as: Phoenix, Volcana, Valkyrie?

18. What color are the distinctive streaks in Rogue's hair?

19. Peter Parker is raised by his Aunt May and Uncle Ben because his parents died when he was a child. How did they die?

20. Who is Thor?

ART & LITERATURE

Great Paintings

1. Who was the 1942 painting *Nighthawks* painted by?

2. Which object can you see on Van Gogh's *Chair*?

3. Which objects can you see on Gauguin's *Chair*?

4. In Ruben's *The Judgement of Paris*, whose face can you see on Minerva's shield?

5. When did Michaelangelo paint the Sistine Chapel ceiling?

6. One of the "four Great Masters" of Chinese painting of the Ming dynasty, Qiu Ying, was known for: animals, flowers, landscapes and palace life?

7. Who painted *Mr. and Mrs. Andrews* in about 1750?

8. *The Death of Marat* depicts a murder victim where?

9. *Wanderer above the Sea of Fog* is a Romantic painting by which German?

10. Seurat made at least 70 drawings and oil sketches of the scene at La Grande Jatte. True or False?

11. What color is the balloon in Paul Klee's 1922 oil painting?

12. The Qingming Scroll is the only surviving work by Zhang Zeduan, one of the greatest painters of the Northern Song period. True or False?

13. What creatures feature in Pablo Picasso's antiwar painting *Guernica*?

14. How many elephants can be seen in *Akbar's Adventures with the Elephant Hawa'i in 1561*?

15. In Christian art, a cross should always point upward when on top of a globe. What is wrong with the globe in *Netherlandish Proverbs*?

16. Which large distorted object is at the bottom of Hans Holbein's portrait *The Ambassadors*?

17. Edouard Manet painted a white cat at the foot of Olympia's bed. True or False?

18. Complete the title of Goya's famous revolutionary painting: *The Third of May...*

19. *The Metamorphosis of Narcissus* was inspired by a poem by which classical poet?

20. *The Lamentation of Christ* on the wall of the Scrovegni Chapel was painted by which Renaissance artist?

     (Answers on page 481)

The Brontës

1. Where did the Brontë sisters grow up in England?

2. Charlotte Brontë wrote *Jane Eyre* under which pseudonym?

3. What was the name of the Brontës' only brother?

4. How many novels did Anne Brontë write and publish?

5. Jane Austen wrote a posthumous biography of Charlotte Brontë. True or False?

6. In which Brontë novel does the female protagonist slam the bedroom door against her husband, causing controversy in 19th-century England?

7. How many Brontë siblings were there in total?

8. In which year was *Wuthering Heights* published under the author's real name?

9. Which Brontë sister wrote *Wuthering Heights*?

10. William Crimsworth is a character in which Brontë novel?

11. Which novelist and contemporary wrote *The Life of Charlotte Brontë*?

12. Emily Brontë married at the age of 20. True or False?

13. *Wuthering Heights* was originally published as part of a three-volume set. The third volume was another Brontë novel—which one?

14. Who are the narrators of *Wuthering Heights*?

15. What is the name of Mr. Rochester's first wife in *Jane Eyre*?

16. As children, the Brontës would often write articles and poems about an imaginary kingdom called what?

17. Charlotte, Emily, and Anne all died of tuberculosis. True or False?

18. Which Brontë novel is set during the industrial depression?

19. What is the name of Mr. Rochester's estate in which Jane Eyre takes up employment as a governess?

20. As well as novels, the Brontë sisters also published a volume of poems together in 1846. True or False?

21. Which popular magazine of the day did the Brontës read?

22. Which city was the model for the fictional Villette in Charlotte's novel?

23. What is Agnes Grey's job?

24. In *Jane Eyre*, where is St. John Rivers going as a missionary?

25. "Reader, I married him." Who got married?

ART & LITERATURE

Twilight: Eclipse

1. How does Jacob let Bella know that he can't be friends with her any more?

2. Bella gets her acceptance letter for the University of Alaska. Where does Edward want her to go?

3. In which city are there a series of murders that the Cullens suspect are vampire-related?

4. Who tells Bella that the evil vampire Victoria has returned?

5. What was the name of Sam's girlfriend before he imprinted on Emily?

6. Jacob's werewolf friend Quil imprints. How old is the lucky lady?

7. Jacob invites Bella to La Push for a bonfire. Who tells the story of how werewolves came to be?

8. What was the name of the vampire who turned Jasper?

9. Why does Bella punch Jacob and crack her hand?

10. Why is someone stealing Bella's clothes?

11. Who decides that the vampires and werewolves should work together to protect Bella and Forks?

12. Who trains newborn vampires?

13. Where are newborn vampires trained?

14. How many werewolves turn up?

15. Jasper wants Bella to be present at the battle, as her smell will drive the newborn vampires wild. True or False?

16. Who does Jacob assign to protect Bella during the battle?

17. Edward gives Bella a crystal that once belonged to his mother. What shape is it?

18. How does Jacob find out that Bella and Edward are getting married?

19. What's the name of the young newborn who surrendered to Carlisle?

20. Bella and Edward plan to get married a month before her birthday. True or False?

A Christmas Carol

1. What is Scrooge's first name?

2. Who was Scrooge's dead business partner?

3. It took Charles Dickens six weeks to write *A Christmas Carol*. True or False?

4. Which day does the book begin on?

5. Who is the first ghost to visit Scrooge?

6. And what does he bring him?

7. How long has Marley been dead before he pays a visit to Scrooge?

8. Where does Scrooge first see Marley's face?

9. Which time does the clock strike when the Ghost of Christmas Past appears to Scrooge?

10. What is the first vision that the Ghost of Christmas Past presents to Scrooge?

11. When the Ghost of Christmas Present meets Scrooge he is holding a what?

12. What is Scrooge desperate to know from the Ghost of Christmas Present?

13. Two children come out from under the garments of the Ghost of Christmas Present. He says they are whom?

14. Who is the final ghost?

15. The Ghost of Christmas Yet to Come shows Scrooge what kind of shop?

16. What is the final scary image that convinces Scrooge to change his ways?

17. What does Scrooge send to the Cratchit family on Christmas Day?

18. Where does Scrooge spend Christmas Day?

19. Scrooge gives Bob Cratchit a bag of coal when he arrives at work after Christmas. True or False?

20. In *The Muppet Christmas Carol*, what part does Miss Piggy play?

21. Who was Scrooge's early love?

22. Who says, "God bless us, everyone"?

23. How is the Ghost of Christmas Yet to Come represented?

24. What is the lifespan of the Ghost of Christmas Present?

25. When was *A Christmas Carol* first published?

ART & LITERATURE

Charles Dickens

1. Charles Dickens's parents' names were what?

2. Which year was *A Tale of Two Cities* written in?

3. Where was Charles Dickens born?

4. Where is Charles Dickens buried?

5. Which character was based on Charles Dickens's father?

6. Dickens was a natural showman. True or False?

7. Charles Dickens once said: "I only ask to be free. The butterflies are free." True or False?

8. How many times has *Great Expectations* been adapted for stage and screen?

9. Which pen name did Dickens use in his earliest works?

10. How many children did Charles Dickens have?

11. What was Charles Dickens's first published story?

12. What was the name of Charles Dickens's mistress?

13. Which is the last novel Charles Dickens completed?

14. How many times did Charles Dickens visit America?

15. The illustrator of Charles Dickens's books was known as "Phiz." What was his real name?

16. Which pet animals did he name Grip?

17. *A Tale of Two Cities* deals with mobs, riots, and revolution. Which other novel also deals with these?

18. Charles Dickens suffered from which condition?

19. What is the name of the eccentric spinster in *Great Expectations*?

20. Dickens was paid by the word. True or False?

(Answers on page 481)

Great Literary Journeys

1. Which Jack Kerouac novel features the travel exploits of Sal and Dean?

2. *Life of Pi* features an ocean-borne boy, a raft, and a tiger. Who wrote it?

3. Who wrote *A Little Tour in France* in 1884?

4. Which Cormac McCarthy thriller features the postapocalyptic journey of a boy and his father?

5. Which classic American novel details the downriver journey of a boy and a runaway slave?

6. Who wrote the popular 1975 travel work *The Great Railway Bazaar*?

7. What is the name of the whaling ship in *Moby-Dick*?

8. In which James Hilton novel does an interrupted journey end in Shangri-La?

9. Antoine de Saint-Exupéry's classic children's book spans space and the Sahara. What's its title?

10. From the violent and unnatural musings of Hunter S. Thompson came which 1971 road classic?

11. *The Call of the Wild* details one dog's journey through the Yukon. Who wrote it?

12. Which Stephen King novel details one man's descent into insanity at the Overlook Hotel?

13. Who wrote *In Cold Blood*, a journey into the Midwest and the minds of two murderers?

14. *The Odyssey* is an ancient tale by Virgil. True or False?

15. Which Virgil poem covers one man's wanderings from Troy to Italy?

16. Which American novelist wrote a travelogue about his travels in Hawaii?

17. *The Lord of the Rings* follows Bilbo and Sam's journey into Mordor. True or False?

18. Who wrote the tale of three boys riding into Mexico and manhood in *All the Pretty Horses*?

19. Which Robert M. Pirsig novel takes the reader on a trip across America with his young son, Chris?

20. Which Joseph Conrad novel takes the reader downriver into deep Africa?

ART & LITERATURE

Postmodern Literature

1. Which novel written by Flann O'Brien in 1939 is often considered a pioneer of the postmodern genre?

2. Which Philip K. Dick novel is venerated as a postmodern classic because of its shifting view of reality?

3. Which William S. Burroughs novel did the author advise could be read in any chapter order?

4. Which Irish writer was seen as pivotal in making the shift from modernism to postmodernism in literature?

5. During which decades is postmodernist literature often thought to have peaked?

6. Which classic postmodern novel immerses itself in warfare paradoxes?

7. Which David Foster Wallace novel is riddled with endnotes and footnotes?

8. Which 1985 Don DeLillo novel is considered his "breakout" work?

9. Irony and black humor are considered two classic elements of postmodern novels. True or False?

10. Which Margaret Atwood novel describes a world controlled by Christian zealots?

11. Postmodernism is skeptical about which type of narratives?

12. Which Kurt Vonnegut novel explores the typical postmodern attribute of paranoia?

13. Paul Auster's 1985 collection of short stories is what?

14. Which group of 1980s postmodern writers included Bret Easton Ellis, Tama Janowitz, and Jay McInerney?

15. Who wrote *Generation X: Tales for an Accelerated Culture* in 1991?

16. Which W. G. Sebald novel is written entirely without paragraphs?

17. Which violent thriller by Bret Easton Ellis follows the life of a yuppie New Yorker?

18. Along with William S. Burroughs, who employed the "cut-up" technique of writing?

19. After which major conflict did the genre of postmodern literature begin?

20. Which Gabriel García Márquez novel was awarded the 1982 Nobel Prize for Literature?

Poets Laureate

1. Who was the first official Poet Laureate of England?

2. In which year did he become Poet Laureate?

3. The position of US Poet Laureate is officially titled: Poet Laureate Consultant in Poetry to the Library of Congress. True or False?

4. Nobel Prize winner Gabriela Mistral was Poet Laureate in which country?

5. Who declined to be the English Poet Laureate in 1850 because he was too old?

6. Who did the post of Poet Laureate go to in 1850?

7. How much is the US Poet Laureate paid annually?

8. Who turned down the position of English Poet Laureate in 1984?

9. Who was the first person to hold the position of New Zealand Poet Laureate?

10. What is the Irish equivalent of a Poet Laureate?

11. The Canadian Poet Laureate holds the title: Canadian Parliamentary Poet Laureate. True or False?

12. For how many years do Poets Laureate hold office in Canada?

13. Saint Lucia does not have a Poet Laureate. True or False?

14. Nigeria does not have a Poet Laureate. True or False?

15. Tsegaye Gabre-Medhin was a Poet Laureate of where?

16. Who was the Poet Laureate of Nazi Germany?

17. The title of the Dutch Poet Laureate is: *Dichter des Vaderlands*. What does this mean?

18. William Wordsworth was a Poet Laureate. True or False?

19. The salary of the British Poet Laureate has always included which type of alcohol?

20. Who followed Carol Ann Duffy as Poet Laureate of Britain?

21. For how long does a Poet Laureate hold the title in England?

22. Which poet was paid a pension by James I as the unofficial Laureate?

23. Which Poet Laureate also wrote crime-fiction novels under the name Nicholas Blake?

24. Who was the British Poet Laureate between 1930 and 1967?

25. Alfred, Lord Tennyson was made the Poet Laureate by Queen Victoria. Which famous poem did he write about the Battle of Balaclava?

ART & LITERATURE

Canterbury Tales

1. When did Geoffrey Chaucer write *The Canterbury Tales*?

2. Why are the pilgrims going to Canterbury?

3. Chaucer often uses sonnets in the telling of *The Canterbury Tales*. True or False?

4. How many pilgrims are going to Canterbury?

5. How many tales did Chaucer originally intend that each pilgrim would tell?

6. *The Pardoner's Tale* tells of three men seeking what?

7. Who are the most honest and righteous pilgrims?

8. Whose motto is: "Love Conquers All"?

9. Which inn is the Host the proprietor of?

10. The Knight's Yeoman tells the longest tale. True or False?

11. Which pilgrim is a con artist trying to pawn off his "holy relics"?

12. Who has a love of garlic, onions, leeks, and wine?

13. Who claims to have "four dead husbands"?

14. Who is responsible for teaching the Crow how to speak?

15. Which tales take place in the Orient?

16. Who does Satan become friends with before casting him into Hell?

17. Which young hero impresses the ladies with his singing and poetry?

18. The Reeve is a calm, fat man. True or False?

19. Who is the daughter of the Roman Emperor?

20. How many "tales" did Chaucer write?

21. What does the Squire wear?

22. "The Miller's Tale" is a fabliau. True or False?

23. Which character is given a mechanical horse that can transport him anywhere across the globe?

24. The Merchant has a thick bushy beard. True or False?

25. Which tale features someone being branded with a red-hot poker?

(Answers on page 482)

Famous Photographers

1. Who was Ernő Friedmann better known as?

2. Which photo agency did he co-found?

3. Charles Negre is famous for his photos of which city?

4. Don McCullin memorably covered war in which country in 1964–1965?

5. What did William Henry Fox Talbot describe his early photography as?

6. Which photographer was an inspiration for Dennis Hopper's character in *Apocalypse Now*?

7. Lee Miller was a man. True or False?

8. Which photographer took a famous portrait of the Kray twins?

9. Which photographer fled Armenia for Canada and worked in Ottawa?

10. What is Rankin's first name?

11. In which year did Eve Arnold die?

12. The Daguerreotype process was invented by Louis-Jacques-Mandé Daguerre. True or False?

13. Which former Chancellor of the Exchequer was an accomplished photographer?

14. Bert Hardy made his name with which magazine?

15. When was *Life* magazine founded?

16. Which female photographer helped shape the look of *Rolling Stone* magazine?

17. Photographer Lord Snowdon was married to which princess?

18. What was the name of film star Errol Flynn's photographer son?

19. What is the name given to photographers who pursue celebrities?

20. Helmut Newton was born in which German city?

21. Which photographer coined the term "the decisive moment"?

22. What was the subject of the book published by photographer Robert Frank in 1958?

23. The "rayograph" was invented by whom?

24. What sort of photography does Annie Leibovitz specialize in?

25. Diane Arbus is known for her landscapes. True or False?

ART & LITERATURE

Everything Shakespeare

1. Who has his or her eyes gouged out in *King Lear*?

2. Tybalt is a member of the House of Capulet. True or False?

3. "Though this be madness, yet there is method in't" is a quote from which play?

4. *Much Ado about Nothing* is set on which island?

5. Ralph Fiennes starred in a film adaptation of which tragedy?

6. Which "second-best" item did Shakespeare bequeath to his wife?

7. Shakespeare's Globe Theater burned down during a performance of which play?

8. Who tells Romeo that Juliet has died?

9. "Is this a dagger which I see before me, The handle toward my hand?" is a quote from *Romeo and Juliet*. True or False?

10. Which monarch, other than Elizabeth I, reigned during Shakespeare's lifetime?

11. Who drinks the "poison'd cup" in *Hamlet*?

12. *10 Things I Hate about You* is based on which of Shakespeare's plays?

13. What is the name of Sebastian's twin sister in *Twelfth Night*?

14. How many of Shakespeare's plays have "Henry" in the title?

15. How does Othello kill Desdemona?

16. Shakespeare was an actor as well as a writer. True or False?

17. In which play does Shylock appear?

18. How many witches are featured in *Macbeth*?

19. All of which planet's satellites share the same names as characters from Shakespeare's plays?

20. Hamlet is the prince of which Scandinavian country?

ART & LITERATURE

Pop Art

1. What was the name of Andy Warhol's studio?

2. Pop Art first emerged in London or New York?

3. In which decade did Pop Art develop?

4. Who designed the cover for the Beatles' album *Sgt. Pepper's Lonely Hearts Club Band*?

5. What was the name of the 1955 pioneering British Pop Art exhibition?

6. Which brand of soup can did Warhol depict in *32 Soup Cans*?

7. What was the name of the founding British Pop Art movement?

8. Eduardo Paolozzi designed mosaics for which London Underground station?

9. Who created the collage *Just What Is It That Makes Today's Homes So Different, So Appealing*?

10. Warhol's first film was *Kitchen*, in 1963. True or False?

11. In which gallery is Roy Lichtenstein's *Drowning Girl* on display?

12. The Museum of Modern Art (MoMA) is in which US city?

13. Robert Rauschenberg based a series of works called *Stoned Moon Series* on which Apollo space mission?

14. Marilyn Monroe's face is featured in a famous series of images by which artist?

15. Where did David Hockney paint *A Bigger Splash*?

16. Whose autobiography is titled *Autorotella*?

17. Which cult rock band did Warhol work with from the mid-1960s?

18. Which medium did Lichtenstein often parody?

19. In which year did Lichtenstein create *Whaam!*?

20. What did Valerie Solanas do to Warhol in June 1968?

(Answers on page 482)

Classic Novels

1. Which children's author founded a cricket team?

2. Which Jane Austen heroine is first described as "handsome, clever, and rich"?

3. How long does Robinson Crusoe spend on his island?

4. Which Dickensian hero is permanently of the opinion that "something will turn up"?

5. In *Vanity Fair*, which word does Thackeray use to demonstrate a social snub?

6. *The Turn of the Screw*'s narrator is employed as what?

7. Toward the end of *Tess of the d'Urbervilles*, where is Tess arrested?

8. Which philosopher wrote *Candide*?

9. Wilkie Collins's novel *Armadale* has been called the earliest detective book in English. True or False?

10. After Jane Austen's death, *Persuasion* and which other book were published as a set?

11. In *Middlemarch*, where in Europe does Will Ladislaw re-encounter Dorothea Casaubon?

12. Which drugs does Sherlock Holmes use?

13. "Quadruped… Forty teeth, namely twenty-four grinders, four eye-teeth, and twelve incisive" defines which animal in *Hard Times*?

14. In *Cold Comfort Farm*, Mr. Mybug is convinced that Branwell Bronte did what?

15. During Tristram Shandy's conception, his mother interrupts her husband to ask if he's remembered to wind the clock. True or False?

16. *Pamela*, the first novel in English, was initially intended to be what?

17. Which Joseph Conrad novel is considered to be a response to *Crime and Punishment*?

18. In *Far from the Madding Crowd*, Bathsheba Everdene's interest in Francis Troy is started by what?

19. In *The Gold Bug*, Edgar Allan Poe uses which branch of cryptography to solve the story's central mystery?

20. Who travels with Don Quixote on his adventures?

21. Who wrote *Of Mice and Men*?

22. In which novel by Franz Kafka does a man change into a giant insect?

23. *Swann's Way* is part of which series?

24. What is the title of Samuel Butler's 1872 novel that satirizes Victorian ideals of Utopian progress?

25. Set in Harlem and Greenwich Village during the 1950s, *Another Country* is by which author?

ART & LITERATURE

DC Comics

1. In which year was National Allied Publications, now known as DC Comics, founded?

2. What does the "DC" in DC Comics stand for?

3. Who was the first hero to appear in a comic book?

4. What was the name of the comic that Superman first appeared in?

5. In which comic did Batman make his debut in 1939?

6. In which comic did Mister Mxyzptlk make his debut in 1944?

7. *Western Comics #1* included characters such as the Wyoming Kid, Cowboy Marshall, and Rodeo Rick. It was published in 1948. True or False?

8. In which year did Superman and Batman join forces for the first time in comics?

9. Aquaman made his first appearance in *More Fun Comics #73* in January 1962. True or False?

10. In 2010, the epic *Blackest Night* came to its conclusion. What is the name of the following series?

11. What is the first name of Bruce Wayne's butler?

12. What is the name of Bruce Wayne's son?

13. What were the names of Bruce Wayne's parents?

14. *Watchmen #1* was published in 1986. Written by Alan Moore, who was the artist?

15. In which year was *John Constantine: Hellblazer* first published?

16. Who is the artist responsible for *V for Vendetta*?

17. Who wrote the second series of *The Sandman*, which published in 1989?

18. What is the title of the first Batman comic that DC produced using entirely computer-generated illustrations?

19. In which year was the imprint Vertigo born?

20. Who said: "You get the best seat in the house for Armageddon"?

ART & LITERATURE

Banned Books

1. Why was *Doctor Zhivago* by Boris Pasternak banned in the former Soviet Union?

2. Which Steinbeck novel was banned in California for portraying its "area residents in an unflattering light"?

3. Why was *Tarzan* by Edgar Rice Burroughs banned?

4. Which book was banned in apartheid South Africa in 1955 for containing "obscene" material?

5. Which anti-slavery novel was banned in the American South and Russia?

6. Why was the same novel banned in Russia?

7. Which author was prosecuted for "offenses against public morals" in 1857?

8. For which book?

9. Which Dr. Seuss children's book was banned in China in 1965 but was allowed to be sold in 1991 after the author's death?

10. Why was it banned in China?

11. In which year was Machiavelli's *The Prince* banned for being anti-Christian?

12. Why was the children's book *And Tango Makes Three* banned in much of America?

13. Which book featuring the Queen of Hearts was banned in China in 1931?

14. Why was it banned in China?

15. Which book by MI5 officer Peter Wright was banned in the UK even before it was published?

16. *The Metamorphosis* by Franz Kafka was banned in Nazi Germany. True or False?

17. Bangladesh, Egypt, India, Iran, Kenya, Kuwait, Liberia, Pakistan, Senegal, Sri Lanka, Tanzania, and Turkey all banned *The Satanic Verses*. True or False?

18. Stalin banned George Orwell's *Nineteen Eighty-Four* because it satirized his leadership. True or False?

19. Why was the novel *The Well of Loneliness* banned?

20. *Black Beauty* was banned in South Africa because of the words in the title. True or False?

Sherlock Holmes

1. Who is Sherlock Holmes's brother?

2. What is found on the body in *A Study in Scarlet*?

3. *In the Adventure of the Copper Beeches*, Violet Hunter is wondering whether to accept a job as a what?

4. Holmes says, "Elementary, my dear Watson" 25 times throughout the full works of Arthur Conan Doyle. True or False?

5. Sir Hugo, Sir Charles, and Miss Beryl Stapleton are all characters from which case?

6. Many of Doyle's works were originally serialized in which magazine?

7. Which short story involves a Miss Sutherland, who is abandoned at the altar on her wedding day by her fiancé?

8. Dr. Watson's future wife, Mary Morston, is introduced in which novel?

9. How many Sherlock Holmes short stories are there?

10. Who is the woman whom Holmes is said to refer to as "The Woman"?

11. How many pipes will Holmes need while solving his trickiest problems?

12. What hobby does Holmes take up when he retires?

13. *A Study in Scarlet* was originally titled *A Tangled Skein*. True or False?

14. Which weapon does Holmes not use while solving cases?

15. Who are the Baker Street Irregulars who often aid Holmes in solving his cases?

16. What is significant about *The Final Problem*?

17. Where does Holmes grapple with Moriarty and fall to his supposed death?

18. *The Valley of Fear* features an informant named… ?

19. In which story does Holmes return, after being presumed dead?

20. What is the name of the final collection of short stories?

ART & LITERATURE

(Answers on page 483)

Who Created This?

1. *The Grand Odalisque*

2. *Luncheon of the Boating Party*

3. *Broken Column*

4. *Primavera*

5. *Olympia*

6. *No. 5 1948*

7. *The Son of Man*

8. *Royal Red and Blue*

9. *In the Loge*

10. *Massacre of the Innocents*

11. *American Gothic*

12. *The Persistence of Memory*

13. *Jimson Weed/White Flower No. 1*

14. *The Third of May 1808*

15. *Las Meninas*

16. *Cataract 3*

17. *Bubbles*

18. *The Scapegoat*

19. *My Bed*

20. *Girl with Balloon*

21. *The Night Watch*

22. *The Arnolfini Portrait*

23. *Flaming June*

24. *The Garden of Earthly Delights*

25. *The Thinker* (sculpture)

       (Answers on page 483)

Modern American Literature

1. Which American author's first novel was *Moon Palace*?

2. Author Thomas Pynchon is often credited as being at the forefront of modern American writing. What was his celebrated third novel?

3. Which 1970 Toni Morrison novel examines identity in a racist society?

4. The title of the John Irving novel is *The World According to* what?

5. Published in 1971, Don DeLillo's first novel was what?

6. The American novel that features 388 endnotes is David Foster Wallace's what?

7. American novelist Michael Chabon's novel about the comic industry is called what?

8. Who wrote satirical family drama *The Corrections*?

9. *The Tree of Smoke* by American author Denis Johnson focuses on the Gulf War. True or False?

10. *Fight Club* is best known for the movie adaptation starring Brad Pitt, but who wrote the novel?

11. Author Cynthia Ozick often writes about life within Jewish-American families. True or False?

12. Which multi-award-winning author's last novel was *Nemesis*?

13. The movie *Brokeback Mountain* was originally based on a short story by which author?

14. This author's 1998 *The Hours* won the Pulitzer Prize for Fiction.

15. Out of this author's many novels, his most famous feature "Rabbit" in the title.

16. Which E. B. White novel is about a spider and a pig?

17. Which American author wrote *The Lovely Bones*?

18. What is the name of Charles Frazier's novel about an epic walk back from the American Civil War?

19. Donna Tartt's best-selling 1992 novel is what?

20. Which Pulitzer Prize–winning author commonly writes about American Indians?

ART & LITERATURE

(Answers on page 483)

The Lord of the Rings

1. Whom did Gollum kill to get his "precious"?

2. Which dwarf joins the Fellowship of the Ring?

3. The…Pony is the inn where the hobbits stay in Bree under Bree-hill.

4. The rings were made by the Elven-smiths of where?

5. Frodo changes his name to Master Took after he leaves the shire. True or False?

6. Which creature rescues Gandalf when he is stranded on the pinnacle of Orthanc?

7. Who cuts the ring from Sauron's hand?

8. Mount Doom has another name—what is it?

9. Who is sent by Saruman to summon Gandalf to him?

10. When the Sword of Elendil is reforged, what does Aragorn name it?

11. Arwen commands the flood that sweeps away the Nazgûl. True or False?

12. Which word does Gandalf have to speak in the Elvish language Quenya to open the Doors of Durin outside the Mines of Moria?

13. Whose tomb does the Company of the Ring find in the Mines of Moria?

14. Frodo sees many things when he gazes into the Mirror of Galadriel, but what does he see first?

15. The Rohirrim are well known for their horses. What is the name of King Théoden's horse?

16. What is Durin's Bane?

17. What does Pippin cast aside when he's been captured by the Orcs so the others can follow their path?

18. Whom does King Théoden hold prisoner for rebelling against his commands?

19. What are you not meant to do in the Dead Marshes?

20. Cirith… is the perilous high pass that Frodo, Sam, and Gollum decide to take before Gollum leads them into a dangerous trap.

Literary Sequels

1. How many sequels are there to C. S. Lewis's *The Magician's Nephew*?

2. Which title follows *Alice's Adventures in Wonderland*?

3. Kingsley Amis continues the lives of Patrick and Jenny Standish in his *Take a Girl Like You* sequel titled what?

4. Which sequel is the next in line after Alexandre Dumas's *The Three Musketeers*?

5. Which J. R. R. Tolkien title follows *The Two Towers*?

6. Which officially recognized sequel to Daphne du Maurier's *Rebecca* was written by Sally Beauman?

7. Which book follows *Harry Potter and the Sorcerer's Stone*?

8. What is the second and final sequel in Philip Pullman's *His Dark Materials* trilogy?

9. *Women in Love* picks up where D. H. Lawrence leaves off in which novel?

10. *Portrait in Sepia* is a sequel to Isabel Allende's *Daughter of Fortune*. True or False?

11. What is the sequel to John Scalzi's science-fiction novel *Old Man's War*?

12. What precedes the 2007 thriller sequel *The 47th Samurai*?

13. William Goldman's thriller novel *Brothers* is a sequel to what?

14. *Beggarman, Thief* is a 1977 Irwin Shaw sequel to *Banker, Philanthropist*. True or False?

15. Which is the fourth sequel in the *Chronicles of Prydain* series?

16. Which Hergé title follows Haddock and Tintin's exploits in *Destination Moon*?

17. Which title picks up where Tom is left in *Tom Brown's Schooldays*?

18. What is the second title in the *Noughts and Crosses* series by Malorie Blackman?

19. John Braine's sequel to *Room at the Top* is what?

20. Tom Sharpe's *Grantchester Grind* is the sequel to what?

CHAPTER 4

GEOGRAPHY

Explore rivers, mountains, volcanoes, and deserts. From national dishes to festive holidays, from the biggest and the longest to the most famous, these quizzes will send you on a journey of discovery.

What on Earth?

1. How old is Earth?

2. Which mountain range divides Europe and Asia?

3. What large-scale ecosystem is at the equator?

4. Lyell formulated the idea that geological processes happen at the same rate today as they did in the past. What is this idea called?

5. What is the igneous rock formed from volcanic lava that often forms pencil-like columns?

6. The outer mantle is one of Earth's layers. True or False?

7. The inner core of Earth is made of lead and iron. True or False?

8. Which of the following is NOT a type of rock: igneomorphic, igneous, sedimentary, metamorphic?

9. Which phenomenon provides an accurate method for calculating Earth's age?

10. Which rocks were formed underwater by layers of minerals and organic remains?

11. Igneous rocks are formed by what?

12. What does high tension and pressure change igneous and sedimentary rocks into?

13. What do we call the stone remains of once-living things found in rocks?

14. Fossilized tree sap is called what?

15. Earth's continents are constantly shifting. True or False?

16. Is Earth at its widest at the equator or pole to pole?

17. Our sun is a planet. True or False?

18. The Pyrenees mountain range forms the border between which two countries?

19. What term is used by geographers to describe a pointed mountain peak formed by glacial erosion?

20. Our solar system does NOT contain which of the following: planets, stars, galaxies, comets?

GEOGRAPHY

Rivers

1. Which is the longest river in the United States?

2. The bottom of a waterfall is called what?

3. The start of a river is called its what?

4. What are small rivers flowing into a larger main river called?

5. What is the world's greatest river in terms of both volume of water and the size of its basin?

6. On which river does Paris lie?

7. Rivers shape the landscape by erosion and deposition. True or False?

8. What forms when a loop of river becomes cut off from the main flow?

9. What is the Thames Barrier on the Thames River for?

10. A river and its tributaries collect all the surface water within a drainage basin. True or False?

11. Which is the world's longest river?

12. The weight of a glacier can make a river underneath the ice flow uphill. True or False?

13. Which of these rivers is NOT in South America: Orinoco, Amazon, Ebro?

14. Which famous river runs more than 400 miles (650 km) eastward across northern Italy?

15. What is the area around a meandering channel called?

16. A floodplain landscape is subject to constant what?

17. What is the solid material carried by the river called?

18. What percentage of the world's electricity is provided by dams built on rivers?

19. The erosive power of a river is greatest during a what?

20. Which is the world's highest waterfall?

21. Which is the world's widest river?

22. Where is the Irrawaddy River?

23. In which African country would you meet people who live along the Omo River?

24. What is the name of Australia's longest river?

25. The Desaguadero River flows from which high Bolivian lake?

Don't Blow Your Top

1. Where in the world is the volcano Krakatoa?

2. Volcanoes can be active, dormant, or… ?

3. Cinder is a type of lava. True or False?

4. All volcanoes have runny lava. True or False?

5. Volcanoes can form under the sea. True or False?

6. Rocks that form from either magma or lava are known as what?

7. Herculaneum and which other city were destroyed by Vesuvius in the year 79 CE?

8. A pyroclastic flow is a fast-moving current of superheated gas and rock. What temperature can it reach?

9. Volcanoes are often surrounded by human settlements. What lures people to settle there?

10. There were once active volcanoes in Britain. True or False?

11. All volcanoes lie on plate boundaries. True or False?

12. Volcanic ash can disrupt air travel. True or False?

13. Which of these volcanoes is NOT in Mexico: Fuji, El Chichon, Paricutin?

14. There are volcanoes in Antarctica. True or False?

15. A hole in the ground emitting steam or smoke in a volcanically active area is called a what?

16. A blob of lava thrown out of a volcano that solidifies in mid-air and lands as a rock is called a what?

17. On which planet is the tallest volcano in the solar system?

18. The depression in the peak of a volcano is called what?

19. Granite comes from volcanoes. True or False?

20. Volcanoes have existed throughout Earth's history. True or False?

GEOGRAPHY

Deserts

1. All deserts are sandy. True or False?

2. What is a watering hole in the desert called?

3. Cacti are native to the Sahara Desert. True or False?

4. Which animal is known as the "ship of the desert"?

5. Which is the world's smallest desert?

6. A desert is defined as a place with less than 10 in (250 mm) of what each year?

7. What is the common name for the desert plant opuntia?

8. Which of these is NOT a type of sand dune: seif, castle, barchan?

9. Where is the Gobi Desert?

10. Much of Antarctica can be classed as a desert. True or False?

11. During which time of day are animals most active in the desert?

12. Rivers cannot flow through deserts. True or False?

13. Where is the Patagonian Desert?

14. What is a group of camels carrying goods and traveling together called?

15. What adaptations help protect desert plants from being eaten by animals?

16. Semiarid lands, which have an annual rainfall between 10 in (250 mm) and 20 in (500 mm) are generally referred to as what?

17. What kind of desert people move frequently in search of fresh grazing for their animals?

18. What does a camel have to help it to walk on sand?

19. How many humps does a Bactrian camel have?

20. All deserts are hot. True or False?

21. What problem is caused by irrigation in the desert?

22. What can cause soil erosion in the desert?

23. What is the name of Australia's vast desertlike area?

24. In the desert, what do plant seeds do during dry periods?

25. Desert plants that hold water are called what?

 (Answers on page 484)

Where Am I?

1. I can see the Trevi Fountain. Which Italian city am I in?

2. I'm looking at a large sandstone pyramid and a large statue of a lion with a human head—which country am I in?

3. I've just sailed past a large green lady holding a torch, heading toward a city full of skyscrapers—where am I?

4. I'm staring down at a city while standing next to a huge statue of Jesus with outstretched arms—which city am I in?

5. I've just climbed the highest mountain in England—which mountain am I on?

6. I'm waiting for my plane 15 miles (24 km) west of Central London—which airport am I at?

7. I'm watching an eruption of the geyser Old Faithful—which national park am I in?

8. I'm standing outside a building with a roof like ship's sails, and in the distance is a large bridge over the harbor—where am I?

9. I'm in the world's northernmost capital city—where am I?

10. I'm standing next to a geyser, and I've just visited the volcano of Hekla—which country am I in?

11. I've just climbed an extinct volcano, the highest mountain in Africa—which mountain am I on?

12. I'm on the northernmost of the four main islands of Japan—where am I?

13. I'm on Devon Island, which is more than 20,000 sq miles (52,000 sq km) in area, but has no one living there. Which country is it a part of?

14. I'm staring down into the Grand Canyon—which state am I in?

15. I'm on the main island of this place, looking at the volcano of Mauna Loa and wearing a flower garland—where am I?

16. I'm cruising along a river and can see the Luxor Temple from the boat—which river am I on?

17. I'm watching the monsoon rains fall in the capital of Bangladesh—which city am I in?

18. I'm standing in the Mayan ruins of Chichén Itzá on the Yucatán Peninsula—which country am I in?

19. I am on the eastern side of the Caribbean island of Hispaniola—where am I?

20. I am on the western side of the Caribbean island of Hispaniola—where am I?

GEOGRAPHY

Mountain High

1. How long are the European Alps?

2. Which are highest usually, fold mountains or block mountains?

3. Kilimanjaro—Africa's highest mountain—is a volcano. True or False?

4. Approximately what percentage of the world's surface is covered by mountains?

5. The top 100 highest mountains in the world are all in the Himalayas. True or False?

6. In which continent are the Atlas Mountains?

7. Measured from base to peak, the world's tallest mountain is Mauna Kea in which country?

8. What is the highest mountain in the Alps?

9. Observatories are often situated on the peaks of remote mountains because the high altitude gives a clearer view of the stars. True or False?

10. Which is the world's highest peak?

11. Any hill higher than 2,000 ft (610 m) qualifies as a mountain. True or False?

12. Fold mountains generally have which sort of peaks?

13. Some fold mountains are still growing. True or False?

14. How fast are the Himalayas currently growing?

15. Where are the Drakensberg Mountains?

16. Which is the highest peak in the Rocky Mountains?

17. In which mountainous area is the ruined Inca settlement Machu Picchu situated?

18. Which is the highest and largest plateau in the world?

19. In which country can the Sierra Madre Oriental be found?

20. The study of mountains is called: orthography, topography, or orography?

21. Which Australian range stretches from the Grampians to Cape York Peninsula?

22. Mount Ras Dejen is in which African mountain range?

23. The Ural Mountains mark the boundary between which two continents?

24. Where are the Blue Ridge Mountains?

25. By which name are Scottish mountains of more than 3,000 ft (914 m) known to climbers?

European Essentials

1. Which European country is famous for chocolate and yodeling?

2. Which colors are seen on the Spanish flag?

3. Spain has coasts on which seas?

4. Switzerland is landlocked. True or False?

5. With an area of 140,000 sq miles (360,000 sq km), which country is the largest in Europe?

6. Which country in Europe has the smallest area?

7. In which country is Monte Carlo?

8. Which country is known as "the Land of Fire and Ice"?

9. Which country has islands in the Aegean and Ionian Seas?

10. Which European country is famous for tulips, clogs, and canals?

11. The United Kingdom is made up of how many nations?

12. What connects Sweden and Denmark?

13. What is the capital city of Spain?

14. What is the capital city of Italy?

15. About 10% of the world's population lives in Europe. True or False?

16. Which European country is famous for feta cheese, the Olympics, and ancient philosophers?

17. France is bordered by how many countries?

18. Poland has a North Sea coast. True or False?

19. In which European capital does the Brandenburg Gate stand?

20. Which two countries border Andorra?

21. Which country does NOT contain part of the Alps mountain range: Hungary, France, Slovenia?

22. Tallinn is the capital city of which country?

23. Which of these countries does NOT have a border with Germany: Italy, Denmark, Czech Republic?

24. Which country created the dessert tiramisu?

25. Where is Bucharest?

GEOGRAPHY

(Answers on page 484)   **151**

African Adventure

1. Which world-famous monuments would you see at Giza?

2. On the border between Zambia and Zimbabwe lies which waterfall?

3. The construction of what in Egypt in 1869 allowed boats to travel between the Mediterranean Sea and the Red Sea?

4. When on safari in South Africa, the lion, leopard, buffalo, elephant, and rhino are known as what?

5. Where do the Tuareg live?

6. Madagascar is the fourth-largest island in the world. True or False?

7. The Koutoubia Mosque is in which city?

8. What is the capital of Sudan?

9. In which country is Timbuktu?

10. Who built the temples of Abu Simbel?

11. In what year was the FIFA World Cup hosted in South Africa?

12. Yamoussoukro is the capital of which nation of western Africa?

13. Which country's flag features half a gear wheel, a machete, and a star?

14. Which of the Seven Wonders of the Ancient World was located in Alexandria?

15. What is a *hammam*?

16. Lemurs are found in the wild only on which island?

17. What is the currency of Malawi?

18. Which peak in Egypt is where Moses received the Ten Commandments, according to the Biblical tradition?

19. Guinea-Bissau was the first Portuguese colony to gain independence. True or False?

20. Equatorial Guinea is the only French-speaking country in western Africa. True or False?

GEOGRAPHY

Megacities

1. What is a megacity?

2. Which Japanese metropolitan area is home to more than 37 million people?

3. Mumbai in India used to be called what?

4. Lagos is a megacity in which African country?

5. The population of London rose by 500% between 1801 and 1891. True or False?

6. In 2017, how many cities in the world had a population of 10 million or more?

7. What is the name of the slum settlements attached to many major cities?

8. How many Indian cities are in the "Top 20 megacities" by population?

9. In addition to London, which are the two other European megacities?

10. Which American megacity covers 34,000 sq miles (87,000 sq km)?

11. What is the biggest city in Brazil?

12. Which megacity straddles two continents?

13. What is the capital of Pakistan?

14. The megacity formerly known as "Calcutta" is now known as what?

15. Approximately how many Mumbai families live on the city's sidewalks?

16. Which city had a population of more than one million around 2,000 years ago?

17. More people around the world now live in the countryside rather than in cities. True or False?

18. The most crowded megacity is Manila in the Philippines. True or False?

19. Which megacity is said to have the most beautiful underground system?

20. The biggest megacities are found on which continent?

21. In which city was the first skyscraper built?

22. How many megacities are there in North America?

23. Megacity Seoul is the capital of which country?

24. What is the biggest megacity in China?

25. More than half of Africa's population live in megacities. True or False?

GEOGRAPHY

Name That Day

1. January 1 is... ?

2. In the US, the third Monday in January is... ?

3. February 14 is... ?

4. In the US, the third Monday in February is... ?

5. March 17 is... ?

6. In the UK, April 23 is... ?

7. In Australia, April 25 is... ?

8. In the US, the fourth Thursday in November is... ?

9. In Canada, June 21 is... ?

10. In Canada, July 1 is... ?

11. In the US, July 4 is... ?

12. In France, July 14 is... ?

13. In Spain, the last Wednesday in August is... ?

14. For the British Navy, October 21 is... ?

15. In India, October 2 is... ?

16. In Germany, October 3 is... ?

17. October 31 is... ?

18. In a number of countries, November 11 is... ?

19. In Brazil, November 15 is... ?

20. December 25 is... ?

National Dishes

1. A tagine from this country is meat braised slowly with fruit, vegetables, and a heady mix of spices, including saffron, cumin, coriander, and nutmeg.

2. The Balmain Bug is a type of what food, eaten regularly in Sydney?

3. The city of Bologna, famous for its pasta sauce, is located in which European country?

4. Which dish of melted cheese and cubes of bread is a national dish of Switzerland?

5. Originally a Spanish dish, chili con carne has spread around the world and is the official dish of which US state?

6. Pho is a hot noodle soup, brimming with vegetables and meat, that is traditionally eaten in Vietnam for which meal?

7. The Polish stew *bigos* traditionally contains at least five different kinds of meat. True or False?

8. What is the name of the sausage formed in a continual spiral that is popular in South Africa?

9. A famous dish in China involving paper-thin pancakes is called Peking what?

10. *Moules-frites* literally translates to mean "mussels–French fries" and is the national dish of which country?

11. A phrase often used to describe someone as typically American is "as American as" what?

12. Which European country is famous for desserts such as tarte tatin, crème brûlée, and crêpes?

13. The tandoor oven is widely used in India. What is it traditionally made from?

14. What kind of food is bratwurst, particularly popular in Germany?

15. Rice noodle roll, steamed dumplings, and pork buns are all part of which Chinese style of food?

16. A taco traditionally describes food wrapped in a corn tortilla and is a famous dish from which country?

17. Which dish is traditionally associated with the British seaside?

18. *Nasi Goreng* is a traditional dish of Indonesia. What does the name literally mean?

19. What is the name of the Spanish dish consisting of rice, seafood, and vegetables?

20. Baklava is made with layers of puff pastry, honey, and pistachio nuts. True or False?

GEOGRAPHY

World Superlatives

1. Which is the highest mountain in the world?

2. Which is the longest river in the world?

3. Where is the deepest lake in the world?

4. Which is the longest mountain range in the world?

5. Which is the world's largest country?

6. Which is the smallest country in the world?

7. There are more member nations in FIFA than the United Nations. True or False?

8. Where are the highest waterfalls in the world?

9. Which is the longest river in England?

10. Which is the most populous and richest state in the United States?

11. Where is the driest desert in the world?

12. Which is the largest desert in the world?

13. Where is the lowest exposed land point below sea level?

14. Which is the world's highest volcano?

15. Which is the world's biggest rain forest?

16. Which is the world's largest glacier?

17. Which is the world's biggest island?

18. Which is the largest continent in the world?

19. Which is the highest capital city in the world?

20. Which is the world's largest freshwater lake by surface area?

21. Which is the world's highest continent?

22. Which is the smallest continent?

23. Which city has the world's largest plaza or square?

24. Which is the biggest and deepest ocean: Pacific, Indian, or Arctic?

25. Where is the world's longest railroad platform?

GEOGRAPHY

(Answers on page 484)

Famous Landmarks

1. In which city would you find an opera house by the harbor that was built in 1959?

2. In which city is the Colosseum?

3. Measuring over 13,000 miles (21,000 km) long, where is the Great Wall?

4. The Unknown Soldier lies beneath a landmark in Paris. Which one?

5. What is the name of the most famous baroque fountain in Rome?

6. The Bridge of Sighs is in which Italian city?

7. Which city in the desert is famous for casinos and chapels for speedy marriages?

8. In which Tuscan city would you find a Leaning Tower?

9. Gaudí buildings are a landmark of which city?

10. This beautiful building in Agra, India, was commissioned by Emperor Shah Jahan. What is it?

11. In which English seaside city was an Oriental-style Royal Pavilion built for the prince regent?

12. Which castle and royal residence is in Berkshire, England?

13. In which country can the Great Pyramid of Cholula be seen?

14. In which city would you find the Golden Gate Bridge?

15. In which city can you walk beside the Liffey River?

16. The Teatro alla Scala Opera House can be seen where?

17. Where is the Little Mermaid?

18. Mumbai's oldest landmark is the what?

19. In which European city is Notre-Dame Cathedral?

20. Which well-known London department store was rebuilt after a fire in 1880 and is now a popular attraction for many visitors?

GEOGRAPHY

Famous Skyscrapers

1. Where is the Burj Khalifa, the tallest skyscraper in the world?

2. The 1889 Rand McNally Building was the first steel skyscraper ever built. In which city does it stand?

3. In which year was the Empire State Building completed in New York?

4. Which towers in Kuala Lumpur stand 558 ft (170 m) high?

5. Which skyscraper was nicknamed "the big boxer shorts" by a Beijing taxi driver?

6. The Bitexco Financial Tower skyscraper sits in the capital city of which Asian country?

7. Standing at 269 ft (82 m) high, in which year did New York's Flatiron Building become the tallest skyscraper in the world?

8. In which country is the 991-ft (302-m) Kingdom Center?

9. When was the Tokyo Mode Gakuen Cocoon Tower completed?

10. Which skyscraper that looks like a ship's sail is sometimes called "the world's only seven-star hotel"?

11. Which Taiwanese skyscraper has been designed to look like a bamboo stalk?

12. In which city is the Spanish skyscraper Torre Agbar?

13. London's skyscraper at 30 St. Mary Axe is more commonly known as what?

14. In which Scandinavian country is the Turning Torso skyscraper?

15. In which year was New York's iconic World Trade Center destroyed by terrorists?

16. Where would you find the Hotel & Casino Grand Lisboa skyscraper?

17. The 1,450-ft (442-m) Willis Tower in Chicago, the tallest building in the Western Hemisphere, was formerly named the Sears Tower. True or False?

18. Which building replaced New York's Twin Towers?

19. Which Hong Kong building was criticized by feng shui masters for its sharp corners?

20. The Tour First in Paris is higher than the Eiffel Tower. True or False?

All about the Americas

1. Where was the earliest known use of chocolate, around 1100 BCE: Mexico, Honduras, or Peru?

2. Which state did the US buy from Russia in 1867?

3. How many stripes does the American flag have?

4. What is the official language of Brazil?

5. The widest road in the world, Avenida 9 de Julio, is in Buenos Aires. After what is it named?

6. What kind of vegetation grows on the salt lake in Uyuni, Bolivia?

7. Which state has the fewest counties?

8. In which country is the road that, in 1995, was christened "the world's most dangerous road" by the Inter-American Development Bank?

9. Estado Unidos Mexicanos is the official name of Mexico. True or False?

10. The Northern Lights, or aurora borealis, can be seen from which state?

11. By what name are the grassy plains of Argentina known?

12. How is almost 90 percent of Brazil's electricity generated?

13. Venezuela was named after which city?

14. Which islands off the coast of Ecuador are famously connected to Charles Darwin's theory of evolution by natural selection?

15. Which is the only US state that borders only one other state?

16. Who was the first European to reach what is now Costa Rica?

17. What is the name of one of the highest freshwater lakes in the world, which is also the largest lake in South America?

18. Which is the only island state in the US?

19. Name the two countries in South America that do not border Brazil.

20. Alaska was the last state to join the union of the United States of America. True or False?

21. Which animal is on the flag of California?

22. When was the Declaration of Independence signed?

23. Disneyland is a national park. True or False?

24. In which state are the Bonneville Salt Flats?

25. In which state is the Liberty Bell?

GEOGRAPHY

Shaking Planet

1. Name the scientific scale most commonly used to measure earthquakes.

2. Name the fault that runs through California.

3. Buildings constructed from which material are most likely to remain standing during an earthquake?

4. How much stronger is an earthquake of 6 on the Richter scale than one of 5?

5. What term refers to the point on Earth's surface that lies directly over the site of the ruptured fault in an earthquake?

6. What term refers to the point deep inside Earth's crust where an earthquake starts?

7. What name is given to geologists who specialize in the study of earthquakes?

8. What instrument is used to measure earthquakes?

9. Following an earthquake in 1906, much of the city of San Francisco was destroyed by what?

10. A large wave triggered by an earthquake is called what?

11. Off which country's coast was was the 2011 Tōhoku earthquake?

12. During a 2011 earthquake, the coast of North America was shifted 8 ft (2.4 m). True or False?

13. Which country experiences the most earthquakes?

14. Name the observational scale used to record earthquake impact.

15. Which state experiences the most earthquakes?

16. The fastest type of shockwave is known by which letter?

17. Where do earthquakes usually occur?

18. Which country experienced the strongest earthquake ever recorded (9.5 on the Richter scale) in 1960?

19. What term is used to describe a small quake following the main earthquake?

20. What term do geographers use to describe a wave of energy released by an earthquake?

　　　　(Answers on page 485)

River Deep

1. On which river would you find the Hoover Dam?

2. How many capital cities does the Danube River flow through?

3. What name is used by geographers to describe the deep pool that forms at the bottom of a waterfall?

4. Which river has the Chinese government tried to tame with the Three Gorges Dam project?

5. Which is the largest river system?

6. The shortest river in the world is only 201 ft (61 m) long. It is the Roe River in Montana. True or False?

7. Which river forms part of the border between the United States and Mexico?

8. What term refers to a small river that flows into a larger river?

9. What term describes the point where two rivers meet?

10. In which country would you find the world's tallest waterfall?

11. Which is the largest river in China?

12. How many countries does the Mekong River flow through?

13. Into which sea does the Volga flow?

14. What process makes the rocks on the bed of a fast-flowing river become smooth over time?

15. Which river flows through Memphis, Tennessee?

16. With a drop of 590 ft (180 m), what is England's highest waterfall?

17. The Mississippi River flows into the Mediterranean Sea. True or False?

18. In 2010, what was the world's largest hydroelectric power station?

19. Pebbles and sand deposited by rivers are known as what?

20. An area of land formed where sediment is deposited in the mouth of a large river is known as a what?

GEOGRAPHY

Capitals

1. Which country's filmmaking capital is called Nollywood?

2. Which capital city can be reached on the *shinkansen* or "bullet train"?

3. Which of these capitals is farther north: Amsterdam, Helsinki, Bucharest?

4. Which city is closest to the equator: Buenos Aires, Havana, Dakar?

5. The capital of Ukraine lies on which river?

6. Which capital city was created from two cities lying on either side of the Danube?

7. In which capital city is there a historic flat-topped rock called the Acropolis?

8. Which African capital city lies farthest north: Accra, Harare, Algiers?

9. Which island, also the name of a popular cartoon film, has a capital called Antananarivo?

10. Doha is the capital of which Gulf Arab state?

11. What is the capital of North Korea?

12. Madrid has never hosted the Olympic Games. True or False?

13. Which of these capitals is farther south: Madrid or Ottawa?

14. What is Croatia's capital?

15. What is the capital of the South American state of Uruguay?

16. Where would you find the capital city Paramaribo?

17. Port Stanley is the capital of which group of islands?

18. What is the name of Canada's capital city, which lies north of New York State?

19. Which South American country's capital is La Paz?

20. Which capital city lies farther north: Edinburgh or Copenhagen?

21. The Australian capital Canberra comes from an Aboriginal word meaning: meeting place, eating place, dancing place?

22. What was the first capital of Egypt under Muslim rule?

23. The Tiber River flows through which capital city?

24. Of which country is Bogotá the capital?

25. Near which Asian capital city is the temple of Kalaniya, reputedly visited by Buddha?

GEOGRAPHY

Agriculture around the World

1. Rice is the only crop grown in paddy fields. True or False?

2. Reindeer herding is one of the few forms of nomadic or shifting husbandry practiced outside the tropics. True or False?

3. In which country was maize first cultivated?

4. About when did agriculture begin?

5. Approximately how many people are actively involved with farming?

6. What percentage of the world's surface is used for agriculture of some sort?

7. The land used for agriculture was originally grassland. True or False?

8. Agriculture can cause soil erosion. True or False?

9. What name is given to the form of agriculture that raises only crops?

10. There are 2 million wild plant species on Earth. How many of them produce food that humans can eat?

11. Does soil form naturally very slowly or at relatively fast rate?

12. Agriculture contributes to the production of greenhouse gases, including which gas in particular?

13. What is commercial horticulture?

14. What sometimes happens to damage the soil when crops are irrigated?

15. Which are the world's most numerous farm animals?

16. What do the initials "GM" stand for in crop production terminology?

17. Barley is not one of the top five food staples (providers of energy) in the world. True or False?

18. Which country is the leading producer (not exporter) of rice?

19. Sugar beet is not normally grown on a plantation. True or False?

20. Viticulture refers to growing what crop?

GEOGRAPHY

Extreme World

1. What is the height of the mountain K2?

2. In which country are the world's deepest mines?

3. Which sea is 1,388 ft (423 m) below sea level?

4. Of the 109 tallest mountains on Earth, 96 are in which mountain range?

5. Which is the largest island in the Caribbean?

6. What is the highest mountain in South America, standing 22,841 ft (6,962 m) high?

7. The longest river system in Australia is named after which two explorers?

8. In which year in the 1980s was the Great Storm that swept across the south of England, causing great damage?

9. Top hotels are listed as five-star hotels. How many stars did the Burj al Arab hotel in Dubai award itself?

10. In which Asian country does the world's largest lizard, the Komodo dragon, live in the wild?

11. What is unusual about the hotel in Jukkasjärvi in Sweden?

12. Europe's tallest mountain is what?

13. Where is the deepest point in the Pacific Ocean?

14. What might you find in the Lascaux caves of France?

15. Which of these cities receives the lowest annual rainfall: New York, London, Tangiers?

16. Which butterfly migrates from the northern US to Mexico and back every year?

17. Europe's longest road and rail bridge is the Øresund Bridge. Which two countries does it connect?

18. The highest inhabited place on Earth is where?

19. When it's noon in Moscow, what time is it in Magadan in the Russian Far East?

20. In which country is Fraser Island, the world's largest sand island?

21. Where is the deepest continental shelf?

22. Where is the world's highest capital city?

23. Where are the Nazca Lines?

24. Where has the highest temperature on Earth been recorded?

25. Why is Kamchatka in Russia called "Valley of Death"?

GEOGRAPHY

Populations

1. With around 1.4 billion people, which country has the highest population in the world?

2. With around 800 people, which country has the smallest population in the world?

3. Approximately how many people live on Earth?

4. Which country had a "one-child policy" to cut down on overpopulation?

5. During the last 40 years, the world's population has what?

6. In 2020, approximately how many people are there for every square kilometer in the world?

7. What is the world's population estimated to be in 2055?

8. Approximately how many people live in the United States?

9. With around 13,000 people, what is the world's smallest independent republic?

10. In which year did the world's population reach five billion people?

11. The population of some countries, such as Nigeria, is not even known to the nearest million. True or False?

12. What is the world's population estimated to do before the end of the 21st century?

13. Which country has the second-largest population in the world?

14. India is the country with the highest sex ratio (number of males for each female) in the world. True or False?

15. By which year will a decline in the world's population have begun?

16. According to estimates, how many people have been born in the last 2,000 years?

17. Which is the most populated continent in the world?

18. Which country has the fastest-growing population?

19. Which was the first country in the world to reach a population of one billion?

20. Since which decade has a worldwide population-control movement been active?

(Answers on page 485)

GEOGRAPHY

Language in Africa

1. How many languages are there in Africa?

2. Where in Africa are Austronesian languages spoken?

3. When was the "Year of African Languages"?

4. How many people are thought to speak Swahili?

5. How many official languages does the Republic of South Africa have: 2, 4, 10, 16?

6. What is the official language spoken in Benin?

7. A number of the world's creole languages are spoken in Africa. True or False?

8. What are the official languages of Chad?

9. Tonal languages are virtually nonexistent in Africa. True or False?

10. Along with Swazi, what is the official language spoken in Swaziland?

11. Tigrinya is an African language spoken where?

12. What is the official language spoken in Guinea-Bissau?

13. Algerian Sign Language was officially recognized by law in which year?

14. What is the official language of Gambia?

15. Which of these languages is NOT spoken in the Democratic Republic of the Congo: German, Kikongo, Lingala?

16. How many speakers of the Somali language are there?

17. Amharic is the Semitic language spoken in which African country?

18. How many languages are spoken in Nigeria?

19. Where in Africa is the Berber language most frequently spoken?

20. Apart from English, what is the official language of Botswana?

(Answers on page 486)

Island Nations

1. Which island nation has the most islands?

2. Which island nation is made up of the North Island and the South Island?

3. Which Pacific Island nation is ruled by a monarchy?

4. In 2011, what percentage of UN members were island nations?

5. Nuuk is the capital of the world's biggest island, which is?

6. Bahrain is an island nation in which body of water?

7. Which island nation is famous for its cigars?

8. Which island nation is also a continent?

9. What is the approximate population of the Pacific Ocean's Marshall Islands?

10. Which island nation's closest neighbor is Korea?

11. In which body of water is the island nation of Taiwan located?

12. The Republic of Maldives is situated in the Pacific Ocean. True or False?

13. How many main islands does the island nation of Bahrain feature?

14. Situated off the southern tip of the Malay Peninsula is which island nation?

15. The capital city of the island nation of Jamaica is what?

16. The Philippines includes more than 7,000 islands. True or False?

17. Which island nation is home to the boiling-hot Geysir?

18. Which island nation is home to the ring-tailed lemur, the lacewings, and the fossa?

19. Which island nation has Greek and Turkish residents?

20. In which island nation did the flightless moa once roam?

21. Which Caribbean island nation was invaded by the US in 1983?

22. Which European language is spoken in New Caledonia?

23. This island nation's capital is Port of Spain, and it consists of 23 islands.

24. This island occupies half of an island that was Indonesian. It declared independence in 2002.

25. How many island nations are part of Africa?

GEOGRAPHY

Famous Natural Landmarks in the US

1. Which colossal natural landmark was formed 17 million years ago by the Colorado River?

2. Which mammoth monolithic rock stands 236 ft (72 m) high on Oregon's Cannon Beach?

3. How many tourists does Niagara Falls attract every year?

4. Nearly 7,000 years ago, the collapse of Mount Mazama created Crater Lake. In which state can it be seen?

5. Which national park spans Wyoming and parts of Montana and Idaho?

6. How high are the Yosemite Falls?

7. Richard Nixon is shown on Mount Rushmore. True or False?

8. Which state has 36 landmarks, more than any other in the US?

9. What is the name of the national park in Maine?

10. The Alaska Range is home to which glacier?

11. The Rainbow Bridge is 275 ft (84 m) across and 289 ft (88 m) high. Where can you go to see it?

12. Established in 1929, in which state is Grand Teton National Park?

13. What is the name of Yellowstone National Park's most famous geyser?

14. The highest mountain in the United States is what?

15. Hawaii's Makalawena Marsh dried up in 2010 and was removed from the list of US National Natural Landmarks. True or False?

16. Which of these is NOT a rock formation in the American Southwest's Monument Valley: Camel Butte, Lady Luck's Ladder, the Three Sisters?

17. Which president designated Devils Tower as the first National Monument in the United States?

18. It is estimated that 300 tourists go missing in Indiana's Pinhook Bog every year. True or False?

19. On the border of which two states does the Hoover Dam sit?

20. Mono Lake has large limestone spikes sticking out of the water. In which state is it located?

GEOGRAPHY

Iceland

1. In which year did Iceland become an independent republic?

2. Iceland has been a nuclear-free zone since 1985. True or False?

3. In which century did Norse chieftain Ingólfur Arnarson settle in Iceland?

4. What is Iceland the only NATO member not to have?

5. What is the name of Iceland's parliament?

6. Where did Iceland's parliament first meet, now a national park?

7. Geographically, which is Iceland's closest neighbor?

8. Iceland's most famous geyser is called what?

9. How many counties does Iceland have?

10. What is Iceland's main form of transportation?

11. Approximately what is the population of Iceland?

12. Along with Nordic, what is the common ancestry of native Icelanders?

13. Only one person from Iceland has received a Nobel Prize. What was it for?

14. Which form of sea hunting is traditional in Iceland, though largely abandoned elsewhere?

15. According to the Global Peace Index, Iceland is what?

16. Iceland has the highest per-capita consumption in Europe of which popular drink?

17. What is Iceland's only native land mammal?

18. Which of these is NOT an Icelandic volcano: Hekla, Kópavogur, Eldfell?

19. What is the main religious denomination in Iceland?

20. In which year did the Icelandic government take control of the country's three banks?

21. Iceland is the most sparsely populated country in Europe. True or False?

22. What is the native language of Iceland?

23. Two disasters of the same kind hit Iceland in 1995, killing many people. What were they?

24. What is the traditional covering for Icelandic houses?

25. What is the highest waterfall in Iceland?

GEOGRAPHY

(Answers on page 486)   **169**

Wild Weather

1. Where do tropical cyclones form?

2. How fast can the winds get in a large tornado?

3. What is the scientific term for a storm cloud?

4. What term do meteorologists use to describe the noise made by a lightning bolt?

5. Light travels more slowly through water than through air, which causes it to be refracted. The result is a what?

6. What weather hazard is created by the buildup of static in storm clouds?

7. What falls from the sky at 87 mph (140 kmph) and can weigh up to 1.5 lb (0.7 kg)?

8. Which ocean current is associated with floods in America and droughts in Australia?

9. Roughly how many tornadoes occur in the US every year?

10. What is measured using the Beaufort Scale?

11. What name is given to a tornado that forms over water?

12. What scale is used to measure the strength of a hurricane?

13. What term is used to describe whirlwinds of sand that form in deserts?

14. What term do meteorologists use to describe a heavy snowstorm?

15. Storm surges are hazards linked to tornadoes. True or False?

16. What are periods of extremely low rainfall known as?

17. When pollution and fog mix, what is created?

18. At what temperature is snow most likely to fall?

19. What hazard becomes more likely after several days of snowfall?

20. What term is used to describe sustained winds of above 40 mph (64 kmph)?

Lakes, Rivers, and Mountains

1. What is the longest river in Europe?

2. The Danube River flows through Sofia. True or False?

3. Which partly submerged mountain is higher than Everest?

4. The Amazon River is home to more species of fish than the Atlantic Ocean. True or False?

5. The Himalayas cross five countries, including Pakistan, Bhutan, India, and which other two countries?

6. Lake Superior has its own tide. True or False?

7. Which is the world's third-longest river?

8. Which river carries the greatest volume of water?

9. How old is the youngest person to reach the peak of Mount Everest?

10. What nationality was Edmund Hillary, one of the first two people to climb Everest?

11. What is the largest salt lake in Australia?

12. There are roughly 96 major rivers on Earth. True or False?

13. In which country is Mount Fuji located?

14. Lake Baikal contains roughly 20 percent of the world's surface fresh water. True or False?

15. What is South America's longest mountain range?

16. Where are the Atlas Mountains?

17. How many bridges are there over the Amazon?

18. The highest peaks in the Western Hemisphere are found where?

19. What is the name given to the study of lakes?

20. Which country contains roughly half of the world's lakes?

21. Which lake is bordered by Germany, Austria, and Switzerland?

22. Lake Chad in Africa crosses four countries. True or False?

23. What is the name of the group of long, thin lakes near New York City?

24. In which part of a river does water flow the fastest—lower, middle, or upper course?

25. Where is Mount Sinai?

GEOGRAPHY

Wild Extreme Earth

1. Where are there more toxic species per square mile than anywhere else in the world?

2. Tristan da Cunha is the most remote inhabited archipelago on Earth. How far away is it from the nearest continent?

3. What is the name of Tristan da Cunha's capital?

4. Where is the hottest place on Earth, with a record temperature of 136°F (57.8°C)?

5. Where is the coldest inhabited place on Earth, with the temperature once dropping to -96.2°F (-71.2°C)?

6. It is so cold in Oymyakon that locals say birds freeze to death in mid-flight. True or False?

7. Which country would you stay away from to avoid meeting the giant huntsman spider, the largest spider on Earth?

8. Gansbaai in South Africa is a popular beach resort. Its waters are also home to the largest number of what in the world?

9. What is the name of deepest point of the world's oceans, at 35,840 ft (10,924 m)?

10. What is the world's highest waterfall, at 3,230 ft (984 m)?

11. The fattail scorpion is so poisonous that one sting can kill a man in minutes. Is it found in Australia, the Middle East, or Brazil?

12. Which US state has the most alligators, with a population of more than one million?

13. In which US state do alligators and crocodiles live side by side?

14. What is home to the largest collection of living plants and animal species in the world?

15. The Amazon Rain Forest is 2,123,562 sq miles (5,500,000 sq km) in size. True or False?

16. Where in Africa are there 45 species of mammals and almost 500 species of birds in one area?

17. What is the driest and coldest place on Earth and generally considered the wildest to visit?

18. In which country is the wettest place in the world, with the highest average yearly rainfall?

19. Antarctica's Dry Valleys are the driest in the world. How long has it been since the valleys last had rainfall?

20. Which country has more venomous snakes than any other country in the world?

The Americas

1. Which mountain chain runs down the western side of North America?

2. More than 60 percent of the Amazon Rain Forest lies in which country?

3. Humans first settled in the Americas between which years?

4. When did Christopher Columbus first land in the Americas?

5. What is the highest lake in the Americas?

6. South America broke off from the supercontinent Gondwana about how many years ago?

7. Aconcagua of Argentina is the highest peak in South America. True or False?

8. What is the southernmost point of the Americas?

9. The Mississippi–Missouri river system drains how many of the states in the US?

10. More people live in Brazil than in the United States. True or False?

11. Canada's population is less than a quarter of the US population. True or False?

12. Where is the largest urban area of the Americas, with a population of around 21 million people?

13. How many sovereign states lie within the Americas?

14. What religion has the largest number of followers in the Americas?

15. Tornado Alley in the US ironically has never been hit by a tornado. True or False?

16. What links the continents of North and South America?

17. What is the northernmost point of the Americas?

18. The Cascades are a range in which North American mountain group?

19. What proportion of the world's animals can be found in the Amazon Rain Forest?

20. Río de la Plata Basin in South America is one of the smallest river basins on Earth. True or False?

21. How many stripes are on the American flag?

22. What is the address of the White House?

23. Which US state is known for its Extraterrestrial Highway?

24. Which city had the first Starbucks?

25. Where would you eat gumbo?

GEOGRAPHY

Natural Disasters on Earth

1. Which natural phenomenon can produce the fastest winds on Earth?

2. Up to what speed can the winds reach in a tornado?

3. What is a tsunami sometimes incorrectly called?

4. What natural disaster has a hypocenter and an epicenter?

5. What is a tornado commonly known as?

6. Cyclones always form over water. True or False?

7. Based on the number of reported incidents, what are the odds of being struck by lightning?

8. What happened to Hog Island, New York, in 1893?

9. What was invented by Benjamin Franklin to protect buildings from lightning strikes?

10. What is it called when snow suddenly flows down a slope?

11. What is the most dangerous type of avalanche, which can reach speeds of up to 80 mph (129 kmph)?

12. Where was the strongest recorded earthquake?

13. What did it measure on the Richter scale?

14. How many active volcanoes are there on Earth?

15. Volcanoes exist only on land. True or False?

16. The Mediterranean island of Thera devastated by a volcanic eruption around 1600 BCE is now known as… ?

17. Which volcano erupted in Washington State in 1980?

18. For what purpose was the Thames Barrier put into operation in 1982?

19. Floods are often caused by a river's banks being broken. True or False?

20. Which city in Europe was hit by a catastrophic earthquake in 1755?

GEOGRAPHY

Deep Blue Sea

1. What is the Sea of Cortez also known as?

2. What term is used to describe a ring of coral islands?

3. Coral reefs are made of what type of rock?

4. Life on the ocean floor can be supported by hydrothermal vents. These volcanic features are also known as what?

5. On average, what is the salinity of the world's oceans?

6. Whirlpools form alongside powerful tidal currents. Where is the world's largest whirlpool?

7. Below which depth is the ocean entirely dark?

8. Which is the saltiest water body?

9. What name has been given to the calm zone in the North Atlantic, famous for enormous "rafts" of floating seaweed?

10. What is the name of the cold Pacific current that allows penguins to live on the tropical Galápagos Islands?

11. Which term is used to describe the swarms of tiny animals that drift among surface algae?

12. Below which depth is there insufficient light to support photosynthesis?

13. Which ocean accounts for 40 percent of the world's oil?

14. Some deep sea creatures that live in total darkness create their own light. What is it called?

15. Which marine ecosystem is able to sustain the greatest diversity of life?

16. Which at is the heaviest marine invertebrate?

17. Which term is used to describe an underwater plain at depths greater than 9,850 ft (3,000 m)?

18. Which of these are found in the deep sea: vampire fish, giant spider crab, anglerfish?

19. Drinking sea water will kill you faster than dehydration. True or False?

20. With an average depth of just 23 ft (7 m), which is the world's shallowest sea?

GEOGRAPHY

Natural Wonders

1. Monument Valley is famous for its sandstone rock formations, called mesas and buttes. Where is it?

2. In which South American country would you find the tallest waterfall on Earth, named after an aviator who flew over the site?

3. If you were a "spelunker," which natural feature would you like exploring?

4. Mitre Peak in Milford Sound is one of the most distinctive peaks in the world. In which country is it located?

5. The northern lights are also known as the "aurora borealis." What are the southern lights called?

6. The Egyptian resort of Sharm el Sheikh is famous for its diving. In which body of water does the diving take place?

7. Which natural feature on the coast of northern Ireland was produced by a volcanic eruption?

8. Dome, pinnacle, edge, and dry-dock are all types of which natural feature?

9. Iguazu Falls are made up of 275 different waterfalls and lie on the border between Brazil and which other country?

10. Which island is famous for the annual migration of millions of red crabs?

11. South America's largest and highest navigable lake is what?

12. Which member of the whale family grows a single tusk up to 8 ft (2.4 m) long on its head?

13. The lowest point in Australia is also the site of its largest lake, which fills only two or three times a century. What is it called?

14. The waterfall Mosi-oa-Tunya, or "the smoke that thunders," was renamed by David Livingstone after which queen?

15. Nearly half of the continental US is drained by which mighty river?

16. How deep is the Grand Canyon at its deepest point?

17. Fjords are deep, steep-sided valleys carved by glaciers. Which Scandinavian country is the best place to see them?

18. Japan's tallest mountain is a symmetrical, snow-capped volcanic cone. What is it called?

19. Which Australian tourist attraction can be seen from space?

20. Which tree, found in several locations in Africa, is also known as the "bottle tree" or "upside-down tree"?

Erupting Earth

1. Which term is used to describe a steep-sided volcano made from eruptions of ash and lava?

2. Which volcanic hazard consists of deadly superheated gas and rock particles?

3. Which rock, which erupts from spreading rifts and hotspots, forms the bedrock of the ocean floors?

4. Which geological term refers to an area of unusually high volcanic activity?

5. Mount Sidley is the highest volcano in which continent?

6. Who was the American seismologist in the 1930s who gave his name to the scale he invented for measuring earthquakes?

7. What name is given to the volcanic zone encircling the Pacific?

8. Which kind of volcanic rock forms when lava cools too quickly for crystals to grow?

9. Which of the following in 1980 were signs that Mount St. Helens was about to erupt: volcano's side bulging, increase in local air temperature, animals leaving the area?

10. Which term is used to describe a volcano that rarely erupts?

11. Mount Fuji is dormant. True or False?

12. Where is the volcano Mount Rainier?

13. How often does Old Faithful, Yellowstone's most famous geyser, erupt?

14. What forms when silica-rich lava solidifies with gas bubbles trapped inside?

15. Australia has no active volcanoes. True or False?

16. Mauna Kea is the largest volcano in the world. True or False?

17. A catastrophic volcanic eruption in the second millennium BCE is associated with the collapse of which legendary city?

18. The eruption of which volcano in 1815 led to widespread famine?

19. Which is the most active volcano on Earth?

20. Snowdon in Wales is an extinct volcano. True or False?

GEOGRAPHY

Lakes and Wetlands

1. Which area of wetlands covers much of southern Florida?

2. With depths of 1 mile (1.6 km), which is the world's deepest lake?

3. Which is the highest navigable lake in the world?

4. Which is the deepest lake in England's Lake District?

5. Name the African lake that has shrunk to one-fifth of its original size over the past 50 years.

6. Which is the largest freshwater lake in the world?

7. What percentage of the world's fresh surface water is in Lake Baikal?

8. Four countries have a coastline on Lake Victoria. True or False?

9. Which inland water body is the lowest point on Earth's surface?

10. In which wetland region does much of the White Nile's water evaporate?

11. Which is the smallest of the Great Lakes?

12. With an average depth of 62 ft (19 m), which is the shallowest of the Great Lakes?

13. Georgian and Saginaw Bays are part of which Great Lake?

14. Which is the largest man-made lake in the world?

15. Which is the largest wetland area in the world?

16. Europe's largest area of marshland straddles the border of Belarus and Ukraine. What is it called?

17. New Zealand's largest lake lies in the crater of an extinct volcano. What is its name?

18. What is the name of the man-made lake that was created by the construction of the Hoover Dam?

19. The Volga River starts in which upland marshy region?

20. Instead of flowing into the sea, Africa's Okavango River ends in the desert, forming the world's largest inland delta. True or False?

21. More than half the world's wetlands have disappeared since 1900. True or False?

22. Which gas do wetlands trap from the atmosphere and store, helping protect Earth from global warming?

23. What is the Ramsar Convention?

24. Peat bogs are a type of wetland. True or False?

25. Which of the Great Lakes is the only one entirely in US territory?

(Answers on page 487)

Glaciers

1. The end of a glacier can be called a what?

2. What is happening when a glacier calves?

3. Glaciers cannot exist at the equator. True or False?

4. Which of these is NOT a name for a hollow formed at the head of a glacier: torrie, carn, panhole?

5. A tributary valley cut off by a deeper glacial valley is called a what?

6. How much of Earth's land surface is covered by ice masses?

7. What percentage of the world's fresh water is held in ice masses?

8. Some glaciers contain colonies of what?

9. What feature might you find at the place where three or more glaciers begin?

10. What are the layers of debris that may appear as black stripes in a glacier called?

11. What is the name for a giant boulder dumped by a glacier far from its site of origin?

12. Parts of the Antarctic ice sheet are more than $2\frac{1}{2}$ miles (4 km) thick. True or False?

13. What is the upper part of a glacier known as?

14. What color is dense glacial ice?

15. What are the mountains that protrude from an ice sheet called?

16. What is the name of a coastal glacial valley that has been flooded by a rise in sea level?

17. Where is the world's fastest-flowing glacier?

18. The deepest ice core yet drilled revealed evidence from how many years ago?

19. The East Antarctica ice sheet overlies several lakes. What is the largest of these called?

20. We are still in an Ice Age. True or False?

21. Which is the only continent that doesn't have glaciers?

22. The biggest icebergs in the world are found where?

23. What makes a glacier move: gravity, flow of water, wind?

24. What is "surging"?

25. What are the cracks in glaciers called?

GEOGRAPHY

People of the World

1. According to the United Nations, what might the population of Earth be in the year 2025?

2. Capital cities always have the largest population in the country. True or False?

3. Many languages in Amazonia have fewer than 500 speakers. True or False?

4. Sherpas are a people who live in Tibet. True or False?

5. The past 200 years have seen the most radical shift in world-population patterns in history. True or False?

6. On which continent is life expectancy the lowest?

7. Which is the most densely populated country?

8. Which is the most sparsely populated part of the world?

9. Which language is spoken by more people than any other?

10. When one town grows and merges with another, it is called a "conurbation." True or False?

11. When was the UN Declaration on the Rights of Indigenous Peoples passed?

12. What is the approximate population of New York City's total urban area?

13. Large urban areas do not affect the climate around them. True or False?

14. Which name is given to a graph that illustrates the age groups in a country's population?

15. What is the center of a city or town called where most of the commerce goes on?

16. According to the 2009 Happy Planet Index, run by the New Economics Foundation, which country is the world's happiest?

17. What is the name of the settlements that are built when large numbers of people come to towns and there is not always room for them?

18. An Inuk is a member of which people?

19. The majority of countries have a higher population of females than males. True or False?

20. Which country is considered to be the world's wealthiest?

21. Which is the most populous country?

22. How many languages are spoken in the world: 5,000, 6,000, 7,000?

23. Is there a set of criteria for people to qualify as indigenous?

24. In which country is First Nations used to describe the predominant indigenous people?

25. Which language is the most widely spoken in India?

 (Answers on page 487)

GEOGRAPHY

Mixed Bag

1. Which of these countries does NOT lie on the Tropic of Capricorn: Zimbabwe, Namibia, Botswana?

2. Which island group 40 miles (64 km) west of North Uist in the Hebrides was inhabited until 1930 but is now a seabird colony?

3. What is the sandy strip called that joins some islands to the mainland?

4. What other (Russian) name is given to the belt of boreal conifer forest encircling the Arctic region?

5. Which sea is surrounded by the countries Egypt, Sudan, Saudi Arabia, Eritrea, and Yemen?

6. Which African country used to be known as the Gold Coast?

7. Where did Christopher Columbus think he'd arrived when he landed in the Americas in 1492?

8. What is the name for a stretch of very deep ocean along the boundary between two tectonic plates?

9. Which mountain ridge marks the eastern edge of the continent of Europe?

10. Which island nation in the central Pacific Ocean is especially threatened by rising sea levels?

11. On which continent are the Drakensbergs, or "Dragon Mountains"?

12. The island of Iwo Jima lies in a chain of volcanic islands stretching south of which country?

13. The semiarid zone directly south of the Sahara Desert is called the what?

14. Europe's fastest eroding coastline is on which coast of England?

15. Which English county has several gritstone "edges" (including Stanage and Curbar Edge)—cliffs that are popular with rock-climbers?

16. Which country in the Indian Ocean has a capital city called Malé?

17. The most common feature created by wave deposition is what?

18. Mungo Park was a Scottish explorer who traveled into uncharted territory in search of the source of which river?

19. Which Antarctic explorer led his party to safety via Elephant Island and South Georgia after their ship was crushed by ice?

20. Climbers attempting Mount Everest reach which zone when they climb above 26,000 ft (8,000 m)?

GEOGRAPHY

Volcanoes, People, and Gods

1. Which volcanic island was formed in 1963 off the coast of Iceland?

2. One of the most active volcanoes in Europe, situated in Sicily, is called what?

3. Which name is given to molten rocks that are produced underneath Earth's crust and sometimes rise to the surface?

4. The ocean floors are made of a dark, heavy rock called what?

5. What is the center of Earth called?

6. The ancient Romans believed that the god Atlas carried the world on his head. True or False?

7. A Hindu myth says that the world rests on the back of six giant what?

8. The fluid lava of a volcano is sometimes blown into fine strands. Hawaiians call this what?

9. Volcanic hot springs at the bottom of the oceans are referred to as what?

10. In Japan, it is a custom to be buried up to your neck in warm volcanic ashes to help what?

11. Which European country is almost entirely made up of volcanic rocks?

12. The edges of the plates that form the floor of the Pacific Ocean are called what?

13. The world's most-visited volcano is Mount Vesuvius in Italy. True or False?

14. Agate is volcanic rock. True or False?

15. One of the only two survivors of the 1902 volcanic eruption on the island of Saint Pierre survived thanks to what?

16. The most famous plate boundary in the world is what?

17. The Transamerica Pyramid has been designed to withstand earthquakes. In which city is this unusual building?

18. The point where two plates meet at an odd angle is called what?

19. In North America, the machine used to measure small movements along a fault line is known as a "creepmeter." True or False?

20. After the eruption of the Nyamuragira volcano in the Democratic Republic of the Congo in 2010, many people got cholera. Why?

GEOGRAPHY

(Answers on page 487)

US States

1. How many states make up the United States of America?

2. Which is the southernmost state?

3. Which state is known as "the First State" because it was the first to ratify the Constitution in 1787?

4. Which was the last state to join the United States, in 1959?

5. North Carolina is south of West Virginia. True or False?

6. Which state is the most populous?

7. Which state is the largest by area?

8. Tallahassee is the capital of which state?

9. Alaska contains the most northerly, westerly, and easterly points of the US. True or False?

10. In which state would you find a giant monument depicting faces carved into the side of a hill?

11. In which state is Harvard University?

12. Which state is known as "the Garden State"?

13. The Green Bay Packers football team is based in which state?

14. How many states start with the letter "W"?

15. Yellowstone National Park is located primarily in which state?

16. How many states do not border any other state?

17. Mount McKinley is the highest peak in the US. In which state will you find it?

18. What is the state capital of California?

19. Niagara Falls straddles Ontario, Canada, and which state?

20. The Mississippi River drains into the Gulf of Mexico in which state?

21. Jousting is the official state sport of Maryland. True or False?

22. Sioux Falls is in which state?

23. How many states start with the word "New"?

24. The "Hollywood" sign is located on which mountain?

25. Which state has the longest coastline?

GEOGRAPHY

Native Tongues

1. *Hakuna matata* (no worries) is from which language?

2. Kalaallit Nunaat is the name of which country in the native language of its indigenous population?

3. Which term refers to a language used by people whose native languages are mutually incomprehensible?

4. The constructed international auxiliary language Esperanto is the first language of business magnate George Soros. True or False?

5. Cleopatra was the famous final pharaoh of ancient Egypt. But what was her native language?

6. What was the native language of Christopher Columbus?

7. Hausa, Igbo, and Yoruba are recognized national languages in which country?

8. What was Queen singer Freddie Mercury's native language?

9. Tagalog is spoken as a first language by one-third of the population (and as a second language by most of the rest) in which country?

10. Roughly how many indigenous languages are there in the largest oceanic country?

11. Author Roald Dahl's parents were native speakers of which language?

12. Aotearoa is the name of which country in the native language of its indigenous population?

13. Along with French and German, one of the official languages in Luxembourg is Luxembourgish. True or False?

14. Which is NOT an official language of Switzerland: English, German, Italian?

15. Napoleon Bonaparte's native language was what?

16. There is a colony of Welsh speakers where in South America?

17. Which beat generation writer spoke in a French-Canadian dialect (Joual) until he was six years old?

18. What was the native language of the Aztecs?

19. In which country will you find native speakers of Maasai and Gikuyu?

20. What is the official language of Suriname?

(Answers on page 488)

The Mediterranean

1. In which modern country on the Mediterranean Coast lay the ancient city of Carthage?

2. "Mediterranean" comes from the Latin word *mediterraneus* meaning what?

3. Which ancient civilization had a wide network of trading routes around the Mediterranean?

4. Which strait connects the Mediterranean and the Atlantic Ocean?

5. Which is the largest island in the Mediterranean?

6. Where is the historic city of Dubrovnik?

7. Is coconut a typical product of the Mediterranean region?

8. Which Italian city is often flooded annually by Mediterranean water?

9. In total, the Mediterranean coastline extends for 29,000 miles (46,000 km). True or False?

10. Approximately how many merchant shipping vessels travel the Mediterranean waters every year?

11. Mediterranean fish stocks have declined by about a third in the past 50 years. True or False?

12. Rising sea levels as a result of climate change are soon expected to submerge parts of the Mediterranean island of Malta. True or False?

13. In which country is Alicante, on the Costa Blanca?

14. Which is the largest city by the Mediterranean Sea?

15. How many modern states have a Mediterranean coastline?

16. The Mediterranean island of Rhodes belongs to which country?

17. The Suez Canal connects the Mediterranean to which sea?

18. The ancient Romans called the Mediterranean *Mare Nostrum*. What does it translate to in English?

19. The African country Niger has a coastline by the Mediterranean Sea. True or False?

20. Kefalonia is part of which Mediterranean country?

GEOGRAPHY

(Answers on page 488)   **185**

What a Wonderful World

1. The word "geology" is based on the Greek for "earth-talk." True or False?

2. How old are the Alps?

3. A geologist could tell the age of a rock by measuring the amount of radioactive minerals it contains. True or False?

4. Earth's crust is divided into huge plates that float on the hot rock below. When these plates move, what can happen: earthquakes, volcanoes, or both?

5. Earth is made partly of metal. True or False?

6. What term is used to describe a river of ice flowing from snowcapped mountains?

7. What is strange about the metal mercury?

8. Both copper and tin are quite soft, but if they are mixed together, they make an alloy that is much harder than either. What is it called?

9. Most islands in the oceans are, or were, volcanoes that have erupted from the ocean floor. True or False?

10. Most mountains are formed by the great plates of Earth's crust being pushed together. True or False?

11. You can find fossils of shellfish on mountains at least 3 miles (5 km) above sea level. True or False?

12. The Grand Canyon was made by rocks being pushed upward at the same time as what was cutting a path through the rock?

13. The walls of the Grand Canyon are made up of layers of rock, with the youngest at the bottom and the oldest at the top. True or False?

14. Water covers how much of our planet?

15. Which desert in South America has had no rain at all since records began?

16. Most of Earth's water is in the oceans and therefore salty. Approximately how much of Earth's water is "fresh" and not salty?

17. How are most caves formed by water?

18. Water from the ceiling of a cave interacts with the air, which crystallizes the dissolved calcite to form hanging… what?

19. What was the length of the biggest-known free-hanging stalactite found in Mexico?

20. Slate is a metamorphic rock. True or False?

More Volcanoes

1. What does the Greek word "tectonic" mean?

2. How tall is the Hawaiian volcano Mauna Kea?

3. What is the highest temperature of the rivers of lava that flow from Hawaiian volcanoes?

4. The Olympus Mons on Mars is the largest-known volcano in the solar system. True or False?

5. Pahoehoe is a type of what?

6. Historically, which country has the most active volcanoes?

7. How many estimated active volcanoes are there on Earth?

8. What is "lahar"?

9. What is the largest volcano on Earth?

10. In which year was the great eruption of Mount Vesuvius?

11. Is Mount Kilimanjaro a dormant or active volcano?

12. For roughly how many years has Mount Etna been constantly erupting?

13. Which Icelandic stratovolcano is nicknamed the "Gateway to Hell"?

14. The Ring of Fire has 452 volcanoes. True or False?

15. How many people died in the 1883 eruption of Krakatoa?

16. A volcano is classified as dormant when it hasn't erupted for how many years?

17. The word "volcano" comes from the name of the Roman god of fire, called what?

18. The North American Plate has a boundary with the Eurasian Plate. True or False?

19. In which state is Mount St. Helens?

20. In what country is the Pinatubo volcano located?

GEOGRAPHY

Human Geography

1. Which country's overseas territories include New Caledonia and Réunion?

2. Where is the largest Buddha statue in the world, and what is its name?

3. In 2010, Japan had the longest life expectancy in the world. How old could most Japanese people expect to live to?

4. Throughout the 20th century, which of the following countries had the largest population: Brazil, China, Russia?

5. Which of the following countries has the smallest population: Denmark, Bulgaria, Luxembourg?

6. In 2020, which city was the world's largest, with a population of 37 million people?

7. In 2010, which of the following countries had the shortest life expectancy: Zimbabwe, India, Indonesia?

8. At the millennium, which country had the greatest percentage of its people living in urban areas: Germany, Argentina, Belgium?

9. At the Millennium, which country had the largest percentage of its people living in rural regions: Papua New Guinea, Mongolia, Canada?

10. Where is the final destination for Muslims taking part in the Hajj pilgrimage?

11. Which French town is a popular destination for Christians seeking cures?

12. In which city is the Blue Mosque?

13. Which is the European Union's biggest city by population?

14. In 2011, what was the most common male first name in the world?

15. What was Europe's newest country when it was created in 2008?

16. Which of the following countries has a population of more than one billion: Brazil, Russia, India?

17. In which city is the landmark the Wailing Wall?

18. Which is the smallest country in the world by area?

19. Which of the following European countries had, as of 2020, a population of more than one million: Iceland, Luxembourg, North Macedonia?

20. Approximately what percentage of the world's population lives in urban areas?

          (Answers on page 488)

Violent Earth

1. What is the name for material thrown out by a volcano?

2. The Soufrière Hills volcano has forced the evacuation of the majority of which Caribbean island?

3. Which name is given to tropical storms that affect the coast of Japan?

4. Which Icelandic volcano erupted in 1963 and created a new island?

5. What is the Corryvreckan, which lies off the coast of Jura in the west of Scotland?

6. Which storm devastated New Orleans and other Gulf Coast areas in 2005?

7. What job do "pisteurs" have in the Swiss Alps?

8. The name of which natural hazard comes from a Japanese word meaning "harbor wave"?

9. If you are going whitewater rafting and your route is given a rating of Class 1, it is what?

10. Which natural hazard is measured on the Saffir-Simpson scale, with 5 being the highest value?

11. In which part of Earth's atmosphere is the ozone layer?

12. The Ring of Doom refers to the line of volcanoes that runs around the coastline of the Pacific Ocean. True or False?

13. Which of these volcanoes is NOT on the Italian island of Sicily: Stromboli, Vesuvius, Etna?

14. Crater Lake in the United States has formed inside an extinct volcano. Which of these records does it hold for the US: largest, saltiest, deepest?

15. The Netherlands has been flooded many times. What is the name of the flat, reclaimed areas of land that make up much of the country?

16. What do scientists believe flattened millions of trees at Tunguska in Siberia on June 30, 1908?

17. The Great Alaska Earthquake that struck the Anchorage area and registered 8.6 on the Richter Scale took place in which year?

18. Which of these people did NOT give his name to a scale for measuring earthquakes: Wegener, Richter, Gutenberg?

19. "Duck, cover, and hold on" is advice given to people on how to react when which kind of natural phenomenon occurs?

20. Which flood-prone Asian country is 80% flood plain, with almost of all it fewer than 16 ft (5 m) above sea level?

GEOGRAPHY

CHAPTER 5

MUSIC

Cast your mind back to Christmas songs, boy bands, and Top 10 girl singers. From classical music and Christmas carols to reggae, rap, heavy metal, and musicals, these questions will challenge your musical memories.

Musical Instruments

1. Where does the percussion section sit in the orchestra?

2. What is a "tabla"?

3. The Polynesian nose flute is played using the nose because it is believed that breath from the nose is purer than that from the mouth. True or False?

4. Fender Stratocaster is a make of what?

5. What is the national musical instrument of Scotland?

6. Unlike many other wind instruments, the bassoon has a double reed rather than a single reed. True or False?

7. The pipa is a four-stringed, pear-shaped instrument that looks like a lute. Where does it come from?

8. How is a xylophone played?

9. Which class of musical instruments does a theremin belong to?

10. There are four pedals on a standard piano. True or False?

11. Why are mutes added to a trumpet's bell?

12. In which country might you find an alpenhorn?

13. What is a "high hat"?

14. What is one of the main differences between a violin and a viola?

15. What is a "balalaika"?

16. Which harplike instrument is associated with the ancient Romans and Greeks?

17. How many strings does a violin have?

18. Piccolos belong in the brass section of the orchestra. True or False?

19. The sousaphone is a type of what?

20. How many notes are there in an octave on a keyboard (white and black keys)?

21. What is a "sackbut"?

22. "Timpani" is the Italian word for drums. True or False?

23. A modern orchestra is usually made up of strings, woodwind, percussion, and what?

24. What is another name for a mouth organ?

25. Which musical instrument is the national symbol of Ireland?

(Answers on page 488)

World Music

1. What is the general term used to describe African popular music from the mid-20th century onward?

2. The bagpipes were first made by herdsmen using a goat or sheepskin for the bag and a couple of reed pipes. True or False?

3. Which country has won the Eurovision Song Contest the most times?

4. Ravi Shankar received international fame as a sitar player when who became his student in 1966?

5. In which country was Johann Sebastian Bach born?

6. What sort of wood is used to make a didgeridoo?

7. With which type of music is Bob Marley most commonly associated?

8. The traditional Chinese instrument known as an "erhu" has only two strings. True or False?

9. Before the 20th century, most music in Japan was played by blind musicians who were monks. True or False?

10. What traditional music influenced the development of blues, gospel, and jazz?

11. The sitar, tabla, and tampura are a group of instruments that originated from which country?

12. Which percussion instrument is often heard in Latin American music?

13. The gum-leaf is a very simple instrument made from a single eucalyptus leaf. True or False?

14. Which type of music originated in the Bronx area of New York City in the 1970s?

15. The Japanese koto is said to resemble the shape of which creature?

16. Which percussion instrument is used mainly in Spain but is also heard in Latin American music?

17. To which class of instrument does a pan flute, also known as panpipes, belong?

18. The world's shortest opera is Darius Milhaud's *The Deliverance of Theseus*, which is only 7 minutes and 27 seconds long. True or False?

19. American composer John Cage composed a work entitled *4' 33"*, which consists of four minutes and thirty-three seconds of silence. True or False?

20. Which huge music festival takes place in fields in Somerset, England?

Rockin' All Over the USA

1. Pioneering grunge label Sub Pop was founded in which American city?

2. Which artist pioneered the Minneapolis sound?

3. Southern rock band Lynyrd Skynyrd wrote which song in an angry response to a Neil Young tune?

4. Chuck Berry wrote "Back in the USA" after a trip to the former USSR. True or False?

5. Whose signature tune is "Midnight Train to Georgia"?

6. Which city is known as the capital of country music?

7. Where was folk-rock legend Bob Dylan born?

8. Which popular song, written for singer Dionne Warwick by Burt Bacharach, is about a Californian city?

9. The classic folk song "City of New Orleans" tells the tale of a journey on which form of transportation?

10. Detroit is one of the most influential cities in American music. Which famous record company was founded there?

11. From which state did the band R.E.M. originate?

12. What style of music is Chicago known for?

13. What was the Philly Sound of the late 1960s and 1970s?

14. Where did the Beatles perform their final American concert?

15. "American Woman" was a hit for Canadian band the Guess Who. True or False?

16. Who wrote the classic country-rock song whose protagonist was standing on a corner in Winslow, Arizona?

17. In 1966, folk duo Simon and Garfunkel recorded a song referencing a particular bridge. What was the song called?

18. The Rock and Roll Hall of Fame is located in which American city?

19. Bryan Ferry, Bing Crosby, Tom Petty, and Frank Zappa all sang about a valley in California. What is its name?

20. The raucous 1960s garage-rock classic "Dirty Water" by the Standells mentions several places of local interest in which city?

MUSIC

Christmas Songs

1. "Happy Xmas (War Is Over)" is a song written by which ex-Beatle and his wife?

2. This Canadian singer released a whole album of Christmas songs in 2011 called *Christmas*. What is his name?

3. Which Christmas song recorded by Bing Crosby in 1942 is the best-selling single of all time?

4. In this Christmas carol, the narrator sings about the many presents their true love bestowed upon them during the holiday season. What is its name?

5. In 2011, Justin Bieber released a Christmas song about standing under what type of foliage waiting to be embraced?

6. Sung by Judy Garland, the song "Have Yourself a Merry Little Christmas" featured in what 1940s movie?

7. Which R&B singer released her song "All I Want for Christmas is You" in 1994?

8. Name the Christmas carol based on the story of a benevolent Bohemian king who became a saint after this death in the 10th century.

9. Elvis Presley had a Christmas steeped in what color following a bout of unrequited love?

10. The Singing Cowboy had a US No. 1 hit with "Rudolph the Red-Nosed Reindeer" in 1949. What name is he better known by?

11. In this holiday tune, Brenda Lee sings about doing what around a Christmas tree?

12. Which New Jersey rocker is known for his version of "Santa Claus Is Coming to Town"?

13. This classic song from "A Charlie Brown Christmas" features solo piano. What is its name?

14. Which Canadian songstress covered the classical Christmas carol "O Holy Night" in 1997?

15. Josh Groban included his version of "It Came Upon a Midnight Clear" on which six-time platinum album from 2007?

16. Which Christmas song performed by Eartha Kitt was considered controversial and banned in some states when it was first released in 1953?

17. Which 1980s duo had an enduring megahit with the song "Last Christmas"?

18. "Do You Want to Build a Snowman?" is a song from which animated movie set in a frosty world?

19. "Feliz Navidad" was written and performed by singer and songwriter José Feliciano. The lyrics include words in both Spanish and English. True or False?

20. "Baby, it's Cold Outside"—covered in 2018 by John Legend and Kelly Clarkson—first debuted in a 1940s movie. True or False?

MUSIC

Christmas Carols

1. In which country were the original words to "Silent Night" written?

2. When Good King Wenceslas looked out, how was the snow?

3. What do the "Herald Angels" sing?

4. Who is thought to have introduced Christmas carols into church services?

5. What is *Adeste Fidelis* Latin for?

6. What stood in Royal David's city?

7. Which famous poet wrote the words that are now used for the carol "In the Bleak Midwinter"?

8. What are the halls "decked" with?

9. Finish the next line in this popular carol: "Good tidings we bring…"

10. What is a "Tannenbaum"?

11. What was the original name of the Christmas song "Jingle Bells"?

12. Of all the trees that are in the wood, what does the holly bear?

13. What gift was given on the eighth day of Christmas?

14. Who composed "A Ceremony of Carols"?

15. Which carol does the following line come from: "The cattle are lowing, the baby awakes…"?

16. In the "Carol of the Bells," what do the bells seem to say?

17. In the carol "We Three Kings," which gift has a "bitter perfume"?

18. "It came upon the midnight clear." What was "it"?

19. How many ships came sailing in on Christmas Day?

20. What did the little lamb say to the shepherd boy?

21. In "Ding Dong Merrily on High," where are the bells ringing?

22. Who was first to hear the First Noel?

23. Which carol includes the line: "Peace on earth and mercy mild, God and sinners reconciled"?

24. While shepherds watched their flocks, who came down?

25. In the carol "I Saw Three Ships," where did the ships sail into?

(Answers on page 489)

MUSIC

Bach Soon, Gone Chopin

1. Chopin is most famous for writing music for which musical instrument?

2. A standard musical staff is made up of how many lines?

3. Which "magical" musical instrument is featured in an opera by Mozart?

4. In the *Carnival of Animals* by Saint-Saëns, which musical instruments represent the elephant?

5. Which section of a symphony orchestra traditionally leads the rest of the orchestra?

6. J. S. Bach was a famous composer during which period of music?

7. The word *pizzicato* tells the musician to what?

8. Who wrote the opera *Porgy and Bess*?

9. Which instrument usually provides the note to tune the rest of the orchestra?

10. Which Italian composer wrote the concerto *Le quattro stagioni*?

11. In Gustav Holst's epic orchestral suite *The Planets*, which planet is the "bringer of peace"?

12. How long was American composer John Cage's infamous entirely silent piece?

13. What does the *clef* indicate on a musical staff?

14. In Prokofiev's musical story *Peter and the Wolf*, which instrument denotes Peter?

15. How many strings are there on a traditional classical guitar?

16. *Forte* means "play loudly." What signals a musician to play quietly?

17. Which male "voice" sings at the highest pitch?

18. Vanessa Mae is a famous British musician. Which instrument does she play?

19. Mozart was an early starter. How old was he when he wrote his first symphony?

20. In musical theory, a *semibreve* is worth what?

(Answers on page 489)

MUSIC

Reggae

1. Which song was the first No. 1 reggae hit in the UK?

2. Who wrote the Bob Marley hit "No Woman, No Cry"?

3. "Rivers of Babylon," which was a hit for Boney M, was previously recorded by whom?

4. The Clash once covered "Police and Thieves," but who wrote it?

5. Who announced "You Can Get It If You Really Want"?

6. Which instrument is associated with Augustus Pablo?

7. What was a 1964 hit for the Wailers?

8. Who first sang "A Message to You Rudy"?

9. Who sang "007 Shanty Town"?

10. Who was born Osbourne Ruddock?

11. Who wrote "54–46"?

12. Which 1969 song by Toots and the Maytals used the word "reggae" for the first time?

13. Which reggae band do Sly and Robbie belong to?

14. What was Burning Spear's real name?

15. Who has used the pseudonyms "Pipecock Jackxon" and the "Upsetter," among others?

16. Where did Desmond Dekker die?

17. Who was known as the "Cooler Ruler"?

18. The album *Jah Son of Africa* made which artist a hit in the UK in the 1970s?

19. What was his nickname?

20. What was Bob Marley's middle name?

21. Where does the word "reggae" come from?

22. Which group had a No. 1 hit with the reggae song "The Tide Is High"?

23. What is the real name of Beenie Man?

24. Who is best known for the hit record "Night Nurse"?

25. Who is Ziggy Marley?

MUSIC

1980s Music

1. Which band was "Too shy-shy" in 1983?

2. Which singer dreamed of an "Uptown Girl"?

3. Which band reinvented rock with its 1987 *Appetite for Destruction*?

4. Who was "Like a Virgin" in 1984?

5. Which band led the mainstream Goth movement?

6. Which comic book did the Thompson Twins get their name from?

7. What is Bruce Springsteen also known as?

8. The Cars sang "Drive" about losing a girlfriend in a car accident. True or False?

9. Which rock act did Billy Duffy play guitar for?

10. Which band felt "Hungry Like the Wolf" in 1982?

11. Who is the lead singer of the Pet Shop Boys?

12. Which 1960s prog rock band had a 1980s comeback with "Owner of a Lonely Heart"?

13. Whose single "Just a Gigolo" caused this singer's exit from Van Halen?

14. Who didn't "Need Another Hero"?

15. Which singer created "Footloose"?

16. Which band told its listeners to "Relax"?

17. Which pop act got caught lip-syncing?

18. Who broke chart records with "The Final Countdown"?

19. Who raged: "We're not going to take it"?

20. Which band was from "A land down under"?

21. Which hit song by Madness does this line come from: "Father wears his Sunday best"?

22. Which rock band released an album titled *Brothers in Arms*?

23. Who sang "Islands in the Stream" with Kenny Rogers?

24. Which male singer sang the line: "How can you just leave me standing? Alone in a world that's so cold (so cold)"?

25. Which American group abbreviated its name to NKOTB?

Hip Hop & Rap

1. Which singer is often credited as being the first to perform a rap in a number-one hit?

2. Which Memphis rap group won an Academy Award for "Best Original Song" in 2006?

3. Which band sang about celebrating Martin Luther King Jr.'s birthday in Arizona?

4. Who recorded "Rapper's Delight"?

5. Which 1980s act does the acronym UTFO stand for?

6. Which artist performed the song "Hey Ya"?

7. What is the name of 50 Cent's band?

8. Andre Young is better known as which rapper?

9. Which rapper is usually seen wearing a large clock around his neck?

10. In which song did Eminem say he was being picked on?

11. Who tells listeners to "Drop It Like It's Hot"?

12. What is the title of Jay-Z's first album?

13. Chuck D gave Trevor Tahiem Smith the stage name "Busta Rhymes". True or False?

14. Who were the two bands that made rap and metal collide with "Bring the Noise"?

15. What was Eazy-E's real name?

16. Under which stage name does Donald Glover perform and record?

17. Snoop Dogg was a member of the Crips gang before becoming one of Dr. Dre's proteges. True or False?

18. Which female rapper had a public feud with Foxy Brown in the 1990s?

19. Which was the first American Latino hip-hop group to have platinum-selling albums?

20. Who broke into the mainstream charts with "Fight for Your Right"?

MUSIC

Famous Musicals

1. Which members of ABBA wrote the music for *Chess*?

2. Which musical based on *Pygmalion* follows a professor trying to turn a common flower seller into a lady?

3. Which musical is based on *Romeo and Juliet*?

4. Which former movie-turned-musical is about a town where dancing was banned?

5. Who wrote the music and lyrics for *Kinky Boots*?

6. In which musical does an American soldier ditch his Asian love for a fellow countrywoman?

7. On which opera by Puccini is *Miss Saigon* based?

8. Which musical set in the Wild West is about the search for a famous singer to perform at a small-town saloon?

9. Which musical is set in a New York performing-arts school?

10. Which musical that stars fairy-tale characters such as Cinderella and Little Red Riding Hood does not have a happy ending?

11. Which musical features the song "I'm Flying High Defying Gravity"?

12. Another musical that became a movie, this story follows a gambler's relationship with a girl from the Salvation Army. What is its name?

13. A French plantation owner and an American nurse fall in love. What's the musical?

14. This animated musical landed Elton John a host of awards. What is it?

15. Which rock musical is a product of the hippie era?

16. Which musical made into a movie is set in early Nazi Berlin?

17. Which musical features the Von Trapp family?

18. In which musical do characters known as the Pink Ladies appear?

19. What "Age" do the characters of *Hair* live in?

20. Which musical features characters named Skimbleshanks, Macavity, and Grizabella, among many others?

21. Which is the longest-running musical in the world?

22. Which musical set in the 1920s features two murderesses in jail awaiting trial?

23. Which musical has the characters Caractacus Potts and the "Child Catcher"?

24. "No Place Like London" and "The Worst Pies in London" are songs from which musical?

25. The musical *Hamilton* features R&B, pop, soul, and hip-hop as well as traditional show tunes. True or False?

2000s Music

1. Who got *Back to Basics* in 2006?

2. Who was the drummer for the White Stripes?

3. What year was the eponymous Gorillaz album released?

4. Which former Blur member did *Gorillaz* feature?

5. Robin Pecknold is the singer in which band?

6. Beyoncé was a member of which girl group before going solo?

7. In which year was Rihanna's debut album *Music of the Sun* released?

8. In which country was Rihanna born?

9. In 2006, MTV included Ghostface Killah in its list of "The Greatest MCs of All Time." True or False?

10. Which singer won five Grammy Awards for her *Back to Black* album?

11. Franz Ferdinand hail from which UK city?

12. Which band's debut album became the fastest-selling in British music history?

13. Lauryn Hill was one of the best-selling hip-hop artists of the 1990s. True or False?

14. will.i.am, Taboo, and apl.de.ap are members of which chart-topping group?

15. The best-selling UK album of the 2000s was James Blunt's *Back to Bedlam*. True or False?

16. In which year did Britney Spears release her third No. 1 hit "3"?

17. Which artist took the decade by storm with her 2008 album *The Fame*?

18. Who recorded her first solo album *Love. Angel. Music. Baby.* in 2004?

19. Thom Yorke is the lead singer of which English band formed in 1985?

20. Which Kid Rock album went platinum in 2003?

(Answers on page 490)

MUSIC

Very Heavy Metal

1. Released on Friday, February 13, 1970, which album is considered the first true heavy-metal record?

2. Which of these bands was NOT part of the New Wave of British heavy metal: Def Leppard, Iron Maiden, Flower Fairies?

3. Three Van Halens featured in the band's original lineup. True or False?

4. Which band was in the Big Four of thrash metal: Clunk, Tin Gods, or Anvil?

5. Who was the first original member to leave Guns N' Roses in 1990?

6. New York is the spiritual home of grunge. True or False?

7. Bass player Lemmy was most associated with which heavy-metal act?

8. In which decade did heavy metal become the most listened to music in the world?

9. Which member of Judas Priest is credited with introducing studs, chains, and leather to the heavy-metal wardrobe?

10. Which drummer brought double-kick drum pedals into the heavy-metal mainstream?

11. Which heavy-metal record became the best-selling debut album of all time?

12. What is the real first name of "Ozzy" Osbourne?

13. Which heavy-metal singer popularized the "evil horns" hand gesture?

14. Angus Young has appeared on stage for several decades dressed in a schoolboy uniform. To which band does he belong?

15. "Ace of Spades" is a song by which British band?

16. Heavy-metal band Megadeth has sold more albums than rival band Metallica. True or False?

17. Iron Maiden's mascot is called Eddie the what?

18. Which heavy-metal band's stage show features fire breathing, blood spitting, smoking guitars, shooting rockets, and levitating drum kits?

19. Which song is sometimes described as the first heavy-metal song?

20. What did Def Leppard drummer Rick Allen lose in a 1984 car accident?

Great American Rock 'n' Rollers

1. Which American rock and roller wrote "Peggy Sue"?

2. Who was the rock-and-roll subject of *La Bamba*?

3. Who was Richard Wayne Penniman better known as?

4. Which member of the Beach Boys was not a Wilson brother?

5. Who kicked rockabilly into the mainstream with "Be-Bop-a-Lula"?

6. Which teen rock and roller was also a TV idol?

7. Which rock and roller was known as "Mr. Excitement"?

8. How did the Big Bopper and Ritchie Valens die in 1959?

9. Which Eddie Cochran song includes these lines: "I'd like to help you son, but you're too young to vote"?

10. What was Bobby Darin's first million-selling single, released in 1958?

11. Chuck Berry was credited with developing rock and roll from rhythm and blues. In which year did he release "Johnny B. Goode"?

12. What was rock-and-roll singer Carl Perkins's best-known song?

13. Which rock-and-roll band was responsible for the surf anthem "Wipe Out"?

14. Singer Roy Orbison was also known as "The Big O." True or False?

15. In which year did Elvis Presley die?

16. Which singer is sometimes called "rock and roll's first great wild man"?

17. What was Elvis Presley's first hit, released in 1956?

18. Rock-and-roll singer Ricky Nelson said in 2001 that he'd like one more number-one hit. True or False?

19. In which state was rock-and-roll singer Buddy Holly born?

20. Which rock-and-roll band sang "Rock around the Clock"?

MUSIC

Music News Pop Idols

1. Which singer, who hit the big time in 2005 with the single "You're Beautiful," used to be an officer in the British Army?

2. Which pop superstar shocked the world in 2010 by turning up to an awards ceremony dressed in an outfit made entirely of raw meat?

3. Beyoncé is one of the world's most famous female pop stars. Her rapper husband is equally famous, but who is he?

4. Every year since 2005, the UK *X Factor* show winners have gone on to take the Christmas No. 1, except in 2009. Which band took the spot?

5. Which superstar "Man in the Mirror" died in 2009?

6. Which singing Ohio schoolkids hold the record for having the most singles in a single year?

7. Which Black Eyed Peas song was pronounced by Apple in 2010 to be the biggest-selling iTunes download of all time?

8. Who became only the third British female to have a debut No. 1 single in America with the song "Bleeding Love" in 2007?

9. Which popular nineties boy band broke up but got back together in 2005?

10. What was the name of the band formed from the five winners of the original TV talent show *Popstars* in 2001?

11. Who sang alongside Jay-Z about New York in the massive hit 2009 single "Empire State of Mind"?

12. Which former N'Sync member found international success as a solo artist and appeared in the film *The Social Network* in 2010?

13. From which country do the members of the band Westlife come from?

14. Which TV show featuring singing and dancing teenagers was not made by Disney?

15. Which rock band stormed to the top of the UK charts with its debut single "I Bet You Look Good on the Dance Floor" in 2006?

16. After leaving Destiny's Child, Beyoncé was propelled to global superstar status with which huge hit single in 2001?

17. Who was the best-selling female artist of the first decade of the 21st century?

18. Justin Bieber was discovered on YouTube. True or False?

19. Whose debut album was called *Music of the Sun*?

20. Which US TV talent show debuted in June 2002?

Famous Musicians

1. Which band's songs were used in the films *Mamma Mia* and *Mamma Mia! Here We Go Again*?

2. Bob Marley was the lead singer with whom?

3. *The Four Seasons* was written by which classical composer?

4. Plácido Domingo and Luciano Pavarotti were two of the Three Tenors. Who was the third?

5. Dean Martin was part of which group of actors?

6. As well as being a prolific composer, Bach also fathered 20 children. True or False?

7. What is Lady Gaga's real name?

8. What was Mozart's middle name?

9. With which form of dancing is Tchaikovsky associated?

10. Shirley Manson is the lead singer of which group?

11. The electronic music band Kraftwerk is from Sweden. True or False?

12. The musician John Williams is associated with which instrument?

13. Who was Adolf Hitler's favorite composer?

14. *Sgt. Pepper's Lonely Hearts Club Band* was the Beatles' first album. True or False?

15. With which musical genre is Duke Ellington associated?

16. Nicole Sherzinger is famous for being in which band?

17. Madonna performed at the London Live Earth concert. In which year did this take place?

18. Who was the lead singer of Led Zeppelin?

19. "White Christmas" was a 1942 hit for which artist?

20. Which state was the title of a Bee Gees No. 1 song?

21. Who composed the opera *Carmen*?

22. Chrissie Hynde is the lead singer of which group?

23. Which 1990s singer had a comeback in 2016 with "When the Bassline Drops"?

24. Who released the album *Fever* in 2001?

25. Which city's streets did Bruce Springsteen sing about in 1994?

Classical Music

1. In which country was the first tuba made?

2. Guillaume de Machaut, a 14th-century priest, wrote many songs based on what theme?

3. In which year did Wolfgang Mozart die?

4. In Vincenzo Bellini's *I Capuleti e i Montecchi*, Romeo's part is written for a female voice. True or False?

5. Who composed *Ein Deutsches Requiem*?

6. How many strings does a modern orchestral harp have?

7. A conductor's only job is to keep time. True or False?

8. What did George Frederic Handel study before he devoted himself to music?

9. Gaps between notes are known as what?

10. How many movements does a nocturne piece have?

11. What physical ailment severely afflicted Johann Sebastian Bach toward the end of his life?

12. Twelve of Franz Joseph Haydn's later symphonies are known as the what?

13. The music of Mark-Anthony Turnage is influenced by which musical style?

14. Concerts gained popularity in England during which war?

15. Music structured according to the "Sonata Structure" begins with what?

16. In which year did the ballet of Tchaikovsky's *Swan Lake* have its premiere?

17. The overture is which part of a musical movement?

18. *Allegretto* means "leisurely" in Italian. True or False?

19. Opera was first performed in which period?

20. A lute is an early version of which instrument?

Motown

1. Who founded Motown Records in 1959?

2. Which Motown singer married Berry Gordy's sister, Anna?

3. Which was the first act signed to Motown, which later became the Miracles?

4. How many top-ten hits did Motown have between 1961 and 1971?

5. What age was "Little" Stevie Wonder when he signed to Motown?

6. Stevie Wonder only ever recorded on one label. True or False?

7. What was the name of Michael Jackson and his band of brothers?

8. How old was Michael when he and his brothers signed with Motown?

9. Who backed Diana Ross?

10. What was the name of Gladys Knight's backing group?

11. Which influential album did Marvin Gaye record for Motown in 1971?

12. In which year did Motown move all of its operations from Detroit to Los Angeles?

13. Why did Motown move its location?

14. What was a hit for the Commodores in 1974?

15. Which Commodore branched out on his own and hit number one in 1982 with "Truly"?

16. Who was the top hit-making producer for Motown in the late 1960s and early 1970s?

17. Boyz II Men was one of Motown's most successful acts of the 1990s. True or False?

18. What did Berry Gordy originally do to Marvin Gaye's recording of "I Heard It through the Grapevine"?

19. In which year did Berry Gordy sell his interest in Motown Records to MCA?

20. How much did Berry Gordy sell Motown Records for?

21. In which city was Motown founded?

22. Which Motown song was the first to reach No. 1 on the charts?

23. Stevland Hardaway Morris is which famous Motown singer's real name?

24. Smokey Robinson was a member of which Motown band?

25. Which was the first female group to sign for Motown records?

Famous Folk

1. Which 1960s folk singer once said: "I've never written a political song. Songs can't save the world. I've gone through all that."

2. Who said in 2010 that Bob Dylan was a "fake" and a "plagiarist"?

3. Certain types of folk music are also called "world music." True or False?

4. Which folk trio had success with a cover version of Bob Dylan's song "Blowin' in the Wind"?

5. From where does Cajun music originate?

6. Which banjo-playing singer was investigated by the House Un-American Activities Committee?

7. What is the name of the instrument commonly known as the "hubcap guitar"?

8. An autoharp is often used by folk musicians from the Appalachia region. How many strings does it have?

9. What is the name of the instrument that Beatle George Harrison was taught to play by Ravi Shankar?

10. On which Fairport Convention album is the track "Tam Lin"?

11. In which year was the most famous Newport Folk Festival held?

12. Who sang: "This land is your land, this land is my land…"?

13. Which group epitomized the folk rock sound with its version of "Mr. Tambourine Man"?

14. There is no copyright on the majority of traditional folk songs. True or False?

15. What did Bob Dylan do that created a storm of controversy at the 1965 Newport Folk Festival?

16. Which duo's music is featured in the 1967 movie *The Graduate*?

17. Which folk singer was later celebrated as "the Grandfather of Grunge"?

18. Which song includes this line: "Well I feel so broke up, I wanna go home"?

19. Before he recorded his first album, what career did Leonard Cohen have?

20. Who wrote the influential song "Woodstock," although she was persuaded not to attend the event personally?

(Answers on page 491)

The Color of Music

1. What kind of big taxi did Joni Mitchell once sing about?

2. What was Prince's ode to colorful weather?

3. The seminal album from jazz legend Miles Davis is a *Kind of* what?

4. Following the death of lead singer Bon Scott, AC/DC soon announced they were *Back in* what?

5. The challenging 1968 Beatles double album with no name is commonly known as what?

6. For chefs, its varieties are Turbinado, Muscovado, and Demerara. For the Rolling Stones, it was simply what?

7. Featuring Northumbrian smallpipes, this song is Sting's 1993 "Fields of" what?

8. The band is Booker T. & the M.G.'s, and the colorful hit they cooked up was what?

9. Dancing cheek to cheek with Chris de Burgh in 1986 was his "Lady in" what?

10. The 1980s song "Pretty in Pink" was so popular that a movie was named after it. Which band wrote it?

11. With shades of punk and ska, what color were Sublime's "Begonias"?

12. Where was Linda Ronstadt hoping to go back to?

13. Who sang about a "Little Red Corvette"?

14. "Strawberry Blonde" is a tune by English Indie outfit the Subways. True or False?

15. Country boy John Conlee scored his first chart success in 1978 with what?

16. "Touch of Grey" was the most commercially successful hit for these epic aging 1960s rockers. Who were they?

17. A sentiment shared by workers of the world, what color was New Order's "Monday"?

18. Which multi-colored effort was created by the Who?

19. Which Van Morrison song includes these lyrics: "Hey, where did we go, days when the rain came"?

20. Maxwell is a Beatles character with a lethal hammer. What color is it?

21. What color was the signal ribbon that Tony Orlando and Dawn were hoping to see?

22. What color was the Manalishi with the two-prong crown that creeps around Fleetwood Mac?

23. Which shoes did the angels want to wear, according to Elvis Costello?

24. Who was known as "the Man in Black"?

25. Texas born and bred, Kelly Clarkson is well-known for watching from what?

MUSIC

Great Opera

1. Which Verdi opera is set in Egypt?

2. Which operatic tenor had great commercial success with his recording of an aria from *Turandot*?

3. What famous sacred song did Charles Gounod compose?

4. Which tear-jerker features the characters Rodolfo, Musetta, Marcello, and Mimi?

5. Who composed *The Pearl Fishers*?

6. Which opera is based on a novel by Alexandre Dumas?

7. Which opera by Puccini includes torture, murder, and suicide?

8. Who created *The Barber of Seville*?

9. The composer responsible for *The Marriage of Figaro* was?

10. Which British composer wrote operas based on works by Shakespeare and Herman Melville?

11. In which opera did soprano Kiri te Kanawa give her final performance before retiring?

12. Which gypsy goes off with a bullfighter and suffers a tragic end?

13. Who wrote the music for *Don Giovanni*?

14. In which opera does a henchman lose his daughter while plotting the downfall of his master?

15. Which opera features a US military officer and his Japanese bride?

16. Which opera was based on a Greek legend and had its first performance in 1762?

17. Which famous composer wrote only one opera?

18. Which opera by Richard Wagner was inspired by a stormy sea crossing he made?

19. Borodin spent nearly 20 years working on his opera *Prince Igor* but died before he completed it. True or False?

20. Which opera was based on a play by Oscar Wilde, which was written in French and based on a story from the Bible?

Famous Drummers

1. Foo Fighters frontman Dave Grohl used to play the drums in Nirvana, but who is the current Foo Fighters drummer?

2. Metallica drummer Lars Ulrich was one of the band's original members. True or False?

3. Neil Peart is the drummer for prog rockers Rush. What is his other role with the band?

4. When did Chad Smith join the Red Hot Chili Peppers as their drummer?

5. After Cream disbanded, drummer Ginger Baker joined Blind Faith with which other former Cream member?

6. Which drummer was an extra in the Beatles film *A Hard Day's Night*?

7. Beatles drummer Ringo Starr was the original narrator for which TV show?

8. When Keith Moon died in 1978, who took over as drummer for the Who?

9. Why didn't Velvet Underground drummer Maureen Tucker play on their 1970 album, *Loaded*?

10. Who played the drums on AC/DC's album *Highway to Hell*?

11. "Back in the USSR" had which Beatle on drums?

12. Who was the drummer for Iron Maiden in 1984?

13. As well as being a singer, Karen Carpenter was also an accomplished drummer. True or False?

14. Rick Allen overcame the complete amputation of his left arm and went on playing as the drummer for which band?

15. Who was the drummer for the Smiths?

16. How old was Led Zeppelin drummer John Bonham when he died?

17. What is English rock drummer Cozy Powell's birth name?

18. Who is the drummer for Aerosmith?

19. Nick Mason is the only Pink Floyd member who wasn't part of the original lineup. True or False?

20. When was drummer extraordinaire Bill Bruford born?

MUSIC

Classical Composers

1. Which country was Frederic Chopin from?

2. Who wrote *The Planets*?

3. Who composed the symphonic suite *Scheherazade*?

4. At 44 years of age, Beethoven was almost completely deaf. True or False?

5. *The Lark Ascending* was composed by which British composer?

6. Complete the title of Charles-Camille Saint-Saëns's famous work: *The Carnival of the…*

7. Which composer was the subject of the film *Amadeus*?

8. George Frideric Handel wrote "Music for Royal Birthdays." True or False?

9. From which oratorio does the famous *Hallelujah* chorus come?

10. Wagner's wife Cosima was the daughter of which pianist and composer?

11. Whose Symphony No. 8 was "Unfinished"?

12. Who wrote the series of piano pieces called the *Gymnopédies*?

13. Who wrote *Le quattro staggioni*?

14. Of which composer was it said, "He did not write 400 concertos; he wrote the same concerto 400 times"?

15. Tchaikovsky's *The Nutcracker* was what kind of composition?

16. Which American wrote *Fanfare for the Common Man*?

17. Who wrote the opera *Dido and Aeneas*?

18. Which one of Puccini's operas is based on a play about a geisha from Nagasaki?

19. Who wrote *The Dream of Gerontius*?

20. Richard Strauss was appointed as a head of music in Nazi Germany. True or False?

21. Who wrote a symphony in which the musicians stop playing one by one until only two are left?

22. Which composer's pianist wife became known as the "Queen of the Piano"?

23. Three of J. S. Bach's pieces were sent into space on the *Voyager* spacecraft as part of a representation of human life in case of extraterrestrial interception. True or False?

24. Which renowned composer was also a professor of chemistry?

25. Which composer's Symphony No. 6 includes the ringing of cowbells off stage?

The Rolling Stones

1. In which year did the Rolling Stones form?

2. Which song begins with the lyrics: "I was born in a cross-fire hurricane"?

3. How is the group sometimes described in fun?

4. Where did Mick Jagger and Keith Richards first discover they shared a love for the same music?

5. In total, how many band members have there been in the Rolling Stones?

6. Keith Richards has a son named after which Hollywood actor?

7. In which year did the band release the album *Exile on Main St.*?

8. Who is the oldest member of the band?

9. Which song contains the lyric: "We're gonna vent our frustration, if we don't we're gonna blow a 50-amp fuse"?

10. In which year did Brian Jones die, one of the band's founding members?

11. Who came up with the idea for the album cover of *Sticky Fingers*?

12. What is Mick Jagger's full name?

13. The Stones' first single was a cover of a Chuck Berry song. What was it?

14. The Stones' second single was "I Wanna Be Your Man." Who wrote it?

15. Which band was Ronnie Wood with immediately before joining the Rolling Stones?

16. Who designed the band's famous lips-and-tongue logo?

17. The Rolling Stones have had a total of 21 UK Number-1 singles. True or False?

18. How many nervous breakdowns are mentioned in the famous song?

19. The music video for the track "Anybody Seen My Baby?" featured which Hollywood actress before she was famous?

20. In which country did the band record some of the tracks for *Exile on Main St.*?

MUSIC

1950s Music

1. Which 1950s singer claimed to be "the architect of rock and roll"?

2. Who performed "Rock around the Clock" in 1955?

3. Which song includes this line: "When the moon hits your eye like a big pizza pie"?

4. When did Johnny Cash make his first recording—"Cry! Cry! Cry!"—with Sun Records?

5. Which singer had a hit with "Rockin' around the Christmas Tree" in 1958?

6. What was Elvis Presley's middle name?

7. Complete the name of this classic 1958 rocker: "Johnny… "

8. Buddy Holly & the Wickets are responsible for "Peggy Sue." True or False?

9. Who recorded "Wake Up Little Suzie" in 1957?

10. Who reached No. 2 on the US charts with "Great Balls of Fire"?

11. What was Julie London's most famous song and biggest-selling single of her career?

12. What was the name of Little Richard's first big hit in 1956?

13. Tony Bennett sang "Cold, Cold Heart" in 1951. True or False?

14. What year was Cliff Richard's first hit "Move It" released?

15. Who was known as "the Girl with the Giggle in her Voice"?

16. Who found his thrill on "Blueberry Hill"?

17. The Everly Brothers once sang "Bye Bye Love." True or False?

18. Who recorded "Be-Bop-a-Lula" in 1956?

19. Complete the title of this Ricky Nelson song: "Poor Little…"

20. Who hit the charts with "That'll Be the Day" in 1957?

21. Who tried to "Mambo Italiano" in 1955?

22. Who was the first singer to have three number-one hits in the same year on the UK singles chart?

23. What item worn by singer Pat Boone became his trademark?

24. Whose debut hit record was "Maybellene"?

25. Who was the first British female singer to have a number-one hit record?

Jimi Hendrix

1. What were James Marshall Hendrix's original first and middle names?

2. Jack Bruce was NOT a member of the Jimi Hendrix Experience. True or False?

3. How many Jimi Hendrix studio albums have been released posthumously?

4. Jimi Hendrix, Billy Cox, and Buddy Miles were known collectively as the what?

5. Jimi formed his first band in 1965. What were they called?

6. On which album did "Purple Haze" first appear?

7. On which album was Hendrix working when he died?

8. What 1950s rock-and-roller claimed to have taught Jimi Hendrix how to be "freaky"?

9. What was Jimi Hendrix's first hit?

10. In which city was Electric Lady Studios built?

11. Jimi Hendrix was upset by the UK issue of the album *Electric Ladyland* because he had not authorized its cover art. What did it show?

12. *Rolling Stone* magazine once named Jimi Hendrix No. 1 on its list of the 100 greatest guitarists of all time. True or False?

13. Which Bob Dylan song did Hendrix famously cover?

14. With which military division did Jimi Hendrix train?

15. Alongside which future band member did Jimi Hendrix serve in the military?

16. Hendrix once played in the Isley Brothers' backup band. True or False?

17. Frank Zappa was responsible for introducing Jimi Hendrix to the wah-wah pedal. True or False?

18. In which year was *Are You Experienced* released?

19. How many members of the Jimi Hendrix Experience are alive today?

20. Which classical composer had also lived in the London house where Jimi Hendrix lived for two years from 1968?

(Answers on page 492)

Boy Bands from the 1980s

1. Which European boy band threesome suggested the world "Take on Me" in 1988?

2. Which Puerto Rican boy band did not allow members over the age of 16?

3. Which US boy band invited their listeners to "Cool It Now" in 1984?

4. Which 1980s boy band featured two sets of brothers?

5. British boy band Bros was made up of brothers Sam and Luke Goss. True or False?

6. Nigel Martin-Smith decided to form which boy band after seeing the success of 1980s act New Edition?

7. After finding fortune with Bros in the 1980s, which boy band did Tom Watkins form as rivals to Take That?

8. Formed in 1988, which was British boy band Big Fun's big hit?

9. Which English boy band hit the charts with: "I Should Have Lied" and "How Many Times"?

10. Which boy band, formed in 1988 in Philadelphia, Pennsylvania, went on to sell more than 60 million albums?

11. Which two members of boy band 'N Sync first found fame in the late 1980s and 1990s on the *New Mickey Mouse Club* TV show?

12. Which original boy band had chart success with "Can You Feel It?" in 1980?

13. British band Boyzone was formed in 1987 but did not make a public appearance until 1993. True or False?

14. Which boy band formed in 1988 is also the most successful R&B group of all time?

15. Which 1980s boy band suggested "I Owe You Nothing" in 1987?

16. Boy band A-ha's best-selling album was what?

17. Which boy band was singer Bobby Brown fired from in 1985?

18. Now seen more often in films than a recording studio, with which boy band did actor Mark Wahlberg sing in the 1980s?

19. Ricky Martin made his start in which 1980s boy band?

20. Eg White was a founding member of Brother Beyond and went on to form pop duo Eg and Alice. True or False?

The Best of 2012

1. Which number-one single had almost 1 billion views on Youtube?

2. What jewel was Rihanna's top song in 2012?

3. Who won New Artist of the Year at the American Music Awards 2012?

4. The British retailer John Lewis used whose vocal for their Christmas commerical?

5. Which artist revealed on her website in November 2012 that she was singing again after undergoing vocal cord surgery?

6. In Taylor Swift's song "We Are Never Ever Getting Back Together" how does her ex "find his piece of mind"?

7. What is the name of Edward Scissortongue's debut solo album?

8. Which movie theme do these lyrics come from? "This is the end / hold your breath and count to ten / Feel the earth move and then / hear my heart burst again."

9. Having composed "The Bassarids" and "Elegy for Young Lovers," which major opera composer died in 2012?

10. Which Scottish singer-songwriter performed in both the opening and closing ceremonies of the London 2012 Olympics?

11. In their duet, featured on his album *18 Months*, what have Calvin Harris and Rihanna discovered?

12. Which song are these lyrics from: "You'll never love yourself / half as much as I love you / you'll never treat yourself right darlin' / but I want you to"?

13. Which well-known music festival did not take place in 2012?

14. Which rapper is featured in Olly Murs's song "Troublemaker"?

15. Which artist topped the Spotify streaming chart of 2012?

16. In the song "Hall of Fame" by the Script, which film character is mentioned?

17. What was the official finale event of the London 2012 Festival?

18. Which artist performed at the 2012 Super Bowl halftime show?

19. According to *Forbes Magazine*, who was the highest-paid musician of 2012?

20. Which veteran guitarist did Jessie J perform with at the closing ceremony of the London 2012 Olympic Games?

(Answers on page 492)   **217**

MUSIC

All Things Grunge

1. Which independent record label is most associated with grunge?

2. Which Mudhoney member is credited with first using the term "grunge"?

3. In which American city was grunge first created?

4. Without which item of clothing would no grunge rocker be complete?

5. Which "quiet, loud" band did Kurt Cobain cite as his major influence?

6. Henry Rollins is sometimes called the "Godfather of grunge." True or False?

7. Which group had a hit with its cover of the disco classic "We Are Family"?

8. Which Screaming Trees member released his first solo album *The Winding Sheet* in 1990?

9. Which grunge band featured the late Layne Staley on vocals?

10. Which grunge album replaced Michael Jackson's *Dangerous* at number one on the Billboard 200 in 1992?

11. Which grunge band recorded a cover of Spinal Tap's "Big Bottom"?

12. Which supergroup featured members from Soundgarden and Pearl Jam?

13. Which grunge band did Courtney Love front?

14. Which 1992 Cameron Crowe film featured cameos from popular grunge rock band members?

15. Which grunge band was the first to sign to a major record label in 1989?

16. Who was the singer of grunge band the U-Men?

17. Tad Doyle was the founder, singer, and guitarist with grunge band Tad. True or False?

18. How many albums have Nirvana sold worldwide?

19. Which Soundgarden member was formerly in Skin Yard?

20. Which Nirvana member went on to form the Foo Fighters?

Genre, Lyrics, and Musicians

1. Which famous album cover features four members of the band walking across a zebra crossing?

2. Which Spice Girl auctioned her famous Union Jack dress?

3. What is the name of the third studio album by American hip-hop artist Kanye West, which features a bear on the album cover?

4. The British rap/hip-hop artist Dylan Kwabena Mills is better known as whom?

5. Complete these lyrics from Queen's "Bohemian Rhapsody": "Is this the real life? Is this…"?

6. What is the missing word from this Led Zeppelin classic: "And she's… a stairway to heaven"?

7. According to Guinness World Records, what is the most covered song in history?

8. Which legendary rock musician had hits including "Hey Joe," "Fire," "Bold as Love," and "Purple Haze"?

9. Which US singer-songwriter won the Nobel Prize for Literature in 2016?

10. Complete these lyrics from Lady Gaga's "Bad Romance": "I want your love, and I want your revenge, you and me…"?

11. Which famous band, led by Chris and also including Guy, Jonny, and Will, plays the songs "Yellow" and "The Hardest Part"?

12. Which legendary blind soul musician rose to fame when he told everybody to do the "mess around"?

13. Which Motown soul superstar "Heard It through the Grapevine"?

14. The musical *Little Shop of Horrors* was written by Andrew Lloyd Webber. True or False?

15. What is the popular name for Debussy's Suite Bergamesque III, the romantic piece featured in the films *Ocean's 11* and *Twilight*?

16. Who wrote *Eine Kleine Nachtmusik*?

17. When crooner Frank Sinatra sang, "Start spreading the news, I'm leaving today," where would he be "makin' a brand new start of it"?

18. Which New Orleans jazz musician lit up the early 20th century with his famous trumpet solos and distinctive gravelly voice?

19. Which classic musical, set in London, features an orphanage, an undertaker, an underground pickpockets' lair, and a pub?

20. Which Lloyd Webber musical is based on the life of an Argentine dictator's wife?

MUSIC

(Answers on page 492)   **219**

Punk

1. When was punk rock said to have started?

2. Iggy Pop was asked to lead the Sex Pistols, but he wasn't able to because he was what?

3. What bird do the Ramones have on their logo?

4. Sid Vicious was named after John Lydon's hamster. True or False?

5. What was the name of the best-known British punk fanzine?

6. Which US singer tumbled into the orchestra pit during a gig, seriously injuring herself on the concrete floor below?

7. Which band did Joe Strummer leave to join the Clash?

8. Who wrote the album *Valley of the Dolls*?

9. Paul Simonon from the Clash was so strapped for cash, he once ate the glue he'd been using to hang flyers. True or False?

10. Punk's style is said to originate from two tiny clothes shops on Chelsea's King's Road. One was "Acme Attractions"—what was the other?

11. Where did the Sex Pistols perform their last gig?

12. Who was charged with murdering his girlfriend in 1978?

13. Rat Scabies was the drummer of which band?

14. Before finding fame as the lead singer of Blondie, Debbie Harry tried her luck as a game show host. True or False?

15. Who was responsible for the Sex Pistols' influential cut-and-paste artwork?

16. When was the first edition of the magazine *Punk* published?

17. Whose performance at Woodstock in 1994 descended into chaos?

18. "My guitar is not a thing. It is an extension of myself. It is who I am." Who said this?

19. Susan Janet Ballion changed her name to become whom?

20. Who was the leader of the New York Dolls?

21. Which British punk rock band was Captain Sensible most associated with?

22. Which Dead Kennedys album was released after they split up?

23. Which album by the Clash featured the song "English Civil War"?

24. Which 1989 Stephen King film featured a Ramones song on the soundtrack?

25. After leaving the Sex Pistols, John Lydon went on to form which postpunk band?

Unusual Instruments

1. In which country would you find a rubber glove bagpipe?

2. Bethanien Kunstlerhaus was the first person to invent the 10-string double violin in 1986. True or False?

3. What natural element plays the Aeolian harp instead of human hands?

4. The Aeolian harp was named after the Greek god Aeolus. True or False?

5. What is the name of the traditional Indian instrument that was sometimes played by Beatle George Harrison?

6. What is a type of dulcimer played with long attachable fingernails and often found in Greece and Eastern Europe?

7. What buzzing mouth instrument did Dion play on his 1962 hit "Little Diane"?

8. The theremin is one of the first fully electronic musical instruments which can be played without touching it. What year was it invented?

9. Which Beach Boys song featured an electric theremin?

10. What is the world's largest instrument, which is housed in a cave and is played by hitting rubber mallets against stalactites?

11. What percussive instrument is featured on the 1975 hit "Moonlight Feels Right"?

12. What is the 24-string stainless-steel harp created by Robert Grawi?

13. What is the name of the instrument made up of glass bowls and glasses of different sizes?

14. A type of bow played by Creole musicians is the cigar box what?

15. What is a five-string double bass with a five-octave range, 29 sympathetic, and four drone strings?

16. When did musician Mark Deutsch finish creating the Bazantar?

17. In which country might you find a crocodile zither?

18. The Japanese kaisatsuko is a type of bow that is played with a small rotating wheel. True or False?

19. Tod Machover is an American musician and inventor of "Hyperinstruments." True or False?

20. What instrument is Martin Žák known for playing with his Old-Time Country band?

(Answers on page 492)

MUSIC

Guitar Lovers

1. What bar is a vibrato unit found in many electric guitars?

2. Which famous guitarist was left-handed and compensated by playing a right-handed guitar upside-down?

3. The second string of a guitar is the D string. True or False?

4. How many notes does the pentatonic scale have?

5. Billie Joe Armstrong is the lead singer and guitarist for which band?

6. Famous blues artist B. B. King gave all his guitars the same name. True or False?

7. Often used for playing the blues, how is a slide guitar played?

8. What are guitar-makers known as?

9. Les Paul collaborated on design with which company?

10. "Noodling" is a guitar term. True or False?

11. Who was known for his famous "duck walk"?

12. What is a capo used for?

13. The sides of the guitar are known as the what?

14. The guitarist Paul Weller led which UK band?

15. What does "arpeggio" mean?

16. "Sweep picking" describes a type of picking that emphasizes off-beats. True or False?

17. What was the first model guitar produced by Fender?

18. How many notes are there in a blues scale?

19. "Scoops," "doops," "gargles," and "vibrato" are all guitar techniques. True or False?

20. A plectrum is also called a pick. True or False?

21. Which type of guitar, which first appeared in 1954, is considered the most played in rock history?

22. How are guitars usually tuned, starting from lowest to highest?

23. In an electric guitar, what are the "microphones"?

24. What was the stage name of Lester William Polsfuss, pioneer and designer of electric guitars?

25. Who created the first fretless bass?

(Answers on page 492)

Opera

1. The Three Tenors famously brought "Nessun dorma" to the masses, but which Puccini opera was it from?

2. In Hades, who appeals to her husband Plutone to grant Orfeo's prayers?

3. Which composer wrote an opera that partly follows the story of *The Little Mermaid*?

4. Which style of opera is associated with silly plots and light-hearted music?

5. Who wrote *Die Fledermaus*?

6. Which operetta is about a trip to the moon in a hot-air balloon?

7. *Dido and Aeneas* is considered to be the first full-length English opera, but who was it written by?

8. In which opera does a devious count try to seduce his wife's chambermaid?

9. Oratorios are different from operas because they are generally not performed with scenery or costumes. True or False?

10. What was Gluck's most famous opera?

11. What is the name of the lieutenant who marries a Japanese geisha in *Madama Butterfly*?

12. Where is *Porgy and Bess* set?

13. Which opera features the "Flight of the Bumblebee"?

14. With whom did Robert Wilson collaborate in creating *Einstein on the Beach*?

15. Which revered 20th-century Greek-American soprano was known as La Divina, "The Divine One"?

16. "Be still, stop chattering" by J. S. Bach is a miniature comic opera about the addiction to which substance?

17. Which 18th-century castrato had such a following that he was able to make outrageous demands, including entering the stage on a horse?

18. Victorian operatic soprano Helen Porter Mitchell is better known by what name?

19. When did the Sydney Opera House open its doors?

20. Rigoletto the hunchbacked jester appears in an opera by Bellini. True or False?

(Answers on page 493)

MUSIC

The Beatles

1. Whom did Ringo Starr replace as drummer?

2. Which Beatle crossed Abbey Road first?

3. In the song "Revolution," John Lennon wanted his vocals to have an unusual sound. How did he achieve this?

4. Which band did Ringo leave to join the Beatles?

5. How long is the book in "Paperback Writer"?

6. What was the Beatles' first mainstream successful single in 1962?

7. Who became the band's manager in 1962?

8. Who famously said the Beatles were "more popular than Jesus"?

9. The final note on the Beatles song "A Day in the Life" is the longest recorded single note in music history. True or False?

10. What was the last song that John Lennon played before a paying audience?

11. What was the working title of the song "With a Little Help from My Friends"?

12. What was the Beatles' first album?

13. Whom did Paul McCartney write "Hey Jude" for?

14. Elton John and Abraham Lincoln are on the cover of *Sgt. Pepper's Lonely Hearts Club Band*. True or False?

15. Which Beatle wrote "If I Needed Someone"?

16. The working title for "Yesterday" was "Scrambled Eggs" until Paul could figure out the lyrics. True or False?

17. Which Beatle sang "Say, Say, Say" with Michael Jackson?

18. Which Beatles song was released 25 years after the band broke up?

19. *Sgt. Pepper's Lonely Hearts Club Band* is the first British rock album to have the lyrics for every song printed on the back cover. True or False?

20. Which was the last album released by the band?

21. Which album required more than 700 hours of recordings?

22. In which Beatles song did George Harrison first play the sitar?

23. What did John Lennon change his middle name to?

24. Which Beatles song has inspired the most cover versions?

25. Who played bass guitar with the early Beatles, left, and died in 1962?

Musicals

1. Who was Alexander Hamilton, the inspiration behind the hit musical *Hamilton*?

2. The Sharks and the Jets are the gangs in which musical?

3. Whose memoirs formed the inspiration behind the musical *The King and I*?

4. Which musical comedy is adapted from the film *Monty Python and the Holy Grail*?

5. Who was the star of the movie *Singin' in the Rain*?

6. Marlon Brando does not sing in *Guys and Dolls*. True or False?

7. Who did Dan Aykroyd and John Belushi play?

8. *Secret Superstar* (2017) was a product of which moviemaking hotspot?

9. Which city is the setting for *On the Town*?

10. Which British musical won six Oscars in 1968?

11. Who created the 1975 musical *The Rocky Horror Picture Show*?

12. *The Greatest Showman* is based on the life of which circus owner?

13. *Cabaret* is set in which European city?

14. What was the name of the Broadway star on whom the musical *Funny Girl* is based?

15. Which musical is based on the life of a female sharpshooter who joined Buffalo Bill's Wild West show in 1885?

16. *The Boys from Syracuse* is based on which Shakespeare play?

17. Who sang "Wand'rin' Star" in *Paint Your Wagon*?

18. Elvis Presley's first film was *GI Blues*. True or False?

19. Which musical includes the songs "If I Loved you" and "You'll Never Walk Alone"?

20. Which musical was based on a sewing machinists' strike at a Ford factory in 1968?

21. Who wrote both the music and lyrics for *Blood Brothers*?

22. "If I Were a Rich Man" is a song from which musical?

23. In which musical do the actors perform the entire show on roller skates?

24. When *Phantom of the Opera* opened in London in 1986, who starred in the title role?

25. Which musical tells the story of two drag queens and a transgender woman who are to play a drag show at Alice Springs?

Gods of Rock

1. Which 1960s band had a 22-year gap between number-one hits, from 1966 to 1988?

2. Who played lead guitar for Black Sabbath?

3. What number did Deep Purple's "Smoke on the Water" reach on the US charts?

4. For which band has Steve Tyler sung lead vocals?

5. In which country was AC/DC formed?

6. Who replaced David Lee Roth for Van Halen?

7. Complete the name of this Iron Maiden hit: "Bring Your Daughter to the… "

8. Which band is famous for its outrageous black-and-white make up?

9. Which guitar hero was nicknamed "God"?

10. Ginger Baker was the drummer for which rock supergroup?

11. Who recorded *Exile on Main St.*?

12. Who replaced Syd Barrett in Pink Floyd?

13. Jimi Hendrix played guitar mainly right-handed. True or False?

14. Which band was Eric Clapton in when he wrote "Layla"?

15. Which band did David Coverdale form when he left Deep Purple?

16. "Pinball Wizard" is featured in which rock opera?

17. Where has the Monsters of Rock festival usually been held?

18. Who recorded the original "Stairway to Heaven"?

19. What was Thin Lizzy's first top-ten hit record?

20. What is Alice Cooper's real name?

1960s Music

1. What was the biggest-selling single in the US in the 1960s?

2. What was the name of the park that the Small Faces sang about in 1967?

3. Which Scottish singer was responsible for the psychedelic pop of "Sunshine Superman"?

4. Which instrument did Beach Boy Dennis Wilson play?

5. What was the name of Jimi Hendrix's backing band?

6. Who released *Beggars Banquet* in 1968?

7. Who wrote the song "Woodstock"?

8. Jim Morrison was the lead singer with the Doors. True or False?

9. "The House of the Rising Sun" was a transatlantic No. 1 hit single for which group?

10. Sly and the Family Stone was formed in 1967 by Brothers Sly and whom?

11. American rockers Blue Cheer are often credited as being the pioneers of heavy metal. True or False?

12. Denny Doherty was not a member of the Mamas and the Papas. True or False?

13. Who was "Born to Be Wild"?

14. In which year did Marvin Gaye make "I Heard It through the Grapevine" a smash hit?

15. Jerry Garcia was the lead singer for which group?

16. Who was the lead singer for the Velvet Underground?

17. Which band sang "A Whiter Shade of Pale"?

18. Which band that wanted to be the Beatles had its own TV show?

19. Neil Young and Steven Stills were once both members of which group?

20. Who was the Who's bass player?

21. Which comedian had the biggest-selling UK single of 1965?

22. What was the name of the backing group for Billy J. Kramer?

23. What was the Shadows' first No. 1 without Cliff Richard in 1960?

24. Which song features a lyric about a cake that was left out in the rain?

25. Whose hits included "One Way Love" and "Got to Get You into My Life"?

MUSIC

Classical Music

1. Which movement began to supersede Classicism around the year 1830?

2. Which conductor always appeared wearing a white carnation?

3. Why did Domenico Scarlatti name one of his compositions "Cat Fugue"?

4. In Purcell's *Dido and Aeneas*, where is Dido queen of?

5. What does the classical music term "andante" mean?

6. The crumhorn is a reed instrument. True or False?

7. How many strings does the modern orchestral harp have?

8. Sarah Chang is associated with which instrument?

9. How old was Giuseppe Verdi when he wrote his Requiem?

10. Barbara Strozzi was a female singer and Baroque composer. Where was she from?

11. What did Benjamin Britten use to simulate raindrops in his opera *Noye's Fludde*?

12. During a performance of *Boris Godunov* at the Sydney Opera House, what fell off the stage and onto a cellist?

13. While touring in 1781, Muzio Clementi had a piano competition against which famous composer?

14. Who completed his *A Midsummer's Night's Dream* composition in 1842, 16 years after writing the overture?

15. Pachelbel was responsible for composing canons and what?

16. How is the piano significantly different from the harpsichord?

17. Which dance is associated with the piece of music "On the Beautiful Blue Danube"?

18. Who wrote *The Nutcracker*?

19. Who wrote a piece called "Skittle Alley Trio"?

20. In which country is Delibes's opera *Lakmé* set?

21. What happened during a performance of Stravinsky's *Rite of Spring* in 1913?

22. Franz Liszt was hugely popular, and his fans demanded clippings of his hair. How did Liszt respond?

23. What does "a cappella" mean?

24. What is a variation?

25. Which conductor founded the Promenade Concerts in London?

Top of the Pops

1. Between 1962 and 1969, John Lennon and Paul McCartney wrote around 180 jointly credited songs. True or False?

2. Which influential figure in jazz co-wrote "Mood Indigo" with Barney Bigard?

3. Which Bryan Adams hit was No. 1 on the US charts for seven weeks?

4. Howard, Mark, Gary, and Robbie are members of the famous pop band Take That. Who is the missing member from this list?

5. Which UB40 hit stayed on the charts for more than 100 weeks?

6. Known as one of the first entertainment superstars, who won 11 Grammys, three Golden Globes, and two Oscars?

7. How is singer Robyn Fenty better known?

8. In 1981, which rock band sang the hit "Down Under"?

9. In 2009, who became the first artist to sell more than one million download songs in a week?

10. Top guitarist Jimmy Page sometimes uses a violin bow with his guitar. True or False?

11. In the film *Muriel's Wedding*, with which pop group is Muriel obsessed?

12. Which girl band sang "Viva Forever"?

13. Which group had a successful album entitled *Reggatta de Blanc*?

14. What is the name of Bon Jovi's highest-selling single?

15. Who originally released the single "Don't Stop Believin"?

16. Elvis recorded more than 600 songs in his music career but wrote or co-wrote only 10 of them. True or False?

17. In 2009, who won two Academy Awards for Best Original Score and Best Original Song for the film *Slumdog Millionaire*?

18. The Beatles performed on the very first *Top of the Pops* broadcast. What did they sing?

19. One of the biggest-selling albums of all time, what is Led Zeppelin's fourth album called?

20. According to the *Guinness Book of World Records*, who is the top-selling female recording artist of all time?

MUSIC

1970s Music

1. What was the best-selling single of the 1970s in the UK?

2. Who sang the title song for the 1970s Bond film *The Man with the Golden Gun*?

3. Who did John Joseph Lydon become in the mid-1970s?

4. Errol Brown was the lead singer of which band?

5. What was the best-selling film soundtrack in the 1970s?

6. Which Bad Company singer was formerly the lead singer in Free?

7. Bob Dylan's 1978 album was called *Street...* ?

8. Which outrageous arena act were best known for its makeup and pyrotechnics?

9. Every member of the Ramones shared the last name "Ramone." True or False?

10. Which Cars member sang "Just What I Needed"?

11. The 1978 song "Who Are You?" was recorded by whom?

12. Which Led Zeppelin song makes references to Norse mythology?

13. How long did it reportedly take Van Halen to record its debut album?

14. Which band released the album *Parallel Lines* in 1978?

15. Which American punk forefathers wore lipstick and women's clothing onstage?

16. Who played bass for Parliament and Funkadelic?

17. Thin Lizzy was named after the Model T-Ford, nicknamed the "Tin Lizzie." True or False?

18. Prog rockers Rush were originally from Canada. True or False?

19. Which hard rockers produced *Highway to Hell* in 1979?

20. In which year did the Clash release *London Calling*?

Guess the Year

1. The world is a colorful blur of spandex, leg warmers, and Rubik's cubes, and Madonna has just released "Like a Virgin." The year is?

2. Nirvana bring grunge to the mainstream stage with "Nevermind." What year is it?

3. The Beatles change the world forever with the release of "Please Please Me." What's the year?

4. In which year did the Bee Gees unleash their seminal disco single "Stayin' Alive"?

5. "Thriller" took Michael Jackson around six months and $750,000 to make. In which year was it released?

6. In which year did Guns N' Roses reinvent rock music with their debut album *Appetite for Destruction*?

7. Dylan's six-minute single "Like a Rolling Stone" was often thought to have changed ideas about popular music. When was it released?

8. In which year did Jimi Hendrix release a cover of Bob Dylan's "All along the Watchtower"?

9. The Sex Pistols demanded that "God Save the Queen" in which year?

10. The highly influential album *The Cars* by the Cars was released in which year?

11. Seattle rockers Soundgarden first released an album in 1982. True or False?

12. In which year did Miles Davis release what is thought to be the best-selling jazz album of all time, *Kind of Blue*?

13. In which year did metal monsters Iron Maiden first form?

14. *She's So Unusual* made Cyndi Lauper the first female artist to have four top-five singles on one album. In which year did it come out?

15. Roy Ayers is a funk, jazz, and soul composer whose hit record *Everybody Loves the Sunshine* was released when?

16. The Psychedelic Furs' "Pretty in Pink" would go on to be featured in a 1986 John Hughes movie of the same name. In which year was the single first released?

17. In which year was Mark Ronson's "Uptown Funk" the best-selling single?

18. "Knights in White Satin" was a hit for the Moody Blues. When was it released?

19. In which year did Elvis Presley make his first recording, "My Happiness," with Sun Records?

20. When did Ed Sheeran release his first album?

MUSIC

Guitar Experts

1. What part of a guitar supports the strings?

2. Where does the guitar brand Ibanez originate?

3. Where in the world is the "tiple" traditionally found?

4. The Telecaster was originally known as the what?

5. Which virtuoso classical guitarist was born in Melbourne in 1941?

6. Who was nicknamed "The Originator"?

7. Which guitar did Jimmy Page famously use for the live performance of "Stairway to Heaven"?

8. What is the name of the famous Spanish classical guitarist who died in 1987?

9. What type of guitar is Joe Bonamassa's favorite?

10. Rage against the Machine's Tom Morello nicknamed his guitar what?

11. "Every time you pick up your guitar to play, play as if it's the last time." Who said this?

12. James Hetfield is associated with which genre?

13. How many types of acoustic guitar are there?

14. Albert King, Stevie Ray Vaughan, and Gary Moore are associated with which genre of guitar playing?

15. Who was the lead guitar player in the Police?

16. Playing two notes simultaneously is called a "duo-pitch." True or False?

17. What distinctive picking technique developed from a banjo-playing style and was used by guitarists such as Johnny Cash?

18. What is Slash's real name?

19. How many frets are there on a standard classical guitar?

20. What does a "humbucker" do?

Orchestras

1. How many different instrument sections are included in a standard orchestra?

2. How many instruments usually make up an orchestra?

3. Which instrument does the rest of the orchestra tune to?

4. Which horn is not part of an orchestra's brass section?

5. Which orchestra section boasts more instruments than all the others?

6. As what is the principal violinist also known?

7. In an orchestra, which section sits behind the strings?

8. In an orchestra, which instrument sits between the violins and the cellos?

9. Compared to a standard orchestra, chamber orchestras are usually what?

10. In which section would you find an orchestra's tamtam?

11. In an orchestra, who is considered the leader of the entire brass section?

12. An orchestra conductor is also known as "the first chair." True or False?

13. In which ancient civilization is the modern orchestra thought to have its roots?

14. Which American was the first woman to conduct a Last Night of the Proms at the Royal Albert Hall in London?

15. Is the celesta a woodwind, brass, string, percussion, or keyboard instrument?

16. With which British orchestra was Sir John Barbirolli most closely associated?

17. In accordance with Marxist ideals, the Soviet Persimfans symphony orchestra was formed in 1922 without a conductor. True or False?

18. How many conductors does Evgeni Kostitsyn's Third Symphony require?

19. Which instrument is sometimes used in addition to a core orchestra?

20. Which stringed instrument did Bach, Mozart, and Beethoven all occasionally play in an orchestra?

(Answers on page 494)   **233**

MUSIC

Keeping the Beat

1. What material was used to cover some of the first known drums?

2. As what is the traditional drumstick grip more commonly known?

3. What is the most well-known African drum called?

4. What is the smallest drum kit cymbal called?

5. Common hand drums that come in a set of two are called what?

6. What is Dee Dee Chandler of New Orleans credited with inventing around 1904?

7. On recordings in the 1920s, the brass instruments were placed the farthest away from the drum kit, to reduce distortion. True or False?

8. What was the name of the mad drummer in the Muppets?

9. Which drummer led an orchestra and was famous for his drum solos?

10. Macaque monkeys drum on objects to display social dominance. True or False?

11. Which part of a drum kit suffers most commonly from cracks?

12. An early drum kit dating from the second century BCE was recently discovered in a Polish salt mine. True or False?

13. Which drummer was the first to use double bass drums in the 1940s?

14. Which group did drummer Lars Ulrich play with?

15. More than 90 percent of drummers develop tinnitus within the third year of playing the instrument. True or False?

16. Are brushes used on drums?

17. Which drummer was famous for blowing up his drum kits onstage?

18. Where does the drum called a "bodhran" originate?

19. Which drum kit cymbal is used to keep a steady rhythm?

20. Early drums dating from 5500 to 2350 BCE have been found in which country?

1990s Music

1. Which band released the double *Illusion* albums in 1991?

2. Which label were Seattle grunge bands most associated with?

3. Which band was responsible for the album *Automatic for the People*?

4. Which 1990s artist used to call himself Romeo Blue?

5. Which rap act sang about celebrating Martin Luther King Jr.'s birthday in Arizona?

6. Which Icelandic singer made a riot with "It's Oh So Quiet" in 1995?

7. Which 1990s act sometimes played live while bouncing on trampolines?

8. Which threesome recorded the theme song for the *South Park* TV show?

9. Which two bands battled it out for the Britpop throne?

10. Which Spice Girl was nicknamed "Sporty Spice"?

11. Which ex-Nirvana member went on to form the Foo Fighters?

12. What is Beck's last name?

13. On which album did the Beastie Boys play their own instruments?

14. With which band is Mike Patton most associated?

15. Which band did Courtney Love front in the 1990s?

16. Which instrument is Tori Amos usually seen playing?

17. Which album did Soundgarden release in 1991?

18. Jerry Cantrell is best known for his time with Alice in Chains. True or False?

19. Who was the singer for the Screaming Trees?

20. Who produced all of Metallica's albums in the 1990s?

21. What was the title of Britney Spears's first single, released in 1998?

22. Who is the lead singer of Pearl Jam?

23. "Everybody's Free to Wear Sunscreen" was a 1999 hit for which Australian artist, best known as a film director?

24. According to Natalie Imbruglia in 1997, "Nothing's right, I'm… ": what was she?

25. Which band had a 1997 hit with the song "The Drugs Don't Work"?

MUSIC

CHAPTER 6

THE NATURAL WORLD

Bugs, beasts, birds, and plants.
See how much you know about
how animals move, eat, and live.
Discover the wonders of
wildlife in trees, the ocean,
underground, and in your backyard.

Bugs and Beasts

1. I have a sting in my tail, and I am related to spiders. What am I?

2. Some female spiders eat the male spider after mating. True or False?

3. Millipedes have 1,000 legs. True or False?

4. What are antennae for?

5. In the US, it's called a "ladybug." What is it called in the UK?

6. Which of these is an insect: ant, earthworm, woodlouse?

7. Which of these is NOT an insect: butterfly, bee, shrimp?

8. Social wasps make their nests from what material?

9. I can build a nest up to 23 ft (7 m) high; what am I?

10. How many flowers can a bee visit in one minute?

11. Maggots are the young of… ?

12. When are ant eggs usually laid?

13. How does a leech feed?

14. What order do butterflies belong to?

15. What name is used for a male bee?

16. How long does it take for a snail to grow up?

17. How does a cricket make a sound?

18. What is the wing covering on a ladybug called?

19. Which of these is NOT the real name of a type of spider: jumping, fishing, singing?

20. How do wasps differ from bees regarding stinging?

Marvelous Mammals

1. Which of these is NOT a group of mammals: tortoises, bats, primates?

2. Which of the following do sea otters eat: plankton, seaweed, sea urchins?

3. What is a female elephant called?

4. Which of these is the loudest land mammal: lion, hyena, howler monkey?

5. Which of these is the smelliest mammal: musk ox, raccoon, skunk?

6. Which of these mammals lives the longest: dolphin, chimpanzee, rabbit?

7. Which of these is NOT a feature common to all mammals: hair, warm blood, four legs?

8. Why do hippopotamuses wallow in mud?

9. Mammals are the only animals with true hair. True or False?

10. Some mammals carry their young in pouches in their bodies. What is this group called?

11. What is the main function of the large ears of a desert mouse?

12. When cats pick up their kittens to move them, where do they grab hold of them?

13. How long can camels go without water?

14. The world's smallest mammal is a species of what?

15. Giraffes only sleep around 4.5 hours every day. True or False?

16. Which of these mammals is NOT a carnivore: leopard, tamarin monkey, meerkat?

17. Macaques like to take hot baths to keep warm. Where in the world are they found?

18. When did the first mammals appear?

19. The capybara, the world's largest rodent, is found where?

20. The biggest mammal on the planet is the elephant. True or False?

21. Why do vampire bats produce the protein draculin in their saliva?

22. Shark teeth fall out often and have to be regularly replaced. How long do most shark teeth last?

23. What is the rattle on the tail of a rattlesnake made of?

24. Why do crocodiles and alligators sometimes rest with their mouths open?

25. Which members of the snail family can inject a deadly neurotoxin when picked up?

Birds of a Feather

1. How do song thrushes break the shells of snails they eat?

2. What common group name applies to birds such as quail, pheasant, and grouse?

3. What is a baby swan called?

4. What is in an owl pellet?

5. What kind of bird was the extinct dodo?

6. What talent do lyrebirds, starlings, parrots, and mynahs have in common?

7. What word is used to describe a group of eggs in a nest?

8. Where do king penguins incubate their eggs?

9. Which bird can dive at 175 mph (282 kmph) in pursuit of prey, making it the world's fastest animal?

10. Which bird often seen on Christmas cards is a member of the order Passeriformes?

11. In which hemisphere do wild penguins live?

12. What bird is traditionally kept in the Tower of London?

13. What word is used to describe a group of chicks in a nest?

14. Where are a kiwi's nostrils?

15. Black swans have been widely introduced, but where are they from originally?

16. How did shrikes come by their alternative name of butcher birds?

17. How do bee-eaters avoid being stung by their prey as they eat it?

18. How do brown pelicans catch fish?

19. What is a barn swallow's nest made of?

20. Where do Atlantic puffins lay their eggs?

(Answers on page 494)

THE NATURAL WORLD

Great and Small

1. This slow-mover lets moss grow on its fur. What is it?

2. Which is the most intelligent mollusk?

3. How many different species of shark are there?

4. Which of these objects have been found in sharks' stomachs: a cannon ball, a newspaper, a barrel of nails?

5. Why is the ladybug sometimes called "the gardener's friend"?

6. What does a frog use to help push food down its throat?

7. When a crocodile shovels down a large meal, what does it appear to do?

8. Vultures have a peculiar way of keeping cool. What is it?

9. The cheetah is the fastest land animal. How fast can it run?

10. What is a nocturnal animal?

11. The aardvark eats termites and ants. How long is its tongue?

12. A kangaroo could leap over your head. True or False?

13. An owl can swivel its head almost all the way round. True or False?

14. Vampire bats are misnamed because they don't eat blood. True or False?

15. At up to 109 ft (33 m) in length, what is the biggest animal in the world?

16. Relative to its size, which is the loudest animal in the world?

17. What can a tiger, a lion, a leopard and a jaguar do that a cheetah can't?

18. Mice like cheese. True or False?

19. What is a duck-billed platypus?

20. Which snake sprays venom directly into the eyes of its enemies?

21. What part of a shark's body was once used to make sandpaper?

22. Which big cat lives only in the high mountains of Central Asia?

23. Which is the largest lizard in the world, at up to 10 ft (3.1 m) long?

24. The largest living member of the crocodile family can reach about 23 ft (7 m) in length. What species is it?

25. Which lizard feeds by firing out its long sticky tongue?

       (Answers on page 495)

Getting Around

1. A shark skeleton is made of what?

2. Why does the parrot fish inflate its body?

3. Flamingos can bend their knees backward. True or False?

4. How many times its own height can a flea jump?

5. Which one of the following animals walks on one toenail per leg: horse, cow, snail?

6. Which of the following groups of animals does NOT hunt for food in packs: leopards, orcas, lions?

7. How far can an elephant jump?

8. Which animal sings with its legs?

9. Which group of animals flies in a V-formation?

10. The whale's flipper is a modified what?

11. Which insect can run the fastest: millipede, ant, cockroach?

12. Which one of the following permanently hitches a ride on another organism: humpback whale barnacle, tick, suckerfish?

13. Which of these birds cannot hover: kestrel, pigeon, hummingbird?

14. When the sidewinder snake moves across a hot desert, how many parts of its body touch the ground?

15. Jellyfish use jet propulsion to move. True or False?

16. Which one of the following moves using water-filled tube feet: sea urchin, maggot, slowworm?

17. What makes lemmings start to move down from high ground?

18. Which of these animals can move tripedally: sloth, human, kangaroo?

19. Which animal accelerates the fastest from a standing start?

20. Bees perform a waggle dance in the hive. About which one of the following does the waggle dance NOT give information: flower color, distance, location?

THE NATURAL WORLD

Plants

1. Which member of the carrot family, commonly found in fields, sunny areas, and roadsides, is highly toxic?

2. What is the function of the bubblelike bladder seen in some seaweeds?

3. What are the "leaves" of ferns more correctly called?

4. How is grass pollen usually transported?

5. Plants convert water, carbon dioxide, and energy from sunlight into sugar. What is this process called?

6. Which plant associated with disturbed ground is used to commemorate World War I?

7. What characteristic do deciduous trees have in common?

8. Which pigment gives plants a green color?

9. Why don't dairy farmers like buttercups?

10. Why do water lily stems contain large air spaces?

11. How long does it take for a Venus flytrap to close on its victim?

12. Which flowers prompted an economic boom and collapse in the Netherlands in the 17th century?

13. Some plants are pollinated at night by moths and bats. What color do such flowers tend to be?

14. Dock leaves are used as a traditional country remedy for what problem?

15. The stems of common reed are traditionally used for what purpose?

16. Which part of a sugar cane plant is processed to produce sugar?

17. What do the plants known as succulents store in their swollen leaves?

18. What plant forms the rather dull diet of the giant panda?

19. What is the fruit of a rose called?

20. Which part of the tree does olive oil come from?

21. The name of which flower originates from the ancient Greek for star?

22. Ericaceous plants like acid soil. True or False?

23. Which king created the Hanging Gardens of Babylon?

24. Burpless, pickling, and slicing are varieties of which fruit?

25. Plums, apricots, and apples are members of which family of flowering plants?

In the Jungle

1. How many of the world's species of plants and animals can be found in the rain forest?

2. It is estimated that there are many millions of insects and plants in the rain forest that are yet to be discovered. True or False?

3. Which is the largest rain forest in the world?

4. The loudest land animal in the world lives in the rain forest. What is its name?

5. Which creature that flies above the rain forest canopy is so bright that it can be seen by airplane pilots?

6. How many different species of poison dart frogs are there: 1,750, 175, 75?

7. What rain forest creature has jaws so powerful that it can pierce the skulls of its prey?

8. The jaguar catches fish by flicking its tail onto the water to lure them to the surface. True or False?

9. Which rain forest insect can carry up to 50 times its own body weight?

10. Are binturongs related to civets, cats, or bears?

11. The rain forest hummingbird is the only bird with the ability to do what?

12. The hummingbird can also hover in mid-air. True or False?

13. The red-eyed tree frog uses its bright eyes as a defense mechanism. True or False?

14. The jungles of which three countries would you visit to see mountain gorillas?

15. Which slow-moving jungle creature eats, sleeps, and gives birth hanging from the branches of the rain forest canopy?

16. How often does the sloth climb down to the forest floor to defecate?

17. Which country would you visit to explore the rain forest of the Monteverde Nature Reserve?

18. Which book does the term "The Law of the Jungle" come from?

19. Are lianas birds, mammals, or plants?

20. What percentage of Earth do jungles cover?

THE NATURAL WORLD

Australian Animals

1. One of the most poisonous creatures in the sea, the Australian box jellyfish, can deliver a fatal sting. What do beachgoers often carry to treat such a sting?

2. The Australian snake with the most toxic venom in the world is the what?

3. Often dragging its prey into a fatal "death roll" is the highly aggressive Australian what?

4. One of the most toxic sea creatures in the world, found in Australian seas, is only the size of a golf ball. What is it?

5. A spiky animal that lives in Australia is an echidna, a quokka, or a Tasmanian devil?

6. Australia has more venomous than nonvenomous snake species. True or False?

7. The most venomous fish in the world lives its life camouflaged as a rock on the bottom of Australian reefs. What is it called?

8. The poisonous Australian spider that bites thousands of people every year and practices cannibalism on its mate is what?

9. This popular killer from movies and books is found in large numbers off the southern coast of Australia. What is it?

10. Although considered humorous in appearance, this Australian mammal has highly venomous spurs on its webbed feet. What is its name?

11. This Australian spider has venomous fangs that can bite through fingernails and shoes. What is it called?

12. The Australian wolf spider is responsible for around one dozen human fatalities a year. True or False?

13. What kind of Australian scorpion is often found in houses?

14. There is no antidote for the sting of a marbled scorpion. True or False?

15. What is Australia's wild dog called?

16. Often seen on outback roads in Australia, this animal's skin is covered in highly toxic venom. What is it?

17. The Australian spectacled flying fox bat is considered more of a threat to human survival than nuclear war and airborne viruses. True or False?

18. If left untreated, a bite from an Australian funnel-web spider can kill a human in two hours. True or False?

19. Shy but deadly, the Australian tiger snake is one of the world's most venomous snakes. Around what percentage of people die every year from an untreated bite?

20. Echidnas are one of the few mammals that lay eggs. True or False?

Wacky Animal Behavior

1. Elephants have the longest gestation period of any animal. How long does their pregnancy last?

2. Fireflies have a special organ inside their abdomens that produces flashes of light. Fireflies are which type of insect?

3. How much krill can a blue whale eat in a day?

4. Sharks have a sixth sense that allows them to detect weak electrical signals generated by their prey. True or False?

5. How does a sloth swim?

6. Which type of crab camouflages itself by collecting tiny shells, bits of seaweed, and sea anemones and attaching them to its shell?

7. The golden poison frog contains enough venom to kill up to how many people?

8. How does a sea anemone expel waste?

9. Which of these is a species of elephant: African Bush, Asian, African Forest?

10. Which of these things do horses and cows have in common: jump great heights, doze standing up, have four stomachs?

11. How does a nesting northern fulmar protect itself from attack?

12. A chameleon's eyes move independently, so it can look in two directions at once. True or False?

13. Which of these animals can produce the loudest noise: African lion, vampire bat, blue whale?

14. Ants never sleep. True or False?

15. Other than navigation, what does a cat use its whiskers for?

16. Shrews are always hungry. Approximately what percentage of their body weight in food do they need daily?

17. Some doctors have used specially bred blowfly maggots to treat flesh wounds, because they eat dead tissue and harmful bacteria. True or False?

18. How many insects can certain bats eat in a single night?

19. Koalas only eat one thing. What is it?

20. An aphid can reproduce asexually by producing clones of itself. True or False?

21. Which type of mammal has the largest eyes relative to its body size?

22. What is special about a mudskipper?

23. Where do young seahorses hatch?

24. Why does the olm or cave salamander have no eyes?

25. Which crustaceans spend their whole adult life standing on their heads?

(Answers on page 495)   **245**

Creepy Crawlies

1. Where are a butterfly's taste receptors located?

2. Roughly for how long have insects existed?

3. What are the three parts that make up an insect's body?

4. If you cut off a cockroach's head, when will it die?

5. For every human being, there are 200 million insects. True or False?

6. How many species of beetle are there?

7. Insects have eyelids. True or False?

8. Which type of spider kills the male during mating?

9. What is the name of the process by which certain insects transform into others, for example, a caterpillar to a butterfly?

10. There is a species of caterpillar that grows to over 3 ft (1 m) long. True or False?

11. What material makes up part of an insect's exoskeleton?

12. What do earwigs avoid?

13. Of all the species of animal on Earth, approximately what percentage are arthropods?

14. Cicadas only emerge from an underground hiding spot every 13 or 17 years, depending on the type. True or False?

15. Approximately how many species of spiders are there?

16. An aphid can give birth without mating. True or False?

17. How many times its weight can the rhinoceros beetle lift?

18. Only full-grown male crickets can chirp. True or False?

19. Which of the following is NOT an insect: spider, beetle, ladybug?

20. What is the study of insects called?

21. What do ordinary spiders like to eat?

22. Wood lice produce defensive chemicals to make them taste foul to most predators. True or False?

23. Although water boatmen live in the water, they breathe air. True or False?

24. What do wood lice need to do in order to grow?

25. What are the stages of metamorphosis?

Secretly Deadly Animals

1. Which insect is responsible for the disease malaria in humans?

2. Which is the deadliest scorpion in North America?

3. Which slow-moving creature has roamed the seas for more than 500 million years and can deliver a fatal sting?

4. An Australian box jellyfish commonly known as the "sea wasp" can kill a grown man in minutes with one sting. True or False?

5. What large mud wallower can easily outrun a human and is known to be extremely temperamental?

6. Usually smaller than a human hand, which variety of scorpion is the most venomous in the world?

7. The slow loris is a harmless-looking primate. What is its deadly secret?

8. Tsetse flies can cause what type of illness?

9. It is small, but the vampire bat has a big reputation for being deadly. Why?

10. This "red-bellied" fish variety looks harmless on its own, but together with its friends, it can strip a whole cow. What is it?

11. The most painful bite inflicted by an animal is said to come from which tiny creature?

12. Racoons are known to attack humans as a group. True or False?

13. A common household pet, cats can carry the parasite *Toxoplasma gondii*, which is very dangerous for pregnant women. True or False?

14. This slow mover usually hides under the sand of the ocean bottom but also has a deadly sting. What is it?

15. Small and yellow, this creature is considered the most poisonous vertebrate in the world. What is it?

16. Up to how many humans could 1 milligram of its poison kill?

17. The toxin from a stonefish can cause temporary paralysis and death if left untreated. True or False?

18. If eaten raw, a common earthworm can kill a grown man in 30 minutes. True or False?

19. Although I am considered a food delicacy in some countries, I am the second-most-poisonous vertebrate in the world. What am I?

20. A meal of the pufferfish can be lethal if not served properly, and only specially trained cooks can prepare it. True or False?

Living Spaces

1. Which of these deserts is NOT in Africa: Namib, Sahara, Gobi?

2. The giant sequoia is a type of what?

3. How many legs does a jerboa have?

4. What physical process causes sand to build in dunes in sandy deserts?

5. The Amazon Rain Forest is being attacked by garimpeiros. What are these people after?

6. Wild dromedaries (one-humped camels) are found in Australia. True or False?

7. Namibia's Skeleton Coast desert is known for which type of weather phenomenon?

8. Which mountain range is home to the Berbers of Morocco?

9. Which of these countries does NOT contain a part of the Amazon Rain Forest: Paraguay, Bolivia, Peru?

10. Which large ape is known in Malaysia as the "man of the forest" and is threatened by forest clearance?

11. Where is the Sonoran Desert?

12. Which of these wetland areas is the largest: the Camargue, Florida Everglades, Okavango Delta?

13. People from which European country were the first to explore the Amazon Rain Forest (after the indigenous people)?

14. What is the name of the large roots that splay outward from the trunk of rain forest trees?

15. The soil in a rain forest is usually shallow and poor in nutrients. True or False?

16. What type of environment is often found close to a desert?

17. The "New Forest" was so called by which king of England in the 11th century?

18. Which tree is traditionally used to make cricket bats?

19. Which fuel was traditionally made in British woodlands by burning coppiced poles?

20. Leaf peeping is popular among tourists in North America. What does it involve?

(Answers on page 496)

Innovating Nature

1. Which animals identify each other by a special whistle?

2. Which animal makes a sound that can be heard 1,000 miles (1,600 km) away?

3. A narwhal is a small whale with one long straight tusk. What is the tusk?

4. Spiders make their webs from a type of silk. What is special about it?

5. Bats make ultrasound noises to catch their prey. Humans cannot hear these because ultrasound is what?

6. The peregrine falcon is the fastest flying bird. Its top speed is about what?

7. Angler fish live in darkness at the bottom of the ocean. They make parts of their body glow to attract prey. What is the glow called?

8. A fish can rise or sink in the water by adjusting its buoyancy. What else uses this technique?

9. A helicopter can fly backward. Which of these can also fly backward: a seagull, a duck, a dragonfly?

10. A bird's wing has a special curved shape, like the wing of an airplane. What is this special shape called?

11. A dolphin finds fish using a technique that has been copied by humans. What is the technique called?

12. A pistol shrimp has a special way to catch its prey. What does it do?

13. The sperm whale's head contains a big bubble of oil. What is this called?

14. Each time a kangaroo lands after hopping, it saves some energy for the next bounce. How do its legs accomplish this?

15. Which fish stuns its prey with a 500-volt shock?

16. Humans did not invent recycling. Which of these is an example of recycling: a spider eating an old web, a squirrel burying a nut, a bat sleeping through winter?

17. Cooperation started long before there were people. Insects pollinated plants and got nectar in return. What is this called?

18. The bubbles in bread come naturally from a microbe. What is that microbe called?

19. We can control rivers with dams. Which animal showed us how?

20. Which plant snaps shut on its prey?

Mammals

1. Which type of primate is an indri?

2. What is the correct name for a group of wolves?

3. What is a group of lions called?

4. What animal rears its young in a nest called a drey?

5. What name is given to the interconnected burrows of rabbits?

6. How soon after birth can a wildebeest calf get to its feet and run?

7. What is the flap of furry skin along a sugar glider's flanks used for?

8. What does a pangolin do when it feels threatened?

9. What is stored in the hump of a camel?

10. What important job do bacteria do in the stomach of a cow?

11. Where do koalas live?

12. What is the correct name for the chisel-like front teeth of rodents and other mammals?

13. The puma is known by many names. Which of these is NOT one of those names: cougar, mountain lion, jaguar?

14. Which great ape is found on the islands of Sumatra and Borneo?

15. What kind of markings typify a tabby cat?

16. Where do armadillos come from?

17. Which type of animal is only found in Australia?

18. Which part of the human body do parasitic whipworms infect?

19. What other common name is often used for the bonobo?

20. The capybara is an excellent swimmer. True or False?

(Answers on page 496)

Top and Bottom Sea Life

1. Which of these is the correct name of a deep sea fish: snaggletooth, toothface, fangtooth?

2. Which creature takes its name from a famous monster and has the ability to turn itself inside out?

3. Many deep-sea creatures make their own light called "bioluminescence." True or False?

4. The barreleye fish is also known as the spookfish, spectre eel, or wraith?

5. What is the name of the deep-sea fish that has a glowing "lure" at the end of its nose?

6. The anglerfish devours its catch whole as soon as it touches its lure. True or False?

7. Which eel was named after the size of its huge mouth?

8. The deep-sea blue hake and spiny eel are on the verge of extinction. Why?

9. Why does the hatchetfish have eyes at the top of its head?

10. How far can a flying fish travel in one glide?

11. Which long and very thin fish spends its whole life in the total darkness of the sea floor?

12. The deep sea is an extremely hostile environment, with temperatures that rarely exceed 37°F (3°C). True or False?

13. What is considered the most common deep-sea fish?

14. There are many more deep-sea creatures that are yet to be discovered. True or False?

15. Deep-sea creatures have eyes that are how many times more sensitive to light than human eyes?

16. The viperfish has such long teeth that it cannot close its mouth. True or False?

17. How does the cookiecutter shark get its name?

18. Many deep-sea creatures are blind. True or False?

19. How do many blind creatures detect food?

20. What do most deep-sea creatures rely on to survive?

21. Which reproductive changes happen to a spotted grouper as it grows up?

22. What advantage does the hammerhead shark's strange head give it?

23. Some sea cucumbers can eject their guts through their rear ends and then grow a new one. But why do they do it?

24. Scallops have up to 200 eyes. True or False?

25. What determines the body temperature of most fish?

THE NATURAL WORLD

Mad about Plants

1. An abundant growth of lichens is usually a sign of what?

2. The monkey puzzle is the national tree of which country?

3. Ferns reproduce using spores. Where do the spores develop?

4. What name is sometimes given to the curled fronds of developing ferns?

5. What kind of plant is the prickly pear?

6. What can slow the reaction time of a Venus flytrap?

7. Which plant produces the world's largest flower?

8. Where might you find sea lettuce?

9. Liverworts reproduce using spores and cell clusters called gemmae. How are these spread?

10. Why do some holly trees never produce berries?

11. The strange desert plant known as welwitschia produces only two leaves in its lifetime. How long does it live?

12. Bamboo is the fastest-growing plant known. How much can a stem grow in one day?

13. What color are wild daffodils?

14. What plant is the main component of natural peat?

15. Horsetails are among the oldest-known land plants. When did they first appear?

16. The king protea is the national flower of which country?

17. What name is given to blooms of toxic diatoms that sometimes appear at sea?

18. What color are the flowers of watercress?

19. What is the world's most widespread conifer?

20. The bristlecone pine is the longest-living tree known. How many years can one live?

Climate Change

1. Which country emits the most carbon dioxide?

2. For how long have there been reliable written climate records?

3. Climate change can cause the extinction of animals and plants. True or False?

4. The two main greenhouse gases that contribute to global warming are methane and carbon monoxide. True or False?

5. What has happened to ice shelves on the Antarctic Peninsula over the last 50 years?

6. Climate change is felt equally all over the world. True or False?

7. Which of these sources of energy is NOT a fossil fuel: coal, oil, light?

8. What percentage of the world's wood harvest is burned for fuel?

9. When was the Kyoto Protocol introduced, which sought to bring carbon-dioxide emissions under control?

10. Climate affects volcanoes. True or False?

11. How does polar ice and snow help to keep the planet cooler?

12. What is fracking?

13. If Earth's surface temperature increases, the amount of seawater that evaporates can trigger storms. True or False?

14. Deforestation and changes in land use account for what percentage of carbon released into the environment?

15. What does the secondary footprint measure?

16. Which of these is NOT a result of climate change: population increase, more storms, raised sea levels?

17. How much of the Arctic Sea ice could disappear by 2050?

18. What is the name of the warm current that brings heavy rain to western South America every few years and causes flooding?

19. The world's average temperature has risen by 1 degree every decade since 1960. True or False?

20. Which scientific organization assesses the information relevant to the understanding of climate change?

21. The weather is the same as climate. True or False?

22. Which of these indicate climate change: more rain, increased population, higher humidity?

23. The richest half of the world is responsible for what percentage of overall global emissions?

24. Floods and droughts are hydrometeorological disasters. True or False?

25. Wasting less food helps cut down greenhouse gases. True or False?

Humongous Fungus

1. How do mushrooms reproduce?

2. Tuber magnatum is one of the world's most expensive foods. What is it commonly known as?

3. What color is the sulfur tuft fungus?

4. What does a chanterelle mushroom smell of?

5. What name is given to the black or white fungus that often grows on objects in damp rooms?

6. What is the study of mushrooms called?

7. What name is given to the rootlike fibers from which mushrooms and toadstools grow?

8. Marmite (Vegemite) is an extract of which type of fungus?

9. The smell of the stinkhorn fungus attracts which type of animal to help carry its spores?

10. What gas produced by yeast fungi helps bread to rise?

11. The fly agaric mushroom is generally associated with which type of tree?

12. A lichen is a combination of a fungus and what other kind of organism?

13. What kind of ant cultivates a fungus within its nest to make food?

14. Glow-in-the-dark fungi were used for indoor lighting in early submarines. True or False?

15. Which medical condition is caused by a fungus growing on the human body?

16. Which type of drug was first discovered in a fungus?

17. Where are you likely to find the fungus mucor?

18. Which of the following cheeses does NOT contain the fungus penicillium: Stilton, Gouda, cottage cheese?

19. What carbohydrate is found in both the fungal cell walls and the outer body cases of insects?

20. Which fairy-tale mushroom was traditionally used to attract and kill flies?

Wonderful Animals

1. Which of these is a very poisonous spider found in Australia: funnel web, black widow, huntsman?

2. Dogs can smell whether someone has cancer. True or False?

3. Insects have tiny holes covering their bodies to let air in. True or False?

4. Roughly how many species of insects have been identified?

5. Which animal can survive the freezing process?

6. What animal can dig 66 ft (20 m) of tunnels a day?

7. What are young whales called?

8. Which is the world's smallest bird at 2½ in (6 cm) long?

9. How fast can an emu run?

10. Which bird species has the biggest beak?

11. Which of these sharks can swim the fastest: nurse, leopard, mako?

12. What do opossums do to fool their attackers?

13. Which animals use echolocation?

14. How long is a giraffe's tongue?

15. Which of these fish contains enough poison to kill 30 people: sunfish, bamboo shark, pufferfish?

16. The strange beak of the crossbill is specially adapted for what purpose?

17. In which of these species does the male become pregnant; octopus, seahorse, ant?

18. Which animal has learned to open a jar of food: dog, seal, octopus?

19. Which animal can hear the highest-pitched sound: moth, dolphin, bat?

20. What is special about the barnacles of the genus *Coronula*?

21. What substance, produced by cave swifts, is the main ingredient in bird's nest soup?

22. Which is the only group of crustaceans able to breed on land?

23. Why don't razorbill eggs roll off cliff ledges where they are laid?

24. The world's deepest-diving bird has been recorded at depths of 1,770 ft (540 m). What is it?

25. Why is the green basilisk lizard sometimes called the "Jesus Christ lizard"?

Size Matters

1. How big is a newborn red kangaroo?

2. What is the largest owl?

3. What is the largest living toothed mammal?

4. What is the world's largest jellyfish?

5. The heaviest invertebrate ever recorded was a mollusk weighing 1,100 lb (495 kg). What species was it?

6. Which is the largest living species of penguin?

7. Which fierce little mammal is the smallest species of carnivore?

8. What is the largest species of dolphin?

9. What is the largest living marsupial meat-eater?

10. Which is the world's heaviest monkey, at up to 82 lb (37 kg)?

11. What is the world's largest wild cat?

12. Tapeworms live in the gut of larger animals and steal their food. How long can a tapeworm grow?

13. Which is the smallest member of the penguin family?

14. The Flemish Giant is the largest breed of which domesticated mammal?

15. On average, a blue whale's tongue weighs around 3 short tons (2.7 metric tons). True or False?

16. How long are the stinging tentacles of a Portuguese man o' war?

17. How much blood can a typical leech consume in one meal?

18. The largest species of ray has a fin span of about 23 ft (7 m). What is it?

19. The world's biggest spider grows up to 11 in (28 cm) across. What is it called?

20. Rhinoceros beetles are immensely strong. How much weight can they lift?

21. Which bird can see small rodents on the ground from a height of 15,000 ft (4,572 m)?

22. The bootlace worm can reach 190 ft (58 m) in length. True or False?

23. The largest carnivorous dinosaur was thought to be the what?

24. Which bird lays eggs the size of a pea?

25. Approximately what percentage of DNA do humans and chimpanzees share?

Birds Are Brilliant

1. The stork has the world's biggest beak. True or False?

2. Weaver birds build the world's biggest tree nests. True or False?

3. Rüppell's vulture is the highest flying bird. How high can it fly?

4. How deep can emperor penguins dive?

5. Which bird has the loudest call? It can be heard 4½ miles (7 km) away.

6. How fast can a roadrunner run? Beep, beep!

7. Only birds have feathers. True or False?

8. Which of these do birds NOT use to help guide them during migration: wind, landmark, the sun?

9. Turkeys have wattles. What are wattles?

10. What are feathers made from?

11. How long ago did birds evolve?

12. What bird makes a meowing sound and a clucking sound?

13. Ian Fleming named James Bond after a famous ornithologist, who was an expert on Caribbean birds. True or False?

14. This owl has the best hearing of any bird. Which species of owl is it?

15. Ducks and geese follow the first thing they see. What is this behavior called?

16. A cygnet grows up to be what?

17. Why are flamingos pink?

18. The kiwi is the national bird of which country?

19. Ostrich eggs are poisonous. True or False?

20. What makes up most of a hummingbird's diet?

21. What is guano?

22. *Aptenodytes forsteri* is the name for which tall nonflying bird?

23. *Pica pica* is the scientific name for which bird?

24. Which birds are sometimes called sea parrots?

25. *Columbidae* are commonly known as what?

Making Sense of It All

1. Bats prevent damage to their ears by what?

2. Flies taste sugary food with their what?

3. A bear's brain is one-third the size of a human's, but how many times better than ours is its sense of smell?

4. What are the taste receptors on a butterfly's feet called?

5. Some fish have a sixth sense called the "lateral line." It is involved in assessing what?

6. Which mammal has the biggest ears for its body size?

7. Turtles can echolocate. True or False?

8. Crickets hear using their legs. True or False?

9. Which of these animals cannot move its eyes independently of one another: seahorse, chameleon, sheep?

10. Does a penguin have a flat or curved cornea so it can see clearly underwater?

11. Which of the following has the greatest number of different types of color receptors in its eyes: bird, mantis shrimp, bull?

12. The mammal with the best sense of touch is the what?

13. Which of these animals cannot close its nostrils: camel, otter, penguin?

14. The colossal squid has an eye about the size of a what?

15. Which mammal can "hear" with its feet?

16. Some animals have infrared sensors which they use to identify what?

17. Some species of fish produce electrical discharge to communicate with each other. True or False?

18. Which of the following can have the most eyes: earthworm, spider, starfish?

19. Which animal can hear the lowest frequency of sound?

20. Jacobson's organs are found in snakes. What does this organ help a snake to do?

21. How many eyes does the box jellyfish have: 8, 12, 24?

22. Each eye on a fly has 3,000 lenses. True or False?

23. Can a four-eyed fish see in air and water at the same time?

24. Which tongue has the most taste buds: human, pig, rabbit?

25. Which animal has a "nose leaf" to help it find food?

Sea Creatures

1. How long are the tusks of a male walrus?

2. What is the cuttle of a cuttlefish?

3. What is the alternative common name of the beluga whale?

4. What does the thresher shark use its enormous tail for?

5. What is the longest ray-finned fish in the world, at up to 36 ft (11 m)?

6. Why do baby angelfish have different markings than adults?

7. At what age do baby hooded seals become independent?

8. Bowhead whales are thought to be the longest-lived mammals. What age was the oldest one known?

9. How do walruses find food in murky water?

10. How long can the tusk of a male narwhal grow?

11. The largest species of seal reaches almost 23 ft (7 m) in length. What is it?

12. The Mediterranean monk seal is the world's rarest seal. True or False?

13. Which mammal has the longest annual migration?

14. How many eggs can a female oyster produce in a lifetime?

15. The Japanese spider crab is the world's biggest arthropod. What is its leg span?

16. The ink produced by a squid is brown. True or False?

17. Which group of invertebrates has larvae known as nauplii, cyprids, and zoea?

18. What is the chalky shell of a sea urchin called?

19. What kind of animal is a Venus's flower basket?

20. Where are the gills of a sea slug?

(Answers on page 497)

Animal Magnetism

1. What term is used to describe an animal that is genetically identical to its parent?

2. If a turtle's eggs are incubated in low temperatures, they will mostly hatch as males. True or False?

3. Giraffes usually give birth to twins. True or False?

4. What are gametes?

5. Massive timed egg release by animals such as corals and fish is called what?

6. What animal remains a juvenile its whole life?

7. How do snakes find their partners?

8. There is a particular way a sea bird called the booby attracts its mate. Which of the following is the most important: its blue feet, its dance, its song?

9. Which birds are well-known for their dazzling courtship displays?

10. Which of the following animals is NOT a hermaphrodite: spider, slug, snail?

11. Which bird collects brightly colored sticks and stones to woo its mate?

12. What is it called when an insect such as a caterpillar turns into an adult butterfly?

13. What are frogs called at the stage between tadpoles and frogs?

14. What is the term used for a young seahorse?

15. The jawfish keeps its eggs safe from predators by doing what?

16. How long do young orangutans stay with their mothers?

17. In some bird and insect species, males gather to compete for the female. What is this called?

18. What is sexual dimorphism?

19. What do cuttlefish do after laying their eggs?

20. Swans are known to have one mate for life. What name is given to this kind of relationship?

Creature Features

1. What is the biological term for a bird, such as a cuckoo, that lays its eggs in another's nest?

2. What kind of bird is an avocet?

3. How many eggs does a female cuckoo lay in each host nest?

4. How do ring-tailed lemur troops settle boundary disputes?

5. What bird migrates farther than any other animal, visiting both the Arctic and Antarctic circles each year?

6. What bird has a call known as a "boom"?

7. Which bird of prey is nicknamed "windhover," because of its hunting technique?

8. How far in an hour could a garden snail travel at top speed?

9. What kind of animal is a slow worm?

10. What alternative name is sometimes used for the European bison?

11. What kind of animal is a silverfish?

12. Are centipedes vegan, omnivorous, or carnivorous?

13. What color is the breast of a male bullfinch?

14. The hellbender is a large member of which group of animals?

15. Nematode worms are the most abundant animals in many soils. How many can 10 sq ft (1 sq m) contain?

16. In 1767, Gilbert White described a species of tiny mouse found in corn fields. What did he call it?

17. The white rhino is actually gray. The name comes from the Afrikaans word *widje*, meaning what?

18. The American millipede *Illacmé plenipes* is thought to have the most legs of any animal. How many?

19. The dormouse gets its name from the French word *dormir*, meaning "to sleep." How long does this dozy rodent hibernate?

20. What are American marmots also known as?

21. For how long does the mayfly live?

22. Which animal sleeps for nearly 22 hours a day?

23. Which animals never sleep like other animals, though they can take rests?

24. Which animal feeds but has no gut?

25. In what unusual way do starfish digest their food?

THE NATURAL WORLD

A Gaggle of Geese

1. What is the word for a group of swans flying in V formation?

2. Which word describes a group of elk?

3. Which amphibian does the collective noun "knot" describe?

4. Groups of rats, wolves, grouse, and hounds can all be described by which word?

5. "Sleuth" is the collective noun for which mammal?

6. A group of penguins is called a "rookery." True or False?

7. Which of the following does NOT refer to a group of ducks: raft, waddle, paddle?

8. What is the collective noun for moles?

9. Which musical term describes a group of gorillas?

10. A "charm" is the collective noun for what?

11. Which of the following does NOT refer to a group of bees: buzz, hive, swarm?

12. "Stand" is a collective noun for which kind of bird?

13. "Irritation" is a collective noun for head lice. True or False?

14. Which word cannot be used to describe a group of zebras: herd, cohort, stripe?

15. What is the collective noun for starlings?

16. Which of these describes a group of badgers: cete, crate, crete?

17. "Barren" is a collective noun for which animals?

18. A "smack" describes a group of which ocean creatures?

19. Which do NOT live in colonies: ants, bees, bats, bears?

20. A group of larks is called an "exaltation." True or False?

Birds

1. Which of these birds is flightless: condor, osprey, kiwi?

2. An ostrich can reach speeds of up to 45 mph (72 kmph) when running. True or False?

3. What is the name of the place where penguins mate and raise their young?

4. The peregrine falcon in flight is the fastest animal in the world. True or False?

5. The wandering albatross is famous for a specific trait. What is it?

6. Which of these birds of prey is the heaviest in the world: golden eagle, Andean condor, spotted harrier?

7. In which season do swans typically mate?

8. How can you tell a male from a female song thrush?

9. What is the term given to the study of birds?

10. Approximately how many red-billed quelea, the world's most abundant wild bird, are there in the world?

11. Which is the heaviest bird in the US?

12. There may be 18,000 bird species, double the number previously thought. True or False?

13. What is the name for a male duck?

14. Which species of bird can fly high enough to soar over Mt. Everest?

15. What is the collective noun for a group of owls?

16. An ostrich's eyeball is larger than its brain. True or False?

17. Which bird is the national symbol for the United States?

18. What country does the King of Saxony bird of paradise come from?

19. What does the Indian tailor bird use to sew leaves to make a nest?

20. A bird's sense of smell is stronger than its sense of hearing. True or False?

21. What is the function of the gizzard in seed-eating birds?

22. A cassowary egg is bigger than an ostrich egg. True or False?

23. How do seabirds regulate their salt intake?

24. How many eggs do puffins lay?

25. Which is the heaviest flying bird?

On the Seashore

1. What is the seashore also known as: the foreshore, the littoral zone, the intertidal zone?

2. Only creatures that can cope with harsh extremes can survive life on the seashore. True or False?

3. What is the most common vegetation found on the seashore?

4. What is a type of seashore crab that uses discarded seashells as its home?

5. Which creature would you commonly find in a rock pool: starfish, mussels, clams?

6. Some species of starfish can regrow lost arms. True or False?

7. Which seashore creature waits for its prey to climb onto it and then paralyzes it with stinging harpoons?

8. A sea anemone can clone itself to reproduce. True or False?

9. I live on the rocky shallows of the seashore and crawl along using my arms. I am a what?

10. This seashore creature is small, is round, floats in the water, and has a translucent color. It is a what?

11. Jellyfish are carnivorous and sting any suitable prey, such as small crustaceans and fish. True or False?

12. Black sandy beaches in the Canary Islands are what?

13. Sea slugs have both male and female reproductive organs. True or False?

14. I have a conical shell and cling tightly to seashore rocks. I am a what?

15. There are "True" and "False" limpets. True or False?

16. Mexico has more seashores than any other country. True or False?

17. Seashores almost always have three zones: a high-tide zone, a middle-tide zone, and a low-tide zone. True or False?

18. Which seashore zone is home to the most life?

19. What are coral animals called?

20. Because the water is shallow in seashore rock pools, it allows photosynthetic activity to take place beneath the surface. True or False?

21. A stretch of sea water separated from the open sea by a narrow strip of land is a…?

22. About half the world's population lives within 60 miles (100 km) of a coast. True or False?

23. What name is given to the process whereby the waves hit the beach at an angle and move material along the coast?

24. Which of these does NOT affect global sea level rise: melting glaciers, melting sea ice, ocean temperatures?

25. Sea level can change regionally. True or False?

Endangered Species

1. The endangered pangolin is found in Asia and which other continent?

2. Which Arctic animal is predicted to become extinct within a century if global warming continues at today's rate?

3. In which year was the Javan rhinoceros added to the critically endangered list?

4. Which endangered creature migrates every winter from North America to Mexico?

5. Which fish commonly used in sushi is on the World Wildlife Fund's endangered list?

6. The kakapo is a flightless bird found in New Zealand. In 2020, how many were left in the wild: 200, 147, 50?

7. Oil spills and warming ocean currents have made the Magellanic penguin an endangered creature. True or False?

8. How many endangered snow leopards are thought to still exist in the wild?

9. As what is the endangered creature *Balaenoptera musculus* more commonly known?

10. Which country is the native habitat of the endangered Komodo dragon?

11. How many endangered species of animals are there worldwide?

12. The leatherback turtle has existed for more than 23 million years but now faces extinction. True or False?

13. The Siberian tiger is an endangered subspecies of tiger. How many other subspecies are already extinct?

14. There are estimated to be only around 250 crested ibises still in existence. From which continent is the bird?

15. The tapir of which country is on the endangered list?

16. What part of the world is the native habitat for the endangered mountain gazelle?

17. Which of these creatures is NOT yet extinct in the wild: red howler monkey, Catarina pupfish, Wyoming toad?

18. The Yangtze river dolphin was removed from the critically endangered list in 2009. True or False?

19. How many Javan rhinoceroses are there left in the wild?

20. Only around 1,000 of this large primate remain in the wild. What is its name?

(Answers on page 498)   **265**

Plants

1. What is the name of the male parts of the flower that make pollen?

2. Foxgloves have dots on their petals to direct pollinators to their nectar. What are these called?

3. Eucalyptus leaves are poisonous. True or False?

4. "Fly agaric" is the name of a mushroom. True or False?

5. *Allium sativum* is the botanical name for which plant?

6. The sap of which plant can be used to treat burns and inflammation because of its cooling properties?

7. Where in the world would you find baobab trees?

8. Out of the following, which of these trees grows catkins: willow, poplar, birch?

9. The male cones on a conifer tend to be soft and smaller than female cones. True or False?

10. How many species of cactus are there?

11. Which plant catches insects by using drops of sticky liquid on its leaves?

12. An angiosperm is a plant that what?

13. Roses can be almost every color of the spectrum apart from what?

14. The difference between herbs and spices is the part of the plant they come from. True or False?

15. Agaves are able to withstand drought, heat, and full sun. Where did they originate?

16. Peanuts are part of the legume family. True or False?

17. What is the technique called when you put a new variety of plant onto an existing plant?

18. The process where plants drop their leaves is known as what?

19. Where are you most likely to find a beech tree?

20. Which part of the globe artichoke plant is eaten?

(Answers on page 498)

Extinct Animals

1. The largest-ever eagle once flew over the skies of New Zealand until it became extinct. What was it called?

2. The aurochs became extinct in the early 17th century. What kind of animal was it?

3. What extinct bird had a huge beak and couldn't fly?

4. Coelodonta is a now-extinct Ice Age mammal. What is its more common name?

5. The European lion is thought to have died out around 100 BCE. In which country was it last sighted?

6. A now-extinct fierce predator from the Ice Age was the what?

7. Moschops was a giant plant-eating animal that became extinct before the dinosaurs even existed. True or False?

8. How many times bigger than a great white shark was the now-extinct Megalodon?

9. There have been no sightings of the rain forest's golden toad since 1989. True or False?

10. The great auk was a Northern Hemisphere equivalent of which marine bird?

11. The Cape warthog is extinct in which continent?

12. The big-eared hopping mouse was last seen on Earth in 1843. In which country was this?

13. What type of animal was a Meganeura?

14. The kronosaurus is a now-extinct reptile that existed during the dinosaur age. In which habitat did it live?

15. Dinichthys was a family of armored fish that died out around 400 million years ago. True or False?

16. What is the Red List?

17. Becoming extinct in the early 20th century, the thylacine is also called the what?

18. An extinct African zebra that only had stripes on half of its body is known as a what?

19. Now extinct, one of the largest flightless birds was found in New Zealand. What was it called?

20. The glyptodon was a car-sized mammal with armor plating that died out after the Ice Age. What type of creature was it?

All about Horses

1. A draft horse with powerful hooves derived from Scottish farm horses is called what?

2. The great war horse of the Middle Ages was the what?

3. Which horse's bloodline can be found in almost every modern breed of riding horse?

4. The horse with the leopard-spotted coat is called what?

5. American Indians were responsible for breeding the Appaloosa in North America. True or False?

6. I am a rare and endangered subspecies of wild horse found on the steppes of Central Asia.

7. The "wild" American mustang was once a domesticated horse. True or False?

8. The British hackney horse was considered well-suited for pulling what?

9. Which famous riding school puts on shows around the world with Lipizzan horses?

10. Complete the name of this horse breed: "Kentucky Mountain…"?

11. The Namib desert horse is the only feral horse in Africa. True or False?

12. The tarpan is an extinct subspecies of wild horse. True or False?

13. Which horse found in the mountainous regions of western Norway is "dun" in color?

14. A miniature horse is usually 34–38 inches (86–97 cm) in height. True or False?

15. Which American breed is known for its unique four-beat running walk?

16. This hard-working draft horse has a chestnut color and is often found in the east of England.

17. The Lokai is a mountain riding horse bred in Mexico. True or False?

18. The Shire horse was often used to pull wagons that delivered ale to customers. True or False?

19. Which pony shares its name with the region of Ireland it came from?

20. Which small pony is popular with young riders and was made famous by the Thelwell cartoons?

21. In which region of France are wild horses still found?

22. A typical adult male horse has how many teeth?

23. What name is given to a female horse under the age of four?

24. What is a stallion technically?

25. Put these in the right order from slowest to fastest: trot, gallop, walk, canter.

Poisonous Plants

1. Curare is a poison obtained from plants. What did South American hunters once use it for?

2. A single cassava tuber can contain enough cyanide to kill a herd of cows. What is it commonly used for in South America?

3. Undercooked kidney beans can be five times more poisonous than raw beans. True or False?

4. Which part of the rhubarb plant is poisonous to humans?

5. Atropa belladonna, one of the most toxic plants around, is more commonly known as deadly what?

6. Tomato plants belong to the highly toxic nightshade family of plants and are therefore poisonous. True or False?

7. In ancient Greece, hemlock was used as a poison for capital punishment. Who was the most famous victim of hemlock poisoning?

8. The plant that gave us digitalis as a medicine is the poisonous what?

9. It is NOT possible for a human to ingest enough poisonous apple seeds to be fatal. True or False?

10. Which poisonous tree was used to make longbows in medieval Britain?

11. In which comic book would you find the villain Poison Ivy?

12. The seeds of the wisteria plant are poisonous. True or False?

13. Potatoes, especially wild potatoes, contain chemicals that produce toxic effects in humans. True or False?

14. In the Harry Potter stories, a potion made from which real poisonous plant is taken by werewolves to maintain rationality and conscience.

15. The bulbs of which common garden plant have been known to poison humans mistaking them as onions?

16. Once it has trapped its prey, a Venus flytrap contains a cocktail of poisons that kill it. True or False?

17. Castor oil, used in food additives and candy production, is produced from castor beans. Which extremely deadly poison is found in the beans?

18. The leaves and nuts of which common tree are poisonous for some animals?

19. Oleander is so toxic that a human can be poisoned by eating honey made by bees that have ingested its nectar. True or False?

20. In the James Bond film *Moonraker*, Hugo Drax cultivates poison from which household plant?

(Answers on page 498)   **269**

Insects and Spiders

1. Which is the only state where termites do not live?

2. What is the scientific term for molting or casting off an old skin?

3. The world's largest butterfly has a wingspan of up to 12 in (31 cm). What is it?

4. What remarkable natural material is produced from organs known as "spinnerets"?

5. What name is given to the stage in a butterfly's life cycle between caterpillar and adult?

6. The fruit fly is the one of the world's most-studied animals. What sort of research is it used for?

7. What food is given to the caterpillars of the silk moth in silk farms?

8. What crop is attacked by the infamous Colorado beetle?

9. What do the caterpillars of monarch butterflies eat?

10. What stinging substance do ants squirt in self-defense?

11. What familiar insects belong to the order Coleoptera?

12. What purpose is served by the long "tail" of the water scorpion bug?

13. Why do raft spiders tremble their legs on the surface of still pools?

14. What do stick insects eat?

15. Flies soften their food by spitting on it and then ingest it with mouthparts that work like a what?

16. Beetles, crabs, spiders, and centipedes are all arthropods. What does *arthropoda* mean?

17. Which group of insects is distinguished by having scaly wings?

18. When fully stretched, spider silk has the equivalent strength of what man-made material?

19. Which group of butterflies are the fastest fliers?

20. What is an egg-laying bee called?

(Answers on page 498)

Mammal Mania

1. What is a young hare called?

2. By which other name is the indri known?

3. What animal is traditionally used to find the precious fungi known as truffles?

4. What special name is given to the otter's den?

5. What is a "numbat"?

6. What unusual hunting method is used by velvet worms to immobilize prey?

7. Many bats are described as crepuscular. What does "crepuscular" mean?

8. Why are African sengis also known as elephant shrews?

9. What escapee from English fur farms became established in the wild but was eradicated in the 1980s?

10. Which anatomical feature allows squirrels to descend headfirst and hang from their back feet?

11. What name is given to a stoat in its white winter coat?

12. How many living species of rhinoceros are there?

13. The word "rodent" comes from the Latin verb *rodere*, describing which action that rodents do well?

14. What food do gelada baboons specialize in eating?

15. The feisty African ratel goes by what other common name?

16. What is the main difference between mammal horns and antlers?

17. How does a chinchilla keep its fine fur clean?

18. Lemmings are described as subniveal animals. What does "subniveal" mean?

19. The honey possum is an Australian marsupial with a tongue shaped like a brush. How much does the male weigh?

20. Which domestic cat breed is characterized by long fur and a very flat face?

21. How long does it take to hard-boil an ostrich egg?

22. How much milk does a baby blue whale drink in a day?

23. Some primates, such as galagos and bushbabies, frequently urinate on their hands and feet. Why?

24. Antlers grow on both males and females of which species of deer?

25. The hippopotamus produces a greasy pink substance from pores in its skin. What function does it have?

Animal Challenge

1. What kind of fish is the freshwater burbot?

2. What kind of mammal is an aardwolf?

3. Which family of fish do humans eat most of?

4. What do scientists count to determine how old a fish is?

5. The goliath frog is the world's largest frog. How much do the biggest specimens weigh?

6. Which of these animals has the best color vision: bumblebee, dog, dolphin?

7. What is the collective term for a group of tadpoles?

8. What kind of animal is the quokka?

9. What kind of animal is a tuatara?

10. What is a zyzzyva?

11. How does the fire salamander defend itself from attack?

12. What name is given to the drumstick-shaped balancing organs used by flies in flight?

13. If a fossorial animal burrows and a natatorial animal swims, how does a saltatorial animal move?

14. Bryozoans, or moss animals, are minute colonial invertebrates. Where do they live?

15. How big is the tardigrade or water bear?

16. How many species of snake are vegetarian?

17. What is the special name given to the rasping tongue of the mollusk?

18. Which other arthropod group are horseshoe crabs most closely related to?

19. Which reptile was traditionally most hunted for tortoise shell?

20. Which is the world's largest turtle, at up to 5 ft (5.5 m) long and 1,500 lb (680 kg) in weight?

Evolution Revolution

1. In which decade did the quagga become extinct?

2. The beaks of which birds particularly interested Darwin on the Galápagos Islands?

3. What were pterosaurs?

4. Darwin kept birds that he studied to help him come up with his theories; which species of bird were they?

5. Which other British naturalist prompted Darwin to publish his theory?

6. Which of these animals has evolved the best eye: octopus, cat, human?

7. How many chromosomes do humans have?

8. Which scientist did experiments on inheritance in pea plants?

9. DNA is a code using four bases; which letters are used to represent this code?

10. A change in DNA is known as a what?

11. What were plesiosaurs?

12. "Hominidae" means what?

13. Which prehistoric era came first: Carboniferous or Cambrian?

14. When did modern humans evolve?

15. What is it called when unrelated species develop along similar lines due to similar selection pressures?

16. Which of these is NOT a close living relative of the elephant: hyrax, dugong, monitor?

17. During which period did pterosaurs live?

18. When was Charles Darwin's *On the Origin of Species* published?

19. The Coelophysis had a special feature to help it be a light and agile predator. What was this special feature?

20. All the genes of a particular species are known as the what?

THE NATURAL WORLD

Social Animals

1. Which of these is NOT found in a bee colony: worker, hunter, queen?

2. How many eggs can a queen honeybee lay in a day?

3. Worker honeybees are always female. True or False?

4. A group of gorillas is known as a what?

5. About how many birds are in a typical king penguin colony?

6. Which order of insects are the highly social ants and bees?

7. Which of these mammals lives in a similar way to ants and bees, with a queen and workers: naked mole rats, meerkats, beavers?

8. Locust birds are so called because they congregate in massive flocks. What is their correct name?

9. The individual animals that make up a coral reef are known as what?

10. Leafcutter ants can emit squeaks audible to the human ear. Why do they do this?

11. Elephants can communicate with very low-pitched noises known as what?

12. What name is given to the dance performed by honeybees to indicate to their fellows the direction of flowers?

13. What is the collective term for a group of dolphins?

14. Which of these is a strategy used by groups of whales working together to catch fish: line fishing, splash herding, bubble netting?

15. Which ape has shown the greatest aptitude for learning sign language?

16. What do ghost knife fishes use to communicate?

17. Ant colonies have their own trash dumps. True or False?

18. What are the names of chemicals that trigger a behavioral response in other individuals of the same species?

19. Which social species of bird lives in groups of up to 500?

20. What is a female-dominated society known as?

21. For approximately how many days does the average worker ant live?

22. The slavemaker ant steals the pupae from other ant colonies to use as ready-made slaves. True or False?

23. What is the average lifespan for a healthy queen honeybee?

24. How does an ordinary worker honeybee become the queen of a colony?

25. Orcas hunt in a team. True or False?

Hunter and Hunted

1. Which of the following has the best hearing: eagle, kestrel, barn owl?

2. Flying fish can glide at 63 mph (100 kmph) to escape predators. True or False?

3. How does a stonefish defend itself against predators?

4. What do some adult birds do to draw hunters away from their young?

5. The porcupine fish can expand its stomach to 100 times its normal size when threatened. True or False?

6. What does the armadillo lizard do when threatened?

7. Which type of poisonous fish is named after a feline?

8. Which insect is considered to have the most painful sting?

9. Belugas are well camouflaged for life in the ice caps. What are belugas?

10. What do plaice do to aid their survival?

11. Which of these animals was so well camouflaged in coral that it was not discovered for years?

12. Crypsis and mimesis are types of camouflage. True or False?

13. Leafcutter ants grow their own food, feeding exclusively on a fungus that grows only within their colonies. True or False?

14. What do Texas horned lizards shoot from their eyes when threatened?

15. How far can a skunk shoot foul-smelling chemicals from its anal glands?

16. Which spider uses a trip line to help it catch prey?

17. What is the scientific name of the relationship between clownfish and sea anemones?

18. Which insects, in huge colonies, have been known to attack and eat much larger animals, such as chickens?

19. What does a snapping turtle do to attract prey?

20. Layers of cells called chromatophores help some animals to do what?

All about Birds

1. What is a male turkey called?

2. How fast can a roadrunner run?

3. How long can a flamingo live?

4. On which remote island can you find the endangered pink pigeon?

5. The tawny frogmouth is a nocturnal bird. What sort of call does it have?

6. To which group of birds does the American chickadee belong?

7. What is a group of budgerigars called?

8. What is the bony crest on the head of some birds and reptiles such as cassowaries and chameleons called?

9. What is the wingspan of the wandering albatross?

10. What kind of bird is a merganser?

11. Where might you find the night parrot?

12. Which birds have males called cobs and females called pens?

13. Which species of goose is the ancestor of farmyard breeds?

14. What does a tufted duck eat?

15. How fast can an ostrich run?

16. Where does the wandering albatross sleep during its long journeys?

17. Which bird has claws on its wings?

18. What is the smallest bird in Europe?

19. What is a group of crows called?

20. What is a group of nightingales called?

21. The comblike platelets used by flamingos to sieve food particles from water are called what?

22. Which sense does the kiwi use to find food?

23. A group of herons is known as a what?

24. An osprey's diet mainly consists of what?

25. The large ridge on the breastbone of a bird is known as the keel. True or False?

Amazing Adaptations

1. The elephant's trunk is made up of its what?

2. The animal with the most acidic conditions in its stomach is the what?

3. If fish tend to have two-chambered hearts and reptiles four-chambered hearts, which group of animals has three-chambered hearts?

4. The Syrian brown bear is actually more cream-colored. True or False?

5. Brightly colored flowers attract bees for what?

6. Which animals possess organs called ampullae of Lorenzini?

7. Which group of animals is likely to have hollow bones?

8. Some fish in Arctic waters would freeze if they didn't contain what?

9. Why do some ants sometimes look after aphids?

10. Which animals use heat sensors to find their prey?

11. How does a jerboa survive without drinking?

12. Which mammal has the longest tail?

13. The pistol shrimp disables its prey by what?

14. What is the function of a fish's swim bladder?

15. Giant pandas hold their food between what?

16. The bombardier beetle defends itself from predators by what?

17. Why is the hoverfly coloration black and yellow to mimic the coloration of a wasp or bee?

18. Which answer is NOT a reason why parrotfish produce a mucous "sleeping bag" for themselves each night: protection from parasites, for warmth, to keep their scent in?

19. Which one of the following cannot change its skin color: Arctic fox, cuttlefish, chameleon?

20. Which of the following is NOT an adaptation for predation: strong jaw, wide cheekbones, all-around vision?

21. Two male birds displaying to a female is a form of what?

22. In the relationship between an anemone and a clownfish, the anemone provides what?

23. The name given to the relationship between two species where both gain is what?

24. When an oxpecker removes ticks from a giraffe, the relationships of the oxpecker to the tick and giraffe are, respectively, what?

25. In some frogs, young tadpoles are herbivorous but then become carnivores and even cannibals. True or False?

(Answers on page 499) **277**

How Many?

1. How many quills does a North American porcupine have?

2. How many purebred Scottish wildcats remain in the wild?

3. What is the approximate strike rate of a woodpecker drumming on a tree?

4. The world's largest bat colony is at Bracken Cave in Texas. How many Mexican free-tailed bats live there?

5. The millipede has 1,000 legs. True or False?

6. About how many species of insect have scientists identified so far?

7. How many individual lenses make up the large compound eyes of a dragonfly?

8. How many species of ladybugs are there?

9. Despite being insects, some butterflies only have 4 legs. True or False?

10. The bristlecone pine is the longest-living tree known. How many years can one live?

11. The 50 trillion cells in a human body are outnumbered how many times by the bacteria in our guts?

12. How many toes does an ostrich have on each foot?

13. How many eggs can a chicken lay in 24 hours?

14. Most mammals have seven bones in their necks. How many does a giraffe have?

15. There were once about 30 million bison in North America. By the late 1800s, how many were left?

16. How many breeds of domestic dog are there: about 200, 400, 600?

17. A desert locust swarm can cover 460 sq miles (1,200 sq km). How many locusts make up such a swarm?

18. Sixty European starlings were introduced to New York's Central Park in 1890. How many live in the US now?

19. How many eggs can a queen bee lay in a day?

20. Which plant family has the most known species (about 25,000)?

Mad about Mammals

1. How long does it take an elephant baby to develop in the womb?

2. Approximately how far across deep oceans can the low-frequency calls of great whales be tracked?

3. Which European animal did early white settlers in Australia mistake the wombat for?

4. Which land mammal has the densest fur?

5. The offspring of a male donkey and a female horse is a mule. What is the offspring of a female donkey and a male horse?

6. What is a baby alpaca called?

7. The Mongolian wild horse is named after a Russian, Nikolay Przhevalsky. What was he?

8. Members of the Afrotheria animal group live mostly in or originated from Africa. True or False?

9. To which family of mammals does the kinkajou belong?

10. What shape are the pupils in the eyes of big cats?

11. How many species of bat are there?

12. Which is the smallest species of rhinoceros?

13. In which continent would you find the giant otter?

14. Which kind of marsupials typically have backward-opening pouches?

15. Which mammal has the warmest fur?

16. Black bears are always black in color. True or False?

17. Which symptoms suggest a cow is infected with the fluke *Schistosoma nasale*?

18. Solenodons are large cousins of moles and shrews. On which two islands do they live?

19. Which type of mammal are pudus and brockets?

20. The aardvark was named by Afrikaans settlers. What does "aardvark" mean?

(Answers on page 500)

Animal Randomizer

1. Where do the legless reptiles known as amphisbaenians normally live?

2. What does the Madagascan aye-aye use to extract grubs from crevices in dead wood?

3. What is a group of trout called?

4. Which mammals have males known as hobs and females known as jills?

5. In which habitat would you look for kangaroos of the genus *Dendrolagus*?

6. Which rhinoceros species has only one horn?

7. What name is given to the fine wool produced by the angora goat?

8. What are male and female guinea pigs called?

9. Where might you find the rare red wolf?

10. How many toes does a horse have on each foot?

11. The colugo or flying lemur glides from tree to tree on a web of skin. How far can a colugo travel in this way?

12. What is the scientific word for the wing membrane of a bat?

13. What color is yak milk?

14. What is the scientific term for an animal that walks with its feet flat on the ground?

15. Most golden hamsters now live in captivity, but where did the species come from originally?

16. The vicuña is thought to be the wild ancestor of which domestic species?

17. Which breed of domestic cattle is famous for its creamy milk?

18. What is the only part of a gazelle carcass a hyena won't try to eat?

19. What kind of animal is a gaur?

20. What name is given to a roosting colony of fruit bats?

21. What term is used to describe the deep energy-saving sleep that takes place over winter?

22. How many feet does a snail have?

23. What word is used for an animal that walks on four legs?

24. The blood pigment hemoglobin gives the sludgeworm tubifex what color?

25. Why do tortoises sunbathe?

(Answers on page 500)

Rain Forests

1. Which of these is NOT a type of rain forest: mangrove, chaparral, lowland?

2. How tall are the tallest rain forest trees?

3. Which rain forest snake can grow to 33 ft (10 m) in length?

4. What is the name given to rain forest plants that grow on trees?

5. Which of these is NOT an adaptation of a rain forest plant: drip tip leaves, large leaves, succulent leaves?

6. What are lianas?

7. Rain forest covers 6 percent of Earth's surface; what percentage of its species does it contain?

0. In 10 sq ft (1 sq m) of leaf litter, how many species of ants have been found?

9. The Amazon rain forest's biggest cat species is the tiger. True or False?

10. How much rain forest is cut down every minute?

11. Approximately what percentage of today's medicines are derived from rain forest plants?

12. Which of these rivers would you be in if a piranha were nibbling your toes: Amazon, Ganges, Nile?

13. What does the pitcher plant feed on?

14. Plants in rain forests release water into the atmosphere through a process called what?

15. This type of rain forest plant has a pool of water at its center that acts as a habitat for animals such as frogs. What is it?

16. The golden poison frog is venomous. It contains enough poison to kill how many people?

17. Are epiphytes plants or insects?

18. Montane rain forests can be found where?

19. How many different species of plant may be found living on one rain forest tree?

20. Which type of farming can accelerate deforestation?

(Answers on page 500) **281**

CHAPTER 7

SPORTS & LEISURE

Keep your brain active with these lively quizzes covering a wide range of everyone's favorite sports. Wrestling, swimming, golf, tennis, baseball, track and field, skiing, and much more to keep your brain in shape.

FIFA World Cup

1. Which nation has won both the men's and women's World Cup?

2. Who won the World Cup in 2018?

3. By 2020, which country had won the World Cup a record five times?

4. Who is the record scorer in a single World Cup, with 13 goals?

5. Who was the team captain for England when they won the World Cup in 1966?

6. When was the first World Cup held?

7. Which is the largest soccer stadium in the world?

8. The original World Cup trophy was named after which administrator?

9. No African team has won the World Cup. True or False?

10. Where was the 1994 World Cup held?

11. The 1970 World Cup final was held in which stadium?

12. By which name is Edson Arantes do Nascimento better known?

13. Who played in the 1974 winning team and also managed West Germany to victory in 1990?

14. In which city did the 2018 World Cup Final take place?

15. Who missed a penalty during the opening ceremony for the 1994 finals, held in the US?

16. Pelé was 17 when he first won the World Cup. True or False?

17. Where was the 2014 World Cup held?

18. How many times has Italy won the World Cup?

19. How many times has Uruguay won the World Cup?

20. Only 13 teams took part in the first World Cup. Where was it held, and who won?

21. The 2002 World Cup was held in South Korea and where?

22. How many World Cup finals have been won on a penalty shootout?

23. The year 2018 saw the highest-scoring World Cup final since 1966. True or False?

24. Which country has lost the World Cup Final the most times?

25. Which country has appeared at the World Cup Finals 8 times but never advanced past the 1st round?

SPORTS & LEISURE

Wrestling

1. What does "WWE" stand for?

2. When was the first WrestleMania held?

3. Which former heavyweight boxing champ fought Stone Cold Steve Austin in 2006?

4. Wrestling was included as an Olympic sport in the London Games of 2012. True or False?

5. Complete the name of this wrestler: Giant Hay…

6. What is Brett Hart's nickname?

7. Which actor played the hero in the 2008 film *The Wrestler*?

8. Who was the first person to become WWE Universal Champion?

9. The most popular Japanese form of wrestling is called what?

10. Which British wrestler was famous for wearing a mask he never took off?

11. Complete the full name of this Olympic wrestling style: Greco–…

12. What is the real name of film star and famous ex-wrestler the Rock?

13. What was the Rock's signature catchphrase?

14. Hulk Hogan was inducted into the WWE Hall of Fame in which year?

15. Gorgeous George was a flamboyant wrestler who influenced which boxing champ?

16. Which country has won the most Olympic wrestling gold medals?

17. What is the top weight class in Olympic wrestling?

18. Who has the most championships in WWE only?

19. "The Party Foul" is the signature move of which wrestler?

20. Sumo wrestlers purify the ring by throwing salt before a bout begins. True or False?

Track and Field

1. A standard 400m racetrack has eight lanes. True or False?

2. What do people in the UK call track and field?

3. Usain Bolt ran for which country?

4. Who was the men's world pole-vault champion between 1983 and 1999?

5. Which track and field race involves a water jump?

6. How many events are there in a heptathlon?

7. Who ran the first sub-four-minute mile?

8. What is the stick handed between runners in a relay race called?

9. Complete the list of jumping events: high, long, pole vault, and what?

10. Barack Obama is a former 100m national champion. True or False?

11. 26 miles, 385 yards (42.195km) is the distance for which event?

12. Bob Beamon held the world record for 23 years in which event?

13. How many hurdles are there in a 100m race?

14. Long jumpers and triple jumpers land in a pit filled with what?

15. Katerina Johnson-Thompson specializes in which event?

16. Usain Bolt set the world 100m record in August 2009 with what time?

17. How many events are there in a decathlon?

18. At which Olympics did Kelly Holmes win two gold medals?

19. The modern Paralympics joined the Summer Olympics in which year?

20. How often are the World Athletics championships held?

Baseball

1. Which team has won the most World Series titles?

2. What is the most common pitch in baseball?

3. Where did Babe Ruth start his major league career?

4. Which major league general manager is the subject of the *New York Times* best-seller *Moneyball*?

5. Mark McGwire holds the record for most home runs hit in a single season. True or False?

6. What is the name of the statue outside Fenway Park in Boston?

7. In the film *Bull Durham*, which actor portrays minor league veteran "Crash" Davies?

8. Who holds the major league record hitting streak of 56 games?

9. Joe Nuxhall was 15 years old when he made his major league debut for the Cincinnati Reds. True or False?

10. Who is the youngest ever player to join the "500 home run club"?

11. What is the name of the Boston Red Sox's mascot?

12. Which team's home is Turner Field?

13. Which country won the inaugural World Baseball Classic tournament in 2006?

14. Which country holds the most Olympic gold medals for baseball?

15. In 2001, the Baltimore Orioles retired the No. 8 jersey in honor of which player?

16. Which type of pitch will the pitcher deliver if the ball is held off-center?

17. How many times was Willie Mays named Most Valuable Player?

18. Which player has a type of headfirst slide named after them?

19. In which year did Ichiro Suzuki win "Rookie of the Year" and "Most Valuable Player"?

20. Which writer pitched against the National League before the 1960 All-Star game?

(Answers on page 500)

Olympic Games

1. How many rings are there on the Olympic flag?

2. Which Olympic stadium was nicknamed "the Bird's Nest"?

3. Which athlete won four gold medals at the 1936 Games?

4. How many countries took part in the 2008 Games?

5. Who is Britain's most successful Olympian?

6. Which city hosted the 2000 Olympic Games?

7. What are starting blocks used for?

8. The Olympic motto *citius, altius, fortius* means what?

9. What were the prizes for ancient Olympics winners?

10. The 1980 and 1984 Games were marked by political what?

11. Horse racing used to be a modern Olympic sport. True or False?

12. In 1984, Mary Decker tangled with which opponent in the 3,000 meters, before falling out of contention?

13. With what was the Olympic flame lit at the 1992 Barcelona Games?

14. Which European city hosted the first Olympic Games in which women took part?

15. Which country hosted the 2016 Olympics?

16. What is the final event of the men's decathlon?

17. What do the Olympic rings represent?

18. Including 2012, how many times has London hosted the Olympics?

19. Who lit the Olympic flame at the 1996 Atlanta Games?

20. In which year were the modern Olympics first held?

SPORTS & LEISURE

Hole in One

1. How many holes are there on a standard golf course?

2. Eldrick Woods is better known by his nickname of what?

3. Where is the "home" of British golf?

4. Who won the Ryder Cup in 2018?

5. Golf is the only sport that has been played on the moon. True or False?

6. What color is another name for a putting surface?

7. Which club does a golfer usually use to get out of a bunker?

8. Who was PGA Tour Player of the Year in 2012, 2014, and 2019?

9. Links golf is traditionally played on which geographical feature?

10. How is a game of golf started?

11. Where does former Masters champion Bernhard Langer come from?

12. A score of one under par is called a what?

13. Who won the US Open in 2019?

14. Who has won the most golf majors?

15. What color jacket does the winner of the US Masters wear?

16. The modern game of golf originated in which century?

17. A flag indicates the position of what on a green?

18. The dimples in a golf ball are to make it travel farther. True or False?

19. Where can players practice their swing technique?

20. The person who carries a player's golf bag and clubs is called a what?

Gymnastics

1. Olga Korbut competed for the USSR at the 1972 and 1976 Olympics. True or False?

2. Trampolining made its debut at which Olympics?

3. The word "gymnastics" comes from the Greek, meaning "to exercise naked." True or False?

4. Gymnast Mary Lou Retton won how many medals at the 1984 Olympics?

5. Only women compete in artistic gymnastics. True or False?

6. Who scored the first perfect 10, at the 1976 Olympics?

7. When was gymnastics first included as an Olympic sport?

8. Which piece of equipment is suspended 19 ft (5.8 m) from the floor?

9. Who won the gold medal for his floor exercises in the 2016 Olympic Games?

10. Colored ribbons are used in which exercises?

11. If a gymnast falls off a piece of apparatus, what is the minimum reduction in his or her score?

12. Which nation's men's team won gold in the 2016 Olympics?

13. Great Britain won both gold and silver medals in the pommel horse event for men in the 2016 Olympic Games. True or False?

14. Which female gymnast won the gold medal for her vault in the 2016 Olympics?

15. The pommel horse was first introduced by the Romans to teach mounting and dismounting horses. True or False?

16. In which position must trampolinists begin and end their routines?

17. When did rhythmic gymnastics become an Olympic sport?

18. A forward somersault with a half twist is better known as what?

19. USSR and Russian gymnasts hold the record for most Olympic gold medals. True or False?

20. Whose nickname was "the Sparrow from Minsk"?

SPORTS & LEISURE

Anyone for Tennis?

1. How many sets do male players have to win to win a match?

2. What is the maximum number of sets in a women's match in the Grand Slams?

3. Who has won the most Wimbledon men's singles titles?

4. The Australian Open final is held in which stadium?

5. Who was the last British woman to win the Wimbledon singles final?

6. Which official beginning with "U" controls a tennis match?

7. What is the name given to the electronic line-judging device?

8. Which Grand Slam tournament is held every January?

9. Before Andy Murray first won the men's Wimbledon title in 2013, who was the last British player to win the event?

10. Which "F" word does a line judge shout when a serving player's footwork is illegal?

11. Who is Serena Williams's tennis-champion sister?

12. To whom did Andy Murray lose in the 2011 Australian Open final?

13. Martina Navratilova won how many Grand Slam singles titles?

14. Which Grand Slam tournament has the longest history?

15. The French Open is played on what surface?

16. What is the line that runs parallel to the base line called?

17. What is a zero called in tennis points?

18. What is a tennis ball covered with?

19. The frame of a traditional racket was made from what?

20. When players are tied at 40/40 in a game, what is this score called?

21. Which current tennis player is nicknamed "the King of Clay"?

22. What does an ace mean?

23. What does an umpire say at the end of a match to indicate that a player has won?

24. Billie Jean King played male tennis player Bobby Riggs in 1973. Who won?

25. What do we call a shot in which a player hits the ball before it bounces on court during a rally?

Boxing

1. What did ancient Greek boxers protect their hands with?

2. What did ancient Roman boxers wear around their hands?

3. When was boxing first included as an event in the modern Olympic Games?

4. What is another name for a boxer?

5. 1350 BCE wall paintings from ancient Egypt show early boxers in action. True or False?

6. Who became the first great British boxing champion in 1719?

7. Which fight became known as "the Bite Fight"?

8. What are the rules first introduced in boxing in 1867 called?

9. World heavyweight champion Rocky Marciano had 49 professional fights. How many did he lose?

10. How old was George Foreman when he became the oldest heavyweight champion?

11. Which American president advocated for boxing, especially for those in the armed forces?

12. Which boxing class is heaviest: flyweight, bantamweight, featherweight?

13. Who was the heavyweight boxing champion of Uganda from 1951–1960?

14. Who suffered his first defeat in 1936 to the darling of the Nazi party, Max Schmeling?

15. Which boxer won Olympic gold as a middleweight and then went on to capture the heavyweight title twice?

16. Which fighters starred in the 1971 bout that was later known as the "Fight of the Century"?

17. The "Sound and Fury" was a notorious match fought in 1997 between which two fighters?

18. By which name was Walker Smith Jr. better known?

19. Which super middleweight fighter retired in 2008 with 46 wins, no draws, and no defeats?

20. Who won 11 world titles at different weights between 1946 and 1960?

SPORTS & LEISURE

Unusual Sports Festivals

1. Where in the world do competitors gather to throw a 22-lb (10-kg) tuna as part of the annual Tunarama Festival?

2. The World Sauna Championships, which test how long one person can withstand a 230°F (110°C) sauna, are held in which country?

3. What do contestants carry in a race at Olney that is said to be 600 years old?

4. The annual Redneck Games are held in the state of Georgia. True or False?

5. In which country have the Bog Snorkeling Championships taken place every August for the last 25 years?

6. What are thrown in a peculiar annual world championship held in Finland?

7. In which year were the British Lawn Mower Racing World Championships created?

8. The Hell Blues Festival takes place every year in which country?

9. What are the boats made from in an annual regatta held in Darwin, Australia?

10. The world record for Haggis Hurling is 217 ft (66 m). True or False?

11. Where does the World Stone Skimming Championship take place?

12. Which sporting festival takes place every October in the English market town of Oundle, Northamptonshire?

13. Which type of food is rolled down Cooper's Hill in an annual festival held in Gloucestershire, England?

14. What is the name of the food-fight festival held in the town of Buñol in Valencia, Spain?

15. One of the events in the annual Cotswold Olimpick Games is shin kicking. True or False?

16. There is no such thing as the World Black Pudding Throwing Championships. True or False?

17. In which English county is the title of World Champion Toe Wrestler fought for every year?

18. Dragon boat racing festivals have been held for thousands of years. How many team members are allowed in each boat?

19. Men competing in a strange annual Finnish sports race have to run through grass, water, and sand obstacles. What do they also have to carry on their backs?

20. How many times has a human won the 22-mile (35-km) Man Versus Horse Marathon—held in Llanwrtyd Wells, Wales— since its inception?

Swimming

1. In which year did swimming become part of the modern Olympic Games?

2. In which Asian country was swimming made compulsory in schools by the 17th century?

3. Swimming champion Mark Spitz came from Germany. True or False?

4. When was the butterfly stroke developed?

5. An Olympic swimming pool is 164 ft (50 m) long. True or False?

6. How many main styles are there in competitive swimming?

7. Which swimming move helps increase the speed of a turn at the end of the pool?

8. Who was nicknamed the "Thorpedo"?

9. Who won the gold medal in the 100 m breaststroke event at the Rio Olympics in 2016?

10. The World Aquatic Championships were first held in 1973. True or False?

11. Which country won every swimming event in the 1948 Olympics?

12. Captain Matthew Webb of England was the first person to swim across the English Channel by using the what?

13. At the 1900 Olympic Games, an underwater swimming race was introduced. True or False?

14. For which swimming stroke is diving off at the start not done?

15. Which two additional events combine with swimming to form a triathlon?

16. During which Olympics were goggles first used in swimming events?

17. Olympic swimming took place in a pool rather than open water for the first time in 1908. True or False?

18. In the individual medley event, which stroke is used first?

19. Swimming has recently been introduced at the Winter Olympic Games. True or False?

20. Which swimming aid did Benjamin Franklin invent?

21. In which year did the 10 km open-water swim appear in the Olympics?

22. Which of the four competitive strokes usually produces the slowest time?

23. Why was the Australian women's 4 x 200 m freestyle relay team disqualified at the 2001 World Championships?

24. Swimmers can perform a tumble turn when swimming breaststroke. True or False?

25. Which swimmer holds the all-time record for winning the most Olympic gold medals?

Skiing

1. Where did Franz Klammer win the 1976 downhill gold medal?

2. Which Italian skier was the star of the slalom and giant slalom in the 1990s?

3. The origin of the word "ski" comes from which language?

4. Downhill skiers can race at up to what speed?

5. In how many James Bond films does 007 ski?

6. Slalom skis are longer than downhill skis. True or False?

7. In which city did Japan host the 1972 Winter Olympics?

8. What is the French word for a marked ski run?

9. The longest indoor slope is in which country?

10. Ski jumpers can leap distances of up to 475 ft (145 m). True or False?

11. What is the name of the legendary downhill course at Kitzbuhel?

12. Which ski resort was the venue for the 2017 Alpine World Ski Championships?

13. The Whistler Ski Resort is in which country?

14. Janica Kostelic won 4 gold and 2 silver Winter Olympic skiing medals. What is her nationality?

15. What is the name of the long-running BBC skiing highlights show?

16. How many gold medals did Jean-Claude Killy win at the 1968 Winter Olympic Games?

17. The "snowplow" is a move that can be performed on skis. True or False?

18. Ski boots can be worn on either foot. True or False?

19. In Europe, ski runs are graded in four categories. Which is the most difficult?

20. I was more famous for failure than for being a great ski jumper. But I was given a nickname that suggested more success than I ever had. What was it?

21. What is a twin tip ski?

22. What is the fastest type of skiing?

23. Which ski area in North America was the first to host the Winter Olympics?

24. Biathlon skiing includes rifle shooting. True or False?

25. Which of these countries has a ski slope: Lesotho, Morocco?

SPORTS & LEISURE

Basketball

1. James Naismith, the inventor of basketball, also introduced the helmet into football. True or False?

2. In which year did basketball become an Olympic sport?

3. How does a referee signal a jump ball?

4. What was Michael Jordan's jersey number (now retired) when he played for the Chicago Bulls?

5. Who is the NBA's all-time leading points scorer?

6. Which is the most successful team in NBA history?

7. Which is the most successful British men's basketball team?

8. Who holds the NBA all-time record for rebounds?

9. Which country won gold in the women's basketball tournament at the 2016 Olympics?

10. Who holds the NBA all-time record for playoff points?

11. When was the Women's British Basketball League founded?

12. Who is the shortest player to have played in the NBA?

13. The circumference of the women's basketball is bigger than the men's. True or False?

14. Who has won the NBA MVP award most often?

15. The baskets are lower for women's basketball than they are for the men's game. True or False?

16. Leonardo DiCaprio, Demi Moore, and Pete Sampras are all fans of which NBA team?

17. Who invented the game in 1891?

18. Which was the first NBA team to win more than 70 games in a regular season?

19. How many NBA titles did Magic Johnson win with the L.A. Lakers?

20. Which NBA MVP was nicknamed "the Mailman," because he always delivered?

21. How many players are allowed on court at the same time?

22. Which term describes an unblocked shot that misses the basket, the rim, and the backboard?

23. In which British city are the Giants based?

24. Which new kind of shot did Joe Fulks introduce in basketball in one game in 1949?

25. When would a player be awarded a free throw?

Famous Soccer Players in History

1. How old was Stanley Matthews when he retired?

2. Jimmy Greaves scored 266 goals for which club?

3. Which player was nicknamed "the Lion of Vienna"?

4. Tom Finney trained for which trade?

5. Billy Meredith signed for Manchester United from which club?

6. Who was the captain for England in the historic home 6–3 defeat by Hungary in 1953?

7. Which Busby Babe survived the Munich air crash to star for England in the 1966 World Cup?

8. In which position did Tommy Lawton mainly play?

9. In Len Shackleton's autobiography, what did he write for the chapter "What the average director knows about football"?

10. Len Shackleton was known as the "Clown… of football"?

11. Which playing formation did Herbert Chapman popularize at Arsenal?

12. Which club did Jimmy Hill manage between 1961 and 1967?

13. Johnny Haynes was the first player to earn how much per week?

14. Which club did Bobby Moore play for in 1975?

15. How old was Alan Ball when he played in the 1966 World Cup Final?

16. Which former England goalkeeper lost an eye in a car accident?

17. Liverpool is home to Liverpool and which other club?

18. Sir Bobby Robson played for Blackpool. True or False?

19. The 1982 FA Cup final went to a replay. True or False?

20. Which club's badge features a reference to the Manchester Ship Canal?

21. Which former Northern Ireland and Manchester United player has an airport named after him in Belfast?

22. What was Stanley Matthew's nickname?

23. When did Jimmy Greaves win his first England cap?

24. For which country did Denis Law win international caps?

25. Which Welsh player joined Juventus in 1957 and was known as the "Gentle Giant"?

       (Answers on page 502)

SPORTS & LEISURE

The Beautiful Game

1. In which year was Roy Hodgson made the manager of England?

2. Which soccer player was named Premier League Player of the Year in 2019?

3. Which club did Robin van Persie play for during the 2011/2012 season?

4. Brazilian Neymar moved from Barcelona for a world-record fee in 2017 to which club?

5. Which manager quit Barcelona after losing in the 2012 Champions League semifinal?

6. Who won the 2019 Champions League?

7. Who managed England in the 2018 World Cup finals?

8. The top league of German soccer is called the *Bundesliga*. True or False?

9. Which controversial technology was first used in 2012?

10. Who became the owner of Chelsea F.C. in 2003?

11. Inter and AC are clubs based in which Italian city?

12. Which team did David Beckham play for in 2011?

13. Which national team does Lionel Messi play for?

14. Who is the most-capped England goalkeeper of all time?

15. Which English soccer club did Cristiano Ronaldo play for before moving to Real Madrid?

16. The 2016 European Championships took place in Portugal. True or False?

17. Who once said, "[Soccer] is a simple game. Twenty-two men chase a ball for 90 minutes and at the end, the Germans always win"?

18. Who won the English Premier League in 2015–2016?

19. The top soccer league in Spain is called *La Liga*. True or False?

20. How many years was Arsene Wenger the manager of Arsenal Football Club?

21. Which Russian, nicknamed the "Black Panther," is widely regarded as the greatest goalkeeper in the history of soccer?

22. Which former Liverpool and England player became the manager of Rangers F.C.?

23. Who is the first person in Scottish soccer history to win five league titles as a player and a manager?

24. Which English soccer team used to play at Maine Road?

25. Which nation won the first World Cup?

(Answers on page 502)

Winter Sports

1. Briton Amy Williams won Olympic gold in 2010 in which event?

2. Which structure that is used in extreme sports such as snowboarding and skateboarding resembles a cross section of a swimming pool?

3. The legendary Hahnenkamm downhill ski course is in which country?

4. The target zone in curling is known as what?

5. Cross-country skiing is also known as "Nordic" what?

6. The Winter Olympics were first held in which year?

7. In which city did Torvill and Dean win Olympic ice-skating gold in 1984?

8. Which sport has been contested at every Winter Olympics since 1936?

9. The Cresta Run racing track is located where?

10. Visors, gloves, and finger spikes are worn in which Olympic sport?

11. Super G combines downhill-style speed with which other skiing discipline?

12. When was snowboarding first included as a sport in the Winter Olympics?

13. Which nation's ice hockey team was known as the Big Red Machine?

14. Ski-jump contests are measured solely by distance achieved. True or False?

15. Complete the name of this famous Austrian skier: Franz K. …

16. An expert-graded slope in Europe is denoted by which color?

17. Curling stones are traditionally made from which rock?

18. Which Briton stole the ski-jumping show in the 1986 Olympics?

19. Snowboarder Shaun White is known as "the Flying" what?

20. Name the sport in which "body checking" is allowed?

21. One minute may be added to a competitor's time for failing to hit targets in which sport?

22. Which country has won the most gold medals at the Winter Olympics for speed skating?

23. Which Olympic sport has a two-men and two-women variation?

24. Who won a gold medal for Great Britain at the 2018 Winter Olympics and in which sport?

25. In ice hockey, which team won the Stanley Cup in 2019?

Tennis Challenge

1. The US Open is played where?

2. Who was the youngest man to win the US Open, at age 19 in 1990?

3. What was the score in the final set of the 2010 Wimbledon match between John Isner and Nicolas Mahut?

4. What word is used in tennis for "zero"?

5. Which two players met in three consecutive Wimbledon finals in 1988, 1989, and 1990?

6. In which Grand Slam event has Rafael Nadal had the most success?

7. How many Olympic gold medals has Andy Murray won?

8. What is the most prestigious international men's team competition?

9. Which Czech-American won 94 men's singles titles?

10. Who is the youngest player ranked in the top 100 by the Women's Tennis Association?

11. How many weeks did Martina Navratilova reign as women's world No. 1?

12. Ashleigh Barty comes from New Zealand. True or False?

13. Which is the only Grand Slam tournament played on grass?

14. Complete John McEnroe's famous on-court outburst: "You cannot be… "

15. What is the name of a soft shot that drops just over the net?

16. What is the women's equivalent of the Davis Cup?

17. In which year were the first Wimbledon Championships held?

18. How high should a standard tennis net be at the posts?

19. Most modern rackets are made of what?

20. It is illegal to serve underarm. True or False?

21. How many kilos of strawberries are eaten at Wimbledon during the tournament fortnight?

22. What is the "Venus Rosewater Dish"?

23. When was tennis first included as a sport in the Olympic Games?

24. What is the minimum number of points needed to win a tennis tie-break?

25. What are the names of the American identical twins who are the most successful men's doubles players of all time?

SPORTS & LEISURE

Water Sports

1. When did synchronized swimming become an Olympic sport?

2. Which event features up to 25 "gates"?

3. Which British diver won bronze in the men's synchronized 10 m platform event at the 2016 Olympics?

4. The Oxford-Cambridge Boat Race starts at which bridge?

5. When did windsurfing become an Olympic sport?

6. The swimming distance of 2.4 miles (3.86 km) belongs to which form of triathlon?

7. Who partnered Steve Redgrave to 1992 Olympic gold in the coxless pairs?

8. A wishbone boom is a part of which equipment?

9. Name the teams in the infamous and violent 1956 Olympic Water Polo semifinal.

10. Which diver hit his head on the springboard in the 1988 Olympics prelim rounds?

11. The modern pentathlon includes swimming, running, and pistol shooting. True or False?

12. Which stroke is used in the pentathlon swimming event?

13. Tanya Streeter was a famous competitor in skin diving. True or False?

14. The venue for the swimming stage in the 2016 Olympics triathlon was what?

15. In rowing, competitors cross the finish line backward. True or False?

16. Synchronized diving made its Olympic debut in which year?

17. How many players are there on a water-polo team?

18. Water-skiing originated where in 1922?

19. What are the two canoeing disciplines in the Olympics?

20. Synchronized swimmers perform their routines to music. True or False?

Slam Dunking

1. Luol Deng was born in which country?

2. Which team has "Sweet Georgia Brown" for its theme tune?

3. How long did the USSR team take to score the winning points in the 1972 Olympic basketball finals?

4. What are the initials of basketball's world governing body?

5. At the start of 2011, who held the record as the NBA's all-time leading scorer?

6. In which position did Wilt Chamberlain excel?

7. What is the panel behind a hoop called?

8. What did Dennis Rodman wear in a PR stunt for his autobiography?

9. FC Barcelona is a basketball team. True or False?

10. John Amaechi played for which team in the 2000–2001 season?

11. What is the optimum length of a basketball court?

12. Which area of a basketball court is sometimes called the "key"?

13. When was the decision made to allow pros to play in the Olympics?

14. In 1936, the I.B.F. proposed a rule banning players taller than 6 ft 3 in (1.9 m). True or False?

15. Women's basketball became an Olympic event at which Games?

16. Larry Bird played for which team as a pro?

17. How high from the ground is the rim of the basket?

18. How tall is Houston Rockets star Yao Ming?

19. Basketball is a contact sport. True or False?

20. When did basketball become an Olympic sport, and who won the first game?

21. When was women's basketball included in the Olympics, and who won?

22. Complete the name of this basketball movie: *White Men Can't*

23. Who has played the most games in his lifetime?

24. An NBA basketball game has four quarters of how many minutes each?

25. How many substitutes are allowed during the course of a game?

Swimming

1. How long is an Olympic-standard pool?

2. Anita Lonsbrough won the 200m breaststroke gold for Britain at which Olympics?

3. What are the platforms called from which swimmers dive in competitive swimming?

4. The minimum depth for an Olympic and World Championship pool is what?

5. The flip turn is used in only two of the four strokes in swimming. Which are they?

6. Under FINA rules, goggles may not be worn. True or False?

7. In 2015, at the age of 10, who became the youngest competitive swimmer in World Championship history?

8. Which world record did Katie Ledecky (USA) set at the 2016 Olympics?

9. What does the "NA" in governing body FINA stand for?

10. The 14th World Swimming Championships were held in Shanghai. True or False?

11. Great Britain won a silver medal in the men's 4 x 200m freestyle relay at the Rio Olympics in 2016. True or False?

12. Which endurance swim did Sarah Thomas achieve in 2019?

13. Which innovation contributed to 29 world records in the 2009 World Championships?

14. How long did Ben Lecomte take to swim the Atlantic unaided in 1998?

15. Which swimmer set new Games records in the men's 50m and 100m butterfly at the 2018 Commonwealth Games?

16. Who won a record seven gold medals at the 1972 Olympics?

17. Who broke that record with eight golds at the 2008 Games?

18. Backstroke, breaststroke, freestyle... Which stroke completes the medley list?

19. How many gold medals did Ian Thorpe win in the 2000 Sydney Olympics (solo and team)?

20. How many world records did Thorpe set (solo and team)?

Rugby

1. What is the name of the Rugby Union World Cup trophy?

2. Complete the name of this French rugby union legend: Serge…

3. What is the mascot of RL Wakefield Trinity Wildcats club?

4. In which year did the Barbarians famously beat New Zealand 23–11 in Cardiff?

5. What specialty equipment do players wear to protect their mouths and teeth?

6. How many ways are there to score in Rugby Union?

7. Who was the top try scorer in the RL Super League in 2019?

8. England's Jonny Wilkinson kicked the 2003 World Cup–winning drop goal with his left foot. True or False?

9. When did the split between Rugby League and Rugby Union take place in England?

10. Who was the famous BBC Rugby League commentator in the 1960s and 1970s?

11. Which Rugby Union club plays at the Stoop?

12. The Calcutta Cup is a competition between which RFU nations?

13. Which team has won the Rugby League Challenge Cup a record 19 times?

14. What is Rugby League great Martin Offiah's nickname?

15. Which team won the Super League Grand Final in 2019?

16. Welsh legend J. P. R. Williams is also a qualified what?

17. Where did Wales play their home RU matches before the Millennium Stadium?

18. Whose autobiography is titled *Beware of the Dog*?

19. The newly rebuilt Twickenham stadium opened in which year?

20. Established in 1926, which English rugby league side plays at Wheldon Road?

21. Which nation joined the Five Nations Championship to make it six in 2000?

22. Kicking the ball while it is in play in rugby is illegal. True or False?

23. Which player was the first to score 200 tries in the RL Super League?

24. The Rugby League Challenge Cup was first contested in which year?

25. Who is the leading try scorer in All Blacks' history?

(Answers on page 503)

Olympic Gold

1. Ed Moses won 400 m hurdle gold medals in which years?

2. How long is the cross-country run in the Pentathlon?

3. When was the first Olympic-torch relay run?

4. When tennis was reintroduced in 1988 as an Olympic event, who won the women's gold?

5. Los Angeles held the Olympics in 1984 and which other year?

6. What was Ben Johnson's time in the 1988 100 m final before he was disqualified?

7. Who won 5000 m, 10,000 m, and marathon golds in the 1952 games?

8. "Clean and jerk" is a class in which sport?

9. In 1980, which British swimmer won gold in the 100 m breaststroke?

10. What is the nickname of Equatorial Guinea swimmer Eric Moussambani?

11. Leni Riefenstahl's film about the 1936 games was titled *Olympia*. True or False?

12. What was the name given to the USA's all-star basketball team in 1992?

13. Who won three gymnastics golds in 1972?

14. What was the main stadium for the 1908 games?

15. Alberto Juantorena won gold in the 1976 400 m and 800 m for which nation?

16. When were the games canceled due to World War I?

17. How high is the highest Olympic diving platform?

18. Rome hosted the Olympics in which year?

19. How many points are awarded for hitting the inner gold circle in archery?

20. Abebe Bikila won the 1960 Marathon running barefoot. True or False?

F1

1. How many times did Juan Manuel Fangio win the F1 world championship?

2. At which racetrack did Niki Lauda suffer a near-fatal crash in 1976?

3. Which was the first purpose-built F1 track?

4. How old was Sebastian Vettel when he became the youngest world champion in 2010?

5. Name the two American winners of the F1 driver's championship.

6. Slick tires will have zero grip in which track condition?

7. What distinguished the 1976 Tyrrell P34 car?

8. What is Ferrari's famous racing symbol?

9. What Italian name is given to Ferrari fans?

10. Ayrton Senna won how many Grand Prix races?

11. The Monaco Grand Prix was first held in which year?

12. The initials "BAR" stand for which team?

13. Which Italian track was famous for its banked bends?

14. A yellow warning flag means what?

15. Which modern Grand Prix is raced at night?

16. Michael Schumacher won the first of his seven titles with which team?

17. Which form of engine, not used since 1988, reappeared in F1 in 2014?

18. Which type of construction is the Kurtis-Offenhauser racing car?

19. What is the record for the fastest F1 pit stop, recorded in 1993?

20. The Monaco circuit includes the slowest corner in Formula One. True or False?

21. How fast can F1 cars travel while qualifying for a race?

22. How many points are awarded to the winning driver in a Formula 1 race?

23. How many times did Michael Schumacher win the F1 World Championship?

24. What were introduced to F1 cars in the 1960s to increase aerodynamic downforce?

25. How many teams competed in Formula 1's debut season in 1950?

SPORTS & LEISURE

It's All about the Bike

1. Chris Boardman rode a bike manufactured by which sports car maker?

2. In which race does the sprint leader wear a pink jersey?

3. How many gold medals did Chris Hoy win at the 2012 Olympics?

4. Which year was the first Tour de France held?

5. Which is a former name for the Tour of Britain: Milk Race, Coffee Tour, Round Britain Whizz?

6. Which mountain in the Tour de France is named after the peak's often windy conditions?

7. Which cyclist dominated the classic Milan–San Remo race in the 1960s and 1970s?

8. How many cycling medals did Team GB win at the Rio Olympics in 2016?

9. Bradley Wiggins was first British rider to win what in 2012?

10. How many gold medals did Laura Trott (Laura Kenny) win in the 2012 Olympic Games?

11. What does "BMX" stand for?

12. In which cycling disciplines do bikes have no brakes?

13. What color jersey does the leader of the Vuelta a Espana wear?

14. In a road race, what is a "peloton"?

15. What does "KOM" mean?

16. What is a 100-mile bike ride called?

17. Which kind of bike is used for off-road cycling?

18. What was the first "modern" bike of 1886?

19. What is the name for the variable-ratio transmission gearing used on many bikes?

20. In mountain-biking ratings, what do two black diamonds mean?

A Game of Two Halves

1. Which British club won the European Cup in 1967?

2. The pre-eminent club competition in South America is called the Copa what?

3. Emmanuel Adebayor played for which African nation?

4. Who was top scorer in the 1982 World Cup Finals?

5. The defensive strategy *catenaccio* translates to what?

6. Which player has made the most appearances in Premier League history?

7. Which Scottish club plays at Pittodrie?

8. Which team plays at Estadio da Luz?

9. Which team captain led France to World Cup victory in 2018?

10. Alf Ramsey's England side in 1966 were dubbed the "Wingless" what?

11. Who managed Barcelona in the 1986 European Cup final?

12. Who was the last Manchester United player to win the Ballon d'Or before Cristiano Ronaldo?

13. Jack Charlton managed which side in the 1994 World Cup?

14. Ruud Gullit made his debut for which Dutch club?

15. Gullit, Marco Van Basten, and which other Dutch player completed a famous trio at AC Milan?

16. José Mourinho succeeded whom as Chelsea's manager?

17. What is the diameter of the center circle?

18. Which two teams play in the Giuseppe Meazza?

19. Until 2010, the English National Football Stadium was based where?

20. What was Rio Ferdinand's first professional club?

SPORTS & LEISURE

(Answers on page 503) **307**

American Sports

1. How many players are there on a baseball team?

2. In which year was the first Super Bowl played?

3. Which team won the first Super Bowl?

4. On December 19, 2010, the New York Giants beat the Philadelphia Eagles by seven points. True or False?

5. Which sport do the Buffalo Sabres play?

6. Who is the latest Major League Baseball player to reach 3,000 hits?

7. At 7 ft 10 in (239 cm), Romanian Gheorghe Muresan is the tallest player in NBA history. True or False?

8. In 1997, which golf pro was the youngest male to be Masters champion?

9. Who was the 2019 women's US Open tennis champion?

10. In which year was Michael Jordan drafted by the Chicago Bulls?

11. Which African-American Olympian won four gold medals for the US at the Berlin Olympic Games in 1936?

12. The Vancouver Canucks shut out the Boston Bruins in the final game of the 2011 Stanley Cup Final. True or False?

13. Which city does the Redskins football team come from?

14. In which year did Serena Williams beat Venus Williams in the US Open quarterfinals?

15. Which tennis player won the men's US Open in 1990, becoming the youngest-ever champion?

16. Barry Bonds broke Roger Maris's record for the most home runs hit in a season. True or False?

17. How many perfect games were thrown in the 2012 Major League Baseball season?

18. Which was the first American city to host the Summer Olympic Games?

19. In which sport is it sometimes said the term "home run" originated?

20. In 1972, which football team hired the first professional cheerleading squad?

21. Which was the first South American city to host the Olympic Games?

22. Which team won the Super Bowl in 2020?

23. Which two American women skaters had a battle on and off the ice rink in 1994?

24. Where is the Astros baseball team from?

25. Which game do the Detroit Pistons play?

Sports Records

1. Jade Jones won gold medals for Great Britain in both the 2012 and 2016 Olympics. Which sport does she compete in?

2. At which Olympic Games was women's boxing included for the first time?

3. Which baseball player holds the record for the most consecutive games in a career?

4. A marathon was once run in under two hours. True or False?

5. After retiring from professional cycling, which other sport did Bradley Wiggins briefly try to make a career in?

6. How quickly did Larry Lewis, the world-record holder for runners 100 years or older, run the 100-yard dash?

7. What is the world-record time for the mile run?

8. Which WWE superstar did Tyson Fury wrestle in 2019?

9. Ken Bradshaw surfed the tallest wave yet recorded in 1998. How tall was it?

10. Which NFL team has won the most Super Bowl trophies?

11. Who is the last non-British, non-German Formula 1 driver to win the World Driver's title?

12. How many gold medals did US swimmer Michael Phelps win at the 2008 Olympics?

13. Which NFL quarterback holds the record for most passing yards in a single season?

14. In 2012, London became the first city to host the modern Olympics for the fifth time. True or False?

15. The Indianapolis Motor Speedway is the largest sporting venue in the world. At maximum capacity, how many people can it hold?

16. At his peak, how much did Konishiki Yasokichi, the world's heaviest sumo wrestler, weigh?

17. In which sport do competitors refer to "catching a crab"?

18. More than 5,000 single strokes have been recorded in one squash rally. True or False?

19. In which sport do competitors use equipment known as a "foil"?

20. What is the approximate distance run by a midfielder during a soccer game?

SPORTS & LEISURE

Surfing

1. What word is used to describe a fall from a wave?

2. Complete the name of this surfing trick: "Hang…"

3. Complete the name of this classic surfing film: *Big…*

4. Which kind of surfer is a "Hodad"?

5. Which coast is famous for surf in Australia?

6. The European expedition that first encountered surfing in Tahiti was led by which seafarer?

7. Who has won the ASP World Surfing title 11 times?

8. The famous Waikiki surfing beach lies close to which city?

9. Which town is a hub for surfing in England?

10. Chris Martin of Coldplay is an avid surfer. True or False?

11. Surfers Paradise is in which country?

12. Which band recorded the album *Surfer Girl*?

13. Who plays the leader of the bank-robbing surfer gang in the film *Point Break*?

14. Surfing is an Olympic sport. True or False?

15. Jeffreys Bay is a famous surf beach in which country?

16. What name is given to the legendary pipeline break off Oahu?

17. Women are not allowed to surf competitively. True or False?

18. What is the name of a famous Hawaiian surfing island?

19. What do surfers apply to their boards to improve performance?

20. Which word beginning with "T" describes the wave feature that surfers aim to speed through?

     (Answers on page 504)

Diving

1. Which professional diver famously hit his head on the springboard in the 1988 Seoul Olympics?

2. What are the two disciplines in Olympic diving?

3. When did synchronized diving become an Olympic event?

4. In which is a diving accident most likely: deep or shallow water?

5. The highest platform in Olympic diving is 33 ft (10 m). True or False?

6. After which Olympic Games was plain high diving discontinued?

7. Solomon Islander Alex Wickham set the record for a high dive at 205 ft (62 m) in 1918. True or False?

8. The impact of Alex Wickham's world-record 205-ft (62-m) high dive ripped off his bathing suit and knocked him unconscious. True or False?

9. Shallow diving is an extreme sport that involves diving from the greatest height into the shallowest depth of water. True or False?

10. In which awkward dive does the abdomen and chest bear the impact?

11. In which country do the La Quebrada Cliff Divers dive 125 ft (35 m) into the sea?

12. Who won a gold medal in the 3 m springboard event at the 2012 Olympic Games?

13. In which year did diving become an Olympic event?

14. As what was Olympic platform diving first known?

15. Which country has won more 10 m platform-diving Olympic golds than any other?

16. A diver's splash on entry affects his or her score in professional diving. True or False?

17. When a diver enters the water without a splash, this is called what?

18. In which position should the body enter the water during a professional dive?

19. How many Olympic Gold medals did US diver Greg Louganis win during his career?

20. A diver takes off in the forward position but then reverses the spin toward the board. What is this dive called?

NFL

1. Which country hosted the first regular NFL season game to be held outside the US?

2. How many yards is a false start penalty?

3. Who holds the NFL record for quarterback sacks?

4. Who is the only player to appear in the NFL and CFL halls of fame?

5. Who holds the NFL all-time record for touchdowns?

6. In what year was the NFL formed?

7. What part of NFL uniform are the cleats worn?

8. The mascot of the Baltimore Ravens is named Poe, after the writer Edgar Allan Poe. True or False?

9. Who holds the NFL all-time record for touchdown passes?

10. Which is the highest-grossing football movie of all time in the US?

11. The Dallas Cowboys are the most valuable sports franchise in the world. True or False?

12. Which NFL team plays at the venue Soldier Field?

13. What is the highest number of fumbles recorded by one player in a single game?

14. Which is the most successful team in the history of the Super Bowl?

15. Which city has held the Super Bowl most often?

16. Which coach has made the most Super Bowl appearances?

17. How long is a regulation NFL football?

18. Who is the only NFL player to have a star on the Hollywood Walk of Fame?

19. Which player has won the Super Bowl MVP most times?

20. Which was the first NFL team to have cheerleaders?

Soccer's Top Prize

1. Which name was used for the World Cup Trophy before it was named in honor of Jules Rimet?

2. How many times has England hosted the World Cup?

3. How many countries have won the tournament a total of five times?

4. Cameroon's Roger Milla is the oldest player to have scored a goal at the World Cup. How old was he when he scored his last goal in 1994?

5. Which country has had the most red cards since the tournament began?

6. No European team has won a World Cup played outside Europe. True or False?

7. Which is the only country to appear in the knockout stage of every tournament?

8. Which is the only host country to be eliminated in the first round of the tournament?

9. Which country has had the most success in penalty shootouts?

10. Which two teams played the first-ever World Cup match in 1930?

11. What is the highest-ever score in a World Cup match?

12. How many times has France lifted the trophy?

13. Which is the only year in which the previous winner did not open the tournament?

14. Who scored the most goals during the 1966 World Cup?

15. The most goals scored in a single World Cup by a single player is 19. True or False?

16. In which year was the first World Cup tournament held?

17. How many times has New Zealand won the World Cup?

18. Who won the first World Cup tournament?

19. Which country hosted the 2018 tournament?

20. How many of the tournament's 32 teams are from Europe?

(Answers on page 504)

Extreme Sports Challenge

1. Parkour originated in which country?

2. Which kind of turn do parachutists perform to land at high speed?

3. Waves in big-wave surfing can be up to what height?

4. Free climber Alain Robert suffers from vertigo. True or False?

5. Who won the first Monster Energy Cup championship in 2011?

6. Iconic 1970s skateboarder Tony Alva's nickname is what?

7. The world's first permanent bungee-jump site is in which country?

8. The Dangerous Sports Club was based in which English university city?

9. White-water rafting is a 2012 Olympic sport. True or False?

10. How fast can speed skiers travel?

11. What does the "B" in BASE jumping stand for?

12. How many times was Björn Dunkerbeck World PWA Windsurfing Champion?

13. The initials "MTB" stand for what?

14. Who was the first woman to climb the north face of the Eiger in the Alps?

15. Hanggliders utilize which weather feature to stay airborne?

16. When a surfer crashes, it's called a what?

17. For how long did free diver Peter Colat hold his breath in a dive in February 2010?

18. In kiteboarding, which term is used to refer to a "very early morning session"?

19. Bungee jumping is illegal in the US. True or False?

20. What is the main objective of wingsuit flying?

21. What is the name of the sport where competitors roll downhill inside an orb?

22. Which extreme sport is similar to tightrope walking?

23. Vertigo bungee is an extreme sport. True or False?

24. What power does a kiteboarder use to move?

25. When do the X Games take place?

Sports Records

1. By turnover, which football club was the richest in 2018–2019?

2. The world high-jump record of 8.04 ft (2.45 m) was set in 1993 by which athlete?

3. Which is the world's richest horse race?

4. In 2011, the world-record distance for a hole in one in golf was what?

5. In 2009, Usain Bolt broke the 100 m and 200 m world records. True or False?

6. As of 2011, who was the leading points scorer in Welsh International Rugby Union?

7. By 2011, the New York Yankees had won the World Series how many times?

8. Henry Cooper was the first (and, as of 2020, the only) boxer to win a Lonsdale Belt three times. True or False?

9. As of 2011, which NFL team had won the Super Bowl six times?

10. The 4 × 100 m men's swimming medley world record was set in 2009 by which country?

11. Bob Beamon held the world long-jump record for how many years?

12. Who was the first—and, to date, the only—man to win the tennis Grand Slam twice?

13. Andy Green broke the world land-speed record in 1997 in a vehicle called what?

14. The women's marathon world record is faster than the men's. True or False?

15. In 1962, Wilt Chamberlain achieved a record number of points for an NBA game. How many did he score?

16. Which constructor has won the most F1 Grand Prix?

17. The world's fastest go-kart can reach speeds of up to what?

18. The clean-and-jerk world weightlifting record was set at which Olympics?

19. The men's world hammer record distance is shorter than the javelin. True or False?

20. What is the record for the highest dive from a diving board?

SPORTS & LEISURE

Sailing

1. Joshua Slocum was the first person to sail around the world single-handed. True or False?

2. Zig-zagging through the eye of the wind to change direction describes which maneuver?

3. Name the type of boat that features two parallel hulls of equal size.

4. In which year did Robin Knox-Johnston become the first person to circumnavigate the globe nonstop?

5. Bruno Peyron and his crew won which prize in 2005?

6. How many sailing events were held at the 2016 Olympics?

7. The Fastnet Race takes place over how many nautical miles?

8. What was the name of Sir Francis Chichester's famous yacht?

9. How many Olympic gold medals has Ben Ainslie won?

10. A "yngling" is a cross between a planing dinghy and a what?

11. Which record did Ellen Macarthur set in 2005?

12. In which yacht did PM Edward Heath win the 1971 Admirals' Cup?

13. When was sailing included on an Olympic program for the first time?

14. What is a "halyard"?

15. In 2016, Thomas Coville sailed solo around the world in how many days?

16. The America's Cup was first won by which country other than the US in 1983?

17. What is a rudder used for?

18. The America's Cup dates back to which year?

19. Which sailor was capsized for five days during the 1997 Vendée Globe?

20. On a sailboat, what is a sheet?

21. The large, often colorful triangular sail used when the wind is coming from behind is called a what?

22. What is a tiller used for?

23. What is the main body of a boat called?

24. Which type of sailing yacht was the original *America*, which gave its name to the America's Cup?

25. A trimaran has four hulls. True or False?

Motorsports

1. Who holds the record for all-time most pole positions in F1 racing?

2. Motorcycling was a competitive event at the 1908 Olympics. True or False?

3. Engine capacity in MotoGP is limited to what?

4. Drag races are usually held over what distance?

5. The Le Mans 24 Hours race was first held in which year?

6. By 2019, how many motorcycling world constructor titles had Honda won?

7. In which year did Barry Sheene win the Motorcycle Grand Prix World Championship?

8. Which former F1 driver is known as "the Flying Scot"?

9. Colin McRae won the world rallying championship in which year?

10. How many times did McRae's father Jimmy win the British rally title?

11. The "S" in NASCAR stands for what?

12. The Borg-Warner Trophy is awarded to the winner of which race?

13. Porsche won the Le Mans 24 Hours race how many times in the 1980s?

14. Who is the only man to win motor racing's Triple Crown?

15. Valentino Rossi won the 2009 world motorcycle title on which make of bike?

16. Which character did Steve McQueen play in the 1971 film *Le Mans*?

17. Whose autobiography is titled *Winning is not Enough*?

18. "ATV" stands for what?

19. The most famous TT race takes place on which island?

20. The waving of the French flag is used to start the Le Mans 24 Hours. True or False?

21. How many times has Lewis Hamilton won the Formula 1 World Championship?

22. Approximately how many cars compete in Le Mans every year?

23. What was the color of the first Indian motorcycles?

24. In which year was NASCAR founded?

25. What is the corporate color for Kawasaki motorcycles?

SPORTS & LEISURE

Opening Overs

1. What is an umpire signaling if he stands with both arms out horizontally?

2. Which side won the first Cricket World Cup in 1975?

3. The Big Bash League is based in which country?

4. Who scored a record 501 not out for Warwickshire in 1994?

5. What are the horizontal pieces of wood on top of the cricket stumps called?

6. The initials "MCC" stand for what?

7. In which year did Ben Stokes make his Test debut for England?

8. West Indies captain Clive Lloyd was nicknamed what?

9. The Brisbane Cricket Ground is also known as what?

10. A batsman can be out in 10 ways. True or False?

11. Who hit a record six sixes in one over in 1968?

12. Who partnered Jeff Thomson in the Australian pace attack of the 1970s?

13. Which team won the ICC Cricket World Cup in 2019?

14. Which cricketer has been called by these different nicknames: The Big 'Un, the Old Man, the Champion, and the Doctor?

15. Andrew Flintoff captained England in the victorious 2010–2011 Ashes series. True or False?

16. Who has scored the most runs for England in Test Match cricket?

17. Which cricket team is known as the Black Caps?

18. In which country is the IPL played?

19. What ground has been the "home" of English cricket since 1787?

20. What name is given to the Test series between England and Australia?

(Answers on page 505)

Horse Racing

1. Who rode Desert Orchid to Cheltenham Gold Cup victory in 1989?

2. The film *Champions* relates the real-life success of which Grand National–winning horse and jockey?

3. What is the course distance of the Epsom Derby?

4. How many times did Lester Piggott win the Epsom Derby?

5. The Kentucky Derby is not open to geldings. True or False?

6. The Prix de l'Arc de Triomphe is run at which course?

7. Willie Shoemaker's nickname was what?

8. Which type of horse race is the Melbourne Cup?

9. How many times did Red Rum win the Grand National?

10. Who was the Grand National's winning jockey in 1981?

11. In which year did Phar Lap win the Agua Caliente Handicap?

12. Which horse won both the 2018 and 2019 Grand National races?

13. Which English artist is recognized as the pre-eminent painter of horses?

14. The famous Il Palio is held in which Italian city?

15. Thoroughbred racehorses can trace ancestry to just three Arabian stallions. True or False?

16. Where is the Sha Tin racecourse?

17. Newmarket, the home of English racing, is in which county?

18. Which horse mysteriously fell just yards from winning the 1956 Grand National?

19. In which year did the first woman jockey ride in the Grand National?

20. The Kiplingcotes Derby is the oldest horse race in the world. True or False?

21. Horse-racing jackets and helmets are known as what?

22. Which father and son trained and rode the winning horse in the 2000 Grand National?

23. The queen has her own thoroughbred breeding stud. On which of the Royal Estates is this situated?

24. Jockey Frankie Dettori famously won 7 out of 7 races at which race course in 1995?

25. Which English king rode in several races at Newmarket?

Golf

1. How old was Tiger Woods when he won his first professional major?

2. Which course has hosted the most US Open tournaments?

3. In which year did Brooks Koepka win his first major?

4. How many dimples are there on a regular golf ball?

5. Who won the 2019 Women's British Open?

6. Despite playing golf left-handed, Phil Mickelson is actually right-handed. True or False?

7. Since 1979, how many Ryder Cup tournaments has the United States won?

8. Which player holds the record for PGA Tour career wins?

9. Which major has Rory McIlroy not won?

10. Tom Watson won how many consecutive PGA Player of the Year awards?

11. How old was Raymond Floyd when he became the oldest player to finish second in a Masters?

12. Holes 11, 12, and 13 at Augusta National are known as what?

13. Which nationality is Inbee Park, the youngest winner of the US Women's Open?

14. Which golfer was nicknamed "the Walrus"?

15. Which player has accrued the most points in the history of the Ryder Cup?

16. Tiger Woods won all five of his matches in the 2009 Presidents Cup. True or False?

17. What is the average hitting distance for a 3-wood golf club?

18. Who was the USA team captain in the first five Ryder Cup tournaments?

19. Which player holds the record for most Masters victories?

20. In which year did Europe first compete against America in the Ryder Cup?

21. Which PGA Tour golfer was hospitalized after injuring himself with his own putter?

22. Which course has been used more often than any other for the Open Championship?

23. What is the maximum number of clubs a player is allowed to carry in a golf bag?

24. In which year was the first round of women's golf played?

25. The first golf balls were made of feathers wrapped in leather. True or False?

SPORTS & LEISURE

Formula One

1. The "K" in KERS stands for what?

2. Who was the first Australian to win the F1 World Championship?

3. How many points are awarded to the winning driver in a Formula One race?

4. Which American track held F1 races between 1961 and 1980?

5. Prior to 2011, which was the last year in which a woman attempted to qualify for a Grand Prix?

6. Formula One cars travel at speeds of up to 220 mph (350 kmph). True or False?

7. Ferrari was originally a works team for which manufacturer?

8. Who was Renault's driver for their and his first world championship?

9. How many times will a driver change gear in an average race?

10. How many races did Ligier win between 1976 and 1996?

11. Jaguar Racing placed what in the nose cones of their cars in the 2004 Monaco Grand Prix?

12. How many Grand Prix races did Alain Prost win?

13. For which team did Juan Fangio and Stirling Moss both race in 1955?

14. The 1960 Ferrari D246 was the last front-engined car to win a Grand Prix. True or False?

15. With which team did James Hunt begin his F1 career?

16. Which car did Mario Andretti drive for his 1978 F1 title?

17. How many drivers can each Formula One team use in one season?

18. Cockpit temperatures in an F1 race car can reach 140°F (60°C). True or False?

19. Lewis Hamilton's first Grand Prix race win was in which country?

20. What does the "P" on the pit board indicate?

SPORTS & LEISURE

(Answers on page 505)   **321**

Soccer

1. With which club did Harry Redknapp begin his managerial career?

2. Who managed Brazil in the 2018 World Cup?

3. The Kop at Anfield is named after which Boer War battle?

4. The laws of the game were first devised in which year?

5. Which club side was formed as an arm of the Yugoslav Army in Belgrade?

6. Diego Maradona won two World Cup winner's medals. True or False?

7. Which English club's motto is *Nil satis, nisi optimum*?

8. Who was the first England player to reach 100 caps?

9. For which US team did Wayne Rooney play in 2019?

10. How far is the penalty spot from the goal line?

11. Goalkeeper Dave Beasant once severed a tendon by dropping what onto his foot?

12. Manchester United has played home games at Maine Road. True or False?

13. Which German striker was nicknamed "Der Bomber"?

14. Spain's Copa del Rey competition was known as what during Franco's dictatorship?

15. The 2018 World Cup final was played in which stadium?

16. Who managed Hungary to the 6–3 defeat of England in 1953?

17. Which striker to date has scored the most goals for Italy?

18. "Viola" is the nickname of which Italian club?

19. When was the Dutch Eredivisie league founded?

20. Which 14th-century English king banned soccer?

Boxing Clever

1. Whom did Mike Tyson beat to win his first world heavyweight title?

2. Who was the last British world heavyweight champion before Lennox Lewis?

3. Which body governed British boxing until 1929?

4. Who was Cassius Clay's first opponent as a pro?

5. Who was known as "the Clones Cyclone"?

6. Whose nickname was "Manos de Piedra" ("Hands of Stone")?

7. Where was Charlie Magri born?

8. How many times did Sugar Ray Robinson win the world middleweight title?

9. What was Sugar Ray Robinson's real name?

10. Which British promoter survived a murder attempt in 1989?

11. What is the name of Emanuel Steward's famous Detroit gym?

12. What are left-handed boxers called?

13. What part or parts of Evander Holyfield's body did Mike Tyson bite in the 1997 fight?

14. Henry Cooper never won a world title. True or False?

15. Boxer Rocky Graziano was known for which boxing skill?

16. The person who advises a boxer during a fight is called a corner man. True or False?

17. How old was Muhammad Ali when he first regained his world heavyweight title?

18. The common weight for a competition glove is how many ounces?

19. Boxing was never part of the ancient Olympics. True or False?

20. What does "TKO" stand for?

(Answers on page 506)   **323**

SPORTS & LEISURE

SPORTS & LEISURE

Running

1. What should a runner ideally eat for breakfast before a marathon: oatmeal and honey, baked beans, fried eggs and bacon, nothing?

2. Who broke the women's marathon world record in 2019 with a time of 2:14:4?

3. When was the first Olympic marathon of modern times?

4. According to the Oxford English Dictionary, how many meanings does the word "run" have?

5. Who won the women's 100 meter in the 2016 Olympic Games?

6. How many runners (approximately) have run in recent London marathons?

7. The steeplechase combines the skills of distance running, hurdling, and long jumping in one race. True or False?

8. Based on the number of participants, what is the world's largest running race?

9. People suffering from patellofemoral pain syndrome have pain where?

10. Today's marathon distance is 26.2 miles. When was this distance first set?

11. Who ran the first sub-four-minute mile?

12. Who set the men's marathon world record in 2018 with a time of 2:01:39?

13. Who is the first-known marathon runner in history?

14. How is a runner's pace calculated?

15. What is running cadence?

16. Where is the world's highest marathon held?

17. On average, how many calories does a person burn during an hour of jogging?

18. What is the main difference in gait between running and walking?

19. After several heart procedures, which US president famously took up jogging?

20. What causes sore muscles after running?

From Surf to Turf: Australian Sports

1. The Australian national women's netball team is nicknamed what?

2. Which team won the 2019 AFL premiership?

3. Who won the 2019 Melbourne Cup?

4. The day of the Melbourne Cup is a public holiday in Victoria. True or False?

5. The Sydney–Hobart yacht race begins on which day?

6. Who was the captain of the Australian cricket team in summer 2019?

7. Who won the 2020 men's singles title at the Australian Open?

8. Which teams entered the AFL competition prior to the Gold Coast Suns?

9. How many field umpires officiate an AFL game?

10. Who competes against NSW in the State of Origin series?

11. How many times has Australia hosted the Olympic Games?

12. Where is the Bathurst 1000 raced?

13. In which state capital is the Australian F1 Grand Prix held?

14. Cycling's Tour Down Under is held in which Australian state?

15. The main race at the Stawell Gift is over how many meters?

16. The AFL best and fairest player is awarded which medal?

17. How many teams compete from Australia in the A-League?

18. What was Sir Donald Bradman's batting average?

19. Who won the 2019–2020 Women's Big Bash League?

20. Which Australian won the Women's Singles tennis title in the 2019 French Open?

SPORTS & LEISURE

Medieval Sports

SPORTS & LEISURE

1. What is the medieval ancestor of ten-pin bowling?

2. Which modern game does the medieval stoolball most closely resemble?

3. Which of these is a stick-and-ball game of Gaelic origin: lacrosse, badminton, hurling?

4. Today it's an Olympic sport, but to which century does the hammer-throw date in Europe?

5. What was a "mêlée" in medieval jousting?

6. Colf is the medieval forerunner to golf. True or False?

7. In the Middle Ages, what was a joust *à plaisance?*

8. Where would a bowman practice archery in medieval England?

9. In the Middle Ages, only boys participated in sport and games. True or False?

10. In which century did jousting tournaments begin to die out in Europe?

11. What was commonly used in the medieval sport of stick fighting?

12. Which medieval people indulged in falconry?

13. By law in 1252, who in England was required to be equipped with a bow and arrows?

14. Which country began medieval mock battles called *carrousels?*

15. The modern sport of bowls was first developed in the Middle Ages. True or False?

16. How many arrows could a medieval longbow archer fire every minute?

17. In the Middle Ages, what was a joust *à l'outrance?*

18. Gameball was a medieval form of football. True or False?

19. How many crossbow bolts could a medieval archer fire every minute?

20. What equipment does the medieval game of horseshoes require, other than the horseshoes?

Horse Riding

1. When did dressage become an Olympic sport?

2. How many riders are there on a polo team?

3. Approximately when were horses first ridden: 10,000 BCE, 4,500 BCE, 500 BCE?

4. Which form of horse racing is the most popular worldwide?

5. Endurance riding usually features what breeds of horse?

6. Equestrian events became part of the Olympic Games when?

7. Name the show-jumping event where horses must jump a very high wall that gets higher with each round.

8. Western riding style was brought to the Americas by the Spanish conquistadors. True or False?

9. Which British rider won the equestrian individual jumping Olympic gold medal in 2016?

10. Where does the CHIO show-jumping tournament take place?

11. What country's national horse-riding sport is called Buzkashi?

12. The competition of endurance riding often takes place over a 100-mile (160-km) radius. True or False?

13. Which former winning track cyclist made her competitive debut as a jockey in 2015?

14. In which year were the first Badminton Horse Trials held?

15. At the 1956 Olympic Games in Australia, all the equestrian events were held in Sweden. True or False?

16. During what historical period could you see horses involved in jousting?

17. Who was the first female jockey to ride in the Grand National?

18. Equestrian Olympic events are governed by the rules of the International Federation for Equestrian Sports. True or False?

19. In the 1932 Olympics in Los Angeles, the show-jumping course was so tough that what happened?

20. Until the 1952 Olympics in Helsinki, only which people were allowed to compete in Olympic dressage events?

CHAPTER 8

FOOD & DRINK

If you think you know your *udon* from your *bakmi*, then this is for you. Travel the world as you learn about exotic and everyday dishes and their origins, including cakes, pickles, herbs, pies, and shellfish... with vegetarian options!

Have You Got a Taste for It?

1. Sushi is basically what: raw fish and rice, pasta, mashed vegetables?

2. What is penne?

3. Is a sweet potato a vegetable or a fruit?

4. What is daal made from?

5. What is pasta made from?

6. What is a tarte tatin?

7. Which country first gave consumers Oreos?

8. Which British chef started with a restaurant called The Fat Duck?

9. Root beer is a popular fizzy drink. What was it originally made of?

10. Butter is added to tea to make butter tea (*po cha*) in which country?

11. Which type of cooking uses a tandoor: North Indian, Thai, Mexican?

12. In which country would you most likely be served food in a dish known as a "tagine"?

13. Tortillas are Mexican flat breads used in wraps, but the same word is also used for a different type of food. What is it?

14. Moussaka is the national dish of which country?

15. Where was Gouda cheese first made?

16. What is the most succulent part of Peking duck?

17. Where would you most likely be given a California roll?

18. Which type of pickle is in a Big Mac?

19. Where were deep-fried Mars bars invented?

20. What name is given to a Spanish doughnut that is dipped in melted chocolate?

FOOD & DRINK

Best of British

1. Which of these is a type of sweet suet pudding: Sussex pond, Norfolk royal, Shetland sassermeat?

2. What is an Aberdeen rowie?

3. Which Scottish delicacy did Robert Burns describe as "Great chieftain o' the puddin'-race"?

4. The main ingredient of Welsh rarebit is rabbit. True or False?

5. Which county is home to the Melton Mowbray pork pie?

6. What are usually offered with a traditional "cream tea," apart from a pot of tea?

7. Gloucester Old Spot is a breed of which British farm animal?

8. At which British sporting event are strawberries and cream traditionally served?

9. Fill in the missing word in this dish: "_____ in the hole."

10. Which of these ingredients is included in Mrs. Beeton's 1861 recipe for mince pies: minced lamb, minced pork, minced beef?

11. Marmalade is named after Mary, Queen of Scots, who enjoyed its health-giving properties: *pour* Marie *malade*. True or False?

12. What is NOT traditional in a British fry-up: eggs, hash browns, bacon?

13. Which small tree's flowers is traditionally used to flavor gooseberry jam and used to make cordial drinks?

14. There are recipes for cooking gray squirrel. True or False?

15. Which English county is noted for its oatcakes as well as for ceramics?

16. The Welsh baked delicacy Bara brith translates as…?

17. Which of these foods is regularly eaten in the UK: bangers and mash, fish and chips, chicken tikka marsala?

18. Name the British cheese that is the favorite of Wallace and Gromit.

19. What links Yorkshire pudding and the fish sold in chip shops?

20. When is the British asparagus season?

Oodles of Noodles

1. Noodle comes from the word *nudel*. From which language does it derive?

2. The world's oldest bowl of noodles was found preserved along the Yellow River in China. How old are the noodles estimated to be?

3. The first written record of dry pasta can be traced to Arab travelers from which century?

4. Udon is a wheat noodle associated with which country?

5. How is the noodle dish *Mie goreng* cooked?

6. With which country is the glass noodle salad most associated?

7. The term "chow mein" refers to a range of stir-fry noodle dishes. Which is its country of origin?

8. From what are cellophane noodles made?

9. In Korea, to which kind of noodles does *olchaeng-chi guksu* refer?

10. *Reshteh* noodles come from which ancient empire?

11. To which kind of noodles does the Chinese *bakmi* refer?

12. When did ramen noodles, which are based on Chinese noodles, become popular in Japan?

13. What are knife-cut Korean noodles called?

14. *Chilk naengmyeon* are chewy, transparent noodles. True or False?

15. What is the main ingredient of vermicelli?

16. *Lo mein* is a noodle casserole. True or False?

17. In which year were instant noodles first marketed in Japan?

18. During which dynasty did noodles become a staple for the Chinese people?

19. Acorn noodles are made from acorn meal. True or False?

20. Which country is most associated with the noodle dish Pad Thai?

21. Noodles and other pasta are what type of carbohydrate?

22. *Kugel* is a traditional Jewish dish featuring noodles. Is it a soup, a pudding, or a drink?

23. Which form of pasta takes its name from a Latin word meaning feather or quill—and hence a writing instrument?

24. What are Japanese buckwheat noodles called?

25. March is National Noodle Month in the US. True or False?

FOOD & DRINK

Easy Cheesy

1. What do cheeses require less of when made in cooler climates?

2. A lover of cheese is called a what?

3. In which European country is there archaeological evidence of cheesemaking dating from 5500 BCE?

4. Eating cheese before and after meals is thought to reduce what?

5. On the 4,000-year-old wall paintings of which African country have images of cheesemaking been found?

6. Where is manchego cheese from?

7. Which character from Homer's *Odyssey* makes cheese?

8. According to the British Cheese Board, how many varieties of cheese exist in the UK?

9. Roquefort is a blue cheese from which country?

10. What is the main feature of *casu marzu* cheese?

11. With which European country is *casu marzu* cheese most associated?

12. Fresh cheeses without additional preservatives will not spoil in a matter of days. True or False?

13. Which *Treasure Island* character asks Jim Hawkins: "You mightn't happen to have a piece of cheese about you, now"?

14. Which country is most associated with feta cheese?

15. Cornish *yarg* is wrapped in nettles. True or False?

16. According to a 2005 British Cheese Board study, cheese consumption before bedtime causes what?

17. Cheese in aerosol cans can commonly be found in the US. True or False?

18. Which popular Italian cheese is often made from domesticated water buffalo milk?

19. According to *The Proverbs of John Heywood* of 1546, the moon is made from what color of cheese?

20. Feta cheese can come from goat's or sheep's milk. True or False?

21. Monterey Jack cheese is from which state?

22. Roquefort is made with ewe, cow, or goat's milk?

23. What is distinctive about how Edam cheese looks?

24. You can make cheese from reindeer milk. True or False?

25. You cannot freeze hard cheese. True or False?

Regional American Cuisine

1. Where is Key lime the official state pie?

2. Which state is most associated with clam chowder?

3. Where did James Dewar first come up with the Twinkie in 1930?

4. Where are boiled peanuts not traditionally enjoyed in the US?

5. In which decade did fajita taco stands begin appearing at rodeos in Texas?

6. Where are Johnny cakes traditionally cooked in the US?

7. Which part of the United States is most associated with biscuits and gravy?

8. Which European immigrants introduced the Texan favorite of chicken-fried steak to America?

9. Which French dish is San Francisco's cioppino most like?

10. The American Indians of which state are thought to have discovered popcorn around 6,000 years ago?

11. Where in New York were Buffalo wings invented?

12. Which city does NOT claim to have invented barbecue ribs: Chicago, Dallas, Seattle?

13. The phrase "as American as apple pie" is not exactly accurate. Why?

14. Po' boy is a meat sandwich from which state?

15. What has been called the "queen of the New Mexican winter table"?

16. Where were chocolate chip cookies invented?

17. The cheeseburger allegedly derives from where in Los Angeles?

18. Chicago-style pizza comes with a thick crust. True or False?

19. On average, how many pizza slices are eaten in the US per person per year: 37, 42, 46, 50?

20. Which state boasts the sourest sourdough bread?

FOOD & DRINK

Shellfish

1. What kind of shellfish forms the heart of a clambake?

2. Whelks are bivalves, gastropods, or cephalopods?

3. Which kind of shellfish is often served in a cocktail?

4. What is opening an oyster shell called?

5. Which of these is NOT another name for the shellfish langoustine: Bernie Bay shuckler, Norway lobster, scampi?

6. Shellfish mostly eat phytoplankton and zooplankton. True or False?

7. Spaghetti alle vongole is made with which shellfish?

8. Which country is responsible for creating the lobster bisque?

9. Which dish features raw shellfish and fish marinated in lemon or lime juice?

10. Which of these is a type of prawn: tiger, lion, leopard?

11. Shellfish that smells strongly of ammonia should not be eaten. True or False?

12. The pipi is a shellfish found in which country?

13. Usually served on crushed ice, these are what?

14. Which region of the US is often associated with crabs?

15. Shellfish is one of the main ingredients of the South American curanto. With which country is it most associated?

16. More people died from oyster poisoning in 2006 than all of the global conflicts combined. True or False?

17. How is the French *plateau de fruits de mer* served?

18. She-crab soup is a favorite in the south of which country?

19. With which state are clams traditionally associated?

20. Moules are…?

21. Which part of a lobster is the tomally?

22. Shrimp and prawns are different species. True or False?

23. What is surf and turf?

24. What is a quahog?

25. Which bivalve might Mary Mary Quite Contrary have had in her garden?

     (Answers on page 507)

Healing Foods

1. Which vegetable is a great reliever of colds, bronchitis, and coughs, especially when eaten raw?

2. Which simple fruit can help relieve stress and anxiety?

3. Which sweet food has antibacterial and antiviral effects?

4. Which berries are thought to lower cholesterol, reduce the risk of diabetes, slow the aging process, and improve motor skills?

5. Which food is rich in protein and omega-3 fatty acid but low in calories and saturated fat?

6. Which drink is thought to lower the risk of cancer and helps treat inflammatory bowel disease?

7. Which green vegetable superfood is loaded with vitamins A, B6, and K, folic acid, and minerals such as calcium and potassium?

8. Which nut has been proven to reduce the risk of coronary heart disease?

9. Once considered a dietary no-no, which food is now thought to provide cancer-preventive properties and mood-enhancing effects?

10. In which dairy product can probiotics be found?

11. Which bulb was praised by the ancient Greeks and Egyptians for its beneficial properties?

12. Which root vegetable is thought to increase fertility in men?

13. Which tropical fruit has been shown to reduce the likelihood of blood clots?

14. A diet high in cheese consumption has been shown to reduce gallstones. True or False?

15. What has root ginger been shown to reduce in humans?

16. Which herb can help reduce intestinal cramps?

17. Which fruit can relieve constipation and diarrhea?

18. Which fruit has been proven to help prevent urinary tract infections?

19. Which vegetable helps stabilize blood pressure and has nerve-soothing properties?

20. Bananas are a good source of potassium. True or False?

FOOD & DRINK

Pickles and Preserves

1. Which famous English sponge cake named after a queen has jam in the middle?

2. Meat during the Middle Ages was preserved in salt. True or False?

3. When making jam, which fruit juice helps draw out the pectin, making it set?

4. Vinegar is mainly used to preserve what?

5. You cannot preserve meat by wet-curing it. True or False?

6. The natural gelling agent agar, used in jam making, comes from which country?

7. The main ingredients of fruit curd are?

8. Membrillo is a fruit cheese from which country?

9. What is used to strain the juice of simmered fruit to make jelly?

10. Fruit cheese contains cheese. True or False?

11. What are a demijohn, an airlock, and a siphon used for?

12. Burying food underground is a method of food preservation. True or False?

13. Fresh fruit bottled in alcohol, if left unopened, will keep for how long?

14. What is the name of the traditional Scandinavian salted salmon?

15. What is sugar mainly used to preserve?

16. Dehydration is one of the oldest-known methods of food preservation. True or False?

17. Brine is a solution made up of what?

18. Malt, balsamic, and pickling are types of which preserving agent?

19. At which temperature does jam reach its setting point?

20. Fruit cheeses date back to pre-Roman times. True or False?

21. What is the origin of the word "marmalade"?

22. Where did the word "chutney" come from?

23. What is the name of the good bacteria involved in pickling?

24. Sauerkraut is pickled what?

25. Which salad vegetable becomes a pickle or a gherkin when preserved?

(Answers on page 507)

Piece of Cake

1. What fungus is added to flour and water to make bread rise?

2. What is a *sfingi*?

3. Which area in Germany is famous for its sweet baking?

4. When is stollen traditionally eaten?

5. The name of the German cake *bienenstich* translates as "bee sting cake." True or False?

6. Madeleines were made famous by which French author?

7. Florentines and *canestrelli* are biscuits from which country?

8. Baking powder produces carbon dioxide when combined with heat. True or False?

9. Shortbread is a traditional biscuit from which country?

10. A meringue-based dessert is named after which famous ballerina?

11. Shortcrust, double-crust, puff, and choux are all types of what?

12. Which Italian cheese can be used as an alternative to cream cheese in baking?

13. Profiteroles are normally filled with what?

14. Panettone is traditionally eaten at Halloween. True or False?

15. Which baked item is traditionally associated with afternoon tea?

16. *Pastel de Leches* is a sponge cake from which country?

17. From which part of the world does the nutty dessert *halwa* come?

18. Complete the following phrase: "the greatest thing since…"

19. Pastry was originally made by the Egyptians. True or False?

20. What is the process of baking a pie crust without the filling known as?

FOOD & DRINK

Food Origins

1. Which bean was once used as a form of currency in Mesoamerica?

2. The humble potato was first farmed where?

3. What food was found buried with Egyptian pharaoh Tutankhamen?

4. From which continent did the banana originate?

5. Where did the pineapple first come from?

6. When is the Bavarian weisswurst traditionally eaten?

7. When the avocado was introduced to the US in the early 19th century, it was called the what?

8. The croissant is a breakfast staple of which country?

9. Which vegetable was first grown in Mesoamerica around 3500 BCE?

10. How long does it take a hen to create and lay an egg?

11. What fruit was a staple in the diets of the ancient Romans, Greeks, and Egyptians?

12. A famous English hot pot comes from which county?

13. The Brazil nut is native to the country of Brazil. True or False?

14. How many types of sausage are there in Germany?

15. The pear is a native fruit of which region?

16. Parma ham originally comes from which country?

17. The snack made of cheese sauce on toast is called Welsh what?

18. In which Asian country did the apricot originate?

19. Olives were first grown in Barcelona, Spain. True or False?

20. Which starchy tuber is a common crop of African origin?

21. Sweet potatoes originated in which region?

22. The Crusaders brought what food back to Europe with them after their exploits abroad?

23. Which sort of thin sausage first appeared in a French recipe in 1903?

24. From when does the British nickname "banger" originate?

25. Where is the *sheftalia* sausage from?

Festive Treats and Other Eats

1. Which green vegetable is a traditional British accompaniment to the Christmas Day meal?

2. At which celebration in the US is pumpkin pie usually served?

3. What is traditional German Christmas cake called?

4. Chocolate eggs are a treat for young and old at which seasonal holiday?

5. Candy canes were supposedly invented to keep children quiet during 19th-century Christmases. True or False?

6. On what festive day would workers and servants be given presents and leftover food?

7. What is traditionally eaten on Christmas Day in the UK: fish, turkey, lobster?

8. Toffee apples are often made at Halloween, shortly after the apple harvest. True or False?

9. What food is eaten on Shrove Tuesday, the day before Lent?

10. Mulled wine is consumed at Christmas and generally served hot or cold?

11. "One a penny, two a penny..."— what Easter treats are these?

12. What type of pie is often served during festive holidays in America?

13. In which country might you be if served a pavlova on Christmas Day?

14. A traditional Scottish fruit cake is a what?

15. Fried chicken is such a great favorite for Christmas dinner in this country that takeout orders are placed months in advance. Which country is it?

16. What was the original ingredient of "nog" in eggnog?

17. *Köttbullar* is a festive food most commonly associated with which country?

18. What coin was traditionally cooked inside a Christmas pudding?

19. Roast turkey is sometimes accompanied by a sauce made from which tangy fruit?

20. What fruit was often placed inside children's Christmas stockings?

21. Which two traditional condiments are served with roast beef?

22. Brandy butter doesn't actually contain any brandy. True or False?

23. In Germany, what is a *Pfefferkuchenhaus*?

24. Figgy pudding contains figs. True or False?

25. Bread sauce is usually served with what?

FOOD & DRINK

An Apple a Day

1. How many varieties of apples are there?

2. Who is the Bramley apple named after?

3. Most modern apples are closely related to the crab apple. True or False?

4. Is a quince an apple or a pear?

5. Where did Cox's Orange Pippin apples originate?

6. Which country produces the biggest apple crop?

7. A peck and a bushel are ways to weigh apples. True or False?

8. The Java apple belongs to the species *Malus domestica*. True or False?

9. Pacific Rose is a pinkish apple grown in which country?

10. A type of slightly sour apple is called Granny…?

11. On which continent did the apple originate: Australia, Asia, Europe?

12. Which of these is NOT an apple variety: Jonathan, Red Delicious, King Edward?

13. The apple genome was recently decoded. The apple was found to have around 57,000 genes. True or False?

14. Apples contain about 85% water. True or False?

15. The first Bramley apples came from seeds planted by a girl in: 1777, 1809, 1901?

16. The apple belongs to the same family as a popular garden flower. Which one?

17. Which alcoholic drink is made from pressed apples?

18. Which area of England is well-known for producing apple-based drinks?

19. What is the apple called "Mother" also known as?

20. Which American folk hero is noted for planting apple trees wherever he went?

FOOD & DRINK

Puddings

1. Spotted Dick is so called because of which ingredient?

2. Cream puffs are known in the UK as what?

3. Haggis, a Scottish dish, is traditionally served with mashed potatoes and what?

4. *La Galette des Rois* is a cake eaten in France to celebrate which feast day?

5. Christmas pudding emerged in medieval England as a way of preserving meat at the end of the season. True or False?

6. Black pudding, a kind of blood sausage, is usually eaten with which meal in the UK?

7. *Ile flottante* is a French pudding consisting of vanilla custard and what?

8. Tiramisu, an Italian pudding, literally means what?

9. Which English school gives its name to a dessert of strawberries, meringue, and cream?

10. In Scandinavia, which dessert is traditionally eaten at Christmas?

11. *Crème brûlée* literally translates into English as what?

12. Pumpkin pie is a traditional dessert at which celebration?

13. What is a clootie, a traditional Scottish dessert?

14. The fruit and meringue-based pavlova was named after a well-known Russian. What was she famous for?

15. Sticky toffee pudding allegedly originated in which country?

16. Sussex Pond pudding is a steamed dessert consisting of suet pastry encasing which whole fruit?

17. February 1 is National Baked Alaska Day in the US. True or False?

18. Which British tart consists of a pastry shell spread with jam and a custard filling topped with coconut flakes and glazed cherries?

19. *Crêpes Suzette* is a French pancake pudding made with which fruit?

20. Summer pudding consists of a selection of berries and fruit and what other ingredient?

FOOD & DRINK

Herb Garden

1. The ancient Egyptians used herbs as medicine. True or False?

2. What are the two types of tarragon?

3. What happens to basil when it gets frozen?

4. By what name is the herb *Salvia officinalis* more commonly known?

5. When is the best time to sow lemongrass seeds?

6. Which herb resembles thin blades of grass?

7. Dried bay leaves have stronger taste than fresh bay leaves. True or False?

8. Which is the best kind of place to grow herbs?

9. In *Hamlet*, Ophelia gives which herb for remembrance?

10. Which herb has seeds that are used as a spice?

11. Horseradish was once used to cure which ailment?

12. Peppermint is a hybrid of water mint and spearmint. True or False?

13. In the Middle Ages, women would give thyme to warriors for what?

14. How long does parsley take to germinate?

15. Which herb is marjoram's closest relative?

16. Which herb is often added to pickles?

17. In medieval times, fennel was used to ward off witchcraft and evil. True or False?

18. Is French or Russian tarragon normally used in cooking?

19. Which religion are myrrh and frankincense associated with?

20. Herbs are generally split into three categories: perennials, biennials, and what?

21. Chamomile tea is said to help you do what?

22. What kind of angelica is used in baking?

23. What herb is traditionally used to flavor pizza toppings?

24. Mint sauce traditionally accompanies which roast meat?

25. Which herb do cats love?

FOOD & DRINK

Vegetarian Options

1. Quinoa, a grain, is a complete protein. True or False?

2. Which meat substitute is made from vital wheat gluten?

3. Where did carrots originate?

4. In India, vegetarian food is marked with which image?

5. A vegetarian doesn't eat animal meat, so what doesn't a vegan eat?

6. In which year was the first vegetarian cookbook supposedly written?

7. A 2002 poll in the US showed what as the reason that most people became vegetarians?

8. How many animal lives does one vegetarian spare in a year?

9. Many crops yield up to ten times more protein per area than meat. True or False?

10. Roughly how much of the world is vegetarian?

11. Fruitarians eat a diet of what?

12. The earliest record of vegetarianism came from which country?

13. A Hindu law book called the *Manusmriti* condemns the killing of animals in all but what instance?

14. Vegans sometimes eat fish. True or False?

15. Which sea vegetable is commonly used to wrap sushi?

16. The "Bambi Effect" promotes vegetarianism by implying what?

17. Buddhist vegetarians don't eat vegetables from which genus?

18. What is tofu also known as?

19. Quorn is sold as a substitute for meat. True or False?

20. PETA, the animal rights organization, is an acronym for what?

FOOD & DRINK

Feeling Fruity

1. According to research, eating which fruits can help prevent eye problems (macular degeneration): bananas, blueberries, oranges?

2. Strawberry is a member of the rose family. True or False?

3. Which fresh fruit stops jelly from setting: pineapple, kiwi, papaya?

4. You can create a natural deodorant by rubbing a lemon under your armpits. True or False?

5. Coconut water is a suitable blood plasma extender and can be used when other IV solutions run out. True or False?

6. What used to be called a Persian apple?

7. A fruit is the part of a plant that contains its what?

8. Which of these is a variety of apple: Discovery, Red Sensation, Blue Mist?

9. Strawberries are the only fruits that grow seeds on the outside. True or False?

10. Which of these fruits does NOT have an edible skin: lemon, mango, melon?

11. Which of these is not a fruit: tomato, cucumber, carrot?

12. Bananas shouldn't be kept in the refrigerator. If you do, what will happen?

13. Which fruit is used to make the Spanish fruit "cheese" membrillo?

14. Which fruit is believed to have been cultivated 1,000 years before wheat?

15. What is the minimum number of servings of fruit and vegetables you should eat each day to stay healthy?

16. What is the kiwi fruit named after?

17. An unripe pineapple is poisonous. True or False?

18. Which of these is an edible fruit: rainberry, cloudberry, snowberry?

19. According to legend, which fruit tree did the Buddha cause to sprout instantly from seed?

20. Which of these is a type of orange: Valencia, Pamploa, Salamanca?

21. What percentage of a watermelon is water?

22. Apple seeds contain cyanide. True or False?

23. A kiwi is also called what?

24. The gooseberry plant has sharp thorns. True or False?

25. Which fruit juice should you not drink with some medication?

Going Greens

1. Which country has the highest percentage of vegetarians?

2. Where did potatoes originate?

3. Albert Einstein was a vegetarian. True or False?

4. What kind of plant is a Jerusalem artichoke?

5. Which cabbage is also known as Dutch cabbage?

6. What is a Turk's turban a variety of?

7. If you ate a whole dandelion, you would be ill. True or False?

8. Which is broccoli's closest cousin?

9. Who in *The Simpsons* is a vegetarian?

10. Which of these girl's names is also a variety of potato: Susan, Charlotte, Sophie?

11. Chard is closely related to spinach. True or False?

12. Slices of cucumber can be applied directly to the face to treat puffy eyes. What other vegetable could also be used?

13. Which vegetable is also known as "lady's finger"?

14. Which vegetable reputedly gave the cartoon character Popeye his strength?

15. Which vegetable is normally the main ingredient in borscht?

16. Garlic is a member of the onion family. True or False?

17. Cacti are used in Mexican cuisine. True or False?

18. Which of these can a carrot NOT be: purple, black, red, yellow, pink?

19. How long do asparagus plants take to mature from seed?

20. Which flower-headed brassica has been claimed to have significant anti-cancer properties?

21. What is South American cassava also known as?

22. Leeks are the national vegetable of which country?

23. What is bok choy?

24. Broccoli, cauliflower, and sprouts all belong to which vegetable family?

25. Why do onions make people cry when preparing them?

FOOD & DRINK

All about Herbs and Spices

1. What herb is included in the French pistou sauce?

2. Which is milder, American mustard or Dijon mustard?

3. Which herb is known as the "Royal Herb"?

4. Parsley can be used to deodorize pans that have a garlic or onion smell in them. True or False?

5. Which of these herbs is a member of the onion family: mustard, borage, chive?

6. Is sumac an herb or a spice?

7. Of which herb are these all varieties: Greek, lemon, sweet, and purple?

8. Which herb is a key flavor in the Scandinavian dish gravlax?

9. The herb smallage is the leaves of the wild variety of which vegetable?

10. The seeds of the herb anise taste of what?

11. Which part of the ginger plant does the spice come from?

12. Peppermint products can alleviate which of these: headaches, stomach-aches, sore muscles?

13. Which two herbs are traditionally used in tabbouleh?

14. Of which herb are these all varieties: orange-scented, lemon, common, silver?

15. The banana plant is a type of herb. True or False?

16. Which herb's Latin name means "dew of the sea"?

17. Which herb was a symbol of immortality in ancient Rome?

18. What is the main herb used in the Argentinian sauce *chimichurri*?

19. The Mediterranean fines herbes mix comprises chives, parsley, tarragon, and which other herb with a mild licorice flavor?

20. What color flowers does the curry plant have?

(Answers on page 508)

Behind the Chopsticks

1. Traditionally you drink apple juice with Chinese meals. True or False?

2. The correct way to eat rice from a bowl is to perch the bowl on your lower lip. True or False?

3. Tea is served with dim sum. True or False?

4. Five-spice powder is often used in Chinese cooking. True or False?

5. As a symbol of longevity, what is always served for a Chinese birthday celebration?

6. What is the most basic and important seasoning for Chinese food?

7. What is the most essential cooking utensil in Chinese cookery?

8. What are you doing if you are "going through the oil"?

9. What is the traditional way to sit down to a Chinese meal?

10. Which of these teas might be served with a Chinese meal: Jagertee, Assam, Oolong?

11. Why are knives and forks not traditionally used at Chinese tables?

12. Which of these Chinese ingredients is traditionally eaten fresh: bamboo shoots, edible jellyfish, bird's nest?

13. Drunken chicken is a dish marinated overnight in: wine, whisky, beer?

14. In Chinese cooking, vegetables are cut into uniform small pieces. Why?

15. How can you make the ends of spring onions curl up after cutting them?

16. What is the best heat source when cooking in a wok?

17. Which of these is actually a traditional Japanese dish: fugu, wontons, Peking duck?

18. Which of these is the odd one out: pilau rice, plain fried rice, beef fried rice?

19. Which of these is a fake ingredient: sea aubergine, cloud ears, hair algae?

20. How is rice usually prepared for consumption in Chinese cooking?

21. A *jiaozi* is a small boiled dumpling. True or False?

22. Noodles are never served in soup in traditional Chinese cooking. True or False?

23. Wrapped in bamboo leaves, a *zongzi* is what?

24. Soba is a Chinese dish from the 15th century. True or False?

25. What kind of nut is a main feature of Kung Pao chicken?

FOOD & DRINK

Breakfast

1. What is the Indian breakfast of flattened rice and seasoned potato?

2. In Scandinavia, *filmjölk* is often served for breakfast. What is it?

3. In which country might your breakfast consist of sheep offal and oatmeal wrapped in a sheep's stomach?

4. What does the Mexican breakfast food known as *huitlacoche* contain?

5. Served with fish, ackee is a fruit that might poison you if not prepared correctly. Which country prepares the dish for breakfast?

6. *Siri paya* is a soup that features the head and feet of a lamb, sheep, or goat. In which country would you be served it for breakfast?

7. In Iraq, honey, butter, and cheese are enjoyed with which bread for breakfast?

8. Polish breakfasts are hearty affairs, featuring eggs, cold meats, tomatoes, and pickles. What is the *twarog* that also accompanies it?

9. It's breakfast time and you're being served kimchi, a dish of fermented vegetables and red peppers. Where are you?

10. Spicy rice noodles are never eaten for breakfast in Thailand. True or False?

11. *Loco moco* is a dish of rice, with a hamburger and fried egg on top. Where in the world is this served for breakfast?

12. In which country would you enjoy the steamed egg dish of *chawanmushi* for breakfast?

13. *Syrniki* is a pancake filled with soft cheese. In which country would you be served this for breakfast?

14. What is the Vietnamese breakfast soup of noodles, basil, lime, bean sprouts, and beef called?

15. In which country would you eat Chocoleca spread on a baguette for breakfast?

16. The offal of which animal is mixed together and fried up for an American breakfast of scrapple?

17. Which country commonly serves open sandwiches for breakfast?

18. Second breakfast is traditional in some parts of Germany. True or False?

19. *Chocolate con churros* is a traditional breakfast of which country?

20. What else is in the Chinese breakfast of congee with century egg?

(Answers on page 508)

Teatime Traditions

1. Which English monarch set the trend for tea drinking in England when she chose the beverage instead of ale for her morning drink?

2. Between what hours is the traditional French tea party, or *thé*, held?

3. At what hour did the duchess of Bedford, Anna Maria Stanhope, hold afternoon tea?

4. British sailors and soldiers used the word "char" for tea. Which language did this slang term come from?

5. American iced tea originally featured green tea and what?

6. In which century was high tea introduced to England?

7. What form of green tea is served in Japan and China in formal tea ceremonies?

8. What traditional English snack often accompanies a formal afternoon tea?

9. In the 1910s, what activity often took place in America's tearooms?

10. Lu Yu was the author of 600 CE *Cha Jing* or "Tea Classic." From which country did he hail?

11. What did Thomas Sullivan successfully market in 1908?

12. Portuguese priests were first introduced to tea drinking in China during the 16th century. True or False?

13. Moroccan tea drinking is often considered an art form. What is the tea's main ingredient?

14. Which of these is NOT one of the reasons a Chinese tea ceremony is held: a declaration of war, an apology, a sign of respect?

15. What year did Catherine of Braganza, wife of Charles II, introduce tea drinking to the English court?

16. Which country declared tea as its national drink in 2013?

17. Singapore is the only country in Asia where tea is not sold. True or False?

18. Which was the first tea to be drunk in China, sometime in the 10th century BCE: green tea, white tea, black tea?

19. In which century CE was the Japanese tea ceremony first developed?

20. In England, which of these is NOT a feature of a Cornish cream tea: scone, golden syrup, cream?

FOOD & DRINK

Super Sausages

1. Pepperoni takes its name from the Italian word for what?

2. Where does the square sausage also known as Lorne sausage come from?

3. British black pudding traditionally contains oatmeal. True or False?

4. In which former Portuguese colony would you find Chouriço?

5. Botifarra blood sausage comes from which Mediterranean cuisine?

6. What is currently the world's spiciest sausage?

7. Similar to American hot dogs, frankfurters are made of pork smoked in a specific way. What is their full, protected German name?

8. Which of these is NOT a part of the traditional haggis: chicken liver, sheep pluck, ox bung?

9. Which country does Lap Cheong sausage come from?

10. From which seasoning's Latin name is the word "salami" derived?

11. Kiełbasa means "sausage" in Polish. True or False?

12. Droëwors is a dried sausage snack popular in which country?

13. In which year was the Cumberland sausage granted protected geographical status by the European Union?

14. Where does chorizo get its distinctive color from?

15. What Italian sausage is made with pork-fat cubes and flavored with spices?

16. The American version of mortadella is called "bologna," and US regulations require that there are no visible pieces of lard. True or False?

17. Fuet is a thin, cured sausage from which country?

18. What is the origin of the word "sausage"?

19. Cervelas is a kind of cooked sausage produced mainly in which country?

20. Measuring 4,921 ft (1,500 m), and containing more than 10,000 pieces, the world's longest sausage chain was produced in which country in 2009?

21. Why did the Roman Emperor Constantinus I ban sausages in 320 CE?

22. Where does the chipolata come from?

23. What sausages would you most likely find at a sports stadium?

24. Reputedly the most expensive sausage contained black truffle shavings. True or False?

25. Weighing a whopping 34,172 lb (15,500 kg) and measuring more than 35 miles (56 km), when was the world record for the longest single sausage established?

Something Fishy

1. Which of these fishing methods are sustainable: handline fishing, fishing with large-mesh nets, diver caught?

2. Which fish product is traditionally used in taramosalata?

3. Which of these fish is endangered: pollock, Arctic cod, barracuda?

4. At 2 years old, a sardine ceases to be a sardine. What does it become?

5. What is the name of the Portuguese dish of salted cod?

6. Which of these is a freshwater fish: perch, tuna, flounder?

7. How do you get to the oyster flesh?

8. The eyes of a fish sold for food can tell you if it's fresh. What sort of eyes should the fish have?

9. What's the most expensive edible fish in the world?

10. Which fish cut comes from just behind a fish's head?

11. Which part of a crab is called the "dead man's fingers"?

12. When you remove an oyster from its shell, it must be alive or it may not be safe to eat. True or False?

13. Kippers are a smoked version of which fish?

14. What should you use to serve Beluga caviar in order not to damage the eggs?

15. From which continent does the dish of ceviche come?

16. The word "fish" comes from which language?

17. Nuoc mam is fish sauce from where?

18. What typically distinguishes freshwater fish from saltwater fish?

19. Sea cucumber is edible. True or False?

20. Sockeye and chinook are types of what?

FOOD & DRINK

Souped Up

1. A popular accompaniment to soup, croûtes are what?

2. Which of these Italian soups contain meat: zuppa Toscana, ribollita, minestrone?

3. Which famous artist created a picture of soup cans?

4. What is the key ingredient in bird's nest soup?

5. A mirepoix forms the base of many classic soups. What does it consist of?

6. The earliest evidence of our ancestors eating soup dates from when?

7. What ingredient other than beetroot does borscht often contain?

8. Vichyssoise is traditionally served hot. True or False?

9. Chicken soup is also known as Jewish what?

10. From where does the soup bouillabaisse come?

11. Which soup would you expect to find prunes in?

12. In the court of Louis XI, ladies' meals were mostly soup because they were afraid chewing would give them facial wrinkles. True or False?

13. Italian wedding soup is traditionally served at Italian weddings. True or False?

14. The world's most expensive soup, "Buddha Jumps over the Wall," is a variety of which Chinese soup?

15. Fruit soup should always be served cold. True or False?

16. Al Capone ran a soup kitchen. True or False?

17. What is the radical weight-loss soup diet called?

18. What is the main ingredient of mock turtle soup?

19. Consommé is always what?

20. What does the Anglo-Indian dish mulligatawny mean in Tamil?

21. What is soup usually served in?

22. What is used to thicken gumbo?

23. What is the main ingredient of daal soup?

24. Where does avgolemono come from?

25. *Tshoem* is an Asian soup from which country?

My Thai

1. This Thai word can mean "rice," "nine," or several other things, depending on how it is spoken. What is the word?

2. What part of the kaffir lime is NOT used in Thai cooking?

3. Krating Daeng is what type of drink in Thailand?

4. In which region of Thailand would you find the spiciest food?

5. What are the most common utensils used to eat Thai food?

6. What green fruit is often used to flavor Thai food?

7. When or how is Thai soup eaten: a snack, breakfast, dinner?

8. What is the main ingredient of *Som Tam*?

9. In what way is galangal different from fresh root ginger?

10. Thai people eat a lot of baked food. True or False?

11. Thai desserts sometimes include rice, pumpkin, corn, tomatoes, and sweet potato. True or False?

12. Which of these is NOT a type of Thai curry: brown curry, red curry, green curry?

13. Most of the herbs used in Thai cooking have health benefits. True or False?

14. Nam pla is very commonly used in Thai cooking. What is it?

15. Shrimp paste is often burned in Thai homes because of its sweet fragrance. True or False?

16. If you found these dishes on a Thai menu, which would you expect to taste hottest: green chicken curry, mussaman beef curry, yellow prawn curry?

17. Agar-agar is used as a setting agent in Thai cooking. What is it derived from?

18. Is licking fingers at the table after a meal in Thailand bad manners or a sign that the meal was excellent?

19. In Thailand, what food is it OK to eat with your fingers?

20. If you give your host a gift in Thailand, you shouldn't wrap it in the colors green, black, or blue. True or False?

In Praise of Pies

1. What is blind baking?

2. What is a flan?

3. A sonker—a deep dish fruit pie—is unique to which state?

4. Crimped, fluted, arrowhead, and feathered are all types of what?

5. Where did the recipe for cobbler originate?

6. In the rhyme "Sing a Song of Sixpence," how many blackbirds were baked in a pie?

7. What was the 12th-century word for a pie crust?

8. The first cherry pie in English history is reported to have been made during the reign of which monarch?

9. Roman statesman Cato the Younger was a big fan of pies. What was the name of his preferred pie?

10. The Bedfordshire clanger is a British elongated pie that has savory filling at one end and sweet filling at the other. True or False?

11. The first cookbook to have recipes for pies and tarts is from which year?

12. A pie is also an American term for which Italian dish?

13. The dessert Apple Brown Betty was named after the women who created the recipe, Angela Brown and Betty Johnson. True or False?

14. Buko pie is a type of pie that consists mainly of young coconuts. Where did this pie originate?

15. Which pie is typically filled with salmon, rice, hard-boiled eggs, mushrooms, and dill?

16. A Boston cream pie is actually a type of cake. True or False?

17. In which season are mince pies cooked and eaten?

18. In the US, where is the shoofly pie most common?

19. What vegetable is commonly found in a spanakopita pie?

20. During the reign of King Charles V, at a banquet a chef created an immense pie that held what inside?

21. Calzone is a type of pie made with what sort of dough?

22. In which Shakespeare play do two characters end up in a pie?

23. The Cornish stargazy pie features what on the top?

24. Melton Mowbray is known for which type of pies?

25. In ancient Roman times, pie crust was so tough that it was thrown away. True or False?

FOOD & DRINK

Forbidden Foods

1. Which popular Scottish delicacy is now forbidden to enter the US?

2. Which popular American condiment has been banned in French primary schools?

3. Which country banned samosas for being "offensive" and "too Christian"?

4. Which European drink that contains wormwood is banned from entering the US?

5. Which country has not banned the sale of shark fins?

6. Where has the Japanese puffer-fish been banned?

7. Which gummy candies were banned from the UK for containing a thickening agent called konjac?

8. How many states have banned unpasteurized milk?

9. Which Sardinian delicacy has been banned across the European Union for containing the larvae Piophila casei, which can cause gastric lesions?

10. Although banned in France, ortolan often still shows up on menus. What is it?

11. Which of these countries still produces foie gras: Belgium, Switzerland, Sweden?

12. Which country banned sassafras oil in the 1960s because of its links to liver damage?

13. While banned everywhere else in the world, kiwi meat is still served in New Zealand. True or False?

14. Although banned in the US, which country and creator of pig's blood cake still considers it a delicacy?

15. Pommac, by Dr. Pepper, was banned in the US for containing the sweetener sodium cyclamate. What is Pommac?

16. Which 1980s American dish became so popular it had to be banned before its main ingredient was made extinct?

17. Kangaroo meat is banned in Australia but sold widely in the rest of the world. True or False?

18. The UK banned stevia as a food but allowed its use as a sweetener in 2011. What is it?

19. The raw version of which Jamaican fruit was once banned from the US?

20. Which confectionery with a non-nutritive object embedded in it has been banned in the US?

FOOD & DRINK

Failed Foods

1. Which short-lived 1963 McDonald's burger was aimed at Roman Catholics who were not allowed to eat meat on Fridays?

2. Which Coca-Cola drink didn't impress consumers, despite having double the amount of caffeine and a coffee flavor?

3. What was the name of the Coca-Cola Company's biggest product failure, launched in 1985?

4. How many grams of fat are there in a McDonald's Big Mac hamburger?

5. Wow! Chips by Frito-Lay promised to be fat free, but instead they caused stomach upsets and were soon removed from supermarket shelves. True or False?

6. Which of these is NOT a McDonald's food idea that didn't take off: McPizza, McHotdog, McCaviar?

7. Which heat-resistant chocolate bar did Hershey's produce briefly in 1990?

8. What long-lasting, carbonated, orange-flavored milk was a great flop with consumers?

9. Which color M&M was abandoned in the mid-1990s?

10. Which Coca-Cola flavor was short lived: New Coke, Pineapple Coke, Ginger Cola?

11. Fruit Brute and Fruity Yummy Mummy were both failed Monster cereals. True or False?

12. Which failed McDonald's burger featured a separately packaged hot and cold side?

13. Who marketed the short-lived BK Baguette Sandwich?

14. Did Jell-O try introducing a mixed vegetable flavor? Yes or No?

15. The McDonald's Arch Deluxe was released in 1996 but didn't make it into 1998. True or False?

16. Despite having Britney Spears advertise it, which Pepsi drink just couldn't be saved?

17. What was Kellogg's failed 1998 ready-made cereal called?

18. Launched in 1992, Crystal Pepsi flopped in every country except China, where it is still sold today. True or False?

19. Which failed soft drink was marketed as the "texturally enhanced alternative beverage"?

20. Which of these was NOT a color available in the failed condiment Heinz EZ Squirt: blue, yellow, purple?

Tea and Coffee

1. In which country did coffee drinking originate?

2. What is often sprinkled on a cappuccino?

3. Which two countries each claim to have invented the "flat white"?

4. Which type of coffee is thick, black, short, and strong?

5. From which Italian port city was coffee introduced to the rest of Europe?

6. Which of these is NOT one of the ingredients of caffè Medici: orange, whipped cream, mint?

7. In which country was the first recorded instance of tea drinking?

8. England's Queen's Lane Coffee House was founded in 1654. In which city can it still be found today?

9. What is added to steamed milk and coffee to make a caffè mocha?

10. During which 19th-century war did coffee become an everyday commodity?

11. During the Age of Sail, what did sailors dissolve in hot water as a coffee substitute?

12. The type of coffee made from espresso, steamed milk, and cocoa powder is called what?

13. Which country produces the most tea?

14. From which Caribbean island is most of the world's Arabica coffee descended?

15. Slices of what fruit are featured in the coffee guillermo?

16. A green eye contains dripped chocolate and three shots of espresso. As what is it also known?

17. In which country would you be most commonly served a *mazagran*?

18. Which of these countries is NOT a leading producer of coffee: Brazil, Colombia, Mali?

19. Where is 80 percent of tea consumed cold?

20. Coffee has been proven to be the leading cause of heart attacks in American men over the age of 50. True or False?

21. A zebra mocha with added raspberry flavoring is known in coffee circles as a what?

22. Turkish coffee never leaves ground coffee beans in the bottom of the cup. True or False?

23. In which country was coffee drinking banned in the 17th century?

24. Tea is the second-most-consumed liquid on Earth after water. True or False?

25. What species of plant does tea come from?

FOOD & DRINK

Some Like it Hot

1. Which explorer brought the chili pepper to Europe?

2. Flavored with lime juice and chilies, this hot Thai soup is called what?

3. How many different varieties of chili peppers are grown in Mexico?

4. Evidence of the first-known curries dates back to around 2600 BCE. Which civilization was cooking these dishes?

5. Which country is the leading producer of spice, with around 1,212,542 tons (1,100,000 metric tons) annually?

6. Vindaloo derives from a Portuguese dish from which part of India?

7. The unit for testing heat in spicy foods is the what?

8. The smaller the chili pepper, the hotter it is. True or False?

9. Which creatures do not suffer from the hot effects of chili peppers?

10. People who love hot, spicy food are called what?

11. What did Doctor Ian Rothwell suffer from after eating the "Widower," supposedly the hottest curry ever made?

12. What compound gives chili peppers their hot taste?

13. *Wat har bo* is deemed to be one of the hottest dishes in the world. From which continent does it originate?

14. The Moruga Scorpion is the hottest chili pepper in the world. Where is it grown?

15. How many Scoville heat units does the hottest curry in the world, the "Widower," allegedly contain?

16. Which spicy dish from Louisiana is made with fresh chili peppers, cayenne pepper, and tomatoes?

17. How many different varieties of chili peppers are used in the legendary *phall* curry?

18. Veeraswamy claims to be the oldest curry house in England. On which London street is it located?

19. Chili peppers have been proven to contain antimicrobial properties. True or False?

20. Hot and sour soup is a favorite food from which cuisine?

(Answers on page 510)

Just Desserts

1. A tub of ice cream weighs 13 lb (6 kg) plus half its weight. How much does it weigh?

2. A classic French dessert means "burned cream." What is it?

3. What is the Italian name for the dessert sabayon?

4. Which dessert was mentioned unfavorably in J. D. Salinger's novel *The Catcher in the Rye*?

5. To whom is the quote "Let them eat cake" attributed?

6. Cat's tongues are meringue treats from where?

7. What type of pastry are cream puffs made from?

8. How would you expect cherries jubilee to be cooked?

9. Which dessert is also known as Norwegian omelette or omelette surprise?

10. What was a traditional English pudding originally steamed in?

11. Which fruit is traditional in French *clafoutis*?

12. What old English dessert is made from milk or cream curdled with alcohol?

13. Culinary legend says this dessert was concocted after a schoolboy dropped a basket. Its name?

14. A *Bienenstich* cake is also known as what?

15. When he was head chef at the Savoy, Auguste Escoffier created the recipe peach Melba for whom?

16. What is "couverture" in confectionery?

17. Traditionally in Ireland, if you receive a piece of barmbrack on Halloween containing a pea, what does it signify?

18. Clafoutis comes from which country?

19. Is chocolate good for dogs?

20. What four ingredients do you need to make a traditional *crème anglaise*?

FOOD & DRINK

(Answers on page 510)   **359**

Meat Matters

1. What meat would you find in a traditional Hoppin' John?

2. Which fast-food chain launched a $119 Wagyu beef burger in 2008?

3. What cut of veal is normally used in osso buco?

4. Bresaola is a type of beef from Italy. How has it been prepared?

5. Which meat is banned in Islam and Judaism?

6. Which animal's meat is used to make bacon?

7. Why do you sear meat in a hot pan?

8. If you request your meat to be cooked "blue" in a restaurant, what will you get?

9. Tripe is a type of what?

10. Farming cattle releases methane and adds to global warming. True or False?

11. Rump, filet, and T-bone are all cuts of what?

12. What meat would you find in a traditional quiche lorraine?

13. The Guinness World Record for the longest hot dog was set in 2011. How long did it measure?

14. Which animal gives us mutton?

15. What is *boudin noir*?

16. Which of these is NOT sold as game: partridge, pheasant, grouse, buzzard?

17. Lean meat is made up of how much water?

18. From what part of the pig do you get the pork butt?

19. What are the traditional ingredients in steak tartare?

20. What meat do you usually spatchcock?

(Answers on page 510)

Cakes

1. With which country would you associate brioche?

2. The world's most expensive cake, the Pirates Fantas or Pirate's Fantasy, was created by chef Dimuthu Kumarasinghe. How much was it worth?

3. The Knave of Hearts stole which tasty teatime treats made by the Queen?

4. Which vanilla dessert's name means a "thousand sheets"?

5. If you were tucking into a slice of *Bebinca* in the home of this 16-layered cake, where would you be?

6. What is the filling in a Baked Alaska?

7. What distinctive colors would you find in a check-pattern if you cut a slice of Battenberg cake?

8. The Australian Frog Cake actually contains frogs. True or False?

9. The pound cake is so called because the traditional recipe includes one pound of four essential ingredients: flour, sugar, eggs, and… ?

10. Which of these is NOT a type of icing: glossy icing, royal icing, buttercream icing?

11. What is a whoopie pie: a sponge cake with buttercream, jelly, peanuts?

12. What type of cake is traditionally served on the Christian festival of Epiphany?

13. The idiom "a piece of cake" is popularly thought to have come from the 19th century. True or False?

14. Who started the tradition of putting candles on birthday cakes?

15. What type of fruit would you find in Eve's pudding?

16. What kind of pastry would you use to make an éclair?

17. The Japanese cake *yōkan* contains which essential ingredient?

18. The first mention of the cupcake can be traced as far back as 1796. True or False?

19. Which of these sugars is the darkest in color: muscovado, demerara, palm?

20. Which of these is the best cream to use for piping: sour cream, clotted cream, double cream?

FOOD & DRINK

Foods of the World

1. In Korean cuisine, the main ingredient of *baechu* kimchi—the most common type of kimchi—is what?

2. Which Japanese dish consists of wheat noodles, served in a meat/fish-based broth with various toppings?

3. The Chinese dipping sauce hoisin sauce has traditionally been made with which type of potato?

4. The long, thin loaf of French bread commonly made from basic lean dough is called what?

5. In Berlin, hot pork sausage served with either curry ketchup or a tomato paste with curry powder is called what?

6. Muktuk is a traditional Inuit meal made from what?

7. Jollof rice is a popular dish all over West Africa, especially in Nigeria and Ghana. True or False?

8. *Suya* is a meat kebab coated with peanuts, chili powder, and other local spices. Where is the origin of this famous delicacy?

9. Couscous is a staple food throughout which region?

10. Hummus is a dish popular throughout the Middle East. It is blended with tahini, salt, lemon juice, garlic, olive oil, and what?

11. Green tea historically goes back to China, but how old are the first references to it in Chinese literature?

12. Falafel is traditionally served in what?

13. Cornbread is a common bread associated with the South and Southwest regions of where?

14. Which country is the world's largest producer of maple syrup?

15. *Cocada* is a traditional Brazilian sweet made mainly from cocoa beans. True or False?

16. Sandwiches de Miga are popular in Argentina. They are single- or double-layered sandwiches made from which type of bread?

17. Coconut milk, paste, rice, and seafood are the main ingredients of Goan delicacies. True or False?

18. Found on African trees, *mopane* is eaten as a dried, crispy snack. What is it?

19. Ackee and salt fish is the national dish of which country?

20. Guacamole is an avocado-based dip that originated where?

Baking

1. Before the eraser was invented, people would rub out pencil marks with breadcrumbs. True or False?

2. Tipo 2 is a type of what?

3. What is the optimal temperature range for yeast fermentation?

4. What kind of reaction helps to create a bread's crust?

5. According to *Guinness World Records*, ten slices of bread were buttered in the fastest time ever in 2018. How long did it take?

6. Yeast is never an ingredient used in making flatbread. True or False?

7. What is the French equivalent of the Italian focaccia?

8. Making soda scones, do you divide the dough in half or into four?

9. The pocket in a pita bread is made by steam. True or False?

10. The first single-loaf breadmaker was released in Japan in what year?

11. Where do Stottie cakes originate from?

12. What kind of pan are chapati cooked in?

13. What type of fat is traditionally used in hot water crust pastry?

14. Are *pooris* cooked by steaming, grilling, or deep-fat frying?

15. In Belgium, what is bread pudding called?

16. Which American religious community is said to have invented whoopie pies?

17. Similar to a baguette, what is this bread called?

18. Which type of brioche is traditionally eaten in France on January 6?

19. What type of flour is used in a *torta margherita*?

20. *Spritzgebäck* is a cookie traditionally served at Christmas. Where?

FOOD & DRINK

Outdoor Eating

1. What is the origin of the word "barbecue": French *barbe à queue*, Spanish *barbacoa*, Taino *barabicoa*?

2. A Maori barbecue is also known as what?

3. Souvlaki is a type of… ?

4. Barbecues have been a White House tradition since which US president was in office?

5. Once your food is over the coals, when should you add a glaze to it?

6. In his seminal book *Ma Cuisine*, who recognized grilling as "the remote starting point, the very genesis of our art"?

7. Which of these is the key ingredient in a jerk marinade: Scotch bonnet chili pepper, chipotle, cayenne pepper?

8. New York was once famous for its turtle barbecues. True or False?

9. Ribfest, a festival with vendors selling barbecue beef, pork ribs, pulled-pork sandwiches, chicken, coleslaw, and more, occurs where in the world?

10. What is a classic kettle?

11. What is ash-roasting also known as?

12. What is a wood-fired oven's typical cooking temperature?

13. When the fat ignites on the coals, what is it called?

14. You should never cover the grill when doing direct heat grilling. True or False?

15. What is a rub?

16. Which nation invented the picnic, which means "to pick/peck"?

17. When making barbecue, when do you apply a mop?

18. In Australia, if someone brings "Yabbies" to a barbecue, what would they be?

19. What barbecue favorite is often called the "poor man's lobster"?

20. Which is the most environment-friendly barbecue fuel?

Perfect Pasta

1. Which of these is NOT a type of pasta: balam, barbina, bucatini?

2. In Italy, how is the flour best suited to making pasta labeled?

3. What ingredient is added to pasta to make it black?

4. What shape are rotelle?

5. What shape are rigatoni?

6. Well-cooked pasta that is firm but not hard is described as "al dente." What is the literal translation of this phrase?

7. Semi di melone are traditionally cooked as part of what?

8. Ancient Romans cooked a form of pasta. True or False?

9. Which of these is commonly used to color pasta: arugula, spinach, basil?

10. Marco Polo discovered pasta. True or False?

11. In October 2010, a Guinness world record was set for the longest strand of pasta ever made. How long was it?

12. What shape is cavatappi pasta?

13. Which of these types of pasta comes in tiny, rice-shaped noodles: ditalli, stelle, orzo?

14. What pasta dish is made from fettuccine, butter, cream, Parmesan, and parsley?

15. The Italian saying *gli spaghetti amano la compagnia* is a reminder to do what when cooking spaghetti?

16. The name of which pasta literally translates as "little ears"?

17. What is the Italian name for angel-hair pasta?

18. What shape is farfalle pasta?

19. Fresh pasta cannot be frozen. True or False?

20. What does the word "gnocchi" mean?

FOOD & DRINK

Spicy Secrets

1. What is the world's most expensive spice?

2. Cardamom is the third-most-expensive spice in the world. True or False?

3. Which of these is the odd one out: rosemary, nigella, poppy?

4. What grows on a curry tree?

5. What's the most-cultivated spice crop in the world?

6. Which spice is the main ingredient of the Middle East candy halva?

7. What is the hottest part of a chili?

8. Mace spice is an ingredient in mace spray tear gas. True or False?

9. What kind of pepper grows on a Brazilian pepper tree?

10. Which spice would you find in Worcestershire sauce?

11. Coriander is commonly used as both a herb and a spice. True or False?

12. Licorice is used to flavor tobacco and toothpaste. True or False?

13. Cardamon seeds are native to which countries?

14. Which of these spices doesn't grow on trees: tar anise, cloves, nigella?

15. Zedoary is also known as what?

16. Which spice still comes almost exclusively from Central America and the West Indies?

17. Nutmeg and mace grow together in the same fruit. True or False?

18. What is the literal translation of garam masala?

19. Which spice is said to have anti-cancer properties?

20. In February 2011, which chili was briefly recognized as the world's hottest by Guinness World records?

21. What is chorizo spiced with?

22. From which part of a tree is cinnamon obtained?

23. What is barbed wire grass, fever grass, and oily heads also known as?

24. On what do nutmegs grow?

25. What color is ground sumac?

(Answers on page 511)

Edible Mushroom

1. Caesar's mushroom was a favorite with Roman emperors. True or False?

2. Giant puffballs regularly weigh more than 9 lb (4 kg). True or False?

3. In the spring and summer months, what type of weather indicates the best time to look for mushrooms?

4. What is the best time of day to search for fungi?

5. Which of these mushrooms can you eat raw: field, wood, morel?

6. Which of these fungi would be easiest to spot due to its bright yellow or orange coloring: chicken-of-the-woods, horn of plenty, honey fungus?

7. Which of these would you find growing on tree stumps: parasol mushrooms, cauliflower fungus, red-staining mushrooms?

8. Which of these would you find growing on patches of bare soil: shaggy parasols, common puffballs, hedgehog fungus?

9. Which mushroom is also known as the "fried-chicken mushroom"?

10. Which of these could help you to identify types of mushroom: cetologist, entomologist, mycologist?

11. Which mushroom is thought to be the largest living organism on Earth?

12. Which of these mushrooms is NOT poisonous: deceiver, lawn funnel cap, brown roll rim?

13. White truffle is a mushroom. True or False?

14. White truffle is one of the most expensive foods in the world. Where would you find it?

15. When might you find a chicken-of-the-woods mushroom?

16. Mushrooms create their own wind. True or False?

17. A morel mushroom is safe to eat only if cooked. True or False?

18. Which of these mushrooms is better suited to breaking rather than cutting, due to its brittleness: hedgehog fungus, boletes, giant puffballs?

19. Which of these fungi does NOT grow in fairy rings: St. George's mushroom, summer truffle, fairy ring champignon?

20. Which of these mushrooms should be cleaned by washing rather than wiping: saffron milk cap, cauliflower fungus, wood blewit?

The Tomato Story

1. Where did tomatoes originate?

2. Tomatoes grow wild in the Galápagos Islands. How are they thought to have arrived there?

3. How many varieties of tomato exist today?

4. The tomato is also called a "love apple." True or False?

5. Standard tomatoes are also known as what?

6. Tomatoes are usually classified according to what?

7. A bush-type tomato is a plant that grows to a fixed height. True or False?

8. Which beneficial carotenoid hydrocarbon is found in tomatoes?

9. Which of these is NOT a variety of tomato: Pink Ping Pong, Legend, Hidden Rose?

10. How many seed chambers does a standard tomato have?

11. Which of these sauces is NOT tomato-based: salsa romesco, marinara, alfredo?

12. What is the knuckle of a tomato?

13. Along with tomato, what are the other classic ingredients used in *insalata caprese*?

14. What are you doing with young plants when you are "hardening them off"?

15. What can irregular watering of a tomato plant lead to?

16. What are green tomatoes?

17. The optimal temperature for pollination is 65.3°F (18.5°C). True or False?

18. Which fruit encourages green tomatoes to ripen if you place them in a bowl together?

19. When drying tomatoes, you should keep the seeds in. True or False?

20. How are fried green tomatoes cooked?

(Answers on page 511)

What's in Season

1. Honey contains a high percentage of water—how high?

2. How long can you freeze oriental greens for?

3. La Tomatina—a tomato-throwing festival held each year in Spain—celebrates the end of the tomato-growing season. True or False?

4. Which of these is NOT in season in the autumn: cucumbers, carrots, pumpkins?

5. If you were clamping potatoes, what would you be doing?

6. When are hazelnuts gathered?

7. Many root vegetables can be left in the ground through the winter months. True or False?

8. You should harvest the central flower head of a broccoli when it is as big as a child's head. True or False?

9. When is the asparagus season, spring or autumn?

10. Runner beans are in season in the spring. True or False?

11. Bottling fruit in alcohol is a good way to preserve your harvest. Which of these fruits wouldn't work well: grapes, pears, apples?

12. Which of these is NOT in season in the winter: onions, leeks, parsnips?

13. When should you pick cranberries?

14. Dull or wrinkled skin on an eggplant indicates what?

15. In which month of the year do grouse begin to appear on restaurant menus?

16. At what time of year are soft fruits ready to be picked?

17. Which of these is NOT in season in the summer: apricots, strawberries, rhubarb?

18. What are new shoots on seed potatoes called?

19. When are bananas in season?

20. Chivers Delight is a variety of which fruit?

FOOD & DRINK

World Cuisine

1. Fugu is a deadly seafood. What is it?

2. Ortolans are a now-banned "delicacy" eaten with a napkin over the head to preserve the aroma. In which country were they mainly eaten?

3. Why is it unwise to eat large barracuda fish?

4. Why are durian fruits banned from public transportation in Singapore?

5. Jansson's temptation is made from potatoes and anchovies. In which country is it popular?

6. Which city has a street named Snake Alley because it specializes in snake-based dishes?

7. Kimchi is served with almost every meal in which country?

8. *Methi* is a popular herb in India. What is it?

9. What is real bird's nest soup made from?

10. What is the main ingredient of the Swedish speciality *surströmming*?

11. Manchego is a hard cheese often served with quince jelly in which country?

12. What is the name of the traditional Greek dish of slow-cooked lamb on the bone, marinated in garlic and lemon, originally cooked in a pit oven?

13. *Onglet*, popular in France, is a type of what?

14. What is the main ingredient of *amchoor* powder, used in North Indian dishes such as *chana* masala?

15. Piri piri is a very hot chili sauce first made in which country?

16. What is ceviche made from?

17. Alinea is one of the best restaurants in the US. Which city is it in?

18. *Kopi luwak*, originally from Indonesia, is the world's most expensive type of what?

19. How old is a thousand-year egg?

20. What is *Oh-toro*?

21. In which country would you find deep-fried tarantula on the menu?

22. What does the Mexican dish *escamoles* contain?

23. Which of these is NOT a nickname of the highly toxic, foul-smelling Norwegian lutefisk: fork destroyer, eating death, weapon of mass destruction?

24. Where would you find raw blood soup, consisting of chicken gizzards and congealed duck blood, topped with peanuts and herbs?

25. *Casu marzu* is an Italian sheep's-milk cheese crawling with live fly larvae. True or False?

Global Cheeses

1. Which of these animals' milk is NOT used to make cheese: buffalo, reindeer, pig?

2. Which of these is NOT part of the traditional cheese-making process: steaming, maturing, fermenting?

3. Valdeon blue cheese is also known as what?

4. Which is the most consumed cheese in the world?

5. Which of these is a soft cheese: Tunworth, Beaufort, Pecorino Sardo?

6. What are the features of a "washed" cheese: white with no rind, sticky and pungent, blue mold?

7. Which of the following is a type of blue cheese: Blue Heaven, Blue Mon, Blue Monday?

8. What cheese would you have in a Greek salad?

9. What is traditionally drunk with Langres?

10. You should not eat the rind of Camembert. True or False?

11. Any flavoring can be added to cheese. True or False?

12. In which region of Italy is Gorgonzola mostly made?

13. Which of these cheeses is NOT made in England: Stinking Bishop, Wigmore, Gubbeen?

14. What are curds?

15. What is distinctive about Emmental cheese?

16. Which cheese is traditionally made from buffalo's milk?

17. What is Halloumi usually preserved in?

18. Which of the following British cheeses has PDO (Protected Designation of origin) status: Dorset Blue Vinny, Celtic Promise, Ragstone?

19. Which cheese was the 2011 Supreme Champion at the International Cheese Awards?

20. Evidence of cheese making has been found as far back as what?

21. The word "cheese" comes from the Latin word *caseus*. True or False?

22. In what year was cheese rationed during World War II in Britain?

23. Stilton is produced in which three counties of England?

24. In what year was Port Salut first produced by Trappist monks?

25. What did French philosopher Diderot call the "King of Cheeses"?

FOOD & DRINK

Food Culture

1. Georges Auguste Escoffier wrote *Le Guide Culinaire*. True or False?

2. Who is credited with establishing a distinctive French cuisine in the 17th century?

3. Marie-Antoine Carême was the chef for which French emperor?

4. What is the literal definition of "haute" in haute cuisine?

5. What kind of beans are a main ingredient of cassoulet?

6. Coq au vin is traditionally a dish from which region?

7. In what year was the first *Michelin Guide* published?

8. The English translation is "mouth amuser." What is the French culinary term?

9. What kind of dish is bouillabaisse?

10. Which French chef founded *Le Manoir aux Quat'Saisons*?

11. Modern Nouvelle Cuisine appeared in which decade?

12. What was medieval chef Guillaume Tirel known as?

13. Occupying Russian troops in 1815 requesting food "quickly" are purported to have given the name to which French cuisine term?

14. What are escargots?

15. Paul Bocuse's *l'Auberge du Pont de Collonges* is in which city?

16. What is the meat traditionally used in pot-au-feu?

17. Foie gras is made from which kind of geese or duck offal?

18. Truffles grow aboveground. True or False?

19. Which of the following is NOT a usual ingredient of *Herbes de Provence*: chive, thyme, rosemary?

20. Fougasse is a type of what?

Travelers' Tastes

1. Huhu is an endemic beetle and a traditional food that is said to taste like buttery chicken from which country?

2. Cicadas can be eaten deep-fried or stir-fried. True or False?

3. Witchetty grubs were the staple diet for many Aboriginal women and children. When eaten raw, they possess a taste similar to almonds. True or False?

4. Which Japanese delicacy consists of small pieces of meat in a brown viscous paste made of the internal organs of marine animals?

5. *Shā guō yú tóu* is what kind of soup?

6. *Hákarl*, fermented shark hung out to dry for four to five months, is a dish native to which country?

7. In the Philippines, this condiment is made of partially or completely fermented fish/shrimp and salt. What is it called?

8. The swim bladder is an organ that fish use to control their buoyancy and is also a delicacy often used in soups in which country?

9. Pig's blood cake from Taiwan doesn't really contain any pig's blood at all. True or False?

10. Nicaraguans are known to eat which type of eggs?

11. Scorpion soup is a delicacy in which country?

12. *Balut* is a fertilized duck embryo that is boiled alive and eaten in the shell. It is commonly sold as street food in which Southeast Asian country?

13. *Raake orret* is trout left in water containing sugar and salt, which is then stored at a cool temperature. Which country does this dish belong to?

14. What does the Peruvian dish of *cuy* contain?

15. Which bugs toasted with garlic, lime juice, and salt are commonly eaten in certain areas of Mexico?

16. *Svio* is a dish of boiled sheep's head, prepared in which country?

17. Various glands of an animal are used in a Latin American dish called *Mollejas*. What is its culinary name?

18. In Jewish cuisine, rendered chicken, goose, or pork fat is used for frying or as a spread on bread. What is it called?

19. Which dish includes pork, mushrooms, and bamboo shoots wrapped in a pancake?

20. Alligator on a stick is chunks of deep-fried alligator found in which continent?

FOOD & DRINK

CHAPTER 9

FILM & TV

Film buff? TV titan?
From Australian and Indian cinema
to Hitchcock and Bond films,
The Simpsons to *Iron Man*,
see just how much you really know
about the small and big screens.

American Soap Operas

1. How many soap operas have been produced in the US?

2. On which ranch does the action on *Dallas* take place?

3. Who played the character of Amanda Woodward on 1990s soap opera *Melrose Place*?

4. Which TV soap opera revolved around feuding factions in the Californian wine industry?

5. In which glamorous 1990s soap opera did *Dallas* actress Linda Gray star for its brief duration?

6. TV soap opera *Santa Barbara* first hit TV screens in 1983. In which year did it air its final episode?

7. In which soap opera did Joan Collins star between 1981 and 1989?

8. Which character on *Dallas* was dubbed "the poisoned dwarf"?

9. Which long-term soap opera focused on couples and conflicts in a Californian cul-de-sac?

10. Which soap opera was the main rival to *Dallas* in the 1980s?

11. Which medical soap opera began in 1963 and is still running today?

12. American soap opera *As the World Turns* aired on television for 54 years. True of False?

13. Which *Dallas* character was the original protagonist in soap opera spinoff *Knots Landing*?

14. The soap opera *All My Children* first aired in 1970 and played its final episode when?

15. The *Young and the Restless* began life in 1973 and is still running today. True or False?

16. Which TV soap opera is "like sand through the hourglass"?

17. Which actor played Bobby on the soap opera *Dallas*?

18. What happened to the 2009 remake of popular 1990s soap opera *Melrose Place*?

19. In which year did soap opera *Dallas* make a return to TV screens?

20. Which red-headed actress has appeared on both the *Melrose Place* and *Desperate Housewives* soap operas?

FILM & TV

Downton Abbey

1. The Crawleys' estate is located in what part of England?

2. Which building is used for the exterior shots?

3. Who is the creator of *Downton Abbey*?

4. Which character was asked to go to America to cook for the Levinson family?

5. Who is the middle daughter of Lord and Lady Grantham?

6. What were seen atop some of the village houses in the first season?

7. Which character does Hugh Bonneville play?

8. Who faces a cancer scare in the second season?

9. Rose's father has a well-known nickname. What is it?

10. Who plays the role of Violet Crawley?

11. Which tragic event leads Matthew Crawley to become heir to the Downton estate and title?

12. Who rescues Lady Edith when a fire breaks out in her bedroom?

13. What is Mrs. Hughes's first name?

14. What is the name of the Crawley family dog?

15. What is Violet Crawley's title?

16. What was Miss O'Brien's job in the household?

17. What momentous news does Lord Grantham announce at his annual garden party?

18. Who jilts Lady Edith at the altar?

19. Which character had a budding romance with a grocer?

20. Which real-life opera singer made an appearance in the fourth season?

British Sitcoms

1. Complete the name of this hit sitcom: *Only Fools and…*

2. Who played Ben Harper in *My Family*?

3. In which branch of the armed forces was *Dad's Army* set?

4. Which sitcom features three precocious children and their mom and dad?

5. Name the sitcom that portrayed the French Resistance.

6. Who played the Vicar of Dibley?

7. What was the name of the hotel run by John Cleese in the sitcom of the same name?

8. What was the name of the character played by Ronnie Barker in *Porridge*?

9. Who did Ronnie Barker play in *Open All Hours*?

10. Who co-starred with Ronnie Barker in the same sitcom, playing the part of Granville?

11. *Red Dwarf* was the name of which type of transportation?

12. How many seasons of *Blackadder* were made?

13. *Men Behaving Badly* was first shown on ITV. True or False?

14. Which sitcom featured a different celebrity in each episode who played an exaggerated version of him- or herself?

15. *Porridge* was filmed in Irish Kilmainham Gaol. True or False?

16. Patsy in *Absolutely Fabulous* was played by which actress?

17. Where did the priests in *Father Ted* live?

18. Who played Tom Good in *The Good Life*?

19. What was the name of the department store in *Are You Being Served?*

20. *It Ain't Half Hot Mum* was set in which Asian countries?

21. Which show featured the character Daffyd Thomas?

22. Which elderly character could clear a room just by saying "During the war…"?

23. The catchphrase "I don't believe it!" comes from which sitcom?

24. In *Rising Damp*, what is the name of the miserly landlord?

25. In *The Young Ones*, what sort of pet does Vivian own?

FILM & TV

Animated Films

1. What is the name of the cowboy hero in *Toy Story*?

2. The film *Inside Out* features five emotions: Joy, Sadness, Anger, Fear, and Disgust. True or False?

3. What is Shrek?

4. In *Happy Feet*, what is Mumble's special talent?

5. Who wrote the book that *Horton Hears a Who!* is based on?

6. What is the name of the studio that made films such as *Toy Story* and *The Incredibles*?

7. Jackie Chan voiced a character in *Kung Fu Panda*. True or False?

8. Asterix is an animated hero created in Belgium and which other country?

9. *Watership Down* featured a cast of rabbits. True or False?

10. What is the Japanese term for animated films?

11. Who was Roger Rabbit married to?

12. What was the first fully computer-animated feature film?

13. What kind of fish was Nemo?

14. Which film features the villain Cruella De Vil?

15. Complete the name of this animated duo: Wallace and...

16. Who is the hero of *A Bug's Life*?

17. What does Carl tie to his house to travel to South America in *Up*?

18. Lemurs are featured in which hit animated film from 2005?

19. Which new main character was introduced in *Toy Story 4*?

20. What is the name of the kingdom where Anna and Elsa live?

21. Which film features singing and dancing penguins?

22. Which was the first full-length animated film to be released?

23. In which film do the characters Sebastian, Eric, and Ursula appear?

24. What are the names of the main character and his helpers in the *Despicable Me* films?

25. *The Lord of the Rings* has never been made into an animated film. True or False?

Billy Wilder

1. Billy Wilder won two Academy Awards for Best Director. True or False?

2. One of the Academy Awards Billy Wilder won was for *The Apartment*. For which film did he win the other?

3. Wilder's grave features the epitaph: "I'm a writer, but then nobody's perfect." Which of his films is this line adapted from?

4. Who plays aviator Charles Lindbergh in *The Spirit of St. Louis*?

5. Which Wilder film is narrated by a dead man?

6. Billy Wilder's first directorial project was in German. True or False?

7. Apart from *Some Like It Hot*, which other film starring Marilyn Monroe was directed by Billy Wilder?

8. What is Marilyn Monroe's character name in *Some Like It Hot*?

9. Which song does Ariane hum repeatedly in *Love in the Afternoon*?

10. Who stars alongside Shirley MacLaine in *Irma la Douce*?

11. In which year was *The Apartment* first released in cinemas?

12. Which team does Luther "Boom Boom" Jackson play for in *The Fortune Cookie*?

13. Shirley MacLaine plays a receptionist in *The Apartment*. True or False?

14. Who plays C. R. "Mac" MacNamara in *One, Two, Three*?

15. Where is *Stalag 17* set?

16. Which item of clothing does the gang boss in *Some Like It Hot* take for his nickname?

17. In which film does Ginger Rogers disguise herself as a young girl named Su-Su?

18. *Sabrina* features which actress caught between the affections of Humphrey Bogart and William Holden?

19. Which Wilder film is based on an Agatha Christie short story?

20. When was Billy Wilder's final film *Buddy Buddy* released?

FILM & TV

Disney Films

1. As of 2019, how many animated feature films had Disney made?

2. What was the name of Mickey Mouse's debut film (with sound)?

3. In *The Princess Diaries*, Mia Thermopolis is the heir to the throne of which fictional European country?

4. What happened to Pinocchio when he lied?

5. Timothy Q. Mouse helped which character to fly?

6. Who was Bambi's best friend?

7. Who wrote the book that *Alice in Wonderland* was based on?

8. The music in *Sleeping Beauty* was based on work by which composer?

9. On which traditional fairy tale was the film *Tangled* based?

10. Who wrote the music and lyrics for *The Lion King*?

11. What did King Louie desire in *The Jungle Book*?

12. Complete the title of this live-action Disney hit movie: *Honey, I Shrunk the...*

13. In *Beauty and the Beast*, which wing of the castle is Belle forbidden from going to?

14. *Toy Story* was a Disney production. True or False?

15. Walt Disney provided the original voice for Mickey Mouse. True or False?

16. What is Sully's full name in *Monsters, Inc.*?

17. In *Winnie the Pooh*, what type of animal is Eeyore?

18. What is the name of the dog in *Up*?

19. Which planet gave its name to a Disney character?

20. What is the name of Mickey Mouse's long-term sweetheart?

21. What is the name of the wicked queen in *Enchanted*?

22. In *Robin Hood*, what is the name of the snake?

23. How many sisters does Ariel have?

24. What were Mickey and Minnie Mouse's original names?

25. In *Aladdin*, for how many years does the genie say he's been trapped in the lamp?

Horror Films

1. In *The Omen*, the central character was named Damien. True or False?

2. Name the British film studio that specialized in horror during the 1960s and 1970s.

3. Jamie Lee Curtis starred in which horror movie?

4. Which horror star provided the rap for Michael Jackson's "Thriller" single?

5. In which city was *The Exorcist* set?

6. Who directed the zombie classic *Dawn of the Dead*?

7. *The Amityville Horror* claimed to be based on real events. True or False?

8. Who wrote the story on which the film *Carrie* was based?

9. Which 1986 film stars Jeff Goldblum as a scientist who invents "telepods"?

10. Complete the name of this film: *The Blair_____ Project.*

11. What was the name of the killer in the *Friday the 13th* series?

12. Who directed *The Shining*?

13. How did Jack Nicholson's character die in *The Shining*?

14. *Arachnophobia* featured which killer creepy-crawlies?

15. Who played the monster in the 1931 *Frankenstein* film?

16. Which 1999 film starred Brendan Fraser and Rachel Weisz?

17. Where was Bela Lugosi born?

18. Complete the name of this film: *An American Werewolf in...*

19. Which British horror veteran said, "There seems to be an insatiable audience for this type of film"?

20. Which film features the story of two policemen who go after a serial killer with a Biblical theme to his murders?

21. Which *Friends* star appears in the film *Scream*?

22. In *A Nightmare on Elm Street*, what animal is seen in Tina's nightmare?

23. Who is the main character in the film *Psycho*?

24. In which film does a young boy get dragged under his bed by a clown doll that comes to life?

25. In *Friday the 13th VI*, how does Jason come back to life?

FILM & TV

Kids' Films

1. Complete the name of this series of movies: *Home…*

2. Who stars as the daughter in the 1976 *Freaky Friday*?

3. Lionel Jeffries directed which 1970 children's classic?

4. Who are Carmen and Juni Cortez?

5. *The Night at the Museum* is set in the American Museum of Natural what?

6. Miley Cyrus stars in which 2009 film adapted from her hit TV series?

7. In which Harry Potter film do giant spiders appear?

8. What happens to Nigel Thornberry in *Rugrats Go Wild* to make him act like a young child?

9. What was special about one of E.T.'s fingers?

10. Who plays Willy Wonka in the 2005 version of *Charlie and the Chocolate Factory*?

11. Which cat character, featured in a newspaper cartoon strip, has starred in a number of films?

12. *Babe* tells the story of a sheep-herding piglet. True or False?

13. *James Bond* novelist Ian Fleming wrote a book that inspired which movie about a car?

14. *Super Mario Bros.* is based on a computer game. True or False?

15. In what year was the original *Wizard of Oz* film made?

16. Complete the title of this film: *Diary of a Wimpy…*

17. A Volkswagen Beetle stars in which film series?

18. What kind of animal is Aslan in *The Chronicles of Narnia*?

19. Who stars as Gulliver in the 2010 adaptation of *Gulliver's Travels*?

20. Which of these painters did NOT give their name to a Teenage Mutant Ninja Turtle: Leonardo, Rubens, Raphael?

Comedies

1. *Shaun of the Dead* is a spoof of what kind of horror genre?

2. Who is the bumbling detective in *The Pink Panther*?

3. What is Marilyn Monroe's character's name in *Some Like It Hot*?

4. *The Hangover* is set in Las Vegas. True or False?

5. In *Trading Places*, what job is given to Eddie Murphy?

6. Who stars in the film *Groundhog Day*?

7. What was "Baby" in *Bringing Up Baby*?

8. Who are Walter Matthau and Jack Lemmon in a 1968 film?

9. Steve Martin made his name with which movie?

10. Charlie Chaplin was born in London. True or False?

11. Which London suburb gave its name to a studio that made a series of comedies between 1947 and 1957?

12. Nigel Tufnel is the guitarist in which film band?

13. Complete the name of this Monty Python film: *Life of…*

14. Mike Myers, the star of *Austin Powers*, was born in Scotland. True or False?

15. *Duck Soup* stars which band of brothers?

16. What type of music is on the soundtrack of *O Brother, Where Art Thou*?

17. Which actor plays Alex "Hitch" Hitchens in *Hitch*?

18. Who directed *Manhattan*?

19. What is the name of the pilot hero in *Airplane!*?

20. What words linked the titles of 29 British comedy films produced between 1958 and 1979?

FILM & TV

James Bond

1. James Bond's gun is a Walther PPK. True or False?

2. What is M's assistant called?

3. James Bond could never manage without his gadgets. What is the code name of the man who supplies them to him?

4. What is James Bond's code name?

5. Which villain does James Bond come up against in Crab Key, Jamaica?

6. What is the name of Auric Goldfinger's manservant, who has a fondness for hats?

7. Emilio Largo, the villain in *Thunderball*, has a fondness for which underwater menace?

8. In which film does James Bond fall in love with and marry Teresa di Vicenzo?

9. The Man with the Golden Gun is also known as whom?

10. What is the name of the main villain in *A View to a Kill*?

11. Kara Milovy, James Bond's love interest in *The Living Daylights*, is famous for playing the violin. True or False?

12. What is the name of the base that is attacked at the beginning of *GoldenEye*?

13. What is Alec Trevelyan's MI5 code name in *GoldenEye*?

14. What make is James Bond's remote-control car in *Tomorrow Never Dies*?

15. What is the name of the American physicist who helps James Bond in *The World Is Not Enough*?

16. What is the name of the character played by Madonna in *Die Another Day*?

17. What is the name of the Treasury agent who accompanies James Bond in *Casino Royale*?

18. What kind of car does James Bond win at cards in *Casino Royale*?

19. Who does James Bond team up with in *Quantum of Solace*?

20. How many James Bond films did Roger Moore make?

War Films

1. Complete the name of this war movie classic: *Saving Private...*

2. Steve McQueen was reportedly the original choice to play Willard in *Apocalypse Now*. True or False?

3. *Enemy at the Gates* portrays the battle for which city?

4. *All Quiet on the Western Front* is set during which conflict?

5. Who plays Cromwell in the 1970 film of the same name?

6. Complete the name of this war movie classic: *The Charge of the Light...*

7. During which war is the above film set?

8. *The Initiation Game* tells the story of how Alan Turing and his team cracked the Enigma code during World War II. True or False?

9. Complete this title: *Bridge on the River...*

10. Which African people gave its name to a film that portrays a huge battle in 1879?

11. Mel Gibson's film *The Patriot* is set during the American Revolution. True or False?

12. Which commander is the main character in *The Desert Fox*?

13. Who directed the film *1917*?

14. Which film tells the story of a Jewish musician's struggle to survive in war-torn Poland?

15. Which film tells the story of a US helicopter crash and rescue in Somalia in 1993?

16. *The Longest Day* is about which day?

17. Who plays Achilles in 2004's *Troy*?

18. Which film celebrates a black Civil War regiment?

19. The Allied operation Market Garden in World War II is portrayed in which 1977 film?

20. John Wayne stars in the 1960 version of *The Alamo*. True or False?

TV Trivia

1. For how many years did Johnny Carson host *The Tonight Show*, the most successful late-night network talk show?

2. What are the last ever words that Frasier Crane says in the final episode of *Frasier*?

3. What is Mike Brady's profession in *The Brady Bunch*?

4. Which *All in the Family* spin-off ran for four seasons until 1983?

5. The *Mary Tyler Moore Show* was one of the first to feature an independent career woman. What is the name of Mary's boss?

6. Which long-running character from the *M*A*S*H* television series is played by another actor in the pilot episode?

7. A record-breaking fifty million American households tuned in for the final episode of *M*A*S*H*. What is its name?

8. In the eighth season of *Roseanne*, Dan and Roseanne have a fourth child named Jerry Garcia Conner. True or False?

9. Who shoots J. R. in *Dallas*?

10. The affable drinker Norm Peterson who props up the bar at *Cheers* is actually named Hillary; Norman is his middle name. True or False?

11. In *South Park*, the trip over Niagara Falls in a barrel finally kills Kenny. True or False?

12. *The Simpsons* became the longest-running prime-time animated series in US television history in 1997. What show previously held the record?

13. Who is the lead guitarist in *The Partridge Family*?

14. On the hit sitcom *Friends*, what are Rachel's favorite flowers?

15. Which high school do the talented kids from *Glee* attend?

16. What are Sheldon's and Leonard's last names on *The Big Bang Theory*?

17. In which year was *Breaking Bad* first shown?

18. In *Sabrina the Teenage Witch*, Sabrina has a magical talking cat that sometimes gives her advice. What is the cat's name?

19. Which classic *Seinfeld* episode from season five revolves around a particular item of clothing?

20. What is the name of the local hangout in *Happy Days*?

Classic Christmas Movies

1. In *White Christmas*, where is the inn that the couples try to save?

2. In the 1966 animated classic *How the Grinch Stole Christmas*, Boris Karloff is the voice of the Grinch but does not do the singing. True or False?

3. In the 2004 animated box-office hit *The Polar Express*, what is the name of the young boy?

4. In *A Christmas Story*, what does the narrator Ralphie want for Christmas?

5. The title song of *White Christmas* was written by Irving Brecher. True or False?

6. In *Home Alone*, where are Kevin's family going on vacation when they leave him "home alone"?

7. In *The Muppet Christmas Carol*, Kermit the Frog plays the part of which Dickens character?

8. While shooting the 1944 film *Meet Me in St. Louis*, Judy Garland met and later married whom?

9. In *Planes, Trains and Automobiles*, Del Griffith is a salesman who sells what?

10. In the 1947 movie *Miracle on 34th Street*, what do Kris Kringle's lawyers use to prove that he is really Santa Claus?

11. Who is the voice of Scrooge in the 2010 animated version of *A Christmas Carol*?

12. In *It's a Wonderful Life*, George Bailey's guardian angel is named what?

13. In *Elf*, Buddy ends up in the North Pole because as a baby he stowed away in Santa's sack. True or False?

14. In *Frosty the Snowman*, what garment brings the snowman to life?

15. The 1944 film noir *Christmas Holiday* is based on a book by which author?

16. In the 1996 film *Jingle All the Way* starring Arnold Schwarzenegger, what present does he need to find for his son?

17. During the filming of the 2000 adaptation of *How the Grinch Stole Christmas*, how many candy canes were used?

18. Billy Bob Thornton stars in the film *Bad Santa*. What is the name of the boy he befriends?

19. How many characters does Tom Hanks play in *The Polar Express*?

20. How many couples do we follow in Richard Curtis's film *Love Actually*?

FILM & TV

1980s Films

1. Who stars as Ferris Bueller in *Ferris Bueller's Day Off*?

2. What is the name of Bill and Ted's band in their Excellent Adventure?

3. Who directed *The Outsiders*?

4. Who plays Andie Walsh in *Pretty in Pink*?

5. *Diner* is set in which city?

6. What is the theme tune to *Flashdance*?

7. What is the name of Prince's 1984 film?

8. Tom Cruise was born in Canada. True or False?

9. Who does Val Kilmer play in *Top Gun*?

10. Where do the "Breakfast Club" students meet for detention?

11. What name was given to the group of young actors who starred in many of the 1980s teen films?

12. What has been banned in the film *Footloose*?

13. *Stand by Me* is based on a story by which novelist?

14. The first Indiana Jones movie is *Raiders of the Lost Ark*. True or False?

15. Who is the real Susan in *Desperately Seeking Susan*?

16. What does the "E" in *E.T.* stand for?

17. Which actress stars as Lisa in the 1985 film *Weird Science*?

18. In which 1984 film do Dan Ackroyd and partners set up a unique removal firm?

19. Who stars as Axel Foley in *Beverly Hills Cop*?

20. What year did Marty McFly go back to in *Back to the Future*?

21. Who directed *Indiana Jones and the Temple of Doom* and *The Color Purple*?

22. Michael Keaton, Alec Baldwin, and Geena Davis star in which classic directed by Tim Burton?

23. "Greed Is Good" is the motto from which 1980s Michael Douglas film?

24. In which film is Jennifer Beals a steel-mill welder by day and a dancer by night?

25. Which film sees a robot called "Number 5" escape from a secret research center?

Children's TV Shows

1. Who created *The Muppet Show*?

2. What is the name of Muppet Dr. Bunsen Honeydew's long-suffering assistant?

3. Who lives in a burrow on Wimbledon Common, London?

4. What is the motto of the Wombles?

5. Which show features the characters Dipsy, Laa-Laa, Po, and Tinky Winky?

6. Which 1970s TV show stars Big Bird?

7. Which cartoon takes place in the underwater city of Bikini Bottom?

8. When did *The Simpsons* first appear on TV?

9. Who created *The Simpsons*?

10. What instrument does Zak play in *Zingzillas*?

11. What children's production company is represented by an orange "splat" and with its name in white?

12. When did Scooby-Doo first bound onto our TV screens?

13. Which show features puppets Zippy, George, and Bungle, and Geoffrey's attempts to calm them down and keep the peace?

14. Who is an average teenager by day and a secret pop superstar by night?

15. What is Dora?

16. What is the purpose of Mickey Mouse's Clubhouse?

17. What are inhabitants of Waverly Place?

18. Who communicate with whistles and eat green soup supplied by the Soup Dragon?

19. Who travels in a blue police box?

20. What is the name of the character first created from an old coat and ping-pong-ball eyes?

(Answers on page 513)

The Oscars

1. The Oscar statuette is made of solid gold. True or False?

2. How old was Tatum O'Neal when she won the Best Supporting Actress award?

3. How many times has a single film won 11 Oscars?

4. Who won the Best Actress award four times?

5. Which film won the first Best Animated Feature award in 2001?

6. How many Oscars did the film *Citizen Kane* win?

7. What links George C. Scott and Marlon Brando?

8. *La Dolce Vita* won which Oscar in 1960?

9. What other name are the Oscars known as?

10. Who won Best Actor for 1934's *It Happened One Night*?

11. Who was the female star in *It Happened One Night*?

12. Who was the first African American man to win the Best Actor award?

13. Which movie was the first sequel to win the Best Picture award?

14. *The Wizard of Oz* lost out to which movie for Best Picture in 1939?

15. Who plays the lead role in the Oscar-winning film *Rocky*?

16. Complete the name of this Oscar-winning movie: *Dances with...*

17. Oscar winners are not allowed to keep their awards. True or False?

18. How many Oscars did the science-fiction classic *Metropolis* win?

19. Which movie won Best Picture in 2011?

20. How many Oscars did *Titanic* win?

Science-Fiction Films and TV Shows

1. Who directed *2001: A Space Odyssey*?

2. The theme music from which film can be heard being played by the mother ship in *Close Encounters of the Third Kind*?

3. What is the name of the planet in *Avatar* where the Na'vi live?

4. Who stars as Barbarella?

5. Which popular 1980s band was named after one of the characters in *Barbarella*?

6. In which 2013 film does Sandra Bullock star with George Clooney?

7. *Forbidden Planet* is based on which Shakespeare play?

8. The original *Star Trek* series is set in which century?

9. With what fighting move did Mr. Spock knock out his enemies?

10. Jeff Bridges plays Tron in the original film of the same name. True or False?

11. The line "You have 20 seconds to comply" comes from which film?

12. Complete the film name: *Close Encounters of…*

13. What are the alien enemies in *Starship Troopers* called?

14. Which series of hit films is based on the books of Pierre Boulle?

15. Who does Mark Hamill play in *Star Wars*?

16. What does Charlton Heston find at the end of the first *Planet of the Apes* film?

17. From which planet do the aliens in *War of the Worlds* come from?

18. *Transformers* originated as a Japanese toy. True or False?

19. Which film stars Gort the robot?

20. What is the name of the robot in *Futurama*?

21. What is the name of the island in the film *Jurassic Park*?

22. In the *Alien* film series, what is the name of Ellen Ripley's pet cat?

23. *Blade Runner 2049* is set how many years after the original film?

24. In *Spaceballs*, what does Lonestar use to disable the enemy's radar?

25. In *The Martian*, what event separates Matt Watney from the original crew, making them think he's dead?

FILM & TV

Monsters in the Movies

1. Exposure to what causes Gremlins to die?

2. Complete the movie title: *Night of the Living...*

3. Béla Lugosi's most famous role was what?

4. The astronauts in *2001: A Space Odyssey* are threatened by their onboard computer named what?

5. Complete the following movie title: *Attack of the 50-Foot...*

6. Which movie features a monster that turns its victims into trees and foliage?

7. Complete the following quote from *King Kong*: "It was _____ killed the Beast!"

8. Which character turns out to be the werewolf in the film *Silver Bullet*?

9. Which pop star plays a vampire opposite Catherine Deneuve in *The Hunger*?

10. What is the name of the red-haired male doll that would rather kill than play?

11. Which film released in 2019 has the tagline: "...King of the Monsters"?

12. Complete the following movie title: *I Walked with...*

13. Complete the following quote from *An American Werewolf in London*: "Have you ever talked to a corpse? It's _____!"

14. What is unusual about the monsters in *A Quiet Place*?

15. The mysterious "Soylent Green" wafers that people survive on in the film of the same name are made from a type of man-eating alien spinach. True or False?

16. In *Halloween*, the murderer's name is the same as a leading comedy star. What is it?

17. Complete the following movie title: _____ *from the Mummy's Tomb.*

18. In *Cloverfield* (2008), a monster attacks which city?

19. Both versions of *Clash of the Titans* include the same line: "Release the..."

20. In *Monsters vs. Aliens* (2009), what happens to Susan Murphy on her wedding day?

(Answers on page 514)

Disney Princesses

1. Snow White is the only princess to get a star on the Hollywood Walk of Fame. True or False?

2. What are the names of Cinderella's two ugly stepsisters?

3. To protect Princess Aurora from the wicked queen, the three fairy godmothers raise Aurora without magic and call her what?

4. In *The Little Mermaid*, Ariel saves Prince Eric from drowning. True or False?

5. In *Beauty and the Beast*, how does Belle prove to the townsfolk that the Beast exists?

6. In *Aladdin*, what is the name of Princess Jasmine's pet tiger?

7. Pocahontas has a dream about an object that is linked to her future. What is the object in her dream?

8. In *Mulan*, what item does Grandmother Fa give to Mulan for serenity?

9. What is the name of Tiana's restaurant, which she opens at the end of *The Princess and the Frog*?

10. In *Sleeping Beauty*, when Aurora takes her place as a princess, her dress is made by hand by her fairy godmother Flora. True or False?

11. Pocahontas is the only princess based on a real person. True or False?

12. What is the name of Belle's friend the talking teapot in *Beauty and the Beast*?

13. Where does Princess Jasmine go when she escapes from the palace disguised as a commoner?

14. In *The Princess and the Frog*, Tiana's father is her biggest inspiration. What is his name?

15. In *The Little Mermaid*, what is a "dinglehopper" used for?

16. In *Tangled*, what is Flynn Rider's real name?

17. What reason does Gaston give for wanting to marry Belle in *Beauty and the Beast*?

18. In *Mulan*, what kind of creature is Mushu?

19. What is the name of Pocahontas's tribe in America?

20. In *Tangled*, what happens to Rapunzel's hair when it is cut short?

FILM & TV

Westerns

1. John Wayne made his breakthrough in which film?

2. Steven Spielberg directed *The Outlaw Josey Wales*. True or False?

3. Complete the name of this classic Western: *The Man Who Shot _____ Valance*

4. How many Best Director Oscars did Western legend John Ford win?

5. The song "Do Not Forsake Me Oh My Darling" featured in which film?

6. Elvis Presley stars in the Western titled *Flaming Star*. True or False?

7. Which valley has provided the backdrop for many Westerns?

8. Bob Dylan plays Billy in *Pat Garrett and Billy the Kid*. True or False?

9. Tombstone, the setting for several Westerns, is in which state?

10. Kirk Douglas plays which sharpshooting legend in *Gunfight at the O.K. Corral*?

11. *The Magnificent Seven* is based on which Japanese film?

12. Who plays Rooster Cogburn in the 1969 version of *True Grit*?

13. Roy Rogers rode the same famous horse in all his pictures. What was its name?

14. Clint Eastwood directed the Western *Unforgiven*. True or False?

15. Who plays the villainous Sheriff Daggett in the *Unforgiven*?

16. What is the title of John Wayne's last film?

17. *Blazing Saddles* was directed by whom?

18. In early Westerns, the hero tends to wear a white hat. True or False?

19. Paul Newman plays the Sundance Kid in *Butch Cassidy and the Sundance Kid*. True or False?

20. Which film was made to rival *Butch Cassidy and the Sundance Kid* at the box office?

21. Who plays "the ugly" character in *The Good, the Bad and the Ugly*?

22. Which actress is rescued as an adult in *The Searchers*, a film said to be based on a real-life incident?

23. What is the title of the Western directed by Quentin Tarantino and released in 2013?

24. Which Western stars Humphrey Bogart as a gold prospector?

25. Which actor directed *Dances with Wolves*?

American TV

1. Which main character in *Grey's Anatomy* dies in the season 5 finale?

2. In the season 7 premiere of *Weeds*, where do we find four of the main characters?

3. Why does Sookie, from *True Blood*, have magical powers?

4. Which character in *Glee* dies in the second season?

5. Which character gets the courage to ask out Pam of *The Office* in the final episode of season 3?

6. Tina Fey from *30 Rock* was also the head writer of *Saturday Night Live*. True or False?

7. Who leaves Ashley in season 7 of *The Bachelorette* because he was only there to promote his business?

8. Who is Squidward Q. Tentacles?

9. Which Walker gets cheated on in season 5 of *Brothers and Sisters*?

10. Which celebrity makes a guest appearance in the season 6 finale of *Entourage*?

11. Which one of Elena's friends turns into a vampire at the beginning of season 2 of *The Vampire Diaries*?

12. Who wrote the book on which the show *Westworld* is based?

13. With what is Silver from *90210* diagnosed in season 1?

14. What happens to Jason Street in season 1 of *Friday Night Lights* that leaves him paralyzed?

15. Mitchell and Cameron of *Modern Family* are raising a baby named Lawrence. True or False?

16. In which year was *Arrested Development* canceled, before it was later relaunched by Netflix?

17. Who is the first and only person to win two editions of *Survivor*?

18. Which Desperate Housewife is a former cheerleader for the San Francisco 49ers?

19. Which two countries have been visited most by contestants on *The Amazing Race*?

20. Who hosts the first season of *Top Chef*?

21. Which star of *Sex and the City* was a last-minute casting decision?

22. Who stars with Jane Fonda in *Grace and Frankie*?

23. How are the shows *Better Call Saul* and *Breaking Bad* connected?

24. Who plays the character of Maeve Millay in *Westworld*?

25. How many seasons of *Dancing with the Stars* have there been?

FILM & TV

Gangster Movies

1. Who plays the original Godfather?

2. On what day does British screen villain Harold Shand face his demise?

3. How many versions of *Scarface* have been filmed?

4. Which film is this quote from: "All my life, I wanted to be a gangster"?

5. Complete the name of the gangster classic: *Angels with Dirty...*

6. According to the film title, there are things to do in Denver when you're what?

7. Which gangster does Johnny Depp play in *Public Enemies*?

8. Which film pairs Robert De Niro and Al Pacino on screen for the first time?

9. What kind of gangster is Denzel Washington in Ridley Scott's 2007 film?

10. *Donnie Brasco* is based on the real-life story of an undercover FBI agent. True or False?

11. "Made it, Ma. Top of the world!" is a line from which 1940s classic?

12. Who plays Jack Carter in *Get Carter*?

13. Who plays the lead roles in 1967's *Bonnie and Clyde*?

14. Who directed *Once Upon a Time in America*?

15. Complete the name of this cult classic: *Reservoir...*

16. The crime family in *The Godfather* trilogy take their last name from which Sicilian city?

17. Complete the name of this film about low-level villains: *Brighton...*

18. Las Vegas is the setting for which Martin Scorsese film released in 1995?

19. In which city is the film *The Untouchables* set?

20. James Cagney never says, "You dirty rat!" in any of his films. True or False?

(Answers on page 514)

MI-5

1. Which government agency does *MI-5* follow?

2. What is the name given to the secure office where the officers are based?

3. The season 7 cliffhanger involves Harry Pearce being held prisoner by whom?

4. Where are the headquarters of MI5?

5. What is the code name given to the Counter-Terrorism Department of MI5?

6. Which character from *MI-5* has not been a Technician and Data Analyst?

7. In which season was Harry Pearce told that the queen wishes to give him a knighthood?

8. In season 8, which organization attempts to provoke a nuclear war between India and Pakistan?

9. What is the name of the spin-off series set in 2013 following a nuclear bomb in London?

10. Harry Pearce is the only person to have interacted with every single one of the show's main characters. True or False?

11. What is Lucas North's real name?

12. In season 9, what is Albany?

13. In Russia, who are the FSB?

14. Who takes on the role of Section Chief at the start of season 10?

15. At the start of season 10, Harry receives a note from a former MI6 agent. What is his name?

16. The identity of five assets is stored in a laptop that is stolen at the start of episode 2 of season 10. Which former MI5 operative is found with the laptop?

17. What is the usual occupation of John Grogan, the first spy uncovered on the stolen laptop in season 10?

18. What is the caller ID on Martha Ford's cell phone when she receives a call from MI5?

19. In what hotel room does Sasha Gavrick hide the cell phone that he retains from his mother?

20. At the end of episode 2 season 10, Tariq takes a minicab to Millbank to alert Harry of a "remote intrusion" on his home server. True or False?

FILM & TV

Modern Movies

1. Julia Roberts won the Academy Award, Golden Globe, and a BAFTA for her role in which 2000 film?

2. In which Austin Powers film does Beyoncé make her movie debut?

3. Which Rolling Stone appears in the *Pirates of the Caribbean* films?

4. Director Tim Burton has cast which actress in seven of his films?

5. Which Jane Austen classic was adapted into a film that stars Keira Knightley?

6. Who is Thomas A. Anderson better known as?

7. *The Lord of the Rings: The Return of the King* won every one of the 11 Oscars it was nominated for in 2003. True or False?

8. *The Shawshank Redemption* is based on work by which author?

9. Who became the first woman to win a Best Director Oscar in 2010?

10. What is the name of the character played by Robert De Niro in Martin Scorsese's *Taxi Driver*?

11. Who plays Chewbacca in 1977's *Star Wars*?

12. How many Academy Awards did Steven Spielberg's *E.T. the Extra-Terrestrial* win?

13. Who plays Deckard in Ridley Scott's *Blade Runner*?

14. *Reservoir Dogs* was directed by Quentin Tarantino in 1992. True or False?

15. Who plays Mildred Hayes in *Three Billboards outside Ebbing, Missouri*?

16. Who directed the *Lord of the Rings* trilogy?

17. Who directed *Titanic*, *Avatar*, and *The Terminator*?

18. *Walk the Line* is a biopic based on the life of which singer?

19. Cameron Diaz got her big break by being cast as the lead female in which film?

20. Which three films have Meg Ryan and Tom Hanks starred in together?

21. For which film did Sandra Bullock receive an Oscar?

22. Who directed the first foreign-language film to win the Academy Award for Best Picture, and what is its title?

23. Which 2020 remake tells the story of a doctor who can talk to animals, and who is the star?

24. Which 2017 film directed by Christopher Nolan features a mass rescue by small civilian watercraft?

25. *Birds of Prey* starring Margot Robbie features which DC Comics character?

FILM & TV

Book to Movie Adaptations

1. What character does Kermit the Frog play in the Muppet version of Robert Louis Stevenson's *Treasure Island*?

2. Which infamous movie villain was originally created by American horror/thriller author Thomas Harris?

3. Which actors play vampires in an adaptation of the book *Interview with the Vampire* by Anne Rice?

4. Complete the inscription from *The Lord of the Rings*: "One Ring to rule them all; One Ring to find them; One Ring to bring them all…"

5. What brand and model of car can be seen flying across London and the British countryside in the second *Harry Potter* film?

6. Alice Walker's *The Color Purple* became a hit Steven Spielberg film in 1985. Which star got her big break in the lead role?

7. In Rudyard Kipling's and Disney's *The Jungle Book*, what is the name of the python?

8. Sean Connery commands a submarine in which 1990 film based on a Tom Clancy book?

9. After five nominations, Kate Winslet won her first Oscar in 2008 for her role in an adaptation of which book by Bernhard Schlink?

10. Which Disney film adaptation of a classic book features playing cards, hares, cats, rabbits, dodos, and door knobs?

11. Part of the action in 1985's *A Room with a View* takes place in which Italian city?

12. *Breakfast at Tiffany's* has transitioned from novella to film to Broadway musical to famous song; who wrote the original book?

13. Meryl Streep stars in the 2006 film based on which novel about the fashion world by Lauren Weisberger?

14. Charles Dickens's *Oliver Twist* has proved popular with filmmakers. Who plays Fagin in the David Lean version?

15. Name the book by Ian McEwan that was filmed in 2007 with Keira Knightley and James McAvoy.

16. Who wrote the courtroom drama on which the Susan Sarandon film *The Client* is based?

17. What is the name of the book that became the influential Steven Spielberg film about the Holocaust?

18. C.S. Lewis's *The Chronicles of Narnia* have now been made into three successful movies, but how many books are there in the series?

19. Who wrote the books that became the successful *James Bond* spy film franchise?

20. *The Leopard* with Burt Lancaster is a 1963 film version of the novel by whom?

FILM & TV

From Stage to Screen

1. Which military movie starring Jack Nicholson was originally a play by Aaron Sorkin?

2. The play *Pygmalion* by George Bernard Shaw was adapted to become an Oscar-winning film musical. True or False?

3. The 1982 movie *Annie* came from a musical of the same name. True or False?

4. The film *My Own Private Idaho* re-imagines two of Shakespeare's plays in a radically new setting in the 1990s. Which two plays are involved?

5. A stage play by C. G. Bond was turned into a stage musical and then a musical film starring Johnny Depp and Helena Bonham Carter. What are the titles of the play and the musical?

6. The successful 1928 play *The Front Page* by Ben Hecht and Charles Macarthur was adapted for the cinema. What is the title of the film?

7. Which 1926 play by Maurine Dallas Watkins set in prohibition-era America became a stage musical and then an Oscar-winning musical movie in 2002?

8. *Romeo and Juliet* by William Shakespeare was adapted and updated for which blockbuster film musical?

9. *Carousel* is a 1956 movie adaptation based on a Rodgers and Hammerstein stage musical of the same name. Which year did it hit the stage?

10. Frederick Knott wrote the play *Dial M for Murder* in 1952. When was the film released?

11. *Who's Afraid of Virginia Woolf?* won the 1963 Tony Award for Best Play. True or False?

12. The film *Forbidden Planet* is a modern take on which play by Shakespeare?

13. Elizabeth Taylor stars in the 1958 film adaptation of Tennessee Williams's play *Cat on a Hot Tin Roof.* True or False?

14. The 1954 play *The Matchmaker* by Thornton Wilder was adapted to become which successful musical film?

15. Which 1975 musical film based on the play of the same name introduced actor Tim Curry?

16. *Glengarry Glen Ross*, a play by David Mamet, was released as a film in 1992. The story depicts the lives of four real-estate agents. True or False?

17. Who plays King Arthur in the 1967 film based on the stage musical *Camelot*?

18. Cyndi Lauper was Eva Peron in the film version of the musical *Evita*. True or False?

19. Which Oscar-winning film is based on the stage play *I Am a Camera*, set in the early years of Nazi Germany?

20. Who is its star?

FILM & TV

Avengers Assemble, from Comic and Screen

1. *The Avengers* was created by Stan Lee and Jack Kirby and first appeared in 1963. True or False?

2. Captain America is one of the original Avengers in the film series. True or False?

3. In which film does Captain America first appear as an avenger?

4. Who is the first supervillain the Avengers face?

5. Loki once turned Thor into a girl. True or False?

6. Who writes the Avengers Charter?

7. What is the name of Thor's hammer?

8. What is the Hulk's full name?

9. Odin once imprisoned Loki in a tree. True or False?

10. What is the name of the project that transforms Steve Rogers from a 98-pound weakling into Captain America?

11. Who plays Tony Stark in the film series?

12. What is the name of the metal that makes up Captain America's shield?

13. Iduun's apples help keep Thor immortal. What are they called?

14. What is Hawkeye's real name?

15. Baron Zemo founded which supervillain team?

16. Where is the Avengers Mansion located?

17. Natasha Romanova, the Black Widow, was originally a spy from where?

18. Which member of the X-Men was once a member of the Avengers?

19. Which additional superhero makes an appearance in *Avengers: Infinity War*?

20. What special powers does Hawkeye have?

21. When describing the Avengers to Loki, how does Tony Stark describe Thor?

22. Where does Natasha Romanoff find Bruce Banner in *The Avengers* (2012)?

23. In *Avengers: Infinity War*, who saves Dr. Strange from being sucked out into space?

24. Which of the Avengers does Loki plan to use to bring down S.H.I.E.L.D.?

25. What does S.H.I.E.L.D. stand for?

FILM & TV

Captain America

1. Captain America makes his first appearance in what comic book?

2. What classification does young Steve Rogers receive at his physical before he becomes Captain America?

3. What does Steve tell the doctor is his reason for enlisting?

4. What is the name of the doctor in charge of "Project: Rebirth"?

5. The Project physician is the only person who knows how the enhancement process works. True or False?

6. What turns Steve Rogers into Captain America?

7. In which year is Steve Rogers frozen?

8. What symbol is on Captain America's shield?

9. Who is Captain America's best friend?

10. In which year is Steve Rogers unfrozen?

11. In the film *Captain America: Civil War*, who does Captain America fight?

12. How did Captain America feel about the Superhuman Registration Act?

13. In *Captain America: The Winter Soldier*, with which S.H.I.E.L.D. agent is Steve Rogers sent on a mission?

14. Who is the Winter Soldier?

15. What is Captain America's shield made out of?

16. In *Captain America: The First Avenger*, who is the Red Skull?

17. In *Captain America: Civil War*, which teenage superhero does Tony Stark recruit to the team to oppose and capture Captain America?

18. Which agent was in love with Steve Rogers in the 1940s?

19. In *Captain America: The Winter Soldier*, what are the giant flying S.H.I.E.L.D. vehicles called?

20. Which role does Tommy Lee Jones play in *Captain America: The First Avenger*?

FILM & TV

Batman: The Dark Knight

1. At what age does Bruce Wayne embark on his journey to learn all the skills he will need to become Batman?

2. What outing ends in disaster for the Wayne family?

3. What is the full name of Batman's butler?

4. What villain does Harvey Dent become?

5. Who directed *The Dark Knight*?

6. Which villain appears in every film in *The Dark Knight* trilogy?

7. Which villain once broke Batman's back?

8. Jason Todd is the third Robin. True or False?

9. When Jason Todd returns from the grave, under what name does he fight crime?

10. By what other name is Jean-Paul Valley known?

11. Which of the following does NOT exist: Batboy, Batman, Batgirl, Batwoman?

12. Bane has brown eyes and brown hair. True or False?

13. Jonathan Crane, aka Scarecrow, suffers from chiropteraphobia. This is the fear of what?

14. What is the Penguin's real name?

15. What is Harley Quinn's job when she first meets the Joker?

16. Batman is a founding member of the Justice League of America. True or False?

17. Barbara Gordon, the first Batgirl, went on to become whom?

18. Barbara Gordon is the biological daughter of Commissioner Gordon. True or False?

19. Selina Kyle's first catsuit as Catwoman is which color?

20. What is the name of the gangster who throws the acid in Harvey Dent's face?

FILM & TV

The Oscars: An Encore

1. In which year was the first Academy Awards ceremony?

2. Which three films have won 11 Oscars, the most by a single film?

3. Which film won the Academy Award for Best Picture in 1994?

4. Which three animated films have been nominated for the Best Picture Oscar, the only three to have been nominated?

5. Who has won the highest number of Oscars for acting?

6. Jean Dujardin was the first-ever French actor to win a Best Actor Oscar in 2011. True or False?

7. Two actors have posthumously won Oscars for acting. One was Peter Finch. Who was the other?

8. Walt Disney has won the highest number of Oscars ever by an individual. How many nominations did he receive?

9. How old was the youngest-ever Oscar winner, Tatum O'Neal, when she won Best Supporting Actress for *Paper Moon*?

10. Which director has won the most Academy Awards for directing?

11. *The Godfather II* is the first sequel to have ever won an Oscar for Best Picture. True or False?

12. Who was the first person to host the Oscars?

13. How many actors have won two Best Actor in a Leading Role Oscars?

14. Who won an Oscar for portraying an Oscar winner in 2005?

15. It was cheaper to build the *Titanic* than it was to make a film about its sinking. True or False?

16. How many times did Gwyneth Paltrow say "Thank you" in her acceptance speech for the Best Actress Oscar for *Shakespeare in Love*?

17. Marlon Brando refused his Best Actor Academy for which film?

18. Which is the only X-rated film to have won Best Picture?

19. What was Roberto Benigni thankful for in his acceptance speech for his film *Life Is Beautiful*?

20. The Academy Award for Best Original Musical has not been awarded since 1984 due to there being an insufficient number of eligible films. True or False?

Art in TV, Music, and Film

1. Which famous artist appeared in the BBC's *Doctor Who* in 2010?

2. The murderer in Wes Craven's *Scream* horror movies wears a Halloween mask inspired by a painting by which artist?

3. What kind of dancer is featured in the 1998 movie *Degas and the Dancer*?

4. Which painting does Thomas Crown steal in the movie *The Thomas Crown Affair*?

5. The television drama *Desperate Romantics* focuses on the lives and loves of which type of artists?

6. In the 1997 movie *Titanic*, Rose has a collection of art on board. Which of these is part of her collection: *Water Lilies* (Monet), *The Kiss* (Klimt), *Sunflowers* (van Gogh)?

7. In 1968, which band paid tribute to Lowry in their single "Pictures of Matchstick Men"?

8. Which British movie starring Bob Hoskins is about a petty criminal who becomes entangled in the life of a high-class call girl?

9. Who stars in the 1996 movie *Surviving Picasso*?

10. Whose painting does Libby use to track down her husband Nicholas Parsons in the 1999 film *Double Jeopardy*?

11. Which artist is at the heart of the book and film *Girl with a Pearl Earring*?

12. Which movie starring Charlton Heston covers the story of Michelangelo's troubles while painting the ceiling of the Sistine Chapel?

13. In *Entrapment* starring Sean Connery and Catherine Zeta-Jones, which artist's painting is stolen at the beginning?

14. Who sang the song "Mona Lisa" in the 1950s?

15. The 1952 movie *Moulin Rouge* is a fictional account of which French artist?

16. *Factory Girl* starring Sienna Miller is about a socialite's relationship with a folk singer and whom?

17. The logo for surf equipment company Quiksilver is inspired by which painting?

18. *Little Ashes* starring Robert Pattinson is a movie about— among others—which artist?

19. Leonardo da Vinci's *The Last Supper* plays a central role in Dan Brown's *The Da Vinci Code*. True or False?

20. Who stars in the silver-screen biopic *Pollock*?

FILM & TV

Film Buff

1. Who directed the 1927 classic *Metropolis*?

2. "It wasn't the airplanes. It was Beauty killed the Beast." Which iconic film does this quote come from?

3. Which famous actor-director plays Cardinal Wolsey in *A Man for All Seasons*?

4. The 1941 film *The Maltese Falcon* is based on the book of the same name. Who wrote the book?

5. Who plays Ilsa in *Casablanca* opposite Humphrey Bogart's Rick?

6. How many Hollywood musicals did Gene Kelly dance in between 1942 and 1957?

7. Which of these actors stars in Alfred Hitchcock's *Vertigo*: James Stewart, Gary Grant, Humphrey Bogart?

8. What year did Disney's *Snow White and the Seven Dwarfs* premiere?

9. What year marked the release of the first-ever 3-D film, *Bwana Devil*?

10. Which 1946 film stars Rita Hayworth and is directed by Charles Vidor?

11. *Frankenstein*, *King Kong*, and *Dracula* were all originally screened in which decade?

12. What is the name of James Dean's final movie before his premature death in 1955?

13. Norma Jeane Mortenson is the real name of which Hollywood icon?

14. Which subgenre of film would you most associate with director Sergio Leone?

15. Who plays Mrs. Robinson in *The Graduate*?

16. What character does Clint Eastwood play in Sergio Leone's *Dollars* trilogy?

17. The 1950s science-fiction classic *The War of the Worlds* stars Gene Barry and which actress?

18. Who is Leo the Lion?

19. Horror-film and Western icon John Carradine is the father of David Carradine. True or False?

20. What is Marlon Brando's debut film?

21. *The Shawshank Redemption* is based on a work by which author?

22. *Star Trek*, directed by J. J. Abrams and premiered in 2009, marked how many motion pictures for the franchise?

23. What is the name of the character played by Robert De Niro in Martin Scorsese's *Taxi Driver*?

24. *Reservoir Dogs* was directed by Quentin Tarantino in 1992. True or False?

25. Who plays Marge Gunderson in *Fargo*?

FILM & TV

BFI on Film

1. What is the name of the first film Ken Loach directed, which premiered in 1967?

2. Who directed the 1949 British classic, *The Third Man*, which went on to win the Best Film award at Cannes?

3. Which British actor first portrayed Darth Vader in *Star Wars* in 1977?

4. What is the subject matter of Lindsay Anderson's 1957 film *Every Day Except Christmas*?

5. Richard Attenborough directed *Gandhi* in 1989. True or False?

6. What year did *Kes* first appear on the big screen?

7. Where in London was Charlie Chaplin born?

8. Which of the following films is NOT directed by Stephen Frears: *Four Weddings and a Funeral*, *Mrs. Henderson Presents*, *Prick Up Your Ears*?

9. What year did Alfred Hitchcock die?

10. What is the name of Guy Ritchie's first film?

11. What is the name of Kate Winslet's character in the 1998 film *Hideous Kinky*?

12. What year was Monty Python first televised?

13. *The 39 Steps*, as directed by Alfred Hitchcock, premiered when?

14. Which British director was responsible for *Brief Encounter* in 1945?

15. Mike Hodges, director of *Get Carter* and *Flash Gordon*, was born in 1966. True or False?

16. How many of the 9 BAFTA nominations did *Four Weddings and a Funeral* win in the 1995 ceremony?

17. Anthony Minghella directed *Truly, Madly, Deeply* in 1991 for which major British television company?

18. What is the name of Sam Mendes's first feature film, which premiered in 1999?

19. Alfred Hitchcock completed his last film in 1976. What is the title?

20. What two films directed by Quentin Tarantino and Robert Rodriguez in 2007 make up *Grindhouse*?

FILM & TV

Bond Villains

1. In which film does Blofeld build himself a new face?

2. Alec Trevelyan gives James and Natalya "six minutes" to escape on his train in *GoldenEye*. What's special about these six minutes?

3. "I gave orders that Bond should be killed. Why is he still alive?" Who says this?

4. What physical difference singles out Le Chiffre, Bond's nemesis in *Casino Royale*?

5. SPECTRE stands for Special Executive for Counter-Intelligence, Terrorism, Revenge, and Evil. True or False?

6. In which film does James Bond first meet Blofeld?

7. What are Blofeld's first and middle name?

8. What is the name of the virus that Blofeld's "Angels of Death" will unleash on the world in *On Her Majesty's Secret Service*?

9. In which film is Dr. Kananga the bad guy?

10. What physical difference does Bond know about Francisco Scaramanga when M first mentions him in *The Man with the Golden Gun*?

11. James Bond and Major Anya Amasova of the KGB come up against which villain in *The Spy Who Loved Me*?

12. Max Zorin famously says, "James Bond. You appear with the tedious inevitability of an unloved season" in *A View to a Kill*. True or False?

13. What is the name of the assassin who breaks into the MI6 safe house in *The Living Daylights* and kidnaps General Georgi Koskov?

14. Which Bond villain says, "The distance between insanity and genius is measured only by success"?

15. In the film *Tomorrow Never Dies*, the villain is Doctor Kaufman. What is he considered a master in?

16. What happened to Renard that resulted in him not being able to feel pain?

17. What poisonous creature do Wint & Kidd use to kill their victim when they first appear in *Diamonds are Forever*?

18. Who says, "Mr. Bond is indeed a very rare breed. Soon to be made extinct"?

19. In *Die Another Day*, the villain Gustav Graves was formerly known as whom?

20. Elektra King hates MI6 because they advise her father not to pay her ransom money. Who does she target specifically?

Iron Man in Words and Pictures

1. Which of the following does the Iron Man suit NOT have: jet boots, gauntlets, wings?

2. Iron Man makes his comic book debut in *Tales of Suspense #39*. What year was it?

3. The first Iron Man suit is gray, and Tony Stark finally settles on a suit of red and gold. What color is the suit in-between?

4. What color are Tony Stark's eyes on film?

5. Tony Stark says, "Being a man in a metal suit doesn't solve any problems… It just gives you a whole lot of new ones to think about." True or False?

6. Which of the following has Stark Industries NOT been known as over the years: StarkCorp, Stark Enterprises, Stark International?

7. What is Pepper Potts's full name?

8. What is Rhodey's name when he puts on the Iron Man suit?

9. Who of the following is a long-standing enemy of Iron Man: Titanium Man, Bethany Cabe, War Machine?

10. Wolverine once borrowed an Iron Man suit from Tony Stark. True or False?

11. What age does Tony Stark enroll at MIT?

12. In what circumstances does Tony Stark decide to go public with his dual identity?

13. What government act causes the last rift between Iron Man and Captain America?

14. Where is the *Dragon Seed Saga* set?

15. When the West Coast Avengers disband, Iron Man sets up Force Works. Who is also a member: Spider-Man, Spider-Woman, Storm?

16. Tony Stark once says, "Hiding? Is that what it's come to? Hiding my feelings, my life behind this iron face?" True or False?

17. Who of the following has Iron Man NOT teamed up with: The Thunderbolts, the Thundercats, Ms. Marvel?

18. What is the super serum that gives superhuman strength, melding man and machine?

19. Which of the following heroes is NOT a member of the Illuminati: The Human Torch, Black Bolt, Mr. Fantastic?

20. Tony Stark designs a special suit of armor for Spider-Man, the Iron Spider costume. True or False?

(Answers on page 516)

FILM & TV

Star Wars

1. At which convention was *Star Wars* first revealed?

2. Who is responsible for creating the beep-boops, blips, and buzzes of *Star Wars*?

3. George Lucas witnessed the blockbusting lineup for the premiere of *Star Wars* while eating lunch where?

4. The story of Mace Windu, a revered Jedi-bendu of Ophuchi, is told in… ?

5. Padme Amidala is Senator of… ?

6. In the original and prequel trilogies, R2-D2 is mostly operated from the inside by which actor?

7. Steven Spielberg thought *Return of the Jedi* was the greatest *Star Wars* film of them all. True or False?

8. Which of the following action figures were NOT offered with Kenner's February 1978 early bird mail-in offer: R2-D2, Luke Skywalker, Darth Vader?

9. E.T. pines for his home world when he recognized a Halloween costume of which character?

10. The final episode of the 2004 *Clone Wars* micro-series introduces which villain?

11. On January 31, 2005, Lucas called "Action" for the last day of *Episode III* shots where?

12. *Star Wars* won the Best Picture Academy Award in 1978. True or False?

13. *Howard the Duck*, also by George Lucas, although poorly received by critics, managed to make back its $37 million budget. True or False?

14. Which of the following megapopular movie theaters did not show *Episode III*: Grauman's Chinese Theater, the Ziegfeld, Leicester Square (London)?

15. The 501st Legion is established as a part of the *Star Wars* universe in which novel?

16. Star Wars Celebration (1999) was the first official *Star Wars* convention. True or False?

17. The voice of a Neimoidian general in *The Clone Wars* is provided by which *Star Trek* actor?

18. In 1996, screen-accurate lightsaber-hilt replicas were released by which collectibles company?

19. The design of C-3P0 is partly inspired by that of another famous droid called what?

20. The Strategic Defense Initiative, the controversial space-based missile defense program of the 1980s, was nicknamed what?

The Simpsons

1. What is the name of Lionel Hutz's law firm?

2. What is the descriptive anagram Lisa's rival creates to describe a famous actor in a game with her father?

3. What class does Lenny teach at the Adult Education Annex?

4. Sherry is older than Terry by 10 seconds. True or False?

5. In "Treehouse of Horror V," what dish is Üter cooked into?

6. What is the name on Bart's fake credit card?

7. How old is Hans Moleman?

8. Which of the following is NOT a kind of Duff beer: Duff Peanut Butter Lager, Duff with Penicillin, Duff Amber Fire?

9. How many times has the creator Matt Groening appeared in *The Simpsons*?

10. Who is Fat Tony's son named after?

11. Who is Señor Ding Dong?

12. In the Springfield Film Festival, there were seven entries. What is the name of Apu's film?

13. How many puppies does Santa's Little Helper sire with She's the Fastest?

14. Who does Bart talk to after a failed prank call made to Moe in the episode "Flaming Moe"?

15. Which of these products is NOT endorsed by Krusty the Klown: Krusty's Kosher Karaoke Machine, Krusty-Brand Home Pregnancy Test, Krusty-Brand Lo-Cal TV Dinner?

16. What is the first film Scratchy the cat appears in?

17. What is the age difference between Bart and Lisa?

18. What is the title of the fourth film in the McBain series?

19. What is the worst name Moe has ever heard?

20. Which of the following is NOT one of Dr. Nick Riviera's degrees: Club Med School, Downtown Drive-Thru Doctors, Female Body Inspector?

FILM & TV

Bond Girls

1. What is the name of the girl who first appears walking out of the sea in a bikini in *Dr. No*?

2. What is significant about Jill Masterson's untimely death in *Goldfinger*?

3. Who says of Bond, "When the time is right, he will be killed"?

4. What is the name of the boss of the Japanese Secret Service in *You Only Live Twice*?

5. Bond and Teresa di Vicenzo first meet in *On Her Majesty's Secret Service* when he does what?

6. What is Tiffany Case obsessed with?

7. In which film does Rosie Carver, intrepid CIA agent, appear?

8. Major Anya Amasova, who appears in *The Spy Who Loved Me*, wants to kill Bond because he betrayed her with another woman. True or False?

9. Naomi works for Karl Stromberg in *The Spy Who Loved Me*. What is her job?

10. What is the signature weapon of Melina Havelock, the heroine in *For Your Eyes Only*?

11. Magda is the cool, enigmatic, and sinuously athletic ringmaster of Octopussy's circus. True or False?

12. When Bond says, "Whoever she was, I must have scared the living daylights out of her," who is he talking about?

13. What is Natalya Simonova's profession in *GoldenEye*?

14. Who says, "You know, this job of yours"?

15. In which country do Bond and Dr. Christmas Jones first meet?

16. In which film does Agent Goodnight appear?

17. What is Jinx wearing when she and Bond first meet in *Die Another Day*?

18. Miranda Frost is an Olympic gold medal winner in which sport?

19. From what agency does Vesper Lynd, Bond's love interest in *Casino Royale*, come?

20. What is the name of the girl Bond teams up with in *Quantum of Solace*?

21. In *Dr. No*, what is Sylvia Trench playing when Bond finds her in his apartment?

22. What secret weapon does Rosa Klebb have in *From Russia with Love*?

23. Who plays Pussy Galore in *Goldfinger*?

24. Who plays Teresa di Vicenzo in *On Her Majesty's Secret Service*?

25. In *Diamonds Are Forever*, what color is Tiffany Chase's mustang?

The BFI on Hitchcock

1. What is Hitchcock's first Hollywood release?

2. What style of film is Hitchcock most notable for?

3. Where was Hitchcock born in the UK?

4. In which film does Hitchcock make his first cameo appearance?

5. Grace Kelly stars in *Rear Window* with Cary Grant. True or False?

6. Which one of these actors does NOT star in a Hitchcock film: Gloria Swanson, Tippi Hedren, Joseph Cotten?

7. How many Laurel Awards did Hitchcock win in his career?

8. In what year was *Psycho* released?

9. Who wrote the script for *North by Northwest*?

10. Hitchcock was knighted in 1979. True or False?

11. How long did it take Hitchcock to progress from Title Designer to Film Director?

12. What is the name of Hitchcock's wife?

13. Which American composer is most notable for his collaborations with Hitchcock?

14. What is Hitchcock's middle name?

15. Ingrid Bergman, while trying to get into character, told Hitchcock she couldn't grasp her character's motivation. To which Hitchcock replied what?

16. What is the name of Alfred Hitchcock's first television series?

17. Hitchcock was raised as a Roman Catholic. True or False?

18. What causes the birds to be aggressive in *The Birds*?

19. During his cameo in *Strangers on a Train*, what does Hitchcock board the train with?

20. What was the date of Alfred Hitchcock's death?

Indian Cinema

1. In which year did commercial cinema begin in India?

2. How many National Film Awards did Satyajit Ray, regarded as one of the greatest auteurs of 20th-century cinema, win?

3. The first Indian talkie movie is what?

4. Known as "The Golden Age of Indian cinema," which era produced some of the most critically acclaimed Indian films of all time?

5. Which was the first Hindi movie to receive the National Award?

6. Who is known as "The Father of Indian Cinema"?

7. Which film was India's entry at the Oscars in 2003?

8. *Kisan Kanya* is India's first color film. True or False?

9. Who is the only Indian to have won the Lifetime Achievement Award at the Academy Awards?

10. Naushad Ali brought Indian classical music into the film medium. True or False?

11. Which 2009 film is based on the terrorist attacks of 9/11?

12. In which year were the Filmfare Awards given for the first time?

13. What was the first Bollywood film to be nominated for the Best Foreign Film Award at the Oscars?

14. In the Indian film world, Begum Ayesha Sultana Khan is popularly known as whom?

15. The lead female role in the popular Hindi movie *Mother India* is played by who?

16. In the overseas market, *My Name Is Khan* is the top lifetime-grossing Bollywood film. True or False?

17. *Monsoon Wedding* won no awards at the 13th Valenciennes International Film Festival in France. True or False?

18. Sunny Deol's real name is what?

19. Jawaharlal Nehru was a die-hard fan of her and even wrote her a fan letter. Who is she?

20. *Raja Harishchandra* is the first full-length Indian motion picture. True or False?

21. Tollywood films are in what regional language?

22. Which Bollywood actor stars in *Life of Pi*?

23. Which actress was awarded the Padma Shri in 2016?

24. Masala films mix genres, such as musicals, romance, and drama. True or False?

25. In which film does Anil Kapoor first appear without his moustache?

FILM & TV

Famous Locations in Film

1. Where was almost all of zombie romp *Shaun of the Dead* shot?

2. In which country was the *Lord of the Rings* trilogy shot?

3. Kubrick horror flick *The Shining* was almost entirely filmed where?

4. Which movie borrows unused footage of the Glacier National Park, in Montana, from *The Shining*?

5. What building is used as the headquarters of the sinister OCP Corporation in *Robocop*?

6. Over which city is Neo flying at the end of futuristic fantasy *The Matrix*?

7. The Tribeca Firehouse at 14 North Moore Street, New York City, was used for which film?

8. Lois Lane is left dangling from a building on which street in New York in the original 1978 *Superman*?

9. Where is the fictional town square in the police spoof *Hot Fuzz*?

10. Where does the opening shoplifting chase take place in *Trainspotting*?

11. In the Bruce Willis thriller *Die Hard*, who does the building belong to?

12. Where can the planet of Tatooine from *Star Wars* be found on Earth?

13. *The Sound of Music* was shot in the studios of 20th Century Fox and where else?

14. Where was romcom *Notting Hill* filmed?

15. Where was the Palantine Rally filmed in the 1970s classic *Taxi Driver*?

16. Where was the main set constructed for the most expensive movie ever made at the time, *Waterworld*?

17. Where can Elliot's house in the 1982 movie sensation *E.T. the Extra-Terrestrial* be found?

18. Antarctic 1982 horror movie *The Thing* was actually shot in British Columbia. True or False?

19. Where was the quirky comedy *Napoleon Dynamite* shot?

20. In which part of London does a coffee-shop explosion take place in the 2006 film *Children of Men*?

FILM & TV

Period Dramas

1. Which period drama starring Jennifer Ehle and Colin Firth hit British TV screens in 1995?

2. Which UK television drama features the ongoing sagas at 165 Eaton Place?

3. Which period drama set in the American West starred Jane Seymour?

4. Between what years did the *Little House on the Prairie* TV show run?

5. *Middlemarch* is a 1994 television adaptation from the novel of the same name by… ?

6. Stanley Kubrick's period film featuring the exploits of a fictional 18th-century Irish adventurer is… ?

7. Who plays the detective tracking Jack the Ripper in *From Hell* (2001)?

8. Where was the 2007 TV period drama *The Tudors* filmed?

9. In what decade is American Western television series *Deadwood* set?

10. Who directed the epic movie *Gladiator*?

11. *Marie Antoinette* is an early period movie starring Norma Shearer. When was it released?

12. Which 2002 miniseries was one of the last filmed with actor Richard Harris before he died?

13. The 2004 epic film *Troy* was based on Homer's… ?

14. The first British television adaptation of *Robin Hood* was produced in 1953. True or False?

15. In which TV series does Alan Rickman play a clergyman named Slope?

16. *Boardwalk Empire* is an American TV period drama set during which era?

17. Which of these is a 2008 movie set in the prehistoric era: *10,000 BC*, *Caveman*, *The Ice Age*?

18. Which 2010 period television drama is set on a post-Edwardian-era Yorkshire country estate?

19. Which 1995 Mel Gibson period flick picked up five Academy Awards?

20. *Jidaigeki* is a type of Japanese television drama set during the time of the samurai. True or False?

21. Who plays Thomas Cromwell in *Wolf Hall*?

22. Which long-running period drama series is based on the novels of Winston Graham?

23. In which British city is *Peaky Blinders* set?

24. Which TV series based on a Gaskell book is set in a Cheshire town in 1842?

25. *Sanditon* is based on an unfinished novel by… ?

Australian Films

1. The popular quote "That's not a knife..." comes from which 1980s Aussie hit?

2. Which 1975 period drama features panpipes and missing schoolgirls?

3. *A Cry in the Dark* is the true-life story of mother Lindy Chamberlain, whose baby was taken by a... ?

4. Toni Collette won a Golden Globe Award nomination for her 1994 role in... ?

5. A violent skinhead biopic starring Russell Crowe is the 1992 film... ?

6. Nicole Kidman first broke into mainstream movies in which 1989 thriller?

7. Which drama about a musician on the verge of a nervous breakdown won Geoffrey Rush a Best Actor Oscar?

8. Which 2000 film features the prison antics of Mark Brandon Read?

9. Which film that centers around the animal action on Hoggett's farm was shot in New South Wales?

10. Winning two Oscars, which 2001 jukebox musical is set in France and stars Ewan McGregor?

11. Which movie follows the 1,500-mile (2,400-km) trek of two Aboriginal girls?

12. The Anzac battlefield movie starring Mel Gibson is what?

13. *Samson and Delilah* is about two Aboriginal children who steal a car to drive to Perth. True or False?

14. Which 1979 road thriller introduced Mel Gibson to an international audience?

15. The 2006 animated comedy about Antarctic hi-jinks is... ?

16. What 2005 horror flick is about every backpacker's nightmare?

17. Which 1992 romcom centers around making it to the Pan-Pacific Grand Prix Championship?

18. Which affectionate suburban satire had Darryl Kerrigan say, "This is going straight to the pool room"?

19. Men dressed as women singing their way through the Outback can be seen in the musical... ?

20. *The Story of the Kelly Gang* was the first feature-length Australian film. It was released in 1906. True or False?

FILM & TV

Superhero Villains

1. Which supervillain waddles into view in *Batman Returns*?

2. Xander Drax is the villain charged with battling "The Ghost Who Walks," better known as whom?

3. Dr. Hector Hammond is a supervillain usually associated with which superhero?

4. Dr. Doom is the terrorizing supervillain from which film?

5. Selena is the archenemy of which superhero?

6. Which bald supervillain is obsessed with destroying Superman?

7. The Red Skull is the villain trying to kill which popular US superhero?

8. Bullseye and Kingpin are on the list of which film superhero?

9. Venom is the shapeshifting nemesis of Spider-Man. True or False?

10. The Abomination is the supreme supervillain set on crushing whom?

11. He's handy if you drop a fork, but not so great if you're having dinner with Charles Xavier. Who is this supervillain?

12. In which movie does bad girl Poison Ivy appear?

13. The Green Goblin spends most of his time trying to kill off which well-known superhero?

14. Which Fantastic Four villain likes to devour planets?

15. Doomsday is the only villain in the universe to have killed Superman. True or False?

16. Once, he loved this superhero like a son, but later Professor Trevor "Broom" Bruttenholm sets out to destroy him. Who is he?

17. Which supervillain is played by Jim Carrey in *Batman Forever*?

18. Which villain has a contract for Johnny Blaze's soul in *Ghost Rider*?

19. Juggernaut makes an appearance in which X-Men movie?

20. Who battles with Superman in space during *Superman IV*?

FILM & TV

(Answers on page 517)

Pixar

1. What year did *Toy Story*, Pixar's first feature-length film, come out?

2. What is the name of the lamp that is the official mascot of Pixar?

3. Pixar was originally the computer graphics division of Lucasfilm Ltd. True or False?

4. What does Sid's sister Hannah call Buzz when they're having tea together in *Toy Story*?

5. Who steals Woody's hat and says: "I'm Woody! Howdy, howdy, howdy!"?

6. What game does the main character in *Geri's Game* play in the park?

7. In which Pixar film would you find Cornelius?

8. What year was the film *Cars* released?

9. Andy's dog is called Bounder. True or False?

10. How many small birds are sitting on the wire in *For the Birds* before the big bird lands?

11. How many years does it take for Sully to be promoted from trainee Scarer to Scarer?

12. What does Boo call Sully?

13. In *Finding Nemo*, Dory is a regal tang, also known as a hippo tang or blue surgeonfish. True or False?

14. What is Team Dinoco's color in *Cars*?

15. In *Finding Nemo*, what is Nemo's dad named?

16. In *The Incredibles*, evil mastermind Syndrome's real name is what?

17. In *One Man Band*, which of the following instruments does Bass NOT play: tuba, violin, drums?

18. In *Cars*, what make is Sally, Lightning McQueen's love interest?

19. What is the name of Linguini's restaurant in *Ratatouille*?

20. *WALL-E* is set in the future, in which year?

21. What does Russell name his giant bird friend in *Up*?

22. In *Toy Story 3*, what is Lotso's full name?

23. In *Cars*, what is the name of Ramone's company?

24. In *Brave*, Merida's father is named Fergus. What does "Fergus" mean?

25. Of what type of wood is Fergus's leg made?

CHAPTER 10

POTLUCK

More of everything mixed up
in this wide-ranging collection of
quizzes covering all subjects from
fashion, cars, and mad emperors to
space, rock pools, and how to survive
in the wild. Take a chance and
see what you get...

Musical Instruments

1. Which keyboard instrument can be carried and squeezed?

2. The didgeridoo comes from which country?

3. Queen Elizabeth I of England was highly musical and played which keyboard instrument?

4. Fender Stratocaster is a make of what?

5. What is a theremin?

6. Unlike many other wind instruments, the bassoon has a double reed rather than a single reed. True or False?

7. The *pipa* is a four-stringed, pear-shaped instrument that looks like a lute. Where does it come from?

8. The saxophone was first used for military music. True or False?

9. Miles Davis is best known for playing which instrument?

10. The theme for the film *The Third Man* is played on which instrument?

11. Mutes are added to a trumpet's bell to do what?

12. A triangle can always be heard above an orchestra. True or False?

13. Which of these is a type of cymbal: hi-hat, snare, tom-tom?

14. Which of these is NOT a sound effect that you can make with a saxophone: trilling, growling, squawking?

15. What sort of instrument is a balalaika?

16. Which instrument to the ancient Greeks symbolized universal harmony?

17. The ukelele was invented in 19th-century Hawaii. True or False?

18. Piccolos belong in the brass section of the orchestra. True or False?

19. The sousaphone is a type of what?

20. How many notes are there in an octave on a keyboard (white and black keys)?

21. What part of a horn is the bell?

22. How many pedals does a harp have?

23. A lute needs a reed to be played. True or False?

24. In *Peter and the Wolf*, what instrument is used to represent the cat?

25. Which instrument is used to represent the duck in *Peter and the Wolf*?

POTLUCK

Dinosaur Attack

1. What does the word "dinosaur" mean?

2. The giant, plant-eating sauropods had incredibly long what?

3. What is the name of the dinosaur famous for the plates along its back?

4. Dinosaurs laid eggs. True or False?

5. What is Archaeopteryx's claim to fame?

6. Pterosaurs were not dinosaurs. How were they different?

7. Ichthyosaurs lived where?

8. What is a paleontologist?

9. Oviraptorids were thought to be egg stealers because the first fossil was found near a group of eggs. True or False?

10. Some experts think the skull of Giganotosaurus was 6 ft (1.8 m) long. True or False?

11. How do scientists think a stegosaur's back plates helped it to keep comfortable?

12. All dinosaurs were huge. True or False?

13. No complete Supersaurus neck is known, but experts think it was more than 52 ft (16 m) long (seven times longer than a giraffe's). True or False?

14. What color was Tyrannosaurus rex?

15. When do experts think the first dinosaurs appeared?

16. Velociraptors are thought to have been fully feathered. True or False?

17. Velociraptors were no bigger than a wolf. True or False?

18. What does "velociraptor" mean?

19. Most dinosaurs were herbivores, carnivores, or omnivores?

20. Tyrannosaurus rex was the largest of all the carnivorous dinosaurs. True or False?

21. What do experts think might have brought about the end of the dinosaurs?

22. What was the first dinosaur to be discovered?

23. What dinosaur was the size of a chicken?

24. Who was the famous female fossil hunter who died in 1847?

25. I have four paddle-like flippers, a tiny head, sharp teeth, and a pointed tail. Which dinosaur am I?

All about You

1. Humans have just one stomach. How many stomachs does a cow have?

2. How many bones are there in an adult skull?

3. Where would you find the smallest bone in the body?

4. To what food group do potatoes belong?

5. What is the largest organ in the body?

6. The brain is soft and squishy. What keeps it safe from damage?

7. How many dead skin cells fall off the human body every day?

8. What is the hardest-working muscle in the body?

9. What does trichromacy refer to?

10. The dangling structure at the back of the mouth is called the what?

11. What gas do we need from the air for respiration?

12. The elbow is an example of which sort of joint?

13. Which of these animals is the slowest runner: brown bear, human, wolf?

14. Which system in the body is part of the immune system and is responsible for carrying white blood cells to the bones?

15. How many teeth does an adult have?

16. Approximately how much food will you eat in your lifetime?

17. There are enough blood vessels in the human body to wrap around Earth's equator twice. True or False?

18. How many years of their life does an average person spend asleep?

19. Where does the aorta travel from, and to where?

20. What is the outside of a cell called?

POTLUCK

(Answers on page 518)

Planet Earth

1. What is Earth's center called?

2. Which of the following has been declassified as a planet: Neptune, Pluto, Mars?

3. How many days does it take for Earth to orbit the sun?

4. How many days does it take for the moon to orbit Earth once?

5. Earth rotates on its axis. How long does one rotation take?

6. The North Pole always faces the sun. True or False?

7. When it is winter in the Southern Hemisphere, what season is it in the Northern Hemisphere?

8. On June 21, the South Pole receives 24 hours of continuous sunlight. True or False?

9. What happens when two tectonic plates move apart?

10. Which of these is NOT caused by the movement of Earth's plates: volcanoes, sedimentation, earthquakes?

11. Earth's surface is split into plates that are always moving. True or False?

12. What is the hardest mineral on Earth?

13. Limestone is a sedimentary rock that dissolves in acid. True or False?

14. The three main types of rock are igneous, sedimentary, and metamorphic. What type of rock is granite?

15. Longitude lines run from pole to pole. True or False?

16. What is the softest mineral on Earth?

17. A scientist who studies rocks is called a what?

18. Precious stones form by crystallization of minerals deep underground. Which of these is NOT a precious stone: coral, ruby, topaz?

19. What percentage of Earth's surface is covered by oceans?

20. Which is the largest ocean on Earth?

21. Pure topaz looks clear or muddy?

22. Which US state produces the most coal?

23. Which gemstone's name translates as "dark red"?

24. Amethyst is a type of what?

25. What is the most common rock on Earth?

Infinity and Beyond

1. How many planets are there in the solar system?

2. Which planet is named after the Roman god of the seas?

3. About how old is the universe?

4. Which toy figure travels "to infinity, and beyond!"?

5. Which is the third planet from the sun?

6. How many signs of the zodiac are there?

7. What happened on April 12, 1961?

8. Crux, the smallest of the 88 modern constellations, is commonly known by what name?

9. A shooting star is also known as an asteroid. True or False?

10. Which was the first shuttle orbiter into space?

11. Which is the best-known galaxy orbiting the Milky Way?

12. Who was the first woman in space?

13. What is the communication cap worn by astronauts called?

14. What type of galaxy is the Milky Way?

15. How long does it take sunlight to reach Earth?

16. Who first proposed that the Earth and planets revolve around the sun?

17. Sputnik was the first man-made object to orbit Earth. True or False?

18. The constellation name "Aquarius" comes from the Latin word meaning what?

19. When did Galileo first use the telescope?

20. The Big Dipper is part of which constellation?

POTLUCK

A Hop through History

1. Stonehenge was built about 5,000 years ago. True or False?

2. What are hieroglyphs?

3. After death, rich Egyptians were mummified and buried with things they might need in the afterlife. This even included food. True or False?

4. In the mummification process, what did the embalmers do with the brain?

5. Which ancient culture invented the stone wheel, a vital aid to transportation?

6. The ancient Romans had a form of central heating. True or False?

7. The calendar we use today was introduced by Julius Caesar. True or False?

8. The first castles to be built in Europe were made of what?

9. When was the first telephone call made?

10. Toilets in castles were in small rooms, at one end of which was a hole with a wooden seat. What happened to the waste?

11. What was the name of the telescope that was launched in 1990 and has provided many photographs of space?

12. In the Middle Ages, people ate food off chunks of bread rather than off plates. True or False?

13. Where was gunpowder invented in the 9th century?

14. On board warships, "powder monkeys" were used to keep the cannons supplied with gunpowder. What were they?

15. Before 1600, which of these would have been familiar to the people of Europe: chocolate, sweetcorn, tomatoes, none of these?

16. Which of these is the odd one out, as it was invented after 1800: postage stamp, printing press, telescope?

17. What was a penny farthing?

18. What disease arrived in Europe in 1347?

19. Before toilet paper was invented, people used all sorts of materials instead. When was the first packaged toilet paper produced?

20. What were trebuchets and mangonels?

(Answers on page 518)

Ice Worlds

1. Penguins live at which pole, North or South?

2. Who led the first successful expedition to reach the South Pole?

3. What kind of ox survives in Arctic conditions?

4. The lowest temperature recorded in Antarctica is -128.2°F (-89°C). True or False?

5. How far can polar bears swim from the shore?

6. The Arctic is shrouded in darkness from October to when?

7. What name is given to open, treeless land that is permanently frozen?

8. The fur of the Arctic fox in winter is what color?

9. What name is given to the people who live in Arctic Canada and Greenland?

10. Which whale that swims in Arctic waters has a long tusk?

11. What is the ferocious seal that preys on penguins in Antarctica?

12. How long will it take for snow falling at the South Pole to reach the coast (as an iceberg)?

13. There are no insects in Antarctica. True or False?

14. The Antarctic Ross ice shelf is about the size of which European country?

15. An average fully grown, male walrus will weigh up to what?

16. In what year did people first set foot on Antarctica?

17. The Lambert Glacier is in the Arctic. True or False?

18. What kind of animal is a south polar skua?

19. Polar bears can prey on whales. True or False?

20. How does a king penguin move its egg around?

POTLUCK

Gothic Literature

1. Horace Walpole is credited with starting the Gothic genre with which novel?

2. What is Doctor Frankenstein's first name in the original book?

3. Which Matthew Gregory Lewis title features debauchery and black magic?

4. German Gothic literature is described by the term *schauerroman*. What does it mean?

5. In which country did Ann Radcliffe set *The Mysteries of Udolpho* although she had never been there herself?

6. Bram Stoker's *Dracula* is influenced by a Sheridan Le Fanu book called what?

7. In which year did Mary Shelley publish *Frankenstein*?

8. Which Jane Austen novel was written as a parody of the Gothic novel?

9. On whom is the character Lord Ruthven based in the novel *Glenarvon*?

10. What is the name of Percy Shelley's first Gothic work, published in 1810?

11. What is the name of John William Polidori's famous Gothic work?

12. Who reinvented the Gothic genre for the Victorian age with *The Fall of the House of Usher*?

13. In which year was Emily Brontë's *Wuthering Heights* published?

14. Complete the title of this Thomas de Quincey novel: *Confessions of...*

15. What grants three wishes in the terrifying 1902 story by W. W. Jacobs?

16. Which Edgar Allan Poe novel describes the horrors of the Spanish Inquisition?

17. What did Lady Caroline Lamb say that Lord Byron was?

18. *The Wanderer* is a novel by which celebrated English diarist?

19. What is the name of Stella Gibbon's character driven mad in the woodshed in the comedy *Cold Comfort Farm*: Grandad Grear, Aunt Ada Doom, Mother Mutter?

20. Author Horace Walpole built his house in a medieval Gothic style. What was the house called?

21. In which century did Gothic novels become popular?

22. Gothic texts rarely have heroic female characters. True or False?

23. Who is the villain in the novel *The Castle of Otranto*?

24. Rearrange these words to make the title of a well-known Gothic novel: *English Old Baron The.*

25. Who wrote *The Woman in Black*?

Underground Animals

1. Moles have poor eyesight, and some are blind. True or False?

2. Badgers live in groups called what?

3. How many legs does an ant have?

4. "Armadillo" translates as what?

5. Gerbils live in burrows in which natural habitat?

6. Rabbits were introduced to Britain by whom?

7. How long can cicada nymphs live underground?

8. A mole eats its own weight in food every day. True or False?

9. Shaving brushes were traditionally made from the fur of which animal?

10. The giant clam burrows under the sea floor and can weigh up to what?

11. Army ant colonies can have up to how many individual ants?

12. The colonies where rabbits live are called what?

13. Some tarantulas live underground. True or False?

14. Worms can live up to how long?

15. Prairie dogs live in underground burrows with special sleeping quarters, nurseries, and toilet areas. True or False?

16. What kind of acid do ants secrete?

17. Chipmunks are good at climbing and digging. True or False?

18. A meerkat is a type of mongoose. True or False?

19. Earthworms are bad for the soil. True or False?

20. Moles can grow up to what length?

21. Prairie dogs are native to which part of the world?

22. How do warthogs prepare their underground burrows?

23. What animal is believed to live deeper underground than any other?

24. Mole crickets have broad shovel-like front legs to help them burrow. True or False?

25. How do pocket gophers carry food from one burrow to another?

Rock Pools

1. The water in seaside rock pools is salty. True or False?

2. How many "teeth" do sea urchins have?

3. Bladder wrack seaweed has bubbles so it can do what in the water?

4. What do starfish have on the ends of their rays?

5. A rock goby is a type of what?

6. How do anemones react when exposed to the air?

7. Cooked mussels are still too poisonous to eat. True or False?

8. Which of these is NOT a bivalve: whelk, oyster, mussel?

9. What do limpets feed on?

10. Barnacles attach themselves to the bottoms of ships. True or False?

11. What do barnacles do when underwater?

12. How much water does a limpet suck up to keep it from drying out?

13. Sea anemones are related to what other creature?

14. Sea lemons are usually yellow but can sometimes be pink. True or False?

15. What covers the body of a blenny fish?

16. Some seaweeds are used to make toothpaste. True or False?

17. Hermit crabs take over empty seashells. True or False?

18. What is kelp?

19. How do limpets move?

20. What is a one-shelled mollusk called?

Things with Wheels

1. How many wheels were attached to Jay Ohrberg's limousine, the longest car in the world?

2. Which alarm clock on wheels beeps and rolls away so its owner has to get out of bed to switch it off?

3. How is the 19th-century high-wheel, ordinary bicycle better known?

4. Which is the smallest car ever made?

5. The ancient Egyptians built their pyramids without the use of the wheel. True or False?

6. A depiction of a wheeled vehicle was discovered on the Bronocice pot dating from around 3500 BCE. In which modern-day European country was it found?

7. Wheels have been found on toys from the Olmec culture that date to around 4500 BCE. True or False?

8. Which country's principal road race is known "the Giro"?

9. With what safety feature is the 4MC bike provided?

10. Who invented the bicycle driven by pedals in 1839?

11. The biggest production car ever made was the 22-ft (6.7-m) Bugatti Royale Type 41. How many of the car were made?

12. What was the name of the first "tank" steam locomotive in the world?

13. Alliott Verdon Roe's triplane was the first airplane built in the UK. How far did it fly on its maiden flight?

14. The YikeBike is a child's motorcross bike. True or False?

15. In which year was the boneshaker bicycle first manufactured in the UK?

16. What is the Antonov An-225 Mriya's claim to fame?

17. Which was the most powerful gear on the Model-T Ford?

18. What can the Gibbs Aquada car do in six seconds?

19. What year was the first Tour de France held?

20. Stuntman Ray Baumann built the biggest motorbike in the world, at 10 ft (3 m) high and how many feet long?

21. The first Rolls Royce car was the Rolls Royce 10. How many were built?

22. The smallest plane ever built is the Mosquito III. True or False?

23. What was a common name for bikes in 1869?

24. What kind of bike is used for off-road cycling?

25. What was the 1817 bike without pedals called?

(Answers on page 519)   431

Famous Best-Sellers

1. With more than 200 million copies sold, which is Charles Dickens's best-selling book?

2. J. R. R. Tolkien's *The Hobbit* has sold more copies than the *Lord of the Rings* trilogy. True or False?

3. Which is crime writer Agatha Christie's all-time best-seller, with more than 100 million copies sold?

4. There were seven books in C. S. Lewis's Narnia series. Which one was the biggest seller?

5. Despite causing great controversy, this Vladimir Nabokov novel went on to sell more than 50 million copies. What is its title?

6. Which 1961 novel describes Yossarian's wranglings with an illogical war machine?

7. H. Rider Haggard's 1887 adventure novel has sold more than 83 million copies in 44 different languages. What is it called?

8. Sometimes taught at school, *Jonathan Livingston Seagull* is on the list of 30 all-time best-sellers. Who wrote it?

9. Brazilian author Paulo Coelho is one of the most widely read authors in the world. Which is his best-selling book?

10. Recounting Miss Shirley's adventures on Prince Edward Island, Lucy Maud Montgomery's best-selling book is what?

11. Published posthumously in 2005, this Stieg Larsson book is called *The Girl with the…* what?

12. Which children's best-selling novelty book ends with a butterfly?

13. *Gone with the Wind* the novel sold millions before it became a film. Who wrote it?

14. Which was George Orwell's best-selling novel?

15. Which Sue Townsend book has sold more than 30 million copies and was the best-selling British book of the 1980s?

16. Kenneth Grahame's 1908 *Wind in the Willows* has sold more than 25 million copies. True or False?

17. Which Richard Adams best-seller focuses on life among rabbits?

18. No list of best-selling authors would be complete without the one who has dedicated himself to horror and sold more than 350 million books. Who is he?

19. *Dream of the Red Chamber* is the highest-selling book in Chinese literature. Who wrote it?

20. *The Little Prince* has sold more than 200 million copies. Who wrote it?

African Wildlife

1. This African animal has no sweat glands, so it needs water or mud to cool down in. What is it: hippopotamus, zebra, lion?

2. Which little African herbivore is related, by name only, to a huge African herbivore?

3. Complete the name of this African flier: the Angolan hairy…

4. How many species of African rhinoceros still exist?

5. Dian Fossey spent her life researching which animal in Rwanda?

6. Which is the closest living relative to the hippo?

7. Which African predator lives along the banks of the Nile River?

8. The African honey badger also goes by what other name?

9. This African animal's special coat pattern is thought to be designed to confuse predators: zebra, cheetah, giraffe?

10. Also called the ant bear, this African animal can commonly be found at the beginning of the dictionary. What is it?

11. To what species of animal does the bongo belong?

12. Which African predators live in groups with up to 100 members?

13. When the male species of the African vervet monkey matures, it moves to a neighboring group. True or False?

14. What is another common name for the African wildebeest?

15. The African dung beetle is now almost completely extinct. True or False?

16. The African animal known as a dik-dik is a what?

17. A giraffe's tongue is 18 in (46 cm) long. True or False?

18. Which small African carnivore likes sleeping inside termite mounds?

19. How many muscles are there in an elephant's trunk: 20,000, 30,000, 40,000?

20. How many toes are on the foot of the African wild dog?

21. Which bird hitches a ride on the backs of hippos and other animals, eating ticks and other insects?

22. After the cobra, what is the second-longest venomous snake in Africa?

23. Hippos can snap a crocodile in half. True or False?

24. Which is Africa's largest eagle?

25. What is a caracal?

(Answers on page 519)   433

Feeling Bendy?

1. Which three religions is yoga associated with?

2. Finish the name of this yoga pose, downward facing…

3. Yoga mainly helps keep which part of the body flexible: legs, arms, spine?

4. Who invented Pilates?

5. Which part of the body does Pilates aim to work: core, shoulders, legs?

6. Pilates trains every part of the body evenly. True or False?

7. Which of the following is NOT used in yoga: weights, block, mat?

8. You should not practice Pilates while pregnant. True or False?

9. Which of the following is the basic principle of yoga: beneficial exercise, positive thinking, relaxation, all of these?

10. What is the vital energy in yoga known as?

11. When is the best time to practice yoga?

12. In yoga, what is the child's pose used for?

13. What is the foundation of yoga: aligning your body, moving in a controlled manner, stretching?

14. Which country did Joseph Pilates come from?

15. Yoga places great importance on breathing. True or False?

16. What did Joseph Pilates call the muscle group comprising the abs, buttocks, lower back, and hips?

17. Which of the following is NOT a Pilates mat exercise: roll down, teaser, one hundreds?

18. Yoga increases muscle tone. True or False?

19. Patanjali is known as "the father of yoga." True or False?

20. Doga is yoga with which animals?

Fashion

1. Which designer is credited with bringing punk fashion into the mainstream?

2. Vivienne Westwood's designs were featured in which 2008 film?

3. Which decade was known as the "anti-fashion decade"?

4. What was a symbol of "power dressing" for women in the 1980s?

5. Which Italian city is often called the "Fashion Capital of the World"?

6. Who created the New Look?

7. What fashion house did Marc Jacobs work for?

8. In 1957, Mary Quant opened her Chelsea shop. What was it called?

9. Of which fashion house was Karl Lagerfeld director from 1983 to 2019?

10. Of which fashion house was Yves Saint Laurent head designer at 21?

11. The word "tuxedo" first appeared in 1889. True or False?

12. Roy Halston Frowick was a famous designer of disco fashion. By what name was he known?

13. Actress Brooke Shields helped Calvin Klein sell his tight-fitting jeans to the world. True or False?

14. Who is credited with inventing "shocking pink"?

15. What is the name of designer Stella McCartney's famous dad?

16. Katharine Hamnett called her 1986 show "Power Dressing." True or False?

17. Which film star famously wore Givenchy?

18. During which decade were leg warmers thought to be a good idea?

19. What sort of woman wore her hair in a "bob" in the 1920s?

20. During what decade was the "poodle skirt" worn?

POTLUCK

Australian Literature

1. Which Australian author won the Nobel Prize for Literature in 1973?

2. Which Australian novelist wrote *Schindler's Ark*, the book that formed the basis for the film *Schindler's List*?

3. What did Australian Henry Lawson do after becoming deaf, an alcoholic, homeless, and suicidal?

4. What honor did Lawson receive in 1922 after his death?

5. Which Australian author has won the Booker Prize twice?

6. Which Australian wrote *The Thorn Birds*, which later became a popular television miniseries?

7. Set in Sydney, *The Harp in the South* is by which Australian author?

8. What pen name did Australian author Nevil Shute Norway use to protect his identity as an aeronautical engineer?

9. His novels, often featuring the Catholic Church, have been published in 27 languages and sold more than 60 million copies worldwide. Who is this Australian author?

10. Who is the author of *The Female Eunuch* and a leading voice for the feminist movement?

11. Which Australian author is better known for his Dame Edna Everage television work?

12. *For the Term of His Natural Life* is a famous 19th-century Australian novel written by whom?

13. Australian author Thea Astley won the Miles Franklin Award in 1962 for which novel?

14. The son of Irish immigrants, which author has been dubbed the "father of the Australian novel"?

15. What Roger McDonald novel is about the Gallipoli campaign?

16. Australian author David Unaipon is famous for being what?

17. After what was Australian author Miles Franklin finally able to publish *My Brilliant Career* in 1901?

18. Thomas Alexander Browne's *Robbery Under Arms* is based on the life of Australian bushranger and killer Ned Kelly. True or False?

19. Who wrote the haunting *Picnic at Hanging Rock*?

20. What is the surname of the Australian author nicknamed "Banjo" who appears on the country's $10 banknote?

Religions of the World

1. How is Siddhartha Gautama commonly known?

2. Who is the prophet of Islam?

3. What year did he die?

4. Which religion are Brahma, Vishnu, and Shiva associated with?

5. Which religion has the most followers?

6. Approximately how many people follow it?

7. Which Chinese teacher, editor, politician, and philosopher was born in 551 BCE?

8. The Rastafari movement began in which country?

9. During which decade was it founded?

10. What is a "menorah"?

11. Where in India does the majority of the Sikh population live?

12. The Harmandir Sahib, or "Golden Temple," is a sacred shrine for Sikhs. True or False?

13. Jainism advocates non-violence toward all living things. True or False?

14. Jainism was founded in which country?

15. Zoroastrianism is a religion most associated with Nepal. True or False?

16. With which faith is the Talmud associated?

17. The rejection of religion is called what?

18. Unitarian Universalism is mostly found in North America. True or False?

19. Maui is a god associated with which Pacific people?

20. Shinto is associated with which country?

21. In which country was voodoo founded?

22. What Christian holiday follows Lent?

23. A sacred text of Zoroastrianism is: the Rig-Veda, the Qur'an, the Avesta?

24. Epiphany is the last day of Christmas. True or False?

25. Shaivism is a sect of which religion?

(Answers on page 519)   **437**

Great Buildings

1. In which decade was the Sydney Opera House completed?

2. Where is St. Peter's Basilica?

3. In which city would you find the Jin Mao Tower?

4. Which of the founding fathers lived in the private house Monticello?

5. Which saint is the great cathedral in Moscow named after?

6. What was the Clock Tower at the Houses of Parliament renamed in 2012?

7. The Neuschwanstein Castle is found in Austria. True or False?

8. Who designed St. Paul's Cathedral?

9. Where would you find the Parthenon?

10. Who designed the great Sagrada Familia in Barcelona?

11. Who did Emperor Shah Jahan have the Taj Mahal built in honor of?

12. In which great building does the British monarchy stay when visiting Scotland?

13. The Chrysler Building is the tallest building in New York City. True or False?

14. Blenheim Palace was built in which UK county?

15. In which city is the skyscraper known as the Shard?

16. Whose statue would you find outside the Palace of Versailles?

17. The Colosseum in Rome can seat 50,000 people. True or False?

18. What is the name of the largest château in the Loire Valley, France?

19. For which religion was the Borobudur Temple in Indonesia built?

20. In which country would you find many stave churches, like the great Borgund Stave Church?

21. Where is the Temple of Heaven?

22. Which famous royal building was bought by George III in 1761?

23. Where can you see the Petronas Towers?

24. Where is the State Hermitage Museum, the second-largest art museum in the world?

25. Which building in Paris has all its pipe work on the outside as part of the decoration?

Political Dynasties

1. When was the House of Habsburg founded?

2. The Habsburg name came from a Swiss castle known in German as the "Hawk's Castle." True or False?

3. Which former US president are former presidents George W. Bush and George H. W. Bush related to?

4. Members of the Bush family include: two senators, a Supreme Court justice, two governors?

5. Which family has dominated Indian politics since its independence in 1947?

6. Of which dynasty was Harun al-Rashid a ruler?

7. What positions of power did the Kaczynski twins hold in the Polish government?

8. What year did President Lech Kaczynski die in a plane crash?

9. What name is associated with the great dynasty of Mongolia?

10. Which emperor from the dynasty once tried to invade Japan?

11. Ruling between 1046 and 256 BCE, what was the longest-running dynasty in China?

12. Iron was first introduced to China during the Zhou period. True or False?

13. Which dynasty did Cleopatra of Egypt belong to?

14. What year did the dynasty come to an end?

15. Which English house ruled between 1485 and 1603?

16. The end of whose reign in 1603 marked a new royal dynasty uniting England and Scotland?

17. James I was the first king of the House of Stuart to reign in England. True or False?

18. Charles I was the last Stuart monarch of Britain. True or False?

19. Between which years did Fidel Castro hold power in Cuba as prime minister and president?

20. Who succeeded him?

World Traditions

1. In which city does the "Running of the Bulls" take place every July?

2. A woman's *nosia* is the traditional folk costume in which country?

3. In which of these countries might you have *ogi*, a fermented porridge, for breakfast: Sweden, Australia, Nigeria?

4. In Japan, it is considered correct etiquette to accept business cards with both hands. True or False?

5. Which Hindu festival is known as the "festival of lights"?

6. In which of these countries might you have an early afternoon siesta: Spain, England, Germany?

7. In which of these countries is giving a clock as a gift considered unlucky: China, Italy, Kenya?

8. Which US city is known for its "Mardi Gras" celebrations?

9. What is the Jewish New Year called?

10. Cremation of the dead is illegal in Singapore. True or False?

11. In which country does the Holi festival take place?

12. In which of these countries do relatives burn special paper money (often called "Hell money") as offerings to the dead: North Korea, Cuba, China?

13. Which meat do Americans traditionally eat at Thanksgiving?

14. In which of these countries is Saint Lucy's Day observed, with a procession headed by a girl wearing a crown of candles or lights: Sweden, Ukraine, Bulgaria?

15. Which of these countries celebrates the Day of the Dead: Finland, India, Mexico?

16. What color robe do monks traditionally wear in Thailand?

17. What is the most popular professional sport in Japan?

18. In which of these countries are pigs considered a sign of good luck: Germany, Argentina, France?

19. In which of these countries are wedding cakes sometimes topped with a small sapling to symbolize new growth: Norway, Bermuda, Iceland?

20. What is the traditional Indian greeting gesture of two hands together known as?

The Night Sky

1. How many constellations are there?

2. How many stars can you see with the naked eye?

3. The closest star to Earth after the sun is what?

4. How far is Alpha Centauri from Earth?

5. How many stars can you see in the Southern Cross?

6. The Southern Cross can only be seen from the Southern Hemisphere. True or False?

7. Approximately how many stars are in the Milky Way?

8. What is an exploding star called?

9. Which distant dwarf planet was discovered in 1781 by William Herschel?

10. The Big Dipper is also known by the same name as a farm implement. What is it?

11. Corona Borealis is more commonly known as what?

12. What is the English name for the constellation Ursa Major?

13. Hyades and Pleiades are two clusters that lie in which constellation?

14. How many constellations did Ptolemy define?

15. The constellation named after the flying horse in Greek mythology is called what?

16. Castor and Pollux are two bright stars from which constellation?

17. What is a binary system in astronomy?

18. The brightest star in Virgo is called what?

19. Galaxies consist of different colored stars. What does the color of the star show?

20. What is the line of three stars that make up part of the Orion constellation called?

21. What kind of star would have a mass of approximately 20 solar masses?

22. How do stars produce energy?

23. What happens to a main sequence star at the end of its life?

24. What color are the hottest stars?

25. Most stars form in nebulae. What is a "nebula"?

POTLUCK

Can You Believe It?

1. Anacondas live in which rain forest?

2. The green anaconda is the heaviest snake. True or False?

3. The planets closer to the sun are composed of heat-resistant, dense material. True or False?

4. Polar bears are thought to have lived on Earth for how many years?

5. The Temminck's courser is a bird that lays its eggs on which kind of ground?

6. The North Pole is a landmass. True or False?

7. Humans journeying through frozen Siberia can travel by train from Moscow to which city?

8. The Sahara is not the world's biggest desert. True or False?

9. Jericho, the world's oldest continuously inhabited city, lies next to which extreme environment?

10. The Ruppell's vulture can fly up to what height above sea level?

11. Which creature has been responsible for half of all human deaths (apart from during warfare) since the Stone Age?

12. Camels can close their nostrils. True or False?

13. The Sonoran Desert toad survives by living in what?

14. A form of microbe can survive the conditions in the hot springs of Yellowstone Park. True or False?

15. Foraminifera can live in the sea at up to what depth under water?

16. Planetesimals are pieces of rock pulled together by gravitational attraction. True or False?

17. A spider released on the surface of the moon in 1969 survived for eight hours. True or False?

18. The roots of some plants in Death Valley are about how many times the height of the average human being?

19. Cockroaches have been shown to survive huge doses of radiation. True or False?

20. What is the name given to huge herds of ruminants that populate the Arctic region?

21. Camels have leathery patches on their knees to stop them from getting burned when they kneel. True or False?

22. What color is a polar bear's skin?

23. What caused the solar nebula to contract and spin faster?

24. What collective term is given to the moon's "seas"?

25. How does the sun produce energy?

Women in Science

1. Marie Curie won the 1903 Nobel Prize for Physics and the 1911 Nobel Prize for what?

2. To which scientific discipline did Caroline Herschel devote her life?

3. Which female scientist helped unravel the structure of DNA?

4. Chair of the Institute of Experimental Physics, Laura Bassi was also the world's first what?

5. Which British woman was a pioneer in the field of paleontology?

6. What is primatologist Jane Goodall best known for studying?

7. What discovery did Danish seismologist Inge Lehmann make about Earth's core?

8. Which female was the first scientist to discover the first fossilized skull of a proconsul, an extinct ape related to humans?

9. In which scientific discipline did Maria Goeppert-Mayer win the 1963 Nobel Prize?

10. She was the 1983 Nobel Laureate in Physiology or Medicine. But in what country was Barbara McClintock born?

11. Gertrude B. Elion won a Nobel Prize for Astrophysics in 1968. True or False?

12. Who was the first female scientist to win a Nobel Prize?

13. In what year did Rita Levi-Montalcini win the Nobel Prize in Physiology or Medicine for discovering nerve-growth factors?

14. Christiane Nüsslein-Volhard won a 1995 Nobel Prize for her studies in embryonic development. True or False?

15. Which female scientist won a Nobel Prize for helping identify the human immunodeficiency virus (HIV) as the cause of AIDS?

16. What animal is zoologist Dian Fossey best known for studying?

17. Which British woman won the Nobel Prize for Chemistry in 1964?

18. What was astrophysicist Jocelyn Bell Burnell the first to discover?

19. The potential of what did scientist Lise Meitner help the world understand: nuclear fission, carbon dating, ammonia?

20. Which female scientist pioneered smallpox inoculation in England?

(Answers on page 520)   443

Italy

1. What is the name of the island near Venice where glass is famously made?

2. The Grand Canal in Venice is 27 miles (44 km) long. True or False?

3. Which is the oldest bridge in Florence?

4. What is the name of the typical Italian Christmas cake, studded with dried and candied fruits?

5. On which Italian island would you find Mount Etna?

6. The balcony of which famous Shakespearean character is found in Verona?

7. In which Tuscan city does the biannual Palio take place?

8. Which Italian pasta is made from potato, flour, and egg in the shape of small dumplings?

9. Which river flows through Florence and Pisa?

10. The Roman Colosseum was first known as the Anfiteatro Flavio. True or False?

11. To which Italian island was Napoleon Bonaparte exiled?

12. Which emperor commissioned the building of the Colosseum?

13. In which city is La Scala?

14. In which month does the Venetian Carnevale take place?

15. In which Italian city is the 1969 version of *The Italian Job* set?

16. How many islands together form the city of Venice?

17. The Vatican City is the world's smallest nation. True or False?

18. Which Roman emperor designed the Pantheon?

19. Which island is the "boot" of Italy kicking?

20. Which volcano destroyed the city of Pompeii?

21. Which strait separates the south of Italy and Sicily?

22. How is the ancient Roman poet Publius Maro known?

23. Cagliari is the largest city in which region of Italy?

24. Which stretch of Italian coastline is a UNESCO World Heritage Site?

25. What is the name of the Italian system of roads?

I'm a Survivor

1. The flare used to signal distress is: orange, blue, green?

2. Which of these is NOT a kind of knot: Siberian hitch, arbor knot, fish hitch ?

3. Which two species of bear are most likely to attack humans?

4. What is the name of the largest hot desert in the world?

5. The hearts of women, children, and the elderly beat faster than those of young adult males. True or False?

6. Which of the following is a symptom of dehydration: tingling limbs, blurred vision, delirium?

7. What is a Finnish marshmallow?

8. Which of the following is a good source of protein: seeds, rice, root vegetables?

9. What does the Beaufort scale measure?

10. Which animal can carry the heaviest load?

11. Which of the following is NOT a type of fire: tepee, snake hole, short log?

12. Vomiting, poor circulation, clammy skin, muscle cramps, rapid dehydration, and increased heart rate are symptoms of cholera. True or False?

13. Which of these is NOT a form of man-made shelter: one-pole poncho, cavern, forest A-frame?

14. What is a "hank"?

15. It is possible to get hypothermia in the desert. True or False?

16. In most cases, how long can the brain survive without oxygen before it suffers irreparable damage?

17. Which chemical can be used to purify water?

18. You have a better chance of surviving an emergency at the top of a mountain than at the bottom. True or False?

19. What is a bow drill used for?

20. Tetanus is caused by what?

21. There are no poisonous seaweeds. True or False?

22. What is the first stage of frostbite called?

23. What is the head covering that Bedouins wear to protect them from the sun?

24. How long can an average healthy adult survive without food?

25. Animal droppings can be used to make a fire in the desert. True or False?

POTLUCK

Around the World in 20 Questions

1. Where is the world's largest mosque?

2. What is the world's oldest inhabited city?

3. In which countries are the Mosi-oa-Tunya falls?

4. What were the falls named during the 19th century?

5. Elvis Presley never set foot in the UK. True or False?

6. Which country has a wind called the "Mistral"?

7. The Sahel region lies close to which desert?

8. The White Nile is the primary source of the Nile. True or False?

9. Which state is Las Vegas in?

10. What was Sri Lanka formerly known as?

11. Which tourist site has the greatest visitor numbers?

12. Who designed the Sydney Opera House?

13. Which two capitals lie on the Plata River?

14. What is the Taj Mahal?

15. Who wrote *Around the World in 80 Days*?

16. Bath was originally founded as a Viking spa town. True or False?

17. On which river was the *Great Eastern* super steamship launched in 1859?

18. What is the name of Richard Branson's Caribbean island?

19. "Machu Picchu" means what?

20. Fill in the blank: The United Nation's Education, Scientific and _____ Organization.

Turbulent Terrors

1. Krakatoa is to the east of what?

2. Which country was hit by a massive tsunami in 2011?

3. What caused the tsunami?

4. Tornado wind speeds can reach 805 mph (500 kmph). True or False?

5. What uncommon event (for the UK) killed eight people in Lewes, East Sussex, in 1836?

6. The Deccan Traps are volcanic features in which country?

7. When was the San Francisco quake that measured 8.25 on the Richter scale?

8. Which volcano erupted in the state of Washington in 1980?

9. How many people were estimated to have been killed in the 2004 Indian Ocean tsunami?

10. What natural calamity killed an estimated 2.5 million Chinese in 1931?

11. According to the National Hurricane Center, where did the deadliest hurricane in US history kill 8,000 people in 1900?

12. What is the literal meaning of the word "tsunami"?

13. Which European city was destroyed by an earthquake in 1755?

14. Mount Etna lies on which island?

15. Which volcano destroyed Pompeii?

16. A meteorite strike of 1908 was centered on which Siberian location?

17. What natural disaster hit eastern England in 1953, also affecting Holland and Belgium?

18. Which of these disasters killed the most people: 1970 Bhola cyclone, 2010 Haiti earthquake, 1976 Tangshan earthquake?

19. What killed an estimated 2,200 people across India, Pakistan, Bangladesh, and Nepal in 2004?

20. Which month of the year sees the most tornadoes in the United States?

(Answers on page 521)   **447**

Chocolate Tasting Club on Chocolate

1. *Chocolat* was a 2000 film starring Juliette Binoche and which actor?

2. Chocolate can increase "good" cholesterol and decrease "bad" cholesterol due to its high levels of what?

3. Which of the following types of bean is the most delicate and sought-after cocoa bean in the world: Arabica, Forastero, Criollo?

4. Chocolate contains tryptophan, a chemical the brain turns into serotonin, also known as the "happiness hormone." True or False?

5. In the chocolate-making process, what are "nibs"?

6. Which continent produces the most factory-made chocolate?

7. Where in the world is the Hotel Chocolat resort?

8. Which country consumes the most chocolate per person per year?

9. The cocoa pod grows from the what on a tree?

10. How many seeds are there in a cocoa pod?

11. *Theobroma cacao* is the scientific name for the cocoa tree. When translated into Greek, it means what?

12. What are the factory workers in *Charlie and the Chocolate Factory* called?

13. What year did the first chocolate shop open in London?

14. To qualify as dark chocolate, it needs to contain at least 60% of what?

15. What year did the first Hotel Chocolat shop open?

16. At what temperature is the cacao bean roasted in the chocolate-making process?

17. Cocoa is a plant native to Hawaii. True or False?

18. In 1870, Daniel Peter developed the process to produce milk chocolate. What nationality was he?

19. White chocolate does not contain cocoa solids. True or False?

20. Chocolate Easter eggs as gifts can be traced back to the 19th century in which two countries?

Christmas Time

1. How many reindeer are said to pull Santa's sleigh (not including Rudolph)?

2. Which popular Christmas carol was written by an Austrian priest as a result of a broken organ?

3. Before turkey, the traditional English Christmas dinner was which bird?

4. Who gives all the presents in "The Twelve Days of Christmas"?

5. In Sweden, St. Lucy's Day is celebrated with candles on which day in December?

6. In what year was the first Christmas card sent?

7. In the Czech Republic, St. Nicholas is called Svaty Mikalas and is believed to climb down to Earth from heaven on a what?

8. The tradition of having a Christmas tree comes from where?

9. Holly berries are poisonous. True or False?

10. If you find a spider's web in your house on Christmas Day in Ukraine, what is it said to bring you?

11. Who banned Christmas in England in 1647?

12. The Magi, also known as the Three Wise Men, were named Melchior, Balthasar, and what?

13. What is a "tannenbaum"?

14. In Victorian times, mince pies were made with what?

15. The letter "x" in Xmas is an abbreviation for Christ in which language?

16. Which country has sent a Christmas tree to London every year since 1947 as a thank you for Britain's help during World War II?

17. On Twelfth Night, the Wassail Bowl was filled with what?

18. In the Netherlands, St. Nicholas is known as Sinterklaas. Which country is he said to sail from on his feast day, December 5?

19. The tradition of kissing under the mistletoe is thought to come from Frigga, the Norse goddess of what?

20. Which famous poet wrote the words that are now used for the carol "In the Bleak Midwinter"?

21. Who is commonly believed to have written the famous poem "T'was the Night before Christmas"?

22. There is a town called Santa Claus in the United States. True or False?

23. What novelty did Tom Smith begin selling in 1847 at Christmas in London?

24. What do Mexican children do with a piñata?

25. Which potted plant is associated with Christmas?

(Answers on page 521)   449

POTLUCK

Really BIG Science

1. From tip to tip, how big is NGC 6872, the biggest galaxy ever detected by astronomers?

2. "Pneumonoultramicroscopicsilicov-olcanoconiosis" is one of science's biggest words. To what does it refer?

3. At 1,300 tons (1,162 tonnes), the Bagger 288 is the biggest mining machine in the world. True or False?

4. The *Armillaria ostoyae* fungus is thought to be the biggest organism on Earth. How many soccer fields would the mushroom cover?

5. What is the MS *Marco Polo*'s claim to fame?

6. What is the biggest celestial body in our galaxy?

7. Where can the biggest thermometer in the world be found?

8. The Large Hadron Collider is the biggest scientific machine built by man. True or False?

9. In 2018, the world's most powerful computer was what?

10. What is the Liebherr T 282B?

11. After nanoscience, which is the likeliest "next big thing": mesoscale, multiscale, hyperscale science?

12. What is VY Canis Majoris best known for being?

13. What is the Overburden Conveyor Bridge F60?

14. Which "big" theory is used to explain the formation of the universe?

15. How much larger than Jupiter is the superplanet TRES4 estimated to be?

16. The cosmic web is widely considered to be the biggest thing in the galaxy. True or False?

17. What is the heaviest plane ever built?

18. The biggest planet in our solar system is what?

19. *Seawise Giant* was the first name for what is the world's longest what?

20. The big science term "Palmitoylole-oylphosphatidylethanolamine" refers to a type of lipid. How is it usually abbreviated?

Guess the Shakespeare Quote

1. Where does Henry V say, "Once more unto the breach, dear friends, once more"?

2. What will turn "the multitudinous seas incarnadine, making the green one red"?

3. What happens after the Earl of Cornwall says, "Out, vile jelly!"

4. What "provokes the desire, but it takes away the performance"?

5. "It is as broad as it hath breadth: it is just so high as it is, and moves with its own organs." What beast is this?

6. Who is a "bolting-hutch of beastliness, swollen parcel of dropsies, huge bombard of sack, stuffed cloak-bag of guts"?

7. "The eye of man hath not heard, the ear of man hath not seen, nor his heart to report what my dream was…" What is this?

8. "I have lost the immortal part of myself, and what remains is bestial." What has Cassio misplaced?

9. "How beauteous mankind is! O brave new world, that has such people in't!" Who gets quite excited at meeting new people?

10. "Exit pursued by a bear" is a stage direction from which play?

11. "Alas, poor Yorick" is from which play?

12. What is the last line of *Hamlet*?

13. Iago was a man "more sinned against than sinning." True or False?

14. "Nor more willingly leaves winter; such summer-birds are…" what, according to Timon?

15. "The first thing we do, let's kill all the lawyers." Which play does this come from?

16. "Hippolyta, I woo'd thee with my sword, And won thy love, doing thee injuries…" Who had an odd approach to romance?

17. Which character in *A Midsummer Night's Dream* says, "Lord, what fools these mortals be!"?

18. "Friendship is a constant in all other things, save in the office and affairs of love?" Claudio says this in which play?

19. Who appears "as doth the blushing discontented Sun from out the fiery portal of the east"?

20. "And as she runs the bushes in the way kiss her face, some twine about her thigh to make her stay." Who is this?

Vital Statistics

1. In which ocean trench is Challenger Deep, the deepest point on Earth, at 35,797 ft (10,911 m) below sea level?

2. Where is Earth's lowest point on land, at 1,320 ft (402 m) below sea level?

3. The tallest tree in the world is 379 ft (115.6 m) tall. What kind of tree is it?

4. What was the world's tallest building (as of August 2019), at 2,717 ft (828 m) high?

5. Roughly how far is it from Earth to the moon?

6. What is the world's largest lake?

7. What is the nearest star to the sun, at about 4.2 light years away?

8. What is the average distance from Earth's center to its surface?

9. What is the highest mountain on Earth, with a peak 29,029 ft (8,848 m) above sea level?

10. Roughly what is the average distance between Earth and the sun?

11. Earth's iron core is roughly the same size as which of these celestial bodies: the moon, Mercury, Pluto?

12. At 2½ miles (3.9 km) deep, TauTona is the world's deepest mine. Where is it?

13. What is the deepest lake on Earth?

14. Approximately how far above Earth's surface is commonly thought of as being the start of space?

15. What is the world's longest river, at 4,132 miles (6,650 km)?

16. What is the closest galaxy to Earth, about 2.3 million light years away?

17. What is the world's longest mountain range, at 4,500 miles (7,200 km) long?

18. Roughly how far is it to the center of our Milky Way galaxy?

19. What is the closest that Venus, the nearest planet to us, ever gets to Earth?

20. Roughly what is Earth's circumference, the distance all the way around the equator?

Color Challenge

1. *Jackie Brown* is a 1997 film by which director?

2. *Back to Black* is an album by which British artist?

3. Who wrote *The Hunt for Red October*?

4. Which football team has won the most NFL league championships?

5. Where would you find the Côte d'Azur?

6. Who was known as the "Black Prince"?

7. Which of the following is an influential human anatomy textbook: *Brown's Anatomy, Black's Anatomy, Grey's Anatomy*?

8. Polar bear fur has no color as it is transparent. True or False?

9. Who wrote the song "Red Red Wine"?

10. Who sang the song "You're the First, the Last, My Everything"?

11. Who plays James Bond in the film *Goldfinger*?

12. Where are the headquarters of the environmental organization Greenpeace?

13. In motor racing, what does the yellow flag indicate?

14. In the novel *The Wizard of Oz*, Dorothy's shoes are red. True or False?

15. What color is Luke Skywalker's lightsaber in *Return of the Jedi*?

16. A red dwarf is a type of what?

17. What is the name of the longest river in South Africa?

18. How many points is the blue ball worth in snooker?

19. What is the name of the sea that borders the east coast of Bulgaria?

20. The Red Baron famously fought in which war?

21. Jack and Meg White from the rock band the White Stripes are brother and sister. True or False?

22. *Carcharodon carcharias* is the Latin name for which large creature?

23. Which organization did Henry Dunant found?

24. In which century did the Black Death ravage Europe?

25. Which vibrant red pigment comes from cinnabar?

Antarctica

1. Which of these countries does NOT administer an Antarctic territory: New Zealand, Australia, Germany?

2. Why do penguins have dark backs and white fronts?

3. Who led the first successful overland crossing of Antarctica in 1958?

4. *The Worst Journey in the World* was written about a trip to Antarctica. What was the point of the journey?

5. What is the lowest temperature ever recorded at Vostok in Antarctica?

6. What is the official currency of Antarctica?

7. Which of these royals doesn't have an Antarctic "land" named after them: Queen Maud, King Edward VII, Queen Elizabeth II?

8. What is the name of the mountain range that runs across the continent?

9. What environmental problem was first identified by scientists working in Antarctica?

10. The southernmost active volcano in the world is in Antarctica. What is it called?

11. One of the sailors on Ernest Shackleton's expedition in 1914 smuggled his pet "Mrs. Chippy" aboard. What kind of animal was she?

12. Scientists working on Antarctic bases sometimes use large yellow barrels to store which liquid?

13. Clothing handed out to people working in Antarctica is labeled "ECW." What do these initials stand for?

14. In what year was the Antarctic Treaty signed, which prevents further claims on it as a territory?

15. Roald Amundsen was the first person to reach the South Pole in 1911. What was his nationality?

16. Finnesko were clothing worn by early explorers. Made entirely from fur, they were worn on which part of the body?

17. What name is given to a crack opening in the sea ice, which ships often follow to save the effort of breaking the ice?

18. What name is given to mountains that are covered with ice, but whose summits stick out above them?

19. Sledding in Antarctica is made difficult by the presence of sastrugi. What are they?

20. Which of these explorers never visited Antarctica: Henry Morton Stanley, Ernest Shackleton, Tom Crean?

Cars

1. What was voted "European Car of the Year" in 1980?

2. What was the nickname of the Austin-Healey Sprite in the US?

3. How many miles per gallon did the 1938 Mercedes-Benz W154 achieve?

4. What is the literal meaning of the name "Volkswagen"?

5. What 1950s vehicle was marketed as "the family car that wins races"?

6. Due to car tax regulations, what was the top speed of the Suzuki Cappuccino?

7. The spokes of the Spyker C8 Aileron are made from ex-propeller blades. True or False?

8. In which country was the Volvo 340 manufactured?

9. What did Jaguar originally manufacture under the name "Swallow"?

10. In which part of the UK was the DeLorean DMC-12 manufactured?

11. What was the nickname of the Chevrolet small-block V8 engine?

12. Whose company developed the Tesla?

13. What is the oldest US sports car still in production?

14. In what year was the current Mazda "M" logo introduced?

15. Which UK-manufactured sports car has an exposed steel frame?

16. How long does it take the Eliica electric car to go from 0–60 mph?

17. The Reliant Robin could be driven on a motorcycle license. True or False?

18. From what source did the Peugeot bbl derive its power?

19. For how many years had Bentley been absent from Le Mans when it returned in 2001?

20. In which year did the Italian government save Alfa Romeo from bankruptcy?

21. What is the top speed of the 1948 Alfa Romeo 158 Alfetta?

22. How long does it take the Bugatti Veyron Super Sport to go from 0–60 mph?

23. What is the top speed of the Hennessey Venom GT?

24. How long does it take the street-legal race car the Ariel Atom to go from 0–60 mph?

25. What was the maximum speed of the Model T Ford?

(Answers on page 522)   455

Unusual Languages

1. Which Native American language was used by the Allies to confuse enemy code breakers in World War II?

2. Where are the 31 Northern Athabaskan languages mostly spoken?

3. Which language was artificially constructed rather than taught at birth and is spoken across Europe, East Asia, and South America?

4. Up to how many people speak this language?

5. Approximately how many languages did author J. R. R. Tolkien create for his Middle Earth characters?

6. Which tonal language uses "click" sounds made with the tongue, teeth, and mouth?

7. How many people speak Votic, a language found in the Kingisepp district of Russia?

8. Which Sami language is spoken not written, making it only possible to learn by living in northern Sweden?

9. Only ten people remaining can speak the Aboriginal Kayardild language of northwest Queensland, Australia. True or False?

10. What language would you be speaking if you said: "Hab SoSlI' Quch!"

11. What does it mean?

12. What is Crimean Gothic an example of?

13. What is an inventor of languages called?

14. Which language was once spoken by Vikings?

15. Which language similar to Old Norse is spoken by around 200,000 people today?

16. An "idioglossia" is a private language developed and spoken by only a few people, often including twins. True or False?

17. What language is spoken by around 140,000 inhabitants of the Yunnan province in southern China?

18. What percentage of the world's 7,000 languages could be extinct by 2050?

19. In *The Hitchhiker's Guide to the Galaxy*, what device is placed in a wearer's ear to enable any language to be translated?

20. What is a language spoken in northern Holland that has a low German dialect but is considered closer to English than any other language?

Greek Mythology

1. Who or what guarded the gates of the Underworld?

2. Who was punished by being forced to eternally push a boulder up a hill, only to have it roll back down?

3. Which of these Greek figures was NOT a child of Zeus: Hera, Aphrodite, Heracles?

4. The winged horse, Pegasus, belonged to the goddess Aphrodite. True or False?

5. Who was the first human woman created by the gods?

6. Who was the Greek goddess of wisdom?

7. How many labors did Hercules have to perform?

0. What was the Titanomachy?

9. What was said to happen if you stared into the eyes of Medusa?

10. Where did Odysseus come from?

11. Which Greek hero killed the Minotaur?

12. Why was Achilles almost invulnerable?

13. Who was the father of Zeus?

14. Poseidon was the brother of Hades. True or False?

15. What is the name of the popular video game series named after the Greek god Ares?

16. What did Prometheus steal from Zeus and give to mankind?

17. What was Dionysus the god of?

18. Who held the world on his shoulders?

19. Which goddess did Hades kidnap?

20. Which of these pairs were twins: Apollo and Artemis, Athena and Ares, Ares and Artemis, Apollo and Athena?

21. Who was the Greek goddess of the rainbow?

22. How many gods lived on Mount Olympus?

23. Who designed the labyrinth of King Minos?

24. Helen of Troy was married to whom?

25. The giant Argos had how many eyes?

(Answers on page 522)   **457**

Cartography

1. The oldest world maps date to approximately the 9th century BCE. The people of which ancient civilization produced them?

2. When do the oldest Chinese maps date from?

3. The early cartography of which country gave the location of the Pole Star?

4. What was Ptolemy's treatise on cartography called?

5. What is an explanation of a map's symbols called?

6. How many medieval Mappa Mundi maps have survived to the present day?

7. Which location was missing from Arab geographer Muhammad al-Idrisi's atlas *Tabula Rogeriana*: Asia, Europe, South America?

8. What was introduced in England around 1620 that improved land-measuring accuracy?

9. A 1715 map of which part of the world is known as the "Beaver Map"?

10. Some maps contain deliberate errors to show the owners if other mapmakers are infringing on their copyright by using the same mistake. True or False?

11. In which year did German cartographer Martin Behaim make the oldest extant globe of Earth?

12. A detail of a map that is shown on a larger scale on the same page is called what?

13. In cartography, "drainage" refers to areas of what?

14. Cartographer and creator of the Mercator projection, Gerardus Mercator, was born in which modern-day country?

15. On a map, what are the interlocking lines of latitude and longitude called?

16. The directional indicator on a map is its compass. True or False?

17. What line of latitude sits at 0 degrees?

18. Although Burma renamed itself Myanmar, most new maps continue to use the name Burma. True or False?

19. How many panels did Martin Waldseemüller's giant 1507 globular world map use?

20. Which line measures distance on a map?

Polluting the Planet

1. How much domestic waste does the city of New York produce each day?

2. Between 1960 and 2010, what percentage of the world's rain forests were felled or burned?

3. NASA estimates that sea levels are rising at what annual rate: $^2/_{100}$ in (0.5 mm), $^4/_{100}$ in (1 mm), $^{12}/_{100}$ in (3 mm)?

4. What is the main cause of smog in modern cities?

5. Which human activity has had the biggest impact on our landscape?

6. What percentage of methane emissions results from rice cultivation?

7. In which ocean is the "Great Garbage Patch"?

8. Air pollution kills about 7 million people each year. True or False?

9. What combines with water vapor to create acid rain?

10. Which of the following greenhouse gases is most potent: CFCs, carbon dioxide, methane?

11. Which rain forest is disappearing the fastest?

12. Which pollutant caused a thinning of the ozone layer over the poles during the 1980s?

13. Climate change has been blamed for "bleaching" the coral reefs. What happens to coral when it is bleached?

14. Since the 1970s, large swathes of mangrove forest have been cleared to make way for what type of development?

15. Which of the following animals is critically endangered: brown bear, African elephant, Amur leopard?

16. What is the main use of deforested land in the Amazon Basin?

17. Which of the following states is most at risk of rising sea levels: Washington, Florida, California?

18. Which toxic material is commonly used in South American mines to extract gold from its ore?

19. What is the most common source of river pollution in the UK?

20. What has been called the most polluted river in the world?

POTLUCK

Another Planet

1. Which planet is sometimes referred to as the "morning star"?

2. Which planets are known as the "inferior" planets?

3. What do astronomers call the brightest meteors?

4. All of the planets are visible to the naked eye except one. Which one?

5. The volcano Olympus Mons is found on which planet?

6. Which planet has the shortest day, under 10 hours?

7. The Babylonians associated which planet with Nergal, their god of war and the underworld?

8. What is the Cassini Division?

9. *Voyager 2* visited which planet on January 24, 1986?

10. At the beginning and end of an eclipse, patches of sunlight breaking through around the edges of the moon are known as what?

11. In degrees, what is Uranus's axial tilt?

12. What do astronomers call the small particles of rocky debris orbiting the sun in interplanetary space?

13. Which planet has the highest wind speeds?

14. What is the brightest object in the Edgeworth-Kuiper Belt?

15. What class of star is our sun at present?

16. Who was the first woman in the US to undergo astronaut testing?

17. Which planet has the longest day?

18. What name do astronomers give for a time when Mercury or Venus appear to move across the face of the sun?

19. Who first described the "canals" on Mars?

20. When two or more planets may be viewed in the same line of sight, what is the phenomenon called?

21. What objects make up the Oort Cloud?

22. What is the name of the largest moon in the solar system?

23. Which is the oldest type of star?

24. Which spacecraft has traveled farthest from Earth?

25. How many galaxies are there in the universe?

Back to Earth

1. On average, Earth's magnetic field switches polarity how often?

2. The axes of polarity and rotation currently differ by how many degrees?

3. Paleomagnetic fields provide a chronological history of what?

4. Aurorae are caused by charged particles trapped in Earth's magnetic field. True or False?

5. There was no oxygen in Earth's early atmosphere. True or False?

6. The intense expulsion of gases from volcanoes is known as what?

7. Microorganisms convert carbon dioxide into oxygen by what process?

8. How do archaea differ from most bacteria?

9. What does ultraviolet radiation NOT split water into: helium, ozone, hydrogen?

10. Stromatolites show that saline oceans formed how long ago?

11. What was the name of the ocean that surrounded the continents before they separated?

12. Early tidal waves traveled at what speed?

13. Whose map showed that the southern continents were once part of a supercontinent?

14. An ophiolite is a part of the ocean floor that has been pushed above sea level by tectonic plates. True or False?

15. The scientific study of rocks is known as what?

16. When oceanic plates of differing ages meet, which one is drawn downward?

17. When two continental plates meet, what is formed?

18. Convergence causes species to do what?

19. What led to the formation of tectonic plates?

20. Adaptation of species to differing conditions was caused by what?

(Answers on page 522)   461

POTLUCK

Energy!

1. What name is given to stored energy?

2. Raising a ball above your head is an example of kinetic energy. True or False?

3. Why is stretching an elastic band an example of potential energy?

4. From where does the potential energy in Huygens's clock come?

5. Into what type of energy is the potential energy in the weight of Huygens's clock transferred?

6. The mainspring in a mechanical clock stores muscle energy as potential energy. True or False?

7. A barrel rolls down a hill: where is its potential energy lowest?

8. To release potential energy in chemical reactions, the activation energy of the chemicals must be exceeded. True or False?

9. If PE = mgh, what is "g"?

10. Which of the following does NOT affect the amount of potential energy an object has: time, weight, height?

11. The energy of movement is known as what?

12. The faster an object moves, and the more mass it has, the more kinetic energy it has. True or False?

13. Kinetic energy is dependent on mass and what else?

14. Energy cannot be created or destroyed, only transferred from one form to another. What is this statement?

15. An object with twice the mass of another traveling at the same speed has half the kinetic energy of the other. True or False?

16. The random movement of particles through a solid, liquid, or gas is known as what?

17. A man fires a pistol. How does heat energy make the bullet leave the gun?

18. Whose experiments proved the principle of conservation of matter?

19. The amount of heat energy needed to raise the temperature of 1 kg of water by 1°C is known as what?

20. Joule spent his honeymoon studying waterfalls to show that heat energy is produced by splashing water. True or False?

Who Am I?

1. Which writer said, "No man is an island"?

2. Who was this Scottish-Jamaican nurse who looked after British soldiers in the Crimea at the same time as Florence Nightingale?

3. Who formed the New Model Army and was Lord Protector when England became a republic?

4. Who was Henry VIII's sixth wife?

5. Whose picture was used on the famous "Your country needs you" recruitment poster?

6. Who led the campaign for Indian independence from Britain?

7. Who is the only person to have been elected president of the US four times?

8. Which group campaigned for parliamentary reform in the mid-19th century?

9. Who is credited with saying "Veni, Vidi, Vici" (I came, I saw, I conquered)?

10. Harriet Tubman and Sojourner Truth worked for the Underground Railroad organization; it was used for helping whom?

11. Who is supposed to have said, "By God they terrify me" when talking about the British Army?

12. Who commanded the English fleet against the Spanish Armada?

13. Why was Dr. James Barry unusual at the time?

14. Which book was based on the experiences of Alexander Selkirk?

15. Who founded the Salvation Army?

16. Whose sons were the princes in the Tower?

17. Who founded Methodism?

18. Who was the leader of the Gunpowder Plot?

19. Who is the only British prime minister to have been assassinated?

20. Who was the first elected secretary-general of the UN?

21. Which mistress of Charles II is supposed to have been the model for the original image of Britannia?

22. Who was Mary Anne Evans better known as?

23. Who made the first nonstop flight across the Atlantic in a Vickers Vimy bomber in 1919?

24. Who was the Greek military leader who conquered as far as India in the fourth century BCE?

25. Who was the English king at the Field of the Cloth of Gold?

POTLUCK

Where Have You Been?

1. Which town in Vietnam is known for its tailors and custom-made clothing?

2. More than one-third of all species in the world live in which rain forest?

3. Manu Chao, the singer who performs in languages including English, Portuguese, French, Arabic, and Spanish, is originally from where?

4. The Great Pyramid of Cheops in Egypt is the oldest of the Seven Wonders of the Ancient World. True or False?

5. What is the highest capital city in the world?

6. The "Benevolent Mountains" of India are geographically known as what?

7. Which mountain is known as "the Tiger of the Alps"?

8. An invasion of which territory caused a war between the UK and Argentina in 1982?

9. In which Australian national park would you find Uluru?

10. The state of Singapore consists of one island. True or False?

11. What is the highest point in New Zealand?

12. The Russian Federation is the world's largest country. Which is the world's second largest?

13. The flag of which country features a blue 24-spoke wheel on a white background?

14. Eureka in Canada is the coldest inhabited place on Earth. What is the daily average temperature?

15. Japan is known for which of the following sports: sumo wrestling, mud wrestling, water wrestling?

16. The Guggenheim Museum in Bilbao, Spain, exhibits what type of art?

17. Where did rhythm and blues music originate: United States, Cuba, Brazil?

18. Which country is famous for its Kabuki performances?

19. Australia's Mount Wycheproof is the smallest registered mountain in the world. True or False?

20. Monaco has the oldest population in the world. True or False?

Famous Last Words

1. "I've never felt better" were the last words of which actor?

2. Which scientist said: "I'd hate to die twice. It's so boring"?

3. "I have a terrific pain in the back of my head." These were the last words of which US president?

4. "I'm tired of fighting! I guess this thing is going to get me" were said to have been the last words of Harry Houdini. True or False?

5. Which artist allegedly said: "Drink to me, drink to my health, you know I can't drink any more"?

6. "I've had eighteen straight whiskies, I think that's a record." This was said by which dying poet?

7. Which author is reported to have commanded: "Go away. I'm all right"?

8. "I wish I'd drunk more champagne" was allegedly the final utterance of which economist?

9. Florence Nightingale's last words were: "Nurse! Nurse!" True or False?

10. Which author is said to have replied, "Nothing but death" when asked if he or she wanted anything?

11. "Oh, I am so bored with it all!" This final statement is attributed to which famous statesman?

12. "Goodnight my darlings, I'll see you tomorrow." Which dying playwright said this?

13. Which dying author is said to have asked: "Does nobody understand?"

14. The last words of philosopher Immanuel Kant were: "It is enough." True or False?

15. Which scientist is reported to have said, "I am not the least afraid to die" before he died?

16. "Last words are for fools who haven't said enough" were supposedly the final words of which influential thinker?

17. A famous actress allegedly said: "Don't you dare ask God to help me!" before she died. Who was she?

18. Inventor Thomas Edison's last words were: "Wait! I've had an idea!" True or False?

19. "Well, if it must be so" were the parting words of which composer?

20. "The sun is God" were the last words of which artist?

(Answers on page 523)

Answers

QUIZ 1

1. Operation Overlord **2.** Hiroshima
3. *Hurricane* **4.** A VI flying bomb
5. Lightning war **6.** Neville Chamberlain
7. Heinrich Himmler **8.** USSR (Russia)
9. An airship **10.** False, the top age was 45
11. In a backyard **12.** A machine gun
13. USSR **14.** A tank **15.** A US bomber
aircraft **16.** May **17.** Rommel **18.** Divine
wind **19.** Poland **20.** Stalingrad **21.** No
22. Enigma **23.** The bombing of Pearl
Harbor in 1941 **24.** France
25. The Soviet Union

QUIZ 2

1. 8th to 11th centuries **2.** Sagas
3. Longships **4.** The handle **5.** False
6. Odin **7.** Bone or antler **8.** Lindisfarne
9. True **10.** Armor made from small iron
rings **11.** A figurehead **12.** Leif Eriksson
13. 600–700 **14.** Axes **15.** Christianity
16. Valhalla **17.** Thor **18.** Creek or inlet
19. Scandinavia—Norway, Sweden, and
Denmark **20.** 1000

QUIZ 3

1. The Falkland Islands **2.** Lord Nelson
3. USS *Yorktown* **4.** *Graf Spee* **5.** Mark
Antony **6.** Duke of Medina Sidonia
7. Admiral Chester Nimitz **8.** *Mary Rose*
9. *General Belgrano* **10.** USS *Nautilus*
11. Jellicoe **12.** HMS *Victory* **13.** John
Paul Jones **14.** *Revenge* **15.** Barbarossa
16. RMS *Lusitania* **17.** Admiral Yamamoto
18. Sir Francis Drake **19.** *Bismarck*
20. Isambard Kingdom Brunel

QUIZ 4

1. Henry VII **2.** Edward **3.** James I
4. Queen Victoria **5.** Elizabeth I
6. William I **7.** King John **8.** Kenneth
MacAlpin **9.** Mary I (Mary Tudor)
10. Stephen **11.** George **12.** Henry V
13. King James **14.** Edward VIII
15. Richard I **16.** Saxe-Coburg-Gotha

17. Llywelyn ap Gruffydd **18.** Edward I
19. Henry VIII **20.** Richard III **21.** Only
1 child survived infancy—Prince William,
duke of Gloucester, who died at age 11
22. Ethelred II **23.** King George II in
1743 **24.** King John **25.** Queen Victoria

QUIZ 5

1. Giza **2.** True **3.** Flood **4.** 3,000 years
5. Sandy white **6.** True **7.** Ramesses II
8. It means "Great House" **9.** Khufu
10. 2.3 million **11.** The Valley of the
Kings **12.** Tutankhamun **13.** Cartouche
14. Hieroglyphs **15** The Rosetta Stone
16. True **17.** Anubis **18.** The Book of
the Dead **19.** True **20.** Cleopatra

QUIZ 6

1. 1991 **2.** East/West **3.** True
4. The Warsaw Pact **5.** Cuba **6.** Berlin
7. The Korean War **8.** The Non-Aligned
Movement **9.** 1949 **10.** President Ronald
Reagan **11.** Hungary **12.** 1961 **13.** True
14. False **15.** KGB **16.** George Marshall
17. 1989 **18.** True **19.** President Richard
Nixon in 1972 **20.** He received two giant
pandas, Ling-Ling and Hsing-Hsing

QUIZ 7

1. The Normans **2.** The Great Hall
3. The Solar **4.** True **5.** Windsor Castle
6. Castle Drogo in 1930 **7.** Latrines
8. The Keep **9.** The moat **10.** Boiling
oil **11.** True **12.** True **13.** True
14. Arrowslits **15.** True **16.** Crenels
17. Portcullis **18.** A castle within a castle
19. The High Table **20.** Pembroke

QUIZ 8

1. King Edward III **2.** Jerusalem
3. Florence **4.** Bank loans **5.** The Black
Death **6.** The Peasants' Revolt **7.** King
Henry II **8.** Dysentery **9.** Gothic
10. True **11.** Marco Polo **12.** Johannes
Gutenberg **13.** Weapon **14.** 4,500

15. The Moors **16.** True **17.** Archery
18. Towers **19.** Eels were used
20. The legs

QUIZ 9

1. Richard III **2.** Two **3.** False
4. The Globe **5.** Virginia **6.** The
Reformation **7.** Spain **8.** Sir Francis Drake
9. Christopher Marlowe **10.** True **11.** Meat
12. Lunch **13.** False **14.** Hans Holbein
15. Lady Jane Grey **16.** The marriage
between King Henry VII (of Lancaster)
and Elizabeth of York **17.** False
18. King Henry VIII and Jane Seymour
19. Groundlings, and in summer they were
also called "stinkards" **20.** King Philip II
of Spain **21.** True **22.** False (knives,
spoons, fingers) **23.** Elizabeth never
married **24.** He is reported to have brought
potatoes and tobacco **25.** A flag was flown
from the top of the building

QUIZ 10

1. Henry VIII **2.** William Shakespeare
3. Margaret Thatcher **4.** Louis Braille
5. Elizabeth I **6.** Charles Dickens
7. Nefertiti **8.** Winston Churchill **9.** Samuel
Pepys **10.** King Arthur **11.** George
Washington **12.** True **13.** Boudicca
14. Blow up Parliament **15.** Leonardo da
Vinci **16.** Descartes **17.** Siddhartha Gautama
18. True **19.** Anne Frank **20.** David
Livingstone **21.** King Charles I **22.** Lenin
23. Captain Scott **24.** Joan of Arc
25. Mother Teresa

QUIZ 11

1. A battleship **2.** Britain and France
3. 1914 **4.** Archduke Franz Ferdinand
5. The Western Front **6.** Russia **7.** King
George V **8.** Trenches **9.** Trench foot
10. Germany **11.** The tank **12.** The Battle
of the Somme **13.** Because Germany
invaded Belgium **14.** Manfred von
Richthofen, also known as the Red Baron
15. The Battle of Jutland **16.** Mining or
tunneling **17.** The area of land between
the fighting armies **18.** United States
19. The ceasefire that ended the war

20. 1918 **21.** Almost one million
22. Zeppelins **23.** True. There wasn't
enough space in the aircraft to carry a
parachute and it would add to the weight
of the plane. It was also thought that they
would encourage cowardice and provide
pilots with an easy escape route
24. The United States. John Joseph
Pershing commanded American armies
in France **25.** Sidney Lewis was just 12
when he enlisted in 1915.

QUIZ 12

1. Oligarchy **2.** City-state **3.** Euclid
4. False **5.** Agora **6.** Training, wrestling,
and running **7.** The Oracle and a temple to
Apollo **8.** A temple of Athena **9.** Sparta
10. Philosophy, science, and government
11. Alexander the Great **12.** Marathon
13. Athens **14.** A type of tunic worn by
both men and women **15.** Homer **16.** Athens
and Sparta **17.** Pythagoras **18.** Mount
Olympus **19.** Zeus, the king of the gods
20. On a battlefield **21.** False—only men
could be full citizens **22.** Stone or clay,
and roofs were covered with tiles or reeds
23. They wore a variety of masks, wigs,
and padded costumes **24.** The Olympic
Games **25.** True

QUIZ 13

1. Ireland **2.** True **3.** Bronze **4.** From
the beaker-shaped pottery they used
5. Stonehenge **6.** Iron **7.** Hill fort
8. Julius Caesar **9.** Claudius **10.** Hadrian's
Wall **11.** Boudicca **12.** Chester or
"Caister" in the name **13.** Ireland and
Scotland **14.** St. Patrick **15.** Angles,
Saxons, and Jutes **16.** Offa's Dyke **17.** The
name given to the northern, central, and
eastern parts of England controlled by
the Danes in the late 9th century
18. Scandinavia **19.** Alfred the Great
20. The Normans

QUIZ 14

1. True **2.** Genghis Khan **3.** Bismarck
4. Benito **5.** Napoleon Bonaparte
6. Saladin **7.** Julius Caesar

8. F. D. Roosevelt **9.** 1979 **10.** True
11. Robert the Bruce **12.** Mahatma
Gandhi **13.** Garibaldi **14.** Mao Zedong
15. Normandy **16.** True **17.** Germany
18. Egypt **19.** Rushmore **20.** Washington,
DC **21.** Defeating Napoleon at the Battle of
Waterloo in 1815 **22.** He won the first
multiracial election in South Africa and
became president **23.** Montgomery
24. Catherine the Great **25.** Oliver Cromwell

QUIZ 15

1. 1917 **2.** Bolsheviks **3.** Czar Nicholas II
4. The Red Guards **5.** Prince Lvov
6. Vladimir Lenin **7.** *Potemkin* **8.** The
White Army (also known as the White Guard)
9. Leon Trotsky **10.** With an ice pick
11. The Red Terror **12.** Collectivization
13. "Man of Steel" **14.** St. Petersburg
15. True **16.** Finland **17.** Alexander
Kerensky **18.** Germany **19.** Joseph Stalin
20. True

QUIZ 16

1. Prince Albert **2.** The Hanoverian
3. Prepaid postage stamps **4.** Black
5. Farmer **6.** Political reform **7.** Canada
8. Suez Canal **9.** Ferdinand de Lesseps
10. The Corn Laws **11.** Queen Victoria
(*Victoria Regina*) **12.** False—Hyde Park
13. Sydenham **14.** Ireland **15.** Four
16. Benjamin Disraeli **17.** Mrs. Beaton
18. Karl Marx **19.** Isambard Kingdom
Brunel **20.** Hyde Park **21.** Florence
Nightingale **22.** Charlotte, Emily, and
Anne Brontë **23.** Charles Darwin
24. The workhouse **25.** True

QUIZ 17

1. Oliver Cromwell **2.** 1861 **3.** The
"Roundheads" often had short haircuts
4. The New Model Army **5.** General
Franco **6.** Gettysburg, in 1863 **7.** Charles
8. Sarajevo **9.** The Vietnam War **10.** 1642
11. Tito **12.** The English royal houses of
Lancaster and York **13.** True **14.** The king
15. Stonewall **16.** American Civil War
17. False **18.** His horse was named Traveller
19. Ulysses S. Grant **20.** Lincoln

QUIZ 18

1. Turkey (Anatolia) **2.** Central America
3. Persian **4.** The handover of Hong Kong
5. Eastern Roman Empire **6.** Egypt
7. India **8.** Japan **9.** Alexander the Great
10. Egypt **11.** 1922 **12.** Genghis Khan
13. Turkey **14.** Augustus **15.** 14th century
16. The Akkadian Empire, in the Middle
East **17.** The Aztec **18.** True **19.** 67 years
20. Timbuktu **21.** A legal code
22. The Mogul Empire **23.** Suleiman
the Magnificent **24.** Cyrus the Great
25. Constantinople

QUIZ 19

1. Ukraine **2.** Smallpox **3.** SARS
4. Athens **5.** 25 million **6.** 60 percent
7. False **8.** Pneumonic plague **9.** True
10. Cats and dogs **11.** Eyam **12.** False
13. Anthrax **14.** John Snow **15.** 200 years
16. China **17.** Syphilis **18.** False **19.** 1348
20. True **21.** Black swellings on the bodies
of bubonic-plague victims **22.** True **23.** No,
only females **24.** India **25.** Smallpox

QUIZ 20

1. Hurling **2.** Rome **3.** True **4.** Wrestling
5. A circlet of wild olive leaves **6.** Persia
(modern-day Iran) **7.** Minoan **8.** 776 BCE
9. None **10.** Funerals **11.** 50,000 people
12. The Circus Maximus **13.** In Egyptian
wall paintings **14.** Boxing **15.** Joe Frazier
16. Tudor **17.** Hockey **18.** 19th century
19. 1840 **20.** True

QUIZ 21

1. Life **2.** Hanging **3.** Tricorne **4.** 1831
5. Australia **6.** Ned Kelly **7.** 18th **8.** Black
Bess **9.** Dalmatian **10.** *The Beggar's
Opera* **11.** Penny dreadful **12.** Alfred Noyes
13. True **14.** Adam and the Ants
15. Charles II **16.** Hounslow Heath
17. The Bow Street Horse Patrol targeted
highwaymen after 1763 **18.** Claude Duval
19. Marble Arch **20.** York

QUIZ 22

1. The *Pequod* **2.** The crew mutinied
3. The right **4.** The *Nimrod*

5. Christopher Columbus **6.** The *Mayflower*
7. USS *Constitution* **8.** The *Cutty Sark*
9. The *Bismarck* **10.** HMS *Invincible*
11. 1912 **12.** True **13.** The *Argo* **14.** Captain
Edward John Smith **15.** Captain Hook
16. It was the last US battleship to be
commissioned and was the site of the Japanese
surrender, which ended World War II
17. False—the back of a ship is the stern
18. Sir Francis Drake **19.** RMS *Carpathia*
20. An oil tanker **21.** *Nautilus* **22.** Thor
Heyerdhal **23.** Greenpeace **24.** The
Fighting Temeraire **25.** *Mary Celeste*

QUIZ 23

1. It was a primitive type of martial art that
combined wrestling and boxing **2.** The
triple jump **3.** Weights **4.** 1896 **5.** England
6. True **7.** Once **8.** 1904 **9.** 1908 **10.** True
11. 1900 **12.** True **13.** A running race known
as the "stadion" or "stade" **14.** Zeus **15.** 1928
16. 1924 **17.** Tennis and golf **18.** Decathlon
and pentathlon (his medals were later restored)
19. Wrestling **20.** Sevens

QUIZ 24

1. Colt **2.** Jim "Killer Miller" **3.** The
Wild Bunch **4.** Dentist **5.** William Henry
McCarty **6.** John Wesley Hardin **7.** Wild
Bill Hickok **8.** In the Long Branch Saloon
in Dodge City **9.** Virgil **10.** Butch Cassidy
and the Sundance Kid **11.** Boot Hill
12. Thumb-busters **13.** The Winchester rifle
14. As the site of the gunfight at the O.K.
Corral in 1881 **15.** Annie Oakley **16.** Billy
the Kid **17.** The Jesse James gang **18.** Pat
Garrett **19.** William Frederick Cody was
nicknamed "Buffalo Bill" after he shot
buffalo under contract to supply Kansas
Pacific Railroad workers with buffalo meat
20. The James-Younger gang **21.** Clay
Allison **22.** Johnny Ringo **23.** Calamity
Jane **24.** Robert Ford **25.** He is thought to
have been 12 years old

QUIZ 25

1. Emperor Commodus **2.** *Munera* **3.** A
venator **4.** *Andabatae* **5.** A freed gladiator
returning to fight **6.** *Charon* **7.** In the

afternoon **8.** Public executions **9.** 123 days
10. 10,000 **11.** Mitte! **12.** 20 minutes
13. False **14.** 36 trapdoors **15.** A weapons
inspection **16.** Thrace, a region east of
Greece **17.** A *retiarius* **18.** A *ludus*
19. True **20.** Emperor Claudius **21.** True.
They were called *Essedarii* **22.** On horseback
23. True **24.** Gladiators mainly ate a
vegetarian diet. This was probably because
it was cheaper than giving them meat
25. Gladiators training for combat used
wooden swords to avoid injury

QUIZ 26

1. Melees **2.** William Marshal (*c.*1146–1219)
3. A rest area **4.** A joust to the death
5. The 11th century **6.** The quintain **7.** False
8. Pope Innocent II **9.** Surrey **10.** Chretien
de Troyes, who wrote *Erec and Enide, c.*1170
11. Coronels were blunted tips on the point of
lances **12.** Bear-baiting **13.** Three **14.** True
15. A funeral **16.** Richard I of England
17. False **18.** Unhorse another knight and
capture him **19.** 1316 **20.** Blunted weapons
21. Tilt **22.** The jousting shield placed on
the shoulder **23.** 12 feet long **24.** True
25. Henry II

QUIZ 27

1. The thick arrows were wrapped in pitch
and set alight. They set fire to wooden hulls
and sails **2.** Galleasses **3.** Robert Whitehead
in 1866 **4.** A ship able to join the line of battle
5. Exocets **6.** Greek fire **7.** Breaking the
French line **8.** A World War II British
biplane torpedo bomber **9.** The Mizzen mast
10. 64–80 **11.** It had three tiers or banks of
oars **12.** His *Turbinia* had steam turbines
13. Q-ships **14.** 18-inch **15.** Wolf packs
16. Torpedo boat destroyer **17.** 7,000 miles
18. Electric batteries **19.** Fighting from the
advantageous windward side **20.** A broadside

QUIZ 28

1. Helmuth von Moltke the Elder **2.** Ramesses
II **3.** Hannibal **4.** Marcus Licinius Crassus
5. William Westmoreland **6.** He lost
his right arm and right eye **7.** Qin Shi
Huangdi **8.** Belisarius **9.** Charlemagne

10. William the Conqueror—King William I
11. King Richard I **12.** Lord Kitchener
13. Genghis Khan **14.** King Edward III
15. True **16.** Oliver Cromwell **17.** Duke
of Marlborough **18.** Robert Clive **19.** Von
Runstedt **20.** General Robert E. Lee

QUIZ 29

1. Arbroath **2.** Robert the Bruce **3.** Fiery
Face **4.** Thistle **5.** True **6.** False. Macbeth
reigned 1040–1057 **7.** Scotland and France
8. In 1707, by the Act of Union **9.** Waverley
Station, Edinburgh **10.** Bonnie Prince
Charles **11.** The MacDonald clan
12. Fotheringhay Castle **13.** Battle of
Stirling Bridge **14.** King James IV **15.** A
poet (1759–1796) **16.** "Painted people"
17. Body snatchers **18.** King Francis II of
France **19.** Holy cross **20.** January 25
21. James Edward Stuart—his son Charles
Edward Stuart was the Young Pretender, also
known as Bonnie Prince Charlie **22.** The
Dress Act of 1746 meant that it was illegal for
the Scots to wear Highland Dress, which
included tartan and kilts **23.** King David I
in the 12th century **24.** Most of the buildings
in the city center were constructed using a
silver-colored granite. Aberdeen is also
called the Silver City **25.** A white X-shaped
cross on a blue background. The flag is
known as "the Saltire"

QUIZ 30

1. New Zealand **2.** 1893 **3.** 1918 **4.** 1920
5. Emily Davison **6.** Mrs. Pankhurst
7. The right to vote **8.** True **9.** World
War I **10.** The UK **11.** Liechtenstein
12. 1984 **13.** The *Daily Mail* **14.** 2015
15. True **16.** Hunger strike **17.** True
18. Imprisoned suffragists who were
seriously weakened by the hunger strike
could be released early **19.** True **20.** 1928

QUIZ 31

1. Whispering Gallery **2.** Lhasa **3.** Lebanon
4. Mexico City **5.** Jordan **6.** Sikh
7. Machu Picchu **8.** The Chrysler Building
9. Sydney Harbour Bridge **10.** Mud bricks
11. The Monument **12.** Pompidou Centre

13. Sky Bridge **14.** St. Basil **15.** NASA
16. The Eiffel Tower **17.** A mausoleum
18. False **19.** Barcelona **20.** Cheops
21. The Empire State Building **22.** Doric
23. Mud brick, known as "earthen
architecture" **24.** Limestone and
granite **25.** True

QUIZ 32

1. Augustus **2.** A giant statue of a
reclining mythical creature with the
head of a human and the body of a lion
3. Poseidon **4.** To channel water into
Roman towns and cities **5.** Ra **6.** *Retiarius*
7. Galen **8.** Nebuchadnezzar **9.** Greek
10. *Aquae Sulis* **11.** Papyrus had a variety
of uses, but it was specially cultivated to be
used as paper **12.** A temple **13.** Spartacus
14. The Yangtze River **15.** Luxor,
Egypt **16.** The Roman **17.** Socrates
18. Thermopylae **19.** Claudius **20.** Greek
21. A ball game called pok-a-tok or
hotchpotch **22.** Benin Bronzes **23.** True
24. For mock naval battles **25** Trepanning

QUIZ 33

1. Anne Boleyn **2.** Pope Adrian VI
3. Richard Cromwell (son of Oliver Cromwell)
4. Eleanor of Aquitaine **5.** King Edward II
6. Lord Darnley **7.** King Alfonso XIII
8. King Manuel II **9.** King Henry VI
10. Marie Antoinette **11.** C. B. Fry
12. False (Holyrood Palace) **13.** Corfu
14. Jordan **15.** Grimaldi **16.** False
17. Simeon II of Bulgaria **18.** The
Netherlands **19.** George IV **20.** Japan

QUIZ 34

1. 866 **2.** 1119 **3.** 1215 **4.** 1922 **5.** 1413
6. 1543 **7.** 1431 **8.** 1635 **9.** 1616 **10.** 1692
11. 1711 **12.** 1796 **13.** 1770 **14.** 1817
15. 1776 **16.** 1846 **17.** 1861 **18.** 1934
19. 1934 **20.** 1905 **21.** 1926 **22.** 1929
23. 1876 **24.** 1875 **25.** 1665

QUIZ 35

1. In the afternoon **2.** Public executions
3. A *retarius* **4.** During the funerals of
wealthy people **5.** Public entertainments

6. Julius Caesar **7.** Criminals or prisoners of war who fought in arenas against wild animals **8.** A *secutor* **9.** He put restrictions on all other games **10.** Six days **11.** The animal hunts **12.** Emperor Caligula **13.** Lightly armored. He wore a large broad-rimmed helmet with a griffin crest, carried a small round or square-shaped shield and thigh-length armor (known as "greaves"), and fought with a curved sword **14.** Emperor Nero **15.** Emperor Commodus **16.** Hercules **17.** Emperor Claudius **18.** To absorb the blood of the dead and wounded **19.** 264 BCE **20.** False

QUIZ 36

1. Venice **2.** China **3.** 1841 **4.** 10 days **5.** Spain **6.** Manchester **7.** Turkey **8.** Galicia **9.** The Grand Tour **10.** *Santa Maria* **11.** Daniel Defoe **12.** True **13.** Up to 120 men **14.** Indonesia **15.** India **16.** 1831 **17.** Kent **18.** 1810 **19.** The Great Western Railway (GWR) **20.** Sedan chair

QUIZ 37

1. Mexico **2.** A jaguar **3.** Warfare **4.** Excrement of the Gods **5.** Spain **6.** True **7.** Swampland **8.** Serpent Skirt **9.** Obsidian **10.** True **11.** Cocoa beans **12.** True **13.** Hernán Cortés **14.** True **15.** The Aztec emperor Moctezuma II **16.** 50% **17.** True **18.** Floating gardens for crop growing **19.** They ran **20.** 16th century **21.** Moctezuma II **22.** The Aztec calendar had 18 months with 20 days in each one **23.** True **24.** Eagles or jaguars **25.** The skin of human sacrifices

QUIZ 38

1. Sagrada Família **2.** Antoni Gaudí **3.** A salt mine **4.** The Church of the Rock **5.** Its monolithic churches carved from rock **6.** Notre-Dame **7.** Canterbury Cathedral **8.** Saint Basil's **9.** Coventry Cathedral **10.** St. Mark's Basilica **11.** St. Peter's **12.** Notre-Dame de Reims **13.** Baptistery of San Giovanni, part of the Duomo in Florence **14.** Lorenzo Ghiberti

15. Norway **16.** St. Paul's **17.** True **18.** True **19.** Westminster Abbey **20.** In the shape of a cross

QUIZ 39

1. 1861 and 1865 **2.** More than three million **3.** True **4.** 2,000 **5.** The Battle of Shiloh **6.** The CSS *Manassas* **7.** False **8.** 1862 **9.** Henry Stanley **10.** Bounty jumpers **11.** 3,500 **12.** Clara Barton, known as "the American Nightingale" **13.** True **14.** 180,000 **15.** 1864 **16.** Three **17.** True **18.** False **19.** 15% **20.** True **21.** Reconstruction **22.** Richmond **23.** Jefferson Davis **24.** Five **25.** Maine

QUIZ 40

1. Tin **2.** A grocer **3.** *Aurifaber* **4.** Higgler **5.** True **6.** A shoemaker **7.** True **8.** Early law enforcement officers **9.** True **10.** Arrows **11.** A crooked lawyer **12.** Sweeping streets **13.** Fish **14.** A puddler **15.** A lavender—a washerwoman **16.** A tapley **17.** True **18.** Cleaned houses **19.** Sweets **20.** True

QUIZ 41

1. Heathen wizards **2.** He wanted to encourage settlement **3.** It was kept in a barrel of brandy **4.** They were held together with coconut rope **5.** True **6.** Ferdinand Magellan **7.** Vitamin C deficiency **8.** The mouth of large whales **9.** 99 days **10.** Steam-powered paddle ships **11.** A navigation aid **12.** Little shirt **13.** Vasco da Gama **14.** Finding latitude **15.** 50 **16.** John P. Holland **17.** His crew didn't want to burn ships **18.** True **19.** Government-sponsored pirates **20.** Portuguese

QUIZ 42

1. Sir Robert Walpole **2.** Ancient Greek Herodotus **3.** Thomas Newcomen **4.** Franklin D. Roosevelt **5.** Harry S. Truman **6.** Tim Berners-Lee **7.** Spain **8.** Barack Obama **9.** Archduke Franz Ferdinand **10.** Lenin **11.** Mao Zedong **12.** Brigham Young **13.** Alessandro Volta

14. John Harington 15. Orville and Wilbur Wright. They made the first powered human flight in 1903 16. Pope Gregory XIII 17. July 21 1969 18. Henry Dunant 19. Dr. Christiaan Barnard 20. Louis Braille 21. Robert Baden-Powell, in 1908 22. Benjamin Franklin 23. Alexander Graham Bell 24. Yuri Gagarin, a Russian Air Forces pilot 25. Karl Benz

QUIZ 43

1. By observing the stars 2. Claudius Ptolemy 3. The Incense Road 4. The Phoenicians 5. The Pacific 6. Henry the Navigator 7. West Africa 8. The lateen sail 9. Map making 10. Spain and Portugal 11. The sextant 12. Christopher Columbus 13. Shorter route to Asia (north of America) 14. Chronometer 15. Abel Tasman 16. To find the Great Southern Continent—Terra Australis Incognita 17. Mungo Park 18. Meriwether Lewis and William Clark 19. David Livingstone 20. Roald Amundsen

QUIZ 44

1. 1747 2. The War of Jenkins' Ear 3. Manchester 4. Cromwell 5. Battle of Towton, 1461, in the English War of the Roses 6. King Edward VIII 7. Crimean 8. Mary, Queen of Scots 9. 1801 10. The eruption of Mount Vesuvius 11. 13 days 12. Boyne 13. Tony Blair 14. The Battle of Hastings 15. Isambard Kingdom Brunel 16. 1999 17. True 18. William Pitt the Younger 19. The Phoney War 20. William Wilberforce 21. 1840s 22. 6 counties 23. Easter 24. Mary I 25. Archbishop Cranmer

QUIZ 45

1. 753 BCE 2. Romulus and Remus 3. Etruscan 4. The toga 5. Set underwater 6. The senate 7. True 8. A legion 9. Bad luck 10. 50,000 people 11. The Carthaginians 12. 80 13. Cruel 14. Stolas 15. Roads 16. Six 17. Being a citizen 18. False 19. Pompeii and Herculaneum 20. A hypocaust 21. 476 CE 22. Julius Caesar 23. Augurs 24. Trajan's Column 25. The Byzantine Empire or Byzantium

QUIZ 46

1. ½ in (1 cm) 2. Pupil 3. Tongue 4. Outer brain 5. Humerus 6. Muscle 7. Liver 8. Spine 9. Ball-and-socket 10. Four 11. False 12. Kidney 13. A grape 14. Mitochondria 15. Skin 16. False 17. Thigh 18. True 19. Thigh 20. Larynx 21. Hands and feet 22. Eyes 23. The lungs 24. Color blindness 25. Colon

QUIZ 47

1. Direct current 2. An electromagnet 3. Water 4. 1920s 5. A plus sign + 6. Milkshake parlors 7. 1921 8. Decode enemy messages 9. Transistor 10. 1946 11. Telegraph 12. Static electricity 13. Kilowatt-hours 14. Zinc 15. Electrical current 16. 1961 17. To insulate against electricity 18. Heart 19. False 20. A circuit

QUIZ 48

1. The sun 2. Solar cells 3. Fossil fuels 4. A very large mirror 5. Carbon dioxide 6. False 7. Pipeline 8. Yes 9. The North Sea 10. Because it is dangerously radioactive 11. True 12. Fracking 13. Nitrogen oxide and sulfur dioxide 14. France 15. True 16. Highland regions 17. Dams are expensive to build 18. True 19. Biomass 20. Yes

QUIZ 49

1. Yuri Gagarin 2. Valentina Tereshkova 3. 15 minutes 4. 1969 5. Buzz Aldrin 6. Edward White 7. Walter Schirra 8. 12 9. *Eagle* 10. The first artificial satellite in orbit 11. 1957 12. Laika the dog 13. To crash-land on the moon 14. The first US satellite 15. Surveyor 16. Sailor of the universe 17. Star sailor 18. Kennedy 19. True 20. Florida 21. Traveler 22. Saturn 5 23. 1958 24. National Aeronautics and Space Administration 25. 12 hours (and 36 minutes)

QUIZ 50
1. 30,000 **2.** In your bones **3.** 206 **4.** 27
5. Tennis court **6.** 10 to 15 times **7.** True
8. Capillaries **9.** 25 million **10.** True
11. 1 minute **12.** Unconscious **13.** To
frown **14.** Red blood cells **15.** Your skin
16. Valves **17.** Beard hair **18.** The brain
19. True **20.** Month **21.** About 35 tons
22. True **23.** 20 **24.** Heart
25. Respiratory system

QUIZ 51
1. True **2.** The London Eye **3.** Race car
driver **4.** The brakes **5.** To improve road-
holding **6.** True **7.** A four-wheel-drive
vehicle **8.** A multi-tool or pocket knife
with other tools attached **9.** True **10.** A lock
for doors **11.** 1971 **12.** A very accurate
watch **13.** Photographic film **14.** Horology
15. Cog wheels **16.** A quartz crystal
17. Perambulators **18.** A widget
19. True **20.** True **21.** The bell inside
the Clock Tower at the Palace of
Westminster **22.** 1700s **23.** A small
manufactured item, a gadget **24.** True
25. 1901

QUIZ 52
1. True **2.** Runway **3.** It has two sets of
main wings **4.** The United States Air Force
(USAF) **5.** Gas engine **6.** *Flyer 1* **7.** Four
engines **8.** Tiredness from changing time
zones **9.** Left **10.** Wood **11.** A plane from
an aircraft carrier **12.** Black box **13.** The
English Channel **14.** Vertically **15.** *Spirit
of St. Louis* **16.** *Voyager* **17.** -58°F (-50°C)
18. True **19.** Concorde **20.** First across
the Atlantic Ocean

QUIZ 53
1. Red **2.** True **3.** False **4.** 10 miles
(16 km) **5.** It sucks extra air into the
engine **6.** It is strong and light **7.** A
red bus **8.** A type of speed camera
9. More than 65 ft (20 m)—in fact, about
75 ft (23 m) **10.** A safety device for
car passengers **11.** 1956 **12.** Horse
13. False **14.** Cat's eye **15.** Ermine
Street **16.** True **17.** True **18.** To reduce

the pressure on the road **19.** John McAdam
20. Mud and snow

QUIZ 54
1. True **2.** Seed **3.** A plow **4.** Hay
5. True **6.** As insulation against the cold
7. No **8.** Chemicals for killing pests
9. Plants are kept warmer **10.** It traps heat
from the sun **11.** To improve traction
12. True (mobile and stationary steam
engines were used) **13.** Tubers **14.** To
stop bacteria from growing **15.** Hydraulics
16. Irrigation **17.** Because plants use
up nitrogen **18.** They get an electric shock
19. Yes **20.** Light from the sun

QUIZ 55
1. Mercury **2.** 5 billion years **3.** Milky
Way galaxy **4.** Mercury **5.** Mars
6. Apollo **7.** Sun **8.** False **9.** Crux
10. Sirius **11.** No **12.** *Apollo 8* **13.** Mars
and Jupiter **14.** Venus **15.** Mars **16.** A
black hole **17.** Halley **18.** International
Space Station **19.** True **20.** Saturn
21. The sun **22.** Pluto **23.** Venus
24. The Roman god of war **25.** Earth

QUIZ 56
1. Energy, stored as sugar or glucose
2. Chlorophyll **3.** True **4.** The sun
5. Marsupials **6.** Vaccinations **7.** Blood
8. Once a month **9.** The mercury
thermometer **10.** In the blood **11.** No
12. False **13.** Hemoglobin **14.** Africa
15. Louis Pasteur **16.** Canines **17.** Linnaeus
18. To facilitate pollination **19.** Birds
20. Mammalia

QUIZ 57
1. Solid **2.** True **3.** Hard **4.** 32°F (0°C)
5. 212°F (100°C) **6.** Crystalline and
amorphous **7.** Liquid crystal display
8. Yes **9.** When a liquid turns into a gas
10. Hydrogen **11.** It sinks **12.** To spread
out **13.** Yes **14.** Nitrogen **15.** Carbon
16. It goes out **17.** Elements **18.** pH scale
19. 10 **20.** Lemon juice **21.** True
22. When a solid changes into a gas
23. Liquid **24.** False **25.** Freezing

QUIZ 58

1. Antiseptics in surgery **2.** HMS *Beagle*
3. A unit of force **4.** True **5.** Radium
6. Leonardo da Vinci **7.** Florence
Nightingale **8.** Seeing an apple fall from
a tree **9.** Bacteria **10.** K **11.** Neil Armstrong
12. False **13.** Radio **14.** Alfred Nobel
15. Alexander Fleming **16.** No **17.** Heredity
18. Ernest Rutherford **19.** Silicon
20. Samuel Morse

QUIZ 59

1. True **2.** His daughter **3.** The pneumatic
tire **4.** Rudolph Diesel **5.** 1911 **6.** Yes
7. Airships **8.** A British flying boat
9. First flight across the Atlantic in 1919
10. By sea in passenger liners **11.** *Titanic*
12. An open-topped motor coach **13.** The
Austin Seven **14.** True **15.** The de Havilland
DH106 Comet **16.** The hovercraft
17. Motorcycles **18.** The two-stroke
motor scooter **19.** The passenger jet
20. 747

QUIZ 60

1. R2-D2 **2.** False **3.** Isaac Asimov
4. A radio-controlled boat **5.** True
6. The elderly and disabled **7.** *Metropolis*
8. Three **9.** It helped build cars **10.** Robby
11. Replicants **12.** Sing **13.** Transformers
14. Pick and place **15.** Surgery **16.** KITT
17. *I, Robot* **18.** Less than 1 percent
19. An android **20.** True

QUIZ 61

1. True **2.** Diffuse reflection **3.** Joule
4. Thermometer **5.** Conduction **6.** They
expand **7.** They contract **8.** Convection
9. Longitudinal **10.** True **11.** Solids
12. 30 degrees **13.** They converge
14. True **15.** Refraction **16.** They diverge
17. Reflection **18.** Retina **19.** Aperture
20. Convex lenses

QUIZ 62

1. A wandering uterus **2.** Austrian
3. Measurements of the human skull
4. True **5.** Analytical psychology
6. Ego, id, superego **7.** Nature and
nurture **8.** False **9.** Memory
10. William Stern **11.** Dogs
12. Willingness to obey authority
13. Hypnosis **14.** Carl Jung **15.** Children
16. Four **17.** That people remember
uncompleted tasks better **18.** Three:
semantic, episodic, procedural
19. James Vicary **20.** Children bond
with parents due to food

QUIZ 63

1. The space shuttle **2.** Venus **3.** Buzz
Aldrin **4.** International Space Station
5. Sulfuric acid **6.** Mars **7.** Craters
8. Saturn **9.** Neptune **10.** *Magellan*
11. Mars Exploration Rover mission
12. The asteroid belt **13.** A cloud of dust
14. True **15.** Volcanoes **16.** Saturn
17. 180 billion **18.** Clouds **19.** Yes
20. Titan

QUIZ 64

1. Joseph Swan **2.** Germany
3. Theory of relativity **4.** Mechanics
5. Hippocrates **6.** Archimedes **7.** True
8. True **9.** Lightning is a form of electricity
10. Michael Faraday **11.** Pressure and
volume **12.** Encrypt and decrypt messages
13. Wilhelm Röntgen **14.** Stephen
Hawking **15.** Smallpox **16.** Sound
amplification **17.** Hot-air balloon
18. Guglielmo Marconi **19.** Johannes
Gutenberg **20.** China **21.** True
22. 23 pairs (46) **23.** Gsregor Mendel,
who was an Austrian monk **24.** A, T, G,
and C **25.** Mutation

QUIZ 65

1. Gyrocompass **2.** Magnetized by
magnet's south pole **3.** Aurora Borealis
4. Lodestone **5.** True **6.** MRI **7.** Hans
Christian Ørsted **8.** Current electricity
9. The direction of force on the conductor
10. Direction the wire moves
11. Alternators **12.** Steam **13.** Step-up
14. Constant flow of electrons
15. Filament **16.** Resistance
17. The free electrons move around
18. Low **19.** 1947 **20.** Velocity

QUIZ 66
1. 18 years **2.** Brick **3.** China
4. Seismometer **5.** Archimedes
6. John Smeaton **7.** 1600s **8.** Robert
Hooke **9.** The refrigerator **10.** Benjamin
Franklin **11.** Pennsylvania **12.** Seine
13. Joseph Paxton **14.** Alexander Graham
Bell **15.** The Parthenon **16.** True
17. The Eiffel Tower **18.** Dubai **19.** John
A. Roebling **20.** 16.7 miles (27 km)

QUIZ 67
1. True **2.** Hummingbirds **3.** Oxygen
4. One hour **5.** 100 million tons (91 million
metric tonnes) **6.** 700 million **7.** Alcohol
8. True **9.** Yes **10.** Venus **11.** 6 miles
(10 km) **12.** Four **13.** Eyeballs
14. Giraffe **15.** 24 hours **16.** 500,000
17. Methane **18.** A flea **19.** True
20. 5 billion **21.** Elasmosaurus
22. Nitrous oxide **23.** Stonehenge
24. Genetics **25.** Developing lobotomy

QUIZ 68
1. A sheep **2.** False **3.** Twig **4.** Yes
5. Less than 10 percent **6.** True **7.** A tadpole
8. Little Nicky **9.** South Korea **10.** A
Tasmanian "tiger" or Thylacine **11.** True
12. *Brave New World* **13.** 2008 **14.** Yes
15. *Star Wars* **16.** Pokémon **17.** True
18. *Jurassic Park* **19.** No **20.** Dolly

QUIZ 69
1. 1981 **2.** The Harvard Mark I
Computer **3.** 1951 **4.** Alan Turing
5. Remington Rand **6.** $1 million
7. 1911 **8.** International Business Machines
9. Spacewar **10.** The mouse **11.** The first
RAM memory chip **12.** 1971 **13.** Steve
Wozniak **14.** The Osborne I 1981
15. Complex number calculation
16. 1985 **17.** The Commodore 64
18. 1982 and 1993 **19.** Linus Torvalds
20. *Doom*

QUIZ 70
1. Galileo Galilei **2.** Aristotle **3.** Charles
Darwin **4.** Ernest Rutherford **5.** The
uncertainty principle **6.** Inventing the
electric battery **7.** Thomas Edison **8.** Louis
Pasteur **9.** Marie Curie **10.** Alan Turing
11. Lise Meitner **12.** Guglielmo Marconi
13. Nicolaus Copernicus **14.** Archimedes
15. Michael Faraday **16.** Leonardo da
Vinci **17.** Penicillin **18.** Alfred Binet
19. Stephen Hawking **20.** Isaac Newton

QUIZ 71
1. False **2.** An aerodynamic shell
3. Yuri Gagarin **4.** True **5.** 3 **6.** False
7. Meteorite **8.** Uranus **9.** True **10.** False
11. They are still there **12.** 1990 **13.** True
14. Mars **15.** 1962 **16.** True **17.** Japan
18. False **19.** They have all investigated
Jupiter **20.** Mars Express

QUIZ 72
1. Hennessey Venom F5 **2.** Ferrari
F40 **3.** True **4.** Lamborghini Miura
5. Diablo **6.** Michael Schumacher
7. Sweden **8.** Bristol Fighter **9.** Panther 6
10. Toyota 2000GT **11.** Ferrari California
12. A fighting bull **13.** Audi **14.** Spyker
15. False **16.** Volkswagen **17.** Juan
Manuel Fangio **18.** DB9 **19.** Koenigsegg
CCR **20.** Ferrari F40 **21.** True
22. First championship for electric
single-seat racing cars **23.** A serpent
24. 959 **25.** Palo Alto, California

QUIZ 73
1. Egyptian **2.** Chloroform **3.** True
4. Babylonian **5.** Hippocrates **6.** An
operation **7.** A 30-volume medical
encyclopedia **8.** The human circulatory
system **9.** Clean hands **10.** A toe
11. 1970s **12.** The Crimean War **13.** True
14. 1920s **15.** True **16.** 1948 **17.** True
18. The sweating sickness **19.** The
Egyptians **20.** That the disease
was waterborne

QUIZ 74
1. Saturn **2.** 63 **3.** Potentially
hazardous objects **4.** Jupiter
5. Nitrogen **6.** Mercury **7.** Apollo
8. Rings **9.** Earth **10.** Sunspots
11. Troposphere **12.** Venus

13. Eugene Cernan **14.** Uranus
15. 1959 **16.** The Kuiper Belt **17.** Neptune
18. Ganymede **19.** Mars **20.** Saturn
21. A blue giant **22.** By nuclear fusion
23. It turns into a planetary nebula
24. Two stars orbiting each other
25. Exoplanets

QUIZ 75

1. Pull **2.** Richard Trevithick **3.** The Maglev
4. *The Rocket* **5.** The roundhouse
6. The caboose **7.** 1863 **8.** Any vehicle
that moves on a railway line **9.** China
10. Sand **11.** A wheeled wagon or trolley
12. The tank car **13.** False **14.** Paris
and Istanbul **15.** The English Channel
16. 28 **17.** A high-speed train **18.** True
19. The United States **20.** *Flying Scotsman*

QUIZ 76

1. Helical **2.** Cytosine **3.** Spindle-shaped
4. Amino acids **5.** 46 **6.** An enzyme
7. Catabolism **8.** A hiatal hernia
9. Diverticular disease **10.** To clean the
blood **11.** 51 oz (1.5 liters) **12.** Lungs
13. Bile **14.** The epiglottis **15.** Stem cells
16. The aorta **17.** Heavy periods **18.** In
the skull **19.** A fertilized egg **20.** Canines
21. The large bowel **22.** The small
intestine **23.** In your nose
24. The pancreas **25.** Ureters

QUIZ 77

1. A diagnosis and treatment manual
2. Insulin to treat diabetes **3.** Fastest
amputation **4.** Coca-Cola **5.** A hot
summer's "Great Stink" caused by
untreated sewage in the Thames
River **6.** Capillaries **7.** Opthalmology
8. To prevent morning sickness
9. Opium **10** A mechanical hand
11. International Red Cross **12.** Aspirin
13. Whip themselves **14.** Edwin
Chadwick **15.** True **16.** The 1930s
17. Oveta Culp Hobby **18.** Mercury
19. The stethoscope **20.** An ice-cream
freezer **21.** Cutting a hole in the skull
22. 1123 **23.** True **24.** Queen Victoria
25. 1895

QUIZ 78

1. Advanced Research Projects Agency
Network **2.** Defense **3.** The Soviet launch
of the Sputnik satellite **4.** J. C. R. Licklider
5. True **6.** Bob Metcalfe **7.** ALOHANET
8. SATNET **9.** Vint Cerf **10.** The Father
of the Internet **11.** 1980s **12.** Ted Nelson
13. The World Wide Web **14.** Marc
Andreessen **15.** Stanford University
16. 1994 **17.** 1998 **18.** 2001 **19.** Web 2.0
20. True

QUIZ 79

1. Alfred Nobel **2.** Water **3.** Nitrous oxide
4. Carbon **5.** Cobalt **6.** Sublimation
7. Potassium **8.** A noble gas **9.** NaCl
10. False **11.** Carbon **12.** False **13.** Au
14. Eats away at materials **15.** Aluminum
16. Nucleus **17.** Tin **18.** The study of
compounds that make up living things
19. Mercury **20.** Two

QUIZ 80

1. The ecliptic **2.** Degrees **3.** Right
ascension **4.** 62 miles (100 km)
5. False **6.** Ursa Major **7.** M81 Bode's
Galaxy **8.** Polaris **9.** Betelgeuse
10. Rigel **11.** M42 **12.** Sirius, in Canis
Major **13.** -1.4 **14.** 88 **15.** First quarter
16. Leonids **17.** Jupiter **18.** Shorter tube,
so more portable **19.** 10 in (250 mm)
20. Arecibo, Puerto Rico **21.** False
22. Four **23.** 6% **24.** Infrared
25. Mercury, Venus, Mars, Jupiter, Saturn

QUIZ 81

1. Marie Curie **2.** Aristotle **3.** Antonie
van Leeuwenhoek **4.** Albert Einstein
5. Sailors **6.** Nagasaki **7.** Joseph Bazalgette
8. Galápagos Islands **9.** The gyrocompass
10. Sir Francis Bacon **11.** Vulcanization
12. Christiaan Barnard **13.** Gillette
14. Artist and architect **15.** Steam engine
16. The aqualung **17.** Poliomyelitis
18. A device used in irrigation
19. Thermostat **20.** Eratosthenes
21. The structure of DNA **22.** The Nobel
Prize **23.** Atomic research **24.** Ferdinand
Cohn **25.** True

QUIZ 82
1. Move **2.** Crustaceans **3.** Itch mite
4. Bacteria **5.** 1896 **6.** Hepatitis A
7. Invade and kill bacteria and archaea
8. Listeria **9.** Edward Jenner **10.** 1978
11. A rhinovirus **12.** Whooping cough
13. Protista **14.** Lyme disease
15. Cinchona **16.** 1928 **17.** A prion
18. Anthrax **19.** Sun animals
20. Plasmodium

QUIZ 83
1. Albert Einstein **2.** The Pythagorean
theorem **3.** Pi **4.** Euler's number
5. The fundamental theorem of calculus
6. Hooke's law of elasticity **7.** An equation
of linear systems **8.** Ohm's law **9.** The
principle of buoyancy **10.** Bernoulli's
principle **11.** Atomic theory **12.** True
13. James Clerk Maxwell **14.** Circumference
of a circle **15.** Newton's Second Law
16. $E = Pt$ **17.** Mitchell Feigenbaum
18. False **19.** A crown **20.** Energy
and mass times the speed of light

QUIZ 84
1. Chernobyl **2.** 18 miles (30 km)
3. 4,375 **4.** The worst-ever industrial
chemical leak **5.** 12,000 **6.** Nuclear
accident following earthquake and tsunami
7. One month **8.** The Aral Sea **9.** 1976
10. 80,000 **11.** A partial meltdown
12. The detonation of an explosives cargo
ship **13.** *Columbia* **14.** A stampede
by pilgrims **15.** The train derailed
16. China **17.** True **18.** More than
seven months **19.** The Pacific Ocean
20. 1989

QUIZ 85
1. 1971 **2.** Pony car **3.** 1987 **4.** Bugatti
Veyron **5.** Tyrrell Racing **6.** True
7. Juventus **8.** Volkswagen Group **9.** AMC
10. 3 **11.** Toyota **12.** CX **13.** Renault RS10
14. True **15.** Midship Runabout two-seater
16. Ford Escort RS Cosworth **17.** Ferrari
Testarossa **18.** Triumph GT6 **19.** 1953
20. Daimler **21.** Sweden **22.** Ferrari F40
23. True **24.** 1906 **25.** Diablo

QUIZ 86
1. Paleogene **2.** *Australopithecus
afarensis* **3.** Living in or among trees
4. 1.20% **5.** A thick femur and short
pelvis **6.** 1995 **7.** The Black Skull
8. He had massive jaws and cheek teeth
9. *Homo habilis* **10.** *Homo ergaster*
11. The hand ax **12.** Migrate **13.** Java,
Indonesia **14.** Pioneer man **15.** Middle
Pleistocene **16.** Liang Bua Cave,
Indonesia **17.** Island dwarfism
18. Germany **19.** Wise man
20. A chin

QUIZ 87
1. Dog sleds **2.** 1820 CE **3.** True
4. Zero **5.** 30% **6.** Aurora Australis
7. True **8.** False **9.** Fabian Bellingshausen
10. 100% **11.** Trapped air contains past
atmospheres **12.** 1961 **13.** Glacial
14. Four **15.** Emperor penguin **16.** True
17. 179 **18.** False **19.** Land surrounded
by sea **20.** Antarctic

QUIZ 88
1. Stephen Hawking **2.** Baikonur
Cosmodrome **3.** 1981 **4.** Payload
Assist Module **5.** True **6.** Five **7.** 23 days
8. Two areas on board the ISS **9.** Sixteen
10. He made the first spacewalk
11. Transmit pictures of Earth **12.** The
service module **13.** Mare Tranquillitatis
14. Apollo 15 **15.** Duststar **16.** The
first Mars rover **17.** Titan **18.** True
19. Pluto **20.** True **21.** Dwight D.
Eisenhower **22.** Fred Hoyle
23. 400 times **24.** Mercury
25. 17,885 mph (28,783 kmph)

QUIZ 89
1. Au **2.** The number of protons and
neutrons **3.** Potential of hydrogen
4. Bakelite **5.** True **6.** Ammonia
7. Linus Pauling **8.** Dmitri Mendeleev
9. Silver **10.** Oxygen **11.** Ionic
12. Protons, electrons, and neutrons
13. True **14.** Sulfuric acid **15.** Robert
Boyle **16.** -ane **17.** Joseph Priestley
18. Transition **19.** Carbon **20.** Two

QUIZ 90
1. Meissner's corpuscles
2. False **3.** Just above your kidneys
4. Destroys harmful substances
5. Limbic system **6.** Pectoralis minor
7. Synesthesia **8.** Saccule **9.** True
10. Temporomandibular **11.** Buttock
12. Rhinoplasty **13.** False **14.** Silver
15. Mouth **16.** Antibodies **17.** True
18. Beta cells **19.** Pyrogen **20.** False
21. Taste it **22.** Blood groups were
discovered **23.** Penicillin **24.** The
poppy **25.** Heart

QUIZ 91
1. Stratford-upon-Avon **2.** False
3. *Hamlet* **4.** Elizabeth I **5.** 36 **6.** *Nothing*
7. The Globe **8.** *Othello* **9.** *Romeo and
Juliet* **10.** Histories **11.** *The Tempest*
12. True **13.** 30,000 **14.** Mark Antony
15. *Macbeth* **16.** Titania **17.** Blank verse
18. *As You Like It* **19.** *Henry V* **20.** 14
21. Gertrude **22.** Anne Hathaway
23. 154 **24.** *A Comedy of Errors*
25. *Twelfth Night*

QUIZ 92
1. *The Hunger Games* **2.** Hilary Mantel
3. Jeff Kinney **4.** *Normal People*
5. *Discworld* series **6.** *The Casual
Vacancy* **7.** False **8.** *The Twilight Saga*
9. Swedish **10.** True **11.** True **12.** Anne
Hathaway **13.** *The Da Vinci Code*
14. Jamie Oliver **15.** *The Handmaid's
Tale* **16.** *The Hobbit* **17.** George R. R.
Martin **18.** False **19.** James Patterson
20. Michelle Obama

QUIZ 93
1. Ian Fleming **2.** *Life of Pi* **3.** Stephenie
Meyer **4.** Philip Marlowe **5.** John
Grisham **6.** Ian McEwan **7.** J. D. Salinger
8. *The Color Purple* **9.** *Animal Farm*
10. Narnia **11.** David Baldacci **12.** *No
Country for Old Men* **13.** Albert Camus
14. *About a Boy* **15.** *The Subtle Knife*
16. Agatha Christie **17.** Bill Bryson
18. Roald Dahl **19.** *The Silmarillion*
20. *Discworld*

QUIZ 94
1. Michelangelo **2.** Campbell's **3.** Constable
4. Cubism **5.** William Hogarth **6.** Greek
7. True **8.** Sunflowers **9.** Leonardo da
Vinci **10.** Salvador Dalí **11.** False
12. Auguste Rodin **13.** Late 18th century
14. False, it is *Angel of the North*
15. Edvard Munch **16.** Monet **17.** Portraits
18. French **19.** Sculpture **20.** Abstract
21. David Hockney **22.** Seurat
23. Jackson Pollock **24.** Theatrical
posters **25.** Toulouse-Lautrec

QUIZ 95
1. Sweet shop **2.** Reading **3.** Frobscottle
4. Boggis, Bunce, and Bean **5.** Tortoise
6. Pheasants **7.** Willy Wonka **8.** Aunt
Spiker **9.** Chocolate **10.** *The BFG*
11. Miss Trunchbull **12.** Quentin
Blake **13.** *The Gremlins* **14.** Yellow
15. Gobblefunk **16.** *Charlie and the
Chocolate Factory* **17.** His beard
18. The Grand High Witch **19.** Billy
20. A monkey **21.** For hunting animals
22. His grandmother **23.** They are
squashed by the giant peach **24.** She is
Miss Honey's aunt **25.** Look round!

QUIZ 96
1. The Blitz **2.** False **3.** Kirke **4.** Parcels
5. 1950 **6.** True **7.** Turkish Delight **8.** Wolf
9. Sword **10.** A new sewing machine
11. Edmund **12.** The snow starts to melt
13. Turns him to stone **14.** Marmalade roll
15. Stone Table **16.** Aslan **17.** Susan
18. False **19.** Cair Paravel **20.** White stag
21. Mr. and Mrs. Beaver **22.** Half man and
half goat **23.** Four **24.** It is always winter
and never Christmas **25.** White

QUIZ 97
1. 11 **2.** Scabbers **3.** Lion **4.** Ollivanders
5. The Mirror of Erised **6.** July 31 **7.** 9¾
8. A Dementor **9.** Gillyweed **10.** An otter
11. Vernon and Petunia Dursley **12.** Professor
Snape **13.** False **14.** Moaning Myrtle
15. Sirius Black **16.** The Little Hangleton
Graveyard **17.** True **18.** A reporter for *The
Daily Prophet* **19.** 142 **20.** Parseltongue

21. Dogs 22. A toad 23. *A History of Magic* 24. Crookshanks 25. True

QUIZ 98

1. Orange 2. Blue 3. Pastels 4. Collage 5. Yellow 6. Charcoal 7. Mix it with their paint 8. A palette 9. Green 10. Printing 11. Stretch it 12. Black 13. False 14. 2H 15. Warm 16. Egg 17. Complementary colors 18. Insects 19. Mosaic 20. Gum arabic

QUIZ 99

1. *New Moon* 2. *Interview with the Vampire* 3. No 4. Bram Stoker 5. True 6. Edward Cullen 7. Whitby 8. Charlaine Harris 9. Vlad III the Impaler 10. Mystic Falls 11. Mountain Lion 12. Garlic bread 13. She is telepathic 14. *Wuthering Heights* 15. Bottled synthetic blood 16. False 17. Renesmee 18. Anne Rice 19. Dracula 20. False

QUIZ 100

1. *Peter Pan* 2. Rabbits 3. Baloo 4. A heart 5. *Next* 6. False 7. Winnie-the-Pooh 8. *Anne of Green Gables* 9. Fairy dust 10. *Through the Looking-Glass* 11. Lilliput 12. Barbecue 13. Edith Nesbit 14. A wolf-dog 15. Neverland 16. Africa 17. *The Lion, the Witch and the Wardrobe* 18. A golden arrow 19. In the Swiss Alps 20. Charles Kingsley 21. *The Railway Children* 22. She cuts off and sells her hair 23. Frances Hodgson Burnett 24. The Banks family 25. Anna Sewell

QUIZ 101

1. False 2. A tent 3. Charles 4. Andy Warhol 5. Blur 6. Ceramics 7. Marc Quinn 8. Chicago 9. Shark 10. 1998 11. Che Guevara 12. The Guggenheim Museum 13. John Lennon 14. Jake and Dinos 15. Fire 16. True 17. 1984 18. David Beckham 19. Diamonds 20. Banksy

QUIZ 102

1. *The Tortoise and the Hare* 2. *The Boy Who Cried Wolf* 3. *The Crow and the Pitcher*
4. True 5. *The Fox and the Crow* 6. *The Bundle of Sticks* 7. Never trust someone who deserts you in need 8. The bear 9. *Mercury and the Woodman* 10. The milkmaid 11. Never count your chickens before they hatch 12. *The Dog in the Manger* 13. A lion 14. In the Roman arena 15. Its bone 16. *The Lioness* 17. Sour 18. Sour grapes 19. *The Nurse and the Wolf* 20. *The Wolf in Sheep's Clothing*

QUIZ 103

1. True 2. 13 3. Blue 4. 1881 5. El Greco 6. Max Jacob 7. Málaga 8. *Young Art* 9. *Guernica* 10. True 11. Georges Braque 12. Fernande Olivier 13. Poetry 14. 40 years 15. Communism 16. Himself 17. 1946–1948 18. False 19. About two years 20. New York 21. The minotaur 22. Barcelona 23. France, 1973 24. Cézanne 25. 9 years old

QUIZ 104

1. Realist 2. De Gas 3. 1834 4. American 5. Absinthe 6. *The Bellelli Family* 7. The National Guard 8. New Orleans 9. True 10. He was going blind 11. The Impressionists 12. True 13. Mid-1880s through 1890s 14. Lamplight 15. Italy 16. Bronze 17. 1917 18. True 19. He became a recluse 20. Dance 21. New Orleans 22. Horses 23. True 24. True 25. False

QUIZ 105

1. *The Great Gatsby* 2. *Don Quixote* 3. False 4. *Frankenstein* 5. *Wuthering Heights* 6. *Moby-Dick* 7. *Alice's Adventures in Wonderland* 8. *Crime and Punishment* 9. *The Adventures of Huckleberry Finn* 10. *Scoop* 11. *Nineteen Eighty-Four* 12. *Catcher in the Rye* 13. *Catch-22* 14. *The New York Trilogy* 15. *Lord of the Flies* 16. *A Bend in the River* 17. *The Lord of the Rings* 18. *Waiting for the Barbarians* 19. *The Trial* 20. *Anna Karenina* 21. *Wolf Hall* 22. *I Know Why the Caged Bird Sings* 23. *Emma* 24. *The Color Purple* 25. Barsetshire

QUIZ 106
1. Vincent van Gogh **2.** Tuscany, Italy
3. *Salvator Mundi* **4.** David Hockney
5. Hans Holbein **6.** John Constable
7. Edgar Degas **8.** *Night* **9.** *Le Chat Noir*
10. Paul Cézanne **11**. Edvard Munch
12. Wassily Kandinsky **13.** Marc Chagall
14. Pop art **15.** Salvador Dalí **16.** L. S.
Lowry **17.** Impressionism **18.** Michelangelo
19. One **20.** Paul Gauguin

QUIZ 107
1. Emily Brontë **2.** Wilkie Collins **3.** Yuri
and Lara **4.** Jamaica **5.** 1960 **6.** False
7. Venice **8.** *Great Expectations* **9.** True
10. *Little Women* **11.** 1949 **12.** He runs
away **13.** Charles **14.** *To Kill a Mockingbird*
15. *Women in Love* **16.** False **17.** *So Big*
18. *First Impressions* **19.** Jack **20.** 19
21. *Frankenstein* **22.** *David Copperfield*
23. Marthas **24.** Aldous Huxley
25. *Middlemarch*

QUIZ 108
1. False **2.** 1874 **3.** The Seine,
France **4.** Paint the effects of light
5. True **6.** Gave the work luminosity
7. Water-lily ponds **8.** Auguste Renoir
9. Open-air painting **10.** Franco-Prussian
War **11.** True **12.** Edgar Degas
13. Claude Monet **14.** Camille
Pissarro **15.** Flags **16.** Alfred Sisley
17. Berthe Morisot **18.** Avant-garde
19. *La Grande Jatte* **20.** Tahiti
21. The Post-Impressionists **22.** Louis
Leroy **23.** Toulouse-Lautrec **24.** True
25. Landscape

QUIZ 109
1. Lydia **2.** In a letter **3.** *Sanditon*
4. Eight **5.** Murdered her **6.** 1775
7. 27 **8.** Six **9.** Half a dozen **10.** True
11. No **12.** True **13.** A Lady **14.** Box
Hill **15.** Longbourn **16.** *Bridget Jones's
Diary* **17.** Emma Woodhouse **18.** Edmund
Bertram **19.** Winchester Cathedral
20. True **21.** Charlotte Lucas
22. Elinor and Marianne Dashwood
23. Four **24.** Four **25.** True

QUIZ 110
1. James Patterson **2.** *The ABC Murders*
3. An orangutan **4.** Cordelia Gray **5.** Ruth
Rendell **6.** Wilkie Collins **7.** Tom Ripley
8. True **9.** Professor James Moriarty
10. A wheelchair **11.** Stephanie Plum
12. True **13.** Jane **14.** Stieg Larsson
15. Raymond Chandler **16.** Inspector Bucket
17. *A Study in Scarlet* **18.** Kathy Reichs
19. A public defender **20.** *The Mousetrap*

QUIZ 111
1. Helena Ravenclaw **2.** His dead sister
Ariana **3.** Gobbledegook **4.** Someone
who has witnessed death **5.** True **6.** Winky
7. A ghoul **8.** A flute **9.** Fawkes
10. Neville Longbottom **11.** True
12. Buckbeak **13.** Five **14.** False **15.** Silver
16. Cornish pixies **17.** Snowy **18.** Female
19. Badger **20.** Professor Snape

QUIZ 112
1. Bloomsbury **2.** Thomas Harris **3.** Anne
Brontë **4.** Gandalf **5.** True **6.** *Hamlet*
7. Ashby-de-la-Zouch, Leicestershire
8. *Blade Runner* **9.** False **10.** Audrey
Hepburn **11.** 1818 **12.** A tiger **13.** True
14. Jeffery Deaver **15.** 42 **16.** Plants
17. *Thirty-Nine* **18.** *Great Expectations*
19. Graham Greene **20.** Sam Spade
21. *Noughts and Crosses* **22.** J. K. Rowling
23. Robert Galbraith **24.** Patrick Ness
25. Gender reassignment

QUIZ 113
1. Captain Abraham Smollet **2.** Hannibal
Lecter **3.** And in the darkness bind them
4. Ford Anglia **5.** Whoopi Goldberg
6. Kaa **7.** On a park bench **8.** *The Reader*
9. *Alice in Wonderland* **10.** Veterinarian
for large animals **11.** Truman Capote
12. *Lord of the Flies* **13.** 12 **14.** Don
Corleone **15.** *To Kill a Mockingbird*
16. *Schindler's Ark* **17.** 7 **18.** *Dr. No*
19. Ian Fleming **20.** The Louvre

QUIZ 114
1. 1990s **2.** Georges Braque **3.** *The Scream*
4. Barbara Hepworth **5.** Paint thickly applied

6. Engraving 7. Antony Gormley
8. Graffiti 9. John Everett Millais
10. Andrew Wyeth 11. Mexico 12. Whistler
13. Jeff Koons 14. Surrealism 15. Venice
16. Horses 17. El Greco 18. Sir Joshua
Reynolds 19. 2000 20. True 21. Bernini
22. Milan 23. True 24. The dove
25. Kate Moss

QUIZ 115

1. 1939 2. *Captain America* 3. True
4. #3 5. False 6. Matt Murdock 7. 1965
8. No 9. False 10. 1980 11. True 12. 1990
13. The Scarlet Spider 14. The Runaways
15. Mark Millar 16. Blue Hulk 17. Phoenix
18. White 19. In a plane crash 20. God
of Thunder

QUIZ 116

1. Edward Hopper 2. His pipe
3. Books and a candlestick 4. Medusa
5. 1508–1512 6. Landscapes and palace life
7. Thomas Gainsborough 8. In his bath
9. Caspar David Friedrich 10. True
11. Red 12. Ovid 13. A horse and a
bull 14. 2 15. The cross points down
16. A skull 17. False 18. *1808* 19. True
20. Giotto

QUIZ 117

1. Yorkshire 2. Currer Bell 3. Branwell
4. Two 5. False 6. *The Tenant of
Wildfell Hall* 7. Six 8. 1850 9. Emily
10. *The Professor* 11. Elizabeth Gaskell
12. False 13. *Shirley* 14. Mr. Lockwood
and Nelly Dean 15. Bertha 16. Gondal
17. False 18. *Agnes Grey* 19. Thornfield
Hall 20. True 21. *Blackwoods* 22. Brussels
23. Governess 24. India 25. Jane Eyre
and Mr. Rochester

QUIZ 118

1. In a letter 2. Dartmouth 3. Seattle
4. Jacob 5. Leah Clearwater 6. 2 years old
7. Billy Black 8. Maria 9. He kisses her
10. To track and kill her 11. Jacob and
Alice 12. Jasper 13. In the forest 14. Ten
15. True 16. Seth 17. A heart 18. He
eavesdrops on them 19. Bree 20. True

QUIZ 119

1. Ebenezer 2. Jacob Marley 3. True
4. Christmas Eve 5. Jacob Marley 6. A
warning 7. 7 years 8. Door knocker
9. One 10. A young Scrooge alone in a
school 11. Glowing torch 12. Whether
Tiny Tim will live 13. Ignorance and Want
14. Ghost of Christmas Yet to Come
15. A beetling shop 16. His name on a
gravestone 17. A turkey 18. At his
nephew's house 19. False 20. Emily
Cratchit 21. Belle 22. Tiny Tim
23. A silent phantom 24. One day
25. December 1843

QUIZ 120

1. John and Elizabeth 2. 1859 3. Portsmouth
4. Westminster Abbey 5. Mr. Micawber
6. True 7. True 8. More than 250 9. Boz
10. Ten 11. *A Dinner at Poplar Walk*
12. Ellen Ternan 13. *Our Mutual Friend*
14. Once 15. Ravens 16. Hablot Knight
Browne 17. *Barnaby Rudge* 18. Epilepsy
19. Miss Havisham 20. False

QUIZ 121

1. *On the Road* 2. Yann Martel 3. Henry
James 4. *The Road* 5. *Adventures of
Huckleberry Finn* 6. Paul Theroux
7. *Pequod* 8. *Lost Horizon* 9. *The Little
Prince* 10. *Fear and Loathing in Las Vegas*
11. Jack London 12. *The Shining* 13. Truman
Capote 14. False 15. *The Aeneid* 16. Mark
Twain 17. False 18. Cormac McCarthy
19. *Zen and the Art of Motorcycle
Maintenance* 20. *Heart of Darkness*

QUIZ 122

1. *The Third Policeman* 2. *VALIS*
3. *Naked Lunch* 4. Samuel Beckett
5. 1960s and 1970s 6. *Catch-22* 7. *Infinite
Jest* 8. *White Noise* 9. True 10. *The
Handmaid's Tale* 11. Grand narratives
12. *Breakfast of Champions* 13. The New
York Trilogy 14. The Literary Brat Pack
15. Douglas Coupland 16. *Austerlitz*
17. *American Psycho* 18. Brion Gysin
19. World War II 20. *One Hundred
Years of Solitude*

QUIZ 123

1. John Dryden **2.** 1668 **3.** True **4.** Chile
5. Samuel Rogers **6.** Alfred, Lord Tennyson
7. $35,000 **8.** Philip Larkin **9.** Bill
Manhire **10.** Saoi **11.** True **12.** Two
13. False **14.** False **15.** Ethiopia
16. Hanns Johst **17.** Poet of the
Fatherland **18.** True **19.** Sherry
20. Simon Armitage **21.** 10 years
22. Ben Jonson **23.** Cecil Day-Lewis
24. John Masefield **25.** *The Charge
of the Light Brigade*

QUIZ 124

1. At the end of the 14th century
2. To visit the relics of St. Thomas
Becket **3.** False **4.** 30 **5.** Four **6.** Death
7. The Ploughman and the Parson
8. The Prioress **9.** The Tabard Inn
10. False **11.** The Pardoner **12.** The
Summoner **13.** The Wife of Bath
14. Phoebus **15.** "The Man of Law's Tale"
and "The Squire's Tale" **16.** The Summoner
17. The Squire **18.** False **19.** Constance
20. 24 **21.** Cloth embroidered with flowers
22. True **23.** Cambyuskan **24.** False
25. "The Miller's Tale"

QUIZ 125

1. Robert Capa **2.** Magnum **3.** Paris
4. Cyprus **5.** Photogenic drawing
6. Tim Page **7.** False **8.** David
Bailey **9.** Yousuf Karsh **10.** John
11. 2012 **12.** True **13.** Denis Healey
14. *Picture Post* **15.** 1936 **16.** Annie
Leibovitz **17.** Princess Margaret
18. Sean **19.** Paparazzi **20.** Berlin
21. Henri Cartier-Bresson **22.** Life in
America **23.** Man Ray **24.** Portraits
25. False

QUIZ 126

1. Gloucester **2.** True **3.** *Hamlet*
4. Sicily **5.** *Coriolanus* **6.** Bed **7.** *Henry
VIII* **8.** Balthasar **9.** False **10.** James I
11. Gertrude **12.** *The Taming of the Shrew*
13. Viola **14.** 7 **15.** Smothers her
16. True **17.** *The Merchant of Venice*
18. Three **19.** Uranus **20.** Denmark

QUIZ 127

1. The Factory **2.** London **3.** 1950s
4. Peter Blake **5.** *Man, Machine and
Motion* **6.** Campbell's **7.** Independent
Group **8.** Tottenham Court Road
9. Richard Hamilton **10.** False
11. Museum of Modern Art **12.** New York
13. 11 **14.** Andy Warhol **15.** California
16. Mimmo Rotella **17.** The Velvet
Underground **18.** Comic strips
19. 1963 **20.** Shot him

QUIZ 128

1. J. M. Barrie **2.** Emma Woodhouse
3. 28 years, 2 months, and 19 days
4. Wilkins Micawber **5.** Cut **6.** A
governess **7.** Stonehenge **8.** Voltaire
9. False **10.** *Northanger Abbey* **11.** Rome
12. Cocaine and morphine **13.** Horse
14. Wrote *Wuthering Heights* **15.** True
16. A conduct manual **17.** *Under Western
Eyes* **18.** A display of his swordsmanship
19. Polyphonic substitution **20.** Sancho
Panza **21.** John Steinbeck **22.** *The
Metamorphosis* **23.** *In Search of
Lost Time* **24.** Erewhon
25. James Baldwin

QUIZ 129

1. 1934 **2.** Detective Comics **3.** Superman
4. *Action Comics 1* **5.** *Detective Comics 27*
6. *Superman 30* **7.** True **8.** 1952
9. False **10.** *Brightest Day* **11.** Alfred
12. Damien Wayne **13.** Thomas and Martha
14. Dave Gibbons **15.** 1988 **16.** David
Lloyd **17.** Neil Gaiman **18.** *Batman:
Digital Justice* **19.** 1993 **20.** The Joker

QUIZ 130

1. It was considered anti-Stalinist
2. *The Grapes of Wrath* **3.** Because
Tarzan and Jane were living in sin
4. *Frankenstein* **5.** *Uncle Tom's Cabin*
by Harriet Beecher Stowe **6.** It was feared
it would cause an uprising **7.** Gustave
Flaubert **8.** *Madame Bovary* **9.** *Green
Eggs and Ham* **10.** For its alleged portrayal
of Marxism **11.** 1559 **12.** It was about
same-sex penguins having a baby and

considered anti-family and not suitable for the age group **13.** *Alice's Adventures in Wonderland* **14.** Animals and humans appeared as equals **15.** *Spycatcher* **16.** True **17.** True **18.** True **19.** It was about sexual love between two women and considered obscene **20.** True

QUIZ 131

1. Mycroft Holmes **2.** A wedding ring **3.** Governess **4.** False **5.** *The Hound of the Baskervilles* **6.** *The Strand* **7.** *A Case of Identity* **8.** *The Sign of Four* **9.** 56 **10.** Irene Adler **11.** Three **12.** Beekeeping **13.** True **14.** A knife **15.** Young street children **16.** Holmes is presumed dead **17.** Reichenbach Falls **18.** Fred Porlock **19.** *The Adventure of the Empty House* **20.** *The Case-Book of Sherlock Holmes*

QUIZ 132

1. Jean-Auguste Ingres **2.** Auguste Renoir **3.** Frida Kahlo **4.** Sandro Botticelli **5.** Edouard Manet **6.** Jackson Pollock **7.** René Magritte **8.** Mark Rothko **9.** Mary Cassatt **10.** Peter Paul Rubens **11.** Grant Wood **12.** Salvador Dali **13.** Georgia O'Keeffe **14.** Francisco Goya **15.** Diego Velázquez **16.** Bridget Riley **17.** Sir John Everett Millais **18.** William Holman Hunt **19.** Tracey Emin **20.** Banksy **21.** Rembrandt **22.** Jan van Eyck **23.** Frederic Leighton **24.** Hieronymus Bosch **25.** Auguste Rodin

QUIZ 133

1. Paul Auster **2.** *Gravity's Rainbow* **3.** *The Bluest Eye* **4.** *Garp* **5.** *Americana* **6.** *Infinite Jest* **7.** *The Amazing Adventures of Kavalier & Clay* **8.** Jonathan Franzen **9.** False **10.** Chuck Palahniuk **11.** True **12.** Philip Roth **13.** Annie Proulx **14.** Michael Cunningham **15.** John Updike **16.** *Charlotte's Web* **17.** Alice Sebold **18.** *Cold Mountain* **19.** *The Secret History* **20.** Louise Erdrich

QUIZ 134

1. Déagol **2.** Gimli **3.** Prancing **4.** Eregion **5.** False **6.** Eagle **7.** Isildur **8.** Orodruin **9.** Radagast the Brown **10.** Andúril, Flame of the West **11.** False **12.** Friend **13.** Balin **14.** A white figure **15.** Snowmane **16.** A balrog **17.** Brooch **18.** Éomer **19.** Look at the lights **20.** Ungol

QUIZ 135

1. Six **2.** *Through the Looking Glass* **3.** *Difficulties with Girls* **4.** *Twenty Years After* **5.** *The Return of the King* **6.** *Rebecca's Tale* **7.** *Harry Potter and the Chamber of Secrets* **8.** *The Amber Spyglass* **9.** *The Rainbow* **10.** True **11.** *The Ghost Brigades* **12.** *Point of Impact* **13.** *Marathon Man* **14.** False **15.** *The High King* **16.** *Explorers on the Moon* **17.** *Tom Brown at Oxford* **18.** *Knife Edge* **19.** *Life at the Top* **20.** *Porterhouse Blue*

QUIZ 136

1. Approx. 4.5 billion years **2.** Ural Mountains **3.** Tropical rain forest **4.** Uniformitarianism **5.** Basalt **6.** False **7.** False **8.** Igneomorphic **9.** Radioactivity **10.** Sedimentary rocks **11.** Cooling molten rock **12.** Metamorphic rock **13.** Fossils **14.** Amber **15.** True **16.** The equator **17.** False **18.** France and Spain **19.** Pyramidal peak **20.** Galaxies

QUIZ 137

1. Missouri **2.** A plunge pool **3.** Source **4.** Tributaries **5.** Amazon **6.** Seine **7.** True **8.** An oxbow lake **9.** Flood control **10.** True **11.** Nile **12.** True **13.** Ebro **14.** Po **15.** A floodplain **16.** Change **17.** Sediment load **18.** 20% **19.** Flood **20.** Angel Falls **21.** Amazon **22.** Myanmar **23.** Ethiopia **24.** Murray **25.** Titicaca

QUIZ 138

1. Indonesia **2.** Extinct **3.** False **4.** False **5.** True **6.** Igneous **7.** Pompeii **8.** 1,830 °F (1,000 °C) **9.** Fertile, mineral-rich soil **10.** True **11.** False **12.** True **13.** Fuji

14. True **15.** Fumarole **16.** Volcanic bomb
17. Mars **18.** The crater **19.** False **20.** True

QUIZ 139

1. False **2.** An oasis **3.** False **4.** Camel
5. Carcross **6.** Rain **7.** Prickly pear
8. Castle **9.** Northern China and southern
Mongolia **10.** True **11.** Night **12.** False
13. Argentina **14.** Caravan **15.** Spines and
thorns **16.** Steppes **17.** Nomads **18.** Large
flat feet **19.** Two **20.** False **21.** Salinization
22. The Sierra Nevada **23.** The Outback
24. Remain dormant **25.** Succulents

QUIZ 140

1. Rome **2.** Egypt **3.** New York City
4. Rio de Janeiro **5.** Scafell Pike
6. Heathrow **7.** Yellowstone **8.** Sydney
9. Reykjavík **10.** Iceland **11.** Kilimanjaro
12. Hokkaido **13.** Canada **14.** Arizona
15. Hawaii **16.** Nile **17.** Dhaka **18.** Mexico
19. Dominican Republic **20.** Haiti

QUIZ 141

1. 650 miles (1,050 km) **2.** Fold mountains
3. True **4.** 20% **5.** False **6.** Africa
7. Hawaii **8.** Mont Blanc **9.** False
10. Everest **11.** True **12.** Pointed **13.** True
14. ¼ in (5 mm) a year **15.** Southern Africa
16. Mount McKinley **17.** Peruvian Andes
18. Tibetan **19.** Mexico **20.** Orography
21. The Great Dividing Range **22.** Ethiopian
Highlands **23.** Europe and Asia
24. Appalachian Mountains **25.** Munros

QUIZ 142

1. Switzerland **2.** Red and yellow
3. Mediterranean and Atlantic **4.** True
5. Germany **6.** The Vatican **7.** Monaco
8. Iceland **9.** Greece **10.** The Netherlands
11. Four **12.** Øresund Bridge **13.** Madrid
14. Rome **15.** True **16.** Greece **17.** Eight
18. False **19.** Berlin **20.** France and Spain
21. Hungary **22.** Estonia **23.** Italy
24. Italy **25.** Romania

QUIZ 143

1. The Egyptian pyramids and the Sphinx
2. Victoria Falls **3.** Suez Canal **4.** The Big
Five **5.** The Sahara **6.** True **7.** Marrakesh
8. Khartoum **9.** Mali **10.** Ramesses II
11. 2010 **12.** Ivory Coast **13.** Angola
14. The Pharos Lighthouse **15.** A northern
African bath-house **16.** Madagascar
17. Kwacha **18.** Mount Sinai **19.** True
20. False

QUIZ 144

1. A city with a population of more
than 10 million **2.** Tokyo **3.** Bombay
4. Nigeria **5.** True **6.** 37 **7.** Shantytowns
8. Three **9.** Paris and Moscow **10.** Los
Angeles **11.** São Paulo **12.** Istanbul
13. Islamabad **14.** Kolkata **15.** 20,000
16. Rome **17.** False **18.** True **19.** Moscow
20. Asia **21.** Chicago **22.** Three
23. South Korea **24.** Shanghai **25.** False

QUIZ 145

1. New Year's Day **2.** Martin Luther King Jr.
Day **3.** Valentine's Day **4.** Washington's
Birthday **5.** St. Patrick's Day **6.** St. George's
Day **7.** Anzac Day **8.** Thanksgiving
9. Indigenous People's Day **10.** Canada
Day **11.** Independence Day **12.** Bastille
Day **13.** La Tomatina **14.** Trafalgar Day
15. Mahatma Gandhi's Birthday **16.** The
Day of German Unity **17.** Halloween
18. Armistice Day or Remembrance
19. Republic Day **20.** Christmas Day

QUIZ 146

1. Morocco **2.** Lobster **3.** Italy **4.** Fondue
5. Texas **6.** Breakfast **7.** True **8.** Boerewors
9. Duck **10.** Belgium **11.** Apple pie
12. France **13.** Clay **14.** Sausage
15. Dim sum **16.** Mexico **17.** Fish
and chips **18.** Fried rice **19.** Paella
20. False; it is made with phyllo pastry

QUIZ 147

1. Everest **2.** Nile **3.** Siberia **4.** Mid-
Atlantic Ridge **5.** Russia **6.** Vatican City
7. True **8.** Venezuela **9.** Severn
10. California **11.** Chile **12.** Antarctic
13. Dead Sea **14.** Ojos del Salado
15. Amazon **16.** Lambert **17.** Greenland
18. Asia **19.** La Paz **20.** Superior

21. Antarctica 22. Australia 23. Beijing (Tiananmen Square) 24. Pacific
25. Gorakhpur, Uttar Pradesh, India

QUIZ 148
1. Sydney 2. Rome 3. China 4. The Arc de Triomphe 5. Trevi 6. Venice 7. Las Vegas 8. Pisa 9. Barcelona 10. Taj Mahal 11. Brighton 12. Windsor 13. Mexico 14. San Francisco 15. Dublin 16. Milan 17. Copenhagen 18. Gateway of India 19. Paris 20. Harrods

QUIZ 149
1. Dubai 2. Chicago 3. 1931 4. The Petronas Towers 5. China Central Television Headquarters 6. Vietnam 7. 1902 8. Saudi Arabia 9. 2008 10. The Burj Al Arab 11. The Taipei 101 12. Barcelona 13. The Gherkin 14. Sweden 15. 2001 16. Macau 17. True 18. One World Trade Center 19. The Bank of China Tower 20. False

QUIZ 150
1. Honduras 2. Alaska 3. 13 4. Portuguese 5. Argentina's Independence Day 6. Cacti 7. Delaware 8. Bolivia 9. True 10. Alaska 11. Pampas 12. Hydropower 13. Venice, Italy 14. Galápagos Islands 15. Maine 16. Christopher Columbus, in 1502 17. Lake Titicaca 18. Hawaii 19. Chile and Ecuador 20. False 21. Grizzly bear 22. July 4, 1776 23. False 24. California 25. Pennsylvania

QUIZ 151
1. Richter 2. San Andreas Fault 3. Steel 4. Ten times stronger 5. Epicenter 6. Focus 7. Seismologists 8. Seismograph 9. Fire 10. Tsunami 11. Japan 12. True 13. Indonesia 14. Mercalli 15. Alaska 16. P 17. At tectonic plate boundaries 18. Chile 19. Aftershock 20. Shockwave

QUIZ 152
1. Colorado 2. Four 3. Plunge pool 4. Yangtze 5. Amazon 6. True 7. Rio Grande 8. Tributary 9. Confluence 10. Venezuela 11. Yangtze 12. Six

13. Caspian 14. Abrasion 15. Mississippi 16. Cautley Spout 17. False 18. The Itapuã Dam 19. Alluvium 20. Delta

QUIZ 153
1. Nigeria 2. Tokyo 3. Helsinki 4. Dakar 5. Dnieper 6. Budapest 7. Athens 8. Algiers 9. Madagascar 10. Qatar 11. Pyongyang 12. True 13. Madrid 14. Zagreb 15. Montevideo 16. Suriname 17. Falkland Islands 18. Ottawa 19. Bolivia 20. Edinburgh 21. Meeting place 22. Al Fustat 23. Rome 24. Colombia 25. Colombo

QUIZ 154
1. False 2. True 3. Mexico 4. 10,000 years ago 5. 2 billion 6. 37% 7. True 8. True 9. Arable 10. About 200 11. Very slowly 12. Methane 13. Raising fruits and vegetables for distribution 14. Salinization 15. Chickens 16. Genetically modified 17. True 18. China 19. True 20. Grapes

QUIZ 155
1. 28,251 ft (8,611 m) 2. South Africa 3. Dead Sea 4. Himalayas 5. Cuba 6. Aconcagua 7. Murray and Darling 8. 1987 9. Seven 10. Indonesia 11. It is made of ice 12. Mount Elbrus 13. The Mariana Trench 14. Prehistoric cave paintings 15. London 16. The monarch butterfly 17. Sweden and Denmark 18. Peru 19. 8:00 p.m. 20. Australia 21. Antarctica 22. La Paz, in Bolivia 23. Peru 24. Death Valley, California, 134°F (56.7°C) 25. Toxic gases from nearby geysers can kill very quickly

QUIZ 156
1. China 2. Vatican City 3. 7–8 billion 4. China 5. Doubled 6. 57 7. 10.5 billion 8. 332 million 9. Nauru 10. 1987 11. True 12. Stop growing 13. India 14. False 15. 2100 16. 100 billion 17. Asia 18. India 19. China 20. 1960s

QUIZ 157

1. Between 2,100 and 3,000 **2.** Madagascar
3. 2006 **4.** More than 140 million **5.** Ten
6. French **7.** True **8.** French and Arabic
9. False **10.** English **11.** Eritrea and
Ethiopia **12.** Portuguese **13.** 2002
14. English **15.** German **16.** Around
15 million **17.** Ethiopia **18.** More than
500 **19.** North Africa **20.** Setswana

QUIZ 158

1. Indonesia **2.** New Zealand **3.** Tonga
4. 25 **5.** Greenland **6.** The Persian Gulf
7. Cuba **8.** Australia **9.** 70,000 **10.** Japan
11. The Pacific Ocean **12.** False **13.** One
14. Singapore **15.** Kingston **16.** True
17. Iceland **18.** Madagascar **19.** Cyprus
20. New Zealand **21.** Grenada
22. French **23.** Trinidad and Tobago
24. Timor-Leste **25.** Six

QUIZ 159

1. The Grand Canyon **2.** Haystack Rock
3. 12 million **4.** Oregon **5.** Yellowstone
National Park **6.** 2,427 ft (740 m) **7.** False
8. California **9.** Acadia National Park
10. Black Rapids Glacier **11.** Utah
12. Wyoming **13.** Old Faithful **14.** Denali
15. False **16.** Lady Luck's Ladder
17. President Theodore Roosevelt **18.** False
19. Arizona and Nevada **20.** California

QUIZ 160

1. 1944 **2.** True **3.** The ninth century
4. An army **5.** Althingi **6.** Thingvellir
7. Greenland **8.** Geysir **9.** 23 **10.** Car
11. 320,000 **12.** Gaelic **13.** Literature
14. Whaling **15.** The most peaceful country
in the world **16.** Coca-Cola **17.** The
arctic fox **18.** Kópavogur **19.** Lutheranism
20. 2008 **21.** True **22.** Icelandic
23. Avalanches **24.** Turf **25.** Glymur

QUIZ 161

1. Over warm ocean water near the equator
2. 250 mph (400 kmph) **3.** Cumulonimbus
4. Thunder **5.** Rainbow **6.** Lightning
7. A hailstone **8.** El Niño **9.** 800–1,200
10. Wind speed **11.** Waterspout

12. Saffir-Simpson **13.** Dust devils
14. Blizzard **15.** False **16.** Droughts
17. Smog **18.** Just below freezing
19. Avalanche **20.** Gale

QUIZ 162

1. Volga **2.** False **3.** Mauna Kea **4.** True
5. China and Nepal **6.** True **7.** Yangtze
8. Amazon **9.** 13 **10.** New Zealander
11. Lake Eyre **12.** False **13.** Japan **14.** True
15. The Andes **16.** Africa **17.** None
18. The Andes **19.** Limnology **20.** Canada
21. Lake Constance **22.** True **23.** Finger
Lakes **24.** Upper course **25.** Egypt

QUIZ 163

1. Australia **2.** 2,000 miles (3,220 km)
3. Edinburgh of the Seven Seas **4.** Al
Azizyah, Libya **5.** Oymyakon, Russia
6. True **7.** Laos **8.** Great white sharks
9. Mariana Trench **10.** Angel Falls,
Venezuela **11.** Middle East **12.** Louisiana
13. Florida **14.** The Amazon Rain Forest
15. True **16.** The Serengeti Plains
17. Antarctica **18.** India **19.** Two million
years **20.** Australia

QUIZ 164

1. Rocky Mountains **2.** Brazil **3.** 40000 BCE
and 15000 BCE **4.** 1492 **5.** Titicaca **6.** 35
million years ago **7.** True **8.** Southern
Thule **9.** 31 **10.** False **11.** True **12.** New
York City **13.** 35 **14.** Christianity
15. False **16.** The Isthmus of Panama
17. Kaffeklubben Island **18.** Western
Cordillera **19.** One in ten **20.** False
21. 13 **22.** 1600 Pennsylvania Avenue
23. Nevada **24.** Seattle **25.** Louisiana

QUIZ 165

1. A tornado **2.** 310 mph (500 kmph)
3. A tidal wave **4.** An earthquake **5.** A
twister **6.** False **7.** One in 700,000 **8.** It
was completely destroyed by a hurricane
9. Lightning rod **10.** An avalanche
11. A dry slab avalanche **12.** Chile
13. 9.5 **14.** 1,500 **15.** False **16.** Santorini
17. Mount St. Helens **18.** Flood protection
for London **19.** True **20.** Lisbon

QUIZ 166
1. Gulf of California **2.** Atoll **3.** Limestone
4. Black smokers **5.** 3.50% **6.** Maelstrom,
Norway **7.** 3,300 ft (1,000 m) **8.** Dead Sea
9. Sargasso Sea **10.** Humboldt Current
11. Zooplankton **12.** 660 ft (200 m)
13. The Indian Ocean **14.** Bioluminescence
15. Coral reef **16.** Giant clam **17.** Abyssal
plain **18.** All of them **19.** True **20.** Sea
of Azov

QUIZ 167
1. The Utah-Arizona border **2.** Venezuela
3. Caves **4.** New Zealand **5.** Aurora
australis **6.** Red Sea **7.** Giant's Causeway
8. Iceberg **9.** Argentina **10.** Easter Island
11. Lake Titicaca **12.** Narwhal **13.** Lake
Eyre **14.** Victoria **15.** Mississippi
16. 6,000 ft (1,830 m) **17.** Norway **18.** Mount
Fuji **19.** Great Barrier Reef **20.** Baobab

QUIZ 168
1. Composite **2.** A pyroclastic flow
3. Basalt **4.** Hotspot **5.** Antarctica
6. Charles F. Richter **7.** Ring of Fire
8. Obsidian **9.** The volcano's side
began to bulge **10.** Dormant **11.** True
12. Washington State **13.** Every 90 minutes
14. Pumice **15.** True **16.** False
17. Atlantis **18.** Mount Tambora
19. Kilauea **20.** True

QUIZ 169
1. The Everglades **2.** Lake Baikal
3. Lake Titicaca **4.** Wastwater **5.** Lake
Chad **6.** Lake Superior **7.** 20% **8.** False
9. Dead Sea **10.** The Sudd **11.** Lake
Ontario **12.** Lake Erie **13.** Lake Huron
14. Lake Kariba **15.** The Pantanal
16. The Pripet Marshes **17.** Lake Taupo
18. Lake Mead **19.** Valdai Hills
20. True **21.** True **22.** Carbon **23.** An
international treaty to protect wetlands
24. True **25.** Lake Michigan

QUIZ 170
1. Snout **2.** A large chunk of ice breaks off
3. False **4.** Panhole **5.** Hanging valley
6. 10% **7.** About 70% **8.** Worms
9. Pyramidal peak or horn **10.** Lateral
moraines **11.** Erratic **12.** True
13. Accumulation zone **14.** Blue
15. Nunataks **16.** Fjord **17.** Greenland
18. 420,000 years **19.** Lake Vostok
20. True **21.** Australia **22.** The Southern
Ocean **23.** Gravity **24.** When a glacier
increases speed **25.** Crevasses

QUIZ 171
1. 8 billion **2.** False **3.** True **4.** False
5. True **6.** Africa **7.** Monaco **8.** Greenland
9. Mandarin Chinese **10.** True **11.** 2007
12. 18.4 million **13.** False **14.** Population
pyramid **15.** Central business district
16. Costa Rica **17.** Shantytowns
18. Inuit **19.** True **20.** Qatar
21. China **22.** 7,000 **23.** No, they
self-identify as indigenous **24.** Canada
25. Hindi

QUIZ 172
1. Zimbabwe **2.** St. Kilda **3.** Tombolo
4. Taiga **5.** The Red Sea **6.** Ghana
7. The Indies (Asia) **8.** Trench **9.** Urals
10. Kiribati **11.** Africa **12.** Japan
13. Sahel **14.** East **15.** Derbyshire
16. Maldives **17.** Beach **18.** Niger
19. Ernest Shackleton **20.** Death Zone

QUIZ 173
1. Surtsey **2.** Mount Etna **3.** Magma
4. Basalt **5.** Core **6.** False **7.** Elephants
8. Pele's hair **9.** Black smokers **10.** Cure
ailments **11.** Iceland **12.** The Ring of Fire
13. True **14.** True **15.** A thick-walled
prison cell **16.** The San Andreas Fault
17. San Francisco **18.** A transcurrent fault
zone **19.** True **20.** There was no sanitation
in the place survivors fled to

QUIZ 174
1. 50 **2.** Hawaii **3.** Delaware **4.** Hawaii
5. True **6.** California **7.** Alaska
8. Florida **9.** True **10.** South Dakota
11. Massachusetts **12.** New Jersey
13. Wisconsin **14.** Four **15.** Wyoming
16. Two **17.** Alaska **18.** Sacramento
19. New York **20.** Louisiana **21.** True

22. South Dakota **23.** Four **24.** Mount Lee
25. Alaska

QUIZ 175
1. Swahili **2.** Greenland **3.** Lingua franca
4. True **5.** Greek **6.** Italian **7.** Nigeria
8. Gujarati **9.** The Philippines **10.** More
than 800 **11.** Norwegian **12.** New Zealand
13. True **14.** English **15.** Corsican
16. Patagonia **17.** Jack Kerouac
18. Nahuatl **19.** Kenya **20.** Dutch

QUIZ 176
1. Tunisia **2.** Between lands **3.** The
Phoenicians **4.** Gibraltar **5.** Sicily
6. Croatia **7.** No **8.** Venice **9.** True
10. 220,000 **11.** True **12.** True **13.** Spain
14. Barcelona **15.** 21 **16.** Greece
17. The Red Sea **18.** Our Sea **19.** False
20. Greece

QUIZ 177
1. True **2.** 65 million years old **3.** True
4. Both **5.** True **6.** Glacier **7.** It is liquid
at room temperature **8.** Bronze **9.** True
10. True **11.** True **12.** A river **13.** False
14. Two-thirds **15.** Atacama Desert
16. 3% **17.** Erosion **18.** Stalactites
19. 39.6 ft (12 m) **20.** True

QUIZ 178
1. Building **2.** 33,480 ft (10,205 m)
3. 2192 °F (1200 °C) **4.** True **5.** Lava flow
6. Indonesia **7.** More than 1,500 **8.** Mud
or debris that flows down from a volcano
9. Mauna Loa **10.** 79 CE **11.** Dormant
12. 3,500 **13.** Hekla **14.** True
15. More than 35,000 **16.** 10,000
17. Vulcan **18.** True **19.** Washington
20. The Philippines

QUIZ 179
1. France **2.** The Leshan Giant Buddha,
China, is 233 ft (71 m) tall **3.** 81 years
4. China **5.** Luxembourg **6.** Tokyo
7. Zimbabwe **8.** Belgium **9.** Papua
New Guinea **10.** Mecca **11.** Lourdes
12. Istanbul **13.** Paris **14.** Mohammed
15. Kosovo **16.** India **17.** Jerusalem

18. Vatican City **19.** North Macedonia
20. 50%

QUIZ 180
1. Tephra **2.** Montserrat **3.** Typhoon
4. Surtsey **5.** Whirlpool **6.** Hurricane
Katrina **7.** Preparing ski runs **8.** Tsunami
9. Very gentle **10.** Hurricane
11. Stratosphere **12.** False **13.** Vesuvius
14. Deepest **15.** Polders **16.** Meteorite
impact on Earth **17.** 1964 **18.** Wegener
19. Earthquake **20.** Bangladesh

QUIZ 181
1. At the back **2.** A percussion instrument
consisting of a pair of hand drums used in
Indian music **3.** True **4.** Guitar **5.** The
bagpipes **6.** True **7.** China **8.** The bars
are struck with sticks or padded mallets
9. Electronic **10.** False. There are two pedals
11. To change the sound **12.** Switzerland
13. A type of cymbal. It consists of two
cymbals and a foot pedal mounted on a
metal stand. It is part of a standard drum
kit **14.** A viola is larger than a violin
15. A *balalaika* is a stringed instrument that
originates from Russia. It has a triangular
wooden hollow body, a fretted neck, and
three strings **16.** Lyre **17.** Four strings
18. False. It's a woodwind instrument
19. Tuba **20.** 12 notes **21.** It's an early type
of trombone. It dates from the Renaissance
period; the late 14th century **22.** True
23. Brass instruments **24.** Harmonica
25. Harp

QUIZ 182
1. Afropop **2.** True **3.** Ireland **4.** George
Harrison from the Beatles **5.** Germany
6. Eucalyptus **7.** Reggae music **8.** True.
An erhu is a two-stringed instrument that
resembles a violin and is played with a bow
9. True **10.** African. The movement of
slaves from Africa to the southern US states
is seen as helping the development of these
different styles of music **11.** India **12.** Bongo
drums **13.** True **14.** Hip-hop **15.** A
dragon **16.** Castanets **17.** It's a woodwind
instrument. Originally from South America,

panpipes consist of cane pipes of different lengths tied or held together by wax or cord and closed at the bottom **18.** False **19.** True **20.** The Glastonbury Festival

QUIZ 183

1. Seattle **2.** Prince **3.** "Sweet Home Alabama" **4.** False **5.** Gladys Knight and the Pips **6.** Nashville **7.** Minnesota **8.** "Do You Know the Way to San Jose?" **9.** Train **10.** Motown **11.** Georgia **12.** The blues and jazz **13.** Soul, funk, and rhythm and blues music that was produced in Philadelphia **14.** Candlestick Park, San Francisco **15.** True **16.** Jackson Browne and Glenn Frey **17.** "The 59th Street Bridge Song" **18.** Cleveland, Ohio **19.** San Fernando Valley **20.** Boston

QUIZ 184

1. John Lennon (and Yoko Ono) **2.** Michael Bublé **3.** "White Christmas" **4.** "The Twelve Days of Christmas" **5.** "Mistletoe" **6.** *Meet Me in St. Louis* **7.** Mariah Carey **8.** "Good King Wenceslas" **9.** Blue ("Blue Christmas") **10.** Gene Autry **11.** Rockin' ("Rockin' Around the Christmas Tree") **12.** Bruce Springsteen **13.** "Christmas Time Is Here" **14.** Celine Dion **15.** *Noël* **16.** "Santa Baby" **17.** Wham! **18.** *Frozen* **19.** True **20.** True

QUIZ 185

1. Austria **2.** Deep and crisp and even **3.** Glory to the Newborn King **4.** St. Francis of Assisi **5.** "O Come All Ye Faithful" **6.** A lowly cattle shed **7.** Christina Rossetti **8.** Boughs of holly **9.** … to you and your kin **10.** A fir tree **11.** One Horse Open Sleigh **12.** The crown **13.** Eight maids a-milking **14.** Benjamin Britten **15.** "Away in a Manger" **16.** Throw cares away **17.** Myrrh **18.** "That glorious song of old" **19.** Three ships **20.** Do you hear what I hear? **21.** Heaven **22.** The first Noel… was to certain poor shepherds **23.** "Hark! The Herald Angels Sing" **24.** The Angel of the Lord came down **25.** Bethlehem

QUIZ 186

1. Piano **2.** Five lines **3.** A flute in *The Magic Flute* **4.** The piano and the double bass **5.** Violins **6.** Baroque **7.** Pluck a string **8.** George Gershwin **9.** The oboe **10.** Antonio Vivaldi **11.** Venus **12.** 4 minutes 33 seconds **13.** The pitch of the notes **14.** Violin **15.** Six strings **16.** *Piano* **17.** Countertenor **18.** Violin **19.** 8 years of age **20.** Four quarter notes

QUIZ 187

1. "Israelites" by Desmond Dekker and the Aces **2.** Vincent Ford **3.** The Melodians **4.** Junior Murvin **5.** Jimmy Cliff **6.** Melodica **7.** "Simmer Down" **8.** Dandy Livingstone **9.** Desmond Dekker and the Aces **10.** King Tubby **11.** Fred "Toots" Hibbert **12.** "Do the Reggay" **13.** Black Uhuru **14.** Winston Rodney **15.** Lee Scratch Perry **16.** In Croydon, England, in 2006 **17.** Gregory Isaacs **18.** U-Roy **19.** The Originator **20.** Nesta **21.** The word is derived from "rege-rege," a Jamaican phrase meaning rags or ragged clothing. It is used to denote a raggedy style of music **22.** Blondie **23.** Moses Davis **24.** Gregory Isaacs **25.** Ziggy is Bob Marley's eldest son. He is a songwriter and musician

QUIZ 188

1. Kajagoogoo **2.** Billy Joel **3.** Guns N' Roses **4.** Madonna **5.** The Cure **6.** *Tintin* **7.** The Boss **8.** True **9.** The Cult **10.** Duran Duran **11.** Neil Tennant **12.** Yes **13.** David Lee Roth **14.** Tina Turner **15.** Kenny Loggins **16.** Frankie Goes to Hollywood **17.** Milli Vanilli **18.** Europe **19.** Twisted Sister **20.** Men at Work **21.** "Our House" **22.** Dire Straits **23.** Dolly Parton **24.** Prince in "When Doves Cry" **25.** New Kids on the Block

QUIZ 189

1. Debbie Harry **2.** Three 6 Mafia **3.** Public Enemy **4.** Sugarhill Gang **5.** Untouchable Force Organization

6. OutKast **7.** G-Unit **8.** Dr. Dre
9. Flavor Flav **10.** Bully **11.** Snoop Dogg
12. *Reasonable Doubt* **13.** True
Boys **14.** Public Enemy and Anthrax
15. Eric Lynn Wright **16.** Childish
Gambino **17.** True **18.** Lil' Kim
19. Cypress Hill **20.** The Beastie Boys

QUIZ 190

1. Benny Andersson and Björn Ulvaeus
2. *My Fair Lady* **3.** *West Side Story*
4. *Footloose* **5.** Cyndi Lauper **6.** *Miss
Saigon* **7.** *Madame Butterfly* **8.** *Calamity
Jane* **9.** *Fame* **10.** *Into the Woods*
11. *Wicked* **12.** *Guys and Dolls* **13.** *South
Pacific* **14.** *The Lion King* **15.** *Hair*
16. *Cabaret* **17.** *The Sound of Music*
18. *Grease* **19.** Aquarius **20.** *Cats*
21. *Les Miserables* **22.** *Chicago*
23. *Chitty Chitty Bang Bang*
24. *Sweeney Todd* **25.** True

QUIZ 191

1. Christina Aguilera **2.** Meg White
3. 2001 **4.** Damon Albarn **5.** Fleet Foxes
6. Destiny's Child **7.** 2005 **8.** Barbados
9. True **10.** Amy Winehouse **11.** Glasgow
12. Arctic Monkeys **13.** True **14.** Black
Eyed Peas **15.** True **16.** 2009 **17.** Lady
Gaga **18.** Gwen Stefani **19.** Radiohead
20. *Kid Rock*

QUIZ 192

1. *Black Sabbath* **2.** Flower Fairies **3.** True
4. Anvil **5.** Steven Adler **6.** False. Seattle
is considered to be its original home
7. Motörhead **8.** 1980s **9.** Rob Halford,
lead singer of the band Judas Priest
10. Lars Ulrich of Metallica **11.** *Appetite
for Destruction* by Guns N' Roses **12.** John
13. Ronnie James Dio **14.** AC/DC
15. Motörhead **16.** False **17.** Head
18. KISS **19.** "Born to Be Wild" by
Steppenwolf **20.** His arm

QUIZ 193

1. Buddy Holly **2.** Ritchie Valens **3.** Little
Richard **4.** Mike Love **5.** Gene Vincent
6. Ricky Nelson **7.** Jackie Wilson **8.** They

were killed in a plane crash, along with Buddy
Holly **9.** "Summertime Blues" **10.** "Splish
Splash" **11.** 1958 **12.** "Blue Suede Shoes"
13. The Surfaris **14.** True **15.** 1977
16. Jerry Lee Lewis **17.** "Heartbreak
Hotel" **18.** False **19.** Texas **20.** Bill Haley
and the Comets

QUIZ 194

1. James Blunt **2.** Lady Gaga **3.** Jay-Z
4. Rage against the Machine **5.** Michael
Jackson **6.** The cast of TV series *Glee*
7. "I Gotta Feeling" **8.** Leona Lewis
9. Take That **10.** Hear'Say **11.** Alicia
Keys **12.** Justin Timberlake **13.** Ireland
14. *Glee* **15.** Arctic Monkeys **16.** "Crazy
in Love" **17.** Britney Spears **18.** True
19. Rihanna **20.** *American Idol*

QUIZ 195

1. Abba **2.** The Wailers **3.** Vivaldi
4. José Carreras **5.** The Rat Pack
6. True **7.** Stefani Germanotta **8.** Amadeus
9. Ballet **10.** Garbage **11.** False. They are
from Germany **12.** Guitar **13.** Wagner
14. False **15.** Jazz **16.** The Pussycat
Dolls **17.** 2007 **18.** Robert Plant **19.** Bing
Crosby **20.** "Massachusetts" **21.** Georges
Bizet **22.** Pretenders **23.** Craig David
24. Kylie Minogue **25.** Philadelphia

QUIZ 196

1. Germany **2.** Unrequited love **3.** 1791
4. True **5.** Johannes Brahms **6.** 47 strings
7. False **8.** Law **9.** Intervals **10.** One
11. Poor vision **12.** London Symphonies
13. Jazz **14.** The English Civil War
15. An Exposition **16.** 1877 **17.** The
opening **18.** False. It means moderately fast
19. Baroque, 17th century **20.** Guitar

QUIZ 197

1. Berry Gordy **2.** Marvin Gaye
3. The Matadors **4.** 110 **5.** 11 **6.** True
7. The Jackson 5 **8.** Ten **9.** The Supremes
10. The Pips **11.** *What's Going On*
12. 1972 **13.** So it could branch out into
motion pictures **14.** "Machine Gun"
15. Lionel Ritchie **16.** Norman Whitfield

17. True **18.** He rejected it **19.** 1988
20. More than $61 million **21.** Detroit
22. "Please, Mr. Postman" by the
Marvelettes **23.** Stevie Wonder
24. The Miracles **25.** The Supremes

QUIZ 198

1. Bob Dylan **2.** Joni Mitchell **3.** True
4. Peter, Paul, and Mary **5.** Louisiana
6. Pete Seeger **7.** A Dobro. This is an
acoustic guitar with a metal resonator
built into it, which resembles a car hubcap
8. At least 36 strings **9.** The sitar
10. *Liege and Lief* **11.** 1965 **12.** Woody
Guthrie **13.** The Byrds **14.** True **15.** He
played an electric guitar **16.** Simon &
Garfunkel **17.** Neil Young **18.** "The
Sloop John B" **19.** He was a poet
20. Joni Mitchell

QUIZ 199

1. Yellow **2.** "Purple Rain" **3.** *Blue*
4. *Black* **5.** White Album **6.** "Brown
Sugar" **7.** Gold **8.** "Green Onions"
9. Red **10.** The Psychedelic Furs
11. Scarlet **12.** "Blue Bayou" **13.** Prince
14. True **15.** "Rose Colored Glasses"
16. The Grateful Dead **17.** Blue
18. "Blue, Red, and Grey" **19.** "Brown
Eyed Girl" **20.** Silver **21.** Yellow
22. Green **23.** Red **24.** Johnny Cash
25. "Behind These Hazel Eyes"

QUIZ 200

1. *Aida* **2.** Luciano Pavarotti with
"Nessun Dorma" **3.** "Ave Maria"
4. *La Boheme* **5.** Georges Bizet
6. *La Traviata*, which is based on the
novel *The Lady with the Camellias*
by Dumas, commonly known as *Camille*
7. *Tosca* **8.** Rossini **9.** Mozart
10. Benjamin Britten: *A Midsummer
Night's Dream* and *Billy Budd* **11.** *Der
Rosenkavalier* by Richard Strauss
12. Carmen **13.** Minstrels **14.** *Rigoletto*
15. *Madame Butterfly* **16.** *Orfeo and
Euridice* **17.** Beethoven: *Fidelio*
18. *The Flying Dutchman* **19.** True
20. *Salome* by Richard Strauss

QUIZ 201

1. Taylor Hawkins **2.** True **3.** Lyricist
4. 1988 **5.** Eric Clapton **6.** Phil Collins
7. *Thomas & Friends* **8.** Kenney Jones
9. She was pregnant **10.** Phil Rudd **11.** Paul
McCartney **12.** Nicko McBrain **13.** True
14. Def Leppard **15.** Mike Joyce **16.** 32
17. Colin Flooks **18.** Joey Kramer
19. False **20.** 1949

QUIZ 202

1. Poland **2.** Gustav Holst **3.** Rimsky-
Korsakov **4.** True **5.** Vaughan Williams
6. *Animals* **7.** Mozart **8.** False. He
wrote "Music for Royal Fireworks"
9. Handel's *Messiah* **10.** Franz Liszt
11. Franz Schubert, Symphony No.8
12. Satie **13.** Vivaldi **14.** Antonio Vivaldi
15. Ballet **16.** Aaron Copland **17.** Purcell
18. *Madame Butterfly* **19.** Edward Elgar
20. True **21.** Joseph Haydn, Symphony
No.45, *Farewell* **22.** Clara Schumann
23. True **24.** Aleksandr Borodin
25. Gustav Mahler

QUIZ 203

1. 1962 **2.** "Jumpin' Jack Flash"
3. The Stolling Bones **4.** At a train station
5. Eight **6.** Marlon Brando **7.** 1972
8. Drummer Charlie Watts **9.** "You Can't
Always Get What You Want" **10.** 1969
11. Andy Warhol **12.** Michael Philip Jagger
13. "Come On" **14.** John Lennon and
Paul McCartney of the Beatles **15.** Faces
16. John Pasche **17.** False **18.** 19
19. Angelina Jolie **20.** France

QUIZ 204

1. Little Richard **2.** Bill Haley & the
Comets **3.** "That's Amore" **4.** 1955
5. Brenda Lee **6.** Aaron **7.** B. Goode
8. False **9.** The Everly Brothers **10.** Jerry
Lee Lewis **11.** "Cry Me a River"
12. "Tutti Frutti" **13.** True **14.** 1958
15. Alma Cogan **16.** Fats Domino
17. True **18.** Gene Vincent **19.** Fool
20. Buddy Holly & the Crickets
21. Rosemary Clooney **22.** Frankie
Lane **23.** White suede shoes

24. Chuck Berry **25.** Lita Roza
with "How Much Is That Doggie in
the Window?"

QUIZ 205
1. Johnny Allen **2.** True **3.** 11
4. Band of Gypsies **5.** Jimmy James
and the Blue Flames **6.** *Are You
Experienced* **7.** *First Rays of the New
Sun* **8.** Little Richard **9.** "Hey Joe"
10. New York **11.** Naked women
12. True **13.** "All along the Watchtower"
14. 101st Airborne **15.** Billy Cox
16. True **17.** True **18.** 1967 **19.** None
20. George Frideric Handel

QUIZ 206
1. A-ha **2.** Menudo **3.** New Edition
4. New Kids on the Block **5.** True **6.** Take
That **7.** East 17 **8.** "Blame It on the Boogie"
9. Brother Beyond **10.** Boyz II Men
11. JC Chasez and Justin Timberlake
12. Jackson 5 **13.** False **14.** Boyz II
Men **15.** Bros **16.** *Hunting High and
Low* **17.** New Edition **18.** New Kids
on the Block **19.** Menudo **20.** True

QUIZ 207
1. "Gangnam Style"—Psy **2.** "Diamonds"
3. Carly Rae Jepsen **4.** Gabrielle Aplin
5. Bjork **6.** In an indie record **7.** *Better.
Luck. Next. Life.* **8.** *Skyfall* **9.** Hans
Werner Henze **10.** Emeli Sandé
11. "Love" **12.** "Little Things"—One
Direction **13.** Glastonbury **14.** Flo Rida
15. Gotye **16.** King Kong **17.** Bandstand
Marathon **18.** Madonna **19.** Dr. Dre
20. Brian May

QUIZ 208
1. Sub Pop **2.** Mark Arm **3.** Seattle
4. A flannel shirt **5.** The Pixies
6. False **7.** Babes in Toyland **8.** Mark
Lanegan **9.** Alice in Chains **10.** *Nevermind*
11. Soundgarden **12.** Temple of the Dog
13. Hole **14.** *Singles* **15.** Soundgarden
16. John Bigley **17.** True **18.** More
than 75 million **19.** Matt Cameron
20. Dave Grohl

QUIZ 209
1. *Abbey Road* **2.** Ginger Spice
3. *Graduation* **4.** Dizzee Rascal
5. "… just fantasy?" **6.** buying
7. "Yesterday" by the Beatles **8.** Jimi
Hendrix **9.** Bob Dylan **10.** "… could
write a bad romance" **11.** Coldplay
12. Ray Charles **13.** Marvin Gaye
14. False **15.** *Clair de Lune*
16. Mozart **17.** New York, New York
18. Louis Armstrong **19.** *Oliver!*
20. *Evita*

QUIZ 210
1. Mid-1970s **2.** Committed to a mental
institution **3.** An eagle **4.** True **5.** *Sniffin'
Glue* **6.** Patti Smith **7.** The 101'ers
8. Generation X **9.** True **10.** David
Johansen **11.** Winterland, San Francisco
12. Sid Vicious **13.** The Damned
14. False **15.** Jamie Reid **16.** 1976
17. Green Day **18.** Joan Jett **19.** Siouxsie
Sioux **20.** Johnny Thunders **21.** The
Damned **22.** *Give Me Convenience or Give
Me Death* **23.** *Give 'Em Enough Rope*
24. *Pet Sematary* **25.** Public Image Ltd.

QUIZ 211
1. Australia **2.** False **3.** The wind
4. True **5.** Sitar **6.** Cymbalom **7.** Kazoo
8. 1919 **9.** "Good Vibrations" **10.** The Great
Stalacpipe Organ **11.** Marimba **12.** Gravikord
13. Glass armonica **14.** Fiddle **15.** Bazantar
16. 1997 **17.** Myanmar **18.** True **19.** True
20. All of them

QUIZ 212
1. Whammy **2.** Jimi Hendrix **3.** False.
The second string is the B string **4.** 5 notes
5. Green Day **6.** True. All of B. B. King's
guitars were named "Lucille" **7.** The
guitarist fits a metal or glass tube, or
"slide," on one of the fingers. The slide is
moved across the strings as they are plucked
8. Luthiers **9.** Gibson **10.** True **11.** Chuck
Berry **12.** A capo placed across the
fretboard changes the key of a song so that it
can be played at a higher pitch **13.** Ribs
14. The Jam **15.** Broken chord **16.** False

17. The "Broadcaster" **18.** Six
19. True **20.** True **21.** Fender
Stratocaster **22.** EADGBE **23.** Pickups
24. Les Paul **25.** Bill Wyman formerly
with the Rolling Stones

QUIZ 213
1. *Turandot* **2.** Proserpina **3.** Dvořák
4. Opera buffa **5.** Johann Strauss **6.** *Frau
Luna* **7.** Henry Purcell **8.** *The Marriage of
Figaro* **9.** True **10.** *Orfeo ed Euridice*
11. Pinkerton **12.** South Carolina **13.** *Tale
of Tsar Saltan* **14.** Philip Glass **15.** Maria
Callas **16.** Coffee—it's also known as the
Coffee Cantata **17.** Luigi Marchesi
18. Dame Nellie Melba **19.** 1973 **20.** False

QUIZ 214
1. Pete Best **2.** John Lennon **3.** He lay on
his back in the studio **4.** Rory Storm and
the Hurricanes **5.** It's a thousand pages,
give or take a few **6.** "Love Me Do" **7.** Brian
Epstein **8.** John Lennon **9.** False **10.** "I
Saw Her Standing There" **11.** "Bad Finger
Boogie" **12.** *Please Please Me* **13.** Julian
Lennon **14.** False **15.** George Harrison
16. True **17.** Paul McCartney **18.** "Free
as a Bird" **19.** True **20.** *Let It Be*
21. *Sgt. Pepper's Lonely Hearts Club
Band* **22.** "Norwegian Wood" **23.** Ono,
to show his "oneness" after marrying
Yoko Ono in 1969 **24.** "Yesterday"
25. Stuart Sutcliffe

QUIZ 215
1. A brilliant politician and one of
the Founding Fathers of the United States
2. *West Side Story* **3.** Anna Leonowens,
who was governess to the children of the
king of Siam in the 1860s **4.** *Spamalot*
5. Gene Kelly **6.** False **7.** *The Blues
Brothers* **8.** Bollywood **9.** New York
10. *Oliver!* **11.** Richard O'Brien
12. P. T. Barnum **13.** Berlin **14.** Fanny
Brice **15.** *Annie Get Your Gun*
16. *The Comedy of Errors* **17.** Lee
Marvin **18.** False **19.** *Carousel*
20. *Made in Dagenham* **21.** Willy
Russell **22.** *Fiddler on the Roof*

23. *Starlight Express* **24.** Michael
Crawford **25.** *Priscilla, Queen of
the Desert*

QUIZ 216
1. The Beach Boys **2.** Tony Iommi
3. No.4 **4.** Aerosmith **5.** Australia
6. Sammy Hagar **7.** "Slaughter" **8.** Kiss
9. Eric Clapton **10.** Cream **11.** The Rolling
Stones **12.** David Gilmour **13.** False
14. Derek and the Dominoes **15.** Whitesnake
16. *Tommy* **17.** Donington Park **18.** Led
Zeppelin **19.** "Whisky in the Jar"
20. Vincent Damon Furnier

QUIZ 217
1. "I Want to Hold Your Hand" by
the Beatles **2.** Itchycoo Park **3.** Donovan
4. Drums **5.** The Experience **6.** The
Rolling Stones **7.** Joni Mitchell **8.** True
9. The Animals **10.** Freddie **11.** True
12. False **13.** Steppenwolf **14.** 1968
15. The Grateful Dead **16.** Lou Reed
17. Procol Harum **18.** The Monkees
19. Buffalo Springfield **20.** John
Entwistle **21.** Ken Dodd with "Tears"
22. The Dakotas **23.** "Apache"
24. MacArthur Park **25.** Cliff
Bennett and the Rebel Rousers

QUIZ 218
1. Romantic (*c.*1830–1900)
2. Sir Malcolm Sargent **3.** He was
inspired when his cat walked across the
keyboard **4.** Carthage **5.** At a walking
pace **6.** True **7.** 47 **8.** Violin **9.** 60 years
of age **10.** Venice **11.** Teacups on a
string **12.** A chicken **13.** Mozart
14. Mendelssohn **15.** Fugues
16. The volume can be controlled
17. Viennese waltz **18.** Tchaikovsky
19. Mozart **20.** India **21.** The audience
rioted because of the unconventional
music **22.** He sent hair from his dog
to fans instead of his own **23.** Singing
without musical accompaniment
24. A new piece of music based on
the original theme of the piece
25. Sir Henry Wood

QUIZ 219

1. True **2.** Duke Ellington **3.** "(Everything I Do) I Do It for You" **4.** Jason **5.** "Red, Red Wine" **6.** Frank Sinatra **7.** Rihanna **8.** Men at Work **9.** Michael Jackson **10.** True **11.** ABBA **12.** The Spice Girls **13.** The Police **14.** "Always" **15.** Journey **16.** True **17.** A. R. Rahman **18.** "She Loves You" **19.** It has no name **20.** Madonna

QUIZ 220

1. "Mull of Kintyre" by Wings **2.** Lulu **3.** Johnny Rotten **4.** Hot Chocolate **5.** *Saturday Night Fever* **6.** Paul Rodgers **7.** *Legal* **8.** KISS **9.** True **10.** Benjamin Orr **11.** The Who **12.** "Immigrant Song" **13.** Three weeks **14.** Blondie **15.** The New York Dolls **16.** Bootsy Collins **17.** True **18.** True **19.** AC/DC **20.** 1979

QUIZ 221

1. 1984 **2.** 1991 **3.** 1963 **4.** 1977 **5.** 1982 **6.** 1987 **7.** 1965 **8.** 1968 **9.** 1977 **10.** 1978 **11.** False **12.** 1959 **13.** 1975 **14.** 1983 **15.** 1976 **16.** 1981 **17.** 2015 **18.** 1967 **19.** 1953 **20.** 2011

QUIZ 222

1. The bridge **2.** Japan **3.** Colombia **4.** Broadcaster **5.** John Williams **6.** Bo Diddley **7.** Gibson EDS-1275 **8.** Andrés Segovia **9.** '59 Les Paul Sunburst **10.** Soul Power **11.** Eric Clapton **12.** Metal **13.** Seven **14.** Blues **15.** Andy Summers **16.** False **17.** Carter picking **18.** Saul Hudson **19.** 19 **20.** Reduce background noise

QUIZ 223

1. Four **2.** Around 100 **3.** The oboe **4.** The English horn **5.** The strings **6.** The concertmaster **7.** The woodwind section **8.** The violas **9.** Smaller **10.** The percussion section **11.** The principal trumpet **12.** False **13.** Egyptian **14.** Marin Alsop **15.** Keyboard—it looks similar to an upright piano **16.** The Hallé **17.** True **18.** Nine **19.** A heckelphone. It is similar to an oboe but is pitched an octave lower **20.** A viola

QUIZ 224

1. Alligator skin **2.** Jazz grip **3.** A Djembe **4.** Splash **5.** Bongos **6.** The drum kick pedal **7.** True **8.** Animal **9.** Gene Krupa **10.** True **11.** The cymbals **12.** False **13.** Louie Bellson **14.** Metallica **15.** False **16.** Yes, drum brushes, sometimes called brooms, are used for softer playing **17.** Keith Moon **18.** Ireland **19.** A ride cymbal **20.** China

QUIZ 225

1. Guns N' Roses **2.** Sub Pop **3.** R.E.M. **4.** Lenny Kravitz **5.** Public Enemy **6.** Björk **7.** Phish **8.** Primus **9.** Oasis and Blur **10.** Mel C (Melanie Chisholm) **11.** Dave Grohl **12.** Hansen **13.** *Check Your Head* **14.** Faith No More **15.** Hole **16.** Piano **17.** *Badmotorfinger* **18.** True **19.** Mark Lanegan **20.** Bob Rock **21.** "… Baby One More Time" **22.** Eddie Vedder **23.** Baz Luhrmann **24.** Torn **25.** The Verve

QUIZ 226

1. Scorpion **2.** True **3.** False **4.** Smelling and touching **5.** Ladybird **6.** Ant **7.** Shrimp **8.** Chewed-up wood **9.** Termite **10.** 40 **11.** Flies **12.** Spring **13.** Sucks blood **14.** Lepidoptera **15.** Drone **16.** 2 years **17.** By rubbing its wings together **18.** Elytra **19.** Singing **20.** Bees can only sting once

QUIZ 227

1. Tortoises **2.** Sea urchins **3.** A cow **4.** Howler monkey **5.** Skunk **6.** Dolphin **7.** Four legs **8.** To cool off **9.** True **10.** Marsupials **11.** Keeping cool **12.** Scruff of the neck **13.** About a week **14.** Bat **15.** True **16.** Tamarin monkey **17.** Japan **18.** 200 million years ago **19.** South America **20.** False **21.** It stops blood clotting **22.** About a week **23.** Old scales **24.** They're trying to cool off **25.** Snails or cone shells

QUIZ 228

1. They smash them on a stone **2.** Game birds **3.** Cygnet **4.** Undigested food **5.** Pigeon **6.** They are excellent mimics

7. Clutch **8.** On their feet **9.** Peregrine falcon **10.** The European robin **11.** Southern **12.** Raven **13.** Brood **14.** At the tip of its beak **15.** Australia **16.** They impale their prey on thorns **17.** They remove the stinger first **18.** Plunge diving from the air **19.** Mud **20.** In clifftop burrows

QUIZ 229

1. Sloth **2.** Octopus **3.** More than 400 **4.** All of them **5.** It eats plant-eating pests **6.** Its eyes **7.** Cry **8.** They pee on their legs **9.** 70 mph (112 kmph) **10.** One that is active at night **11.** 17¾ in (45 cm) **12.** True **13.** True **14.** False **15.** The blue whale **16.** A water boatman **17.** Roar **18.** False **19.** A semiaquatic egg-laying mammal **20.** The spitting cobra **21.** The skin **22.** The snow leopard **23.** The Komodo dragon **24.** The saltwater crocodile **25.** Chameleon

QUIZ 230

1. Cartilage **2.** To deter predators **3.** False **4.** About 200 **5.** Horse **6.** Leopards **7.** They cannot jump **8.** Cricket **9.** Geese **10.** Limb **11.** Cockroach **12.** Humpback whale barnacle **13.** Pigeon **14.** Two **15.** True **16.** Sea urchin **17.** Lack of food **18.** Kangaroo **19.** Cheetah **20.** Flower color

QUIZ 231

1. Poison hemlock **2.** They help the fronds float **3.** Fronds **4.** By the wind **5.** Photosynthesis **6.** Common poppy **7.** Leaves that drop in the autumn **8.** Chlorophyll **9.** The plants poison cattle **10.** To help them float **11.** Less than a second **12.** Tulips **13.** White or pale yellow **14.** Nettle stings **15.** Thatching **16.** The stem **17.** Water **18.** Bamboo **19.** A hip **20.** The fruit **21.** Aster **22.** True **23.** Nebuchadnezzar II **24.** Cucumbers **25.** Rosaceae

QUIZ 232

1. More than half **2.** True **3.** The Amazon Rain Forest **4.** Howler monkey **5.** Blue morpho butterfly **6.** 175 **7.** Jaguar **8.** True **9.** Leaf-cutter ant **10.** Civets **11.** Fly backward **12.** True **13.** True **14.** Uganda, Rwanda, and Democratic Republic of the Congo **15.** Sloth **16.** Once a week **17.** Costa Rica **18.** *The Jungle Book* **19.** Plants **20.** Less than 6%

QUIZ 233

1. Vinegar **2.** Taipan **3.** Saltwater crocodile **4.** Blue-ringed octopus **5.** Echidna **6.** True **7.** The stonefish **8.** The redback spider **9.** The great white shark **10.** Duck-billed platypus **11.** The funnel-web spider **12.** False **13.** The marbled scorpion **14.** False **15.** Dingo **16.** The cane toad **17.** False **18.** False (15 minutes) **19.** 45% **20.** True

QUIZ 234

1. 22 months **2.** Beetle **3.** 8,000 lb (3,600 kg) **4.** True **5.** Breaststroke **6.** Decorator crab **7.** 20 **8.** Through its mouth **9.** All of them **10.** Doze standing up **11.** By vomiting fish oil **12.** True **13.** Blue whale **14.** False **15.** To see whether it can fit through an opening **16.** Up to 300% **17.** True **18.** More than 3,000 **19.** Eucalyptus leaves **20.** True **21.** Tarsier **22.** It's a fish that leaves the water **23.** Inside their father's pouch **24.** It lives in total darkness **25.** Barnacles

QUIZ 235

1. On their legs **2.** 400 million years **3.** Abdomen, thorax, head **4.** Several days later **5.** True **6.** About 1.5 million **7.** False **8.** Black widow **9.** Metamorphosis **10.** False **11.** Chitin **12.** Open spaces **13.** 85% **14.** True **15.** 48,000 **16.** True **17.** 850 **18.** True **19.** Spider **20.** Entomology **21.** Moths and flies **22.** True **23.** True **24.** Shed their external skeleton **25.** Egg, larva, pupa, and adult

QUIZ 236

1. Mosquito **2.** Arizona bark scorpion **3.** Jellyfish **4.** True **5.** Hippopotamus **6.** Deathstalker scorpion

7. It has special glands that produce poison **8.** Sleeping sickness **9.** It spreads diseases such as rabies **10.** A piranha **11.** Bullet ant **12.** True **13.** True **14.** A stingray **15.** The golden poison frog **16.** 20 **17.** True **18.** False **19.** A pufferfish **20.** True

QUIZ 237

1. Gobi **2.** Tree **3.** Four **4.** Saltation **5.** Gold and precious stones **6.** True **7.** Fog **8.** Atlas **9.** Paraguay **10.** Orangutan **11.** Southwest US and northwest Mexico **12.** Okavango Delta **13.** Spain **14.** Buttress roots **15.** True **16.** Scrubland **17.** William the Conqueror **18.** Willow **19.** Charcoal **20.** Watching autumn leaves change

QUIZ 238

1. Dolphins **2.** Blue whale **3.** A long tooth **4.** It is very strong **5.** Too high-pitched to hear **6.** 200 mph (320 kmph) **7.** Bioluminescence **8.** A submarine **9.** A dragonfly **10.** An aerofoil **11.** Echo location **12.** Stuns its prey with a shock wave **13.** The spermaceti organ **14.** Its legs act like springs **15.** Electric eel **16.** A spider eating an old web **17.** Symbiosis **18.** Yeast **19.** Beaver **20.** Venus flytrap

QUIZ 239

1. A lemur **2.** A pack **3.** A pride **4.** A squirrel **5.** A warren **6.** About 5 minutes **7.** As a parachute **8.** Curls into a ball **9.** Fat **10.** Help break down food **11.** In trees **12.** Incisors **13.** Jaguar **14.** Orangutan **15.** Stripes **16.** The Americas **17.** Marsupials **18.** The intestine **19.** The pygmy chimpanzee **20.** True

QUIZ 240

1. Fangtooth **2.** Vampire squid **3.** True **4.** Spookfish **5.** Anglerfish **6.** True **7.** Gulper eel **8.** They are being over-fished **9.** To see what is happening above it **10.** Up to 1,300 ft (400 m) **11.** Black dragonfish **12.** True

13. Lanternfish **14.** True **15.** 100 times **16.** False **17.** It takes cookie-shaped bites out of animals **18.** True **19.** Through smell and changes in water pressure **20.** Organic matter sinking from higher levels **21.** It switches from female to male **22.** All-around vision **23.** To deter an attacker **24.** True **25.** The temperature of the water

QUIZ 241

1. Clean air **2.** Chile **3.** In capsules underneath the fronds **4.** Fiddleheads **5.** A cactus **6.** Lack of sunshine **7.** Rafflesia **8.** In coastal waters **9.** By splashing raindrops **10.** Only female trees produce berries **11.** 1,000–2,000 years **12.** 40 in (100 cm) **13.** Yellow **14.** Sphagnum moss **15.** 400 million years ago **16.** South Africa **17.** Red tides **18.** White **19.** The Scots pine **20.** Over 4,500

QUIZ 242

1. China **2.** 200 years **3.** True **4.** False **5.** They have broken up **6.** False **7.** Light **8.** 51% **9.** 1997 **10.** False **11.** It reflects sunlight back to space **12.** Drilling into the ground to get oil or natural gas **13.** True **14.** About 15% **15.** CO_2 from the life cycle of a product **16.** Population increase **17.** 20% **18.** El Niño **19.** False **20.** IPCC **21.** False **22.** More rain and higher humidity **23.** 90% **24.** True **25.** True

QUIZ 243

1. By producing spores **2.** The white truffle **3.** Yellow **4.** Apricots **5.** Mildew **6.** Mycology **7.** Hyphae **8.** Yeast **9.** Flies **10.** Carbon dioxide **11.** Birch **12.** An alga **13.** The leafcutter ant **14.** True **15.** Athlete's foot **16.** Antibiotic **17.** Moldy bread **18.** Cottage cheese **19.** Chitin **20.** Fly agaric

QUIZ 244

1. Funnel web **2.** True **3.** True
4. Around 1,000,000 **5.** Wood frog
6. Mole **7.** Calves **8.** Bee hummingbird
9. 30 mph (50 kmph) **10.** Toucans
11. Mako **12.** Pretend to be dead
13. Dolphins and bats **14.** 18 in (46 cm)
15. Pufferfish **16.** To open pine cones
17. Seahorse **18.** Octopus **19.** Moth
20. They live only on whales **21.** Saliva
22. Woodlice **23.** Their shape makes
them roll in circles **24.** The emperor
penguin **25.** It can run on water

QUIZ 245

1. The size of a peanut **2.** The eagle
owl **3.** The sperm whale **4.** The lion's
mane jellyfish **5.** A colossal squid
6. The emperor **7.** The least weasel
8. The killer whale **9.** The Tasmanian
devil **10.** The male mandrill **11.** The
tiger **12.** More than 80 ft (25 m) **13.** The
little penguin **14.** Rabbit **15.** True **16.** Up
to 100 ft (30 m) **17.** Ten times its body
weight **18.** The manta ray **19.** The
goliath tarantula **20.** 850 times their
body weight **21.** Buzzard **22.** True
23. Spinosaurus **24.** Hummingbird
25. 98.50%

QUIZ 246

1. False **2.** True **3.** 36,100 ft (11,000 m)
4. 1,650 ft (500 m) **5.** White bellbird
6. 15 mph (24 kmph) **7.** True **8.** Wind
9. Skin flap on the neck **10.** Keratin
11. 150 million years **12.** Gray catbird
13. True **14.** Barn owl **15.** Imprinting
16. A swan **17.** Their diet of shrimp
18. New Zealand **19.** False **20.** Nectar
21. Seabird excrement **22.** Emperor
penguin **23.** Magpie **24.** Puffins
25. Pigeons

QUIZ 247

1. Putting their wings over them
2. Feet **3.** About 2,000 times
4. Chemoreceptors **5.** Movement
and pressure in the water **6.** Fennec
fox **7.** False **8.** True **9.** Sheep

10. Flat **11.** Mantis shrimp
12. Star-nosed mole **13.** Penguin
14. Soccer ball **15.** Elephant **16.** Heat
release from possible prey **17.** True
18. Spider **19.** Elephant **20.** "Taste"
the air **21.** 24 **22.** True **23.** Yes
24. Rabbit (17,000) **25.** Bat

QUIZ 248

1. About 35.5 in (90 cm) **2.** An internal
shell **3.** The white whale **4.** Herding
and stunning prey **5.** The oarfish **6.** So
adults don't attack them **7.** 5 days
8. About 200 years **9.** They feel it with
their whiskers **10.** Up to 9¾ ft (3 m)
11. The southern elephant seal **12.** True
13. The humpback whale **14.** About 100
million **15.** Up to 13 ft (4 m) **16.** False
17. Crustaceans **18.** A test **19.** A sponge
20. On its back

QUIZ 249

1. A clone **2.** True **3.** False **4.** Sperm
and eggs **5.** Spawning **6.** An axolotl
7. From their scent **8.** Its blue feet
9. Birds of paradise **10.** Spider
11. Bowerbird **12.** Metamorphosis
13. Froglets **14.** Fry **15.** Keeping them
in its mouth **16.** 7–8 years **17.** Lekking
18. Males look different from females
19. Die **20.** Monogamous

QUIZ 250

1. A brood parasite **2.** A wader **3.** One
4. With stink fights **5.** The Arctic tern
6. The bittern **7.** The common kestrel
8. About 3.3 ft (1 m) an hour **9.** A lizard
10. Wisent **11.** An insect **12.** Carnivorous
13. Pinkish red **14.** Salamanders
15. Several million **16.** The harvest
mouse **17.** Wide **18.** Up to 750 **19.** Six
to seven months **20.** Woodchucks
21. One day **22.** Koala **23.** Sharks
24. Tapeworm **25.** Outside
their body

QUIZ 251

1. Wedge **2.** Gang **3.** Toads **4.** Pack
5. Bears **6.** True **7.** Waddle **8.** Labour

9. Band **10.** Goldfinches
11. Buzz **12.** Flamingo **13.** False
14. Stripe **15.** Murmuration **16.** Cete
17. Mules **18.** Jellyfish **19.** Bears
20. True

QUIZ 252

1. Kiwi **2.** True **3.** Rookery **4.** True
5. It has the largest wingspan of any
bird **6.** Andean condor **7.** Spring
8. Only the male sings **9.** Ornithology
10. 10 billion **11.** Trumpeter swan
12. True **13.** Drake **14.** Bar-headed goose
15. Parliament **16.** True **17.** Bald eagle
18. Papua New Guinea **19.** Spider silk
20. False **21.** To grind food in the
stomach, for digestion **22.** False
23. Salt glands next to their nostrils
24. One **25.** Kori bustard

QUIZ 253

1. All of these **2.** True **3.** Seaweed
4. Hermit **5.** All of these **6.** True
7. Sea anemone **8.** True **9.** Brittle star
10. Jellyfish **11.** True **12.** Volcanic
13. True **14.** Limpet **15.** True
16. False **17.** True **18.** Low-tide zone
19. Polyps **20.** True **21.** Lagoon
22. True **23.** Longshore drift
24. Melting sea ice **25.** True

QUIZ 254

1. Africa **2.** The polar bear
3. 2009 **4.** The monarch butterfly
5. The bluefin tuna **6.** 147 **7.** True
8. Fewer than 7,000 **9.** The blue whale
10. Indonesia **11.** More than 3,000
12. True **13.** Three **14.** Asia
15. Malaysia **16.** The Arabian
Peninsula **17.** The red howler monkey
18. False **19.** 67 **20.** The
mountain gorilla

QUIZ 255

1. Anthers **2.** Nectar guides
3. True **4.** True **5.** Garlic
6. Aloe vera **7.** Africa **8.** All of
these **9.** True **10.** More than 2,000
11. Sundew plant **12.** Produces flowers

13. True blue **14.** True **15.** The
Americas **16.** True **17.** Grafting
18. Abscission **19.** Deciduous woodland
20. The flower bud

QUIZ 256

1. Haast's eagle **2.** Wild ox **3.** Dodo
4. Woolly rhinoceros **5.** Greece
6. Saber-toothed tiger **7.** True
8. Three times **9.** True **10.** Penguin
11. Africa **12.** Australia **13.** A giant
dragonfly **14.** The sea **15.** True
16. A list of threatened animal species
around the world **17.** Tasmanian
tiger **18.** Quagga **19.** The moa
20. Armadillo

QUIZ 257

1. Clydesdale **2.** Destrier
3. Arabian **4.** Appaloosa **5.** True
6. Przewalski's horse **7.** True
8. Carriages **9.** Spanish Riding
School **10.** Saddle Horse **11.** True
12. True **13.** Fjord horse **14.** True
15. Tennessee Walking Horse **16.** Suffolk
Punch **17.** False **18.** True **19.** Connemara
20. Shetland pony **21.** Camargue
22. 40 **23.** Filly **24.** An ungelded
male horse **25.** Walk, trot,
canter, gallop

QUIZ 258

1. Poison darts **2.** Flour **3.** True
4. The leaves **5.** Nightshade **6.** True
7. Socrates **8.** Foxglove **9.** False
10. English yew **11.** *Batman* **12.** True
13. True **14.** Wolfsbane **15.** Daffodil
16. False **17.** Ricin **18.** Oak **19.** True
20. Orchids

QUIZ 259

1. Alaska **2.** Ecdysis **3.** The Queen
Alexandra's birdwing **4.** Spider silk
5. Chrysalis **6.** Genetics **7.** Mulberry
leaves **8.** Potatoes **9.** Milkweed
10. Formic acid **11.** Beetles
12. It is a snorkel or breathing tube
13. The vibrations attract fish prey
14. Leaves **15.** Sponge **16.** Jointed feet

17. Butterflies and moths 18. Steel
19. Skippers 20. Queen bee

QUIZ 260

1. A leveret 2. Babakoto 3. A pig
4. A holt 5. A marsupial mammal
6. They spray them with sticky slime
7. Active at dawn and dusk 8. They
have a long snout 9. Coypu 10. Double-
jointed ankles 11. Ermine 12. Five
13. Gnaw 14. Grass 15. Honey badger
16. Horns are permanent 17. It takes
regular dust baths 18. Living under
snow 19. Under ½oz (11g) 20. Persian
21. 2 hours 22. About 88 gallons
(400 liters) 23. It aids grip and
makes a scent trail 24. Reindeer
25. An antibacterial sunscreen

QUIZ 261

1. A cod 2. A hyena 3. Herring
4. Rings in the ear bones 5. 7¹/₃ lb (3.3 kg)
6. Bumblebee 7. A cloud 8. A wallaby
9. A lizardlike reptile 10. A tropical
American weevil 11. By secreting
venom from skin pores 12. Halteres
13. Hopping or jumping 14. In water
15. Less than ⁴/₁₀₀ in (1 mm) long
16. None, they all eat meat 17. Radula
18. Spiders 19. The hawksbill turtle
20. The leatherback

QUIZ 262

1. 1880s 2. Finches 3. Flying reptiles
4. Pigeons 5. Alfred Russel Wallace
6. Octopus 7. 46 8. Mendel 9. A, C,
G, T 10. Mutation 11. Prehistoric marine
reptiles 12. Great apes 13. Cambrian
14. About 250,000 years ago 15. Convergent
evolution 16. Monitor 17. Mesozoic
18. 1859 19. Hollow bones
20. Gene pool

QUIZ 263

1. Hunter 2. 2,000 3. True
4. Band 5. 200,000 6. Hymenoptera
7. Naked mole rats 8. Queleas 9. Polyps
10. To attract ants toward a leaf
11. Infrasound 12. Waggle dance

13. Pod 14. Bubble netting
15. Bonobo chimpanzee 16. Electrical
signals 17. True 18. Pheromones
19. Weaver 20. Matriarchy 21. 50
22. True 23. 2–5 years 24. By eating
royal jelly 25. True

QUIZ 264

1. Barn owl 2. False 3. Sharp
poisonous spines 4. They pretend to
be injured 5. True 6. Rolls into a ball
7. Lion fish 8. The bullet ant 9. White
whales 10. Bury themselves in sediment
11. Pygmy seahorse 12. True 13. True
14. Blood 15. 13 ft (4 m) 16. Funnel-web
spider 17. Mutualism 18. Driver ants
19. Wiggles its pink tongue
20. Change color

QUIZ 265

1. A tom 2. About 20 mph (32 kmph)
3. Up to 80 years in captivity 4. Mauritius
5. A repetitive hoot 6. The tit family
7. A chatter 8. A casque 9. Up to 12 ft
(3.7 m) 10. A duck 11. Australia
12. Swans 13. The greylag goose
14. Aquatic invertebrates 15. Up to
43 mph (70 kmph) 16. On the wing
17. The hoatzin 18. The goldcrest
19. A murder 20. A watch 21. Lamellae
22. Smell 23. Siege 24. Fish
25. True

QUIZ 266

1. Nose and upper lip 2. Crocodile
3. Amphibians 4. True 5. Pollination
6. Sharks 7. Birds 8. Contain an
antifreeze 9. Aphids supply a sugary
solution 10. Some snakes 11. Its
water comes from the plants it eats
12. Giraffe 13. Making a loud sound
14. Buoyancy 15. Fingers and modified
wrist bones 16. Squirting a hot noxious
liquid 17. It stops predators from attacking
it 18. For warmth 19. Arctic fox
20. All-around vision 21. Intraspecifc
competition 22. Protection
23. Mutualism 24. Predation
and mutualism 25. True

QUIZ 267

1. About 30,000 **2.** About 400 **3.** 150 pecks a minute **4.** Between 20 and 40 million **5.** False **6.** About 1 million **7.** More than 10,000 **8.** 5,000 **9.** False **10.** More than 4,500 **11.** Ten times **12.** Two **13.** One **14.** Seven **15.** Fewer than 1,000 **16.** About 400 **17.** Up to 80 million **18.** About 200 million **19.** Up to 2,000 **20.** The orchid family

QUIZ 268

1. 22 months **2.** 1,900 miles (3,000 km) **3.** A badger **4.** A chinchilla **5.** A hinny **6.** A cria **7.** A military explorer **8.** True **9.** Raccoons **10.** Round **11.** About 1,200 **12.** The Sumatran **13.** South America **14.** Those that burrow **15.** Arctic fox **16.** False **17.** Constant snoring **18.** Cuba and Hispaniola **19.** Deer **20.** Earth-pig

QUIZ 269

1. Underground **2.** A long, thin finger **3.** A hover **4.** Ferrets **5.** In trees **6.** Javan **7.** Mohair **8.** Mr. and Mrs. **9.** North America **10.** One **11.** More than 330 ft (100 m) **12.** Patagium **13.** Pink **14.** *Plantigrade* **15.** Syria **16.** Alpaca **17.** Jersey cow **18.** The stomach contents **19.** Ox **20.** A camp **21.** Hibernation **22.** One **23.** Quadrupedal **24.** Red **25.** To control body temperature

QUIZ 270

1. Chapparal **2.** 230 ft (70 m) **3.** Anaconda **4.** Epiphytes **5.** Succulent leaves **6.** Climbing plants **7.** 50% **8.** 50 **9.** False **10.** 150 acres **11.** 40% **12.** Amazon **13.** Insects **14.** Transpiration **15.** Bromeliad **16.** Ten **17.** Plants **18.** Altitudes above 3,280 ft (1,000 m) **19.** 80 **20.** Cash cropping

QUIZ 271

1. Germany **2.** France **3.** Brazil **4.** Just Fontaine **5.** Bobby Moore **6.** 1930 **7.** Rungrado 1st of May Stadium in Pyongyang, North Korea **8.** Jules Rimet **9.** True **10.** United States **11.** Azteca **12.** Pelé **13.** Franz Beckenbauer **14.** Moscow **15.** Diana Ross, who was singing during the celebrations **16.** True **17.** Brazil **18.** Four times **19.** Twice **20.** It was held in Uruguay, and Uruguay beat Argentina 4–2 **21.** Japan **22.** Two—Brazil in 1994 and Italy in 2006 **23.** True **24.** Germany **25.** Scotland

QUIZ 272

1. World Wrestling Entertainment **2.** 1985 **3.** Mike Tyson **4.** True **5.** Stacks **6.** "The Hitman" **7.** Mickey Rourke **8.** Finn Bálor **9.** Sumo **10.** Kendo Nagasaki **11.** Roman **12.** Dwayne Johnson **13.** "Can you smell what the Rock is cooking?" **14.** 2005 **15.** Muhammad Ali **16.** Russia/Soviet Union **17.** Super heavy **18.** John Cena **19.** Adam Rose **20.** True

QUIZ 273

1. True **2.** Athletics **3.** Jamaica **4.** Sergei Bubka from Ukraine **5.** Steeplechase **6.** Seven events **7.** Roger Bannister **8.** Baton **9.** Triple jump **10.** False **11.** The marathon **12.** Long jump **13.** Ten hurdles **14.** Sand **15.** Heptathlon **16.** 9.58 seconds **17.** Ten events **18.** Athens, 2004 **19.** 1960 **20.** Every 2 years

QUIZ 274

1. New York Yankees **2.** Fastball **3.** Boston Red Sox **4.** Billy Beane **5.** False **6.** The Teammates **7.** Kevin Costner **8.** Joe DiMaggio **9.** True **10.** Alex Rodriguez **11.** Wally the Green Monster **12.** Atlanta Braves **13.** Japan **14.** Cuba **15.** Cal Ripken Jr. **16.** Slider **17.** Two **18.** Pete Rose **19.** 2001 **20.** George Plimpton

QUIZ 275

1. Five **2.** The main stadium in Beijing for the 2008 Games

3. Jesse Owens **4.** 204 **5.** Sir Steve Redgrave **6.** Sydney **7.** They are used by short-race athletes to push off when starting and are linked to the timing system **8.** Faster, higher, stronger **9.** Olive wreaths **10.** Boycotts **11.** False **12.** Zola Budd **13.** A flaming arrow **14.** Paris, 1900 **15.** Brazil **16.** 1,500 m **17.** The main continents of the world **18.** Three times **19.** Muhammad Ali **20.** 1896

QUIZ 276

1. 18 **2.** Tiger **3.** St. Andrews, Scotland **4.** Europe **5.** True **6.** A green **7.** Sand wedge **8.** Rory McIlroy **9.** Coast **10.** By teeing off **11.** Germany **12.** Birdie **13.** Gary Woodland **14.** Jack Nicklaus **15.** Green **16.** 15th century **17.** A hole **18.** True **19.** On a driving range **20.** Caddy

QUIZ 277

1. True **2.** Sydney 2000 **3.** True **4.** Five **5.** False **6.** Nadia Comaneci **7.** 1896 **8.** Still rings **9.** Max Whitlock **10.** Rhythmic gymnastics **11.** 0.5 **12.** Japan **13.** True—Max Whitlock won gold and Louis Smith took silver **14.** American Simone Biles **15.** True **16.** On their feet **17.** 1984 **18.** Barani **19.** True **20.** Olga Korbut

QUIZ 278

1. 3 out of 5 **2.** Five **3.** Roger Federer **4.** The Rod Laver Arena **5.** Virginia Wade **6.** The umpire **7.** Hawk-Eye **8.** The Australian Open **9.** Fred Perry in 1936 **10.** Fault **11.** Venus **12.** Novak Djokovic **13.** 18 **14.** Wimbledon **15.** Clay **16.** The service line **17.** Love **18.** Felt **19.** Wood **20.** Deuce **21.** Rafael Nadal **22.** A serve that is not touched by an opponent **23.** Game, set, and match **24.** Billie Jean King **25.** A volley

QUIZ 279

1. Strips of soft leather **2.** Strips of hard leather with spikes **3.** 1904 **4.** A pugilist **5.** True **6.** James Figg **7.** The bout

between Mike Tyson and Evander Holyfield in 1987. Tyson bit off part of Holyfield's ear. Tyson was disqualified and lost his boxing license **8.** The Queensberry Rules **9.** None **10.** 45 years old **11.** Theodore Roosevelt **12.** Featherweight **13.** Idi Amin **14.** Joe Louis **15.** Floyd Patterson **16.** Muhammad Ali and Joe Frazier **17.** Mike Tyson and Evander Holyfield **18.** Sugar Ray Robinson **19.** Joe Calzaghe **20.** Sugar Ray Robinson

QUIZ 280

1. Australia **2.** Finland **3.** Pancakes **4.** True **5.** Wales **6.** Cell phones **7.** 1973 **8.** Norway **9.** Beer cans **10.** True **11.** Scotland **12.** The World Conker Championships **13.** Cheese **14.** La Tomatina **15.** True **16.** False **17.** Derbyshire **18.** 20 paddlers, 1 drummer, and 1 steerer **19.** Their wives **20.** Twice

QUIZ 281

1. 1896 **2.** Japan **3.** False **4.** 1930s **5.** True **6.** Four **7.** The dolphin kick **8.** Australian champion Ian Thorpe **9.** Adam Peaty **10.** True **11.** The US **12.** Breaststroke **13.** True **14.** Backstroke **15.** Running and cycling **16.** 1976 **17.** True **18.** Butterfly **19.** False **20.** Flippers **21.** 2008 **22.** Breaststroke **23.** Celebrating team members jumped into the water before all the other competitors had finished **24.** False. They can only do this in front crawl or backstroke **25.** Michael Phelps, with 28 medals

QUIZ 282

1. At the Winter Olympics in Innsbruck **2.** Alberto Tomba **3.** Old Norse **4.** 93 mph (150 kmph) **5.** Five **6.** False **7.** Sapporo **8.** Piste **9.** Germany **10.** True **11.** Streif, Hahnenkamm **12.** St. Moritz **13.** Canada **14.** Croatian **15.** "Ski Sunday" **16.** Three **17.** True **18.** False **19.** Black

20. Eddie the Eagle **21.** A ski with a raised tail so the skier can take off and land backward **22.** Downhill **23.** Lake Placid **24.** True **25.** Both

QUIZ 283

1. True **2.** 1936 **3.** He stands with both thumbs pointing upward and with arms extended **4.** 23 **5.** Kareem Abdul-Jabbar **6.** Boston Celtics **7.** Newcastle Eagles **8.** Wilt Chamberlain **9.** United States **10.** LeBron James **11.** 2014 **12.** Tyrone Bogues, 5 ft 3 in (1.60 m) **13.** False—it's smaller **14.** Kareem Abdul-Jabbar **15.** False. They are both the same height **16.** L.A. Lakers **17.** James Naismith **18.** Chicago Bulls **19.** Five titles **20.** Karl Malone **21.** Ten players: five on each side **22.** Air ball **23.** Manchester **24.** The jump shot **25.** When they are fouled while shooting

QUIZ 284

1. 50 years of age **2.** Spurs **3.** Nat Lofthouse **4.** Plumbing **5.** Ardwick **6.** Billy Wright **7.** Bobby Charlton **8.** Center forward **9.** Nothing **10.** Prince **11.** 3–2–2–3 formation **12.** Coventry City **13.** £100 **14.** Fulham **15.** 21 years of age **16.** Gordon Banks **17.** Everton **18.** False **19.** True **20.** Both Manchester City and Manchester United **21.** George Best **22.** "The wizard of dribble" **23.** May 1959 **24.** Scotland **25.** John Charles

QUIZ 285

1. 2012 **2.** Virgil van Dijk **3.** Arsenal **4.** Paris Saint-German **5.** Pep Guardiola **6.** Liverpool F.C. **7.** Gareth Southgate **8.** True **9.** Goal-line technology **10.** Roman Abramovich **11.** Milan **12.** L.A. Galaxy **13.** Argentina **14.** Peter Shilton, 125 caps **15.** Manchester United **16.** False **17.** Gary Lineker **18.** Leicester City F.C. **19.** True **20.** 22 years, 1996–2018

21. Lev Yashin **22.** Steven Gerrard **23.** Neil Lennon **24.** Manchester City **25.** Uruguay

QUIZ 286

1. Skeleton bobsled **2.** Half-pipe **3.** Austria **4.** The house **5.** Nordic Combined **6.** 1924 **7.** Sarajevo **8.** Alpine skiing **9.** St. Moritz, Switzerland **10.** Luge **11.** Slalom **12.** 1998 **13.** USSR **14.** False **15.** Franz Klammer **16.** Black **17.** Granite **18.** Eddie Edwards **19.** Tomato **20.** Ice hockey **21.** Biathlon **22.** The Netherlands **23.** Bobsled **24.** Lizzy Yarnold in the skeleton bobsled **25.** The St. Louis Blues

QUIZ 287

1. Flushing Meadows, New York **2.** Pete Sampras **3.** 70–68 **4.** Love **5.** Boris Becker and Stefan Edberg **6.** French Open **7.** Two (2012 and 2016) **8.** Davis Cup **9.** Ivan Lendl **10.** Coco Gauff **11.** 331 weeks **12.** False—she comes from Australia **13.** Wimbledon **14.** Serious **15.** A drop shot **16.** The Fed Cup **17.** 1877 **18.** 3½ ft (1.07 m) **19.** Carbon graphite **20.** False **21.** Approximately 62,000 lb (28,000 kg) **22.** The pewter, silver, and gold salver presented to the Wimbledon Ladies Singles Champion **23.** 1896 **24.** Seven points **25.** Bob and Mike Bryan

QUIZ 288

1. 1984 **2.** Canoe slalom **3.** Tom Daley **4.** Putney **5.** In 1984, at the Los Angeles Games **6.** Ironman **7.** Matthew Pinsent **8.** Windsurfing board **9.** Hungary and USSR **10.** Greg Louganis **11.** True **12.** Freestyle **13.** True **14.** Fort Copacabana in Rio de Janeiro **15.** True **16.** 2000 **17.** 7 players **18.** Lake Pepin, Minnesota **19.** Slalom and sprint **20.** True

QUIZ 289

1. Sudan **2.** The Harlem Globetrotters **3.** Three seconds **4.** FIBA—the

International Basketball Federation
5. Kareem Abdul-Jabbar **6.** Center
7. A backboard **8.** A wedding dress
9. True **10.** Orlando Magic **11.** 94 ft
(28.65 m) **12.** The six-foot semicircle used
for free throws **13.** 1989 **14.** True.
This was for the 1936 Olympics, but
the proposal was later withdrawn
15. Montreal 1976 **16.** Boston Celtics
17. 10 ft (3 m) **18.** 7 ft 6 in (2.29 m)
19. True **20.** In 1936, and the USA
won **21.** In 1976, and the USSR won
22. *Jump* **23.** Robert Parish (USA)
1,611 games **24.** 12 minutes
25. Seven substitutes

QUIZ 290

1. 164 ft (50 m) **2.** Rome 1960
3. Starting blocks **4.** 6 ft 6 in (2 m)
5. Freestyle and backstroke events
6. False—goggles were first allowed
at the Olympics in 1976 **7.** Alzain
Tareq from Bahrain **8.** 800 m freestyle
9. *Natation*, the French word for
swimming **10.** True **11.** True
12. She swam the English Channel
four times **13.** Swimsuits made of
polyurethane and elastane-nylon
14. 73 days **15.** Chad Le Clos from
South Africa **16.** Mark Spitz
17. Michael Phelps **18.** Butterfly
19. Three **20.** Three

QUIZ 291

1. The Webb Ellis Cup
2. Blanco **3.** Daddy Cool **4.** 1973
5. A gumshield, also known as a
mouthguard, fits over the teeth and
gums **6.** Five **7.** Tommy Makinson
of St. Helens **8.** False **9.** 1895
10. Eddie Waring **11.** Harlequins
12. Scotland and England **13.** Wigan
14. Chariots **15.** St. Helens beat the
Salford Red Devils **16.** Doctor
17. Cardiff Arms Park **18.** Brian
Moore **19.** 1995 **20.** Castleford
Tigers **21.** Italy **22.** False
23. Danny McGuire **24.** 1897
25. Doug Howlett

QUIZ 292

1. 1976 and 1984 **2.** 1⅞ miles (3 km)
3. 1936 **4.** Steffi Graf **5.** 1932 **6.** 9.79
seconds **7.** Emil Zátopek **8.** Weightlifting
9. Duncan Goodhew **10.** Eric the Eel
11. True **12.** The Dream Team **13.** Olga
Korbut **14.** White City **15.** Cuba
16. 1916 **17.** 33 ft (10 m) **18.** 1960
19. Ten **20.** True

QUIZ 293

1. Five times **2.** The Nürburgring, Germany
3. Silverstone **4.** 23 years of age
5. Phil Hill and Mario Andretti **6.** Wet
7. It had six wheels **8.** A prancing horse
9. Tifosi **10.** 41 races **11.** 1929 **12.** British
American Racing **13.** Monza **14.** Danger
on or near the track **15.** Singapore
16. Benetton **17.** Turbocharged engines
18. Tubular framed **19.** 3.2 seconds
(Benetton) **20.** True—the Loews Hairpin
21. More than 200 mph (322 kmph)
22. 25 **23.** Seven times **24.** Airfoils
25. 18 teams

QUIZ 294

1. Lotus **2.** The Giro d'Italia
3. Six gold medals **4.** 1903 **5.** The Milk
Race **6.** Mont Ventoux **7.** Eddy Merckx
8. 12 gold medals **9.** The Tour de France
10. Four gold medals **11.** Bicycle
motocross **12.** Cycle speedway and Track
13. Red **14.** The main group or pack of
riders **15.** King of the Mountain **16.** A
century ride **17.** Mountain bike **18.** The
Rover safety bicycle **19.** Derailleur
20. A steep climb or descent

QUIZ 295

1. Glasgow Celtic **2.** Libertadores
3. Togo **4.** Paolo Rossi **5.** Door-bolt
6. Gareth Barry, 653 **7.** Aberdeen
8. Benfica **9.** Hugo Lloris **10.** "Wonders"
11. Terry Venables **12.** George Best
13. Republic of Ireland **14.** Haarlem
15. Frank Rijkaard **16.** Claudio Ranieri
17. 20 yd (18 m) **18.** AC Milan
and Inter Milan **19.** Preston
20. West Ham United

QUIZ 296

1. Nine **2.** 1967 **3.** Green Bay
Packers **4.** False **5.** Ice hockey
6. Albert Pujols **7.** False **8.** Tiger
Woods **9.** Bianca Andreescu from
Canada **10.** 1984 **11.** Jesse Owens
12. False **13.** Washington, D.C.
14. 2008 **15.** Pete Sampras **16.** False
17. 3 games **18.** St. Louis **19.** Cricket
20. The Dallas Cowboys **21.** Rio de
Janeiro, Brazil **22.** The Kansas City
Chiefs **23.** Nancy Kerrigan and
Tonya Harding **24.** Houston
25. Basketball

QUIZ 297

1. Tae kwon do **2.** London 2012
3. Cal Ripken Jr., for the Baltimore
Orioles **4.** False **5.** Rowing **6.** 17.8 seconds
7. 3 minutes 43 seconds **8.** Braun
Strowman **9.** 85 ft (26 m) **10.** Pittsburgh
Steelers **11.** Kimi Räikkönen from
Finland (2007) **12.** Eight **13.** Drew
Brees **14.** False **15.** 400,000 people
16. 630 lbs (287 kg) **17.** Rowing
18. False **19.** Fencing
20. 6¾ miles (11 km)

QUIZ 298

1. Wipeout **2.** "Ten" **3.** *Wednesday*
4. A pretender **5.** The Gold Coast
6. Captain Cook **7.** Kelly Slater
8. Honolulu, Hawaii **9.** Newquay
10. True **11.** Australia **12.** The Beach
Boys **13.** Patrick Swayze **14.** False
15. South Africa **16.** Banzai
17. False **18.** Oahu **19.** Wax
20. A tube

QUIZ 299

1. Greg Louganis **2.** Platform and
springboard **3.** 2000 **4.** Shallow
water **5.** True **6.** 1924 **7.** True
8. True **9.** True **10.** The belly
flop **11.** Mexico **12.** Ilya Zakharov
13. 1904 **14.** Fancy diving
15. USA **16.** True **17.** A rip
entry **18.** Vertical **19.** Four
20. A reverse dive

QUIZ 300

1. Mexico **2.** Five **3.** Michael Strahan
4. Warren Moon **5.** Drew Brees **6.** 1920
7. Shoes **8.** True **9.** Peyton Manning
10. *The Blindside* **11.** True **12.** Chicago
Bears **13.** Seven **14.** Pittsburgh Steelers
15. Miami **16.** Bill Belichick **17.** About
11 in (28 cm) **18.** Terry Bradshaw
19. Tom Brady **20.** Baltimore Colts

QUIZ 301

1. Victory **2.** Once **3.** One **4.** 42 years
old **5.** Brazil **6.** False **7.** Brazil
8. South Africa **9.** Germany
10. France and Mexico **11.** 10–1
12. Twice **13.** 2006 **14.** Eusebio
15. False **16.** 1930 **17.** Never
18. Uruguay **19.** Russia
20. 13

QUIZ 302

1. France **2.** Hook **3.** 80 ft (23 m)
4. True **5.** Ryan Villopoto
6. "Mad Dog" **7.** New Zealand
8. Oxford **9.** False **10.** 155 mph
(250 kmph) **11.** Buildings **12.** 12
13. Mountain bike **14.** Alison Hargreaves
in 1988 **15.** Thermals **16.** Wipe out
17. 19 minutes 21 seconds **18.** Dawn
patrol **19.** False **20.** To stay airborne
for as long as possible **21.** Zorbing
22. Slacklining **23.** True
24. The wind **25.** Summer and
winter each year

QUIZ 303

1. Barcelona **2.** Javier Sotomayor
3. Dubai World Cup **4.** 448 yds
5. True **6.** Neil Jenkins **7.** 27
8. True **9.** Pittsburgh Steelers
10. USA **11.** 23 **12.** Rod Laver
13. Thrust SSC **14.** False
15. 100 **16.** Ferrari **17.** 207 mph
(333 kmph) **18.** 2004 **19.** True
20. 192 ft 10 in (58.8 m)

QUIZ 304

1. True **2.** Tacking **3.** A catamaran
4. 1969 **5.** The Jules Verne Trophy

6. Ten events **7.** 608 **8.** *Gypsy Moth IV*
9. Four gold medals **10.** Keelboat
11. The fastest solo nonstop
circumnavigation of the world
12. *Morning Cloud* **13.** 1896
14. A line (rope) used for raising
or lowering sails **15.** 49 days
16. Australia **17.** A rudder steers
the boat **18.** 1851 **19.** Tony Bullimore
20. Line (rope) for controlling and
adjusting the sails **21.** Spinnaker
22. A tiller is a straight piece of
wood or metal that fits into the
rudder and is used to steer the boat
23. The hull **24.** A schooner
25. False

QUIZ 305

1. Lewis Hamilton **2.** False
3. 800 cc **4.** ¼ miles (400 m)
5. 1923 **6.** 71 **7.** 1976 **8.** Jackie
Stewart **9.** 1995 **10.** Five **11.** Stock
12. Indianapolis 500 **13.** Seven
14. Graham Hill **15.** Yamaha
16. Michael Delaney **17.** Jackie
Stewart **18.** All-Terrain Vehicle
19. Isle of Man **20.** True **21.** Six times
22. 50 cars **23.** Blue **24.** 1948
25. Green

QUIZ 306

1. A wide **2.** West Indies **3.** Australia
4. Brian Lara of Australia **5.** Bails
6. Marylebone Cricket Club **7.** 2013
8. "Supercat" **9.** The Gabba **10.** True
11. Gary Sobers **12.** Dennis Lillee
13. England **14.** W. G. Grace
15. False—it was Andrew Strauss
16. Alastair Cook **17.** The New Zealand
Cricket Team **18.** India **19.** Lord's
Cricket Ground **20.** The Ashes

QUIZ 307

1. Simon Sherwood **2.** Aldaniti and
Bob Champion **3.** One mile, four furlongs,
and six yds (2,420 m) **4.** Nine times
5. False **6.** Longchamp **7.** "The Shoe"
8. Handicap **9.** Three **10.** Bob
Champion **11.** 1932 **12.** Tiger Roll

13. George Stubbs **14.** Siena
15. True **16.** Hong Kong **17.** Suffolk
18. 1977 **19.** Devon Loch
20. True **21.** Silks **22.** Ted
Walsh (trainer) and Ruby
Walsh (jockey) **23.** Sandringham
24. Ascot **25.** King Charles II

QUIZ 308

1. 21 years old **2.** Oakmont,
Pennsylvania **3.** 2017 (US Open)
4. 336 **5.** Hinako Shibuno **6.** True
7. Nine **8.** Sam Snead **9.** The Masters
10. Four **11.** 49 **12.** Amen Corner
13. South Korean **14.** Craig Stadler
15. Nick Faldo **16.** True
17. 210–240 yd **18.** Walter Hagen
19. Jack Nicklaus **20.** 1979
21. Ben Crenshaw **22.** St. Andrews
(29 times) **23.** 14 **24.** 1811, in
Musselburgh, Scotland
25. True

QUIZ 309

1. Kinetic **2.** Jack Brabham
3. 25 points **4.** Watkins Glen
5. 1992 **6.** True **7.** Alfa Romeo
8. Fernando Alonso **9.** 2,800 times
10. Nine **11.** Diamonds **12.** 51
13. Mercedes-Benz **14.** True
15. Hesketh **16.** Lotus-Ford
17. Four drivers **18.** True
19. Canada **20.** Position

QUIZ 310

1. Bournemouth **2.** Adenor Leonardo
Bacchi (commonly known as Tite)
3. The Battle of Spion Kop, 1900
4. 1863 **5.** Partizan Belgrade
6. False **7.** Everton—Nothing but
the best is enough **8.** Billy Wright
9. D.C. United, Washington
10. 12 yd (11 m) **11.** A jar of
mayonnaise **12.** True **13.** Gerd
Muller **14.** Copa del Generalisimo
15. Luzhniki Stadium, Moscow,
Russia **16.** Gustav Sebes
17. Luigi Riva **18.** Fiorentina
19. 1956 **20.** King Edward II

QUIZ 311

1. Trevor Berbick **2.** Bob Fitzsimmons
3. National Sporting Club **4.** Tunney
Hunsacker **5.** Barry McGuigan **6.** Roberto
Duran **7.** Tunisia **8.** Five times **9.** Walker
Smith Jr. **10.** Frank Warren **11.** Kronk
12. Southpaws **13.** Both ears **14.** True
15. He is considered one of the greatest
knockout boxers of all time **16.** True
17. 32 years old **18.** 10 oz **19.** False
20. Technical knockout

QUIZ 312

1. Oatmeal and honey **2.** Brigid Kosgei
of Kenya **3.** 1896 **4.** 645 **5.** Elaine
Thompson **6.** More than 40,000 **7.** True
8. Kahit Isang Araw Lang (Even Just for
a Day) Unity Run **9.** The knee **10.** The
London Olympics in 1908 **11.** Roger
Bannister **12.** Eliud Kipchoge of Kenya
13. Pheidippides (490 BCE, Greece)
14. Time divided by distance
15. The number of steps a runner takes
each minute **16.** Nepal **17.** 346 calories
18. In running, both feet leave the
ground regularly **19.** Bill Clinton
20. Microscopic tears in muscle fibers

QUIZ 313

1. "The Diamonds" **2.** Richmond F.C.
3. Vow and Declare **4.** True **5.** Boxing
Day **6.** Tim Paine **7.** Novak Djokovic
8. Port Adelaide and the Brisbane Lions
9. Three field umpires **10.** Queensland
11. Twice **12.** Mount Panorama, NSW
13. Melbourne **14.** Adelaide, South
Australia **15.** 120 m **16.** The Brownlow
Medal **17.** Ten teams **18.** 99.94
19. Brisbane Heat **20.** Ashleigh Barty

QUIZ 314

1. Skittles **2.** Cricket **3.** Hurling
4. The 15th century **5.** A mass
tournament of mounted fighters **6.** True
7. A joust for pleasure **8.** In the butts
9. False **10.** The 17th century
11. A quarterstaff **12.** Royalty and
nobles **13.** English men between
15 and 60 **14.** France **15.** True

16. 12 arrows **17.** A joust to the death
18. True **19.** Two **20.** Stakes

QUIZ 315

1. 1912 **2.** 4 riders **3.** 4500 BCE
4. Thoroughbred **5.** Arab breeds
6. 1900 **7.** Puissance **8.** True
9. Nick Skelton **10.** Aachen, Germany
11. Afghanistan **12.** True **13.** Victoria
Pendleton **14.** 1949 **15.** True. Australian
quarantine laws were so strict that
competitors' horses were banned
16. The Middle Ages **17.** Charlotte Brew
18. True **19.** No team finished the
course, and no medals were awarded
20. Commissioned officers in the
armed forces

QUIZ 316

1. Raw fish and rice **2.** A type of pasta
3. Vegetable **4.** Lentils **5.** Wheat, water,
eggs **6.** Upside-down French apple cake
7. USA **8.** Heston Blumenthal **9.** Roots of
the sassafras plant **10.** Tibet **11.** North
Indian **12.** Morocco **13.** Spanish omelette
14. Greece **15.** Holland **16.** The skin
17. In a sushi bar **18.** Dill **19.** In Scottish
chip shops **20.** Churros

QUIZ 317

1. Sussex pond **2.** A savory bun
3. Haggis **4.** False **5.** Leicestershire
6. Scones with butter and/or clotted cream
and strawberry jam **7.** Pig **8.** Wimbledon
9. Toad **10.** Minced beef **11.** False
12. Hash browns **13.** Elderflower **14.** True
15. Staffordshire **16.** Speckled bread
17. All of them **18.** Wensleydale
19. Batter **20.** May

QUIZ 318

1. German **2.** More than 4,000 years
3. 5th century **4.** Japan **5.** Fried
6. Thailand **7.** China **8.** Mung beans
9. Tadpole noodles **10.** Persian
11. Meat noodles **12.** Around 1900
13. Kalguksu **14.** True **15.** Rice
16. False **17.** 1958 **18.** The Han
Dynasty **19.** True **20.** Thailand

21. Complex **22.** A pudding **23.** Penne
24. Soba **25.** True

QUIZ 319

1. Salt **2.** Turophile **3.** Poland
4. Tooth decay **5.** Egypt **6.** Spain
7. Cyclops **8.** Around 700 **9.** France
10. Live insect larvae **11.** Switzerland
12. False **13.** Ben Gunn **14.** Greece
15. True **16.** Good sleep **17.** True
18. Mozzarella **19.** Green **20.** True
21. California **22.** Ewe **23.** It has a
red rind **24.** True **25.** False

QUIZ 320

1. Florida **2.** Maine and Massachusetts
3. Illinois **4.** Alaska **5.** 1960s **6.** New
England **7.** The South **8.** German and
Austrian immigrants **9.** Bouillabaisse
10. New Mexico **11.** Buffalo **12.** Seattle
13. Neither is native to the US
14. Louisiana **15.** Green chile stew
16. Massachusetts **17.** Pasadena
18. True **19.** 46 **20.** California

QUIZ 321

1. Lobster **2.** Gastropods **3.** Prawns
and shrimp **4.** Shucking **5.** Bernie Bay
shuckler **6.** True **7.** Clams **8.** France
9. Ceviche **10.** Tiger **11.** True
12. New Zealand **13.** Oysters
14. Maryland **15.** Chile **16.** False
17. On a bed of ice **18.** USA
19. Maine **20.** Mussels **21.** Liver
and pancreas **22.** True **23.** A main
course combining red meat and
seafood **24.** An edible hard clam
25. Cockleshells

QUIZ 322

1. The onion **2.** The banana
3. Honey **4.** Blueberries **5.** Fish
6. Green tea **7.** Broccoli **8.** The walnut
9. Dark chocolate **10.** Yogurt **11.** Garlic
12. The sweet potato **13.** The
pineapple **14.** False **15.** Rheumatism
and indigestion **16.** Fennel
17. The apple **18.** Cranberries
19. Celery **20.** True

QUIZ 323

1. Victoria **2.** True **3.** Lemon
4. Vegetables **5.** False **6.** Japan
7. Fruit and sugar **8.** Spain **9.** Piece
of muslin **10.** False **11.** Brewing
12. True **13.** Indefinitely **14.** Gravadlax
15. Fruit **16.** True **17.** Salt and water
18. Vinegar **19.** 221°F (105°C) **20.** True
21. Portuguese word *marmela* meaning
quince **22.** India **23.** Lactic acid
24. Cabbage **25.** Cucumber

QUIZ 324

1. Yeast **2.** Doughnut **3.** Bavaria
4. Christmas **5.** True **6.** Marcel Proust
7. Italy **8.** True **9.** Scotland **10.** Anna
Pavlova **11.** Pastry **12.** Mascarpone
13. Cream **14.** False **15.** Scone
16. Mexico **17.** India **18.** Sliced
bread **19.** True **20.** Blind baking

QUIZ 325

1. Cocoa **2.** Peru **3.** Bread **4.** Asia
5. South America **6.** Before midday
7. Alligator pear **8.** France **9.** The squash
10. Around 24 hours **11.** The fig
12. Lancashire **13.** True **14.** More
than 1,000 **15.** The Middle East
16. Italy **17.** Rarebit **18.** China
19. False **20.** The yam **21.** Central
America **22.** Sugar **23.** Chipolata
24. World War II **25.** Cyprus

QUIZ 326

1. Brussels sprouts **2.** Thanksgiving
3. Stollen **4.** Easter **5.** True **6.** Boxing
Day **7.** Turkey **8.** True **9.** Pancakes
10. Hot **11.** Hot cross buns **12.** Pecan pie
13. New Zealand **14.** Dundee cake
15. Japan **16.** Ale **17.** Sweden
18. A silver sixpence **19.** Cranberries
20. Orange **21.** Mustard and horseradish
22. False **23.** Gingerbread house
24. True **25.** Poultry

QUIZ 327

1. More than 7,500 **2.** Matthew Bramley
3. True **4.** Pear **5.** Britain **6.** China
7. True **8.** True **9.** New Zealand

10. Smith **11.** Australia **12.** King
Edward **13.** True **14.** True
15. 1809 **16.** Rose **17.** Cider
18. The southwest **19.** American
Mother **20.** Johnny Appleseed

QUIZ 328

1. Dried currants **2.** Profiteroles
3. Turnips **4.** Epiphany **5.** True
6. Breakfast **7.** Meringue **8.** Pick me
up **9.** Eton **10.** Rice pudding **11.** Burned
cream **12.** Thanksgiving **13.** A dumpling
14. Ballet dancing **15.** Scotland
16. Lemon **17.** True **18.** Manchester tart
19. Orange **20.** Bread

QUIZ 329

1. True **2.** French and Russian
3. It turns black **4.** Sage **5.** Spring
6. Chives **7.** False **8.** Hot and sunny
9. Rosemary **10.** Coriander **11.** A cough
12. True **13.** Courage **14.** Four to six weeks
15. Oregano **16.** Dill **17.** True **18.** French
19. Christianity **20.** Annuals **21.** Relax
and sleep **22.** Crystallized **23.** Oregano
24. Lamb **25.** Catnip

QUIZ 330

1. True **2.** Seitan **3.** Asia
4. A green dot in a square **5.** Any
products that come from animals
6. 1812 **7.** Health **8.** Between 50
and 400 **9.** True **10.** 5–10% **11.** Fruits,
nuts, and seeds **12.** India **13.** Ritual
sacrifice **14.** False **15.** Nori **16.** Some
animals are too cute to kill and eat
17. Allium **18.** Bean curd **19.** True
20. People for the Ethical Treatment
of Animals

QUIZ 331

1. All of them **2.** True **3.** All of them
4. True **5.** True **6.** Peach **7.** Seeds
8. Discovery **9.** True **10.** Melon
11. Carrot **12.** The skin will blacken
13. Quince **14.** Fig **15.** Five **16.** A
flightless bird from New Zealand
17. True **18.** Cloudberry **19.** Mango
20. Valencia **21.** 92% **22.** True

23. A Chinese gooseberry **24.** True
25. Grapefruit

QUIZ 332

1. India **2.** South America **3.** True
4. A sunflower **5.** White **6.** Squash
7. False **8.** Cauliflower **9.** Lisa
10. Charlotte **11.** False **12.** Potato
13. Okra **14.** Spinach **15.** Beetroot
16. True **17.** True **18.** Pink **19.** 2–3 years
20. Broccoli **21.** Manioc **22.** Wales
23. A type of cabbage **24.** Brassicas
25. They contain a chemical that
irritates the eyes

QUIZ 333

1. Basil **2.** American **3.** Basil **4.** True
5. Chive **6.** Herb **7.** Basil **8.** Dill
9. Celery **10.** Licorice **11.** Underground
rootstalks **12.** All of these **13.** Parsley and
mint **14.** Thyme **15.** True **16.** Rosemary
17. Tansy **18.** Parsley **19.** Chervil
20. Yellow

QUIZ 334

1. False **2.** True **3.** True
4. True **5.** Noodles **6.** Soy sauce
7. A wok **8.** Deep-frying to seal in the
juices **9.** Around a round table **10.** Oolong
11. They are considered weapons
12. Bamboo shoots **13.** Wine **14.** They
cook more quickly **15.** Add them to
iced water **16.** A gas flame **17.** Fugu
18. Pilau rice **19.** Sea aubergine
20. It is steamed **21.** True **22.** False
23. A dumpling **24.** False **25.** Peanut

QUIZ 335

1. Poha **2.** Yogurt **3.** Scotland **4.** Diseased
corn **5.** Jamaica **6.** Pakistan **7.** Khubz
8. Cheese **9.** Korea **10.** False **11.** Hawaii
12. Japan **13.** Russia **14.** Pho
15. Senegal **16.** Pig **17.** Finland
18. True **19.** Spain **20.** Rice

QUIZ 336

1. Queen Anne **2.** 5:00 pm and 7:00 pm
3. 5:00 pm **4.** Cantonese **5.** Alcohol
6. The 18th century **7.** Matcha

8. Cucumber sandwiches **9.** Tea dances **10.** China **11.** Tea bags **12.** True **13.** Mint **14.** As a formal declaration of war **15.** 1662 **16.** India **17.** False **18.** Green tea **19.** The 8th century **20.** Golden syrup

QUIZ 337

1. Bell peppers **2.** Scotland **3.** True **4.** Goa **5.** Catalan **6.** Gamla Stan **7.** Frankfurter Würstchen **8.** Chicken liver **9.** China **10.** Salt **11.** True **12.** South Africa **13.** 2011 **14.** Paprika **15.** Mortadella **16.** True **17.** Spain **18.** The Latin *salsisium* (being salted) **19.** Switzerland **20.** Germany **21.** Due to their pagan connections **22.** France **23.** Hot dog **24.** True **25.** 2000

QUIZ 338

1. All of them **2.** Smoked cod's roe **3.** Arctic cod **4.** A pilchard **5.** Bacalhau **6.** Perch **7.** Pry the shells apart **8.** Bright, convex, and black **9.** Bluefin tuna **10.** Loin fillet **11.** The gills **12.** True **13.** Herring **14.** A round-edge mother-of-pearl spoon **15.** South America **16.** Old English *fisc* **17.** Vietnam **18.** Thinner bones **19.** True **20.** Salmon

QUIZ 339

1. Large croutons **2.** Zuppa Toscana **3.** Andy Warhol **4.** Dried swiftlet saliva **5.** Onions, celery, carrots **6.** 6000 BCE **7.** Potato **8.** False **9.** Penicillin **10.** Provence **11.** Cock-a-leekie **12.** True **13.** False **14.** Shark-fin soup **15.** False **16.** True **17.** Cabbage-soup diet **18.** A calf's head **19.** Clear **20.** Pepper water **21.** A tureen **22.** Sassafras **23.** Lentils **24.** Greece **25.** Bhutan

QUIZ 340

1. Kao **2.** The pith **3.** Energy drink **4.** Northeast **5.** A fork and spoon **6.** Lime **7.** All that and more

8. Papaya **9.** It has a harder, woodier texture **10.** False **11.** True **12.** Thai brown curry **13.** True **14.** Fish sauce **15.** False **16.** Green chicken curry **17.** Seaweed **18.** Bad manners **19.** Sticky rice **20.** True

QUIZ 341

1. Baking a crust or pastry without filling **2.** An open-topped pastry shell with a filling **3.** North Carolina **4.** Decorative edges for pies **5.** Early British-American colonies **6.** Four and Twenty **7.** *Coffyn* **8.** Elizabeth I **9.** Placenta **10.** True **11.** 1545 **12.** Pizza **13.** False **14.** The Philippines **15.** Coulibiac **16.** True **17.** Christmas **18.** Pennsylvania and the Delaware Valley **19.** Spinach **20.** A captive girl **21.** Pizza dough **22.** *Titus Andronicus* **23.** Fish heads **24.** Pork pies **25.** True

QUIZ 342

1. Haggis **2.** Ketchup **3.** Somalia **4.** Absinthe **5.** China **6.** The European Union **7.** Jelly Sweets **8.** 22 **9.** *Casu marzu* **10.** A small songbird **11.** Belgium **12.** America **13.** False **14.** Taiwan **15.** A carbonated soft drink matured in barrels **16.** Blackened redfish **17.** False **18.** A herb **19.** Ackee **20.** Kinder Eggs

QUIZ 343

1. Hula Burger **2.** Coca-Cola BlāK **3.** New Coke **4.** 30 g—38 percent of the DV (daily value) **5.** True **6.** McCaviar **7.** Hershey's Desert Bar **8.** Sip Ups **9.** Tan **10.** New Coke **11.** True **12.** The McDLT **13.** Burger King **14.** Yes **15.** False **16.** Pepsi Blue **17.** Breakfast Mates **18.** False **19.** Orbitz **20.** Yellow

QUIZ 344

1. Yemen **2.** Cocoa powder or dark chocolate **3.** New Zealand and Australia **4.** Espresso **5.** Venice **6.** Mint **7.** China **8.** Oxford **9.** Chocolate **10.** The American Civil War **11.** Burned bread

12. Espressino 13. China
14. Martinique 15. Lime 16. Triple
Death 17. Portugal 18. Mali
19. North America 20. False
21. Red Tux 22. False 23. Turkey
24. True 25. Camellia

QUIZ 345
1. Christopher Columbus
2. Tom yum 3. 140 4. The Indus
Valley civilization 5. India 6. Goa
7. Scoville heat unit 8. True 9. Birds
10. Pyro-gourmaniacs 11. Hallucinations
12. Capsaicin 13. Africa 14. Trinidad
15. More than six million 16. Shrimp
creole 17. Ten 18. Regent Street
19. True 20. Asian

QUIZ 346
1. 19½ lbs (9 kg) 2. Crème brulée
3. Zabaglione 4. Brown Betty
5. Marie Antoinette 6. Spain
7. Choux pastry 8. Flambéed
9. Baked Alaska 10. A cloth
or shirt sleeve 11. Cherries
12. Syllabub 13. Eton mess
14. Bee sting cake 15. Dame Nellie
Melba 16. Rich, high-quality chocolate
17. You won't marry this year 18. Greece
19. No, it can make them very ill
20. Cream (or milk) sugar, vanilla,
and egg yolks

QUIZ 347
1. Pork 2. Burger King 3. Shank
4. Cured 5. Pork 6. Pig 7. To
seal in the juices 8. Seared and
just warm within 9. Offal 10. True
11. Steak 12. Bacon 13. 668 ft 7.62 in
(203.80 m) 14. Adult sheep
15. Blood sausage 16. Buzzard
17. 75% 18. Shoulder 19. Beef, capers,
shallots, egg yolk 20. Chicken

QUIZ 348
1. France 2. $35 million 3. Tarts
4. *Mille-feuille* 5. Goa, India 6. Ice
cream 7. Pink and yellow 8. False
9. Butter 10. Glossy 11. A sponge cake

with buttercream 12. King cake
13. True 14. Ancient Greeks
15. Apples 16. Choux 17. Red bean
paste 18. True 19. Muscovado
20. Double cream

QUIZ 349
1. Chinese cabbage 2. Ramen
3. Sweet potato 4. Baguette
5. Currywurst 6. Frozen whale skin
7. True 8. Nigeria 9. North Africa
10. Chickpeas 11. 5,000 years
12. Pita bread 13. United States
14. Canada 15. False 16. White
17. True 18. A caterpillar
19. Jamaica 20. Mexico

QUIZ 350
1. True 2. Italian flour 3. 77–82.4°F
(25–28°C) 4. Maillard 5. 20.8 seconds
6. False 7. *Fougasse* 8. Four
9. True 10. 1986 11. Northeast
England 12. A tava 13. Lard
14. Deep-fat frying 15. Bodding
16. Amish 17. Ficelles 18. *Brioche
des rois* 19. Potato flour
20. Germany

QUIZ 351
1. All of them are possible sources
2. Hāngi, a pit oven 3. Kebab
4. Lyndon B. Johnson 5. In the
last few minutes 6. Auguste Escoffier
7. Scotch bonnet chili pepper 8. True
9. USA and Canada 10. A type of outdoor
grill 11. Hobo pack cooking 12. 900°F
(480°C) 13. A flare-up 14. False
15. Herbs and spices rubbed onto
meat 16. France 17. During cooking
18. Freshwater crayfish 19. Monkfish
20. FSC charcoal

QUIZ 352
1. Balam 2. OO 3. Squid or
cuttlefish ink 4. Wheels 5. Tube
6. To the tooth 7. Broth 8. True
9. Spinach 10. False 11. 12,388 ft
(3,776 m) 12. Spiral 13. Orzo
14. Alfredo 15. Not leave it unattended

16. *Orecchiette* **17.** *Capelli d'angelo*
18. A bow tie **19.** False **20.** Lumps

QUIZ 353

1. Saffron **2.** True **3.** Rosemary
4. Curry leaves **5.** Chilies **6.** Sesame
7. The white pith veins in the pod
8. False **9.** Pink pepper **10.** Tamarind
11. True **12.** True **13.** India and
Sri Lanka **14.** Nigella **15.** White
turmeric **16.** Allspice **17.** True **18.** Hot
spices or mixture **19.** Turmeric
20. Infinity **21.** Cayenne **22.** Inner
tree bark **23.** Lemongrass
24. On trees **25.** Red

QUIZ 354

1. True **2.** True **3.** Warm, mild
weather after rain **4.** Early morning
5. Field mushrooms **6.** Chicken-of-
the-woods **7.** Cauliflower fungus
8. Common puffballs **9.** Clustered
domecap **10.** Mycologist **11.** Honey
mushroom **12.** Deceiver **13.** False
14. Northwestern Italy **15.** Early
summer to autumn **16.** True **17.** True
18. Hedgehog fungus **19.** Summer
truffle **20.** Cauliflower fungus

QUIZ 355

1. Western South America
2. As seeds in the stomachs of turtles
3. More than 5,000 **4.** True **5.** Globe
tomatoes **6.** Their shape and size **7.** True
8. Lycopene **9.** Hidden Rose **10.** False
11. Alfredo **12.** Where the calyx joins
the stem **13.** Mozzarella and basil
14. Exposing them to the outdoors
15. The fruit splitting **16.** Unripe tomatoes
17. True **18.** Bananas **19.** False
20. Sliced, coated with cornmeal,
and fried

QUIZ 356

1. 80% **2.** Up to nine months
3. False **4.** Cucumbers **5.** Storing
underground for the winter **6.** Autumn
7. True **8.** False **9.** Spring
10. False **11.** Apples **12.** Onions

13. At the end of summer **14.** An
overripe fruit **15.** August **16.** Summer
17. Rhubarb **18.** Chits **19.** They grow
all year round **20.** Apple

QUIZ 357

1. Pufferfish **2.** France **3.** They contain
too much poisonous ciguatoxin
4. They smell so bad **5.** Sweden
6. Taipei **7.** South Korea **8.** Fenugreek
9. Saliva nests made by swifts
10. Fermented herring **11.** Spain
12. *Kleftiko* **13.** Steak **14.** Dried mango
15. Portugal **16.** Raw fish **17.** Chicago
18. Coffee **19.** About 100 days
20. A cut of tuna **21.** Cambodia
22. Giant black Liometopum ants'
eggs **23.** Eating death **24.** Cambodia
25. True

QUIZ 358

1. Pig **2.** Steaming **3.** Picos Blue
4. Mozzarella **5.** Tunworth **6.** Sticky
and pungent **7.** Blue Monday **8.** Feta
9. Champagne **10.** False **11.** True
12. Lombardy **13.** Gubbeen **14.** Coagulated
milk proteins **15.** Its holes **16.** Mozzarella
17. Brine solution **18.** Dorset Blue Vinny
19. Ford Farm Cave-Aged Cheddar
20. 6000 BCE **21.** True **22.** 1941
23. Derbyshire, Leicestershire,
Nottinghamshire **24.** 1816
25. Roquefort

QUIZ 359

1. True **2.** La Varenne **3.** Napoleon
4. High **5.** Haricot **6.** Burgundy
7. 1900 **8.** *Amuse-bouche* **9.** Fish stew
or soup **10.** Raymond Blanc **11.** 1960s
12. Taillevent **13.** Bistro **14.** Snails
15. Lyon **16.** Beef **17.** Liver **18.** False
19. Chive **20.** Bread

QUIZ 360

1. New Zealand **2.** True **3.** True
4. Shiokara **5.** Fish-head soup
6. Iceland **7.** Bagoong **8.** China
9. False **10.** Turtle **11.** China
12. Philippines **13.** Norway

14. Guinea pig 15. Grasshoppers
16. Iceland 17. Sweetbreads
18. Schmaltz 19. Spring rolls
20. North America

QUIZ 361

1. Over 100 2. Southfork 3. Heather
Locklear 4. *Falcon Crest* 5. *Models Inc.*
6. 1993 7. *Dynasty* 8. Lucy 9. *Knots
Landing* 10. *Dynasty* 11. *General
Hospital* 12. False 13. Gary Ewing
14. 2011 15. True 16. *Days of Our
Lives* 17. Patrick Duffy 18. It was
cancelled after one season 19. 2012
20. Marcia Cross

QUIZ 362

1. Yorkshire 2. Highclere Castle in
Hampshire 3. Julian Fellowes 4. Daisy
5. Lady Edith Crawley 6. TV antennas
7. Lord Robert Crawley 8. Mrs. Hughes
9. Shrimpie 10. Dame Maggie
Smith 11. The sinking of the *Titanic*
12. Thomas, the underbutler 13. Elsie
14. Isis 15. Dowager Countess of
Grantham 16. Lady's maid to Lady Crawley
17. The outbreak of World War I 18. Sir
Anthony Strallan 19. Mrs. Patmore
20. Kiri Te Kanawa

QUIZ 363

1. *Horses* 2. Robert Lindsay
3. The Home Guard 4. *Outnumbered*
5. *Allo Allo* 6. Dawn French 7. *Fawlty
Towers* 8. Norman Stanley Fletcher
9. Arkwright 10. David Jason 11. A
spaceship 12. Four seasons 13. True
14. *Extras* 15. False 16. Joanna Lumley
17. Craggy Island 18. Richard Briers
19. Grace Brothers 20. India and Burma
(Myanmar) 21. *Little Britain* 22. Uncle
Albert in *Only Fools and Horses*
23. *One Foot in the Grave*
24. Rigsby 25. Hamster

QUIZ 364

1. Woody 2. True 3. An ogre 4. Tap
dancing 5. Dr. Seuss 6. Pixar 7. True
8. France 9. True 10. Anime 11. Jessica

Rabbit 12. *Toy Story* 13. A clownfish
14. *101 Dalmations* 15. Gromit 16. Flik
17. Balloons 18. *Madagascar* 19. Forky
20. Arendale 21. *Happy Feet* 22. *Snow
White and the Seven Dwarfs* 23. *The Little
Mermaid* 24. Gru and the Minions 25. False

QUIZ 365

1. True 2. *The Lost Weekend* 3. *Some
Like It Hot* 4. James Stewart 5. *Sunset
Boulevard* 6. True 7. *The Seven Year Itch*
8. Sugar Kane 9. *Fascination* 10. Jack
Lemmon 11. 1960 12. The Cleveland
Browns 13. False 14. James Cagney
15. A POW camp 16. Spats 17. *The
Major and the Minor* 18. Audrey Hepburn
19. *Witness for the Prosecution* 20. 1981

QUIZ 366

1. 58 films 2. *Steamboat Willie*
3. Genovia 4. His nose grew
5. Dumbo 6. Thumper 7. Lewis
Carroll 8. Tchaikovsky 9. *Rapunzel*
10. Elton John and Tim Rice 11. Fire
12. *Kids* 13. The West Wing 14. False
15. True 16. James P. Sullivan 17. A
donkey 18. Dug 19. Pluto 20. Minnie
21. Queen Narissa 22. Sir Hiss
23. Six sisters 24. Mortimer and
Minerva 25. 10,000 years

QUIZ 367

1. True 2. Hammer 3. *Halloween*
4. Vincent Price 5. Washington, D.C.
6. George A. Romero 7. True 8. Stephen
King 9. *The Fly* 10. *Witch* 11. Jason
12. Stanley Kubrick 13. He froze to
death 14. Spiders 15. Boris Karloff
16. *The Mummy* 17. Modern-day
Romania 18. London 19. Peter Cushing
20. *Se7en* 21. Monica (Courteney
Cox) 22. A lamb 23. Norman Bates
24. *Poltergeist* 25. With the help of
a bolt of lightning

QUIZ 368

1. *Alone* 2. Jodie Foster 3. *The
Railway Children* 4. *Spy Kids*
5. History 6. *Hannah Montana*

7. *Harry Potter and the Chamber of Secrets* **8.** He hit his head **9.** It glowed red **10.** Johnny Depp **11.** Garfield **12.** True **13.** *Chitty Chitty Bang Bang* **14.** True **15.** 1939 **16.** *Kid* **17.** *Herbie* **18.** A lion **19.** Jack Black **20.** Rubens

QUIZ 369

1. Zombie **2.** Inspector Clouseau **3.** Sugar Kane **4.** True **5.** Stockbroker **6.** Bill Murray and Andie MacDowell **7.** A leopard **8.** *The Odd Couple* **9.** *The Jerk* **10.** True **11.** Ealing **12.** *Spinal Tap* **13.** *Brian* **14.** False **15.** The Marx Brothers **16.** Country music **17.** Will Smith **18.** Woody Allen **19.** Ted Striker **20.** Carry On...

QUIZ 370

1. True **2.** Miss Moneypenny **3.** Q **4.** 007 **5.** Dr. No **6.** Oddjob **7.** Sharks **8.** *On Her Majesty's Secret Service* **9.** Francisco Scaramanga **10.** Max Zorin **11.** False **12.** Severnaya **13.** 006 **14.** BMW **15.** Christmas Jones **16.** Verity **17.** Vesper Lynd **18.** Aston Martin DB5 **19.** Camille **20.** Seven

QUIZ 371

1. *Ryan* **2.** True **3.** Stalingrad **4.** World War I **5.** Richard Harris **6.** *Brigade* **7.** The Crimean War **8.** False—the film's title is *The Imitation Game* **9.** *Kwai* **10.** *Zulu* **11.** True **12.** Rommel **13.** Sam Mendes **14.** *The Pianist* **15.** *Black Hawk Down* **16.** D-Day **17.** Brad Pitt **18.** *Glory* **19.** *A Bridge Too Far* **20.** True

QUIZ 372

1. 29 years **2.** "Wish me luck" **3.** Architect **4.** *Archie Bunker's Place* **5.** Lou Grant **6.** John Patrick Francis Mulcahy **7.** "Goodbye, Farewell, and Amen" **8.** True **9.** Kristin Shepard **10.** True **11.** False **12.** *The Flintstones* **13.** David Cassidy **14.** Lilies **15.** William McKinley High School

16. Cooper and Hofstadter **17.** 2008 **18.** Salem **19.** "The Puffy Shirt" **20.** Arnold's

QUIZ 373

1. Vermont **2.** True **3.** We don't find out **4.** A Red Ryder BB gun **5.** False—Irving Berlin wrote the song **6.** Paris **7.** Bob Cratchit **8.** The film's director, Vincente Minnelli **9.** Shower curtain rings **10.** Letters addressed to Santa **11.** Jim Carrey **12.** Clarence **13.** True **14.** A silk top hat **15.** W. Somerset Maugham **16.** A Turbo-Man action toy **17.** 1,938 candy canes **18.** Thurman Merman **19.** Six characters **20.** Eight couples

QUIZ 374

1. Matthew Broderick **2.** Wyld Stallyns **3.** Francis Ford Coppola **4.** Molly Ringwald **5.** Baltimore **6.** "Flashdance... What a Feeling" **7.** *Purple Rain* **8.** False **9.** Iceman **10.** The Library **11.** The Brat Pack **12.** Dancing **13.** Stephen King **14.** True **15.** Madonna **16.** Extra **17.** Kelly LeBrock **18.** *Ghostbusters* **19.** Eddie Murphy **20.** 1955 **21.** Steven Spielberg **22.** *Beetlejuice* **23.** *Wall Street* **24.** *Flashdance* **25.** *Short Circuit*

QUIZ 375

1. Jim Henson **2.** Beaker **3.** The Wombles **4.** Make Good Use of Bad Rubbish **5.** *Teletubbies* **6.** *Sesame Street* **7.** *SpongeBob SquarePants* **8.** 1987 **9.** Matt Groening **10.** Guitar **11.** Nickelodeon **12.** 1969 **13.** *Rainbow* **14.** *Hannah Montana* **15.** An explorer **16.** To teach through problem solving **17.** Wizards **18.** The Clangers **19.** *Dr. Who* **20.** Kermit the Frog

QUIZ 376

1. False **2.** 10 years old **3.** Three **4.** Katherine Hepburn **5.** *Shrek* **6.** One **7.** Both refused Best Actor awards **8.** Best Costume Design **9.** The Academy Awards **10.** Clark Gable **11.** Claudette Colbert **12.** Sidney Poitier **13.** *Godfather II*

14. *Gone With the Wind* **15.** Sylvester Stallone **16.** *Wolves* **17.** False **18.** None **19.** *The King's Speech* **20.** 11 Oscars

QUIZ 377

1. Stanley Kubrick **2.** *Jaws* **3.** Pandora **4.** Jane Fonda **5.** Duran Duran **6.** *Gravity* **7.** *The Tempest* **8.** 23rd century **9.** A Vulcan nerve pinch **10.** False **11.** *Robocop* **12.** *The Third Kind* **13.** Bugs **14.** *Planet of the Apes* **15.** Luke Skywalker **16.** The ruined Statue of Liberty **17.** Mars **18.** True **19.** *The Day the Earth Stood Still* **20.** Bender **21.** Isla Nubar **22.** Jonesy **23.** 30 years **24.** Raspberry jam **25.** A deadly dust storm

QUIZ 378

1. Sunlight **2.** *Dead* **3.** Count Dracula **4.** HAL **5.** *Woman* **6.** *Troll* **7.** Beauty **8.** The priest **9.** David Bowie **10.** Chucky **11.** *Godzilla* **12.** *A Zombie* **13.** Boring! **14.** They're blind and very sensitive to noise **15.** False **16.** Michael Myers **17.** *Blood* **18.** New York **19.** Kraken **20.** She turns into a giant after being hit by a meteorite

QUIZ 379

1. True **2.** Anastasia and Drizella **3.** Briar Rose **4.** True **5.** She uses the magic mirror **6.** Rajah **7.** A spinning arrow **8.** An apple **9.** Tiana's Palace **10.** False **11.** True **12.** Mrs. Potts **13.** The marketplace **14.** James **15.** To comb hair **16.** Eugene Fitzherbert **17.** Because she is beautiful **18.** A tiny dragon **19.** The Powhaton tribe **20.** It turns brown

QUIZ 380

1. *Stagecoach* **2.** False **3.** *Corral* **4.** Four Oscars **5.** *High Noon* **6.** True **7.** Monument Valley **8.** False **9.** Arizona **10.** Doc Holliday **11.** *The Seven Samurai* **12.** John Wayne **13.** Trigger **14.** True **15.** Gene Hackman **16.** *The Shootist* **17.** Mel Brooks **18.** True **19.** False—he plays Butch Cassidy **20.** *The Wild Bunch* **21.** Eli Wallach **22.** Natalie Wood

23. *Django Unchained* **24.** *The Treasure of the Sierra Madre* **25.** Kevin Costner

QUIZ 381

1. George O'Malley, a long-serving intern **2.** Copenhagen **3.** She's a half-fairy **4.** Jean Sylvester **5.** Jim Halpert **6.** True **7.** Bentley **8.** An octopus in the show *SpongeBob SquarePants* **9.** Kevin **10.** Matt Damon **11.** Caroline Forbes **12.** Michael Crichton **13.** Bipolar disorder **14.** He tackled a defender **15.** False **16.** 2006 **17.** Sandra Diaz-Twine **18.** Teri Hatcher **19.** China and India **20.** Katie Lee Joel **21.** Kim Cattrall **22.** Lily Tomlin **23.** *Better Call Saul* is a prequel to the older series **24.** Thandie Newton **25.** 28 seasons

QUIZ 382

1. Marlon Brando **2.** Good Friday **3.** Two **4.** *Goodfellas* **5.** *Faces* **6.** Dead **7.** John Dillinger **8.** *Heat* **9.** American **10.** True **11.** *White Heat* **12.** Michael Caine **13.** Faye Dunaway and Warren Beatty **14.** Sergio Leone **15.** *Dogs* **16.** Corleone **17.** *Rock* **18.** *Casino* **19.** Chicago **20.** True

QUIZ 383

1. MI5 **2.** The Grid **3.** The Russians **4.** Thames House, London **5.** Section D **6.** Ben Kaplan **7.** Season 6 **8.** Nightingale **9.** *Spooks: Code 9* **10.** True **11.** John Bateman **12.** A genetic weapon **13.** Federal Security Service **14.** Erin Watts **15.** Sharecropper **16.** Victor Elliott **17.** Freelance engineer **18.** St. Josephs **19.** 416 **20.** False

QUIZ 384

1. *Erin Brockovich* **2.** *Austin Powers in Goldmember* **3.** Keith Richards **4.** Helena Bonham Carter **5.** *Pride and Prejudice* **6.** Neo **7.** True **8.** Stephen King **9.** Kathryn Bigelow, for *Hurt Locker* **10.** Travis Bickle

11. Peter Mayhew 12. Four awards
13. Harrison Ford 14. True 15. Frances
McDormand 16. Peter Jackson
17. James Cameron 18. Johnny Cash
19. *The Mask* 20. *Joe Versus the
Volcano, Sleepless in Seattle*, and
You've Got Mail 21. *The Blind Side*
22. Bong Joon Ho directed *Parasite*
23. *Dr. Dolittle*, Robert Downey Jr.
24. *Dunkirk* 25. Harley Quinn

QUIZ 385

1. Captain Abraham Smollett
2. Hannibal Lecter 3. Tom Cruise and
Brad Pitt 4. "And in the darkness bind
them" 5. A Ford Anglia 6. Whoopi
Goldberg 7. Kaa 8. *The Hunt for Red
October* 9. *The Reader* 10. *Alice in
Wonderland* 11. Florence 12. Truman
Capote 13. *The Devil Wears Prada*
14. Alec Guinness 15. *Atonement*
16. John Grisham 17. *Schindler's
Ark* 18. Seven books 19. Ian Fleming
20. Giuseppe Tomasi di Lampedusa

QUIZ 386

1. *A Few Good Men* 2. True—the film was
My Fair Lady 3. True 4. Shakespeare's
Henry IV and *Henry V* 5. The film was
Sweeney Todd, and the play was titled
The Demon Barber of Fleet Street
6. *His Girl Friday* 7. *Chicago* 8. *West
Side Story* 9. 1945 10. 1954 11. True
12. *The Tempest* 13. True 14. *Hello,
Dolly!* 15. *The Rocky Horror Picture
Show* 16. True 17. Richard Harris
18. False 19. *Cabaret*
20. Liza Minnelli

QUIZ 387

1. True 2. True 3. *Captain America:
The First Avenger* 4. Loki 5. False
6. Tony Stark 7. Mjolnir 8. Dr. Robert
Bruce Banner 9. True 10. Project:
Rebirth 11. Robert Downey Jr.
12. Vibranium 13. Golden Apples
of Iduun 14. Clint Barton 15. Masters
of Evil 16. Fifth Avenue, New York
17. Russia 18. Beast 19. Spider-Man

20. He can manipulate his arrows so
that they always hit their targets—he's
a super marksman 21. As a demi-god
22. He's working as a doctor in
Kolkata, India 23. Spider-Man
24. The Incredible Hulk 25. Strategic
Homeland Intervention, Enforcement
and Logistics Division

QUIZ 388

1. *Captain America Comics* (1941)
2. 4F 3. He didn't like bullies
4. Dr. Abraham Erskine 5. True 6. Super
Soldier Serum and "vita-rays" 7. 1945
8. A star 9. Bucky Barnes 10. 2011
11. Iron Man 12. He is opposed
to it 13. Natasha Romanoff, the Black
Widow 14. Bucky Barnes 15. Vibranium
16. Johann Schmidt 17. Peter Parker,
aka Spider-Man 18. Strategic Scientific
Reserve (SSR) Agent Peggy Carter
19. Helicarriers 20. Colonel
Chester Phillips

QUIZ 389

1. 14 years old 2. A visit to the
movies 3. Alfred Pennyworth
4. Two-Face 5. Christopher Nolan
6. The Joker 7. Bane 8. False 9. Red
Hood 10. Azrael 11. Batboy 12. True
13. Bats 14. Oswald Chesterfield
Cobblepot 15. Intern psychiatrist at
the asylum 16. True 17. Oracle
18. False 19. Purple 20. Maroni

QUIZ 390

1. 1929 2. *Titanic, Ben-Hur*, and
*Lord of the Rings: Return of the
King* 3. *Forrest Gump* 4. *Beauty
and the Beast, Up*, and *Toy Story 3*
5. Katharine Hepburn 6. True
7. Heath Ledger 8. 59 9. 10 years
old 10. John Ford 11. True
12. Douglas Fairbanks 13. Nine
14. Cate Blanchett for playing
Katharine Hepburn in *The Aviator*
15. True 16. 12 times 17. *The
Godfather* 18. *Midnight Cowboy*
19. Childhood poverty 20. True

QUIZ 391

1. Vincent van Gogh **2.** Edvard Munch
3. A ballerina **4.** San Giorgio Maggiore
at Dusk **5.** Pre-Raphaelites **6.** *Water
Lilies* (Monet) **7.** Status Quo **8.** *Mona Lisa*
9. Anthony Hopkins **10.** Wassily Kandinsky's
11. Johannes Vermeer **12.** *The Agony and
the Ecstasy* **13.** Rembrandt **14.** Nat King
Cole **15.** Toulouse-Lautrec **16.** Andy
Warhol **17.** *The Great Wave off Kanagawa*
18. Salvador Dalí **19.** True
20. Ed Harris

QUIZ 392

1. Fritz Lang **2.** *King Kong* **3.** Orson
Welles **4.** Dashiell Hammett **5.** Ingrid
Bergman **6.** 19 **7.** James Stewart
8. 1937 **9.** 1952 **10.** *Gilda* **11.** 1930s
12. *Giant* **13.** Marilyn Monroe
14. Spaghetti Western **15.** Anne Bancroft
16. The man with no name **17.** Ann
Robinson **18.** The lion from the MGM
logo **19.** True **20.** *The Men* **21.** Stephen
King **22.** 11 **23.** Travis Bickle
24. True **25.** Frances McDormand

QUIZ 393

1. *Poor Cow* **2.** Carol Reed **3.** David
Prowse **4.** Covent Garden Market
5. False **6.** 1969 **7.** Lambeth **8.** *Four
Weddings and a Funeral* **9.** 1980
10. *The Hard Case* **11.** Julia **12.** 1969
13. 1935 **14.** David Lean **15.** False
16. Four **17.** BBC **18.** *American Beauty*
19. *Family Plot* **20.** *Death Proof* and
Planet Terror

QUIZ 394

1. *Diamonds Are Forever* **2.** They're
actually only three minutes **3.** Dr. No
4. He weeps blood **5.** False **6.** *You Only
Live Twice* **7.** Ernst Stavro **8.** Virus Omega
9. *Live and Let Die* **10.** A third nipple
11. Karl Stromberg **12.** False **13.** Necros
14. Elliot Carver **15.** Undetectable
murder and torture **16.** There's a bullet
in his brain **17.** Scorpion **18.** Kamal
Khan **19.** Colonel Moon, North Korean
Army **20.** M

QUIZ 395

1. All of them **2.** 1963 **3.** Gold **4.** Blue
5. True **6.** StarkCorp **7.** Virginia Potts
8. War Machine **9.** Titanium Man
10. True **11.** 15 **12.** To save the life
of a dog **13.** The superhuman registration
act **14.** China **15.** Spider-Woman
16. False **17.** The Thundercats **18.** The
Extremis formula **19.** The Human Torch
20. True

QUIZ 396

1. San Diego Comic-Con **2.** Ben Burtt
3. Hamburger Hamlet **4.** *The Journal
of the Whills* **5.** Naboo **6.** Kenny Baker
7. True **8.** Darth Vader **9.** Yoda
10. General Grievous **11.** Elstree Studios
12. False **13.** False **14.** Grauman's
Chinese Theater **15.** *Survivor's Quest*
16. False **17.** George Takei **18.** Icons
19. Maria in *Metropolis* **20.** Star Wars

QUIZ 397

1. I Can't Believe It's a Law Firm
2. Genuine Class **3.** How to Chew
Tobacco **4.** False **5.** Üterbraten
6. Santos L. Halper **7.** 31 **8.** Duff
with Penicillin **9.** Eleven **10.** Michael
Corleone **11.** The mascot for the
doorbell company **12.** *Bright Lights,
Beef Jerky* **13.** 25 **14.** Hugh Jass
15. Krusty's Kosher Karaoke Machine
16. *That Happy Cat* **17.** 2 years and 38
days **18.** *McBain IV: Fatal Discharge*
19. Joey Jo-Jo Junior Shabadoo
20. Downtown Drive-Thru Doctors

QUIZ 398

1. Honey Ryder **2.** She is covered in
gold paint **3.** Fiona Volpe **4.** Tiger
Tanaka **5.** Saves her from drowning
herself **6.** Diamonds **7.** *Live and
Let Die* **8.** False **9.** Pilot **10.** Crossbow
11. True **12.** Kara Milovy **13.** Computer
programmer **14.** Paris Carver
15. Kazakhstan **16.** *The Man with the
Golden Gun* **17.** An orange bikini
18. Fencing **19.** The Treasury
20. Camille Montes **21.** Golf

22. A poison-tipped blade in her shoe
23. Honor Blackman 24. Diana Rigg
25. Red

QUIZ 399

1. *Rebecca* 2. Suspense 3. Leytonstone
4. *The Lodger* 5. False 6. Gloria Swanson
7. Eight 8. 1960 9. Ernest Lehman
10. True 11. 5 years 12. Alma
13. Bernard Herrmann 14. Joseph
15. "Fake it" 16. *Alfred Hitchcock Presents*
17. True 18. It is never explained 19. A
double bass fiddle 20. April 29, 1980

QUIZ 400

1. 1913 2. 36 3. *Alam Ara* 4. 1940s to
1960s 5. *Mirza Ghalib* 6. Dhundiraj
Govind Phalke 7. *Devdas* 8. True
9. Satyajit Ray 10. True 11. New York
12. 1954 13. *Mother India* 14. Sharmila
Tagore 15. Nargis Dutt 16. False
17. False 18. Ajay Singh Deol
19. Devika Rani 20. True 21. Telugu
22. Irrfan Khan 23. Priyanka Chopra
24. True 25. *Lamhe*

QUIZ 401

1. North London 2. New Zealand
3. EMI Elstree Studios in Britain
4. *Blade Runner* 5. City Hall, Dallas
6. Sydney 7. *Ghostbusters* 8. 42nd Street
9. Wells, Somerset 10. The Carlton
Street Bridge, Edinburgh 11. Fox Studios
12. Tunisia 13. Salzburg, Austria
14. Notting Hill 15. Central Park
16. Hawaii 17. Tujunga, California
18. True 19. Waldon, Idaho
20. Fleet Street

QUIZ 402

1. *Pride and Prejudice* 2. *Upstairs,
Downstairs* 3. *Dr. Quinn, Medicine
Woman* 4. 1974 and 1983 5. George
Eliot 6. *Barry Lyndon* 7. Johnny Depp
8. Ireland 9. The 1870s 10. Ridley
Scott 11. 1938 12. *Julius Caesar*
13. *The Iliad* 14. True 15. *The
Barchester Chronicles* 16. Prohibition
17. *10,000 BC* 18. *Downton Abbey*

19. *Braveheart* 20. True 21. Mark
Rylance 22. *Poldark* 23. Birmingham
24. *Cranford* 25. Jane Austen

QUIZ 403

1. *Crocodile Dundee* 2. *Picnic at Hanging
Rock* 3. Dingo 4. *Muriel's Wedding*
5. *Romper Stomper* 6. *Dead Calm*
7. *Shine* 8. *Chopper* 9. *Babe* 10. *Moulin
Rouge!* 11. *Rabbit-Proof Fence*
12. *Gallipoli* 13. False 14. *Mad Max*
15. *Happy Feet* 16. *Wolf Creek*
17. *Strictly Ballroom* 18. *The Castle*
19. *The Adventures of Priscilla, Queen
of the Desert* 20. True

QUIZ 404

1. The Penguin 2. The Phantom 3. Green
Lantern 4. Fantastic Four 5. Supergirl
6. Lex Luthor 7. Captain America
8. Daredevil 9. True 10. The Incredible
Hulk 11. Magneto 12. *Batman and
Robin* 13. Spider-Man 14. Galactus
15. True 16. Hellboy 17. The Riddler
18. Mephistopheles 19. *X-Men: The
Last Stand* 20. Nuclear Man

QUIZ 405

1. 1995 2. Luxo Jr. 3. True
4. Mrs. Nesbit 5. Shark 6. Chess
7. *A Bug's Life* 8. 2006 9. False
10. 15 11. 2 12. Kitty 13. True
14. Light blue 15. Marlin 16. Buddy
Pine 17. Violin 18. Porsche
19. Gasteau's 20. 2805 21. Kevin
22. Lots-o'-Huggin'-Bear
23. Ramone's House of Body Art
24. Strong Man 25. Yew

QUIZ 406

1. Accordion 2. Ausralia 3. Virginals
4. Guitars 5. Electronic musical
instrument 6. True 7. China 8. True
9. Trumpet 10. Zither 11. Change the
sound 12. True 13. Hi-hat 14. Squawking
15. Stringed 16. Lyre 17. True 18. False
19. Tuba 20. 12 21. The end that projects
the music 22. Seven 23. False
24. Clarinet 25. Oboe

QUIZ 407

1. Terrible lizard **2.** Necks and tails
3. Stegosaurus **4.** True **5.** It is the oldest
known bird **6.** They flew **7.** In the sea
8. A person who studies fossils **9.** True
10. True **11.** Acting as a cooling system
12. False **13.** True **14.** No one knows
15. About 230 million years ago **16.** True
17. True **18.** Fast thief **19.** Herbivores
20. False **21.** An asteroid hitting Earth
22. Megalosaurus **23.** Compsognathus
24. Mary Anning **25.** Plesiosaur

QUIZ 408

1. Four **2.** 22 **3.** Ear **4.** Carbohydrates
5. Skin **6.** Skull **7.** About a million
8. Cardiac muscle **9.** How we see in
color **10.** Uvula **11.** Oxygen **12.** Hinged
joint **13.** Human **14.** Lymphatic **15.** 32
16. About 35 tons **17.** True **18.** 26 years
19. Heart down to the abdomen
20. Cell membrane

QUIZ 409

1. The inner core **2.** Pluto **3.** 365.25
4. 27.3 **5.** 1 day **6.** False **7.** Summer
8. False **9.** Divergence **10.** Sedimentation
11. True **12.** Diamond **13.** True
14. Igneous **15.** True **16.** Talc
17. Geologist **18.** Coral **19.** 71 percent
20. Pacific **21.** Clear **22.** Wyoming,
at 40 percent of the country's production
23. Garnet **24.** Quartz **25.** Basalt

QUIZ 410

1. Eight **2.** Neptune **3.** 13.7 billion years
4. Buzz Lightyear **5.** Earth **6.** 12 **7.** First
human in space **8.** The Southern Cross
9. False **10.** *Columbia* **11.** Large
Magellanic Cloud **12.** Valentina Tereshkova
13. Snoopy cap **14.** Barred spiral
15. 8.3 minutes **16.** Aristarchus
of Samos **17.** True **18.** Water-bearer
19. 1609 **20.** Ursa Major

QUIZ 411

1. True **2.** Characters in ancient
Egyptian writing **3.** True **4.** Scooped
it out through the nose **5.** Mesopotamians
6. True **7.** True **8.** Wood **9.** 1876
10. It went down a chute into the moat
11. Hubble **12.** True **13.** China
14. Young boys **15.** None of these
16. The postage stamp **17.** A bicycle
18. The Black Death **19.** 1857
20. Siege engines

QUIZ 412

1. South **2.** Roald Amundsen
3. Musk **4.** True **5.** 60 miles (96 km)
6. February **7.** Tundra **8.** White
9. Inuit **10.** Narwhal **11.** Leopard seal
12. 100,000 years **13.** False **14.** France
15. 2,000 lb (1,360 kg) **16.** 1821
17. False (Antarctic) **18.** A bird
19. True **20.** On its feet

QUIZ 413

1. *The Castle of Otranto* **2.** Victor
3. *The Monk* **4.** Shudder novel **5.** Italy
6. *Carmilla* **7.** 1818 **8.** *Northanger
Abbey* **9.** Lord Byron **10.** *Zastrozzi*
11. *The Vampyre* **12.** Edgar Allan Poe
13. 1847 **14.** *An English Opium-Eater*
15. The monkey's paw **16.** *The Pit
and the Pendulum* **17.** Mad, bad, and
dangerous to know **18.** Fanny Burney
19. Aunt Ada Doom **20.** Strawberry
Hill **21.** Late 18th century **22.** False
23. Manfred **24.** *The Old English
Baron* **25.** Susan Hill

QUIZ 414

1. True **2.** Clans **3.** Six **4.** Little Armored
One **5.** Deserts **6.** The Romans **7.** 17
years **8.** True **9.** Badgers **10.** 550 lb
(250 kg) **11.** More than 1 million
12. Warrens **13.** True **14.** 10 years
15. True **16.** Formic **17.** True **18.** True
19. False **20.** 9 in (23 cm) **21.** North
America **22.** They don't—they steal them
from other animals **23.** Devil worm
24. True **25.** In their cheek pouches

QUIZ 415

1. True **2.** Five **3.** Float **4.** Eyes **5.** Fish
6. Close and cover themselves **7.** False
8. Whelk **9.** Algae **10.** True **11.** Open

their shells **12.** A spoonful **13.** Jellyfish **14.** True **15.** Slime **16.** True **17.** True **18.** A type of seaweed **19.** Rippling the muscles in their foot **20.** A univalve

QUIZ 416

1. 26 **2.** The Clocky **3.** The penny-farthing **4.** The Peel P60 **5.** True **6.** Poland **7.** False **8.** Italy **9.** An anti-tilting device **10.** Kirkpatrick Macmillan **11.** Six **12.** *Novelty* **13.** 295 yd (270 m) **14.** False **15.** 1869 **16.** The biggest plane in the world **17.** Reverse **18.** Transform into a boat **19.** 1903 **20.** 30 ft (9 m) long **21.** 16 **22.** False **23.** Boneshaker **24.** Mountain **25.** The dandy horse

QUIZ 417

1. *A Tale of Two Cities* **2.** False **3.** *And Then There Were None* **4.** *The Lion, the Witch and the Wardrobe* **5.** *Lolita* **6.** *Catch-22* **7.** *She* **8.** Richard Bach **9.** *The Alchemist* **10.** *Anne of Green Gables* **11.** *Dragon Tattoo* **12.** *The Very Hungry Caterpillar* **13.** Margaret Mitchell **14.** *Nineteen Eighty-Four* **15.** *The Secret Diary of Adrian Mole, Aged 13³/4* **16.** True **17.** *Watership Down* **18.** Stephen King **19.** Cao Xueqin **20.** Antoine de Saint-Exupéry

QUIZ 418

1. The hippopotamus **2.** The elephant shrew **3.** Bat **4.** Two **5.** The gorilla **6.** The whale **7.** The crocodile **8.** The ratel **9.** The zebra **10.** The aardvark **11.** Antelope **12.** Spotted hyenas **13.** True **14.** The gnu **15.** False **16.** Small antelope **17.** True **18.** The dwarf mongoose **19.** 40,000 **20.** Four **21.** Oxpecker **22.** Black mamba **23.** True **24.** Martial eagle **25.** A lynxlike cat with long ears

QUIZ 419

1. Hinduism, Jainism, Buddhism **2.** Dog **3.** Spine **4.** Joseph Pilates **5.** Core **6.** True **7.** Weights **8.** False **9.** All of these **10.** *Prana* **11.** Early morning or the evening **12.** Resting between poses **13.** Aligning your body **14.** Germany **15.** True **16.** The powerhouse **17.** Rolldown **18.** True **19.** True **20.** Dogs

QUIZ 420

1. Vivienne Westwood **2.** *Sex and the City* **3.** 1990s **4.** Shoulder pads **5.** Milan **6.** Christian Dior **7.** Louis Vuitton **8.** Bazaar **9.** Chanel **10.** Dior **11.** True **12.** Halston **13.** True **14.** Elsa Schiaparelli **15.** Paul McCartney **16.** True **17.** Audrey Hepburn **18.** The 1980s **19.** A flapper **20.** 1950s

QUIZ 421

1. Patrick White **2.** Thomas Keneally **3.** He began writing **4.** A state funeral **5.** Peter Carey **6.** Colleen McCullough **7.** Ruth Park **8.** Nevil Shute **9.** Morris West **10.** Germaine Greer **11.** Barry Humphries **12.** Marcus Clarke **13.** *The Well Dressed Explorer* **14.** Joseph Furphy **15.** *1915* **16.** The first published Australian Aboriginal **17.** Having it rejected by multiple publishers **18.** False **19.** Joan Lindsay **20.** B. Paterson

QUIZ 422

1. Buddha **2.** Muhammad **3.** 632 CE **4.** Hinduism **5.** Christianity **6.** 2.1 billion **7.** Confucius **8.** Jamaica **9.** 1930s **10.** A branched candelabrum used in Jewish ceremonies **11.** Punjab **12.** True **13.** True **14.** India **15.** False **16.** Judaism **17.** Atheism **18.** True **19.** Maori **20.** Japan **21.** Haiti **22.** Easter **23.** The Avesta **24.** True **25.** Hinduism

QUIZ 423

1. 1970s **2.** Vatican City **3.** Shanghai **4.** Thomas Jefferson **5.** St. Basil **6.** Elizabeth Tower **7.** False **8.** Sir Christopher Wren **9.** Athens **10.** Antonio Gaudi **11.** His deceased wife, Mumtaz Mahal

12. Holyrood Palace 13. False
14. Oxfordshire 15. London 16. King
Louis XIV 17. True 18. Château de
Chambord 19. Buddhism 20. Norway
21. Beijing, China 22. Buckingham
Palace 23. Kuala Lumpur, Malaysia
24. St. Petersburg, Russia
25. Centre Pompidou

QUIZ 424

1. 11th century 2. True 3. Franklin
Pierce 4. All of these 5. Nehru–Gandhi
6. Abbasid 7. President and prime minister
8. 2010 9. Khan, Yuan Dynasty 10. Kublai
Khan 11. Zhou Dynasty 12. True 13. The
Ptolemaic Dynasty 14. 30BCE 15. Tudor
16. Elizabeth I 17. True 18. False
19. 1959–2008 20. The Habsburgs

QUIZ 425

1. Pamplona 2. Bulgaria 3. Nigeria
4. True 5. Diwali 6. Spain 7. China
8. New Orleans 9. Rosh Hashanah
10. False 11. India 12. China
13. Turkey 14. Sweden 15. Mexico
16. Orange 17. Baseball 18. Germany
19. Bermuda 20. Namaste

QUIZ 426

1. 88 2. 3,000 3. Proxima Centauri
4. 4.2 light years 5. Five 6. False
7. Up to 400 billion 8. A supernova
9. Uranus 10. The Plow 11. The
Northern Crown 12. Great Bear
13. Taurus 14. 48 15. Pegasus
16. Gemini 17. Two stars orbiting each
other 18. Spica 19. Its surface temperature
20. Orion's Belt 21. A blue giant
22. By nuclear fusion 23. It turns
into a planetary nebula 24. Blue
25. A cloud of dust and gas

QUIZ 427

1. South American 2. True 3. True
4. More than 115,000 5. Scorched earth
6. False 7. Vladivostok 8. True
9. The Dead Sea 10. 36,100 ft (11,000 m)
11. The mosquito 12. True 13. Burrows
14. True 15. 7 miles (11.2 km) 16. True

17. False 18. Ten times 19. True
20. Reindeer or caribou 21. True
22. Black 23. Gravity 24. Maria
25. Nuclear fusion

QUIZ 428

1. Chemistry 2. Astronomy 3. Rosalind
Franklin 4. Female professor 5. Mary
Anning 6. Chimpanzees 7. That it
contained an inner core 8. Mary Leakey
9. Physics 10. United States 11. False
12. Marie Curie 13. 1986 14. True
15. Françoise Barré-Sinoussi 16. Gorillas
17. Dorothy Hodgkin 18. Pulsars
19. Nuclear fission 20. Lady Mary
Wortley Montagu

QUIZ 429

1. Murano 2. False 3. Ponte Vecchio
4. Panettone 5. Sicily 6. Juliet
7. Siena 8. Gnocchi 9. River Arno
10. True 11. Elba 12. Vespasian
13. Milan 14. February 15. Turin
16. 117 17. True 18. Hadrian
19. Sicily 20. Mount Vesuvius
21. Strait of Messina 22. Virgil
23. Sardinia 24. Amalfi Coast
25. Autostrada

QUIZ 430

1. Orange 2. Fish hitch
3. Grizzly and polar 4. Sahara
5. True 6. All of them 7. A method of
melting snow 8. Seeds 9. Wind speed
10. Indian elephant 11. Short log
12. True 13. Cavern 14. A small
coil of cordage 15. True 16. 3 minutes
17. Iodine 18. False 19. Making fire
20. Bacteria in the soil 21. True
22. Frostnip 23. Shemagh
24. About 3 weeks 25. True

QUIZ 431

1. Mecca 2. Jericho 3. Zambia and
Zimbabwe 4. Victoria Falls 5. False
6. France 7. Sahara 8. True 9. Nevada
10. Ceylon 11. Times Square, NYC
12. Jorn Otzon 13. Buenos Aires
and Montevideo 14. A mausoleum

15. Jules Verne **16.** False
17. River Thames **18.** Necker
19. Old Peak **20.** Cultural

QUIZ 432
1. Java **2.** Japan **3.** An underwater earthquake **4.** True **5.** Avalanche
6. India **7.** 1906 **8.** Mt. St. Helens
9. At least 225,000 **10.** Floods
11. Galveston, Texas **12.** Harbor wave
13. Lisbon **14.** Sicily **15.** Vesuvius
16. Tunguska **17.** Storm and
tidal flooding **18.** 1970 Bhola
cyclone **19.** Monsoon
20. May

QUIZ 433
1. Johnny Depp **2.** Antioxidants
3. Criollo **4.** True **5.** Irregular
raw bean fragments **6.** Europe
7. St. Lucia **8.** Switzerland **9.** Flowers
10. 20 to 40 **11.** Food of the Gods
12. Oompa Loompas **13.** 1657
14. Cocoa solids **15.** 2004
16. 210–290°F (99–145°C)
17. False **18.** Swiss **19.** True
20. France and Germany

QUIZ 434
1. Eight **2.** "Silent Night" **3.** Goose
4. My true love **5.** December 13
6. 1843 **7.** Golden rope **8.** Germany
9. True **10.** Good luck **11.** Oliver
Cromwell **12.** Caspar **13.** Christmas
tree **14.** Beef and spices **15.** Greek
16. Norway **17.** 24,902 miles (40,075 km)
18. Spain **19.** Fertility and love
20. Christina Rossetti **21.** Clement
Clarke Moore **22.** True **23.** Christmas
crackers **24.** Break it **25.** Poinsettia

QUIZ 435
1. 522,000 light years across
2. A lung disease caused by silica
dust **3.** False **4.** Around 1,665
5. It is the world's largest container
ship **6.** The sun **7.** California
8. True **9.** Summit supercomputer
10. The world's biggest truck

11. Mesoscale science **12.** The
largest star found by astronomers
13. The world's biggest movable
machine **14.** The Big Bang
15. 70 percent **16.** True **17.** Antonov
An-225 **18.** Jupiter **19.** Supertanker
20. POPE

QUIZ 436
1. Harfleur **2.** King Duncan's blood
3. He blinds the Earl of Gloucester
4. Drink **5.** A crocodile **6.** Falstaff
7. Bottom's dream **8.** His reputation
9. Miranda **10.** *A Winter's Tale*
11. *Hamlet* **12.** "The rest is silence."
13. False **14.** Men **15.** *Henry VI,
Part 2* **16.** Theseus **17.** Puck
18. *Much Ado about Nothing*
19. Richard II **20.** Venus

QUIZ 437
1. Mariana Ocean Trench, Pacific
2. Dead Sea **3.** Coast redwood
4. Burj Khalifa, Dubai
5. 250,000 miles (400,000 km)
6. Caspian Sea, Eurasia **7.** Proxima
Centauri **8.** 3,960 miles (6,370 km)
9. Mount Everest, Himalayas
10. 93 million miles (150 million km)
11. The moon **12.** South Africa
13. Lake Baikal, Siberia **14.** 62 miles
(100 km) **15.** The Nile, Africa
16. Andromeda Galaxy **17.** Andes,
South America **18.** 28,000 light years
19. 24 million miles (38 million km)
20. 24,900 miles (40,000 km)

QUIZ 438
1. Quentin Tarantino **2.** Amy
Winehouse **3.** Tom Clancy
4. Green Bay Packers **5.** France
6. Edward of Woodstock **7.** *Grey's
Anatomy* **8.** True **9.** Neil Diamond
10. Barry White **11.** Sean Connery
12. Amsterdam, Netherlands
13. A hazard on the track **14.** False
15. Green **16.** Star **17.** Orange
River **18.** Five **19.** The Black Sea
20. World War I **21.** False

22. Great White Shark **23.** The Red Cross **24.** 14th **25.** Vermilion

QUIZ 439
1. Germany **2.** For camouflage when underwater **3.** Vivian Fuchs **4.** To collect penguins' eggs **5.** -128°F (-89°C) **6.** There isn't one **7.** King Edward VII **8.** Transantarctic Mountains **9.** Hole in the ozone layer **10.** Mount Erebus **11.** Cat **12.** Their urine **13.** Extreme Cold Weather **14.** 1959 **15.** Norwegian **16.** Feet **17.** Lead **18.** Nunatak **19.** Ridges of snow and ice **20.** Henry Morton Stanley

QUIZ 440
1. Lancia Delta Integrale **2.** Bugeye **3.** 2.8 **4.** People's car **5.** Alfa Romeo 1900 SSZ **6.** 85 mph (137 kmph) **7.** True **8.** Netherlands **9.** Motorcycle sidecars **10.** Northern Ireland **11.** Mighty Mouse **12.** Elon Musk **13.** Chevrolet Corvette **14.** 1997 **15.** Ariel Atom **16.** 4 seconds **17.** True **18.** Lithium-ion batteries **19.** 73 **20.** 1933 **21.** 180 mph (290 kmph) **22.** 2.4 seconds **23.** 260 mph (418 kmph) **24.** 2.5 seconds **25.** 40–45 mph (64–72 kmph)

QUIZ 441
1. Navajo **2.** Alaska and Canada **3.** Esperanto **4.** 200,000 **5.** 20 **6.** Xhosa **7.** 20 **8.** Pite Sami **9.** True **10.** Klingon **11.** Your mother has a smooth forehead! **12.** An extinct language **13.** A conlanger **14.** Old Norse **15.** Icelandic **16.** True **17.** Nakhi **18.** 90% **19.** The Babel fish **20.** Frisian

QUIZ 442
1. Cerberus **2.** Sisyphus **3.** Hera **4.** False **5.** Pandora **6.** Athena **7.** 12 **8.** The 10-year war between the Titans and the Olympians **9.** You would turn to stone **10.** Ithaca **11.** Theseus **12.** He was dipped into the river Styx

as a child **13.** Cronus **14.** True **15.** *God of War* **16.** Fire **17.** Wine **18.** Atlas **19.** Persephone **20.** Apollo and Artemis **21.** Iris **22.** 12 **23.** Daedalus **24.** Menelaus **25.** 100

QUIZ 443
1. The Babylonians **2.** The fourth century BCE **3.** India **4.** *Geographia* **5.** A legend **6.** Around 1,100 **7.** South America **8.** Gunter's chain **9.** North America **10.** True **11.** 1492 **12.** An inset map **13.** Water **14.** Belgium **15.** Grids **16.** True **17.** The equator **18.** True **19.** 12 **20.** The bar scale

QUIZ 444
1. 12,000 tons (12,192 metric tons) **2.** 33% **3.** $^{12}/_{100}$ in (3 mm) **4.** Road transport **5.** Farming **6.** 10 percent **7.** Pacific **8.** True **9.** Sulfur dioxide **10.** CFCs **11.** Sumatra's, in Indonesia **12.** CFCs **13.** Symbiotic algae are expelled **14.** Tourism resorts **15.** Amur leopard **16.** Soybean cultivation **17.** Florida **18.** Mercury **19.** Agriculture **20.** Ganges

QUIZ 445
1. Venus **2.** Mercury and Venus **3.** Fireball meteors **4.** Neptune **5.** Mars **6.** Jupiter **7.** Mars **8.** The dark split in Saturn's rings **9.** Uranus **10.** Baily's Beads **11.** 97.9 degrees **12.** Meteoroids **13.** Neptune **14.** Pluto **15.** Yellow dwarf **16.** Geraldyn Cobb **17.** Venus **18.** A transit **19.** Giovanni Schiaparelli **20.** A conjunction **21.** Comets **22.** Ganymede **23.** White dwarf **24.** *Voyager 1* **25.** 125 billion

QUIZ 446
1. Every 500,000 years **2.** Eleven **3.** Polarity reversals **4.** True **5.** True **6.** Outgassing **7.** Photosynthesis **8.** They are anaerobic **9.** Helium **10.** 3.5 billion years **11.** Panthalassa

12. 298 mph (480 kmph) **13.** Wegener
14. True **15.** Petrology **16.** Older
17. Mountains **18.** Compete
19. Convection **20.** Divergence

QUIZ 447

1. Potential energy **2.** False **3.** Energy
is stored as it stretches **4.** Work in raising
the weight **5.** Kinetic **6.** True **7.** At the
bottom of the hill **8.** False **9.** Gravity
10. Time **11.** Kinetic energy **12.** True
13. Velocity **14.** Principle of energy
conservation **15.** False **16.** Brownian
motion **17.** Expands the air, which pushes
the bullet **18.** Lavoisier **19.** Mechanical
equivalence of heat **20.** True

QUIZ 448

1. John Donne **2.** Mary Seacole **3.** Oliver
Cromwell **4.** Catherine Parr **5.** Lord
Kitchener **6.** Mohandas Karamchand
Gandhi **7.** F. D. Roosevelt **8.** Chartists
9. Julius Caesar **10.** Runaway slaves
11. The duke of Wellington **12.** Lord
Howard of Effingham **13.** He was a
woman **14.** *Robinson Crusoe* **15.** William
Booth **16.** The sons of Edward IV **17.** John
Wesley **18.** Robert Catesby **19.** Spencer
Perceval **20.** Trygve Lie **21.** Frances
Stewart **22.** George Eliot **23.** Alcock
and Brown **24.** Alexander the Great
25. Henry VIII

QUIZ 449

1. Hoi An **2.** Amazon Rain Forest
3. Paris, France **4.** True **5.** La Paz
6. Western Ghats **7.** The Matterhorn
8. The Falklands and South Georgia
9. Kata Tjuta **10.** 54 **11.** Mount Cook
12. Canada **13.** India **14.** -2°F (-19°C)
15. Sumo wrestling **16.** Modern
17. United States **18.** Japan **19.** True
20. True

QUIZ 450

1. Douglas Fairbanks, Sr. **2.** Richard
Feynman **3.** Franklin D. Roosevelt
4. True **5.** Pablo Picasso **6.** Dylan Thomas
7. H. G. Wells **8.** John Maynard Keynes

9. False **10.** Jane Austen **11.** Winston
Churchill **12.** Noël Coward **13.** James
Joyce **14.** True **15.** Charles Darwin
16. Karl Marx **17.** Joan Crawford
18. False **19.** Edvard Grieg
20. J. M. W. Turner

Acknowledgments

Dorling Kindersley would like to thank Anukriti Arora, Shipra Jain, Ankita Das, and Adhithi Priya for design assistance and Arushi Mathur for editorial assistance.